INSIDE
AFRICAN
POLITICS

INSIDE
AFRICAN
POLITICS

Kevin C. Dunn and
Pierre Englebert

LYNNE
RIENNER
PUBLISHERS

BOULDER
LONDON

Published in the United States of America in 2019 by
Lynne Rienner Publishers, Inc.
1800 30th Street, Boulder, Colorado 80301
www.rienner.com

and in the United Kingdom by
Lynne Rienner Publishers, Inc.
Gray's Inn House, 127 Clerkenwell Road, London EC1 5DB

Library of Congress Cataloging-in-Publication Data
Names: Dunn, Kevin C., 1967– author. | Englebert, Pierre, 1962– author.
Title: Inside African politics / Kevin C. Dunn and Pierre Englebert.
Description: 2nd edition. | Boulder, Colorado : Lynne Rienner Publishers,
    Inc., 2019. | Includes bibliographical references and index.
Identifiers: LCCN 2019000101 | ISBN 9781626378070 (pbk. : alk. paper)
Subjects: LCSH: Africa, Sub-Saharan—Politics and government. | Political
    culture—Africa, Sub-Saharan. | Political stability—Africa, Sub-Saharan.
    | Ethnicity—Political aspects—Africa, Sub-Saharan. | Africa,
    Sub-Saharan—Foreign relations.
Classification: LCC DT352.5 .D86 2019 | DDC 320.967—dc23
    LC record available at https://lccn.loc.gov/2019000101

British Cataloguing in Publication Data
A Cataloguing in Publication record for this book
is available from the British Library.

Printed and bound in the United States of America

The paper used in this publication meets the requirements
of the American National Standard for Permanence of
Paper for Printed Library Materials Z39.48-1992.

5 4 3 2 1

Contents

Tables and Figures

Tables

Figures

Acknowledgments

FIRST AND FOREMOST, WE ARE GRATEFUL TO LYNNE RIENNER, who provided the initial impetus for this textbook, and to Peter Lewis, who saw it off the ground and whose mark no doubt remains on the final product. We gratefully acknowledge the insightful reading of the entire manuscript by two anonymous reviewers, whose comments allowed for significant improvements. In addition, we thank Morten Bøås, Deborah Bräutigam, Jim Hentz, Paul Nugent, Anne Pitcher, Ian Taylor, Aili Tripp, and Denis Tull, who kindly provided detailed comments and suggestions on specific chapters of the first edition. Manya Janowitz, Sarah Miller, Evan Roe, and Jeanne Segil, all students at Pomona College at the time, provided excellent research and editorial assistance, as did Kerstin Steiner of Claremont Graduate University. The fall 2011 and fall 2012 students of Politics 162: Comparative Politics of Africa, at Pomona College, helped with early iterations of the text and generously shared their impressions. Finally, we are grateful to our colleagues and our students who gave feedback on the first edition, so that we could improve the text for this new edition.

1

Why African Politics Matter

IN SEPTEMBER 2017, WHILE SPEAKING TO A GROUP OF
African heads of states at the United Nations (UN), US president Donald Trump repeatedly sang the praises of "Nambia," a country that does not exist. Though it was later suggested that he was attempting to reference Namibia (not Gambia or Zambia or an entirely fictitious country he might have spontaneously invented), the diplomatic gaffe went largely uncommented upon. The president's ignorance of African affairs was not noteworthy largely because many, if not most, Americans share it. Imagine if he had invented a European country—"Swedlandia," perhaps—in a speech to the European Union (EU). The outcry and mockery would have certainly been more pronounced.

A few months later, President Trump infamously referred to African countries as "shit-holes" in an outburst related to immigration. While the "Nambia" reference seemingly stemmed from ignorance, Trump's "shit-hole" comment was grounded in both ignorance and well-worn stereotypes about life across the continent. While these comments were offensive and troubling, for the student of Africa this was familiar territory. Not only is the continent often marginalized and its study frequently relegated to the periphery of knowledge about the world, but it also suffers from people's limited knowledge of it being based on stereotypes, many informed by racist tropes and assumptions.

On the one hand, the relative neglect of Africa may be easy to understand. After all, in most regions of the world, geographical proximity, historical affinity, direct relevance, and available expertise largely determine what gets taught. Africa's marginal status is partly a historical artifact that tends to endure. In fact, during the transition period to the Trump administration, his advisers sent a four-page list of questions to the State Department expressing profound skepticism about Africa's relevance to the United States and US interests. On the other hand, the prevalence of stereotypes and misrepresentations about Africa can make this ignorance dangerous when it serves as the foundation for policies and practices.

Since you are reading this book, you might already be convinced of the utility of studying Africa and African politics. The continent, after all, is part of the world and studying it reminds us of the universality of human experiences and of the sometimes hidden relevance of even the most marginal of regions to our own concerns, wherever we may be. Yet, another way to answer the question "Why study African politics?" is to embrace Trump's perspective. If Africa is indeed full of "shit-hole" countries, it would be important to find out why that is and what are the consequences. Trump's language might have been rough, but thinking of Africa as a region of political, social, and economic problems is far from entirely inaccurate. It is common at the outset of textbooks on African politics to warn students against stereotypes of a continent plagued with corruption, conflict, poverty, and famines. But Africa *is* a continent plagued with corruption, conflict, poverty, and famines. It is many other things too, but there is no point denying the breadth and depth of its problems. Understanding these problems, if only to mitigate their possible consequences on countries elsewhere, is a perfectly legitimate motivation for the acquisition of knowledge. After 9/11, most Americans have come to realize how issues intrinsic to societies of the Middle East have greatly affected their own political systems. Likewise, Europeans, facing high levels of migration from Africa, already experience some consequences of Africa's predicaments. Thus, anyone interested in the welfare and security of their own political system would be well inspired to gain knowledge on the functioning of African political systems.

It is more common, however, at least among students in North America and Europe, to be interested in the study of Africa with a view toward helping solve its problems for Africans' sake. From this perspective, Africa is often characterized as existing in some form of crisis and needing external help. Taking this view to its extreme, Africa is portrayed as needing to be "saved." One can certainly question this salvation scenario, but seeking to understand Africa's problems with a view to helping solve them is a generous and altruistic calling and constitutes perfectly sufficient motivation to embark upon the study of the continent. One is unlikely to do much good, however, without a decent understanding of some of the roots of the problem one is trying to solve. Responding to famines by sending food aid is likely to provide some relief to those affected, but solving the problem requires understanding why, after more than sixty years of self-rule, some African governments still regularly appear unable or unwilling to provide the most basic safety nets for their populations. Helping a village by building a school is likely to be cheered by the villagers, but improving educational opportunities for African children requires understanding why such public investment has not been forthcoming in the first place, where resources have gone instead, what the social expectations of the benefits of access to education are, and so forth. Campaigning against sexual violence in conflicts might help mobilize resources for the victims, but finding ways to stop or discourage the practice demands at least understanding the logic of conflicts characterized by decentralized violence, the nature of civilian-military relations, and the goals of the belligerents.

The necessity of knowledge for action is not only true of humanitarian and charitable intervention; it also applies to policymaking at large. Studying African politics with a view to improving policy toward Africa should be well worth the effort. The gap that exists between the relative wealth of our knowledge on how contemporary African states and societies function and the assumptions underlying international policies and foreign aid toward the region is large indeed. While the examples from Trump may be seen as extreme, over and over again one is confronted with analyses of African politics that rely on disembedded assumptions. It seems that to end corruption, for example, one need merely elect a new ruler of personal integrity or appoint a corruption czar (Wrong 2010). The very understanding of African corruption as the consequence of the greed of elites or as a way for impoverished civil servants to deal with their predicament fails to grasp the "political work" corruption does and its centrality in African political systems (Pierce 2016:21). Similarly, rebuilding states in the wake of conflicts is often seen as only requiring large financial commitments from donors, new constitutions inspired from Western models, and committed leadership. That the international reconstruction partners were also those who colonized and thus created those failed states in the first place, that previous Western-inspired constitutions met with little success, that the centralized state is a source of insecurity for much of the populace, and that the former belligerents are often incorporated into the postconflict leadership represent obstacles not easily overcome and usually glossed over in policy design. In fact, one can argue that a large number of Western and international policies in Africa have failed for a lack of proper understanding of the mechanisms of African politics and the rationales of their politicians (Tull 2011). People in the policy world can thus expect a significant payoff from a better understanding of African politics.

It is not difficult to debunk assumptions about Africa's presumed marginality, for there are many ways in which the African continent is central to the concerns and interests of people in other regions, including Europe and North America. Six of the world's ten fastest-growing economies in

2018 were African, with Ghana and Ethiopia at the top, followed by Côte d'Ivoire, Djibouti, Senegal, and Tanzania. Since 2011, Nigeria and Angola have both been among the top ten exporters of crude oil to the United States. With numerous oil fields in development across the continent, global interest in African oil is certain to grow. In 2016, foreign direct investment to Africa totaled $59 billion. Since 2009, China has been Africa's largest single trading partner, with Sino-African trade amounting to roughly $188 billion in 2017. India's trade with Africa was $90 billion in 2015, skyrocketing from $5.3 billion in 2001. Russian trade with Africa has steadily increased, accounting for $3.6 billion in 2017, up from $2.2 billion just two years before. Militarily too, Africa lies centrally on the radars of foreign powers. The United States has a military command for Africa (known as AFRICOM), a permanent base in Djibouti, and military missions deployed in several African countries. As of 2017, the United States maintained roughly 6,000 active US military personnel spread across the continent. France has over 3,000 troops in permanent military bases in Djibouti, Gabon, and Senegal, and missions in Côte d'Ivoire, Chad, the Central African Republic, and across the Sahel. Africa is the home of China's only overseas military base in the world, with its naval facility in Djibouti joining those of France, the United States, Germany, Italy, and Russia. Investing knowledge in the political systems and societies of African countries would of course be a worthwhile exercise for anyone intent on understanding or managing these important relationships.

There are also unusual rewards to the study of African politics for the more academically minded—those interested in political science and particularly comparative politics. Of course, knowledge about African politics is its own reward for anyone directly interested in the region. But even if Africa is not your priority, studying its politics can provide important insights of fairly universal scope, in at least two ways. First, the study of African politics addresses broad, complex, and fundamental questions, going to the core of the discipline of political science. For example, the African experience informs us about the relationship between state formation and political violence. It brings to life, in all their richness and complexity, problems of political legitimacy and social contracts in heterogeneous societies, and their relationship to phenomena such as patronage. The African experience is also a vibrant laboratory of political identity. And it provides insights into the roots of democracy and authoritarianism and the challenges of development.

Thus Somalia might seem like a "shit-hole" to many, but it is also a crucible of politics. Nigeria might be renown for its corruption, but it is also a miracle of national integration (and the two issues are not unrelated). Eastern Congo might be wracked with political violence, but it also bears deep insights into the relation between land, power, and ethnicity; while neighboring Rwanda, which lives with the legacy of genocide, is also a unique experiment in identity transformation and postconflict justice. Benin and Togo might not be known for much, but they provide stunningly contrasting experiences in democratization and reversal to authoritarianism. The list goes on. To study African politics is to learn from the ongoing experiences of Africans with these questions of universal relevance.

Second, and related, the study of African politics is also fascinating for all the ways in which the African experience deviates from patterns in other regions or from what established theories predict. To a significant extent, the study of comparative politics and international relations has historically developed by incorporating materials from regions other than Africa (Dunn and Shaw 2001; Lemke 2003). In part, this came as a result of an occasional perception among non-Africanist scholars that African politics was a matter of regional or area studies rather than bona fide comparative politics.[1] As a result, both comparative politics and international relations theory have been somewhat biased and, not surprisingly, have done a poor job at times of explaining empirical features of African politics. In other words, the political scientist's conventional toolbox has been incomplete when it comes to Africa. Thus, studying Africa leads one to challenge notions, concepts, and theories developed in other contexts, and makes comparative politics better.

Only recently has the African experience more fully contributed to the development of comparative politics and international relations. Should Richard Sklar (1993) rewrite today the article he wrote in the early 1990s, "The African Frontier for Political Science," he undoubtedly would reap a greater harvest than Africanism's contributions to the study of dual authority, cultural relativism, and mixed methodologies. African studies have contributed to theory development in the fields of democratic theory (e.g., Bratton and van de Walle 1997); rationality and culture (e.g., Bates 1983; Schatzberg 2001); economic development and modernization (e.g., Bates 1981; Chabal and Daloz 1999; and a large body of empirical and theoretical literature on growth); elections and democracy consolidation (e.g., Lindberg 2006; Edgell et al. 2018); state theory (e.g., Bayart 1993; Young 1994a, 2012); civil society (e.g., Monga 1996; Kasfir 1998b); class analysis (e.g., Sklar 1979; Boone 1990; Samatar and Oldfield 1995); ethnic politics (Bates 1983; Posner 2005; and many more); civil wars and ethnic conflicts (e.g., Reno 1995; Clapham 1998a; Bøås and Dunn 2007; Williams 2011); governance and political corruption (e.g., Olivier de Sardan 1999; Smith 2007); international relations (Bayart 2000; Clapham 1996; Cornelissen, Cheru, and Shaw 2012; Dunn and Shaw 2001; and Lemke 2003); and more.

There will be ample opportunities to return to these contributions later, but a few examples might be helpful at this stage. Michael Bratton and Nicolas van de Walle (1994, 1997) have shown that conventional theories of democratic transitions that stressed the role of negotiated top-down settlements, honed in the experience of Latin America and southern Europe (e.g., O'Donnell, Schmitter, and Whitehead 1986), failed to explain African transition patterns. They argued instead that to understand African transitions, one had to take into account the nature and structural characteristics of the previous regime and the role of protests. Since then, their insights have become part of the democratization canon and informed the study of transitions in other regions too (e.g., Linz and Stepan 1996; Schedler 2006).

Robert Bates provides another example. In a 1983 article, he highlighted how conventional modernization theory could not account for the growing influence of ethnicity over time in African politics. To solve this puzzle, he offered a new concept of ethnic coalitions and a broad theory of rational policy preferences. His earlier work (Bates 1981), explaining the paradox of why African policymakers seem to make systematically bad economic policy choices, has become a classic of rational choice theory (a methodological disposition to which we return in Chapter 3). Similarly, Richard Sklar (1979) argued that class analysis was not helpful in making sense of African politics unless classes were defined in their relation to the state rather than to the means of production, and unless their behavior was extended beyond class struggle, both heterodox views that nudged this analytical tradition beyond its Marxian roots. And Douglas Lemke's (2002) evidence that conventional theories of war failed to explain the significantly lower probability of interstate conflict on the continent led him to reconsider what constitutes international relations and what actors should be included in its study in order to make sense of the contemporary world across regions. Here too the list goes on.

To study Africa is thus to expose oneself to conditions that challenge established theories of comparative and international politics and, thereby, to enrich both these disciplines and one's grasp of them. By surveying and explaining these many theoretical developments, and putting them into their empirical contexts, we hope this textbook will help the student make sense of this rich body of work.

Explaining African Politics: An Overview

What is it about African politics that we seek to explain? What questions drive our inquiry? At the most elementary level, we want to know how politics is organized on the continent, how things work, how political institutions and behavior in Africa vary from those in other regions and within Africa itself. At the core of such inquiry lies the state. African states are generally deemed to be weak, fragile, and sometimes even failed, yet they are also very good at surviving and retaining significance for their citizens. Despite their ambiguous colonial origins and sometimes hesitant territorial reach, they have evolved, adapted, and been appropriated by Africans. In their own ways, they "work" (Chabal and Daloz 1999). Although the state is the core unit of African politics, it is one of the areas where the knowledge gap between scholarship and policy practice is the widest. Donors insist on state stability, capacity, democratization, and decentralization. Yet they often seem unaware of how these states actually function beyond their formal institutional surface (Trefon 2011a). Therefore, we begin this book with an in-depth discussion of the African state (Chapter 2), including its precolonial and colonial origins; the process of decolonization, the transfer of statehood to Africans, and the degree to which the state was appropriated by Africans at independence; the very notion of African sovereignty; and how the African state compares to states elsewhere and to what states are theoretically supposed to be and do.

Politics also largely takes place outside the state, in the realm of society and at the level of individuals (Chapter 3). Particularly important in this sphere are issues of identity and their political salience. And, of course, it is not possible to speak of identity in Africa without discussing ethnicity. Here too, however, the gap between prejudice and scholarship is wide. Africans are nearly universally seen (including by many Africans themselves) as privileging ethnic (or "tribal") identity over other forms of collective characteristics. Many problems, from corruption to conflict, tend to be attributed to ethnic polarization. The reality is formidably more complex. Yet there is no denying that ethnicity, in all its ambiguity, lies center-stage in African politics. We take great effort to discuss it in depth and nuance, highlighting both its relevance and its propensity to offer misleading explanations. We explore the different ways to conceptualize ethnic identity, from primordial ties of blood to coalitions based on political expediency; look at the connection between ethnic and national identity, including the more recent development of political discourses of autochthony that link ethnicity with place; and discuss the tendency of many regimes to repress, and of others to accommodate, ethnic identity. In each case we look at the explanatory power of different approaches to make sense of actual and highly varied empirical conditions in Africa, from peaceful cohabitation to genocide.

Yet for all the attention it receives, ethnicity is far from being the only dimension of collective action or social cleavage in Africa. For one, religion has gained much momentum as a political force across the continent, as elsewhere. Christian faiths, particularly of the Pentecostal type, have made great inroads and manifested a new political assertiveness. African Islam too, while not gaining as many new converts as the Christian faiths, has been in ebullition, partly caught between worldwide trends and homegrown practices. In addition, despite the penetration of world religions on the continent, spiritual and religious beliefs that are specifically African have continued to thrive and occasionally show deep political significance. In this respect, the practice of witchcraft merits our attention.

Social class has long been a traditional mode of analysis for Western social science, yet it rarely manifests itself in the expected ways in African politics. Because of the historical weakness of many African economies, classes often need to be conceptualized in different ways than they might be elsewhere in order to yield analytical mileage. We discuss class theories of African politics and suggest ways in which they can help explain some empirical patterns. We also focus on gender as an identity category and a mode of analysis. In Africa as in other regions, gender differences and inequalities based on sex matter a great deal. In many dimensions of life, African women are at a significant material disadvantage compared to men. We discuss this and the ways in which African women organize and seek political representation.

Finally, there is a remarkable wealth of associative life outside the state in Africa. Nongovernmental organizations (NGOs) are a very popular form of association. Their activity belongs to civil society, the realm of public life between the household and the state. The concept of civil society in comparative politics is both useful and constraining. Rather Western-centric in its historical origins and normative expectations, it travels with some difficulty to Africa. Yet it is invoked widely by scholars, donors, and African activists alike. We look at its definitions and expected functions, its usefulness and limitations in the context of African politics, and the ways in which some scholars have suggested amending the concept for it to better reflect African realities.

Having laid the historical stage to the state and provided an overview of social forces and cleavages, we turn to how power is actually exercised (Chapter 4). The exogenous origins of African states have combined with precolonial patterns of rule and problems of social heterogeneity to produce a peculiar type of rule that has dominated across the continent since independence. Because it mixes elements of formal institutionalized statehood with more informal and personalized dimensions, it is commonly referred to as neopatrimonialism. Understanding neopatrimonialism might be one of the most important steps in acquiring knowledge about

African politics. It illuminates numerous practices and patterns, from the personalization of power, to the weakness of institutions, to the prevalence of corruption. At the same time, neopatrimonialism has its limitations as an explanatory device of African politics, particularly as it does a poor job of accounting for differences of rule among countries and because its very ubiquity has diluted its conceptual rigor over time.

We also discuss the functioning of formal institutions associated with the exercise of power. First are political parties. Current African political parties differ greatly from their predecessors in the pre-1990 era of single parties and independence movements. In addition, their lack of clear ideological differentiation and of institutionalization makes them very different from parties in many other regions of the world. Next we discuss the political salience of African militaries, which have a long-standing tradition of wresting power away from civilians. We review the empirical record of coups d'état, discuss theories of military takeovers, and paint the profile of military governments. Finally we discuss the functioning of state institutions, paying particular attention to executives and administrations, legislative bodies, and judiciaries. These are areas that have only recently gained more prominence among scholarship on Africa, which has tended to focus on the very top of the state.

Formal state institutions are only part of the story of rule in Africa, however. Formal and informal institutions coexist and mesh as people straddle different worlds. French political scientist Emmanuel Terray (1986) has referred to this duality with the dichotomy of the "air conditioner" and the "veranda," two legitimating spheres with different behavioral expectations in and across which African individuals and politics function. With this important empirical pattern in mind, we dedicate significant space to the study of institutional pluralism—the hybridity of African politics and the shared nature of its governance, which is effectively performed not only by the state, but also by customary authorities (many of which are also, paradoxically, state actors), associations, religious groups, and foreign donors. Thus we go beyond the study of formal institutions and look at the effective existence of authority and governance on the ground, at the ways in which politics surfaces within the social spheres, and at the overlapping and intertwining of the formal and the informal.

The study of political regimes is, of course, one of the most common preoccupations of comparative politics, and we dedicate a chapter to it (Chapter 5). We discuss the authoritarian tendencies of African regimes before the 1990s, the democratic wave that followed the end of the Cold War, the consolidation of democracy in some states and the reversal to authoritarianism in many others, and the particular contribution of African politics to regime typology: the hybrid regime, which blends elements of democracy, such as relative media freedoms and the right to organize political parties, with features of authoritarianism, such as unfree and unfair elections, repression of opponents, manipulation of constitutions, and the like. A particularly interesting feature of African hybrid regimes is that, while harboring features usually associated with transitions to democracy, they are actually stable.

Politics is exercised everywhere within a material world that constrains it. Resource scarcity is an important conditioner of African politics. The relatively widespread prevalence of poverty across the continent colors the nature of people's participation in politics and the exercise of state power. At the same time that many Africans are poor, many African countries are rich in natural resources, which also greatly affect political institutions and behavior. Thus this book allocates considerable space to the study of Africa's political economy (Chapter 6). It discusses the unusual historical, climatic, geographical, and resource-based constraints of African economies; the burden and political effects of epidemics such as AIDS; and the management of African economies by governments and donors. In this respect, the impact of neopatrimonialism on economic policies gets much attention, as do the intended remedies for economic failure, including the multiple iterations of donor-sponsored programs for economic reform. We conclude this political economy survey with an examination of the notable improvement in a number of African economies in the twenty-first century and the degree to which the "Africa rising" narrative carries weight.

While economic crisis is a common African narrative, so are conflict and state failure. And indeed, no amount of "Afro-optimism" will conceal the fact that African countries have been prone to conflict, even though most African societies live in peace most of the time. Given the importance and policy relevance of this topic, we dedicate a large chapter to it (Chapter 7). We help the reader make sense of what often appear to be irrational instances of political violence. Who are the insurgents? What do they want? What do they do? How do they relate to the state, to their environment and resources, and to foreign actors? We are careful to connect these questions to our earlier discussions of state, social forces, economic resources, and forms of governance. We discuss wars of national liberation, interstate wars, secessions, nonseparatist rebellions, and composite conflicts. We also show how conflict has evolved over time in Africa, especially before and after the Cold War, as well as the more recent developments in the twenty-first century. We then review the rich body of literature that deals with the causes of conflict and apply it to cases from across the continent. Here too, the study of Africa has much to teach us and greatly contributes to the existing literature. The chapter concludes with a discussion of conflict resolution and of the notions of human security and insecurity in Africa.

We conclude the book with a discussion of the international relations of African states (Chapter 8). The frequent perception of African states as passive recipients of foreign interventions, from colonialism to humanitarian aid, is largely misleading. However dependent they might appear, they have considerable agency and their rulers often use their situation of weakness to their advantage. We begin by reviewing theoretical perspectives on Africa in the world and the contributions these studies have made to theorizing about international relations in general. We then provide a historical overview of the foreign relations of African states, from colonialism to the post–Cold War era. Particularly interesting are the specific current relations of African countries among themselves and with the dominant actors outside the continent. Among the former, we emphasize dynamics of integration and collective action within the African Union (AU) and its predecessor, the Organization of African Unity (OAU), as well the development of regional economic and security organizations. Among the latter, we stress relations with former colonial powers and with the United States, Russia, China, and other important global actors. In many ways, this chapter will challenge any presumptions of Africa's marginality in world affairs.

Our goal is not only to provide a conceptual overview of African politics but also to help the reader understand the roots of some persistent problems that undermine the quality of life of Africans and have been begging for policy solutions for several decades. Problems such as underdevelopment, poverty, and inequality; violence, conflict, and the breakdown of state structures; authoritarianism, institutional weakness, and political instability; poor governance and widespread corruption; and debt and uneven relations with donors provide focus to our inquiry across chapters.

We also seek to make sense of change. Although there is little point in denying that many Africans face significant political and economic problems, theirs is a continent of rapid and discontinuous change, with trends and dynamics that call for analysis. Why did many countries democratize in the 1990s and how did democracy evolve afterward? How have some countries collapsed or recovered or both over time? What explains variations in economic performance from decade to decade? How did Africa go from being characterized by *The Economist* as the "hopeless continent" in 2000 to the "hopeful continent" in 2013? Change is not just something we need to explain; it is something that permanently challenges what we are explaining or have already explained. Thus the elaboration of neopatrimonial theory does a great job of making sense of the African state until the 1990s, but then runs into some problems. The story of decay that characterizes Africa from the late 1980s onward—that of state failure, collapse, conflict, and ethnic wars, and which has generated a large body of thoughtful literature—finds itself again in question after the turn of the twenty-first century, when Africa seemed to embark upon a new turn, with greater growth and the end of several conflicts. However trite the transition paradigm, Africa is undoubtedly undergoing a transition. In some ways, as with the recent development of an African middle class, this transformation is potentially profound. In other ways, to the extent, for example, that this development reflects a mere commodity boom, it might not be so dramatic. At any rate, accounting for change in the short run is a challenge. We touch upon it but place it in the broader context of more than six decades of postcolonial politics and economics. We focus on analytical and theoretical insights in the hope that the reader will acquire the analytical skill to make sense both of past trends and of developments new and yet to come.

Africa?

This book starts from the premise that there is such a thing as African politics and therefore such a thing as Africa. The subsuming of continent-wide trends and events into a shared conceptual framework can be a stretch, and we do not wish to contribute to the occasional misconception of Africa as a country. There are immense variations in political systems (from Benin's democracy to Eritrea's dictatorship), societal trends (from Tanzania's sense of unity to Rwanda's intense polarization), and economic fortunes (from Botswana's miracle to Zimbabwe's catastrophic decline) across the continent. Some of these are visible to the naked eye. African countries have shopping malls, air-conditioned high-rises, widespread cell phone usage, countless television and radio stations, Internet cafés, and bustling metropolises choked with traffic. At the same time, and often in the same countries, there are entire neighborhoods without water, sewers, or electricity; internally displaced people and refugees living in camps; malnourished and uneducated children; disconnected villages living largely in self-subsistence (or falling short of it); and societies at war with themselves.

Seeing African politics as a conceptual whole does not preclude recognizing such variations. Our first goal is to highlight shared patterns across the region and develop concepts and theories that can help the reader make sense of African politics in general, for African states and societies do share many circumstances, whether embedded in history, nature, or society. Yet it is also our goal to explain the variety of settings, conditions, and outcomes that exist on the continent. These variations are an intrinsic component of African politics, and most theories are able to account for them. Moreover, as this book will make clear, hybridity is an essential characteristic of many dimensions of African politics and economies. As a result, the empirical diversity of the continent need not be an obstacle to its holistic study, for there is much to be learned from observing and understanding variations among and within African countries.

There is also much to be learned from the diversity of perspectives in scholarship on Africa. People study African politics not only from different personal, ideological, and methodological perspectives, but also from diverse disciplines including political science, history, economics, sociology, and anthropology. Our approach is to discuss good scholarship and interesting ideas, wherever they come from. While we seek all points of view, we generally do not care about the origins and personal characteristics of the authors we study. Nor do we believe that the study of Africa requires "pro-African" attitudes or "the championship of Africa's interests in all their ramifications" (Owomoyela 1994:77, 95). Such an approach does not strike us as likely to produce reliable knowledge, and we are not sure what these attitudes or interests might actually be. At the same time, we do not mean to dismiss the concerns of "Afrocentricity," in the sense given to it by Richard Sklar (1993) as a form of cultural relativism that puts at the center of inquiry issues that are of concern to Africans themselves and not only or necessarily to outside observers. Our first goal remains to help students, wherever they might be, understand African politics. Such understanding might require non-African students to learn things that are of importance to Africans, even if such topics did not originally strike them as important. Thus, while we study issues such as corruption, which might sometimes be of greater concern to outsiders than to Africans, we also discuss policies devised by African regimes to deal with cultural heterogeneity or to produce political legitimacy, which might be of greater concern to Africans than to outsiders. Most of the time, we find the distinction moot, but we remain attentive to reining in whatever Western bias we might have.

Although we act largely in this textbook as data organizers by inventorying, categorizing, comparing, and contrasting existing knowledge, one might be legitimately concerned that our own perspectives, as US scholars, could bias our analysis. One could wonder whether thinking of African politics as someone else's politics does justice to the topic or reduces our understanding of it. To some extent, the extraneity of the topic is unavoidable and similar to what it would be for a textbook on European politics or, for that matter, on astronomy (although we at least spend time in Africa, whereas few astronomers ever go to space). There might be ways to study African politics that would be reductionist. If we were, for example, to impute all political patterns that are unusual to Western eyes to some forms of local "tradition" or "culture," we would cheat ourselves of decent knowledge and run the risk of being injurious to many Africans. Yet Africa can be an object of scholarly inquiry without resorting to such shortcuts. We agree with the call of several scholars for considering the "banality" of African politics (e.g., Bayart 1993; Coulon 1997), although we do not want this to undermine any legitimate excitement that the study of the continent might trigger. In other words, Africans are very much the same as people anywhere else. They are born, most go to school, they work, they seek some degree of welfare, and they all eventually die. By the same token, African politics is also the same as politics anywhere else. Africans vote, compete for scarce resources, display political preferences, feel and express sentiments of national and regional allegiances, revolt, and so forth. It is important to ground our study of African politics in this understanding. It need not prevent us, however, from acknowledging that African lives are also different in many ways from those of people elsewhere. Once born, a greater proportion of Africans than people on any other continent never get a chance to live. Fewer also go to school. Many cannot find sufficient employment for survival. As a result, the welfare they long for often eludes them. And most of them die much earlier than people elsewhere. By the same token, African politics also differs from politics elsewhere. There are fewer democracies, more conflicts, and more coups; states are less functional, with greater reliance on primary commodity production; politics is more informal. These differences need not imply any intrinsic difference about people. We subscribe to this point of view and, when trying to explain any specific phenomenon, make similar assumptions about Africans as we would about people anywhere else. We assume that people are fairly rational, that they pursue some degree of self-interest, that they care about their families, that they seek security and predictability. In doing so, however, they face different sets of constraints and possibilities, different realms of the "politically thinkable" (Schatzberg 2001), than do people in the Western world. These differences, the origins of which we discuss, account in part for different politics.

And what about issues of method? The study of African politics has been mired in questions of methods that also relate to the identity of the region. Some scholars have stressed that we should think of African politics as African first, and gain knowledge of the continent's or of its countries' uniqueness (see Dressel 1966; Zeleza 1997; Szanton 2004). These scholars have insisted on the importance of specialized knowledge of countries, on the elaboration of concepts and theories that are useful to make sense of Africa for its own sake, and on being cognizant of specific cultural, linguistic, and historical contexts. They tend, as a result, to offer detailed discussions of specific case studies, but do not necessarily relate them to broader, more universal theoretical questions or discussions. In addition, they are more likely to cut across disciplines while focusing on Africa alone (in contrast to focusing on political science alone and comparing multiple regions). The rise of centers on African studies in Western universities largely embodies this approach.

Others have argued that comparative politics should be of universal relevance and that similar tools should be applied across regions, irrespective of local characteristics. From this perspective, politics in the United States, France, India, and Zambia can be best understood if studied along similar axes. In other words, an explanation that is only regional falls short of being a bona fide explanation. Gary King, Robert Keohane, and Sidney Verba (1994) make the case for universalist methods in comparative politics. Rational choice theory takes this argument a step further by suggesting that the rational maximization of self-interest by individuals is the best behavioral assumption to make sense of politics around the world (see Lichbach and Zuckerman 2009 for a more thorough discussion and comparison to other approaches).

This methodological dispute has raged in the study of all regions, not just Africa. It is far from merely academic and it has divided entire university departments in sometimes acrimonious battles, as resources were reshuffled away from area studies in the wake of the Cold War, when there seemed to be less of a national security interest in knowing about other regions and cultures (Bates 1997). It should be clear from our introduction that we believe in the universality of African politics and in the contributions that the study of the continent can make to political science in general. We think African politics should be studied like politics elsewhere. At the same time, we do not think such study is possible without a grounded knowledge of the region, gained in part from fieldwork and from learning about local histories and cultures. We therefore find the distinction between area studies and rational choice or other universal methods to be unnecessarily divisive. We agree instead with Ron Kassimir (1997:156) that "local knowledge and global knowledge are inseparable and mutually constitutive."[2] And we think students should fill their analytical toolboxes with as many tools as possible.

One last qualification before we move on to more substantive concerns. This is a book about African politics, but it does not deal with all of the continent's fifty-four countries. Our focus is the forty-nine states of sub-Saharan Africa (see the Appendix on pp. 413–417). We do not discuss the politics of Algeria, Egypt, Libya, Morocco, or Tunisia, which are commonly studied with the "Arab world" or together with Middle Eastern countries. This segregation is due partly to historical patterns of knowledge distribution in academia—some of it idiosyncratic—and partly to substantive differences in the politics of these two regions. Because of the limitations of our training and experience, we do not challenge the tradition of studying sub-Saharan Africa separately from North Africa. It is worth noting, however, that there are some remarkable exceptions to this approach, not least Crawford Young's (2012) *The Postcolonial State in Africa*.

Finally, a word about student level. This textbook provides a systematic introduction to African politics south of the Sahara. Its use requires little prior knowledge. However, it does not present information on the basic facts of Africa and its countries, which is easily available from many other sources (e.g., Griffiths 1995; *Africa South of the Sahara 2019*, 2018; CIA 2018), and it is probably best suited to students with some basic knowledge of political science, particularly comparative politics. We also hope that the book will be a companion for further study and act as a work of reference. We regard the book's bibliography to be an invaluable resource in and of itself. For each topic, the textbook reviews a range of theories and arguments, comparing and contrasting the most important contributions in the field, and singling out their implications for policy or for further study. Thus, more advanced undergraduate and graduate students, as well as policymakers and other professionals who focus on Africa, might also find the material here of interest and of assistance in their work.

Notes

1. The view of Africanist scholarship as parochial was contested by James Coleman and C. R. D. Halisi (1983:45), who noted that most Africanist works of the first two decades of independence actually mixed local knowledge with broader theory.

2. For more on this controversy, see the 1997 special issue of *Africa Today* and the 2005 special issue of *Africa Spectrum*. See also Bates, Mudimbe, and O'Barr 1993.

2

The Evolution
of African States

STATES ARE NOT THE ONLY UNIT OR LEVEL OF POLITICS.
But in Africa, just as elsewhere, they are essential containers of politics.
They are often the prize or the cause of political action. Therefore, it is
useful to begin our examination of African politics with a critical interrogation of the African state. Where did they come from? What existed
before them? What of the past has endured and how? What impact did
colonialism have on state formation in Africa? How has the postcolonial
state evolved? Is there a stereotypical African state? What are its defining characteristics? Do African states function in unique ways? These
questions provide the foundations for the study of African politics.

We address them in this chapter in a largely chronological order. We
begin with an overview of the politics of precolonial times, and then
move on to the main characteristics of colonial rule under European
powers. We stress those parts of colonial rule that have the most obvious
relevance to contemporary African politics, and that might help explain
certain features of African states and variations among them, including
the process of decolonization. We next discuss the roots of postcolonial
state power. In doing so, we examine the nature of African states—that
is, the foundations of their authority. If we think of states as a "genus,"
is there an African "species"? If so, what characterizes the species, what
varieties exist, and what differentiates it from others? Specifically, we
compare how much African states derive their existence and authority
from their colonial past or from any other source of legitimacy that may
have historically developed within their societies. Since African states
originated mostly as exogenous colonial creations, how does their
"imported" nature affect contemporary politics? What are the nature and
the effects of the African state's colonially constructed boundaries?

Alternately, to what extent have these originally colonial states become African over time? What kinds of social contracts lie at the root of their appropriation by Africans, if any?

Precolonial Politics

Most of Africa came under European colonial control in the second half of the nineteenth century. But Africans certainly had a lengthy, vibrant, and varied political history prior to the intrusion of Europeans. Before colonization, there was a mosaic of political systems across the continent, some of which had endured and developed over centuries. It is important to recognize that African politics were dynamic. There were conflicts, migrations, slavery, the rise and fall of kingdoms and empires, and substantial contacts—largely based on trade—with other parts of the world. African precolonial societies were generally patriarchal, though women's experience of inequality varied greatly across the continent, as women employed various strategies to create and maintain a degree of autonomy, such as among the matrilineal women traders of Senegambia. There were some areas of organized, relatively centralized political systems, and others with smaller-scale groups that were more anarchical and unstable. In making sense of contemporary politics, it is important to bear in mind that the encounter with colonialism varied as a function of the nature of preexisting systems and that many of these precolonial political formations did not altogether disappear with the colonial episode. Many endured in one form or another and sometimes continue to exercise significant appeal today, whether as political contenders or as references, narratives of mobilization, and frames of representation. The very complexity of contemporary African politics comes in large part from the plural nature of political authority that derives from this mixed historical legacy.

A convenient and commonly adopted typology distinguishes between two basic forms of political organization in precolonial Africa. In the words of the founders of Africanist political anthropology, Edward Evans-Pritchard and Meyer Fortes (1940:5), there were "societies which [lacked] centralized authority, administrative machinery and constituted judicial institutions" with "no sharp divisions of rank, status or wealth," and there were societies with all three features of government "in which cleavages of wealth, privilege, and status [corresponded] to the distribution of power and authority." Over the years, the former have been typically referred to as anarchical, acephalous, or stateless societies, and the latter as kingdoms, empires, and states. In between, anthropologists note the existence of chiefdoms (e.g., among the Ewe of Ghana and Togo) that were not acephalous but that did not form political units larger than a cluster of towns. Indeed, rather than a strict dichotomy, reality corresponded more to a fluid continuum from least to most hierarchical.

African stateless societies were relatively small, in large part because their mode of organization did not lend itself to scale. They consisted of politically unincorporated groups—that is, groups without centralized authority or well-developed political hierarchy, where lineage provided the basis of social organization, and lineage segmentation the principle of political evolution. A lineage is a group of shared descent. In these groups, family or clan elders exercised political authority, often in some collective form. Although lineages recognized their shared culture, there was no centralized authority among them. Lineages established themselves as clans through a process of segmentation. With elders in charge, young men often had to migrate in order to eke out a living and attain some status on their own (Bates 2008). As they did, they took wives and children with them and segmented from their elders, while retaining a shared lineage. Igor Kopytoff (1987) credits the logic of segmentation with a significant effect on the formation of African political systems and identities, beyond lineage clans. He refers to segmentation as a "frontier process": African societies' tendency to fission produced ejected people ("frontiersmen") who formed new social orders, attracting others along the way. These communities could vanish over time or become the foundation of new polities and even new ethnic identities.

There were variations among lineage societies. At the least level of hierarchy, some groups were little more than bands as small as a few dozen people who lived a life of hunting and gathering. The San of the Kalahari (often known as Bushmen), in today's Botswana, provide an example of this now essentially extinct mode of organization. More common were clan societies, where clans could include thousands of people. Before the creation of Somalia, first as a collection of colonies and then as a country, the Somali were a clan society, with no centralized authority among them and, actually, a fair degree of competition with shifting alliances (Lewis 2003). This might not be entirely unrelated to Somalia's current situation, which is still stateless and clan-based in many ways. In some cases, clans of a single nation might be united with cross-clan institutions such as age groups (e.g., the Maasai of Kenya and Tanzania), or they might share a common religious leader (Potholm 1979). Although lineage is central to these stateless societies, the kinship it involves is sometimes as much a political discourse as a physical reality. As Peter Geschiere (1991:31) stresses about the Nuer of South Sudan and the Maka of Cameroon, principles of kinship were very fluid among lineage groups, and unrelated clients or foreigners could progressively become included in clan structures.

At the other extreme, precolonial Africa was not short on states, kingdoms, and even empires. Over several centuries before colonization, state formations had risen and fallen across the continent. Some states were based on conquest, with one migrating group, often herders and warriors, conquering and assimilating sedentary and farming groups, a common pattern in the Great Lakes region of Central Africa. Of course, such a pattern of state formation is not unique to Africa. The invasion of the Gaul by the Germanic Francs in the fifth century led to the creation of France, for example. Other African states developed as a result of local elites controlling trade routes. For example, the Ghana Empire reached from Senegal to the edge of Niger from the eighth to thirteenth centuries, trading across the Sahara in gold and salt. It was succeeded by the Mali Empire, which peaked in the fourteenth century. Finally, some states developed, usually toward coastal areas, as a result of the slave trade. These states, which raided their region in search of slaves, whom they sold to European traders, included the Kongo kingdom (which had developed before the slave trade), Oyo in Nigeria, and Dahomey in Benin.

By the middle of the nineteenth century, right before colonization, there were still some well-established states across the continent. In the west, the Sokoto caliphate of Northern Nigeria ruled over a vast territory and had exchange networks with northern Africa as far as Egypt and the Middle East. In today's Ghana, the Ashanti (also spelled Asante) kingdom exercised authority over many people and managed to produce significant prosperity, to the point that Ivor Wilks (1975) noted the emergence of class politics in nineteenth-century Ashanti, and Basil Davidson (1992) suggested it was developing a bona fide bourgeoisie. When explorer Henry Morton Stanley "discovered" the Buganda kingdom in the 1870s, he was so impressed with its political organization and the peace and security it provided its subjects (Stanley 1988 [1878]) that he wrote back home that all it needed to equal Western civilization was Christianity (upon which the British sent missionaries, whom the Baganda promptly decapitated). And the southern part of the continent counted many more kingdoms, such as those of the Tswana (in today's Botswana and South Africa), the Barotse (in Zambia), the Swazi (in Swaziland [as of 2018, Eswatini] and South Africa), and the Zulu of South Africa, who waged numerous military conquests under the leadership of their king, Shaka, in the first decades of the nineteenth century before losing their war against the Boer settlers—the "Voortrekkers"—in 1838 (which led to the 1843 creation of the colony of Natal). In the east, the dominant political system was the Ethiopian state, which, by the time of the European colonial expansion, was under the authority of Emperor Menelik II. It was an ancient political system with traditions dating back some 2,000 years to the Aksum kingdom, anchored around the Amharic and Tigray peoples, who dominated and assimilated many other regional groups. It was the only sub-Saharan African state to have developed its own written language, facilitating political centralization and administration. Its armies were strong enough to defeat the Italians at the battle of Adowa in 1896, which spared Ethiopia the fate of colonization and brought about its recognition as a state by European powers (and membership in the League of Nations after 1919).

As organized and centralized as they were, most African states differed from Western states in some significant ways. First, apart from Ethiopia, they did not have any permanent impersonal administration, as they lacked written languages. Yet Wilks (1975) notes that Ashanti displayed significant bureaucratic development, while Larry Yarak (1990) shows that the Ashanti state had diplomatic services and relied on Arabic for some of their written correspondence. Usually, however, power was distributed along ritualized lines, and specific roles were recognized to specific individuals. Heredity was an important mode of reproduction of states and leadership. Second, patron-client relationship cemented the unity of these states and the loyalty of lesser chiefs to the ruler. In quasi-feudal fashion, local chiefs and subjects typically paid tribute to the ruler in exchange for his protection. Power was projected from the center to the periphery via multiple levels of clientage, and absolutism was common. At the periphery, local chiefs were more loosely connected to the center, and were able to exercise their authority with more autonomy. Third, as might have become clear already, political authority was exercised not so much over a territory than over people. With perhaps a few exceptions, such as the Sokoto caliphate and Borno in today's Nigeria, there were no fixed boundaries. As Kopytoff (1987) notes, political space within precolonial Africa was best conceived as a multilayered structure of concentric circles of diminishing control, radiating from the various cores. Power emanated outward from the center and diminished as distances increased. The king ruled over his subjects rather than over land. Fourth, as with nonstate societies, kinship and lineage also mattered in states. Many kingdoms were divided into clans and competing lines of succession. Yet lineage played a more secondary role as a principle of societal and political organization among the statelike societies than among the stateless ones. Finally, temporal and spiritual authority were closely connected. The European territorial state, which was exported to the region via colonization, with its bureaucratic ways, its spatial definitions, and its largely formal and impersonal rules, stood in sharp contrast to African experiences of statehood.

In addition to understanding precolonial modes of political organization, it behooves the student of Africa to fully appreciate the role of slavery and of the slave trade in precolonial Africa and its profound impact on the politics of the continent. It is important to grasp the extent to which relations among African polities were often characterized by warfare, conquest, and raiding. From the sixteenth century onward, this was in large part a result of the trans-Atlantic slave trade, which created formidable pressure for the acquisition and sale of slaves. Combining the trans-Saharan and the trans-Atlantic slave trades, probably some 14 million Africans were shipped out as slaves from the fifteenth to the eighteenth centuries.[1] Most likely, another few million were killed in the warfare that accompanied enslavement. In addition to the horrible consequences that slavery carried for its victims at the time, it had very negative long-term political and economic effects (Nunn 2008), to which we return later in this book, undermining the endogenous evolution of African political institutions and the demographic foundations for growth.

There is only so much we can cover of this history in a textbook on contemporary African politics. Yet it is worth bearing in mind that Africa was far from a political and institutional blank page at the outset of colonization. There were multiple and heterogeneous political formations across the continent. As the following sections will show, this diversity may help make sense of different colonial regimes and might even account for contemporary differences in governance. European-imported political practices encountered diverse terrains across the continent where principles of organization, notions of legitimacy, and technologies of power varied greatly, which resulted in different institutional arrangements and degrees of political cohesion. Although the contemporary African state is most obviously the child of colonialism, it has other legacies too, and African politics is best understood as of mixed parentage. From this perspective, some argue that acephalous societies had a harder time adjusting to colonialism than did their statelike counterparts (Geschiere 1991:30). Catherine Boone (2003b) even suggests that this liability has extended to postcolonial states, which have found it more difficult to strike a social bargain and project effective power over lineage societies than over regions with more established hierarchies. One can think of Somalia and wonder whether statelessness might have enduring features. Similarly, Stelios Michalopoulos and Elias Papaioan-nou (2013) find a positive association between the degree of precolonial centralization of Africa's ethnic groups and their contemporary level of development as proxied by satellite images of light density at night. Yet looking at the quality of contemporary governance at the country level, Pierre Englebert (2000a) finds that the more statelike the average level of precolonial systems in a current country, the weaker the quality of its contemporary governance. Maybe countries that harbor communities with stronger political identities, formed in the crucible of precolonial statehood, have greater difficulties engineering nation building?

The Colonial State

The Scramble

First and foremost, colonization was conquest. The late nineteenth cen-tury had not yet developed the norms of human equality and nonag-gression that seem more prevalent nowadays. Many in Europe consid-ered the white race superior and saw few objections in appropriating the land of others and looting their assets (nor did they have, until then, many qualms doing this to each other). For them, empire was good, if not an outright necessity.

Until the mid-1800s, however, European powers had been satisfied with controlling trading centers and ports along the African coast, which they began establishing two centuries earlier. There seemed to be no strong desire to subjugate Africa for its own sake. The continent was only useful for its outposts along the oceans, on the road to somewhere else, or for its trading places, as with the infamous triangular trade in which Euro-peans exported miscellaneous goods (such as textiles, arms, and con-sumer goods) to Africa, where they bought slaves whom they carried to the Americas to load up their ships with commodities (sugar, coffee, tobacco, etc.) to bring back home. Thus, by 1870, there was still no sig-nificant European territorial penetration in Africa, with the exception of South Africa. There, Dutch settlers—the Boers—had arrived as early as the 1650s, attracted by the fertile lands and more temperate climate. Else-where, only a few more or less fortified stations existed along the coast, some of which had already endured for several centuries. The Portuguese had settled many of these beachheads early on, at the peak of their mar-itime empire, and their strongholds marked an itinerary from Portugal to the Indian Ocean: Cape Verde, Guinea-Bissau, Cameroon, Angola, and

Mozambique. The French had been in four communes of Senegal (Dakar, Gorée, Saint-Louis, and Rufisque—all formally incorporated into France) since the seventeenth century and were beginning to push up the Senegal River. They also had a base in Gabon and controlled small islands in the Indian Ocean. The Spanish were in the Canary Islands, and in Annobòn and Fernando Po, two islands that would later form part of Equatorial Guinea. The British had personnel at the mouth of the Gambia River, in Sierra Leone, on the Gold Coast, on Lagos Island, in the Cape, and in parts of Natal colony, Lesotho, and Mauritius. The Ottoman Empire reached in a thin band down the coast of the Red Sea from Egypt to the southern tip of today's Eritrea. The Belgians, Germans (whose own nation-state was still being built by 1870), and Italians (who had also just unified as a country) had yet to set foot on the continent.

There are contending schools of thought as to why what happened next did happen, but all of a sudden, in what Crawford Young (1994a:83) labels "an extraordinary moment of imperial enthusiasm," European states began making sovereign claims over territories they had neglected or ignored for centuries, and Africa found itself almost entirely occupied and partitioned in a matter of two decades. A brief overview of this "scramble for Africa" is necessary to comprehend its current political geography.

It is most likely that a confluence of factors provoked the scramble. Writers in the Marxian tradition (Hobson 1902; Lenin 1999 [1916]) believe that European governments were the instruments of European capital accumulated during the industrial revolution, which, hampered by the limited purchasing power of European workers and in need of new markets, sought to expand into Africa. But there were other economic motivations too. There were rivalries between European trading posts and inland African states over control of the flow and taxation of goods, and the European trading houses and private entrepreneurs frequently demanded support from their states in the form of protection or annexation, which led to progressive territorial encroachments (Press 2015). Economic conditions were also shifting and undermined the principles of free trade that had underwritten the European presence until then. As mass markets expanded in Europe, plantations of palm or cotton in western Africa developed and resulted in a need for greater territorial control (Young 1994a:84–85).

Beyond economic motives, Africa provided the stage where an intensified round of European rivalries played out. The unification of Italy in the 1860s and of Germany in 1871 brought about new significant players at home and abroad, and they too, eager for parity, established outposts in Africa as of the early 1880s. Moreover, King Leopold II of the Belgians, feeling his ambitions constrained by his country's diminutive size, sought territories around the world and eventually settled on central Africa at around the same time, engaging via his envoy Henry Morton Stanley in massive treaty signings (some 450) with local rulers, often through the use of violence and coercion. All these European dynamics somehow projected onto the continent. A sense of rush, of preemptive colonization, emanated. It was compounded by the rise of nationalism in Europe and of a public opinion that demanded empires, fostered by a mentality of racial superiority and the certainty of scientific "progress" that authorized the conquest, if not eradication of, "lesser" species (Lindqvist 1996).

Young European officers, traders, missionaries, and other adventurers were let loose. They mounted expeditions up rivers, through forests, and across deserts, collecting territory for their countries and glory for themselves in this age of "exploration." In practice, there were some military confrontations, such as the defeat of Samory Touré by the French in the Fouta Djallon region of Guinea, or the crushing of the Sokoto caliphate and the defeat of Ashanti by the British in Northern Nigeria and Ghana. Ironically, centralized states might have been easier to defeat because one decisive battle could lead to capitulation (as happened with the battle of Omdurman in 1898, through which Lord Kitchener established British control over Sudan), whereas stateless peoples had to be defeated repeatedly (e.g., Nigeria's Igbo and Senegal's Joola).[2] More often, however, the colonizing troops made progress by seeking alliances in local inter-African conflicts and pressuring local rulers to relinquish their sovereignty in exchange for military assistance against their rivals. In most cases, the display of superior force was sufficient and the process did not involve warfare. Treaties were signed with rulers who might have had no choice, might have seen some benefits in these treaties for their own local political position (Bayart 2000), or might not have fully understood the scope of what was unfolding. At any rate, however violent it was, colonization was also legalistic. To convince each other of their claims, Europeans had to produce treaties with locals as evidence of their territorial advances.

As the scramble provoked tensions among Europeans, they held a conference in Berlin in 1884–1885 to agree upon common rules of colonization. Contrary to frequent characterizations of conference delegates drawing lines across the African map, colonial powers did not literally carve up the continent among themselves in Berlin. Yet the conference adopted several principles that contributed to the subsequent partition of the continent. It recognized Leopold II's claim over the Independent State of Congo (deemed to be the king's private property; in effect he ruled over two states, Belgium and Congo, although he never set foot in the latter), affirmed the principles of free trade and navigation along the Congo and Niger Rivers, and provided for freedom of missionary work (Hochschild 1999). Most important, however, the conference established the principle of effective occupation (Crowe 1942). For a colonial claim to be recognized, it had to be based on a treaty signed with local authorities and on an effective, albeit basic, administrative presence (such as a police station). This principle favored an acceleration of the scramble as the colonizers sought to support their claims through some physical presence. It also produced a pattern of occupation that privileged peripheral border areas, where the territorial claims of others were confronted, while leaving unmanaged space within.

Thomas Packenham (1992) has written a sweeping and compelling account of the colonial scramble for Africa, largely from the perspective of the colonizers, and readers should refer to it for more details on this issue and its multiple dynamics. For our purpose, suffice it to say that by 1910, most of the entire continent had been claimed by European powers. The French held vast swaths of western and central Africa, and the British held equally large amounts of eastern and southern Africa, with additional significant possessions in the west such as the Gold Coast (Ghana) and the colonies that would become Nigeria. The Portuguese had Cape Verde, Guinea-Bissau, São Tomé and Príncipe, Angola, and Mozambique; the Spanish had Western Sahara and Equatorial Guinea; the Belgians had Congo; the Italians had Somalia and Eritrea; and the Germans had Togoland, Kamerun, South West Africa (future Namibia), Tanganyika, and Ruanda-Urundi. Aside from the partition of the French colonial empires into smaller units, the map of Africa as of 1910 (see Figure 2.1) looks remarkably similar to that of a century later, and nothing at all like the one from three decades earlier.

For the student of contemporary African politics, the remarkable brevity of the colonial conquest should be borne in mind. Endowed with technological and material superiority, the Europeans took a mere few years to co-opt, coerce, bring down, or destroy African political systems, some of which had endured for centuries. Hence, colonial conquest represented a dramatic exogenous shock to Africans, a forceful reorientation of their politics away from their own institutions and toward those established by Europeans. These European colonial institutions were, however, surprisingly shallow. This is not to say that colonization was not deeply transformative; interruptive of local political, social, and economic processes; and highly destructive of assets, lives, and lifestyles. But it is to recognize that the colonial reengineering of African politics was hap-

Figure 2.1 Colonial Status of Current African States, 1910

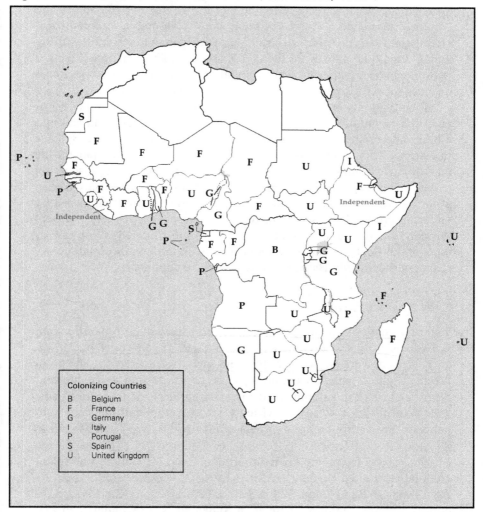

hazard and superficial. New colonial states were created and recognized based on largely bogus treaties and a handful of police administrators. Fearful of the expense, colonial offices were rather reluctant and lacked a master plan. Anthony Kirk-Greene (1980:38, citing data from Michael Crowder) notes that, as of 1904, no more than 135 whites were employed in colonial service in British East Africa; as late as the 1930s, the ratio of colonial administrators to local population was

1 to 54,000 in Nigeria, 1 to 35,000 in Congo, and 1 to 27,000 in French West Africa. Mutual recognition among the colonizers guaranteed the colonies' existence, but most of them were weak and lacked empirical effectiveness. In fact, the construction of African colonies on the cheap would remain a hallmark of the colonial consolidation period. Together with the enduring appeal of precolonial identities, it had lasting consequences for African postcolonial state formation.

Finally, it is worth thinking briefly of the frequent claim that European colonization "Balkanized" Africa, that it divided the continent into a multitude of small, unsustainable states in the manner of the Balkans in Europe. This claim is often brought about by those who lament the lack of African unity (Nkrumah 1970). Yet as the preceding discussion makes clear, this is not an empirically valid argument; it is only true in a normative way, in the sense of an aspiration to unity hampered by enduring colonial divisions. In reality, there never was any political African unity, and colonization actually consolidated a myriad of diverse political systems into some fifty territorial states, dramatically reducing the already Balkanized nature of the continent.

Early Colonial Rule

The first years of colonial rule were mostly dedicated to pacification. Police and military outposts were established, revolts were put down, and Africans were shown who the new rulers were. Rapidly, the colonizers sought to make the colonies pay, to turn them into profitable ventures. The early development of infrastructure, particularly railroads, followed this logic. Many of Africa's contemporary rail lines are remnants of these early colonial projects, such as the train from Matadi to Kinshasa in the Democratic Republic of Congo (DRC) (where the use of dynamite to overcome difficult terrain earned the Belgians and their colonial state the nickname "crushers of rock"—*bula matari*),[3] the train from Dakar to Saint-Louis in Senegal, or the train from Khartoum to the cotton-growing region of Sannar in Sudan. It is no wonder then that many of Africa's railroads to this day remain outward-looking and export-oriented in their design, more likely to bring extracted commodities to the oceans than to link Africans with each other.

Although there were some limited European investments (commercially and governmentally financed), what is particularly stunning in retrospect is the rapidity with which Africans were exploited, and the extent to which this exploitation entailed a dramatic transformation of existing economic structures, one massively disadvantageous to Africans. Colonization, from the outset, translated into forceful extraction. It is facile irony but it bears telling: while the colonizers often invoked a struggle against slavery as justification to invade the continent, the economic regime they installed in the first phase of colonial empire ultimately represented a broadening of enslavement for Africans.

Extraction took many forms. Taxation was possibly the most common, basic, and destructive of past livelihoods. Following the iron rule of self-financing, the colonies raised their funds from the colonized. Almost everywhere, the head tax (which had the benefit of not requiring the sophisticated trappings of nation building, such as cadastral surveys) was rapidly introduced, and with it the cash economy. Africans, required to pay the head tax in cash, were forced to seek employment in colonial projects and to abandon their subsistence crops for commercial ones. In some instances, such as the Wolof Basin in Senegal, local elites and their followers did rather well in the switch to cash crops, peanuts in this case (Cooper 2002:23). In most instances, however, the introduction of cotton, tea, cocoa, or other cash crops spelled increased economic vulnerability for African peasants, a situation yet unresolved today. Many had to abandon agricultural activities altogether and migrate at least seasonally to mining areas, where they became wage laborers.

Africans were also taxed in their bodies. Given the lack of road infrastructure in the first decades of colonial rule, the most basic transportation needs were problematic for the colonizers. On rare occasions, there were river connections (but even then, ships had to be assembled), but hardly any roads, trains, and trucks to rely on. To bring documents, supplies, furniture, and other material necessities to their outposts, Africans were forcefully converted into beasts of burden. Porterage was widely practiced by all colonial powers: chiefs were instructed to round up young men in villages, who were then forced to carry loads for the colonial administration, in chains if need be. It was only one facet of generalized forced labor. Men and women had to give of their time and strength (and, on occasion, their lives) to build roads, dig canals, clear brush, and fulfill other duties for their new rulers. Colonialism took place upon an existing background of inequality and, in cases such as forced labor, reinforced it. Summoned to labor for the colony, the more affluent Africans sent their own slaves to do the job when possible, reproducing with colonial complicity their own system of domination (Young 1994a:137).

Finally, in several instances, colonial extraction amounted simply to theft. Mostly in colonies of European settlement, such as Kenya, South Africa, or Southern Rhodesia (later Zimbabwe), but to some extent everywhere, Europeans appropriated the most fertile land. They set up farms and ranches, and established state-owned or commercial plantations. In many cases, forced labor helped make those endeavors profitable.

Altogether, colonization amounted to a dramatic and forceful transformation of African economic relations and landscape. It was largely based on coercion and undermined subsistence. Colonization forcefully incorporated Africa into the emerging global economic system, and did so by placing the colonies in unequal and subservient positions. African economies were restructured away from self-sufficiency to serving European needs and tastes, creating structural volatility and vulnerability, with control over these processes almost exclusively in the hands of the colonizers. While the colonial state would later justify itself as developmental (as discussed later), it was first and foremost extractive and impoverishing (e.g., see Watts 1983).

Socially, the advent of colonialism initiated a significant change in sub-Saharan gender roles. Whereas established African cultural practices tended to allow women to participate publicly in society, the advent of European interventions greatly curtailed women's status across the continent. During colonization, women's legal status, especially regarding property ownership and inheritance, fluctuated greatly. On the one hand, inheritance rights for widows and children established by the European rulers, grounded in assumptions of Christian monogamy, tended to be more favorable for women than they had been under traditional regimes. On the other hand, colonial systems further entrenched male dominance within marriages and before the law. English common law, for example, treated women as dependents who had no proprietary capacity. As Europeans appropriated arable land for colonial plantations, such as in the Kikuyu region of Kenya, and men migrated to urban centers, the wives who were left behind found it difficult to secure land for subsistence farming. The disenfranchisement of African women in the colonial political economy was largely driven by the gendered assumption of male European colonial agents that men played the primary economic and political roles. This was quite ironic given the primacy of farming in most parts of Africa, and the fact that this activity is often regarded as women's sphere of work. Yet women were generally unable to capitalize either economically or politically on their involvement in this economic sphere, largely due to traditional and colonial gender constraints. As Gwendolyn Mikell (1997:21) notes, "colonial regimes were able to achieve their aims only by using, building upon, and further distorting the gender hierarchy already present in African culture."

Politically, there were some variations across colonizers in the institutions and systems of rule they set up, but these should not be overstated. To some extent, whatever difference existed was a function of the colonizers' purposes, and these could change from place to place for a given colonizer. Whether a colony was designed for settlement by Europeans (as in Kenya) or for pure resource extraction (as in Congo) resulted in different institutional setups. Daron Acemoglu, Simon Johnson, and James Robinson (2001) have argued that, under pressure from the settlers, who wanted to reproduce conditions from home, colonies of European settlement developed better property rights and subsequently better governance than did their more extractive counterparts. Acemoglu and his colleagues also argue that the original designation of a colony as one of extraction or of settlement depended on the degree of settler mortality (see Mahoney 2010 for a cogent critique).

Much is often made of the question of direct versus indirect rule in the colonization of Africa. British colonization is associated with the notion of "indirect rule," designed in 1919 by Lord Lugard, then governor-general of Nigeria. Indirect rule involved capitalizing on the existence of local authorities as relays of colonial rule. Local chiefs were not to be deposed and replaced with external administrators. Instead, they were to retain their authority over their subjects in exchange for loyalty toward the British. They were to exercise their local rule to the benefit of the British, collecting taxes and enforcing colonial policies. But they were to do so while largely maintaining their own legal, institutional, and political order. As a result, "an array of African chiefs were recognized and vested with the authority of the colonial state," as Crawford Young (1994a:107) puts it. This system had several consequences. First, it tended to promote the rise of customary rulers in modern politics. Northern Nigeria was the archetype of indirect rule, with the Hausa-Fulani ruling elite continuing to exercise its local domination throughout colonization. When Nigeria became independent, the prime minister of its northern region was Ahmadu Bello, the sarduna (a position close to caliph) of Sokoto (Sklar 1963; Vaughan 2000). Buganda, in Uganda, provides another example. The British signed the Buganda Agreement of 1900 with the Kabaka (king of Buganda), whereby most of the kingdom's prerogatives over its citizens were recognized (and new ones, over land, were given). The agreement also granted Buganda some territories that it had hitherto contested with other neighboring kingdoms. Not surprisingly, when the independence of Uganda came about, the Kabaka wanted to be president and refused to see national laws and institutions applied to his kingdom (Apter 1967; Oloka-Onyango 1997). Thus it is somewhat more frequent to see so-called traditional authorities play a prominent role in contemporary politics in former British colonies than elsewhere.

By empowering a multitude of chiefs with colonially derived authority, indirect rule also created what Mahmood Mamdani (1996) has called "decentralized despotism." To some extent, the source of power of these local authorities was in part displaced outside the community they ruled, with the consequence that it undermined existing modes of accountability. Thus, local chiefs became more despotic. In addition, in the many areas where there had not been any centralized authority, indirect rule promoted the rise of new chiefs whose authority was not embedded in local societies. Instead of preserving indigenous modes of rule, indirect administration ended up as a multiplier of colonial domination. Mamdani stresses how this situation led to a "bifurcated" notion of statehood. In the cities, "civil society" prevailed, with colonial laws centered on the expatriate colonial community. In the villages, native law dominated. This distinction, Mamdani argues, was reproduced in postcolonial times, with the consequence that the authority structure in rural areas tends to be resistant to reforms of the state.

Finally, and largely related, indirect rule is in part associated with the existence of legal pluralism in Africa, although such pluralism is not unique to British colonies. African states tend to harbor multiple and overlapping legal systems. There is the formal law of the state, which is usually inherited from the metropolitan legal system. Then there is customary law, which tends to have multiple incarnations across the territory. Some problems are typically referred to customary courts (e.g., land disputes, marriage problems, and witchcraft); others are referred to formal courts. Often, cases heard in customary courts can be appealed in formal courts. Sometimes, Africans can benefit from this pluralism by trying the different avenues of legal recourse. Legal pluralism has taken on extreme dimensions in Nigeria, where thirteen northern states adopted sharia as their own law in 2000 in violation of the national constitution. In Sierra Leone, the rise of conflict in the 1990s has been linked to frustration at the resilience of customary legal arrangements by which established elders obtain the servitude of young men accused of having sex with some of their many wives (Mokuwa et al. 2011).

In contrast to the British, the French are said to have practiced direct rule. They partitioned their African colonial empire into two large structures: Afrique Occidentale Française (AOF) and Afrique Equatoriale Française (AEF). Each had a governor-general. Within each the French created distinct administrative territories with governors. Each of these provinces was in turn divided into *cercles,* the main local instrument of colonial rule, which were run by French *commandants de cercle,* who exercised authority over French chiefs of subdivisions. Yet this should not be understood as implying that Africans did not participate in colonial rule in French colonies. With all of AOF counting no more than 300–400 French administrators between the two world wars, co-opting Africans was a matter of sheer necessity. Thus the French too appointed Africans as local agents. The last two levels of administration—cantons and villages—were administered by Africans. The main differences with the British, however, were that these people were not appointed as a function of their customary authority. They could be commoners or even come from different regions of the country, and they were more likely to apply French colonial laws and directives than to apply local customs. They were direct agents of the French colonial state, which operated under a principle of legal unity. Yet in practice it was often expedient not to try to control all facets of life and to delegate some issues to customary law, with the consequence that here too legal pluralism arose. By and large, with respect to administration, the Belgian, Italian, and Portuguese colonial systems were more similar to the French than to the British system.

Everywhere the colonizers had to rely on local African agents, but the distinction between direct and indirect rule is occasionally exaggerated. Does the difference matter, however, in terms of predicting subsequent political evolution? It is hard to say with certainty, since indirect rule cut both ways. On the one hand, it might have had beneficial effects by preserving (while transforming) preexisting forms of rule. On the other, it probably compounded the problem of postcolonial national integration, since it usually subsumed these traditional systems into larger diverse territories. It is hard not to relate the contemporary polarization of Northern Nigeria to its colonial status. Similarly, Buganda proved to be the thorn in the side of Ugandan national integration and directly contributed to the breakdown of Uganda's political system in 1967. Matthew Lange (2004) has shown that the proportion of former British colonies that were under indirect rule as of 1955 negatively and significantly correlates with several contemporary indicators of governance quality as well as with political stability.

Aside from the transfer of power by the British to the white minority in South Africa in 1910, the main event of this first period of colonization probably was World War I, from 1914 to 1918. Although it was largely confined to Western Europe, it involved African colonies in at least two ways. First, particularly in AOF, a large number of Africans (some 135,000) were forcibly recruited to fight in Europe. They became known as the *tirailleurs sénégalais,* from the name of an early African military colonial contingent, although by then they were no longer exclusively Senegalese (Echenberg 1991). They made a significant contribution to the war effort and often returned home both ideologically transformed and more inclined toward reformist activism. In addition, the recruitment efforts often led to riots that shook the still-young colonial structures. Thus, World War I was associated with more unsettled politics in the colonies.

Part of the struggle between Great Britain, France, and Belgium on the one hand, and Germany on the other, also took place in the colonies. More than 60,000 *tirailleurs* fought in Africa. There was significant fighting in Cameroon and Tanganyika, for example. In the end, Germany's defeat resulted in a colonial reshuffle, largely akin to a sharing of the spoils, as its colonies were distributed among the victors. Belgium acquired Ruanda-Urundi; France most of Togoland and the majority of Kamerun; and the United Kingdom the remainder of Togoland, the part of Kamerun that borders Nigeria, South West Africa (future Namibia), and Tanganyika (see Figure 2.2). Technically, the German colonies became "mandates" of the newly established League of Nations. They were to be managed on behalf of the League for the welfare of local populations. In practice, however, they were assimilated into colonies and often were physically merged with them. The Belgians annexed Ruanda-Urundi to Congo, and the British administered Tanganyika with Zanzibar (later to become Tanzania), Western Togoland with Ghana, and Western Cameroon with Nigeria. In a move that would prove highly harmful to local populations and delay their independence by more than thirty years, the British transferred effective management of the South West African mandate to white-ruled South Africa, which later subsumed it under its apartheid system.

Late Colonial Rule and Decolonization

While the interwar years were largely characterized by increased extraction and the further institutionalization of colonial rule, the post–World War II period, from 1945 to 1960, was characterized by decolonization. However, although it can be argued that African decolonization symbolized the success of African nationalism and represented the outcome of liberation struggles, not everyone finds the historical significance of decolonization so compelling. Independence did not represent as massive a transformation of African politics as colonization did. Although it spelled emancipation from rule by Europeans, in many ways it also embraced and reproduced the colonial project. It is indeed essential to

Figure 2.2 Colonial Status of Current African States After 1945

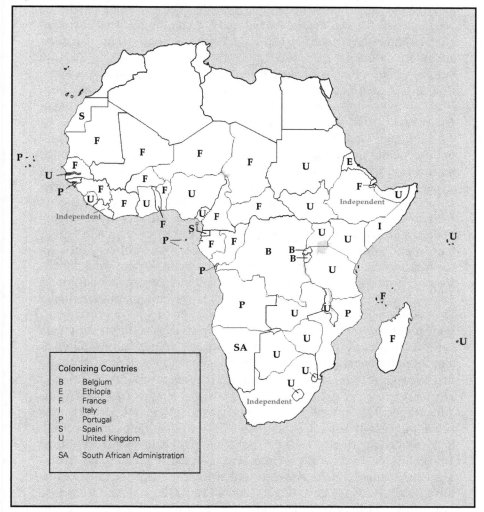

Colonizing Countries

B	Belgium
E	Ethiopia
F	France
I	Italy
P	Portugal
S	Spain
U	United Kingdom
SA	South African Administration

understand the extent to which decolonization made a choice for the postcolonial state and sidestepped once and for all the alternative paths of political evolution. With it, African history changed course forever.

World War II would prove to have a greater impact than World War I on the European colonies in Africa. While Belgium was largely occupied during both wars, France only fell to the Germans in the second war, and rather rapidly so. It had to be liberated, and it subsequently glorified its own resistance to the invader. Although Great Britain avoided the same fate, it nevertheless needed US assistance to win the war. Thus, as the war neared its end in 1944 and the spirit of liberation and resistance pervaded the Allies, a contradiction spread over their subjugated colonies (particularly vivaciously experienced by African veterans). For what distinguished Belgian, French, and British occupation of Africa from the German occupation of many European countries?[4] Why was resistance exalted when applied against German occupation but vilified against French colonialism?

Although the colonizers avoided facing these contradictions head-on, they could not altogether escape confronting them. Right from the termination of World War II, the late colonial period was marked by dynamics of decolonization, which fed on these contradictions. Before France itself was liberated, Charles de Gaulle organized a conference in Brazzaville in 1944 to reform the colonies, which had served as the main platform of his resistance and reconquest effort after mainland France had fallen to the Germans (Yacono 1991). There was still very little for the Africans themselves in this conference, as none of them were invited. Instead, it mostly offered reforms to the colonial governors and French populations. Nevertheless, it opened a path toward reform in the colonies by establishing local assemblies, giving the right to vote in French elections to citizens of colonies (but citizenship itself was tightly rationed), calling for a less exploitative relation between France and its colonies, and formally ending forced labor in the colonies. The British similarly had to make some concessions, although they were still in a position of greater relative strength vis-à-vis their colonial empire than the French. Already in 1941, in what became known as the Atlantic Charter, British prime minister Winston Churchill and US president Franklin Roosevelt had included the right to self-determination of all peoples as part of their envisioned postwar world architecture. Later that decade, the British extended voting rights to Africans in their colonial legislative and executive councils, which gave them a taste of self-rule, albeit under British governors. These reforms led to the rise of a new class of politicians, practicing governance under British watch. Several of them, including Kwame Nkrumah of Ghana (Gold Coast), Jomo Kenyatta of Kenya, Hastings Banda of Malawi (Nyasaland), and Obafemi Awolowo of Nigeria, would gather in Manchester in 1945 for a Pan-African conference that called for additional reforms in the colonies and helped spread ideas of emancipation and decolonization.

At the same time, the United Nations, which was established in 1945, became a sounding board for anticolonial ideas and de-legitimized colonial holdings. Chapter 11 of its Charter, titled "Declaration Regarding Non-Self-Governing Territories," considered self-government the outcome of colonial rule. It also converted the "mandates" of the League of Nations into "trusteeships" whose stated purpose was "to promote the political, economic, social, and educational advancement of the inhabitants of the trust territories, and their progressive development toward self-government or independence." Of course, it was not considered politically feasible for colonizers to recognize these rights to their trust territories without also extending these rights to their regular colonies. Moreover, Article 1 of the UN Charter recognized the "principle of equal rights and self-determination of peoples." Although this is a dimension of international law that has remained plagued to this day with doctrinal disagreements and implementation contradictions, it provided ammunition for those who wanted to escape the colonial yoke.

The post-1945 period was thus characterized by multiple reforms, mostly in English and French Africa, toward the self-government and self-determination of the colonies. However, the idea of independence was not initially part of these reforms. For the British, self-government did not necessarily imply independence. The French for their part did not speak of it until the late 1950s and tried instead to integrate African elites into structures of shared governance. African elites themselves were more often preoccupied with reaching rights equal to those of the colonizers than with outright independence from the colonizers.

In the British colonies, reforms of self-governance proceeded at a rapid pace, pushed in part by the momentum of India's independence in 1947. Their legislative and executive councils were meant to promote African governance and train a generation of politicians, progressively empowering local elites. Interestingly, in view of Great Britain's long dedication to indirect rule, these local assemblies and governments largely sealed the fate of chiefs. As these new institutions developed, they further crystallized the colony as the container of postcolonial politics and contributed to the marginalization of native authorities. Their adoption represented, to some extent, a departure from the previous colonial experiment with self-government that indirect rule had embodied. Largely unaddressed at the time were the implications of this reversal on national integration, particularly in the multiethnic colonies where indirect rule had thrived. Kwame Nkrumah of Ghana limited the Ashanti and other chiefly influences with relative ease (Rathbone 2000). But in Nigeria and Sudan, the question of national unity has dominated politics since independence.

Once begun, British decolonization generally proceeded at a fast pace. Sudan became independent in 1956, and Ghana in 1957, ahead of the big continental wave of 1960 that saw seventeen African countries accede to international sovereignty. Yet things were more complicated and protracted in those British colonies that had large numbers of European settlers. In Kenya, where many whites occupied farms in the Kikuyu plateau, the Mau Mau peasant uprising lasted from 1952 to 1960 and contributed to the deferring of independence until 1962 (Branch 2009; Anderson 2005; Throup 1987). That was nothing, however, compared to what happened in Southern Rhodesia, where many powerful white settlers rejected all ideas of black self-rule. As it became harder and harder to deny self-government to Africans, the white minority government of Ian Smith declared its own unilateral independence in 1965 and embarked upon apartheid-like policies, provoking an African armed insurgency that ended with the eventual victory of the Zimbabwe African National Union (ZANU) and the independence of the country as Zimbabwe in 1980.[5]

The French contrasted with the British in the degree to which they hoped to assimilate their colonial subjects into French culture and political life. Until the mid-1950s, the idea of turning Africans into Frenchmen and Frenchwomen remained at the heart of France's Africa policy. Although the 1944 Brazzaville conference was more intent on renewing France's power after World War II than on granting Africans any kind of voice, the constitutional revision of 1946, which brought about the Fourth Republic in France, created the French Union and provided for some degree of political representation of Africans in an assembly composed half of representatives from metropolitan France and half of representatives from the colonies and overseas territories.[6] This is how some African politicians who would later become presidents of their countries, such as Félix Houphouët-Boigny of Côte d'Ivoire, Ahmed Sékou Touré of Guinea, Léopold Senghor of Senegal, and Modibo Keita of Mali, began their political careers, as members of parliament in France, with some of them even serving as ministers in the French government. The ideas of the French Union, embedded in the 1946 constitution ("France forms, with overseas peoples, a union based on equality of rights and obligations, without distinction of race or religion"), embodied the spirit of assimilation.

Assimilation harbored, however, a massive contradiction: there were more colonial subjects than French citizens, and this could only be managed through unequal representation if the French were to remain in control. As franchise was progressively extended for Africans, the parity of representation in Paris became less and less tenable. The reality was that France could not assimilate its colonies. Demographically, if France were to continue on this path, it would be assimilated by its colonies. This realization led to a retrenchment of the assimilationist agenda and its replacement with the policy of association. In 1956, the Loi-Cadre created territorial assemblies, akin to the British model, and France began encouraging African politicians to pursue their careers at home. Then, in 1958, de Gaulle, who had returned to politics the year before,[7] engineered a new constitution for a Fifth Republic. In domestic French politics this constitution meant to strengthen presidential powers and avoid the governmental instability that had plagued the Fourth Republic. From the perspective of relations with the colonies, it provided for France to recover its own parliament and for the colonies to get theirs, while a "French Community," with its own assembly, would be established for common business, an arrangement that displaced assimilation to a new, largely benign sphere. The new constitution was put up to a referendum in France and in the colonies. The French and all African colonies voted yes, except for Guinea, where Sékou Touré, more radical than his peers, had campaigned for a no vote. A miffed de Gaulle then offered Guinea immediate independence and pulled out all French civil servants.

The French Community was not to last, however. France became mired in the Algerian war in the late 1950s and de Gaulle decided that his country would be better off facilitating a peaceful transition of its African colonies to independence while keeping close influence and control over them. The breakup of AEF and AOF into twelve colonies, put in motion by the Loi-Cadre in 1956 and reinforced in 1958, guaranteed that francophone countries would remain weak and dependent on France. Several African leaders had to be encouraged to agree to independence. Nevertheless, for the majority of them, 1960 witnessed a peaceful transition to sovereignty, marked by the conclusion of "cooperation agreements" with France that maintained Paris's influence.

Djibouti, however, was an exception among the French colonies. A small and strategically placed territory in the Horn composed of Somalis (the Issa) and Ethiopians (the Afar), it voted yes in the 1958 referendum, although a strong minority (mostly Issa) voted no. The French government subsequently tilted the political system in favor of the Afar and retained colonial control in alliance with this group past 1960. Increasing demands for independence led to violent demonstrations during a visit by de Gaulle in 1966, but a 1967 referendum (which today would not be considered free and fair) confirmed the territory's French status. To undermine irredentist Somali views, the French altered the colony's name in 1967 from "French Somali Coast" to "Territory of the Afar and Issa." Continued political agitation for independence led to yet another referendum in 1977, in which more than 98 percent of voters approved independence (Bourges and Wauthier 1979:320–332).

Aside from Djibouti, Cameroon and Madagascar were the only sub-Saharan French colonies where violence accompanied decolonization. In Cameroon, the Union des Populations du Cameroun (UPC), a mainly Bamiléké and Bassa movement led by Ruben Um Nyobe, launched an armed insurrection in 1955 after its peaceful demands for a revision of the trusteeship system and for a reunification of anglophone and francophone Cameroon were rejected by the French. Although Nyobe was killed in 1958, the insurrection survived until 1970, well after Cameroon acquired its independence (Le Vine 1964; Joseph 1977; Deltombe, Domergue, and Tatsitsa 2011). In Madagascar, an anticolonial insurrection took place as early as 1947 and was forcefully repressed by the French, leaving between 10,000 and 90,000 casualties (Tronchon 1986).

Elsewhere on the continent, decolonization was either extremely abrupt or nonexistent. Until the late 1950s, the Belgians did not imagine the independence of Congo taking place for another three decades, if at all. The violent repression of demonstrations for political rights in Kinshasa (then Léopoldville) in 1958, however, led them to abruptly reconsider their position and to rush into a poorly planned transition to independence. Political parties were authorized and mostly took on ethnic dimensions. At that point, there were fewer than two dozen Congolese with college degrees out of a population of over 15 million. A few Congolese elites were invited to Brussels to help draft a constitution, with the understanding that the Belgians would remain involved in much of the country's administration and military after formal independence. Elections were held in May 1960, which saw the Mouvement National Congolais (MNC) of Patrice Lumumba emerge as the dominant party. Yet the Belgians connived to undermine Lumumba. A few days after independence, on 30 June 1960, the Congolese military mutinied and the province of Katanga, whose leader, Moïse Tshombe, had been kept away from the national government, declared its secession. Lumumba was captured and murdered, seemingly with the complicity of Belgium and the United States. The country collapsed into several conflicts that endured in one form or another until 1967 (Young 1965; Weiss 1967; Verhaegen 1966, 1969).

In Spanish Guinea and Sahara, and in the five Portuguese colonies, in contrast, time appeared to stand still. Spain and Portugal, with their dictatorial regimes friendly to Hitler's Germany, had stood mostly on the sidelines as World War II unfolded, and avoided the turmoil for reform that followed. The Portuguese government considered its colonies to be an intrinsic part of Portugal, mere overseas provinces, and favored a policy of migration and settlement. Arguing that it did not have colonies, it refused to decolonize (Bender 1978). As a result, African insurgencies developed in its colonies, first in Guinea-Bissau, and later in Angola and Mozambique (Azevedo 1991; Chaliand 1969; Marcum 1978). The Portuguese colonies became independent after the dictatorship was overthrown in the 1974 "Carnation Revolution," but conflict endured, this time among different domestic factions, in Angola and Mozambique. Spanish Guinea similarly acceded to sovereignty after the death of General Franco in 1975. Things turned more complicated in Spanish (Western) Sahara, over which sovereignty was claimed by Mauritania and Morocco. Both countries invaded it after Spain abandoned it in November 1975. In 1979, Mauritania pulled out and relinquished its claim. To this day, Morocco has continued to occupy large segments of the country and to claim it as Moroccan. A United Nations–planned referendum on independence has been postponed many times (Jensen 2004).

Although elements external to African dynamics were essential, decolonization was far from merely a European affair. After World War II, an increasing number of Africans began to mobilize for emancipation, and generated the first wave of African nationalism. This movement found its origins in a diversity of forms of mobilization, including ethnic associations and religious groups, but its main manifestation after World War II became the political party, particularly "congress" or "convention" types of mass parties in anglophone countries. Run by educated and urbanized leaders, few of these parties wanted independence at first (Buijtenhuis 1991:48), focusing their demands instead on justice and improvements in the lives of Africans. For although development was on the agenda of colonizers in this period, colonialism still treated Africans with great abuse, discrimination, and violence, as powerfully told in the works of Frantz Fanon (1963). Yet the agenda of African parties turned increasingly nationalistic in the years that followed the war (Rotberg 1962). The small, educated minorities that provided their leadership preached development, capitalized on the tensions among ethnic groups to rise as credible nationwide leaders, and called for an "African renaissance" and renewed pride in being African (Coleman 1954:409; see also Hodgkin 1956; Curtin 1966). Kwame Nkrumah's Convention People's Party (CCP) provides a typical example.

The paradoxical feature of this nationalism is that it ended up embracing the colonial state. While resistance to colonialism until World War II had taken the form of specific actions by subnational groups, the newly emerging African political elites laid claim to the colonially created state itself. Of course, there was a significant current of thought that called for the independence of all of Africa as a unified entity. This promotion of Pan-Africanism, however, was more dominant among the African diaspora and certain intellectuals than among the new political elites (Legum 1976; Abdul-Raheem 1996). Even when it was embraced by the latter, as with Kwame Nkrumah (Nkrumah 1970), it was in effect rather shallow, as the siren song of individual sovereignty proved irresistible. In the end, anticolonial activism often was the product of the *évolués,* the new African elites formed by the colonizers whose legitimacy resided within colonial institutions. They often did not hail from chiefly families or did not feel threatened by the residual power of some subnational groups. As Crawford Young (1994a:199) suggests, "the realization took root" among African nationalists and European colonizers in the late colonial period that chiefs "could not provide the leadership for a territorial state." Thus, promoting the post-colony as the nation was politically expedient and served in part to undermine competing sources of power. It is true that, all around the world, nationalism often imagines the nation around which it seeks to mobilize (Anderson 1983). But the imagination of the future nation by African nationalists was a step further than most.

To a large extent, what the new African nationalists wanted was to replace the colonizers. Of course, there were demands for freedom, dreams of liberty, and calls for equality. But ultimately, decolonization was a transfer of power within an enduring institutional arrangement. It modified the relationship between the colony and the colonial power, but it did not destroy the colonial project per se. As Yves Bénot (1969:82) noted, independence was often understood more as a juridical transformation, through which the legal relationship between the metropole and the colonies would be altered to the benefit of African elites, than as a "radical break in this relationship."

Before concluding our discussion of decolonization, it is worth mentioning the rise and role of the notion of development in the later colonial period. Remember that colonization was at first mere exploitation and domination. Yet by the 1950s its continuation was often legitimated by notions of improvement in the lives and welfare of Africans, notions of progress and, in short, of "development." The concept of development was first enunciated in 1922 in British colonies with Lord Lugard's idea of "dual mandates": the British are in Africa not only for their own benefit but also for that of local populations. The French articulated a similar discourse around the time with the idea of *mise en valeur* (improvement) of their colonies: exploitation in a manner that creates value rather than merely extracting it. In retrospect, these are early notions of development and they were used, as is still often the case with the development discourse, as legitimation of the state. By the 1950s, such notions were the staple of colonial rule. Africans were being sent to school in larger numbers, roads and other infrastructure were being built, markets were made, and the colonizers claimed to favor the development of local populations, a claim that was successfully internalized by many Africans and that still is frequently encountered in Africa. Development became the official raison d'être of the colonial state, as it would be for independent states, despite the subsequent relative failure of the state as an agent of development (see Chapter 6).

If colonization was Africa's major transformation, independence was less momentous. It allowed for the reproduction of colonial states, now postcolonial. Essentially, it closed the colonial parentheses by replacing European rulers with African ones. From this perspective, independence can be thought of as a colonial achievement as much as an African one. The natives achieved self-rule, but within the confines of the enduring colonial state. Yes the colonizers were leaving. But in more ways than one, their political project has endured.[8]

Postcolonial States

Whether the colonial origins of African states represent a liability, an asset, or nothing of significance is an important debate among Africanists. Whether these states have remained exogenous to their own societies or have been adopted, adapted, embedded, or otherwise Africanized—and, if so, at what cost—lies at the core of understanding African politics. Similarly, the relationship between African states and their colonially inspired territories, the presumed arbitrariness of their borders, should give us pause. All these questions matter to the extent that they might illuminate some of the roots of the problems experienced by modern states in Africa, such as their difficulties in nation building, their weak capacity, or their relative propensity for internal conflict. To place the discussion in a comparative setting, we begin with a brief survey of ways to think about states and their characteristics. Then we assess how the African experience relates to these ideas. We must be careful, however, not to set up an idealized state and then find the African state wanting in comparison. We need to realize that the African state has its own specificities and its own ways of doing politics.

What Is a State?

The state is both a basic unit and a paramount outcome of politics. There are over 200 states in the world. Sub-Saharan Africa, home to forty-nine of this total, has provided fertile ground for statehood (it has about 12 percent of the world's population but some 25 percent of its states). There are essentially three ways to think about states. We can ask what makes a state, what are its components, and what differentiates it from other public forms of social and political organization. Then we can think of what it is supposed to do, how it is expected to perform. Finally, we can ask how such an institution arises.

Worn as it is, Max Weber's definition of the state as a "human community that (successfully) claims the monopoly of the legitimate use of physical force within a given territory" remains a useful starting point (1978 [1922]). The crucial elements are a people, a territory, monopolized violence, and legitimate use of that violence. "Monopolized violence" refers to the fact that the state is the only institution, agent, or social group that controls the exercise of force. In an ideal state, there cannot be competing militias or rebel groups, alternative lords and rulers, or pockets where central authority cannot reach. The first three elements of Weber's definition are more or less objective; the last one (legitimacy) is in the eye of the beholder. What Weber tries to get at is that there must be some sort of social compliance, a sufficient acceptance of the state for it to exist as a state. If a people, in a given territory, fall under the monopolized violence of a foreign invader, this situation does not constitute a state for Weber, unless the rule of that invader is eventually accepted as legitimate. The 1933 Montevideo Convention on the Rights and Duties of States, which still lies at the core of the international system, echoed Weber's scholarship and identified the constitutive elements of a state as a territory, a permanent population, and a government. It stayed away from legitimacy, however, and added instead an external dimension: the capacity to "enter into relations with other states."

Weber's definition is theoretical and ideal. Some of its dimensions are uncontroversial. It seems indeed that, without a human population, the question of statehood is rather moot. Yet a human "community" is a step further, as it might presuppose some degree of bonding that many contemporary states do not experience. Moreover, some states, such as the Vatican, hardly have any population. The territorial requirement also seems essential, although here too there are a few exceptions, such as the Order of Malta, recognized as a sovereign state by some sixty countries but consisting largely of an office building in Rome. In Africa, Western Sahara is recognized by many other African states and by the African

Union, but it has a diminutive population and no control over its claimed territory, much of which Morocco occupies. Yet other constitutive elements are more problematic. One can wonder, for example, whether any state in the world exercises the monopoly of legitimate violence. In the United States, it is legal for citizens to carry and stockpile guns. Nevertheless, although the constitutive elements of statehood manifest themselves in various degrees, it is worth bearing them in mind: a people, a territory, an effective government, some degree of legitimacy (which does not necessarily imply democracy), and relations with other states.

Instead of asking what states are supposed to be, we can also wonder what they are supposed to do, and for whom. Why do we need them? Of course, these questions have motivated the writing of millions of pages since Plato's *Republic*. Yet we can single out a few crucial contributions to the analysis of African states. Possibly the most important is that of Thomas Hobbes, whose *Leviathan* (1968 [1651]) remains remarkably relevant today. Hobbes offered a thought experiment (largely inspired by episodes of civil war in England in the 1640s) about a society without a state, living in a "state of nature." In such a system, everyone would have to fend and fight for themselves. There would be perpetual violence, looting, theft, and fear. Property and other individual rights could not develop. To escape this conundrum, Hobbes believed that rational individuals eventually would see that they had to collectively surrender the means of violence to some shared institution and agree to live under its authority. This surrendering of individual violence for greater welfare engenders the formation of the state. It is thus the state's main purpose to end violence, to absorb and tame it, and to allow us to live peacefully and safely in society.

Together with John Locke and Jean-Jacques Rousseau, Hobbes is one of several writers who belong to the tradition of the social contract. These authors imagined society coming together to sign a contract, a covenant, whereby they surrendered certain individual rights in order to form the state and protect their lives and property. For all its abstraction, its lack of historical foundation, and its nature as only a thought experiment, the idea of the social contract is an essential foundation of states. It captures the willingness of individuals to surrender some liberties for a greater collective good and is germane to Weber's legitimacy concerns. Can the citizens of a state entertain the idea that they or their ancestors have willingly joined this system? Do they internalize the benefits they derive from the constraints imposed upon them by life within the state? Is there some general consensus on belonging together and on recognizing the legitimate authority of the state? Certainly, the answers to these questions will depend in part on the historical origins of states. They will also partly be a function of the success of states in providing peace, safety, and property rights.

Although they stress very basic ideas of survival and social order, what these social contract thinkers refer to, in broad terms, is the problem of organizing collective action, of providing collective goods.[9] For there are many things we cannot do as individuals or through mere market mechanisms. Not only must security be provided, but laws must be written and enforced, infrastructure developed, taxes raised, and the like. The state is one obvious solution to these problems. As suggested by Mancur Olson (1971 [1965]), the state can force everyone to bear their share of the work or of the financial burden for the public good to be supplied. If the state is indeed intent on maximizing public welfare, it has the formidable tool of its sovereign legitimate force to organize collective action. Thus a society with an effective state will be able to reach a higher level of development than one without an effective state. The notion of "state capacity" refers in part to a state's ability for such collective action.

Even if one does not believe in the necessity for the state to provide many public goods, such as education or healthcare, most believe that states are necessary for providing some basic agreed-upon lawmaking mechanisms to secure property rights and reduce transaction costs (the costs of doing business, such as negotiating and enforcing contracts) so as to make production and exchange among individuals possible.[10] For an economy to thrive, and thus for economic development to occur, it is generally agreed that states must be able to provide and enforce basic rules that all parties can rely on and without which transactions would be seriously impaired. Classical economist Adam Smith had already identified this need for economic governance when he wrote, in 1776, that it took a "well-governed society" for the division of labor to produce its expected productivity gains (1976 [1776]:15). More recently, authors such as James Buchanan (1975) and Douglass North (1990) have highlighted the role of the modern state in reducing transaction costs and securing property rights. Their view of the state might seem economically narrow to some and remains controversial for many Africans and Africanists, yet it is one that is widely endorsed by agencies such as the World Bank and that has significant implications for development.

We can also flip things around and see the state as trouble rather than as a benevolent entity. For Karl Marx (most of the time), the modern state was the instrument of capitalism. As the "executive of the bourgeoisie," it was doing the capitalists' bidding, adopting laws and policing in such a manner that profit would be maximized. In short, the state organized and regulated the exploitation of the masses. This might not be exceedingly relevant to Africa, where capitalist industrialization remains limited and where working classes still are hard to find (as opposed to scattered peasantries), but it raises the question of whether the African state could be conceived as the instrument of exterior economic forces, using it for access to resources and to keep African populations submissive. Such "dependency" arguments, which were particularly popular in the 1970s and 1980s, continue to hold sway among many scholars of Africa (Amin 1976; Ahiakpor 1985; see also Taylor and Williams 2004a).

Finally, we can ask where states come from. Mancur Olson (1993) thinks the state results from increasingly efficient banditry. Things start with societies plagued by "roving bandits" who roam the countryside, looting, stealing, and destroying as they encounter villages (very much as in Hobbes's state of nature). Such a picture might conjure up images of early medieval Europe or of some African "rebel" groups (see Bøås and Dunn 2007). Olson suggests that such bandits progressively realize that they can do better by protecting those villages and their farmers and then taxing their production, as long as they have enough time ahead of them to enjoy the fruits of their system. In short, they have an incentive to become "stationary bandits" if the present value of the sum of their future taxation benefits exceeds the value of looting the assets now. They can give themselves a sufficient time horizon by continuing to invest in violence and protecting themselves and their subjects from other roving bandits. And so the state is born, essentially as a racketeering enterprise in the business of extracting monopoly rents from its subjects. We are far from the social contract indeed. Olson argues that it is only progressively, through accidents of history, that the stationary bandits democratize by broadening their membership to eventually include the majority of citizens, whose "encompassing interest" favors the adoption of policies that increase general welfare. Although the colonial origins of the African state do not conform to the story of the passage from roving to stationary banditry, it is tempting to make sense of the contemporary behavior of multiple African states along the line of stationary banditry. In this respect, insecure leaders with a short time horizon are more likely to loot their countries than are their more stable counterparts.

Using a more empirical historical approach, Charles Tilly (1990) had come to similar conclusions. Looking at the rise of nation-states in medieval Europe, he argued that the exigencies of war, such as purchasing weapons and conscription, led kings to develop administrations in order to tax their populations and draft soldiers. Because the people had to pay tax and surrender their sons, they began making demands on the state, and a state-society relationship ensued that saw the formation of nation-states. In Tilly's now classic formula, "states make wars, and wars make states." As we will return to later, Tilly's theory is particularly relevant to the study of the state in Africa, where the relative absence of interstate wars has been a characteristic of the post-independence era. Some have argued that this absence of warfare prevents the formation of strong African states (Herbst 1990b). Irrespective of war, Tilly brings up the important issue of the state making demands on people, and of people, in turn, making demands on the state. What are the effects of this kind of bargaining, which is largely absent from African state formation, on the subsequent legitimacy and effectiveness of states?

Putting less emphasis on violence, Hendrik Spruyt (1994) showed how material changes, anchored in demographics and trade, gave the territorial state a comparative advantage in western Europe around the eleventh century over alternative forms of collective action. Spruyt sees the late eleventh century as a time of growing economic production, long-distance trade, and rising towns. He notes that the increased importance of towns changed the balance of political order and led to several possible institutional outcomes, one of which was the territorial state. The sovereign state "beat" other possible institutional configurations in western Europe because of its superior features of internal hierarchy and territorial demarcation. Internal hierarchy led to standardization and increased certainty, and helped prevent free-riding, increasing the credibility of the state's commitments. Territorial jurisdiction made it clear where state hierarchy applied and reduced opportunities for defections. Finally, other configurations around Europe followed suit, exiting the system they were in and mimicking statehood.

The African State

How do African states compare to these ideal-types? How do they conform to these general theories? Recall the main constitutive elements of statehood are generally: a territory, a people, an effective government, a degree of legitimacy, and relations with other states.

Territory is one undeniable dimension of African statehood. All forty-nine sub-Saharan African states have clearly delimited (at least on maps) and remarkably stable territories. Some of them might be small, particularly island states, but on average their territories are rather large compared to states in other regions. Elliott Green (2012) calls our attention to the fact that Africa has about the same number of states as Europe, but on more than twice the area. That the territories of African states have endured to this day is quite impressive given the relatively shallow colonial penetration that led to their creation and the threats of breakdown that surfaced soon after independence in some of them, such as Congo with the secession of Katanga, or Nigeria with the secession of Biafra.

African states comprise human populations, but it is debatable whether each forms a homogeneous or cohesive community (Jackson and Rosberg 1982). We will come back to this issue in ample detail in Chapter 3, but it bears noting already that African societies are highly heterogeneous, particularly in ethnic terms. With a few exceptions, the states created by colonization include formerly distinct societies and polities. Many precolonial political formations now subsumed in the same state were distinct systems in precolonial times. Sometimes, they had been at war with each other, which raises doubt as to their status as a unified community. Among the few exceptions are Rwanda and Burundi, which were colonized more or less in their precolonial configurations. Yet their degree of polarization and the amount of violence their people have meted out on each other since independence suggest that they too suffer from deficits of community. Botswana, Lesotho, and Swaziland (as of 2018, Eswatini) also constitute exceptions, as they were precolonial kingdoms that invited British protection to fight off the encroachments of Boer settlers. Finally, Somalia differs in the sense that it is almost entirely populated by ethnic Somalis. To the extent that these Somali clans were not previously politically integrated, however, Somalia conforms more to the modal heterogeneous African state.

However, as we will also discuss in Chapter 3, cultural heterogeneity has not prevented the rise of strong postcolonial national identities in Africa. It is certainly not unreasonable to argue that there are such things nowadays as Chadian, Congolese, or Nigerian nations. It is telling, in this respect, that very few African insurgencies actually aim at dismantling the state. Rather, insurgents tend to fight for control of it and frequently veil themselves in the cloak of nationalism. Hence, though polarized and conflict-ridden as they might be, African states generally meet the human community test.

At least in formal terms, African states have governments—that is, executives, administrations, and security agencies that rule their territories and populations. These governments can be quite visible, whether in coverage by the media, through their public buildings and monuments, or in the routine presence of soldiers and police in the streets. They are generally good at exercising their domination over their population. Chapter 4 focuses on the governing dimension of

African politics. Yet as that chapter will show, the extent to which African governments govern in practice is subject to wide continental variations. As we suggest later, many of them are weak in the sense that they have little capacity to design and implement complex policies, and some do not even seem intent on trying. In addition, they effectively share the responsibility to govern with many other public and private institutions, such as customary authorities, nongovernmental associations, religious groups, foreign governments, charities, and international organizations. In many ways then, the governing of African societies, or what some call the sovereignty of their states (e.g., Chalfin 2010), is delegated upward and downward.

Despite these variations in the degree of effective existence of African governments, all but a couple of African states are recognized by other states as sovereign and legally belong to the international community of states. Unlike states in most other regions, they were not required to demonstrate their existence to others before being recognized (Jackson and Rosberg 1982; Jackson 1990). They received automatic recognition at independence on the principle that former colonies represented the instrument of the self-determination of African peoples. This outside recognition of African states has never wavered, however weak some of them have become in reality. Hence, Somalia retains its seat at the United Nations despite for decades having lost most features of statehood on the ground. In contrast, a couple of African states have failed to obtain widespread recognition. The Frente Popular de Liberación de Saguía el Hamra y Río de Oro (POLISARIO) has demanded sovereignty for Western Sahara since the withdrawal of the Spanish colonizers in 1975. Yet, confronted with Moroccan claims over the same territory, it has been unable to obtain the recognition of its Sahrawi Republic from more than some fifty countries and the African Union over the years. That is nevertheless a lot better than Somaliland, a former British colony that united with the former Italian colony of Somalia in 1960, but seceded in 1991, and has yet to be recognized by a single sovereign state despite more than twenty years of effective existence and a degree of governance that contrasts with the violent anarchy of Somalia next door.

The last dimension of statehood—the monopoly of legitimate violence—is by far the most complicated to assess. Of course, many African states are or have been plagued with political violence, but this does not necessarily imply that such violence is perceived as politically legitimate by significant segments of their populations. However, countries such as Sudan during its civil war with the south, or Nigeria during the Biafra secession, or Chad for all of its existence have had tenuous reservoirs of political legitimacy. Reciprocally, many will find it unquestionable that the violence exercised by the Rwandan state during the 1994 genocide lacked legitimacy. By and large, the complex question of legitimacy is better left unanswered at this early stage. Hopefully, the rest of the text will provide more material to think about it productively. Suffice it to say for now that legitimacy is a controversial dimension of the existence of African states.

Setting this last question aside, we can tentatively conclude that African states are generally recognizable members of the species. If we ask what they actually do, however, we are more likely to conclude that they are outliers compared to states elsewhere. On average, African states are not very successful at providing essential human security to their citizens. In not a few cases, they are the ones that represent a threat to the security of their populations. Even those that do not oppress or terrorize their citizens are generally weak at supplying them with essential collective goods. The majority of African states do poorly at coordinating collective action, reducing transactions costs, providing stable property rights, and offering basic services to their citizens. In a nutshell, they are short on good governance and lack capacity.

A large literature has flourished since the 1990s on the degree to which states "fail" or do not achieve their expected functions. The concept of "state failure," which surfaces in our discussion at several points in this book, has come to represent the status of those with the worst performance, countries that essentially no longer formally function as states (which does not imply, however, that they are devoid of power and domination, or even of institutions). The concept is certainly controversial, with many academics challenging it on theoretical, normative, empirical, and practical grounds (Ezrow and Frantz 2013). Some have suggested that Western policymakers, prioritizing their own security and development agendas, have employed the concept to legitimize various forms of policy interventions (Grimm, Lemay-Hébert, and Nay 2014). Setting these important critiques aside for the moment, if we accept the validity and utility of the concept, there appears to be a greater average degree of state failure in Africa than in other continents. Figure 2.3 shows the range in state capacity across the continent as of 2018, based on the Fund for Peace's "Fragile States Index" (formerly "Failed State Index"), which captures twelve measures of social, economic, and political performance; the figure compares this capacity to the average degree of capacity of other states around the world. Theoretically, the index can range from 0 to 120. The best worldwide score is 17.9, for Finland (the "least failed" state in the world by this yardstick). The worst is 113.4, for South Sudan, which just barely beats out Somalia. The average score for

Africa is 88; for the rest of the world it is 61. Only two African countries—Seychelles and Mauritius—perform better than the average for all other countries of the world. All other African countries exceed this average, and seven of them are among the worst ten.

Despite the African state's weak average performance under these measurements, it is important to note that capacity varies across the region and over time. For every Chad, there is a Botswana; for every Sudan, a Namibia. It is also important to think about the state over time and not only at a specific moment. Some African states, such as Ethiopia and Zimbabwe, have gone from apparent success stories to crisis cases, whereas others that were once lamentable, such as Ghana and Kenya, now count among the most capable ones. Nevertheless, even if we bear in mind variations across the continent, and whether we rely on this particular indicator or other similar ones, there is without a doubt a crisis of the African state, a failure at reaching some ideal of statehood or at performing basic functions of collective action and security provision for its citizenry. There is even to some extent a failure at what Mancur Olson (1993) would call "stationary banditry," or the rational extraction and accumulation of resources in some countries. We return to this failure and seek to explain it at much greater length later in the book. For now, however, we turn to the questions of where African states come from and what is the link, if any, between their largely colonial origins and their postcolonial performance.

Figure 2.3 Index of State Fragility in Africa, 2018

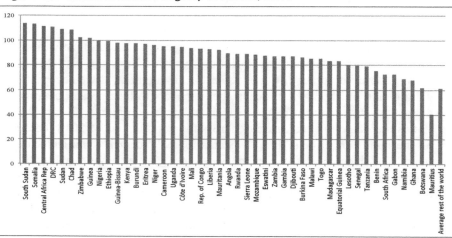

Source: Fund for Peace Fragile States Index 2018 (accessed November 2018).
Notes: Higher numbers indicate greater fragility.

Imported states. Aside from Ethiopia, all African states can be thought of as "imported" to the extent that they are the continuation of colonial creations from the late nineteenth century. Their existence, their authority, their territory, and even their sovereignty are the outcome of political processes in which domestic African forces often played minor roles at best. This is not a particularly African condition, however. One can think of most of the world as having adopted a version of statehood—the sovereign territorial state—that originated in western Europe. Bertrand Badie (1992) has argued that this process of importation of the European rational-legal state has led to a "Westernization" of political order around the world. But the results, he suggests, were not quite as intended, and the universalization of the state has largely "failed." A crucial consequence of this failure is a "loss of meaning" in the relationship between the rulers and the ruled, which "discourages the individual in his efforts to adapt to an institutional life of no concern to him" (227). Badie relies on this insight to account for "new forms of mobilization," including particularisms based on identity (239), which he argues characterize politics in regions where the graft of the Western state has failed. The importance of ethnicity in African politics, to which we will return at great length in the next chapter, comes to mind.

Although of a general scope, Badie's work applies to Africa, and he summons many examples from the continent. It echoes a popular theme in African studies, the notion that the imported nature of the African state bears at least some responsibility for its dysfunctions. There has probably been no more eloquent and engaging statement of the imported state hypothesis in Africa than Basil Davidson's highly readable *Black Man's Burden: Africa and the Curse of the Nation-State* (1992). Davidson suggests that, rather than any inherent African characteristic, it is the European nation-state that is at the root of most contemporary African political problems. African societies, he argues, were largely prevented from continuing their own evolution by the destruction inflicted by the slave trade and colonialism. The latter promoted the rise of alienated African elites largely trained in Europe and oblivious to the historical foundations of political legitimacy. These regimes, severed from their history and people, produced "nation-states" that have been largely inimical to the interests of Africans.

Among others who have focused on dimensions of political alienation inferred from the imported nature of the state, Peter Ekeh (1975), a Nigerian scholar whose work we return to in Chapter 3, suggests that the state is of little concern to many Africans, who see it as an exogenous institution in transactions with which moral behavior is not expected. As a result, no social loyalty to the state develops, and corruption spreads.

This message echoes that of another Nigerian, novelist Chinua Achebe, who has one of his characters in his landmark novel *A Man of the People* declare "in the affairs of the nation there was no owner, the laws of the village became powerless" (1966:30). The work of Ngugi Wa Thiong'o, a Kenyan playwright and essayist, also conveys the alienating nature of the Eurocentric African state and calls for escaping from it by reembracing African languages (see, particularly, Ngugi Wa Thiong'o 1986).

Beyond these works of a rather general scope, there are several more explicit theories in political science on the possible effects of the colonial origins of African states. One possibly important insight is that, in its colonial genesis, the African state was born largely autonomous from African societies (Young 1994a:118) and remained so throughout the colonial period. Evoking the interwar period, Crawford Young (1994a) notes that "the completeness of its domination freed the state from responsiveness to its subjects to a remarkable degree" (159). In the terminal phase of colonialism, it briefly lost its autonomy to the metropolis (204), to the educated nationalist Africans, and to the United Nations and international law. But "the silent revenge of the colonial state was surreptitiously to embed in its post-independence successor [its] corrosive personality." Hence it remains a "superstructure of domination severed from civil society" (242).

This historical autonomy might have biased the African state toward absolutism (Callaghy 1984; Mbembe 2000). Accountability was not part of its design and African social forces, playing but a minor role in its formation, were unable to demand significant concessions from it. In contrast, as we highlighted previously, European states had to bargain for authority and resources with other social groups when they developed (Tilly 1990; Holsti 1996). Even if they took a long time to democratize, they were born embedded in their societies. African leaders, however, inherit relatively unencumbered state power at the end of colonial times.

Yet the process by which the autonomy and absolutism of the colonial state extend to the postcolonial period cannot be taken for granted or just assumed away. How does the commanding nature of the state endure after colonial force recedes? In an influential argument, Robert Jackson and Carl Rosberg (1982, 1986) suggested that the recognition of African postcolonial states in international law reproduced the colonial bias in favor of rulers and voided the necessity for African states to gain internal legitimacy and develop capacity (see also Jackson 1990). Unlike regions where the state acquires its sovereignty in a domestic process of capacity building eventually recognized by its peers and competitors, African states gained their sovereignty at the time of their independence from the mere act of recognition of their existence by other states and by the United Nations. Scholars of international law refer to this type of recognition as constitutive of sovereignty, as opposed to declarative recognition, which merely recognizes the already effective existence of a state. For the majority of African states, it is thus the act of recognition by external actors and institutions that confers the quality of sovereignty.[11]

Jackson and Rosberg built upon this insight to develop the notion that African statehood is "juridical" rather than "empirical." Jackson (1990) later even coined the term "negative sovereignty," or sovereignty awarded as a category to postcolonies without evidence of their capacity to rule themselves. Jackson and Rosberg traced the sources of African juridical or negative sovereignty to the international legal apparatus of decolonization, developed first and foremost within the United Nations, and to the normative implications of the ideology of development, which dominated in the late colonial era and into the 1960s and according to which former colonies have the right to exist as states before they may be able to do so on their own, and even to be assisted in becoming empirical states.

An essential element of their reasoning is that constitutive recognition is not granted to just any African political entity but to former colonies alone. As Jackson (1990:17) summed it up, "To be a sovereign state today one needs only to have been a formal colony yesterday." It bears reflecting upon the fact that past existence as a colony is the unique principle guiding contemporary recognition as a sovereign entity in Africa. This principle was enshrined in UN General Assembly Resolution 1514 (XV) of 1960, which provided sovereignty to former colonies and outlawed their territorial reconfiguration. From this perspective, international law has become the successor to the colonizer as repository of the sovereign power of African states and rulers. It should be noted, however, that while the independence of Eritrea in 1993 followed this principle—it invoked past colonial status to claim statehood—that of South Sudan in 2011 represents an exception that might possibly herald a change in norms of African recognition (Walker 2017).

Jackson and Rosberg suggest that recognition, which comes with entitlements to foreign aid and the benefit of international norms such as noninterference in domestic affairs, gives African rulers a significant advantage over their society and allows for the reproduction of their autonomy and authority while exonerating them of the necessity to build capable states. Jackson and Rosberg link multiple pathologies of African states (lack of democracy, weak capacity, overstretched economies, etc.)

to juridical statehood. Building upon their insight, Pierre Englebert (2009) hypothesized that constitutive recognition grants African states the capacity to command their societies through their monopoly to make laws, which he sees as an unrivaled and unearned source of their authority. In this perspective, African states are able to largely reproduce the colonial blueprint and rule with limited constraint and accountability, practicing their authority as command.[12]

In a different argument but one that also relies on their external genesis, Jeffrey Herbst (2000) suggests that the imported origins of African states have resulted in countries that are too large for their available technologies of power. Contrary to the often-held assumption that the larger the state the better, African states, he contends, suffer from diseconomies of scale (see also Clapham, Herbst, and Mills 2006). Precolonial authority was generally exercised over much smaller territories than nowadays, and postcolonial states face significant hurdles in trying to broadcast their power across their territories, a problem compounded by the frequently uneven geographical distribution of their populations. Yet Herbst notes that international support for these states has prevented them from failing completely, allowing them instead to survive without the foundations for more capacity. Hence he links the historical origins of African states to their shortfall in terms of Hobbesian effectiveness and lack of territorial control.

In a similar vein, Englebert (2000b) sees the imported nature of the African state as resulting in different degrees of structural or historical fitness with precolonial politics. Although there is a general African mismatch between postcolonial states and preexisting forms of authority compared to other regions, some African states match preexisting political configurations better than others. Englebert argues that the greater the mismatch, the greater the relative power payoffs for African elites of resorting to clientelistic policies and corruption compared to the benefits of developmental policies. Similarly, looking at most of the postcolonial world, Joel Migdal (1988) argued in a landmark book that the weak capabilities of some third world states derive from their relative weakness with respect to their "strong societies." This is not true of all postcolonial countries. However, in places such as anglophone Africa, where indirect rule prevailed, Migdal contends that the colonizers reinforced local societies and made it subsequently hard for the states they had created to impose their authority after the colonial era.

The picture that emerges from all these authors captures some of the paradoxical features of African statehood. Although African states appear weak and lack the capacity to properly control their territories and populations, and to implement policies and provide services, they are nevertheless rather powerful domestically and are able to survive and evolve in apparent autonomy from their society. Their imported origins might help account for both of these dimensions.

In another incarnation of the imported state hypothesis, some authors have focused on the configuration of African boundaries and its consequences. A common argument goes that the particular artificiality and arbitrariness of African boundaries make state formation and economic development particularly challenging and conflict more likely. Of course, all around the world, few borders, aside from those of island states, are "natural" in the sense that political geography would follow some uncontroversial pattern of the natural world. The Alps and the Pyrenees are sometimes presented as France's natural borders, but they were not for a long time. As for the Rhine, a cursory look at the history of Europe after the fall of the Roman Empire should suffice to discredit its natural pretensions at separating peoples. Thus, artificiality is the rule when it comes to borders everywhere. Arguments that African borders are particularly artificial do not therefore properly distinguish the continent from others.

Yet, rather than artificiality, it might be their degree of arbitrariness and of exogeneity, as a result of their largely colonial origins, that distinguishes African boundaries (Asiwaju 1985; Brownlie 1979; Davidson 1992; Nugent and Asiwaju 1996). First, as mentioned earlier in this chapter, the concept of territorial delimitation of political control was by and large culturally alien to precolonial African polities, where authority extended over people more than over land (Allott 1974; Herbst 2000). Boundary zones were fluid as jurisdiction faded from the center toward the periphery (when jurisdiction existed, which was not the case for many stateless societies). In addition, Islam, the largest unified religion in Africa, did not recognize sovereignty over specific territories (Joffe 1990). Second, Africans were at best minor participants in the drawing of their territories. For sure, they were not without any agency in the matter. At times the colonizers consulted with them and took the unity of cultural groups into account, as with the partition of Ruanda-Urundi from German East Africa (Griffiths 1986), or with the redrawing of the Niger-Nigeria boundary at the turn of the century to broadly coincide with the upper north limit of Usman dan Fodio's jihad conquest (Thom 1975). In other cases, borders were determined after making treaties with local chiefs (Prescott 1987), or were adjusted afterward to take account of partitioned groups and migration (Barbour 1961; Nugent 1996), as happened between Sudan and Uganda (Prescott 1972). More politically centralized precolonial cultures may also have been more successful at resisting or negotiating partition than were their stateless counterparts (Nugent 1996). But in general, colonial borders were created without knowledge of, or interest in, local territories and populations (Asiwaju 1984; Jackson and Rosberg 1985; Davidson 1992). Treaties among imperial powers and with local chiefs, as well as administrative decisions within single colonial empires, often resulted in straight lines or the use of rivers or other geographical features that previously had been as likely to unite as to separate local populations. Astronomically based straight lines were a particularly popular mode of delimitation, for their expediency suited colonizers whose knowledge of the boundary zones was limited by the minimal definition of effective occupation adopted at the Berlin Conference. In the end, up to 44 percent of African boundaries contained straight lines (Barbour 1961) (see Figure 2.4). In addition, fourteen African states are landlocked, more than in any other region. A. I. Asiwaju (1985) has also found that no less than 177 African cultural or ethnic groups (representing, on average, 43 percent of a given country's population) were partitioned by colonial borders.

Elliott Green (2012) argues that the design of African boundaries was partly a function of the conditions the colonizers encountered on the ground. He suggests that colonizers established larger states in areas that had low population density and low trade, in order to save costs. Because the colonies had to pay for themselves and the main means to do so was the head tax, and because the Berlin Conference had agreed on effective pacification not being necessary for colonial claims, colonizers faced positive returns from increasing state size in low-density environments. Green also finds that the closer the precolonial state was to the sea, the more trade-based it was and the lesser the colonial necessity to increase state size to provide for revenue. Thus, inland countries tend to be larger nowadays than their coastal counterparts. The shape of states too was a function of population density, as colonizers were more likely to draw straight lines in low-density environments, where there were few or weak preexisting systems on which to rely. In high-density areas, colonizers were more attuned to local political realities.

As with the appropriation of the postcolonial state, however, African ruling elites showed little ambiguity or hesitation in embracing the borders they inherited from colonialism and defending them against challenges. The charter of the Organization of African Unity, established in 1963, put the preservation of territorial integrity among its essential principles. At their first ordinary session the following year in Cairo, the OAU heads of state solemnly declared that "all Member States pledge themselves to respect the borders existing on their

Figure 2.4 Map of Africa, 2019

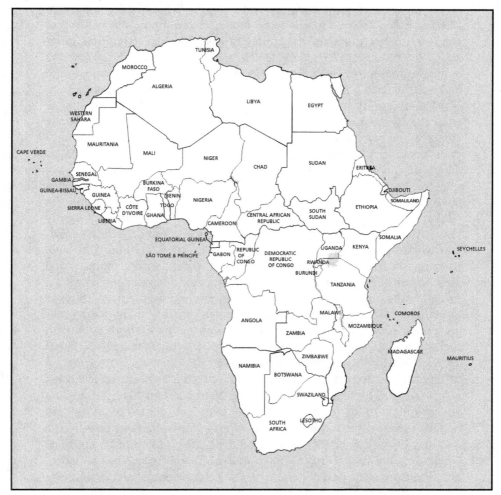

achievement of national independence" (OAU 1964). This principle, known in international law as *uti possidetis,* or "as you found it," characterized the dominant position of all African states (Morocco and Somalia aside) with regard to borders. For African governments, this legal position had the advantage of ruling out any territorial adjustments that could have been manipulated by "neocolonial" interests and of enshrining principles of territorial integrity and noninterference, which they were otherwise incapable of enforcing on their own. It bears noting here that the 1963 founding of the OAU took place at the tail end of the three-year secession of Katanga from Congo, which had begun days after its independence in 1960 and had received more or less discreet support from Belgium and the United States (short of recognition, however). In retrospect, African rulers had legitimate reasons to fear the dynamics that territorial adjustments might unleash, and the decision to make theirs such a physical legacy of colonialism was not irrational.

The essential question for the student of African border issues is what the consequences of *uti possidetis* have been. There is no easy answer. One common claim is that the maintenance of colonial boundaries has at least limited the number of interstate conflicts in Africa, as we discuss in Chapter 8. By choosing not to challenge each other over their borders and the minorities partitioned by them, African states have removed a potential cause of dispute from their foreign policies (Bayart 1996; Joseph and Herbst 1997). This is a claim that can hardly be verified, however, since there is no control group of African countries with flexible borders. Yet it is true that interstate conflicts have been few in Africa, in proportion to both the number of countries and the number of partitioned communities that could ignite such conflicts. Probably the only large-scale case of border conflict in Africa involves Somalia's claim over Ethiopian and Kenyan territory inhabited by ethnic Somalis, which has caused repeated conflicts with both countries, including long-lasting hostilities in Ethiopia's Ogaden region (Boyd 1979). The 1997–1999 border war between Ethiopia and Eritrea is a bit different to the extent that Eritrea separated from Ethiopia in 1993, yet it has colonial dimensions too. Finally, Morocco and Mauritania went to war in the 1970s as they both made historical claims over Western Sahara (not recognized at the time as an independent country by the majority of African states). Apart from that, most other border conflicts (including between Burkina Faso and Mali over the Agacher strip, between Cameroon and Nigeria over the Bakassi peninsula, or between Benin and Niger over the island of Lete on the Niger River) have been about the exact location of the border and stayed rather minor. This is not, altogether, a bad record.

Yet some have argued that the perception that Africa has had few boundary disputes is by and large mistaken. Pierre Englebert, Stacy Tarango, and Matthew Carter (2002) highlight that the majority of territorial dispute cases brought before the International Court of Justice from 1960 to 2000 were African. Furthermore, they identify thirty-four cases of disputes among African countries over border issues from 1960 to 2000. Although these represent only about 29 percent of Africa's 104 borders, they involved no less than two-thirds of all its countries. In addition, these authors provide evidence that the likelihood of international conflict increases with the arbitrariness of the border, which they measure as the average proportion of people on both sides of a boundary who belong to partitioned ethnic groups. Whereas boundaries whose proportion of partitioned people is less than 25 percent are three times more likely to be peaceful than to be disputed, those whose proportions of partitioned people are between 75 and 100 percent are seven times more likely to be disputed than to be peaceful.

There are also mixed arguments and evidence over the effects of African borders on national identity and nation building. On the one hand, after more than fifty years of independence, colonially derived boundaries do not seem to have precluded the formation of national identities, even among groups that straddle borders. Paul Nugent (2002), for example, has shown that the Ewe astride the Ghana-Togo border feel stronger allegiance to their nation-states than to an Ewe nation. Given the number of partitioned peoples, the list of African secessionist groups is indeed remarkably short. Elliott Green (2017) argues, however, that the degree of national identification fluctuates and is often determined by whether or not one's own ethnic group is in power. Of course, there is no intrinsic reason why grouping different people together should necessarily lead to trouble and conflict; most precolonial African states were also multiethnic (Evans-Pritchard and Fortes 1940). On the other hand, here too there is some evidence that border arbitrariness correlates with different political pathologies. For example, there is a positive, significant, and robust relationship between the diversity of precolonial political cultures included in a country and the extent of its instability, as measured by coups, coup attempts, and coup plots. In addition, the degree of variance in an African country's precolonial cultures, the length of its boundaries, and its size are all positively associated with the likelihood of secession (Englebert, Tarango, and Carter 2002).

There are also documented negative effects of boundary arbitrariness on the quality of governance and the level of economic development. Herbst (2000), for example, shows that the variations in the "national design" of states inherited from colonization (e.g., odd boundaries, large territories, uneven distribution of population density, peripheral human settlement) are associated with less development in infrastructure. In the end, students of African politics are encouraged to reflect critically upon the possible implications of the "imported state." Yet as our discussion has illustrated, one would be advised not to overgeneralize or embrace deterministic claims. Rather, there is probably much to be learned from exploring variations in functioning of the "imported state" across time and across the continent.

Africanized states. Despite their colonial origins, African states are also very much African in the sense that Africans themselves have been active agents of their reproduction. They may have started as institutional imports, but they have been adopted, adapted, and appropriated. Some scholars have argued that it may be more useful to conceive of states not as static entities, but as ongoing processes that are constantly being performed. In this approach, the performance of the state by African rulers has structuring effects on political life (Dunn 2009; Doty 2003). Whether one focuses on the state as an institution or a process, however, one can investigate the ways in which Africans have had agency and have contributed to shaping the political structures they have today, from negotiating the terms of the transfer of power from the colonizers to the daily reproduction of their states. Moreover, the exercise of power, in Africa as elsewhere, involves negotiations, bargains, and transfers of resources and authority, all of which have led to a penetration of the state by African societies and vice versa.

This current of thought, which highlights the "banality" of African politics or its lack of exceptionalism and its universal qualities, has been rather dominant in French and francophone scholarship since the 1980s (see Coulon 1997). Jean-François Bayart is a proponent of the idea that imported African state institutions become indigenized and that their imported nature ends up playing a relatively minor role in the long-run history of African societies. He stresses that the imported state is hybridized with local strategies of power, reappropriated by local groups (1996:14). This process began under colonial rule as the metropolitan powers concluded alliances with local groups in a bid to secure the stability of their domination. Thus we should not see Africans as the passive recipients of colonial politics but as participants in the elaboration of a political order derived from the encounter with the colonials. The resulting state, Bayart suggests, is a "rhizome" state, "an infinitely variable multiplicity of networks whose underground branches join together the scattered points of society" (1993:220). Thus the colonial state is Africanized by the local, common practice of politics and power. Hence, Bayart proposes a long-term analysis that acknowledges the ruptures introduced by colonialism, but minimizes their scope and refrains from any deterministic implication.

Few other scholars who stress the African appropriation of the postcolonial state go as far as Bayart in denying that colonialism had a significant impact on the African state, however. Jean-François Médard (1991:358), for example, acknowledges that the colonial state is "reappropriated" by Africans but in the process its "ordinary logic" is "*bouleversée,*" or shaken up. Because the postcolonial state is embedded through mechanisms of clientelism (to which we return in Chapter 4), its adaptation ends up undermining its effectiveness. Similarly, Goran Hyden (2006) notes that African states lack legitimacy compared to "domestic" institutions. The strength of community loyalties has led African leaders to seize the state as prey. The state has become both an arena of communal competition and the goal of this competition. It is appropriated by Africans, but it is unable to become *autonomous* from society, which Hyden sees as a precondition for collective action capacity. Hyden stresses that the postcolonial African state is not the colonial one, because "different social bases of the state . . . emerged after independence" (59). Colonials, for example, did not need to worry about balancing communal interests. But Hyden also identifies the consequences of these new social bases: "the crisis that has come to dominate the political scene on the continent is the inability of the state to operate as a distinct institution free from the constraint of community" (62), with the result that the African state is soft and weak.

Hyden's argument about the limited societal autonomy of the African state stands in sharp contrast to Crawford Young's (1994a) assertion of its colonially derived autonomy. Other authors, such as Thomas Callaghy (1987b) and Peter Evans (1995), have also argued that the African state lacks autonomy, because it is too deeply penetrated by social groups as a result of its predatory appropriation. Whether the state is autonomous or not is a largely unsettled question in African politics (as it seems to be in theories of the state everywhere). Of course, this might be a function of what is perceived as the state, how autonomy is viewed, and what fields of state behavior are considered. The state could be hijacked by some societal interests—thereby lacking autonomy—which would then go on exercising power with no further accountability to anyone else—thereby displaying autonomy. The sources of authority of the state could also be exogenous to society, and thus autonomous from it, while the instruments of its authority could be widely shared among domestic actors.

In an insightful book based on the experience of Sierra Leone before and during its civil war of the early 1990s, William Reno (1995) offered a picture of the appropriated state through his descriptions and analyses of alliances, largely based on informal economic activity, between states and nonstate actors since colonial days. In order to guarantee the compliance of local chiefs, colonial and postcolonial administrators gave them informal access to diamond markets and the use of labor resources. Informal markets are thus intertwined in local strategies of power and accumulation. Rulers use "nonformal state power" to intervene in these markets and seek opportunities and resources for clients, progressively redesigning formal institutions inherited from colonialism and contributing to the rise of a genuinely African "shadow state." Mahmood Mamdani's classic *Citizen and Subject: Contemporary Africa and the Legacy of Late Colonialism* (1996) also probes the nature of the African postcolonial state. Unlike Bayart or Reno, Mamdani does not deny or ignore the significance of colonialism and of the transition to independence. Yet in contrast to scholars who stress the imported nature of the state, he draws an argument about how the accommodation of the colonial and postcolonial state and the types of political alliances it embarked upon have led to a deeply undemocratic state. As with Reno, the alliance between the state and African chiefs lies at the core of Mamdani's analysis. His main thesis is that colonial rule was based on "institutional segregation," a "regime of differentiation" (7), which independence failed to abolish. Faced with the dilemma of establishing minority control over their conquests, colonial powers reserved a space of rights and direct rule to themselves, a white civil society, in urban areas and dominated the local African peasantry through indirect rule (in this book, Mamdani deals mostly with anglophone Africa) by either reconstituting or imposing tribal leadership as the local extension of the colonial state (17). Hence he argues that the colonial state was "bifurcated." After independence, alliances were sought with local tribally designed leadership and the "unreformed Native Authority came to contaminate civil society" (21). Thus the "decentralized despotism" of African chiefs is the consequence of strategies of embedding the colonial and postcolonial state.

Although the writings of Bayart, Reno, and Mamdani stress dimensions of power and domination, one can also conceive of the appropriation of the colonial state along the lines of a social contract. The quest for development, and the organization of social and economic life toward it, were the essential legitimating discourse of the early African state, as they had been of the late colonizer. The exchange of state-provided development for political allegiance can be thought of as the founding social contract of the postcolonial era, a contract that was seriously jeopardized by the widespread failure of the African state to bring about development. Yet the enduring nature of the African state suggests that its authority relied on other consensual bases. For Paul Nugent (2010), there are miscellaneous other social contracts that legitimated the African state at independence, some of which have endured. He contends that there were different combinations of "coercive, productive and permissive" social contracts, with the latter being the most pervasive. Nugent defines permissive social contracts as follows: "While the governing authority claims its sovereign rights, it chooses not to exercise them (or all of them), in return for securing a measure of *de facto* compliance" (44). Thus, in Ghana, the state was forced to curtail its ambitions over land and taxation; in Gambia, it had to allow for open borders; in Senegal, it had to accept the "relative autonomy of the Muslim brotherhoods." In other words, the postcolonial state negotiates its reproduction with society by backing off of a range of its prerogatives. Although several states later revisited the concessions they had granted in the initial social contracts, Nugent sees some permanence in them. Even in Ghana, which went through several coups, state failure, a revolution, and a democratic transition, the original contract, according to Nugent, "never unraveled."

Finally, it is fitting to conclude this section and chapter on a different perspective, one that explicitly claims that the African state must be measured by its own yardstick and not against a Weberian ideal-type that makes it look deficient (Dunn 2001). In one of the most influential books on African politics of the late twentieth century, Patrick Chabal and Jean-Pascal Daloz (1999) make the claim that "Africa works."[13] According to them, what appears like disorder and dysfunctionality is in fact an African type of modernity in which conventional modernization and development do not apply but in which "political actors . . . seek to maximize their returns on the state of confusion, uncertainty, and sometimes even chaos, which characterizes most African polities" (xviii). Yet their argument about what we could label the "African-ness" of the state contrasts greatly with the argument suggesting that the colonial state was appropriated by Africans. For Chabal and Daloz, it is colonialism that never succeeded in displacing precolonial modes of politics: "the colonial administrative experience" did not "eradicate 'pre-colonial' political traditions" (11), and the "strongly instrumental and personalized characteristics of 'traditional' African administration" (13) resisted colonial bureaucratic institutionalization. As a result, the African state "never significantly emancipated from society" (4). This situation of "weak institutionalization" has benefited African political elites. By such standards, therefore, African politics is truly African and the weak state is a measure of African resilience rather than a sign of failure.

The complexity and density of politics in Africa and the limitations of our knowledge make it possible to have rather divergent assessments and theories of the same realities. Arguments about the nature of African statehood provide a telling example at the onset of this book. While some theories make contradictory claims and are hard to reconcile, it is nevertheless often possible to incorporate elements from most of them in order to weave together a more complete and nuanced picture. Thus one can think of the African state as both imported and Africanized, as both colonial and indigenous, as both autonomous and embedded. And we can think of contemporary features of African politics and development as deriving, at least in part, both from the state's exogenous nature and from the processes whereby it has been reappropriated over the years. Moreover, taking a cue from Chabal and Daloz, one can explore how "Africa works" by considering for whom, how, and at what costs.

Notes

1. See Schraeder 2004:52–54 for a useful summary of different sources on the slave trade.

2. We are grateful to Paul Nugent for bringing this pattern to our attention.

3. Crawford Young has written at length on *bula matari* and expanded the notion to the colonial state in general (see Young and Turner 1985; Young 1994a).

4. Portugal and Spain, whose authoritarian pro-Nazi regimes stayed mostly out of the war, suffered less colonial contradiction, to the demise of their colonies, which would have to wait significantly longer to reach independence and fight harder for it.

5. We do not discuss South Africa here, which had become formally independent in 1910. The ruling Afrikaans white minority was no longer colonial in nature, having been established in the country since the 1650s. The struggle of the African National Congress was thus not anticolonial but for majority rule, although it considered the white minority to be colonialists.

6. Forced labor was abolished at the same occasion.

7. De Gaulle served as head of state from the end of the war in 1944 until 1946, and again from 1957 to 1969.

8. We close here the historical narrative. For a historical treatment of the postcolonial period, nothing compares in quality and comprehensiveness to Paul Nugent's *Africa Since Independence* (2012).

9. Collective action does not have to be defined at the scale of the state. It applies to any group. Labor unions, for example, or business lobbies face important questions of collective action.

10. There are, of course, a number of anarchist-leaning thinkers who would question the necessity of the state. James Scott (2009) provides an illuminating study of contemporary stateless societies in Southeast Asia, for example.

11. Note that such constitutive recognition is not that different from the principles of the 1884–1885 Berlin Conference, where recognition of each other's possessions by colonial powers was predicated on the flimsiest notion of "effective occupation."

12. This argument does not preclude the fact that other variables, such as economic crisis or pressure for democratization, might subsequently tone down the inherited absolutism of the African state.

13. In its original French version, the title of Chabal and Daloz's book evoked the notion that Africa was off to a start, in apparent response to René Dumont's (1966) claim that it was off to a "false start."

3

People, Identity, and Politics

STATES DO NOT EXIST OUTSIDE OF SOCIETIES. AN UNDER-standing of African politics requires an examination of how and why people mobilize and act collectively. This exercise is no different than what it would be if we were studying the politics of some other region. Certain dimensions of the social realm, such as class and gender, figure centrally, as does civil society—the realm of formal associative life. Nevertheless, the study of African politics also entails an investigation of a few relatively distinctive features of African social life. Two in particular stand out. First, although civil society is an important conceptual category in Africa, there are reasons to believe that civil society looks and functions differently in Africa than elsewhere. Second, any study of African societies cannot avoid an in-depth investigation of questions of ethnicity. Many Africanists would argue that ethnic groups might be the most important political category in Africa, and that ethnic identity might be the most important driver of individual political behavior. Those who disagree will still recognize the importance of ethnicity, but more as a consequence than as a cause of other features of African politics. One way or another, one must come to grips with the concepts of ethnicity, ethnic identity, and ethnic collective action if one is to acquire a working understanding of African politics.

We thus begin with a discussion of ethnicity, arguably the most fundamental category of political life in Africa. What is the meaning of ethnicity and ethnic identity? Why is ethnic identity so salient in Africa compared to most other regions of the world? How does ethnic diversity affect policy choices and ruling strategies? Why do some countries, such as Nigeria or Ethiopia, seem prone to ethnic conflict while others, such as Tanzania or Burkina Faso, seem to manage their ethnic diversity peacefully? And similarly, why do some countries experience ethnic conflict at one point in time and not at another?

We present three ways to think about ethnicity in a sequence that moves from viewing it as a deep-rooted fixed characteristic to thinking of it as a fluid and changing cultural resource that people, and particularly political elites, can appeal to in some circumstances. For each of these approaches, we confront the theory with instances of ethnic conflicts or ethnic-based policy problems and see how they fare in explaining them. Of course, reality is always complex and it is rare when one single theory can make sense of everything. These should therefore be perceived as "ideal-types," theoretically pure conceptions of the world that may explain some of reality but rarely all of it. Some cases will be better explained by one view, others by another, and still others will require a multidimensional explanation. As with other topics in this book, these theories should thus be construed as analytical tools, bearing in mind that few jobs can be completed with one tool alone. One would be therefore ill-advised to dismiss any part of one's toolbox.

We then take a more policy-oriented track and ask how African governments cope with ethnic diversity. We discuss problems of nation building, and of competing allegiances between national and ethnic identity. We review what mechanisms states have developed to deal with the ethnic question. Historically, approaches have ranged from formal constitutional mechanisms of accommodation to policies of physical destruction of certain groups, with informal co-optation being probably the most frequent solution. One's understanding of ethnicity becomes crucial here, as it dictates or constrains policy preferences.

There are, however, other dimensions to African societies' heterogeneity that are relevant to politics. Other cultural features such as language and religion are occasionally prevalent. Africanists tend to collapse the discussion of language into that of ethnicity, largely because the distinction between ethnic identity and ethnolinguistic identity can be hard to make. A notable exception is Cameroon, where since late 2016 political protests and violence have marked increased tensions between that country's anglophone and francophone communities, reflecting regional structural disparities and crises within the state itself (Pommerolle and Heungoup 2017).

Religion deserves more of its own treatment. Particularly important trends in the twenty-first century include the rise of evangelical churches and political Islam, sometimes within the same country, and the continued political significance of practices of witchcraft across

the continent. While many countries continue to be able to accommodate diverse faiths, religious polarization has generally increased and
represents a serious problem in countries such as Nigeria, and a rising
problem in countries such as Senegal and Tanzania. Western countries,
and particularly the United States, have also become increasingly concerned with the perceived penetration of Islamist movements in the
Sahel and the Horn regions.

Next we turn to a discussion of the analytical relevance of social
classes in Africa. Class analysis has long been a foundational element
of political science and often provides great explanatory mileage in
the study of politics. Yet class-based analyses of African politics have
historically met with limited success because of the absence of well-
defined class categories relative to industrialized societies. The fact
that there are often no clear-cut workers versus owners of capital or
land in Africa should not, however, be an impediment to understanding politics along some adjusted class lines. Some scholars have suggested that relation to the state, as opposed to the means of production, is the relevant factor in distinguishing class identity. Others have
stressed urban versus rural interests. Regardless of how class is
defined, many scholars have observed that class struggles are not
prevalent in Africa, especially when compared to ethnic competition
that seems to cut across classes. Yet there might be other modes of
class action on the continent.

We continue with a discussion of gender in African politics. In general, formal state politics in Africa is overwhelmingly male-dominated.
Yet there are significant differences among countries in the degree of
women's integration into formal political institutions, with a number
of recent experiments aimed at increasing institutional representation.
In addition, women can sometimes act as a political category, particularly at the associative level. Some authors have shown, for example,
that women-based nongovernmental organizations are less likely to
suffer from ethnic divisions than their male counterparts. We discuss
formal policies in relation to gender equality, as well as less formal
gender dynamics in African politics.

We conclude this chapter with a discussion of civil society, its
features in Africa, and its role in African politics. Specifically, we ask
what civil society is and what it is expected to do in politics. We then
show the concept's limitations and potential bias in the study of
African politics and how it has been modified by some scholars to
better reflect the realities of African societies and political mobilization among them.

Ethnicity

Theories of Ethnic Identity

Africa is significantly more ethnically heterogeneous than the rest of the world; no other region comes close to its level of ethnic fragmentation. For all of sub-Saharan Africa, the probability that two randomly selected individuals belong to different ethnic groups is 66 percent.[1] For the world as a whole (including Africa), the average is 36 percent.[2] Yet there are significant variations in ethnic heterogeneity among African countries, as Table 3.1 makes clear. Swaziland (as of 2018, Eswatini), for example, is rather homogeneous, composed of 97 percent ethnic Swazis. Its score on the ethnic diversity index is particularly low, at 6 percent. At the opposite end, Uganda counts some twenty-five highly differentiated and rather evenly distributed groups, including well-established precolonial kingdoms such as Ankole, Buganda, Bunyoro, and Toro, as well as other less centralized groups such as the Karamajongs and the Acholi. As a result, there is a 93 percent chance that two randomly selected Ugandans will belong to different ethnic groups.

For such data to be meaningful, however, the category of "ethnic group" must be well defined. Yet this is hardly ever the case. As is apparent in Table 3.1, there can be widely varying estimates of how many ethnic groups are present in a country. Depending on sources, Angola has from 8 to 100 ethnic groups, Benin from 21 to 31, Ghana from 10 to 75, and the Democratic Republic of Congo from 4 to more than 300. There are two broad reasons for such disparities. On the one hand, there is a relatively simple problem of aggregation. Given the nuances and fluidity of cultural features, where does an ethnic group start and where does it end? One can think of Somalia as almost entirely composed of ethnic Somalis, for example.[3] Or one can consider its eight clans to represent the relevant level of political and cultural aggregation, making for a much more heterogeneous picture. For the Democratic Republic of Congo, one account lists as many as 365 ethnic groups (Ndaywel e Nziem 1998:256–257). One the other hand, these groups are all largely associated with four broad linguistic families: Kikongo, Swahili, Lingala, and Tshiluba. These examples suggest that one obtains different ethnic counts depending on the level of aggregation one chooses.

The other reason for such disparity is that, to some extent, the degree to which a country is perceived as ethnically heterogeneous depends on one's definition of "ethnic group" and one's theoretical understanding of ethnicity. One can consider that ethnicity is a long-standing, precolonial, fixed level of identity. From this perspective, people were Zulu, Hutu, or Kikuyu before they became South African, Rwandan, or Kenyan. In such

Table 3.1 Ethnicity in Africa

	Ethnic Diversity (%)	Politically Relevant Ethnic Groups (%)	Number of Groups	Size and Name of Largest Group (%)
Angola	79	65	8–100	38, Ovimbundu
Benin	79	30	21–31	39.2, Fon
Botswana	41	0	6–13	92, Tswana
Burkina Faso	74	0	8–14	50, Mossi
Burundi	30	26	2–5	85, Hutu
Cameroon	86	71	200+	31, Highlanders
Cape Verde	42	n/a	9	71, Creole
Central African Republic	83	23	10–20	33, Baya
Chad	86	66	19–30	46, Arab
Comoros	0	n/a	5–7	39, Ngazidja
Congo, Democratic Republic of	87	80	4–365	10, Kongo, Luba
Congo, Republic of	87	19	5–25	48, Kongo
Côte d'Ivoire	82	49	60+	42, Akan
Djibouti	80	n/a	4–5	50, Somali (Issa)
Equatorial Guinea	35	2	5–6	85, Fang
Eswatini	6	0	1–4	97, Swazi
Eritrea	65	n/a	8–9	55, Tigrinya
Ethiopia	72	54	11–15	40, Oromo
Gabon	77	21	40	30, Fang
Gambia	79	48	5–9	42, Mandinka
Ghana	67	44	10–75	45, Akan
Guinea	74	59	4–16	40, Peul
Guinea-Bissau	81	5	20	30, Balanta
Kenya	86	57	15–36	22, Kikuyu
Lesotho	26	0	1–4	99, Sotho
Liberia	91	62	15–19	20, Kpelle
Madagascar	88	0	11–20	27, Merina
Malawi	67	55	7–22	32, Chewa
Mali	69	13	11–21	50, Mande
Mauritania	62	n/a	6–15	82, Moor
Mauritius	46	60	4	68, Indio-Mauritian
Mozambique	69	36	29	38, Makhuwa
Namibia	63	55	14	46, Ovambo
Niger	65	51	7–17	55, Hausa
Nigeria	85	66	250+	29, Hausa-Fulani
Rwanda	32	26	3	84, Hutu
São Tomé	n/a	n/a	n/a	n/a
Senegal	69	33	6–10	43, Wolof
Seychelles	20	0	1–5	70, Creoles
Sierra Leone	82	60	18–25	35, Temne

continues

Table 3.1 continued

	Ethnic Diversity (%)	Politically Relevant Ethnic Groups (%)	Number of Groups	Size and Name of Largest Group (%)
Somalia	81	0	3–11	85, Somali
South Africa	75	49	11–14	23.8, Zulu
South Sudan	n/a	n/a	6–17	40, Dinka
Sudan	71	41	5–12	70, Sudanese Arab
Tanzania	74	59	130+	12, Sukuma
Togo	71	49	33–37	44, Ewe
Uganda	93	63	24–34	17, Baganda
Zambia	78	71	8–23	37, Bemba
Zimbabwe	39	41	3–5	82, Shona
Average (unweighted)	66	36		

Sources: Data on ethnic diversity from Alesina et al. 2002. Data on politically relevant ethnic groups from Posner 2004a. Data on number of groups and largest group from Morrison, Mitchell, and Paden 1989; *Africa South of the Sahara 2019* (2018); Encyclopædia Britannica 2013; CIA 2018; Statistics South Africa 2003; and Ndaywel e Nziem 1998.

Note: n/a = data not available.

a case, one may rely on anthropological and ethnographic accounts of identity and end up with a large number of smaller groups. Alternatively, one can think of ethnicity as more flexible, as an identity resource among others that people can use, or not, depending on circumstances. In this case, many cultural distinctions may appear politically irrelevant and not constitute the foundation of ethnic differences. Or they may be relevant at one time or place, and not in another. If one were to think this way, being black might have once been a more relevant ethnic identity in South Africa than being Zulu. And being Hutu or Tutsi might not always have been a meaningful political distinction in Rwanda.

The following pages describe the main theoretical approaches to ethnic identity and salience in Africa. Their differences are not merely a matter of gratuitous theoretical disagreements, for one's understanding of ethnicity has serious policy implications. The choice of constitutional arrangements to accommodate cultural pluralism, electoral rules to promote or repress minority representation, or conflict resolution mechanisms to settle civil wars will largely depend on whether ethnicity is seen as a "hard" or a "soft" constraint, as affecting politics or being affected by it, as deeply ingrained or somewhat superficial.

Primordialism. Primordialism is a view of ethnicity as a deep-rooted, ancestral, irreducible, and nonnegotiable part of one's identity. By and large, it assumes that Africans may be Congolese, Nigerian, Sudanese, or Zambian, but they also have preexisting or even permanent ahistorical ethnic identities that largely define who they are. These identities are perceived as traditional and, from the perspective of this approach, reflect the "real" Africa that is essentially composed of competing ethnic groups.

According to primordialism, Africa's ethnic diversity is understood as a cause of conflict and an explanation for the poor functioning of its states. Interpretations of African conflicts as representing ancestral tribal hatreds fall into this category. For scholars of primordialism, Africans owe allegiance to their ethnic group or "tribe," and they act in the national public sphere in a manner that maximizes their communal interests at the expense of the state and in competition with other communities. Peter Ekeh's (1975) work represents probably one of the most eloquent and sophisticated expressions of the primordial view. Ekeh argues that Africans are faced with two spheres of public life: the "civic public," which is the extension of the colonial state, and the "primordial public," which encompasses traditional village life. The morality that Africans display in their private lives carries to their actions in the primordial public, which is the natural historical extension of the private sphere, but does not carry to the civic public, which is seen as an exogenous structure toward which they have no moral obligation. While the primordial community functions along lines of reciprocity, the civic public is seen as only a resource to be tapped for the benefit of the community.

Ekeh's argument attempts to explain the frequently corrupt behavior of African elites. The "uniqueness of modern African politics," he writes, results from the "tensions and confrontations between these two publics," as elites are expected to "rob the civic public in order to strengthen the primordial one" (1975:108). One of the strengths of his theory is that it provides a moral explanation of corruption based on Africans' allegiance to their primordial identity. It also makes sense of "tribalism," or competition among ethnic groups for access to state resources via their elites in power. Consider, for example, the widespread prevalence of corruption in Nigeria, the country Ekeh focuses on. Primordialism can account for it by presenting Nigeria as an illegitimate structure superimposed upon the primordial political systems of the Yoruba, the Hausa-Fulani, and the Igbo, among others. In the words of another Nigerian, novelist Chinua Achebe (1960:38), the state then becomes "an alien institution and people's business [is] to get as much from it as they [can] without getting into trouble." Hence, corruption.[4] The primordialist view tends therefore to see the state as the problem more than ethnic groups per se. Michela Wrong's (2010) account of the plundering of Kenya's public monies by a group of Kikuyu politicians vividly illustrates this idea of "getting as much as one can" from the state for the benefit of an ethnically defined community.

Clifford Geertz (1973) provides another classic example. Geertz wondered how new African postcolonial states could form national identities as their "people's sense of self [remained] bound up in the gross actualities of blood, race, language, locality, religion, or tradition." He thought the new states were therefore "abnormally susceptible to serious disaffection based on primordial attachments" (258–259). Because he views ethnic identity as so deeply rooted, Geertz did not consider the problem of the new states to be simply one of dealing with cultural heterogeneity, but of facing "competing loyalties of the same general order" as the nation-states. "Primordial discontent," he wrote, "strives more deeply and is satisfied less easily" than other forms of opposition (261).

This perception of ethnicity as representing the core political identity of subnational communities offers a theoretical explanation for phenomena such as some civil wars, separatism, and irredentism. The civil war between South Sudan and the northern-controlled national government from the late 1950s to 2005 can thus be understood as the refusal of the southern black Dinka, Nuer, and other populations to be assimilated by the Arabizing national state. This is what Francis Deng (1995) calls a "war of visions." The war of secession launched by rebels in the Casamance region of Senegal in 1982 can also be interpreted in primordial terms as an attempt by the Dioulas (or Joolas) of Casamance to reject their integration into the Senegalese state, which is broadly controlled by Wolof elites.[5] Primordialism is also the most frequent explanation for the invasion of the Somali-populated Ogaden region of Ethiopia by Somalia in the 1970s. In the words of former Somali president Abdirashiid Ali Shermaarke, "our neighbors are our Somali kinsmen whose citizenship has been falsified by indiscriminate boundary arrangements. . . . We speak the same language. We share the same creed, the same culture and the same traditions. How can we regard our brothers as foreigners?" (Samatar 1985:155).

Although primordialism was a more prevalent approach in the 1960s and 1970s than it is today, it has retained significant analytical currency, especially in juxtaposition with other perspectives. A book by Joshua Forrest (2003:2) analyzes "subnational" movements in many African countries as partly a result of "individuals' conscious or ascriptive adherence to ethnic or regional identity patterns," together with other factors such as regional inequalities and elite identity manipulations. Primordialism has also retained its relevance because it is a view often held by Africans themselves about the nature of their ethnic identity (e.g., Ayittey 1998), particularly at the grassroots, and is capable of accounting for the occasionally intense emotional attachment to ethnic identity (Young 2002).

Constructivism. Since the late 1970s and 1980s, constructivism has progressively displaced primordialism as the mainstream approach to ethnicity among Africanists. For constructivists, ethnic identities are somewhat malleable and very much the outcome of some other factors. Far from being transcendental to contemporary life or otherwise traditional, ethnic identity can be invented, constructed, or rendered more or less salient.

Crawford Young (1976) begins his landmark work *The Politics of Cultural Pluralism* with the question "Are you a Mumbala or a Mupende?" which he was asked by an angry Congolese policeman in 1962. The question was rather surprising to the extent that Young is a white American, yet he wisely decided not to explore "the full meaning of his question" with the policeman, or to "explain my inability to respond within the categories offered" (3). Thankfully, he had no such reservation for his readers. Young does not tell us his eventual answer, but he uses the episode to show how the Mumbala-Mupende ethnic distinction was the dominant "social code" at the time in the polarized Idiofa region of Congo, although it had no particular political meaning before 1959. Rather, it was the politics of independence and the frustrated expectations of what it would bring about that led people of Pende ethnicity to realize that they were less well prepared for access to state positions than were other local groups "who came to be lumped as Mbala." As "discontent . . . cried out for the identification of new social enemies," a Mbala-Pende dichotomy arose, centered on the perceived social advantages of the Mbala (4).[6]

Young's account illustrates how the political salience of ethnic identity can be triggered by changing circumstances. Colonization was one such circumstance. Colonizers imposed or crystallized tribal categories upon Africans. These identities may have existed before and may have carried political meaning, as was the case with the Ashanti of Ghana and the Baganda of Uganda. Yet they may also have existed in rather diluted ways and without representing a political project, as was the case with the Igbo of Nigeria, who shared common cultural features but were politically aggregated by the British colonizers, who through their policies of indirect rule tended to seek out chiefly local counterparts. In some other cases, groups were simply invented. This happened, for example, with the "Ngala" of Congo, a label broadly applied by the colonizers to people from the Congo River area around Mbandaka, which had no historical or social foundation whatsoever (Young 1976:171–174; see also Young 1965:242–246). Colonial anthropological work, which favored the practice of ethnic monographs, further contributed to the creation of ethnic identity, as did religious missions, which consolidated and helped define local languages for the purpose of translating the Bible.

The ethnic inventions of the colonizers, their anthropologists, and missionaries had very tangible consequences. Populations that may originally have been fragmented with complex patterns of cultural identity started identifying with the new categories, in a sort of "feedback effect" (Young 1976:166), as these labels offered avenues to relate to the new prevailing structures of power. Urbanization and the migration of rural Africans to the new cities reinforced these patterns of identity formation. Africans from different groups came into contact with each other in the new colonial cities and became aware of their different identities, especially as they occasionally faced different treatments from the colonizers, who favored some over others. What Young labels urban "social fields" became therefore a locus of ethnic differentiation, and sometimes of polarization, among these groups. As their members migrated back to rural areas, they carried their new identities with them and contributed to ethnicizing Africa's hinterland. In countries where there was no similar pattern of migration from ethnically homogeneous regions to the new urban centers, however, ethnic identity did not develop along equally polarized lines. This has been the case of Tanzania, for example, where big cities developed in zones of diffuse ethnicity and did not witness the significant arrival of migrants from homogeneous regions (Young 1976:218–234).

"Differential modernization," or different rates of access to modern social roles, is another factor in the formation of ethnic identity and in the salience of ethnic polarization (Young 1976:175–181). The importance of external factors in the formation of ethnic identity can also be seen in the progressive formation of ethnic groups that include references to administrative divisions. While the Luba of the DRC existed as a political entity before Belgian colonization (Vansina 1990), their partition across two provinces progressively led to the rise of two groups frequently at odds with each other: the Luba-Kasai in Kasai province, and the Balubakat in northern Katanga province. Similarly, in neighboring Congo-Brazzaville, the populations of the southern regions of Niari, Bouenza, and Lekoumou are often referred to as "Nibolek."

Benedict Anderson's (1983) view of cultural communities is broadly compatible with that of Young. Although he writes neither about Africa nor about ethnicity, he had considerable impact on the study of African ethnicity. Anderson sees the rise of "print capitalism" as lying at the root of national identity, because it promoted certain vernacular languages in which state bureaucracies operated and in which newspapers offered shared experiences to their readership. He also argues that administrative assignments across states promoted the consciousness of a shared identity among bureaucrats. Anderson's view of national identity as derived from the top down offers a constructivist alternative to a previously dominant view that conceived of the origins of nations as lying in some primordial link of blood (e.g., Smith 1986). His criticism of the ethnic theory of origin of nations resonated strongly with constructivist Africanists who were challenging primordialist conceptions of ethnicity.

Pushing constructivism further, Terrence Ranger (1983) addressed not so much the origins of African ethnicity as those of "traditional" structures of power in Africa. He argues that many European traditions were invented at the end of the nineteenth century, including those of empire. Colonials in Africa used their own alleged traditions to create a structure of power and domination, and to establish clear roles of dominant and dominated. Africans were enrolled in these traditions and sought to appropriate some of them, partly as a way of social promotion. More important, Europeans also created African traditions in their attempts to make sense of and control these cultures. In doing so, writes Ranger, they created rigidity where there used to be fluidity. These invented traditions were in turn used by Africans, who also further contributed to their invention. Ranger does not argue that ethnic identity per se was invented, but rather that many features of "traditional" political organization among ethnic groups are creations of the colonial era. Africans, "uprooted" by colonization, used new traditions as "new ways of making a new society" (237).

One advantage of Ranger's argument is that it presents colonized Africans as a dynamic group with its own divisions and differentiated patterns of adjustment. Africans are not uniformly at the losing end of the colonial relation, and some employ the traditionalist discourse of the colonizers. Elders use tradition against youth, men against women, chiefs in order to expand their control over other groups, and indigenous populations in general to fend off immigrants (254–260).[7]

A similar, albeit politically more radical, emphasis on the "traditional" structures of power, as opposed merely to identity, comes out of Mahmood Mamdani's *Citizen and Subject* (1996). Mamdani's main thesis is that colonial rule was based on "institutional segregation," a "regime of differentiation" that independence failed to abolish (7). Faced with the dilemma of establishing minority control over their conquests, colonial powers reserved a space of rights and direct rule to themselves, a white civil society in urban areas, and dominated the local African peasantry through indirect rule by either reconstituting or imposing tribal leadership

as the local extension of the colonial state (17). Mamdani thereby empha-
sizes the "uncustomary" nature of native authorities. Independence succeeded in deracializing the state but failed to "detribalize" it. Moreover,
the need for rulers to bridge the urban-rural gap to extend their hegemony
led them to a retribalization of the state, as they sought alliances with
local, tribally defined leadership. The enduring tribal nature of the local
state has led strategies of resistance to unfold at the same level. The
weakness of "tribalism as revolt," however, is that it reproduces the existing social fragmentation and divisions. Mamdani thereby presents a
remarkable picture of Africa's predicament through a unifying constructivist view of power and resistance. His analytical framework can help us
make sense, for example, of post-electoral violence in Kenya in 2007–
2008. After Mwai Kibaki, a man of Kikuyu ethnicity and the incumbent
president, was fraudulently declared the winner of the December 2007
presidential election, supporters of his cheated opponent, Raila Odinga, of
Luo ethnicity, took to the streets and meted out violent reprisals against
apparent perceived supporters of Kibaki. These actions rapidly descended
into Luo-against-Kikuyu warfare and left more than a thousand dead, and
many more displaced and scattered across refugee camps in the region
(Bøås and Dunn 2013; Cheeseman 2008). Perceptions of the state as controlled by the Kikuyu led to a revolt against electoral fraud based on ethnic lines. Yet there is no predetermined conflict between the Kikuyu and
the Luo or other ethnic groups. It is the manner in which these communities appear to have unequally benefited from the postcolonial state that
has induced polarization among them. The ethnic nature of political
resistance to electoral fraud reproduces ethnic divisions within Kenya and
hampers the spread of substantive democracy.

Not only does constructivism account for the origins of ethnic identity, but it can also help make sense of variations in ethnic salience and
cleavages through time and space, which a primordial understanding of
ethnicity would be unable to accommodate. For example, why has the
Hutu-Tutsi cleavage been so important in Rwanda since the 1990s, providing even the ferment for a genocide of Tutsis in 1994, whereas this
distinction did not carry a potent political significance before the late
1950s (Lemarchand 1970)? In addition, why are "Rwandophones" (a
category that includes both Hutus and Tutsis) jointly shunned and stig-
matized as "non-Bantus" in Congo, but polarized into two distinct
groups in Rwanda and Burundi? Looking elsewhere, why was Somali
identity the prevailing level of ethnic aggregation of Somalis in the
1960s, whereas clans have increasingly taken this role since the 1980s?
Why were the Igbo of Nigeria the force behind the secession of Biafra

in 1967, whereas in the 1990s and 2000s, Niger Delta politics revolved around collective action by the Ijaw, Itsekiri, Ogoni, and others? Understanding the salience of these identities as resulting from other circumstances—whether demographic, political, institutional, or other—allows for the modulation of different ethnic patterns given the same available distribution of ethnic identities. It also helps us make sense of the fact that, most of the time in most places, ethnic groups coexist and collaborate peacefully (Fearon and Laitin 1996).

Finally, constructivism is also capable of explaining the simultaneity of different political identities and the propensity of many Africans to display both ethnic polarization and nationalist fervor. Not only are some ethnic cleavages meaningful at some periods and others at different times, but the same individuals may find themselves part of different groups or cleavages at different points in time or concurrently. This does not mean that a Nigerian can be Yoruba today, Hausa tomorrow, and Igbo next week. What it does mean, however, is that a Congolese can stress her Chokwe identity at one point, privilege the broader Lunda cultural referent at another (of which the Chokwe can be thought of as a subgroup), highlight her Swahili language at yet another, and finally present herself as a Katangan, all the while displaying her Congolese nationalism.

Because constructivism conceives of ethnic identities as malleable and constituting registries from which people can draw according to the circumstances they face, it can reconcile these fluid and overlapping displays of allegiance. Attahiru Jega (2000) shows that national identity and class were prevalent modes of identification in Nigeria during the oil boom of the 1970s, but progressively gave way to ethnic, religious, communal, and regional identities as the economy regressed under the austerity measures of structural adjustment programs in the 1980s. These "identity transformations" responded to the dynamics of the accumulation process as competition intensified for access to state power and resources. Tim Kelsall (2005) uses a constructivist understanding of ethnicity to explain the lack of social movements in Africa. The prevalence of semipermanent, opportunistic work in Africa, he argues, leads to a "fragmentation of the self." In their quest for survival, people develop links to several potential patrons, always on the lookout for the best option: "The ways in which people make a living in Africa encourage them into plural identities, which prevents them from organizing collectively over time, thereby foreclosing certain types of social movement and popular power" (64).

The simultaneous display of subnational and national identity is one of the most puzzling dimensions of identity politics in Africa, and one for which constructivism may offer a plausible answer. Young (2002, 2007, 2012) argues that Africans inherited three levels of subjective identity from the colonial era: racial identity provided the basis for Pan-Africanism, the ideology of continental unity; territorial identity for nationalism; and ethnic identity for tribalism or ethnicity. Nationalism in Africa became the tool for the liberation from colonial rule because it corresponded to the territories that were given sovereignty. As such it was rooted in a "shared experience of common colonial subjugation within a territorial container" (2002:7) rather than in ethnicity or precolonial history. Ethnicity has not competed with this sense of nationalism because its origins are equally recent and shallow. Although it represents shared cultural values and sense of consciousness, ethnicity has not developed into ethnonationalism in Africa, as that ideological field was already occupied by the state. Instead, ethnic solidarity developed as a mobilization resource for political competition within the state.

Constructivism's emphasis on the invented nature of ethnic identity does not imply that these identities or the social cleavages that they produce are not real. Whether the Ngala ethnic group existed from the beginning of history or was accidentally invented by Belgian colonizers does not affect the relevance of the Ngala ethnic category. That the modern version of the Buganda kingdom of Uganda was invented by the 1900 Buganda Agreement, which made it a British protectorate, does not erase anything from Buganda's very real current existence and significance in Ugandan politics. The results of inventions are real, and so are imagination's consequences. From this perspective, some go so far as to argue that constructed identities cannot easily be reconstructed, and that, for all practical purposes, a quasi-primordial treatment of ethnic identity as fixed in any given situation is methodologically legitimate (van Evera 2001).[8]

Instrumentalism. Rather than an altogether new theory of ethnicity, instrumentalism represents a specific variation of the constructivist approach. Yet it takes constructivist insights so far that it deserves to be treated as its own approach. The two key dimensions of instrumentalist texts is their tendency to focus on the uses of ethnicity by political entrepreneurs and their view of ethnic groups as political coalitions like any other.

Robert Bates (1983) adopts a rational choice approach to ethnicity. Rational choice is a methodological disposition according to which political outcomes, including collective action, can be explained based on the assumption that individuals make rational cost-benefit decisions in the pursuit of the maximization of their self-interest. Bates starts from the interesting observation that ethnicity is not some primitive level of identity that disappears in the process of modernization, but a phenomenon of increased salience in contemporary Africa that he sees as a rational response to modernization. Ethnic groups are efficient coalitions, he argues, that come together to stake a claim on the distribution of the resources of modernization. The efficiency of ethnic coalitions derives first from their spatial distribution. Because members of a given ethnic group tend to cluster in space, they have similar preferences with respect to allocation decisions, which are homogeneous and well defined. For example, they are likely to share a desire for schools, roads, or other infrastructure in their region, or to support agricultural subsidies for the crops grown in their region. In addition, because colonial powers often delineated administrative units along loose ethnic lines (which may be truer of British than of other colonies), it became in the interest of colonial subjects to organize ethnically in order to gain control over the administrative mechanisms of the modernization process, which allocate public resources. Finally, it soon became in the interest of modernized groups and elites to sponsor the creation of "traditional" sentiments, because they had to organize collective support to advance their position in the competition for the benefits of modernity, particularly through elections. Ethnic groups persist under modernization and are further consolidated because they are successful at extracting goods and services from the modern sector and at satisfying the demands of their members. Modernization and ethnic conflict (or competition) end up being two sides of the same coin.

Bates's work is striking for the lack of affect it imparts upon ethnicity. From his instrumentalist perspective, Africans find it useful to adopt ethnic identities, and their elites encourage them to do so, but they could just as well have chosen other types of political coalitions had they faced different incentives. Blood, history, and emotion are nowhere in sight. A similar approach was adopted by Nelson Kasfir (1979) in a paper that also highlighted the roles of political entrepreneurs and of rational cost-benefit decisions in the choice of ethnic identity by individuals.

In the same vein, Daniel Posner (2004b, 2005) focuses not only on the rationality of ethnic identity and its coalitional nature, but also and more precisely on the role that the relative size of different identity groups plays in determining the choice of ethnic identity and the nature of ethnic cleavages. In one article, he asked why the Chewas and Tumbukas, who straddle the border between Zambia and Malawi, were allies in the former country and adversaries in the latter while their objective cultural differences were identical on both sides of the border. The essence of his argument is that relative size matters. In Zambia, Tumbukas and Chewas are relatively small groups and can derive benefit from joint collective action, while in Malawi they are relatively large groups and represent "viable bases for political coalition-building" on their own (Posner 2004b:529).

Generalizing some of these insights, and in contrast to primordialists, who would conceive of ethnic identity as affecting the functioning of political institutions, Posner suggests that it is institutions that shape the "repertoires of potentially mobilizable ethnic identities that individuals possess" (2005:3) and their incentives for selecting one identity rather than another. Institutions also coordinate these choices across individuals so as to produce a society-level outcome. Thus, Posner explains that, during one-party rule in Zambia (1966–1990), ethnic identities were more salient, as they represented the foundations of claims of inclusion in the regime. Once the country democratized in the early 1990s, these ethnic identities no longer represented broad enough bases for electoral success, and political identity started to coalesce at the level of the four main national language groups. Hence, the transition from authoritarianism to electoral democracy—an institutional transformation—produced an adjustment in the level of ethnic identity.

While Posner identifies a shift away from ethnicity and toward language groups in the move from single-party to multiparty politics in Zambia, it is also true that ethnic, ethnolinguistic, or regional identities tend to surface and acquire more salience in the context of electoral democracy than under authoritarian or single-party rule (Ottaway 2003). In Burundi, for example, the adoption of multiparty politics before the 1993 elections led to the formation of the Front pour la Démocratie au Burundi (FRODEBU), a Hutu party, and the Union pour le Progrès National (UPRONA), a Tutsi party. This had already been the case in the 1970s with the creation of the Parti pour la Libération du Peuple Hutu (PALIPEHUTU). Ethnic parties were banned in a later constitution. While not as explicit, Ivorian political parties in the 2010 elections were also largely identified with ethnic groups. The Front Populaire Ivoirien (FPI) had a core Bete constituency, the Parti Démocratique de Côte d'Ivoire (PDCI) a mostly Baoulé (Akan) leadership, and most politicians and supporters of the Rassemblement des Républicains (RDR) came from northern groups identified as Dioulas. One can find similar ethnic patterns of party distribution in many African countries.

The fluidity of ethnic identity implied by instrumentalism led Posner to reconsider the usefulness and accuracy of the conventional measure of ethnic heterogeneity with which we started our discussion of ethnicity (see the "ethnic diversity" column in Table 3.1), as it was both static and insensitive to political conditions. Thus Posner (2004a) embarked upon a recoding exercise that sought to identify "politically relevant" ethnic groups, from which he would recalculate new indices of ethnic fragmentation by decades. The resulting PREG index (politically relevant ethnic groups) for the 1980s is reproduced in Table 3.1. In all but two instances (Mauritius and Zimbabwe), PREG yields lower estimates of ethnic fragmentation than the earlier method. The continental average falls from 66 percent to 36 percent. In some countries, such as the Republic of Congo, the drop is dramatic, from 87 percent to 19 percent. Such a reduction captures the fact that, while there are many different cultural groups in Congo, only three broad categories have political significance: the southerners, aggregated around the mostly Bakongo populations of the Niari, Bouenza, and Lekoumou regions (the "Nibolek" referred to earlier), who are a majority; the populations of the "Pool" area around Brazzaville, most of whom are Lari; and the northerners, largely represented by the Mbochi ethnic group, with an estimated 13 percent of the country's population. One could identify subgroups within the broad Bakongo identity, but it would carry little analytical mileage in Congolese politics. Similarly, there are more groups than just the Mbochi in the north, but several decades of rule by dictator Denis Sassou-Nguesso, a Mbochi, have given his group unusual political leverage.

In the neighboring Democratic Republic of Congo, on the other hand, ethnic diversity starts from a similar 87 percent, but barely falls according to the PREG index, to 80 percent. While the DRC does indeed have as many as 365 ethnic groups, and not all of them have political significance, a large amount of them do, particularly at the local level, resulting in a high index number. In the North Kivu region alone, ethnic polarization is pronounced between Rwandophone communities (Hutus and Tutsis) and other groups such as the Nande, Hunde, Bashi, Tembo, and Nyanga, and within these latter groups. In South Kivu, ethnic communities with political relevance include the Vira, Bembe, Fulero, Tembo, and Shi. In that region, there is even a politically differentiated subset of Tutsi, known as the "Banyamulenge," a term (and an identity) that only surfaced around the 1980s (Willame 1997) and that literally means "the people who live around Mulenge." All these ethnicities and their salience are largely maintained by the nature of local administrative divisions and the constitutional powers granted to customary chiefs, providing another instance of institutions shaping identities.

Some of the insights of instrumentalism have been taken further in recent scholarship. Using data from over 35,000 respondents in twenty-two public opinion surveys in ten African countries, Benn Eifert, Edward Miguel, and Daniel Posner (2010) find that the likelihood of ethnic self-identification (as opposed to class or occupational self-identification) increases as one nears a presidential election. They infer from their findings that ethnic identity is an instrument in the competition for political power. Biniam Bedasso (2017) argues that ethnicity has been politically salient in Kenya because elites are able to use it more successfully as a bargaining chip than economic cleavages. And as Dominic Burbidge (2014) notes, ethnic identification often trumps class solidarity among middle-class voters because of the fear that others from different ethnic groups will vote along ethnic lines. Instrumentalist approaches suggest that, rather than reflecting ancestral bonds, ethnicity persists for strategic reasons.

While primordialism is particularly attractive for explaining violent conflicts, instrumentalism, with its focus on competition rather than conflict, is better suited to making sense of politics in electoral environments. As such, it is not surprising that it has gained some currency in the wake of the spread of electoral democracy in Africa since 1990. Its arguments lend themselves well to the study of voting patterns, electoral alliances, and ruling coalitions. An important concept in this respect is that of "minimum winning coalitions," advanced by William Riker (1962), according to which politicians form the smallest possible coalition necessary to win elections, so as to limit subsequent redistributive obligations. Ethnic instrumentalists suggest that politicians and their supporters will promote levels of identity aggregation sufficient for electoral victories. Using this insight, Karen Ferree (2012) argues that when a country's ethnic configuration leads to a single possible minimum winning coalition, political parties are stable over time, whereas when no such coalition emerges or when several are possible, instability ensues. Dominika Koter (2016) points out that politicians utilize different electoral mobilization strategies depending on the political environment. Koter's argument is that the stronger the hierarchical ties between local leaders and their followers, the less the likelihood for direct appeals to ethnicity. She notes that appeals to ethnic identity are generally lacking in countries such as Senegal where politicians can utilize intermediaries such as the marabout and traditional leaders, unlike countries such as Benin, Kenya, and Guinea, where political calculations make ethnic mobilization much higher. While providing useful insights, instrumentalism's assumptions of rationality and fluidity face greater challenges, however, in explaining protracted conflicts among ethnic groups and intense identity polarization, where all parties seem to end up worse off than from collaboration.

By way of conclusion, it is worth pondering how the different theories of ethnicity might help us make sense of the carnage that unfolded in Rwanda from April to June 1994, during which an estimated 800,000 mostly Tutsi citizens were killed at the hands of their mostly Hutu compatriots.[9] Rwanda is one of the handful of African countries that did not originate as a colonial state. It dates back several centuries as a precolonial kingdom, under a traditional structure of Tutsi domination, that, although not necessarily blissful, was nevertheless mostly peaceful. Under German and later Belgian colonial rule, the political domination of the Tutsi was reinforced, in part because the colonizers considered them a superior race. While colonialism did not invent the Hutu and Tutsi categories, it nevertheless reified them by treating them as rigid, primordial identities and crystallized relations of power in a manner that widened the chasm between these two communities. In the late 1950s, in a sudden reversal, the Belgian Catholic clergy, very powerful in all Belgian colonies, encouraged the political rise of the Hutu majority. This shift triggered a social revolution, which saw the political rise of the Hutu as a demographic majority embittered by past discrimination. The period 1959–1962 witnessed the massacres of many Tutsis and the exile of others to Congo and Uganda.

Those who fled to Uganda, and their children, would later contribute to the formation of the Rwandan Patriotic Front (RPF), a Tutsi-based insurgency, which launched a war in 1990 against the Hutu-dominated regime of Juvenal Habyarimana, who had been in power since 1972 at the head of an increasingly radicalized regime that institutionalized discrimination against Tutsis.

By 1994 the RPF was on the brink of overthrowing the regime. A United Nations–brokered peace agreement had provided for power-sharing between the RPF and the government, but its implementation was marred by problems. Hours after the president was killed when his plane was shot down upon returning home from peace negotiations in Tanzania, radical Hutu militiamen who had opposed the peace embarked on a genocide, which by all appearances had been long planned and unfolded until the RPF won the war in June and sent a couple million Hutus into exile in Congo and Tanzania (thousands of whom were also subsequently murdered when the RPF forces invaded Congo in 1996).

Although this and most other depictions of the Rwandan genocide highlight the polarization between Hutus and Tutsis, how did ethnicity factor into it? It must first be stressed that the long and peaceful cohabitation of Hutus and Tutsis in Rwanda over centuries suggests that the genocide was not simply the expression of a primordial enmity. Precolonial life reflected the rather porous nature of identity boundaries. To a large extent, the colonial institutionalization of social and political roles along ethnic lines increased the political salience of ethnic identity. This was later reinforced by the exile of many Tutsis. In this respect, constructivism provides some context and background for understanding the genocide. It has now become clear that Hutu politicians instrumentalized these ethnic identities as means to prevent the continuation of the international peace process that was to lead to enduring power-sharing. They planned the annihilation of Tutsis as a form of "final solution," aimed at resolving once and for all their Tutsi problem and annihilating popular support for the RPF. Incapable of militarily defending their regime, they engineered the destruction of an entire segment of their population, mobilizing Hutus by using a discourse that represented Tutsis as voracious power-grabbers who could not be trusted and as "cockroaches" that had to be crushed.

The Rwandan genocide might thus best be understood as the manipulation of ethnic history and identity for political ends by threatened government elites. They did not invent the Hutu and Tutsi identities. Yet they raised their political salience to a matter of life or death. In the process, they also reinforced these identities and contributed to the reproduction of ethnic polarization in Rwanda. As we discuss later, subsequent efforts by the RPF to ban ethnic identification have made only minimal inroads toward undoing Rwanda's dramatic cleavage.

State Responses to Ethnicity

Whatever its origins, the political salience of ethnic identity in Africa can pose very serious challenges to government. As Geertz (1973:261) noted, the newly independent African states were faced not merely with diversity but also with "competing loyalties of the same general order" as themselves. As we will discuss at great length in Chapter 4, African governments have typically dealt with these competing loyalties through informal mechanisms of co-optation. In this section we focus on formal attempts to either deny or accommodate ethnic identity.[10]

Denial and repression have been easier where ethnic salience was weak to begin with, as in the case of Tanzania discussed below. Yet repressive policies have also been applied where ethnic divisions were more salient, as in Guinea under Ahmed Sékou Touré, where Peuls were persecuted, or in Congo/Zaire under Mobutu Sese Seko, who employed informal ethnic balancing among elites. Despite these efforts, we are not aware of successful instances of eradicating the political salience of ethnicity through repression in ethnically divided societies. On the contrary, the polarizing and paralyzing salience of ethnicity in the first free elections ever held in Guinea, in 2010, suggested that Sékou Touré's policies might have left a greater legacy of ethnic politics than he inherited.

In contrast, some countries have attempted to construct institutional accommodation of ethnic diversity. In cases such as Uganda and Ethiopia, constitutional arrangements have been attempted to reserve a distinct place in the state for ethnic groups and their elites. Many African countries have at least some measure of formal recognition of "traditional" ethnic-based authorities, such as houses or councils of chiefs. As democracy has expanded across the continent, an increasing number of countries have introduced in their electoral laws requirements of cross-country representation, the purpose of which has been to reduce the salience of ethnic candidates and to create incentives for campaigning across ethnic groups. But recent scholarship suggests that ethnic voting might in fact not be as preponderant in Africa as is widely believed (see Chapter 5).

Repression of ethnicity. Julius Nyerere's Tanzania provides one of the most successful cases of ethnic repression and identity transformation in Africa. Despite having an estimated 130 languages and being one of the most ethnically diverse countries in Africa, Tanzania has managed to have few significant ethnic divisions compared to the rest of the continent and has displayed more political stability than most African countries since independence (Bienen 1989:100). Behind this achievement, it can be argued, is a nation-building policy undertaken by the central government at independence, based on a strategy of undermining ethnic ties, forcing the adoption of a unified language policy and a national ideology, and restructuring traditional economic relations. In many ways, Tanzania was not successful. Its economic policies, for example, failed to bring about development and caused much havoc among its populations (Hyden 1980). But Nyerere did succeed in building a Tanzanian identity and reducing ethnicity to relative political insignificance (Miguel 2004), a landmark achievement among his peers.

Nyerere first undermined sources of power associated with ethnicity by abolishing councils of chiefs and reinforcing nonethnic structures such as village and district councils. His Tanganyika African National Union (TANU) also dismantled customary tribal laws and ran campaigns against the notion of multiracialism, or against communal representations for Africans, Europeans, and Asians, and in favor of an "all-African" approach to Tanzanian identity (Glickman 1995:293). Nyerere's efforts were facilitated in this respect by the dispersion of Tanzanian ethnic identities in a country where no single group is large enough to dominate the center (Horowitz 1985:39–40). The erection of TANU as a single party is also often credited with promoting national unity, although single parties were widespread throughout Africa in the 1960s and 1970s with little similar success. Though in many African countries specific ethnic groups tend to be associated with military power, Nyerere kept ethnic representation in the military balanced at all levels of hierarchy (Glickman 1995:293). Additionally, TANU-mandated enrollment in national service further contributed to national integration (Wangwe 2005).

The head-on clash with customary authority was paralleled by the elevation of Swahili to the status of official national language. Swahili has the particular characteristic, and political advantage, of not being associated with any particular ethnic group. It is a vehicular language, widespread throughout much of East Africa, which people often speak together with their local vernacular. The National Swahili Council promoted rapid Swahilization in all spheres of life. Its vocabulary was widened and works of international literature were translated into Swahili. Nyerere went so far as to translate Shakespeare's *Julius Caesar* himself, and he boasted that he could travel throughout the country without interpreters, which few African rulers can. This adoption of an African language as the national language for politics and administration is unique on the continent and permitted the conduct of government to be "vastly more visible and proximate to the mass of the population" (Young 1976:263). Moreover, from a comparative perspective, only a few African countries benefit from such an ethnically neutral vehicular language as Tanzania's Swahili. Even in next-door Uganda, the use of Swahili is significantly more associated with some ethnic groups than with others, which casts doubt on the potential for replication of the Tanzanian experiment.

Ideological activism also played an important role in the formation of a Tanzanian identity. Nyerere developed and promoted a doctrine of "African socialism" that included elements of Pan-Africanism, nationalism, and social equality. He stressed human dignity, equality of opportunity, equal political rights across races, and a commitment to reduce income and wealth disparities beyond the commitment of most other African rulers. These values were spread throughout the school curriculum, which emphasized the commonalities of Tanzanians. Political education was a standard subject from the late 1960s, and teachers were required to serve in the national service, where significant indoctrination took place (Miguel 2004:335). TANU youth leagues, present in many schools, reinforced doctrinal purity (Hyden 1980).

Economic policies, although they largely failed to extract Tanzania from poverty, reinforced the regime's nation-building efforts. Redistributive policies begun in the late 1960s promoted equitable public spending in health and education across regions (Rothchild 1997:80). A program of "villagization" led to the relocation of 60 percent of the population from isolated rural homesteads to larger villages "based on what was seen as the ideal African traditional family . . . which provided and shared basic necessities of life on the basis of mutual respect and obligation" (Wangwe 2005). Although this program led to great misery and social dislocations, it also united Tanzanians in their predicament (Young 1976).

Altogether, the active repression of tribal authority, the development of a coherent national ideology, Swahilization, educational policies, and economic reforms contributed to Tanzania's unique experience in taming the political salience of ethnicity. It should be stressed, however, that Tanzania is not without other significant societal fault lines (a point to which we return later in this chapter). Success on the ethnic front has not prevented the rise of polarization along religious lines between Muslims and Christians. Moreover, the division between the mainland and the island of Zanzibar has not abated. But while the usually peaceful Tanzania witnessed an increase in political violence in 2018, it has not taken on ethnic dimensions.

Despite its relatively far-reaching reforms, the Tanzanian experience pales in comparison to the denial of ethnic identity in post-genocide Rwanda. Upon taking power in 1994, the Tutsi-dominated Rwandan Patriotic Front regime faced two particularly pernicious problems. One was the apparently impossible task of promoting reconciliation in a country where one of two groups had just seen half its population bludgeoned to death by members of the other. The second, more practical, was to consolidate its power despite its own minority status (Tutsis represent no more than 15 percent of Rwanda's population). With a propensity for heavy-handed politics, the RPF attempted to address both problems at once by putting an end, in public discourse and policy, to the Hutu-Tutsi distinction and attempting to engineer a new Rwandan identity, thereby enforcing "ethnic amnesia" as some observers have called it (Lemarchand 1992; Vandeginste 2014). Officially, there no longer are ethnic groups in Rwanda, and the social category of ethnicity is no longer given any currency. In 2013, the RPF government launched the "Ndi Umuyarwanda" ("I am Rwandan") program to foster a nonethnic national identity (Reyntjens 2018:514). To apprehend the radicalism of this approach, it helps to bear in mind that Rwanda had previously been one of the African countries where ethnicity and ethnic difference were most institutionalized, with identity cards listing one's group, and with jobs and certain residency areas apportioned along ethnic lines, in a manner at times reminiscent of apartheid South Africa.

Nowadays, official Rwandan ideology promotes the idea of a new citizen for whom ethnicity, if at all mentioned, is little more than a historical category, a tool to understand the genocide (the term for "genocide" in Kinyarwanda has also been altered to remove its implied reference to ethnicity). Any public mention of ethnicity risks exposing its perpetrator to a 2002 law that prohibits "divisionism," which is punishable by prison sentences of up to five years (Morrill 2006).

Many doubt that Rwandan president Paul Kagame's repression of ethnicity emanates from the same altruistic intentions as Nyerere's. The ban on ethnicism and divisionism has provided the regime with the legal ammunition to deter opponents in general. Some argue that it is also preventing a cathartic national dialogue on the genocide (Lemarchand 2007). For sure, it conveniently shields the current authorities from being held accountable for their own alleged abuses during and after the war against Hutu rebels, opponents, or civilians. Yet it involves a degree of social reengineering rarely matched in Africa and an experiment worth following for the student of ethnicity.

Other African countries have experienced milder forms of institutional tinkering to reduce the salience of ethnicity in politics. Often this has involved redrawing administrative boundaries, such as those of provinces, to prevent their overlap with ethnic identities, so as to limit the incentives for collective action to turn ethnic. Such policies heed Bates's advice that "what is required is a form of correction which exploits the very properties which generate the phenomenon [of ethnic coalition] in the first place: the desire for benefits and the capacity to act rationally in pursuit of them" (1983:165). The expansion of states in Nigeria from three at the time of independence—each capturing one dominant ethnic group—to four, twelve, thirty, and eventually thirty-six partly proceeds from this logic (Alapiki 2005:50). However, as Posner (2005) would have predicted, it has also resulted in the multiplication of localized identities. The same intentions underwrote the splitting of Buganda into four districts in 1966 (Young 1976:263), and the conversion of Burkina Faso's ten departments into thirty provinces in 1984. Elsewhere, as in Uganda and Kenya, the multiplication of local government units has followed a patronage logic (Green 2010; Hassan and Sheely 2017). Electoral rules are also sometimes designed to discourage ethnic voting. In Nigeria, ethnic-based political parties are banned and successful presidential candidates must win a simple majority of total national votes as well as at least one-third of the votes in at least two-thirds of the thirty-six states (Bogaards 2010).

Accommodation of ethnicity. At the other extreme from ethnic repression have been a few experiments in the formal legal incorporation of ethnicity into political systems. In these instances, ethnicity is not only recognized but also legally integrated at the root of the nation-building strategy. It becomes—in theory, at least—a building block of the state rather than a competitor to it. Note that these systems implicitly convey a primordial understanding of ethnicity.

In sharp contrast to Rwanda's denial of ethnicity, neighboring Burundi adopted a postconflict electoral system in 2005 that acknowledges, builds upon, and enshrines ethnicity and ethnic distribution, in what has been called a case of "ethnic consociationalism" (Vandeginste 2014; Lemarchand 2007). The concept of consociationalism was coined by Arendt Lijphart (1977) to define the political systems of nations such as Belgium and the Netherlands, where subnational communities are brought together in a national system through the formal co-optation of their leaders and proportional access to power. Burundi, like Rwanda, has a large (85 percent) Hutu majority and a Tutsi minority. Civil war and political unrest have raged since the 1993 assassination of an elected Hutu president, Melchior Ndadaye, by Tutsi military officers. Burundi's civil war, which only (and tentatively) ended in 2009, was but the last episode in a long series of reciprocal violent flares among its two communities, including peaks in 1965, 1969, 1972 (when the massacre of some 200,000 people led to the decimation of Hutu elites), and 1988. The 1993–2009 civil war was characterized by anti-Tutsi pogroms, bombing of Hutu neighborhoods by the military, ethnic cleansing, and armed Hutu insurgencies.

The 2000 Arusha Accord led the way to the constitution of 2005, which proposed a consociational solution to Burundi's ethnic crisis by aiming to strike a balance in the representation of both groups in executive and legislative organs, as well as in the army, along a principle of "proportionality, combined with minority over-representation" (Vandeginste 2009:76). Although the ethnicity of the president is to be determined by the electorate, the constitution provides for two vice presidents, one Hutu and one Tutsi. The government and the national assembly must be composed of 60 percent Hutus and 40 percent Tutsis. If the elections do not yield such a result, the electoral commission can co-opt additional members. In the senate and the military, the distribution is 50–50 Hutu-Tutsi. Moreover, two-thirds of national assembly members must be present to enact legislation, and laws must be passed by at least a two-thirds majority, implying that at least some Tutsi votes must be obtained. Locally, no more than 67 percent of the mayors of cities and villages can be from the same group.

What have been the effects of this system? The new constitution helped decrease the intensity of the civil war and rallied several fighting factions to peaceful politics. While most opposition parties boycotted the 2010 and 2015 parliamentary elections, leaving the ruling National Council for the Defense of Democracy–Forces for the Defense of Democracy (CNDD-FDD) with a preponderant majority in the national assembly, the electoral commission intervened to restore constitutional order, as it also did in 2005, by co-opting Tutsi representatives. Thus, by and large, the constitution has been successful at reducing effective Hutu hegemony. There is also no evidence that it has increased the salience of ethnic identity and the degree of polarization between Hutus and Tutsis (Vandeginste 2014:272). On the contrary, some evidence suggests that with the ethnic representation question taken out of the political sphere, most conflicts have now become inter-Hutu, while Tutsis benefit from their protected minority status. In this manner, despite the problems, a political model built around ethnicity might have paradoxically evacuated the ethnic question. Thus, René Lemarchand (2007:11) notes that this system has resulted in "an unprecedented de-polarization of the political arena," particularly through the emergence of ethnically mixed parties that attempt to gain majorities within the parameters of the constitutional distribution of ethnicity. Yet success is more mitigated in terms of state capacity, as the ethnic balancing act has prevented effective management of the nation. Rules of representation and voting in the national assembly, for example, have predictably resulted in a "complete standstill" of legislative activities (Vandeginste 2009:77). The system came under considerable strain after President Pierre Nkurunziza's controversial decision to run for a third term in 2015, with the country experiencing intense political violence, particularly in the capital, Bujumbura (van Acker 2018). Irrespective of the intrinsic merits of the Burundi solution, its accommodation of ethnicity provides a fascinating comparison to neighboring Rwanda's attempts at eradicate the Hutu-Tutsi distinction (Vandeginste 2014).

For decades, the Democratic Republic of Congo has employed the practice of *representativité,* a form of ethnic consociationalism, which ensures political representation for ethnic groups of sufficient size and, thus, some degree of access to state resources. But while this approach has been central to maintaining a degree of legitimacy for the Congolese state, there is some evidence that the 2015 restructuring of the Congo's eleven provinces into twenty-six has had the unintended consequence of heightening the political salience of ethnicity (Englebert, Calderon, and Jené 2018). The Congo's new provinces tend to be more ethnically homogeneous than previous ones, with the new provincial assemblies and governments even more homogeneous than the provinces themselves, leading to the exclusion of some groups and threatening the legitimacy of the practice of *representativité*.

Ethiopia provides another example of formal accommodation, though its adoption of ethnic federalism in its 1995 constitution does not make any specific ethnic provision for the sharing of power at the center. Recognizing minority rights to self-determination, Ethiopia created ethnically defined federated regions, such as Tigray, Oromia, Somali, Afar, and Amhara. Titular groups were given "proprietary rights" over their territory (Clapham 2006:29), while "nations, nationalities, and peoples" were given the right to secede. In practice, however, this system has shown its limitations. While minorities were formally granted a large degree of autonomy, the government established pro-regime official organizations to represent them, preventing their effective autonomy. With only one ethnic formation allowed to represent each group in its region and in the government, the rewards of the system in practice remained limited to a coterie of collaborators. Moreover, while theoretically providing for ethnic balance, in practice, the Tigrayan People's Liberation Front has dominated Ethiopian politics for most of the past three decades. While the possibility of secession had largely been seen as theoretical (Abbay 2004:608), Ethiopia entered uncharted waters in 2018 when Prime Minister Hailemariam Desalegn suddenly resigned in the face of popular protests and Abiy Ahmed, the ruling coalition's first Oromo leader in its thirty-year history, became prime minister and launched a series of substantial reforms.

Ethiopia's formal incorporation of ethnicity has not prevented the continued insurgency of several ethnic groups who were forcefully integrated into Ethiopia at the end of the nineteenth century, such as the Somalis of the Ogaden region (Hagmann 2005) or the southern Oromos, the largest group in the country, constituting some 32 percent of its population. Although the post-1995 regime gave Oromia autonomy and allowed for the use of the Oromo language in local schools, its manipulated nature led to the resurgence in 1996 of an Oromo insurgency that had flared with low intensity since the 1970s. The country was shaken by intense political violence in 2017, as Somalis were driven from the Oromia region and Oromos were evicted from the

Somali region in retributive acts that left hundreds of thousands displaced and numerous dead. While the promotion of an Oromo to prime minister heralds a new era for Ethiopia, the country must still contend with a volatile legacy of ethnic-tinged violence and unrest.

In Uganda, the 1962 constitutional system contained an element of ethnic federalism. The problem for Ugandan authorities was to account for the idiosyncratic view of the world of Buganda elites, who refused to see their king, the Kabaka, under anyone else's authority. At the same time, other ethnic constituencies in the country declined to be placed under the authority of a king who was not theirs. An unusual compromise was engineered whereby Kabaka Muteesa II was made the ceremonial president of the entire country, while executive power effectively was vested in the hands of the prime minister, Milton Obote. Simultaneously, the Buganda kingdom was granted a large degree of quasi-federal autonomy for its internal affairs under the authority of the Kabaka, with its own government, parliament, laws, and administration. Other regions did not enjoy the same degree of independence. This arrangement worked very poorly and lasted until 1966, when Obote's troops stormed Buganda's capital, Mengo (a neighborhood of Kampala), and the king went into exile in England. All Ugandan kingdoms (which also include Ankole, Bunyoro, and Toro) were subsequently abolished (Oloka-Onyango 1997).

In 1993, however, President Yoweri Museveni agreed to the restoration of kingdoms across the country, but only as "cultural" institutions, mostly at the urging of Buganda authorities who had provided support to him during the 1981–1986 civil war that brought him to power (Nsibambi 1994). The coronation of Crown Prince Ronald Mutebi that year marked the return of Buganda in Ugandan politics. Subsequent years have been characterized by steady tensions between the government, which seeks to limit Buganda resurgence to nonpolitical matters, and the kingdom, which has steadily pushed for greater authority and for the adoption of an ethnic federal system.

Milder instances of formal accommodation or co-optation of customary authorities by African regimes (which differ from their informal co-optation, which we discuss in Chapter 4) are rather common and have increased since the early 1990s (Vaughan 2003). Richard Sklar (1999) has coined the notion of "mixed government" to refer to such regimes where formal sovereign politics makes room for elements of precolonial authority. According to Sklar, such arrangements provide elements of stability to African political systems. In Ghana, for example, the 1992 constitution guarantees the institution of chieftaincy with its traditional councils, establishes a national house of chiefs, and restricts the state from appointing or refusing to recognize chiefs. Ghanaian authorities also reserve 30 percent of the seats of district assemblies for chiefs and retrocede 22.5 percent of revenue from stool lands to them (Ray 1998), although their participation in politics is limited in other ways. In South Africa, the 1996 constitution recognizes and protects the "institution, status and role of traditional leadership, according to customary law," and allows for the creation of national, provincial, and local councils of traditional leaders. Chiefs have not been shy in trying to exercise their power at the national level, although they regularly feel threatened by the democratizing institutions of the post-apartheid state. In October 2000, the Congress of Traditional Leaders of South Africa (CONTRALESA) forced the Thabo Mbeki government to postpone municipal elections and to convene a committee to address their grievance over the redistricting of municipalities and the resulting control of rural lands. According to Michael Williams (2000:5), this suggests that "traditional leaders have expanded their scope of authority" in the post-apartheid era. In KwaZulu-Natal, for example, Zulu chiefs share power in a manner virtually indistinguishable from that of the local officials of the state. KwaZulu-Natal chiefs occupy 20 percent of the seats on KwaZulu regional councils, a number adopted so that each of the estimated 260 traditional leaders in the province would have a position (M. Williams 2000).

Other countries, particularly in southern Africa and among former British colonies, have developed institutions of chiefly co-optation, although they usually play merely consultative roles. Botswana has a consultative house of chiefs; Namibia a council of traditional leaders, which advises the government on land matters; Somaliland a house of elders as its upper chamber in parliament; and Zambia a national house of chiefs; while Zimbabwe reserves ten seats for chiefs in its national assembly.

Of course, in some instances, the most radical form of accommodation of ethnicity would be the dissolution of existing states, which has been proposed by some, though not necessarily along ethnic lines (Herbst 2000; Englebert 2009). Although it is a recurrent theme in some of the literature, it faces very stiff resistance as a solution to Africa's national integration problem. In general, Africa's subnational component groups do not have any specific rights to self-determination under international law (see Chapter 2). Sudan's comprehensive peace agreement of 2005 is the only instance where such a solution has ever been considered. It allowed for the organization of a referendum in South Sudan in January 2011 in which local populations were given the choice to stay within Sudan or secede and form their own country. Although ethnically diverse, northern Sudan is dominated by populations who identify as Arab and practice Islam. South Sudan comprises black populations such as the Nuer and Dinka, and has a greater prevalence of Christianity. In South Sudan, 98.83 percent of voters chose independence in the January 2011 referendum (with several districts curiously exceeding 100 percent), and the country obtained international sovereignty in July. There is no telling what precedent value South Sudan's independence will have. Not only did the South Sudanese have to cross multiple high thresholds in their quest, but the country's rapid descent into civil war and state collapse may dampen the enthusiasm of other separatists.

Nationalism

For all the talk and the emphasis on ethnicity in Africa, one of the most salient and puzzling features of African politics is actually the surprising degree of national identity that African states have managed to produce among their citizens, and the extent to which the latter profess nationalist sentiments despite their subnational divisions. This postcolonial nationalism might be, surprisingly, one of the few political successes about which African governments can boast. It is a somewhat paradoxical one, given the colonial origins of these states and the occasional intensity of ethnic sentiment.

In an illuminating survey by Amanda Lea Robinson for Afrobarometer (2009b), respondents in sixteen countries were asked to compare the strength of their ethnic and national identities. Only 8 percent answered that they "feel only being a member" of their ethnic group, and 9 percent said they felt more a member of their ethnic group than a member of their country. In contrast, 35 percent responded that they felt an equal sense of belonging at the ethnic and national levels, 9 percent that they felt more national than ethnic, and as many as 32 percent that they felt "only" national (1 percent did not know). In a testament to Julius Nyerere's legacy, national identity was strongest in Tanzania, with 88 percent of respondents feeling themselves to be either only Tanzanian or more Tanzanian than a member of their ethnic group. For Nigeria, in contrast, only 17 percent of respondents felt themselves to be only Nigerian or more Nigerian than a member of their ethnic group, suggesting that nationalism is not evenly distributed across the continent. What comes out strongly in these numbers is that, even if it is intense by itself, ethnicity does not usually appear to compete with or undermine Africans' sense of national identity. On the contrary, identification with the nation occasionally supersedes identification with the ethnic group.

To some extent, these findings undermine a purely primordialist understanding of political identity in Africa. The "competing loyalties" feared by Clifford Geertz (1973) seem instead to have given way to a firm new postcolonial loyalty, or at least to compatible and noncompeting identities. Such a situation might be better explained by a more constructivist view of ethnicity. Since independence, new identities have been relentlessly shaped by African elites, who stand to gain legitimacy from the rise of nationalist sentiment. From the late colonial period onward, African politicians relied heavily on nationalism for their anticolonial struggle, despite the apparent contradiction that they were thereby espousing the structures created by the very colonialism they were opposing (Coleman 1954:419).

The first advantage of nationalism for these elites is that it provided an ideological justification for them to take control of the colonial state, and it did so in the very political language of the colonizers. The second advantage is that it raised their status compared to that of "traditional" leaders associated with ethnicity and with the precolonial period. Thus, in a context of competition for political control, nationalism gave modernized elites an edge over their ethnic competitor, and progressively gained currency as a credible alternative to ethnicity. Young (1994b:69) notes that nationalism promoted the domestic hegemony of the new elites by "legitimat[ing] state power and those that exercised it."

Beyond the efforts of political elites themselves to promote nationalism, the salience of national identity in Africa also no doubt evolved as a function of changing circumstances in the social lives of Africans and as the new states have provided the context and container of much social and political life. Early modernization theorists (Deutsch 1953; Gellner 1964 and 1983; Anderson 1983) suggested that the process of modernization—such as urbanization, universal education, access to mass media, and industrialization—would promote national identification over competing forms of subnational group identification. When such transformations did not immediately occur in the postcolonial era, and in fact ethnic-based fragmentation seemed to increase, some observers suggested the counter claim that these processes of modernization may in fact engender the increased salience of ethnicity (Bates 1983; Melson and Wolpe 1970). Working with her Afrobarometer (2009b) data noted earlier, Amanda Lea Robinson (2014) observes that attachment to the nation, relative to one's ethnic group, increases with education, urbanization, and formal employment at the individual level, and with economic development at the state level, suggesting not only the validity of classic modernization theory but also the expectation that widespread national identification is likely across Africa with greater economic development. Yet Elliott Green (2017) argues that one's embrace of a national identity is contingent on the degree to which one's ethnic group is in power.

In everyday life, contact with the state itself, be it through formal education or accessing official documents, has seemingly worked to progressively reify the nation and bring people of different regions and ethnic backgrounds into contact with each other, shaping their sense of shared identity. This may result regardless of the quality of the contact, for as Young (2002:247; see also Young 2012) has argued, Africans' "narratives of suffering"—shared memories of colonial and postcolonial misery largely inflicted by the state—have been a notable source of African nationalism. One can also conceive of a more instrumentalist view of nationalism and national identity, in which national citizenship enables access to the resources of the state (Keller 2014).

From this perspective, the development of a national identity is partly the outcome of survival strategies based on the instrumentalization of the state (Chabal and Daloz 1999). People embrace the postcolonial signifier in order not to be left out. Africans may have other compelling identities, including ethnicity, but the only identity that gives them access to the state and its opportunities is the national one. Not only is this view compatible with the simultaneous existence of ethnic sentiment, but it might help explain it too. National identity is necessary to support claims for access to the state, while ethnicity provides a principle for the distribution of these benefits. National and subnational sentiments are thus jointly produced.

Religion

For most of the first three decades of independence, religion was usually not a crucial variable of identity mobilization or social polarization in Africa; ethnicity and "tradition" were more frequently the main levers of social mobilization. One of the most dramatic sociopolitical developments in Africa since the wave of democratization and economic liberalization efforts in the 1990s, however, has been the increased presence of religion within the public sphere, particularly the spread of Christianity and the diversification of Islam (Abbink 2014). Specifically, Evangelical and Pentecostal denominations have multiplied, while Islamic fundamentalism has made some inroads, increasing the incorporation of the continent into international religious frameworks. Yet however paradoxical it may seem at first, the rise of imported formal religions has been accompanied by the resilience, if not the spread, of spiritual practices based on local faith systems. The belief in and the practice of indigenous forms of spiritualism, known colloquially as witchcraft, have remained widespread across the continent, including as instruments of power and of political accountability. In many ways, beliefs and practices associated with witchcraft have been more central to politics than broader religious affiliations, in part because African cosmologies and the spiritual practices that derive from them create a unique situation where the spiritual and the temporal overlap, and where the political world derives resources and legitimacy from the world of the spirit.

Table 3.2 provides a snapshot of the distribution of the two main world religions—Christianity and Islam—across Africa, as well as of indigenous beliefs (which are often, however, practiced concurrently with formal religions), subsumed under the label of "animism," in 1970 and in 2010, with projections for 2050. Diversity is the first defining characteristic of religious distribution in Africa. Some nations, such as Angola, are almost entirely Christian (largely Catholic in this case), while others, such as Somalia, are almost entirely Muslim (Sunni in this case, as in most others). There is a regional pattern to this diversity. Countries of the Sahel and along the East Coast of Africa have proportionally larger Muslim populations. As one nears the Gulf of Guinea or goes deeper into central Africa and then southern Africa, Christianity is more prevalent. In general, Islam has remained predominant where it already was at the time of European colonization. Christian beliefs, in contrast, gained ground through colonial and missionary work, especially in previously animist areas. Animism is not a religion per se, but is the label given to indigenous African belief systems, which share quite a number of characteristics. To some extent, dimensions of animism condition the manifestation of other religions and promote the political salience of religion in Africa. Stephen Ellis and Gerrie Ter Haar (2007:386) have argued that, in many African nations, under the influence of animist beliefs, "the sacred and the secular can be said to constitute one organic reality." Animism entails a belief in intertwined invisible and visible worlds. Power exists within the invisible world and lends itself to the outside sphere of politics in terms of legitimacy and accountability. Faith in this spirit world is an essential characteristic of indigenous African religions (see also MacGaffey 1986).

In addition to diversity across countries, there is diversity within quite a few countries, and it can be of great political significance. Some countries, such as Mauritania and Somalia, are almost entirely Muslim, while others, such as Botswana and Namibia, are entirely Christian.

Table 3.2 Religion in Africa (percentages)

	1970			2010			2050		
	Christian	Muslim	Other	Christian	Muslim	Other	Christian	Muslim	Other
Angola	74	0	26	90.5	0.2	9.3	90.5	0.2	9.3
Benin	17	14	69	48.5	23.8	27.7	48.5	27.3	24.2
Botswana	27	0	73	72.1	0.4	27.5	83.9	1.8	14.4
Burkina Faso	8	35	57	22.5	61.6	15.8	19.3	64.6	16.5
Burundi	68	1	31	91.5	2.8	5.7	90.5	3.2	6.8
Cameroon	37	20	43	70.3	18.3	11.3	67.6	22.0	10.7
Cape Verde	96	0	4	89.1	0.1	10.8	89.7	0.1	10.2
Central African Republic	52	3	45	89.5	8.5	2.0	87.9	10.1	12.0
Chad	18	42	40	40.6	55.3	3.9	42.7	53.9	3.4
Comoros	1	99	0	0.5	98.3	1.1	0.5	98.3	0.2
Congo, Republic of	79	0	21	85.9	1.2	12.9	87.8	1.1	11.1
Côte d'Ivoire	25	23	52	44.1	37.5	18.4	41.5	37.3	21.2
Djibouti	7	92	1	2.3	96.9	0.7	2.3	96.9	0.8
Congo, Democratic Republic of	68	1	30	95.8	1.5	2.6	95.7	1.7	2.6
Equatorial Guinea	83	1	16	88.7	4.0	7.2	88.7	4.0	7.5
Eritrea	52	46	2	62.9	36.6	0.5	62.9	36.6	0.5
Eswatini	51	0	49	88.1	0.2	11.5	89.3	0.5	10.2
Ethiopia	51	31	18	62.8	34.6	2.6	58.3	39.9	1.8
Gabon	78	1	22	76.5	11.2	12.3	71.5	16.0	12.5
Gambia	2	84	13	4.5	95.1	0.1	3.3	95.7	1.0
Ghana	41	14	46	74.9	15.8	9.3	67.8	22.3	9.9
Guinea	1	68	31	10.9	84.4	4.5	10.0	85.5	4.5
Guinea-Bissau	12	35	53	19.7	45.1	35.2	16.0	48.8	35.2
Kenya	42	6	52	84.8	9.7	5.5	82.1	13.3	4.6
Lesotho	57	0	43	96.8	0	3.2	97.2	0	2.8

Table 3.2 continued

	1970			2010			2050		
	Christian	Muslim	Other	Christian	Muslim	Other	Christian	Muslim	Other
Liberia	22	19	59	85.9	12.0	2.0	85.4	12.1	2.5
Madagascar	29	2	70	85.3	3.0	11.4	82.8	3.2	5.1
Malawi	36	16	48	82.7	13.0	4.2	84.0	12.9	3.1
Mali	1	78	21	2.4	94.4	3.2	2.3	93.4	4.3
Mauritania	1	99	0	0.3	99	0.6	0.3	99.1	0.6
Mauritius	34	16	50	32.7	17.3	50	32.9	17.6	49.5[a]
Mozambique	26	12	62	56.7	18.0	25.3	60.0	15.1	24.9
Namibia	41	0	59	97.5	0.3	2.1	97.3	0.3	2.4
Niger	0	86	14	0.8	98.4	0.7	1.1	97.9	1.0
Nigeria	30	44	26	49.3	48.8	1.8	39.3	58.5	2.2
Rwanda	48	9	43	93.4	1.8	4.8	93.0	3.2	3.8
São Tomé	96	0	4	82.2	0	17.9	79.6	0	20.4
Senegal	5	90	5	3.6	96.4	0	2.5	97.4	0
Seychelles	91	0	9	94.0	1.1	4.8	—	—	0
Sierra Leone	4	38	58	20.9	78.0	0.9	18.5	80.4	1.1
Somalia	0	100	0	0	99.8	0	0	99.7	0
South Africa	42	1	57	81.2	1.7	17.0	80.0	2.6	17.4
South Sudan	—	—	—	60.5	6.2	33.4	60.5	6.2	33.4
Sudan	5	71	24	5.4	90.7	3.8	5.4	90.7	3.8
Tanzania	25	31	43	61.4	35.2	3.3	66.6	30.8	2.6
Togo	26	13	61	43.7	14.0	42.4	36.7	14.0	49.2
Uganda	55	6	39	86.7	11.5	1.8	84.3	13.9	1.8
Zambia	57	0	42	97.6	0.5	1.8	96.7	1.0	2.2
Zimbabwe	57	1	42	87.0	0.9	12.0	86.1	1.1	12.8
Average (unweighted)	37	28	35	62.9	30.2	6.9	58.5	35.2	6.3

Sources: Robert J. Barro, *Data Sets*, http://scholar.harvard.edu/barro/publications/religion-adherence-data; Pew Research Center 2010b, 2015.
Notes: a. The population of Mauritius was 48.5 percent Hindu in 2010 and predicted to be 47.8 in 2050. Percentages may not sum to 100 due to rounding.

Yet pluralism is the modal religious configuration. Moreover, Africa is unique in the sense that Christians and Muslims live in close proximity in most of its countries (Otayek and Soares 2007:2). In general, religious coexistence is peaceful most of the time, and interfaith marriages are not particularly rare in many countries. There are, however, cases of severe polarization. Nigeria might be the African country where Christian and Muslim communities are the most evenly balanced, with 49 percent each as of 2010, though the 2050 predictions anticipate a substantial shift. Just as it has suffered from ethnic polarization over the years, it also recurrently provides the stage for religious conflict among its communities (or at least religion often provides the narrative for local intercommunal conflicts). It does not help that there is considerable overlap between ethnic and religious identity. The north of Nigeria, where the Hausa-Fulani are dominant, is also majority Muslim. The southeast, where the Igbo form the largest group, is mostly Christian. In between these two regions, in the Middle Belt states such as Plateau, religious patterns are more fluid.[11]

Although pre-partition Sudan had a strong Muslim majority, here too the geographic patterns of distribution of religious beliefs overlapped with ethnic identities—with the north being dominantly Muslim and the south dominantly Christian—in a manner that reinforced cleavages and undermined nation building ever since independence. After the breakup of the country in 2011, the proportion of Muslims in Sudan rose from 71 percent to 91 percent. A similar phenomenon became salient in Côte d'Ivoire in the 1990s, with increased polarization between mostly Muslim northerners and mostly Christian southerners. Although the conflict was not about religion, religious differences became the markers of political identity.

The presence of religious cleavages is in part a function of the sometimes dramatic changes that have taken place in the prevalence and nature of religions within countries over the past half century, the most significant of which has been the rise of Christianity, mainly of the Evangelical and Pentecostal types as previously mentioned. From 1970 to 2010, the unweighted proportion of Christians rose from 37 percent to 57 percent. While Islam appeared to remain steady (with Muslims composing 28 percent of the African population in 1970 versus 31 percent in 2010), the rise of Christianity was compensated by a significant erosion of animism (from 35 percent to 9 percent).[12] Another recent transformation has been the rise of Islamic fundamentalism across much of Africa, particularly after the 1979 Iranian revolution. These rapid transformations have introduced an element of disequilibrium into the politics of many African states, placing Africa in the middle of broader religious patterns and conflicts, and in the middle of religious narratives that increasingly structure relations among countries around the world.

Table 3.2 also reflects the projected distributions for religion across the continent in 2050. It is important to note that these projections anticipate the doubling of Christian and Muslim populations in Africa. Christianity is projected to remain the largest religious group in sub-Saharan Africa, but its proportion of adherents is expected to decline from 63 percent in 2010 to 59 percent in 2050. Islam is expected to grow faster, particularly in West Africa, with Muslims altogether increasing from 30 percent to 35 percent of the population (Pew Research Center 2015). One can note how specific countries, such as Nigeria, are expected to undergo a notable shift demographically, which will potentially have social and political consequences.

Our focus on Christianity and Islam is not meant to imply an absence of other world faiths. Hinduism is prevalent in Mauritius, and there are significant Jewish communities in Ethiopia and Nigeria (Miles 2013). Generally, however, Christianity and Islam are the only established large-scale world religions on the continent.

Christianity

Christianity first arrived on the continent during the first or early second century C.E., with Ethiopia's King Ezana making Christianity the kingdom's official religion in the fourth century. Christianity's major expansion across the continent was tied to colonial conquest, as European powers integrated Christian conversion and anti-Muslim crusading into their colonial project. The growth of Christianity in Africa has continued in the postcolonial era, to the point that today the Christian world is increasingly becoming African. By midcentury a plurality of Christians are expected to be Africans—increasing from 26 percent in 2015 to over 40 percent in 2060 (Pew Research Center 2017).

Christians are sub-Saharan Africa's largest religious group, with an estimated 517 million adherents in 2010 (up from 144 million in 1970) when counting all denominations (Pew Research Center 2015). It is estimated that some 6 million Africans become Christians every year (Freston 2001:107). By 2050, it is assumed that Christians will number around 1.1 billion in Africa. But while they will still be the largest group on the continent, the Christian share of the region's population is actually expected to shrink from 63 percent in 2010 to 59 percent in 2050 due to the faster growth rate of Islam.

Paul Gifford (2016:12) argues that the growth of Christianity is "perhaps the most salient social force in sub-Saharan Africa." But it is important to note the great variation between and within Christian denominations. As Robert Dowd (2015:22) notes, Christianity, like Islam, is not made of unchanging essences and that "there has been a great deal of variation in how leaders of the same religious faith tradition, whether Christian or Muslims, have applied their faith tradition to politics across time and across space at the same point in time." Today, the largest groups among African Christians are Catholics, with about 176 million adherents, followed by Pentecostals, with 107 million practitioners. In 2010, members of all Protestant faiths together added up to 296 million. Although Catholics might still outnumber them, the Pentecostals are witnessing the most "dramatic expansion." Countries with the greatest Pentecostal presence include Zimbabwe, South Africa, Ghana, the Democratic Republic of Congo, Nigeria, Kenya, Angola, Zambia, and Uganda, all of whose populations are more than 20 percent Pentecostal or Charismatic ("Spirit-Filled") Christian (Pew Research Center 2006a, 2006b, 2010a, 2015).

The spread of Pentecostalism in Africa is not unique, as Evangelical faiths have gained considerable ground in many regions of the world. They are popular with people of different cultures and material conditions. Moreover, systematic missionary work has certainly contributed to the success of these religions. In Kenya, for example, "televangelism, prosperity theology and crusades by Western preachers [have] become more prevalent" (Pew Research Center 2006a). And the mostly Pentecostal Christian Association of Nigeria "aggressively" proselytizes in the north of the country (Loimeier 2007:65).

Some authors see enduring economic crisis and widespread African poverty as fertile ground for Christian churches. Kwame Bediako (2000) examines the evolving dynamics of Christianity in contemporary Africa, suggesting that the rapid spread of Christianity has been largely driven by widespread poverty, with the poor turning to evangelicals as a source of strength in times of economic crisis. Christianity in Africa, according to Bediako (2000:314), has become "the religion of the relatively and absolutely poor" and promotes a new "globalization from below." The emphasis on the poverty of Christ and on the extent to which this poverty fed his power against established political authority and the forces of empire might resonate among Africa's poorer communities. The New Testament's equation of misery in this life but happiness in the next, of deprivation now but plenty later, might also constitute a sustaining promise for many. Thus the worsening of Africa's economic environment from the 1980s onward might have favored the growth of faiths associated with Christianity. This might be a matter not only of rationalizing one's misery but also of facilitating agency. Many Pentecostal churches, which have seen some of the greatest progress in membership, have a liturgy of material success in this world and of self-help.

Beyond the appeal of faith per se, however, some Christian churches also offer solidarity networks in times of vulnerability. In the Democratic Republic of Congo, the Catholic Church rose as a near-substitute to the state during the years of chaos that began in the early 1990s. This was not a new pattern. Under colonial rule, and during Mobutu Sese Seko's regime, the church had been largely responsible for the provision of health and education services in Congo. During the years of state collapse, particularly in the east of the country, which was at war, the church became involved in health, schooling, and caring for marginalized populations, and in some limited measure in infrastructure reconstruction (fixing roads and bridges). Similarly, Charles Piot (2010:53) makes a causal link between the retreat of the postcolonial state and the rise of Pentecostalism in Togo. He finds these churches to have an anti-authoritarian message and to offer an alternative to the "traditions" and "gerontocracy" that undergirded colonial political power. Togolese Pentecostal churches are involved in the provision of services. They build schools and clinics. They even provide development based on the donation and taxation of their members, something that few African states have so far been able to do. Piot suggests that these churches are a "total experience" substituting for state and family and making up for anomie. People pray for jobs, to find a house, to receive money. They "enact middle-classness" (Piot 2010:56).

Finally, the particular appeal of what Paul Gifford (2016) calls "enchanted Christianity" may be partly related to its use of a language and beliefs germane to those used in African endogenous spiritual practices, stressing the role of miracles and the world of spirits. Pentecostals' belief that God as well as angels and demons play "direct, active role[s] in everyday life" (Pew Research Center 2006a:3, 26) is not dissimilar to the active role of spirits in African religions. Although Pentecostalism denounces the cults of spirits and witchcraft, Piot (2010) suggests that, in doing so, it also paradoxically reaffirms the existence of spirits and demons. When Frederick Chiluba became president of Zambia in 1991, he invited Pentecostal ministers to "cleanse" the presidential palace of evil spirits (Freston 2001:156–159). Gifford (2016:125) notes the ways that many African Catholics remain "enchanted" despite official church teachings, reifying assumptions about "African authenticity and self-reliance."

Occasionally, Christian churches get directly involved in politics. As nonstate institutions, they are constitutive elements of civil society (a concept to which we return at the end of this chapter), and they might contribute to holding governments accountable. Jon Abbink (2014:84) observes that there has been an "unrelenting growth in the public presence of religion in Africa" since the 1990s, coinciding with the wave of democratization and economic liberalization. Religion is an easily available and accessible instrument of mobilization, and is increasingly a key component of people's identity. As such, some political debates have increasingly been framed within religious terms across the continent, such as in Uganda's highly controversial anti-homosexual legislation, Kenya's 2010 constitution with its legalization of abortion and limits on freedom of worship, and protests against the African state as a general source of "immoral secular order" (Prozesky 2009).

The Church of the Province of Kenya (CPK), the most important religious institution in the country, stood against the one-party regime under President Daniel arap Moi. Because of their religious status, CPK bishops were part of a small minority of citizens who could criticize the government without facing detention, and many bishops took advantage of this role by questioning Moi's regime (Freston 2001). Similarly, in Congo, the Catholic hierarchy stood up to Mobutu in the late 1960s and he punished it by nationalizing Catholic schools. In the more recent Congolese conflict, the Catholic Church stood up to rebels in South Kivu, with its activists forming the crucible of the resistance to the Rwandan invasion and to the rebellion of the Rassemblement Congolais pour la Démocratie (RCD) after 1998, and the bishop of Bukavu was assassinated under mysterious circumstances. In recent years, the Catholic Church has organized pro-democracy protests aimed at pressuring Joseph Kabila to hold elections and leave office. Given that the Catholic Church runs about half of the schools and clinics in the country, it carries enormous weight and enjoys a level of legitimacy lacking by the government and opposition. Beyond the actions of church leadership, religious discourse can also promote political participation. Piot (2010:57) suggests that the Pentecostal churches of western Africa offer narratives that undermine the past authority of the state and make sense of new circumstances in the post–Cold War world.

Some believe therefore that churches can have democratizing virtues in Africa. In his comparative study, Dowd (2015:79) suggests that African religious leaders are "more supportive of democracy in more highly educated and religiously diverse settings than religiously homogenous settings." In several countries since the 1990s, church leaders have played important roles in facilitating transitions to democracy. In Benin and Congo, for example, Catholic archbishops presided over the "sovereign national conferences" that came to symbolize these transitions.

Conversely, political contestation might be a minority position for African churches, which frequently act as accomplices of power, as churches often do elsewhere. In Kenya, Evangelical Pentecostal churches were much more supportive of Moi than was the Anglican CPK. At one service he attended in the Redeemed Gospel Church in 1992, Moi was portrayed as a God-fearing Christian, with the preacher declaring: "In heaven it is just like Kenya. . . . There is only one party—and God never makes a mistake" (Freston 2001:146). Similarly, several politicians have instrumentalized and promoted Evangelical churches as a tool of political mobilization and a convenient means of self-recycling. Former Marxist dictator Mathieu Kérékou, of Benin, manipulated his born-again credentials to return to power in 1995 and unseat opponent Nicéphore Soglo, whom he associated with the occult forces of voodoo, although he had been an assiduous practitioner of voodoo himself while president until 1989 (Strandsbjerg 2000). He had also converted to Islam in 1980, in the wake of surges in oil prices.

Islam

Islam has been present in Africa since it expanded from the Arabian Peninsula in the ninth century, but it was only in the nineteenth century, not long before colonization and the spread of Christianity, that it made major inroads and became a significant political as well as religious force. Nowadays, more than 248 million Muslims, or 30 percent of the world's Muslim population, live in sub-Saharan Africa (Pew Research Center 2010b). But the Muslim population is growing at a faster rate than the Christian population, and is expected to become 670 million by 2050. While Christianity will still be the most populous religion on the continent, the Muslim share is expected to increase from 30 percent to 35 percent (Pew Research Center 2015). Most of them are Sunni (with a significant Shiite minority in Nigeria). Of these, a large number practice Sufism, a variety of Islam that stresses local saints and leaders and provides a certain degree of syncretism with local pre-Islamic beliefs. However, more radical and fundamentalist beliefs have gained favor among a minority of African Muslims over the past couple of decades, and Sufi doctrine itself is undergoing changes in some locales. As a result, African Islam is characterized by a significant degree of pluralism.

Unlike more orthodox versions of Islam, Sufism is not particularly focused on the literate knowledge of the Quran and stresses instead the necessity of adopting a lifestyle that pleases and does not defy God. Many analysts define Sufism as a mystical form of Islam, in the sense that its practitioners seek knowledge of God through meditation, emotion, and incantation. Sufis have multiple saints, whom they honor through pilgrimages to their tombs and other rituals. Normally, a Sufi believer follows a specific founder (considered to be a saint) and his descendants and subsequent teachers of the founder's philosophy, called *marabouts* in Senegal, with the result that Sufi Islam is divided into orders, or brotherhoods, named *turuk*[13] (Otayek and Soares 2007:3). The main Sufi brotherhoods in Africa are the Tijaniyya and the Qadiriyya. In Senegal, although a majority of Muslims belong to branches of the Tijani order, the local Mouride brotherhood is particularly influential, and counts former president Abdoulaye Wade (2000–2012) among its disciples. Mouride brothers follow the teachings of founder Cheikh Amadou Bamba and can substitute a pilgrimage to his birthplace of Touba, in Senegal, for the pilgrimage to Mecca that is usually demanded of Muslims who can afford it (Hassan 2008:4). Some see Sufism as only superficially Islamic, as it appears "less pure" than the versions of Islam promoted by more quranic and Arabic schools. Benjamin Soares (2006) and Roman Loimeier (2007) show that Sufi Islam coexists with fetishist practices in Mali and Nigeria, respectively.

Some dimensions of Islam, such as precepts on social interaction and penal law, lend themselves easily to politics. Yet in general, African practitioners of Islam endorse a secular view of the state and there is no evidence that most African Muslims are interested in the application of sharia law beyond matrimonial and other conventional civil areas. Moreover, the economic returns to a Western-style education have reduced the appeal of *madarsas* (Arabic quranic schools) and other Islamic education institutions. This does not mean that organized Islam is without influence on politics. In Senegal, marabouts are widely seen as kingmakers. They have long been the clients of the state and, particularly, of the Socialist Party, which ruled from independence until 2000. The marabouts have secured political support and legitimacy for the Senegalese state among their followers, and the state in turn supplies them with resources, particularly through price and production support for groundnuts, and allows them to run their own "state within a state" in the holy city of Touba, the aforementioned birthplace of the founder of Mouridism (Behrman 1970; Boone 1992; Copans 1980; Coulon 1981; Cruise O'Brien 1971; Villalón 1995). Typically, the marabouts instruct their followers to vote for the ruling party through *ngidels,* or commands. This practice peaked in 1988 with a forceful endorsement of Abdou Diouf by Serigne Abdou Lahat, the Mouride leader at the time, before the marabouts adopted a more neutral stance in the 1993 elections (Beck 2001:613). In 2000, some important marabouts encouraged their supporters to vote for the opposition, and Abdoulaye Wade won the elections (Villalón 2007:168–176). In addition, African Muslim communities have mobilized at times to lobby for their policy preferences, as in Somalia when religious leaders vocally opposed (without success) a 1975 secular family code (Marchal 2004:118), and in Mali when similar reforms giving greater powers to women were suspended by the president in 2010 after widespread opposition by Muslim organizations (Wing 2012).

Since the 1970s and particularly after 1990, Sufi Islam has been increasingly challenged by a more activist minority fundamentalist current. Recent decades have seen the advance of Salafism, which advocates strict interpretations of Islamic scriptures, rejects esotericism, and seeks to emulate the early Muslim community as a corrective to the corrupt and decadent modern world (Haykel 2009). In particular, Saudi Arabia's conservative Wahabbi school has made inroads through the activities and the financing of preachers and Islamic NGOs (Iddrisu 2013; Kane 2007; Salih 2004), particularly with younger Muslims (Becker 2006). Many of the more recent mosques in Africa, built with money from Saudi Arabia, tend to be Salafist. Similarly, Islamic humanitarian assistance from Arab countries has promoted the development of Islamic health and education services in the wake of state retrenchment (Otayek and Soares 2007:10). A very diverse "Islamic reform" movement has emerged from these initiatives in several African states and has found fuel in the perceived lack of morality of politics. The reformists, many of whom studied in Egypt and Saudi Arabia and are influenced by scholars from the Arabian Peninsula (and sometimes Iran), have promoted the development of quranic schools. These developments have usually not resulted in the creation of Islamic parties (which are banned in several African countries), but have seen the rise of a new Muslim elite. "In most places in sub-Saharan Africa," Otayek and Soares (2007:13) write, "it is the rise of a Muslim counter-elite, often Arabophone and increasingly active in the public sphere (with new Islamic associations, access to liberalized media, and complex transnational interconnections), that helps to explain some of the ways Islam has been politicized." The target of their critiques is the Westernized secularized political elites, and since the 1970s factors such as political corruption, economic inequality and crisis, and the 1979 Iranian revolution have fueled their spread. Not surprisingly, their rise has occasionally clashed with established political and religious authorities; for example, Mauritania, Africa's only Islamic republic, has actually banned Islamic NGOs.

Despite the progress of Islamic reform, it has so far not gained much ground with the general public (Otayek and Soares 2007:6; Becker 2006:599). Apart from Sudan, Somalia, and northern Nigeria, it has not led to many institutional or political changes within the state. However, it is worth paying some attention to developments in these three locales, as well as to the more radical manifestations of the reformist agenda outside the state.

In Sudan, a process of Islamic radicalization began in the late 1970s and was part of the attempt of northern Arabic and Muslim elites, who have dominated Sudanese politics since independence, to extend and reinforce their control over the entire country, including the more heavily Christian south. This movement was historically linked to the penetration in Sudan of the Muslim Brotherhood from Egypt. The coming to power in 1989 of the Revolutionary Command Council, and the subsequent adoption of sharia law in 1991, marked the peak of the government's project of "Islamization of society and state" (Ahmed 2007:193). This political experiment in Sudan has certainly marked so far the most clear-cut attempt to engineer a radical and occasionally violent Islamic revolution in a sub-Saharan African country, and it is no surprise in this context that Osama bin Laden was based in Sudan from 1991 to 1996. Yet the extent of its success and of its popular support is debatable, as it largely backtracked from its earlier ambitions and suffered from intra-regime competition from the late 1990s onward (see de Waal and Salam 2004; Flint and de Waal 2008). The comprehensive peace agreement of 2005, which saw the settlement of the conflict between the north and the south and ushered in South Sudan's independence, suggested at least partial failure of the original agenda, and limited the reach of sharia to the north. To some extent, the radicalization of the regime in 1989 led to the resumption of the war with the Christian south, and eventually to the loss by the Khartoum regime of the southern portion of the country in 2011.

In Somalia, an Afghanistan-like confrontation between a violent Islamic insurgency and no less violent clan militias, some of which have formed a government, has brought a new kind of religious politics to the continent, causing concern and precipitating some degree of intervention by the United States.[14] The rise of political Islam in Somalia must be put in the context of nearly two decades of complete state collapse after the fall of the Siad Barre regime in 1989. To some extent, public religious commitment has been a mechanism for traders and other businesspeople to substitute networks of social trust for the breakdown of state institutions (the necessity of such networks also partly explains the historical spread of Islam along the East Coast of Africa). At different times in the country's civil war, Islam has also displayed a comparative advantage over clans in the provision of security. Widespread banditry in Mogadishu neighborhoods provided the context for the first experiments with Islamic courts in

1994 and 1999 (Marchal 2004). These courts are essentially police organizations composed of militias that patrol neighborhoods and arrest suspected criminals, and judges who hand out sentences based on sharia. Some more fundamentalist organizations, such as al-Itihad, a group with Sudanese roots, and al-Islaah, gained some influence in the context of the courts. Progressively, the courts and the Islamic groups within them grew and seized control of some neighborhoods and ports where they taxed trade. As such they became competitors to clans and clan militias and were either disbanded or assimilated in subsequent years. Some of them provided the initial core of the police force of the transitional federal government, which was established by different clans in 2000. Yet the transitional government was never able to extend its authority beyond a few blocks of Mogadishu, and kept Islamist organizations from joining its coalition. In 2004, different Islamist groups organized into the Council of Islamic Courts (CIC) and wrested power from the hands of the transitional government. According to Ken Menkhaus (2007:371), they enjoyed the support of a large portion of the Somali population as they once again helped ensure stability by eliminating gangs and restoring some form of law. The CIC also broke through the clan identity lines and offered a more unifying ideology of "pan-Somali nationalism and anti-Ethiopianism." Yet Menkhaus distinguishes this support as "broad but not deep" (372), as clan divisions and anxieties could not be erased.

The CIC imposed sharia courts and also maintained a powerful military, which integrated the radical al-Shabaab militia. As power within the CIC began to move away from moderates toward hard-liners, the US government feared an al-Qaeda connection and became involved. Prodded by the United States, Ethiopia invaded in 2006, with dire humanitarian consequences. In 2009, Ethiopian troops departed, and were replaced by a few African Union battalions. Some Islamists subsequently regrouped and fought back. They brought the conflict to African states supporting the AU mission, including bombings in the Ugandan capital in 2010. The following year, Ethiopian troops returned to Somalia, and Kenya invaded in an effort to destroy the capacity of the Islamists. In response, al-Shabaab extended their reach into Kenya, launching several violent attacks, including the 2013 Westgate Mall attack in Nairobi (Menkhaus and Gore 2017). While al-Shabaab has been reduced in power and size in recent years due to the limited success of foreign interventions, the federal government does not have enough control of Mogadishu to last without peacekeepers or foreign military backing.

Northern Nigeria has seen a process of apparent Islamic radicalization since 1999, when the governor of Zamfara state adopted sharia law against the provisions of the federal constitution. Twelve other northern states followed suit, implementing some form of Islamic law (Thurston 2014; Last 2000). Because many non-Muslims also live in the north, the adoption of sharia became the cause of serious tensions and social conflict among religious communities. Yet the political significance of Islam in Nigeria did not begin with the sharia movement of 2000, and this movement itself is more complex than a hypothetical spread of radical Islam.

In 1804, Sufi religious scholars under the leadership of Usman dan Fodio took power in the Hausa kingdoms of today's northern Nigeria and established the Sokoto sultanate (Loimeier 2007:44), thus providing a historical precedent of unified Muslim temporal rule, which continues to appeal to many. Although Islam was separated from power at independence, Sufi leaders continued to carry significant influence, particularly with the numerous military regimes, controlled by northern officers, that ruled Nigeria between the middle 1960s and the late 1990s. Starting in the 1970s, however, there were recurrent attempts at reforming Nigerian Islam, particularly as a result of the widespread corruption associated with power and the perceived hybridity of Sufist practices (Kalu 2003). Izala, a reformist movement sponsored by Saudi donors, gained considerable leverage at the time, until it too succumbed to the "Nigerian curse" and lost influence under accusations of corruption (Loimeier 2007:52–55). After the Iranian revolution in 1979, more radical groups surfaced and called for jihad. Far from unifying Nigerian Islam in a homogeneous struggle, these movements contributed to fragmenting political Islam in Nigeria. The appeal of sharia derived in part from this context and from the election to the presidency in 1999 of Olusegun Obasanjo, a born-again Christian Yoruba. For many Muslim northerners, sharia was seen as a solution to corruption and bad government, whereas for northern political elites, it was also an instrument to weaken the Obasanjo government and the constitution. Thus the immense popularity that accompanied the sharia declaration in Zamfara led other northern politicians to follow suit. Yet the political nature of the movement has left many doubtful, as have misuses of the law and the failure of these northern states to engineer successful reforms (Loimeier 2007:66–67). Alex Thurston (2014:29–30) observes that the sharia project has not resulted in a manifestation of restrictive Islamism, but exacerbated intra-Muslim rivalries and electoral competition within the secular political structures. Although sharia remains officially on the books as of 2018, its implementation is haphazard and its popularity is in decline, even among Muslims.

No other African country has so far embarked upon institutional change based on an Islamic agenda. In several countries, however, there has been a rise in the profile and activities of groups that claim radical Islamist agendas, although not all of them are indigenous to these countries. Numerous countries across the Sahel have had to deal with small insurgencies associated with radical Islam, such as al-Qaeda in the Islamic Maghreb (AQIM), a group founded by Algerian militants who returned from the Afghan war against the Soviet Union in the 1980s. AQIM has claimed responsibility for the killing or abduction of several tourists, aid workers, and expatriates throughout the region. In Mali, AQIM united with other insurgent groups, some Islamist and some secular, to wrest control of the northern half of the country from the government from March 2012 until a French military intervention began in January 2013. During their rule, they applied a strict version of sharia and destroyed several monuments dedicated to Sufi saints (Scheele 2015; Bøås and Dunn 2017).

While AQIM is largely an Algerian export that has grafted itself onto the local communities within the West African countries it operates, Boko Haram in Nigeria is a homegrown Islamic insurgent movement with greater implications for domestic politics. Its name in Hausa means "Western education is a sin," and its agenda is reactionary, opposed to the state, science, education, and democracy, and in favor of complete sharia law in all dimensions of life and for all residents of northern Nigeria. It has been increasingly active since 2009, shifting its aim from police stations and political targets to bars, mosques, and schools, including its infamous kidnapping of several hundred schoolgirls from Chibok in 2014. While Boko Haram frames its actions in the rhetoric of global jihad, including pledging its allegiance to the Islamic State of Iraq and the Levant in 2015 and rebranding itself as Islamic State in West Africa, Virginia Comolli (2015:141) suggests that it is less a jihadist terrorist group than a domestic "insurgency campaign involving a terrorist component."

On the East Coast too, militant Islam, not necessarily of African origins, has taken on increased political salience beyond Somalia and Sudan. In 1998, al-Qaeda detonated bombs at US embassies in Kenya and Tanzania. Kenya has a rather small Muslim minority, at less than 10 percent of the total population, but the presence of transnational Islamic militant groups in its territory has probably been facilitated by its large border with Somalia, especially as al-Shabaab has actively worked to exploit local grievances against the Kenyan government (Menkhaus and Gore 2015; Haynes 2005:1330). Muslims are a larger group in Tanzania, where they make up about 35 percent of mainlanders and 95 percent of Zanzibaris, and a minority among them have indeed experienced greater radicalism (Becker 2006). Yet Jeffrey Haynes (2005:1330),

although he identifies a "gradual hardening of indigenous Muslim identity in Tanzania" as evident in recurrent "armed takeovers of moderate
mosques" in Dar es Salaam, nevertheless suggests that "the notion that
the country has begun to degenerate into a new territorial beachhead for
transnational Islamic extremism is misplaced." Similarly, Felicitas
Becker (2006:593) has noted that conflict between older "traditionalist
Sufi Muslims" and younger "anti-Sufi Islamists" in Tanzania is partly
derived from the arrival of literacy. Oral traditions, being less firm,
accommodated certain variations in religious practice, whereas literate
believers who can follow the Quran are more fundamentalist in their
implementation of its injunctions. In 2017, neighboring Mozambique
experienced its first jihadist violence, inflicted by a previously unknown
group calling itself "al-Shabab." Though the country has a long history
of violence, this is the first time it has taken on religious dimensions.

Altogether, one cannot make proper sense of the increasing appeal
of reformism in African Islam, even within the Sufi tradition, without
coming to terms with the failures of the political and economic structures inherited from Western colonization and with the besieged feelings
of many African Muslims in view of Western policies toward other
Muslim countries. All over the continent, the rise of more radical Muslim groups and their agenda does not come only from the expansionist
schemes of Islamist groups in other countries or regions. It also corre-
sponds to the exhaustion of postcolonial regimes that have offered their
citizens relatively little in terms of development, and with which Muslim establishment has long collaborated. To some extent, their agenda is
one that calls for greater ownership of the postcolonial state and for an
alternative to the many failings of Western modernity. Thus the appeal
of sharia can correspond to the assertion of a genuine local political
identity in contrast to the association of secularism with the postcolonial
project (Abbink 2014). As such, it parallels an international position of
resentment among many Africans at perceived Western imperialism, a
position reinforced in the wake of the US invasion of Iraq, a majority-
Sunni Muslim country, in 2003 (Villalón 2007).

However, in Africa's many religiously plural societies, the radicalization of Muslim faith has caused significant polarization and fears, and
led other communities, particularly Christians, to feel threatened (many
Muslims, likewise, see the formidable expansion of Christian churches
as a threat). Religious polarization between Christians and Muslims has
been worse in countries where these communities live in close proximity
and where religious identity can be instrumentalized for other pursuits.
Such has arguably been the case in Nigeria, where Middle Belt states

such as Plateau frequently provide the stage for what appears to be religious conflict between Muslim and Christian communities. The Middle Belt region is both ethnically diverse and not under any single religious hegemony. As a result, it has become a bit of a battleground in Nigerian identity wars, where most social and political life is processed through a religious lens and has caused numerous occasions for collective violence (Loimeier 2007:64; Reno 2004:232; see also Harnischfleger 2004).

The Spirit World

Historically, Africans have not only been the recipients of imported religions but have also produced indigenous cosmologies that share many characteristics across large parts of the continent. One of these is the belief in a continuum between the material world and the world of the spirits and the dead. These spirits are active, powerful, and influential in our world. As a result, those who can communicate with them have significant influence in this world, and they are courted and used by those who seek political power. In his first tour as president of Benin, for example, Mathieu Kérékou relied heavily on the services of Mohamed Amadou Cissé, a marabout, or spiritual expert.[15] The world of spirits is not necessarily a benevolent place. It is filled with intrigue. Often, spirits manifest themselves in the real world to do evil things, sometimes because they have entered Faustian bargains with the living through the practice of witchcraft, understood as the use of spiritual powers "either to protect and promote the welfare of or to cause harm to" the living (Adinkrah 2015:56).

One of the consequences of such cosmology is the imputation of events to witchcraft or other spiritual practices, and the unfalsifiability of such causality. The spirits of ancestors and their dealings with mortals *explain* specific individual and collective events and outcomes. One gets sick not because one caught a virus or because there are bacteria in the untreated water, but because someone else arranged for it out of spite, jealousy, revenge, or other motives. One wins elections and becomes powerful not because one campaigned well and offered credible and appealing policy solutions to existing problems, but because miscellaneous sacrifices were performed. One wins a soccer game not because of superior talent, but because of a talisman worn around the neck. One avoids death in battle because one performed specific rituals and applied a concoction that prevents bullets from penetrating the skin. Thus the return to Botswana in 2000 of the bones of an African man (known as "El Negro" or the "Negro of Banyoles") who had been displayed, stuffed, in a Spanish museum for decades, was popularly blamed for severe drought the following year (Gewald 2001). For people coming from a more Cartesian tradition, this supernatural dimension of life can be perplexing. For many expatriates involved in missionary or development work on the ground, these practices often seem like obstacles toward greater agency and ownership of one's destiny and environment. Yet they also reflect a mode of adaptation to the natural circumstances faced by Africans, and differ only to a degree from religious interpretations of natural or political events in other countries.

Some suggest that witchcraft has taken on epidemic proportions in Africa. Charles Piot (2010:153) recalls a Togolese village meeting convened to discuss education during which attendees "complained about the high incidence of witchcraft in the schools—of students witching teachers in retaliation for poor grades, of teachers witching recalcitrant students, of students witching other students." Witchcraft also has great political significance. When two of President Mobutu's sons died in quick succession in the mid-1990s, at a time when his power was vacillating under attack from democratic forces, it was widely interpreted by many Congolese as the outcome of witchcraft. He was believed to have indirectly sacrificed his sons in order to stay in power. Similarly, the decision by President Denis Sassou-Nguesso of the neighboring Republic of Congo to rebury the bones of explorer Pierre Savorgnan de Brazza in a mausoleum in 2008 has been interpreted by many as an attempt by Sassou to acquire additional power from magic practices associated with his control of the bones of the colonial ancestor of his country (Bernault 2010). In general, the intermingling of the spiritual and the temporal implies that politicians must often gain some spiritual legitimacy, or be perceived to have spiritual powers, in order to succeed politically (Chabal and Daloz 1999). Yet as Ellis and Ter Haar (2004) show, witchcraft is not just manipulated by the powerful to augment their power; it is also an instrument of resistance by the weak, and can sometimes undermine the domination of the powerful.

Western analysts have a particularly hard time "making sense" of witchcraft, as it stands in contrast with the more rationalized views of the world to which they are accustomed. Because it is often studied by anthropologists, scholarship on the subject tends to be interpretive (Geschiere 2013). Some suggest a rejection of modernity or globalization, as witches are often rumored to fly in airplanes or travel in underground trains. In September 2011, the Nigerian government had to issue a communiqué to counter rumors that cell phone calls originating from certain numbers could kill those who answered them.

Others argue that witchcraft endures because its beliefs and practices can make sense of the helplessness, relative lack of agency, and insecurity that numerous Africans experience. Citizens might resort to witchcraft to cope with the general arbitrariness of life, and politicians to deal with the precariousness of office. Ellis and Ter Haar (2004, 2007) suggest in this respect that the belief in this spiritual world may stem from an omnipresent sense of powerlessness. Similarly, Adam Ashforth (1998) explains the pervasiveness of witchcraft in Soweto, South Africa, by invoking the notion of "spiritual insecurity": South Africans try to control the suffering they undergo, from physical insecurity and lack of economic opportunities, through accusations of witchcraft. In Tanzania, the killing of albinos to make fetishes has been linked to the desire of artisanal gold miners to reduce the risk of their activities and maximize the chances of finding gold (Bryceson, Jonsson, and Sherrington 2010).

More specifically, witchcraft might offer a compelling explanation for the presence of evil in people's lives (Ellis and Ter Haar 2007). Given the precariousness of many dimensions of life in Africa, there might be a greater need to explain evil than in other regions. Edward Evans-Pritchard (1937) was probably the first author to discuss witchcraft as a tool to process misfortune, impute causation for it, and assign responsibility. Charles Piot (2010:127) sees witchcraft narratives as discourses about "hard realities—about unequal access and the failures of European development, about the il/legitimate constitution of political authority, about the temptations of illicit wealth production. They are concise, albeit allegorical, ways of trying to understand shifts in power's operation in today's world." Witchcraft goes well beyond narratives, however, and coping with insecurity and vulnerability might well engender more insecurity and vulnerability for certain groups. Edward Miguel (2005) has shown that the prevalence of drought in Tanzania led to the killings of alleged witches, who were accused of being responsible for the lack of rain. Miguel notes that killing these older, widowed women removed less productive members from the community at a time of food distress. Indeed, Mensah Adinkrah (2015:74) notes the centrality of gender in witchcraft, arguing that women, especially elderly women, are more prone to be accused of witchcraft given the assumption of their relative weakness, though one can also see witchcraft as a vehicle for increased female agency within patriarchal societies.

Finally, witchcraft contributes sometimes to a system of political accountability. Peter Geschiere (1997) was the first to bring the study of African witchcraft away from pure cultural anthropology and into the fold of postcolonial political studies. Relying mostly on examples from the Maka of Southern Cameroon, he showed that witchcraft compensated for the loss of local political control implied by participation in national politics. Local Maka elites who acquired positions of authority at the center remained liable to local communities through the sanction of witchcraft. They may have had political powers that the Maka could do little about, but they could be reined in by the practice of witchcraft, which acted as a restraining mechanism. Similarly, Patrick Chabal and Jean-Pascal Daloz (1999:68) write that "the world of the irrational is one which binds the individual with the community in ways which are not open to choice." As Geschiere (1997) argued, national political figures remain accountable to their local communities through witchcraft, which serves as a means for checks and balances.

In a more recent work, Geschiere (2013:13) reflects on the ways in which the meaning of witchcraft has evolved over time and varies across the continent, warning against "sweeping generalizations about witchcraft omnipresence." He notes that the projects of colonization and modernization worked to denigrate African indigenous spiritual belief systems, a trend that continues with evangelical Christianity's equation of African tradition with "an omnipresent devil" (12). Yet, he argues that modern mass media have contributed to the magnification of witchcraft rather than the weakening of it, a position echoed by Adinkrah (2015) in his examination of witchcraft in Ghana.

All these approaches carry precious insights into African witchcraft, even as some Western observers attempt to make sense of what they may regard as existing beyond comprehension. Ultimately, it is useful to recognize that African witchcraft practices typically derive from cosmologies that link power and material success to the spirit world, that establish a continuum between the world of the living and the world of the dead (MacGaffey 1986). These beliefs have existed, continue to exist, and have implications for African daily and political life. As with religion elsewhere, they are unlikely to disappear with modernization, and they have adapted well to the spread of Islam and Christianity.

Social Classes and Class Politics

Class analysis has traditionally been a powerful mode of understanding social systems and politics across much of the globe. In Africa, because of the lack of industrialization and the limited spread of industrial capitalism (many Africans are independent peasants), class analysis has generally not been as popular or successful. In recent years, however, increased attention has been paid to the supposed "emerging" African middle class and its transformative power for economic development and democratization (Ncube and Lufumpa 2015; Melber 2017). Are there social classes in Africa? Is there a class logic to African politics? What is the relationship between the African state, social classes, and class formation? While traditional understandings of class have been found wanting, many Africanists have found some variations of classical class analysis useful in answering these questions.

For Karl Marx, classes are socioeconomic groups articulated around their relations to the means of production (capital, labor, and land), with the dominant classes changing as the modes of production change (e.g., feudalism, capitalism, communism). Classes become true classes when their members become aware of their specific economic interests as distinct from those of people in other classes. Once this happens, classes conflict with each other and class struggle becomes the engine of history.

Many political scientists are conversant with Marxian thought and accustomed to analyses that explain politics through an analysis of social class. In the first decades of African independence, it was thus common to see scholars use class analysis to try to make sense of what they observed in Africa. Because they could not identify classes in the historical European sense, they looked for alternative class systems. Without proper capitalist production and a capital-owning class, some looked to the state and its elites as representing the modernized nationalist "bourgeoisie." Such parallels were facilitated as the African state progressively acquired many of the existing means of production through frequent nationalizations of land, extractive industries, and whatever little manufacturing existed. But the explanatory power of class analysis was limited by both the lack of systematic exploitation of labor by the state and the lack of class solidarity. Marxian scholars were hard-put to account for collective action along the lines of ethnicity, particularly the overthrow of incumbent regimes by elites of other ethnic background who apparently shared the same material class interests. Ethnic identification seemed to trump class consciousness and solidarity.

Others found greater explanatory power in using a theory partly derived from Marxism, according to which African governments were the local representatives of worldwide capitalism, on which African dominant classes were dependent for their accumulation. This approach, known as dependency theory, was first elaborated in the context of Latin America (Frank 1966; Cardozo and Faletto 1979). Its African version owed its existence to scholars such as Samir Amin (1972, 1976), Walter Rodney (1981), and John Saul (1979). It placed contemporary

African development within the longer historical context of colonization and exploitation, recognizing the structural inequalities within the
global capitalist system and assuming their continuing impact on postcolonial politics. It provided an explanation for the stagnation and
underdevelopment in Africa, at a time when rich countries continued to
thrive with economies often fueled by natural resources extracted from
Africa. It also made sense of the rise and seeming ubiquity of African
authoritarian and military regimes, which were seen as the repressive
local hand of international capital, eager to keep workers subdued and
wages low, and to maintain (and partake in) easy access to commodities
and profits for international capital. It failed, however, to explain why
so many African regimes turned against foreign investments, which they
often nationalized or expropriated.

The "Kenya debate" came to symbolize the dispute between classical Marxists and dependency theorists in making sense of Africa's
political economy (Leys 1996). Kenya offered fertile ground for such
analyses because it had one of the regimes most resolutely engaged on
a capitalist path in Africa, in particular contrast to neighboring Tanzania, which had chosen "African socialism" (the "African" part translated an understanding that conventional relations of production were
not to be found in Africa, where communal ownership of land was historically predominant). Could capitalist development be successful in
postcolonial nations like Kenya?

Dependency theorists, for whom the growth of the core capitalist
countries took place at the expense of the peripheral postcolonial
ones, did not think so. For one, they thought that the colonial organization of production, which had been taken over by local elites at
independence, did not favor the efficient use of national resources. In
addition, foreign capital was too dominant and choked the small
African business class. And finally, the state was too focused on using
resources to buttress the power of the incumbent elites rather than to
foster production (Leys 1996:143–144).

Classical Marxists such as Colin Leys (1975), however, thought
that capitalism not only was possible in Kenya but also could promote
some form of development. They relied on the existence of an indigenous Kikuyu-based capital-accumulating class, which was at the core
of the Kenyan state in the first two decades of its independence and
was able to generate significant economic growth. Yet Kikuyu accumulation suffered some setbacks after the 1970s, and the domestic rate of
capital formation remained much inferior to foreign capital (Kaplinsky
1980). Leys (1996:153) also later acknowledged that, although the

Kenyan bourgeoisie might have been economically efficient, it was not necessarily "competent politically, as a class," in part because of its ethnic divisions.

Do the failings of the Kenyan bourgeoisie imply that class analysis is not helpful in Africa? At the very least, the experience of Kenya and other African countries suggests that a class approach to African politics must avoid dogmatism and show flexibility in the use of class concepts. There may be a class logic to African politics, but it is unlikely to revolve around a conventional capitalist mode of production and to follow a pattern of class struggle (South Africa might be an exception). Richard Sklar (1979) was probably the first author to successfully use class analysis in Africa, but he did so in a rather unorthodox way. In his milestone contribution, Sklar argued that there is considerable class action in Africa and that many things can be understood in class terms, but he suggested that African classes coalesce around the state rather than the means of production, and that class struggles are not the dominant mode of class action on the continent.

The most dominant form of class action in Africa, for Sklar, is class formation. When political parties provide patronage to their supporters, they distribute resources that contribute to class formation. Sklar used the example of Nigerian parties, showing that, in the south, the goods of modernization handed out by parties (education, government jobs, and other means of access to patronage) contributed to the formation of a ruling class, while in the north, traditional authorities were able to use state resources to transform their customary status into a class advantage. All these people, wrote Sklar (1979:167), "exhibit elitist patterns of behavior and acquisitive tendencies that mark the process of class formation." Sklar made one of his most important points in this context. He concluded that in all the cases he reviewed, it was "the exercise of power by those who control various and diverse social organizations" that led to the formation of the dominant class, and not the other way around. Wealth was not acquired in the economic sphere and translated into political power, as Marx would have had it. On the contrary, in Africa, the reverse is true; "class relations, at bottom, are determined by relations of power, not production."

Sklar made another important theoretical contribution to the study of African politics when he noted the occasional alliance between the modernized elites and traditional rulers, who carry a lot of local power and legitimacy. Such alliances usually revolve around relations of clientelism, as we study in Chapter 4. As the state elite distribute clientelistic resources to traditional elites, a dynamic of class formation takes place through a process that Sklar labeled a "fusion of elites." Clientelism becomes thus a mode of class action, a form of class collaboration rather antithetical to class struggle.

Class consolidation constitutes another important form of class action for Sklar, and can be useful in explaining apparent class contradictions in the behavior of African elites, such as their inimical attitudes toward foreign investments. Once a dominant class forms, noted Sklar (1979:168), it tries to "reconstruct the existing organization of authority" in accordance with its perceived needs. From an economic point of view, it makes sense for this incipient class to use state power in order to transfer the assets of foreigners to itself. Nationalizations, expropriations, and other instances of economic indigenization are thus instances of economic consolidation of the African dominant class, seeking shortcuts to accumulation. Politically, the ruling class is likely to embrace authoritarian ways and military rule to protect itself from challenges. Hence, Sklar was able to explain both the anticapitalist and authoritarian tendencies of African regimes within a modified class framework.

The important insight that African classes and class politics revolve around control of the state was reinforced by the work of Larry Diamond (1987), who showed how state employment and expenditure decisions, development plans, patronage, and corruption were central to dominant-class formation in Africa. The African state is "swollen," writes Diamond, as it overemploys people and allocates too much of its expenditures along political lines. Gaining access to the state is therefore how one gains access to resources. In this context, political corruption becomes the primary means of accumulation of wealth. The dominant class then seeks to expand the state as a means to strengthen its economic basis. The dominated class fails to develop class consciousness and to protest because it is either co-opted through patronage or fooled by politicians' use of "tribalism" to divide the lower classes, a clear instrumentalist view of ethnicity. Eventually, economic domination is consolidated as the elites use their power and control of the law to acquire substantial plots of land and provide the best education for their children, the next generation of elites. Diamond concludes by writing that the dominant class acts as a "parasitic character feeding off the revenue of a swollen state" (592).

As interesting as these class analyses of the state might be, they fail, however, to explain why Africa's emergent dominant class has largely failed to promote effective capital accumulation and development. Catherine Boone (1990) addresses this question head-on. Looking at the apparent failure of Africa's dominant class to turn itself into an indigenous capitalist class, she develops the concept of "rentierism." In the parlance of political economy, a rent is an excessive profit, derived from some distortion in markets. Boone defines it as a "politically mediated opportunity for obtaining wealth through non-productive economic activity" (187), such as the acquisition of an import license or production subsidy. She sees two mechanisms by which the rentier state prevents the development of a genuine capitalist class. First, the parasitic nature of the rentier class reduces the likelihood that government will support policies favorable to the development of an independent capitalist class that could have power on its own, independent of the state. Second, the inefficiencies inherent in rentierism eventually erode the capacity of the state to administer the economy and increase the risks faced by investors, who tend to shy away from such environments. Not only are dominant classes in Africa not economically based, as Sklar identified, but their very consolidation takes place at the expense of wealth accumulation.

There have since been other successful attempts to use class analysis in Africa. Abdi Samatar and Sophie Oldfield (1995), for example, use a class framework to make sense of one of the lone economic success stories of Africa: Botswana. In general, they see the lack of a common class project by African elites as a main reason for African underdevelopment. In Botswana, however, there is a dominant class with a development project to foster its economic interests, and this class is building up state institutions to this effect. This contrasts with the use of the state elsewhere in the process of class formation that ruins public institutions, as illustrated by Diamond and Boone. Samatar and Oldfield take the Botswana Meat Commission as a case in point. The commission is very efficient and delivers high-quality meat.

Their explanation is that Botswana elites retained autonomy by resisting British colonial rule and South African attempts at integration. During decolonization, they were also able to maintain their hegemony over the masses and their strong sense of a historical role. These traditional elites were also economic elites, generally being large livestock owners. With few challengers, they inherited the colonial state at independence. The first president, Seretse Khama, set up the Botswana Democratic Party, whose leading members were cattle owners (Khama was the largest owner himself). The Botswana Meat Commission was directly under the control of the president. As such, a crucial state institution was used to favor the reproduction and the growth of the cattle system, not to distribute resources to political supporters as elsewhere in Africa. Hence, accumulation takes place and so does development.

Over the past decade, class analysis has made something of a resurgence in the wake of economic growth and increasing incomes across much of the continent (discussed in Chapter 6). International organizations, such as the World Bank and the African Development Bank, as well as numerous media commentators, have extolled the presence and virtues of an expanding middle class, specifically their assumed role as agents of democratic change and economic development in the region. While the term "middle class" often lacks conceptual clarity, the African Development Bank classifies members of the middle class as those with per capita consumption of $2 to $20. "Upper middle class" refers to those spending between $10 to $20 a day, while the "lower middle class" spend $4 to $10 a day. The largest segment of the African middle class (estimated to be 204 million people) are regarded as part of a vulnerable "floating middle class" that is at risk of falling back into poverty (African Development Bank 2012:13; Ncube and Lufumpa 2015). It is argued that this emerging middle class has enabled African economies to shift away from export-led growth to create dynamic domestic markets, while fostering indigenous entrepreneurialism. Some scholars have argued that the emerging middle class is intrinsic to democratic development, examining such cases as South Africa (Southall 2013) and Kenya (Neubert 2016). Others are critical of what they regard as overly optimistic assumptions about economic growth, pointing to the widening level of inequalities and limited employment opportunities across the continent (Melber 2016). Sirkku Hellsten (2016:159) questions the assumption that an expanding middle class will "somehow automatically steer Africa towards democracy and good governance."

These bourgeoning debates indicate that, despite early misgivings, class analysis offers considerable analytical mileage in Africa as elsewhere, provided one is flexible enough to apply it without undue dogmatism. Inequality and exploitation in Africa may not take familiar Western forms, but they are there nonetheless, and often in particularly acute forms. Exploitation at the hands of the state might not revolve around production, and it might not result in systematic accumulation, but it represents a political and economic system with structural inequality that can be thought of in modified class terms. Even the domination of traditional chiefs, "decentralized despots" in Mahmood Mamdani's words (1996), contains a certain class logic. Class analysis is, at any rate, another important tool in the political scientist's toolbox.

Gender Inequality and Women's Participation

While daily life in Africa is hard for many, it is often particularly so for women. First, many African women face significant daily physical hardship. They work the fields, carry water (more than half of rural house-holds and about a quarter of urban households lack easy access to drinking water), gather wood, cook on open fires, and care for the children. With a fertility rate of 4.8 births per woman, African women face greater maternal mortality rates than women in other regions. They also have less time for leisure, income-generating activities, or self-improvement. Only 57 percent of adult women are literate, as against 72 percent of men.[16] They face unequal opportunities in education and employment, and violence at home and in public spaces. Second, many laws discriminate against women. In many African countries, statutory and customary laws limit their access to land and other types of property, while in some parts of the continent married women have little or no say in how their cash earnings are spent, nor do they fully participate in intra-household decisionmaking on spending, particularly in poorer households. Finally, across the continent, with few exceptions, women are largely unrepresented in politics (United Nations 2010). In Michael Kevane's (2014:17) apt words, for African women these differences "add up to unambiguously diminished welfare and capacity to fulfill life aspirations. The situation is more like comparing a rotten papaya with a lustrous lemon."

Such salient inequalities have begged for a gender study of African politics. Gender refers to the socially defined sets of assumptions and beliefs regarding the accepted roles of men and women that help structure behavior, analysis, and decisionmaking. Therefore, to examine the roles and agency of women and men within African societies requires attention to the complex ways in which gender is constructed, performed, and reified. In short, a gender analysis of politics asks how women and men are placed in the study of formal politics, how political processes affect men and women differently, and how activities that women are typically involved in outside the male-dominated institutional sphere are included in one's analysis of politics (Waylen 1996:4).

As noted in the previous chapter, African precolonial societies were generally patriarchal, though women's experiences varied greatly across the continent. Iris Berger (2016:11) notes that at the outset of colonial rule, African women "were fully engaged in the economic life of their communities" in ways that exceeded European women at this time. But the advent of European interventions greatly curtailed women's status across the continent. Gwendolyn Mikell (1997:11) notes that four factors were significant in redefining gender norms and establishing new forms of gender relations in Africa: "(1) Christianity, with its notions of monogamy and female domesticity and subordination; (2) Westernized education which gave men advantages over women; (3) differential marriage systems, with Western marriage guaranteeing women access to property rights that women married under traditional rites could not claim; and (4) alternative legal systems that supposedly acknowledged African women's independent rights, although colonial magistrates often treated women as jural minors needing male guardians." With the introduction of forced labor for colonial projects, the induced wage-labor migration to pay taxes, male urbanization, and rural cash-cropping, the colonial regimes established a sexual division of labor that would persist into the postcolonial era (Coquery-Vidrovitch 1997).

The form and extent to which these changes affected African women varied according to circumstances across the continent. Yet the general effect was the creation of a colonial social order that was oppressive for nonelite African women, with their economic, political, and social status largely diminished (Romero 2015). Legally the colonial system further entrenched male dominance, treating women as dependents who were often denied the ability to own land necessary for subsistence farming. Colonialism introduced and normalized European assumptions about gender social roles, furthering a gendered division of labor and the marginalization of women in the political sphere. Many women resorted to "spiritual power" to resist this marginalization and carve out new spaces for themselves (Berger 2016:31).

These changes were often resisted, either directly or indirectly. One spectacular case was the "Igbo Women's War" of 1929, which involved thousands of women in Nigeria engaged in a public challenge to the warrant chiefs (traditional leaders used by the British as tax collectors), whom they accused of excessive taxation and political marginalization (Chuku 2005). At least sixteen native courts were attacked and destroyed by women and many warrant chiefs were forced to resign as a result of the disturbance. A major tactic used by the women was the practice of "sitting," which involved following their male targets anywhere and everywhere, while singing, dancing, and publicly challenging and humiliating them. This latter technique is not dissimilar to that employed by the "women in white" movement led by Leymah Gbowee in Liberia in the early 2000s to shame Liberian fighters into ending abuses of civilians (and for which Gbowee received the Nobel Peace Prize in 2011).

Nationalist movements in the era of independence tended to promise a reversal of the colonial practice of excluding women and sought to mobilize all of society by promising greater inclusion and equality for women. Once in power, however, politicians tended to turn their back on such promises, though continuing to rely on support from women and women's organizations for their own nationalist agenda. Often, post-independence nationalist goals were portrayed as negating the need for a separate women's movement. Despite some substantial social gains, such as increased female literacy and education, most African states limited women's access to political parties, ministerial positions, and the reins of power. In Ghana, for example, Kwame Nkrumah's ruling Convention People's Party (CPP) relied on market women to campaign for the party and government policies, but integrated very few women into ruling political institutions. In cases where armed liberation movements emerged—such as in the Portuguese colonies of Guinea-Bissau, Angola, and Mozambique, as well as Kenya and Rhodesia—women were often incorporated into leadership roles, fought alongside men, and helped sustain the liberation forces in myriad ways. Yet at the end of these struggles, there was usually a call for women to abandon their recently acquired leadership roles and return to subordinate roles of domesticity for the sake of post-independence nation building.

In postcolonial Africa, the socioeconomic status of women has continued to vary significantly across space and time. In parts of East Africa, for example, established gender norms have usually meant that women have often been restricted to rural economic activities, while in West Africa more of them are economically active in urban spaces. Yet regardless of their roles in local economies, women across the continent have been particularly exposed to, and suffered from, detrimental economic conditions. The economic crisis of the 1980s, and the African state responses to it, often led to increased dispossession and hardship for women. As Jane Parpart (1989) wrote, many African women regarded the state as a predatory institution that was best avoided. In many ways, the growth of the African informal economic sector during this time was driven by women's survival strategies in the context of avoiding the state (Kinyanjui 2014). The plight of African women was illuminated during the United Nations Decade of Women (1975–1985), which shed light on issues such as the feminization of poverty, rising infant malnutrition and mortality, and rising maternal mortality. Reflecting on the socioeconomic status of African women at the end of the twentieth century, Mikell (1997:1–2) writes: "African women know that they have borne the brunt of the crises of their states over the past two decades. The evidence is apparent in the lower educational levels for women across the continent, the continuing presence of women in agricultural and other rural activities (rather than in the professions and other income-producing activities), and in the higher levels of female malnutrition and maternal and infant mortality so well documented during the 1980s." Powerful fictional accounts of African women's experiences can be found in excellent novels such as Tsitsi Dangarembga's *Nervous Conditions* and Buchi Emechata's *The Joys of Motherhood.*

The use of structural adjustment programs (SAPs) as a response to economic decline (see Chapter 6) might well have exacerbated the socioeconomic predicament of African women. As the burden of social welfare was progressively shifted from the state to the household, women were on the frontline of the effects of SAP-required cuts in social sector spending. As a consequence, many of them were forced to take on the increasing burden of unpaid work in caring for the sick, as well as meeting the basic survival needs of their families in general. The rise of the HIV/AIDS crisis across the continent a few years later also significantly impacted women, who make up over half of the estimated 23 million cases of HIV infection in Africa (see Chapter 6). Women and girls are particularly vulnerable because they often lack control over their own sexuality and reproductive functions.

The relative political opening that has characterized most African regimes since the 1990s (see Chapter 5) has, however, created new opportunities for women. A variety of women's organizations emerged across the continent, from professional and advocacy groups to economic associations. As Carolyn Shaw (2015:2) notes in her examination of female activism in Zimbabwe, these developments have occurred in a context where "feminism" is often regarded as a Western construct at odds with "conventional" notions of women as mothers and obedient wives. Regardless, the past several decades have witnessed increased women's activism and notable successes by African women's movements (Badri and Tripp 2017). Helen Dancer (2015) has shown how substantial changes in land issues in Tanzania have been achieved by women's civil society groups.

More notable has been the extraordinary increase in women's legislative representation in Africa, having tripled between 1990 and 2015, jumping from 1.8 percent to 22.2 percent. Proportionately, Africa has more women in the cabinet (20 percent) than other parts of the world (18 percent) (Tripp 2016:382). This has largely been achieved through the adoption of quotas. Over 65 percent of African countries have some form of quotas to increase female legislative representation, and countries with quotas have an average of 25 percent female representation compared to 14 percent for countries without quotas. These quota systems vary from parties voluntarily adopting a quota to mandated reserved seats for women (eleven countries) to compulsory legislated quotas requiring all parties to include a certain percentage of women on their candidate lists (sixteen countries) (Tripp 2016:383–384; Kandawasvika-Nhundu 2013). These legislative and party quotas have largely helped increase the female representation in elected offices. Rwanda is the leading example, for Africa and the world, with women constituting 63 percent of the parliament's lower house. In October 2018, the Ethiopian prime minister appointed a cabinet composed half of women and the legislature elected Sahle-Work Zewde as president, making her the only female African head of state at the time of writing.

Yet, increased women's representation does not guarantee enacting significant changes in the status of women. Amanda Gouws (2016:401) notes that South Africa failed to develop policies around gender-based violence despite women occupying 42 percent of the government, largely due to the lack of political will among the female members of parliament. This supports the argument by Weldon and Htun (2013) that autonomous women's movements are more important than having women in government.

Kenya has provided insights into the changing role of women in the political sphere. Until 1992, the state engaged in practices of co-optation and control of women's formal and informal mobilization attempts. Instances of women defying male control were exceptional. Wangari Maathai, the renowned environmentalist who challenged the Kenyan state for over two decades and in 1989–1990 famously stopped the government from erecting a skyscraper in the middle of a recreation park in the center of Nairobi, was one such exception. Maathai's husband divorced her for being too educated, too independent, and too successful. After Kenya's first multiparty elections in 1992, Maathai and other Kenyan women became active in electoral politics in the hope that it would engender greater political empowerment, while also capitalizing on other forms of political engagement against the state, including hunger strikes and media campaigns (Nzomo 1996). Although a modest number of women were elected to political office in December 1992, Kenyan women's movements realized that participating in formal electoral politics offered a limited vehicle for political empowerment. Laws and state practices, combined with continuing societal beliefs, meant that Kenyan women continued to face discrimination and deteriorating socioeconomic status. In 2001, for example, Kenyan president Daniel arap Moi explained to a gathering of women that they were hindered from making progress due to their "little minds." After an unsuccessful campaign for parliament, Maathai founded the Green Belt Movement, an environmental NGO focused on conservation and women's rights (which she regarded as intertwined), and in 2004 won the Nobel Peace Prize. Examining the case of Maathai and other Kenyan female activists, Maria Nzomo (1996:181–184) suggests that women's movements in Africa have had to focus on a range of issues concerning capacity building, increasing autonomy, and developing strategies for resisting state co-optation and manipulation.

Uganda offers another illuminating case study for examining women's relationship to the state and political power. In many ways, it illustrates the severity of women's economic marginalization in contemporary African societies. For example, as noted by Aili Tripp (2001:121), Ugandan women own only 7 percent of the land while providing more than 70 percent of all agricultural labor. In addition, when a woman's husband dies, it is frequently the deceased husband's family or clan that inherits his land, rather than his wife. Yet Ugandan women have made significant strides in other dimensions of life, in large part because of their organizational autonomy from the state. As of 2017, there were 154 women out of 449 members of parliament (34 percent) and roughly 30 percent in local government. Tripp notes that the women's movement in Uganda became a substantial political force in the wake of the rise to power of Yoweri Museveni's National Resistance Movement (NRM) in 1986. Unlike elsewhere in Africa, where sections of women's movements had been captured and subverted by the ruling party or regime, the women's movement in Uganda gained momentum from its initial relative autonomy from the state and the NRM. Throughout Africa, major women's movements are often led by relatives of the country's leaders and thus serve to support the ruling party. Uganda has grown to be an exception, yet co-optation has recently emerged as the NRM has tried to use the women's movement for its own advantage. Reserving seats for women in parliament has helped to create a situation where women elites have been more loyal to Museveni than to women's issues. But as Tripp (2000:xvii) argues, "even in the Ugandan case, where the state has been 'relatively' accommodating to women's demands and women have been brought into political leadership at various levels, the rules, structures, and practices continue to promote an older, more exclusionary vision of politics, making it difficult for women to assert their interest. The problem for women is not just one of representation and voice; rather, it is a matter of whether they will have a say in making the rules that determine how politics is conducted."

The Ugandan case illustrates the limited success gained from women's movements even when they have been capable of maintaining relative autonomy vis-à-vis state institutions. In the end, while engagement, disengagement, and assertions of relative autonomy are all part of a repertoire of strategies that women and women's organizations employ to cope with their economic and political contexts (Goetz and Hassim 2003), there is no magic bullet for the improvement of women's lot and their increased representation in Africa. It is nevertheless worth noting a recent rise in the representation of women at the top of the state. Ellen Johnson Sirleaf of Liberia was the first African woman to become president, in 2006, followed by Joyce Banda of Malawi in 2012 and Ameenah Gurib-Fakim of Mauritius in 2015. Women have also been appointed as prime ministers in Mali (2011–2012), Mozambique (2004–2010), Senegal (2013–2014), and Namibia (2015–present). By the beginning of 2019, there had been ten African female heads of state and government, though only two had been popularly elected. The experiences of women—from the formal realm of electoral politics to the informal economy—continue to vary greatly across the continent, confirming the importance of employing a gendered analysis when studying African politics.

Civil Society

"Civil society" means many things to many people. Most commonly, it means the organized social space between the state and the family. Civil society differs from society at large to the extent that it defines specific types of social organizations and social relations, those fostered by organizations such as unions, churches, interest groups, and even recreational associations. For some authors, civil society is also characterized by certain norms: it should be civil and tolerant, and it is supposed to be democratic.

The concept matters in political analysis because characteristics of civil society are often believed to affect characteristics of the political system. For example, ever since the work of Alexis de Tocqueville, the vibrancy of associative life in a country is believed to correlate with the strength of its democracy. People form relations in civil society, develop mutual expectations, and establish bonds of reciprocity and social trust, which then facilitate their interactions in the political system and might help bridge otherwise significant political differences (Putnam 1992). Thus, many political scientists are tempted to look at features of civil society when seeking explanations for different trajectories of a political system.

For the first three decades of African independence, however, civil society was hardly visible in most of Africa and it therefore had little currency in Africanist political science. Civil society organizations had been severely restricted under colonialism. The efforts of the new states to be all-encompassing or "integral" (Young 1994c)—that is, to control all facets of life—left very little room for autonomous social organization, especially in view of the residual control of customary authorities in rural areas. Africans were squeezed between overbearing postcolonial states (Azarya and Chazan 1987) and the local weight of tradition (Mamdani 1996). There were associations, but most of them were orchestrated by the states themselves or their ruling single parties. Unions, youth, or women's groups, for example, were typically centralized under the authority of the state. Independent political parties or unions were often not allowed. Even sport leagues were sometimes state-supervised.

In these circumstances there was very little room for independent associative life and little to be expected from it in terms of effects on the political system. This situation changed abruptly in the early 1990s. The sudden wave of democratization that swept through Africa in the wake of the collapse of the Soviet system opened up new spaces of social organization that were soon inhabited by a multiplicity of groups recognizable to students of civil society. Although the democratic impetus in many cases preceded the organization of domestic civil society, scholars soon hypothesized that the success of African democratic experiments depended in large part on the vibrancy of their civil societies (Diamond 1996). Policymakers, particularly within donor agencies, followed suit and adopted programs to help develop and strengthen African civil societies as part of their democracy-promotion agendas.

In certain ways, these analytical and policy efforts have been well rewarded. Some studies that incorporate features of civil society or social capital, a germane concept, have been very successful at accounting for important dimensions of post-1990 African politics, not least divergent democratic trajectories (see Chapter 5). At the same time, however, civil society analysis has also occasionally constrained our understanding of Africa. As a concept intimately linked to the evolution of Western political systems, civil society has occasionally introduced a bias in our understanding of African politics. It has encouraged us to look for meaning and significance in certain recognizable political forms while neglecting or bemoaning others. Too often, scholars have taken the concept and tried to apply it to Africa, rather than first looking at Africa and conceptualizing from there. From a policy perspective, civil society assistance from external sources might have encouraged Africans to adopt practices and institutional forms that please donors but that might not always reflect local dynamics or represent local aspirations.

These limitations do not imply, however, that the civil society baby should be thrown away with its bathwater. In an interesting development and as a testimony to the contribution of Africanist political science to broader knowledge, several scholars have suggested ways to amend and refine the concept so as to improve its analytical usefulness in Africa (see Obadare 2013). Nelson Kasfir (1998a, 1998b), for example, has developed a cogent argument in favor of integrating customary social structures into a new conception of civil society. And Célestin Monga (1996) has called for attention to more informal and cultural forms of civil society.

What Is Civil Society and Why Is It Relevant?

There are many currents of thought on civil society in Western political science, but it is de Tocqueville's notion of it as the realm of "autonomous, intermediate associations," the purpose of which is to organize citizens and prevent the state from appropriating too much power, that has had the upper hand among Africanist scholars. It is this approach that imbues civil society with a democratizing mission (Bratton 1989a:417).

Larry Diamond (1996:208) provides a fine example of the burdening expectations of the concept when defining civil society as "the realm of organized social life that is voluntary, self-generating, (largely) self sup-porting, autonomous from the state, and bound by a legal order or set of shared rules. It is distinct from 'society' in general in that it involves cit-izens acting collectively in a public sphere to express their interests, pas-sions, and ideas, exchange information, achieve mutual goals, make demands on the state, and hold state officials accountable. Civil society is an intermediary entity, standing between the private sphere and the state." In a similar perspective but with fewer expectations, Peter Lewis (1992:35) defines it as "the arena of private and particular concerns within a given polity, institutionally separate and autonomous from the formally constituted public authority of the state." While embracing a pluralistic perspective, Lewis is careful, however, not to project any spe-cific outlook on civil society: "the constituent elements of civil society freely associate, affiliate or disengage on the basis of perceived interest and preference. . . . Consequently, civil society is neither homogeneous nor cohesive; the particularities within the private realm provide consid-erable basis for conflict and division" (36).

What are civil society's constituent groups in practice? Typically they include trade unions. In fact, in several African countries, organized labor was one of the few types of associations that resisted state control even during the days of authoritarian single-party rule. They also fre-quently cut across ethnic lines, unlike many other associations (on which more later). Some have argued, however, that their retrenchment under donor-sponsored market-based reforms augurs ill for the future promises of civil society in Africa (Bangura 1999). Other groups include churches, student organizations, media outlets, business associations, public intellectuals, and many of the ubiquitous NGOs that populate Africa's institutional landscape.

One possible problem with the Tocquevillian approach to civil society is that it puts very substantive expectations on its member organizations. John Harbeson (1994:1), for example, wrote that grassroots movements were springing up all over Africa in the 1990s to overthrow repressive regimes and empower African citizens, pushing governments to comply with citizens' demands for reform. From such a perspective, it becomes hard, afterward, not to perceive African civil societies as having failed at their historical mission. In general, most civil society scholars in the heyday of this approach to African politics believed that social groups had a substantial role to play in institutional (and democratic) change on the continent (Harbeson, Rothchild, and Chazan 1994; Diamond 1996; Bangura 1999). Some early democratic transitions encouraged such optimism. In Zambia, for example, unions were at the forefront of democratization. Frederick Chiluba, the opposition leader who would become the first president of democratic Zambia, was a union leader. Yet Zambia's later difficulties with democracy, and the ease with which Chiluba adopted the ways of personal rule once in power, subsequently cooled off the democratic expectations of civil society theory in Africa.

Aside from unions, nongovernmental organizations generated, for a while, the greatest hope for transforming African politics and holding states more accountable. Empirically, NGOs exploded as an associative form around the same time that many African regimes were embarking on transitions in the late 1980s. In part, they arose as a result of the very weaknesses and retreat of the state under economic reforms, which left a certain vacuum that NGOs occupied (Bratton 1989a). In addition, their rise was also a response to the dejection of donors toward corrupt and inefficient states and their desire to find new local counterparts as aid recipients. Supply followed demand, and the NGO became a widespread mode of social organization. Soon every village, if not every bureaucrat, had its own NGO bidding for development grants. Yet as weak as they were, governments did not willingly surrender political terrain to NGOs. They harnessed their residual authority and mostly kept them in check politically, allowing them to substitute for the state in terms of service provision, but not to become a political counterpart to state power. Monitoring, coordination, co-optation, and, when necessary, dissolution were frequent strategies used by governments in dealing with NGOs (Bratton 1989b). Eventually, relations between states and NGOs in Africa settled into some sort of equilibrium whereby NGOs were and continue to be recognized as important substitutes to governments, providing public goods and services, while falling short of promoting a genuine reform of the state. In fact, the substitutive role of NGOs partly exonerates the state from being accountable for its failings and may actually reinforce it in the process.

Similarly, media freedom is usually considered an important element of civil society, both because it represents a potential counter-power and because information is crucial to civil society's capacity to operate independently of the state. That there has been, in the wake of the transitions of the 1990s, a significant increase in the availability and range of opinions of media in Africa is indisputable. Where monopolistic government-owned newspapers and broadcasters once dominated the media landscape, a diverse group of public and independently owned media now often stands. Yet according to Reporters Without Borders (2018), few African countries reach the top tier of journalist freedoms. Ghana, Namibia, South Africa, and Cape Verde are the only African countries among the thirty countries with the freest media; Eritrea is the second worst in the world, behind North Korea. Twenty-eight African countries are listed among the world's worst half. African journalists are subjected to multiple threats, including arrest, execution and assassination, violence, and social and family pressure. These threats come from official security forces, but also from militias, private security forces, mercenaries, and armed political militants. According to Marie-Soleil Frère (2011), two phenomena facilitate these abuses. First is the general climate of impunity that prevails in many African countries. Violence against journalists is "almost never punished." The assassination by individuals linked to the presidency of opposition journalist Norbert Zongo in Burkina Faso in 1998, for example, remains unpunished to this day, despite widespread popular mobilization (Hagberg 2002). In the Democratic Republic of Congo, several independent journalists have been murdered since the election of President Joseph Kabila in 2006, with little or no legal consequence. The second factor is what Frère calls the "plasticity of norms," or the fact that the existence of legislation to protect journalists is of limited effect because of haphazard application and weak judiciaries. As a result, many African journalists face self-censorship, and the visibility of a multiplicity of media does not translate into a close watch being exercised on governments. To avoid risks and earn an income, many journalists substitute public relations work and promotional pieces for investigative journalism. Not rarely, they will publish or broadcast pieces entirely produced by the president's or ministers' communication teams.

The rise of social media has been seen as an important tool in empowering civil society across the continent. Activists and citizens have utilized social media platforms such as Whatsapp, Facebook, and Twitter to rapidly share information and organize opposition movements. Social media were credited in helping remove the Central African Republic's President François Bozizé in 2013, organizing resistance to the Seleka rebels that replaced him, and ensuring the legitimacy of the following presidential elections (Smith 2016). In Congo-Brazzavile, journalists and democracy activists used social media to expose human rights abuses and electoral fraud during the 2016 elections. While social media have worked to connect and empower civil society, they have also been utilized to circulate hate speech and fake news, and enflame violence in some contexts. In recent years, several African countries have blocked their citizens' access to social media, including Cameroon, Chad, the Democratic Republic of Congo, Gabon, Gambia, the Republic of Congo, and Uganda.

Limitations of the Concept of Civil Society in African Politics

As the discussion on unions and NGOs makes clear, there is something of a gap between theoretical expectations of civil society and empirical reality in Africa. To a certain extent, both the conventional definitions and the pluralist hypotheses about civil society are poor matches for the conditions on the continent (Lewis 1999).

Some cultural traits widely shared across Africa might represent a first obstacle for the development of Western-type civil society. Goran Hyden (2006:155) has suggested that the role of affective relations in African societies might prevent voluntary associations from transforming into civil organizations. Specifically, Hyden perceives relations of affection within kinship bonds as an important feature of African societies, and suggests that they may in fact generate a lack of trust among Africans across the main structures of affection. Michael Bratton (1989a:415) concurs, noting that "familial affection . . . can create internal cleavage and factional conflict in larger structures." Victor Azarya (1994:92) goes so far as to argue that Africans display a tendency toward "amoral familism," attaching no moral relevance to activities not involving the family. Echoing Peter Ekeh (1975), Azarya claims that "public activity is therefore expected to be a means of diverting general societal resources to private (i.e., family) interests." He concludes that "amoral familism is the normative opposite of civil society. The stronger amoral familism is in a given society, the less civil that society will be." In a similar but distinct vein, Célestin Monga (1996:155) suggests that many African religious and civic groups display a "cult of nihilism and cynicism" that represents a threat to the development of a healthy and vibrant civil society.

Some of these arguments implicitly refer to ethnicity. In general, the salience of ethnic identity in African social relations is perceived as undermining the formation of civil society, since the latter is expected to cut across cleavages and transcend parochialism. Donald Rothchild and Letitia Lawson (1994:255), for example, warn that Africa's "fundamentally divided societies are likely to produce civil societies significantly more segmented than European philosophy would suggest, at least in the short run." Similarly, Peter Lewis (1999) suggests that parochial divisions that exist within society at large are also likely to be reproduced within civil society organizations. Victor Azarya (1994:94) goes further and claims that primordialism within associations is a larger problem, as many of them have membership criteria actually based on ethnic identity or place of origin.

Another demanding assumption is that, for civil society to coalesce, there already exists a well-defined and agreed-upon society and polity. How can associative relations of trust and reciprocity form if members of society do not agree that they belong together in the first place? The lack of historical embeddedness of postcolonial African states is problematic in this respect. African states lack social contracts. As Lewis (1992:36–37) puts it, the requirement that "civil society presupposes a viable political community, in which participants recognize certain boundaries of common destiny and interest," is rarely met in Africa. Kasfir (1998a:131–132) hammers the point home: "the pluralist assumption that all interests can be reconciled through compromise may turn out to depend more on the legitimacy of particular government structures than on the effects of pluralist competition. . . . Where the interests in dispute are intrinsic and not easily divisible, such as questions of morality and identity, there will be fewer opportunities for compromise."

In addition, the dominance of neopatrimonialism as a political system across the continent (see Chapter 4) precludes the rise of a clear distinction between state and society, a necessary first step to the blossoming of a civil society. Neopatrimonialism is particularly inimical to civil society to the extent that it blurs the distinction between public and private. In neopatrimonial societies, the idea of a dichotomy between state and social roles is largely fictitious. As Jean-François Bayart (1993) has suggested, the African state is like a rhizome whose roots penetrate widely underground and resurface throughout the social landscape. Neopatrimonialism manifests itself through a multitude of vertical networks of patron-client relationships that link the holders of state power with the social clients. State and society are deeply intertwined. The absence of a distinct social sphere might preclude, therefore, the rise of a genuine civil society independent from the state (Lewis 1992). Particularly, the use of patronage by African governments can prevent civil society organizations from being autonomous from the state (Kasfir 1998b:9). In recent years, the co-optation of civil society organizations has been a marked characteristic of neopatrimonial regimes such as Museveni's Uganda and Mugabe's Zimbabwe. Of course, state patronage would not necessarily be a problem if civil society organizations were not willing to be co-opted in the first place (Ndegwa 1996).

The pervasiveness of patronage is also symptomatic of deeper economic deficiencies that prevent the rise of an independent civil society. Even after a couple of decades of adjustment programs and despite significant growth since the beginning of the twenty-first century, there is still relatively little economic activity in Africa that is not incorporated into the state domain. Yet associational life is likely to correlate with "indigenous capitalist industrialization," which must be able to benefit from economic foundations independent from the state (Bratton 1989a:427). Paraphrasing Barrington Moore's suggestion that democracy is not possible without a bourgeoisie, we could also write: "no independent bourgeoisie, no civil society."

Ironically, the remedy that most African NGOs have found for their lack of an independent domestic economic basis—foreign funding—has not come without its own share of liabilities for civil society. For Stephen Ndegwa (1996:24–25), the reliance on external funding "seriously undermines NGOs' ability to advance political issues in the long term," as their "agenda may become blurred by that of . . . donors." Kasfir (1998a:134) too is highly critical of the notion that outsiders can stimulate civil society: "an aid-created independent civil organization," he writes, "comes close to being an oxymoron. . . . Unless the new externally funded African organizations can develop effective social roots and local resources of their own, they will die on the vine as soon as their foreign patrons depart or lose interest." Clive Gabay's (2015) examination of civil society in Malawi illustrates how these organizations do not hold the state accountable by representing the interests of the country's population, but rather reflect the interests and agendas of international organizations, on which their funding depends—a view that echoes Harri Englund's (2006) sobering examination of Malawi's human rights activists.

Civil Society and African Realities

While there might be limitations about social structures in Africa that prevent the rise of bona fide civil society, it is also possible that the conventional notion of civil society largely misses the wealth and realities of African associational life. A few scholars have tried to adapt the concept of civil society to African realities (Obadare 2013). Such efforts constitute important contributions to scholarship and offer some redress to the Western bias of much of the existing civil society literature.

Célestin Monga's *Anthropology of Anger* (1996) is a landmark publication in this respect. Monga, a Cameroonian democracy activist turned scholar, strives for a "grassroots" explanation of social dynamics in Africa. He argues that an *informal* civil society has been vociferous and has posed effective challenges to the state for a very long time, yet social scientists have overlooked this civil action because such behaviors are not measurable with classical tools. In contrast, Monga calls for paying more attention to, and theorizing about, alternative forms of engagement, including "indigenous" types of social action, "new spaces for communication and discussion over which the state has no control," and all groups, organizations, and personalities that pursue freedom, justice, and the rights of citizenship against authoritarian states (4). It is not membership in bowling leagues and Rotary Clubs that effectively describes African civil society, Monga argues, but more "banal" forms of informal resistance, including music, linguistic novelty, and tailoring of appearance (hairstyles, postures while walking, standing, or talking) (111). In addition, Monga calls our attention to the many groups Africans are forming to voice their anger at their governments. Most of these groups are informal, however, along "lines of sex, age, kinship, and religion." According to him, "these groupings are a way of reclaiming the right of self-expression, long confiscated by the official institutions of power" (146). It is all these manifestations to manage and steer communal anger that represent genuine African society in Monga's work.

While less experiential, Nelson Kasfir's call for a more inclusive definition of civil society in Africa echoes in many ways Monga's argument. Turning the ethnic problem upside down, Kasfir (1998a) laments that the traditional framing of civil society leaves out ethnic groups as well as neopatrimonial relations and organized protests, which are the most dominant forms and represent the makeup of African civil society today. With civil society supposed to provide the foundation to democracy, Kasfir (1998b) wonders what the social basis of African democracy will be "if large numbers of organizations embedded in long-standing social formations can play no role in achieving it" (3). While others saw ethnicity as a liability to the formation of African civil society, it is exactly ethnicity, among other factors, that Kasfir has in mind when he refers to "long-standing social formations." For Kasfir, rather than an obstacle to civil society, ethnicity is "far more significant than the formally organized civil society promoted by scholars and donors." Ethnic activity contributes to a broad and rich associational life, and "if ethnic demands are excluded from civil society, it will be difficult to expect civil society organizations to represent anything close to the full agenda of citizens' demands" (7). He does not deny that ethnic-based associations (such as ethnic mutual welfare groups or even customary authorities) are likely to polarize civil society; he argues instead that they simply cannot be kept out. A body must not necessarily be civil to belong to civil society, says Kasfir. "Civil" should instead be "public" so as to entail the inclusion of all "citizens acting in common" (11). The work by Kasfir, Monga, and others draws our attention to the fact that the civil society concept, like social class, provides rich analytical value for the study of African politics when one is flexible in its uses and sensitive to the unique ways it is manifested in contemporary African contexts.

Notes

1. Simple average, based on forty-eight states, before the partition of Sudan.
2. Data derived from Alesina et al. 2002. Before this dataset was made available, most researchers used the less reliable ELF index (ethnolinguistic fractionalization), calculated and published by Charles Taylor, Michael Hudson, and Bruce Russett (1972) and based on data collected by Soviet anthropologists in the 1960s (State Geological Committee of the USSR 1964).
3. On ethnicity, language, and politics in Somalia, see Laitin 1977 and Laitin and Samatar 1987.
4. For a more recent and systematic primordialist rendition of the effects of ethnicity on economic policies in Africa, see Easterly and Levine 1997.
5. An example of this approach can be found in Diouf 1988. See also Marut 2002 and, for a more constructivist perspective, Foucher 2002.
6. In many Bantu languages, "Mu" refers to the designation of an individual, with "Ba" occasionally signifying the plural. Hence, for example, one is a Mumbala, while one's group is the Mbala or Bambala. Similarly, one is a Muganda, while one's group is the Baganda. The prefix "Bu," as in "Buganda" or "Burundi," designates the community in its collective personality.
7. Ranger (1993) later somewhat backtracked from his strong constructivist stance and acknowledged greater historical continuities in Africa's political "traditions."
8. For a critique of the primordialism-constructivism dichotomy, see Hale 2004.
9. The following discussion relies largely on Lemarchand 1995 and Mamdani 2001.
10. Despite the prevalence of constructivist literature in the field of theory, policy analyses largely continue to treat ethnic groups as given and exogenous in quasi-primordialist ways. It is hard to incorporate the insights of constructivism into policy, as ethnic identity may well itself be a function of policies and institutions (see Chandra 2001 on the nonincorporation of constructivist findings into the study of ethnic politics).
11. For a fictional and heartbreaking account of religious conflict in Nigeria, see "Luxurious Hearses" by Uwem Akpan (2008).
12. There might be fewer and fewer people who practice animism as their sole religion, but traditional beliefs often continue to find favor among converts to world religions.
13. *Tarika* in the singular.
14. For more details on the extent to which US policy in Africa relates to broader US policy against Islamic "terror," see Chapter 8.
15. Although it also conveys a notion of religious authority, "marabout" in this context should not be confused with the marabouts of Sufi brotherhoods in Senegal.
16. Data for 2016 are from World Bank, *World Development Indicators,* http://data.worldbank.org/indicator.

4

The Practice of Power

WHAT ARE THE KEY COMPONENTS OF STATES IN AFRICA? Are they organized differently from other states? Do they function in ways uniquely African? Which branches of government matter and why? How relevant are political parties? What purposes do they serve? How prevalent are military coups in Africa? How do African elites practice politics? How do African rulers exercise power? These are questions central to the study of comparative politics in general, and when applied to Africa offer interesting results.

In this chapter, we begin by discussing the general mechanisms through which African states reproduce and African rulers keep themselves in power. In doing so, we identify a key concept: *neopatrimonialism*. The word might be cumbersome but its descriptive and explanatory powers are great—although there is a fair amount of controversy over its usage and relevance. Next we examine several important dimensions of politics—parties, militaries, and executive, administrative, legislative, and judiciary authorities—and analyze the effects neopatrimonialism has on them.

The state is not the only provider of rule in Africa. African governance is often effectively exercised by a multiplicity of actors of more or less public standing, and this gives the African state a negotiated quality that is worth investigating. As we discuss levers of power such as executives, administrations, and bureaucracies, we include a survey of nonstate actors involved in the provision of public goods and of their relationship with the formal state. We also investigate whether reforms of the state, such as decentralization, have made it more or less accountable to its population.

141

Neopatrimonial Rule

It is not possible to make sense of contemporary African politics without coming to terms with the notion and the practice of neopatrimonialism. Although there are variations across the continent in the degree to which neopatrimonial rule is implemented, its presence has been a constant across the vast majority of African states for several decades. The concept tries to capture an ensemble of practices and features of African political systems—personal rule and the personalization of politics, patronage, the lack of distinction between public and private realms, institutional weakness, coexistence of bureaucratic and informal politics, corruption, and so forth—and to place them in a historical and comparative perspective. It finds its origins in the work of Max Weber, the German sociologist from the early twentieth century who identified several ideal-types of political rule: charismatic, patrimonial, and rational-legal. Here is not the place to discuss Weber's work in depth—most introductions to comparative politics address his typology—but it is worth digging deeper into the notion of patrimonial rule to see how it informs the concept of neopatrimonialism.

From Patrimonialism to Neopatrimonialism

Max Weber (1978 [1922]) defines patrimonialism as a system in which all political and administrative power relations between the ruler and the ruled are personal relations. Family and family roles lie at the core of this system. All is more or less informal and there is no differentiation between public and private. Specifically, public monies and the private purse of the chief are one. The chief is the central, defining character of the system. Moreover, it is the person of the chief, rather than his office, who carries authority. This feature is often referred to as personal rule. As Christopher Clapham (1985) suggests, patrimonial authority is very similar to the authority a (traditional) father has over his children (unless, of course, they are teenagers). In other words, it is caring but absolute, and the children have next to no recourse against the decisions of the father. As a result, the patrimonial chief exercises his authority with few constraints and next to no institutional setting. He grants positions and resources in exchange for loyalty, which is often secured by the links of kinship that support and undergird such systems. Those who receive these positions (such as subaltern chiefs, "ministers," personal retainers, etc.) use them in part to appropriate the resources of their own subsistence and to extract a surplus for the chief (Médard 1982:178).

There is thus a large element of reciprocity in a patrimonial system: the main patron uses his authority and legitimacy, derived from his dominant family position, to appoint others to positions of authority, from which they can gather resources for themselves in exchange for their loyalty and for transferring some resources back to him. Note, therefore, how governmental authority and the economic rights of rulers translate in this system into "privately appropriated economic advantages" (Médard 1982:179). It is worth noting that, in Weber's argument, the subjects consider these practices as legitimate in the exercise of authority (see Pitcher, Moran, and Johnston 2009; see also Michael Schatzberg's 2001 concept of "matrix of legitimacy").

Initially, in drawing his typology of regimes, Weber reserved the patrimonial type to "traditional" systems such as patriarchies, centered on family structures, which can be found across the world in "premodern" societies. Precolonial Africa had numerous similar political systems, as discussed in Chapter 2. By extension, the system applies to traditional monarchies, where the power of the king is absolute and reproduces patterns of patriarchy.

Several observers of postcolonial Africa soon noticed that many of these features of traditional patrimonialism were present in contemporary regimes: "Big Men" rose to power and did away with institutional or legal constraints; personal bonds of loyalty continued to play a leading role in politics; reciprocal relations of clientelism and apparent use of public authority for private gain appeared widespread; and rulers called themselves "fathers" of their nations while treating their people like children. To help make sense of what seemed to become an increasingly generalized pattern of rule, scholars went back to Weber and called attention to the patrimonial features of contemporary African regimes. As early as the mid-1960s, Aristide Zolberg (1966) evoked the notion of "neotraditional" patrimonial regimes in his study of the new one-party states of West Africa. In 1972, in a book on Mobutu Sese Seko's Zaire, Jean-Claude Willame developed the concept of "decentralized patrimonialism" to account for the lack of central government control over the country's territory in the 1960s (a pattern that recurred in the 1990s and beyond). Willame noted how people regionally appropriate official posts, from which they derive status and resources, which allow them to become local quasi-warlords.[1] Later, Thomas Callaghy (1984) compared the rise of Mobutu to the "patrimonial-administrative" system of the French absolute monarchy in the seventeenth century, highlighting the personal nature of Mobutu's rule and his reliance on bonds of individual loyalty and state resources. It is worth noting how patrimonialism is used in succession by Willame and Callaghy to explain both decentralized chaos and the rise of centralized authority—an analytical ubiquity that might undermine the concept's usefulness, as we discuss later.

All these authors, however, struggled with the fact that these African regimes were not merely patrimonial. Next to the patrimonial behavior of their rulers, there were also formal institutions, laws, apparently neutral bureaucracies and bureaucrats, administrative routines, and the like. In other words, African postcolonial states also contained significant elements of what Weber referred to as "rational-legal" rule—that is, elements of modern bureaucratic states. There were variations, of course, with places such as Botswana or Senegal displaying greater amounts of rational-legal rule, and places such as Chad or Congo/Zaire displaying lesser. But all postcolonial African states were more than mere patrimonial systems and all included visible elements of modern statehood.

The notion of neopatrimonialism was developed to cope with this twofold dimension of African states: an essentially patrimonial rule, exercised upon a background of—and simultaneously with—legal-rational authority.[2] Importantly, neopatrimonial states are modern states with at least a formal distinction between private and public. As Gero Erdmann and Ulf Engel (2007:105) articulate in a study of the concept and its limitations, "neopatrimonial rule takes place within the framework of, and with the claim to, legal-rational bureaucracy or 'modern' stateness. Formal structures and rules do exist, although in practice, the separation of the private and public sphere is not always observed." Clapham (1985:48), another keen student of African politics, highlights the main features of neopatrimonialism: "Officials hold positions in bureaucratic organizations with powers which are formally defined, but exercise those powers, so far as they can, as a form not of public service but of private property. Relationships with others likewise fall into the patrimonial pattern of vassal and lord, rather than the rational-legal one of subordinate and superior, and behavior is correspondingly devised to display a personal status, rather than to perform an official function."

Features of Neopatrimonialism

How is power organized in such a system? The outward appearance of the African state reflects legal institutional arrangements, be they parliamentary, presidential, dictatorial, military, or something else. But in the end, within these formal structures, neopatrimonialism functions as a complex web of patron-client relations parasitically anchored on state offices and resources. At the core of the system is the personal ruler, the all-powerful president whose words sometimes matter more than the country's constitution and laws. Each of his clients (ministers, generals, governors, and so forth) owes the president his position and gives him, in return, complete loyalty. These patrons might have earned their position because they are from the president's region, ethnic group, or family, or because they might represent a threat to the president. Thus neopatrimonialism brings friends and foes together around the table to jointly consume the "pie" of state resources, or the "national cake" to use a Nigerian expression. Each of these clients then in turn becomes the patron of another set of clients, who reproduce his authority by exchanging their loyalty for the resources, positions, and status that the patron has access to by virtue of his formal role in the state system. And so forth, down to the village level, where local chiefs might well represent the last iteration of the system. It is crucial to visualize this pyramid of patron-client relations cutting across formal institutional assignments. Power in Africa emanates from overlapping structures or, to use the words of Emmanuel Terray (1986), from both the "air conditioner" and the "veranda."

The outcome of successful neopatrimonialism is the co-optation, the buy-in, of most significant elites of society and the groups they represent. State resources and offices are given to potential competitors to buy their compliance. Ultimately, the success and longevity of neopatrimonial networks requires political elites to fulfill the expected vertical redistribution of resources through the patron-client relationship. As an important corollary, different sections of society are brought together in a form of social contract via the co-optation of their leaders. Stability is purchased via the state. This phenomenon of "fusion of elites" was identified and characterized early on by Richard Sklar (1963), who illustrated it in the case of Nigeria, where northern customary elites were brought into the national postcolonial project through political parties. Jean-François Bayart (1985, 1993) later elaborated upon the concept and recoined it "reciprocal assimilation of elites." Catherine Boone (1992) has documented its associated patterns in Senegal in the state's co-optation of its religious leaders, the *marabouts,* via their control of the groundnut industry. Cameroon, where the president, Paul Biya, has systematically appointed prime ministers from the restive anglophone region, provides another case in point.

It is important, however, not to overemphasize the universalism and stability of the system. Many would-be clients are left out, temporarily or not, and might actively pursue the destabilization of the system. Sometimes, entire regions or ethnic groups and their leaders are underrepresented or excluded from neopatrimonial redistribution. This produces inequality and favors political instability. Competing factions arise, within and without the system, and might try to dislodge the president so as to recenter the pyramid along a new set of personal relationships. Hence, factionalism is a typical feature of neopatrimonial systems. As Robert Jackson and Carl Rosberg (1984:421) note, "personal rule is a distinctive type of political system in which the rivalries and struggles of powerful and willful men, rather than impersonal institutions, ideologies, public policies, or class interests, are fundamental in shaping political life." In some cases, these factional struggles might be conducive to military coups, palace revolutions, or even civil wars. But while these events have the potential to reshuffle patron-client relations and bring about a turnover among the main characters in the system, they typically do not affect the formal institutional setup, which confers African states with an air of stability despite their obvious weakness (on which more later) and the instability of their daily politics. The dramatic ousting of Zimbabwe's Robert Mugabe in 2017 illustrates this factionalism. After almost four decades in power, Mugabe was deposed when the military stepped in to support ousted vice president Emmerson Mnangagwa against first lady Grace Mugabe and her supporters in a factional struggle that had come to define Zimbabwean politics for several years.

Because neopatrimonialism is based on networks of personal relations, it is also elitist. At the top of the pyramid sits the "Big Man," an autocrat whose main line of accountability follows the vectors of clientage. Other "big men" follow down the pyramid, constructing their own political networks that are reliant on the vertical distribution of resources (Utas 2012). These big men function as central nodes within the networks of vertical redistribution, and it is the constellation of these elites that largely makes up the political system. While Jackson and Rosberg (1984:423) argue that the masses tend to be "unmobilized, unorganized, and therefore relatively powerless to command the action and attention of government," other authors have noted the occurrence and importance of popular mobilization (Branch and Mampilly 2015).

Finally, neopatrimonialism is characterized by arbitrariness. As formal rules are bent, the behavior of public agencies is unpredictable and often abusive (Vansina 1982). Many leaders seem to improvise as they go along: "they have arbitrarily changed the constitution to accommodate their preferred personal roles rather than attempted to draw their roles from the script, which is the way of constitutional government" (Jackson and Rosberg 1984:428). Hence the numerous attempts by incumbent heads of state to change the constitution so as to stay in power beyond their legal terms. Such arbitrariness is replicated down the levels of state hierarchy. In a richly documented ethnography of local state agents in a region of the Democratic Republic of Congo, Theodore Trefon vividly illustrates arbitrary manipulations of the law by officials who use rules to coerce and intimidate citizens while simultaneously suggesting ways to bypass them in exchange for material resources (Trefon with Ngoy 2007).

Origins of African Neopatrimonialism

Why is neopatrimonialism so prevalent in Africa? Where does it come from? There are essentially two schools of thought on this matter. One favors a cultural explanation and anchors contemporary practices in traditional modes of rule. The other is more political-economic and presents neopatrimonialism as the rational response of African rulers to the obstacles they face in ruling their nations. The reality probably has elements of both.

Victor Le Vine (1980) was among the first scholars to offer a cultural interpretation of African neopatrimonialism, arguing that African regimes find their origins in the traditional precolonial patrimonial systems, which have adapted to their new environment. Clapham (1985:49) also contends that neopatrimonialism is similar to the order of things in precolonial tribal societies, where kinship was the principal value. At its base, the modern state is beholden to the same logic, he writes. And Médard (1982) too suggests that clientelism is a traditional mode of political organization in Africa, which has survived in the new postcolonial institutional environment. He stresses that far from dissolving in the new states, some of these traditional clientelistic structures managed to renew themselves thanks to the availability of resources from the state. This harkens back to our discussion of the nature of the state in Chapter 2, with precolonial African patrimonialism merging with the imported institutions of the modern state to produce the distinct features of neopatrimonialism.

Goran Hyden (1980, 2006) provides a particularly salient example of the cultural approach to neopatrimonialism, having focused much of his life's work on showing the particular cultural features of African social life, based largely on ties of "affection," and their effects on development and state formation. According to Hyden (and many cultural anthropologists), personal relations are particularly important in Africa (hence the paramount influence of family) and tend to be based on principles of reciprocity. People invest in social obligations to create interdependence, some of which may play a role of insurance over the long run. In this system, generosity is highly regarded, as sharing wealth cements the bonds of personal relations and creates future obligations for the recipients, which might prove handy in societies based on survival agriculture, where reversals of fortune are common. Redistribution as well as consumption is thus central to African societies and largely proceeds from their prevalent uncertainty and insecurity. To some extent, Africans have imported these features of social life into the formal structures of the modern state. Traditional sharing has fed clientelism. Access to power has come to involve an obligation to redistribute, to exchange one's benefits, but magnified by the propensity for immediate consumption, which has put pressure on those with access to state resources.

In a similar vein, Michael Schatzberg (2001) relates many elements of personal rule to specific African cultural notions of political legitimacy. Family is at the root of the African polity, Schatzberg argues. Nations are represented as families, with presidents as fathers and the people as children. One of the essential duties of fathers is to feed their children. Power and politics are thus about eating (consumption), which is also an essential element in Jean-François Bayart's (1985, 1993) influential analysis of African politics. The president, as father, must provide; he cannot consume alone. Such expectations facilitate appropriation of state resources by the ruler and redistribution to a dependent people. The state is the cash cow of the system; it is perceived as little more than a redistributive mechanism.

In contrast to these arguments, neopatrimonialism can also be thought of as a rational response to the specific political constraints faced by ruling African elites. As we discovered in Chapter 2, independent African states were born fragile and shallow, and with highly heterogeneous societies. Independence brought many unrealistic expectations, which rulers were unable to meet and which soon translated into grievances. The leaders who inherited these states were therefore under great pressure to consolidate their power in the face of contending sources of political allegiance. For the majority of them, the key to staying in power rested not in building institutions and promoting development, but in a mix of repression and co-optation, which in practice translated into neopatrimonial rule. The weaker the state, the more benefits its elites derived from using its resources to pursue their quest for hegemony, either by attempting to reshape their societies into a new state-defined mold or by establishing new networks of support based on patronage, nepotism, regional preferences, and other forms of neopatrimonial policies. The weaker the states were to begin with, the more pressing their leaders' quest for increased power and the greater the relative returns, in terms of power, of neopatrimonial policies.

The work of Richard Sandbrook (1972) adopts this perspective in order to explain the propensity of African regimes to develop factionalism. Unintegrated societies, he argues, are kept together by patron-client networks, which in turn favor factional conflicts among lineages of clients. Factions are "segments of clientage networks" (117) that try to control the top of the patron-client pyramid. Thus factional instability is explained as the outcome of rational strategies of power, rather than as the outgrowth of long-standing cultural practices. Robert Jackson and Carl Rosberg (1984) also subscribe to a rational or contingent understanding of personal rule, which they see as an answer to the inherent instability and arbitrary institutions of postcolonial African states. Rulers such as Bokassa of the Central African Republic, Mobutu of Congo/Zaire, Idi Amin of Uganda, and Sékou Touré of Guinea—all examples of personal rulers unbound by institutional restraints—were essentially responding to the innately arbitrary, unsteady, and insecure foundations upon which they stood. Their repressive tendencies answered their fear of conspiracies from potentially disloyal segments of society. Their lack of institutionalization of power resulted from their distrust of formal institutions largely inherited from the colonial era. Hence, everything became personal, with real power exercised in the shadows of formal structures, a concept later developed by William Reno (1995) as the "shadow state." Even the single parties that they set up and that apparently ruled the country were little more than instruments of mobilization in support of the person of the president, and had little autonomous existence (in significant contrast to single parties in regimes such as the Soviet Union or China). They ruled by decrees and by clientelism, building large, ineffectual bureaucracies and armies as rewards for loyalty and incentives for compliance.

The neopatrimonial nature of bureaucracies and public employment was clearly articulated and illustrated in the landmark work of Richard Joseph (1987) on Nigeria. For Joseph too, *colonial* rather than precolonial features favored the expansion of neopatrimonialism, as well as its economic logic. Joseph coins the notion of "prebendalism" (also adapted from a concept earlier developed by Weber) to refer to the allocation of political and administrative office as political reward, without anticipation of actual bureaucratic performance but for appropriation of a financial rent. Joseph shows that the expansion of the state sector began in Nigeria toward the end of colonialism, with the creation of marketing boards and public enterprises. After independence, the rise of the oil industry favored large expansion of budgets and additional growth of the state, which became the means of accumulation, both personal and communal.

Prebendalism, the appointment of clients to positions of state authority, became the dominant means of accessing the state as a resource.

Consequences of Neopatrimonialism

To some extent, neopatrimonialism has proven a highly successful strategy. In the immediate postcolonial era, neopatrimonial systems of rule proved to be remarkably stable in many countries, even as they produced "strong" regimes in "weak" states such as Zaire, Kenya, Sierra Leone, Malawi, and Côte d'Ivoire. The fact that most African countries have remained unified since their independence, despite their weakness and heterogeneity, might be considered a testimony to the integrative power of patron-client relations and personal rule. The pyramidal nature of neopatrimonial rule has no doubt provided elements of instrumental legitimacy where the historical and moral legitimacy of the state were missing. In this respect, the "fusion" and "reciprocal assimilation of elites" might have prevented the worst-case scenarios of disintegration and violence, and possibly "economiz[ed] the cost of coercion" (Médard 1982:169).

All evidence suggests, however, that this success has come at a very high price. For indeed, neopatrimonialism has often proven profoundly inimical to all things developmental. Almost by definition, it is antithetical to good governance. In a neopatrimonial system, people "occupy bureaucratic offices less to perform public service than to acquire personal wealth and status. . . . The essence of neopatrimonialism is the award by public officials of personal favors" (Bratton and van de Walle 1994:458). Many civil servants (though certainly not all) have obligations to their family, their village, their ethnic kin, their region, and, according to their rank, their patron or clients. Hence, "the notion that politicians, bureaucrats or military chiefs should be the servants of the state simply does not make sense" (Chabal and Daloz 1999:15).

Poor governance is not just an affliction of African states; it is their mode of functioning. This is an important insight for the student of African development, as well as for donors intent on reforming African systems. Corruption is the fuel of neopatrimonialism; theft from the public is one of its organizing principles. In his examination of the "moral economy of corruption," Steven Pierce (2016:222) observes that a "corruption-complex" has come to define Nigerian political and daily life, but notes that it is important to understand corruption not in absolute terms, but as part of a shifting moral terrain within neopatrimonial practices: "corruption cannot be fully appreciated without a relatively systemic attention to the history not just of corrupt practices but of the ways in which corruption functions as means of engaging in politics and political critique." Thus, improving governance in Africa is far from simple. It is much more than a matter of training better bureaucrats, providing them with technology, and otherwise increasing their capacity. Similarly, campaigns against corruption risk undermining the very foundations of regimes and are thus often likely to be little more than lip service. African governance might be poor in developmental terms, but it serves an integrative function and it is relatively good at it (see Chabal and Daloz 1999). Thus, attempts to promote developmental policies and institutions threaten the very core of the foundations of African regimes and entail political costs that are often neglected by those who design these policies.

The negative effects of neopatrimonialism go further than corruption and mismanagement, however. The personal nature of power makes it exceedingly hard to delegate responsibilities and to define positions by their function, as would take place in a rational-legal system. Clapham (1985:49) puts it nicely: "When the boss is away, especially in the case of the head of state, the decision-making process waits on his return. If he is reluctant to make decisions, the entire system sinks into a torpor from which it may only be rescued by his overthrow and replacement by a new boss." Even if the boss is in, technocrats learn quickly that there is little demand for any kind of new or different policy that may "rock the boat." Those who attempt to make changes encounter "indifference if not hostility" (van de Walle 2001:136).

There are significant consequences to such flawed governance. States are inhibited in their most basic functioning. Citing research by the International Monetary Fund (IMF), Christian von Soest (2007:622) notes that "political interference with the process of collecting state revenue" leads to shortfalls of more than 60 percent of potential tax revenue in some African countries. Moreover, there is little capacity of civil society to monitor public agencies and demand accountable governance. As Peter Lewis (1992) has shown, the extensive vertical and unequal patron-client networks that constitute African regimes are inimical to the development of an autonomous civil society. Through them, the state seeps in and pervades society, providing foundations for its own stability at the expense of a societal capacity to articulate interests and make effective governance demands.

Beyond weak governance, the entire institutional development of the state is threatened by neopatrimonialism. Personal rulers fear alternative sources of power (Reno 1997a). As a result, it is against their best interest to let strong ministries, bureaucracies, or judiciaries develop. Instead, they keep their administrations off-balance by rotating personnel and depriving them of the necessary resources to carry on their functions. Moreover, personal rulers do not wish to have their hands tied by rules and laws. Thus they frequently revise their own laws, undermining the stability of the legal system, or freely violate them altogether. In Côte d'Ivoire, Félix Houphouët-Boigny equivocated for many years over the rules of his own succession so as to keep potential challengers on their toes. In Zaire, Mobutu rotated ministers in and out of office (and sometimes in and out of jail) with rapidity and regularity. Needless to say, in such an environment, state institutions tend to remain thwarted. As Erdmann and Engel (2007:105–106) write, "formal institutions cannot fulfil their universalistic purpose of public welfare. . . . Political informality has gained such a dimension that one can even speak of institutionalized informality, which turns into a separate type of political culture." Thus, while it can be successful at building and sustaining the power of the president, neopatrimonialism inhibits the capacity of state institutions.

A country's economic development can be threatened by neopatrimonialism. Instead of facilitating the development of an entrepreneurial capitalist class, neopatrimonialism turns the dominant class, which has formed through the acquisition of clientelistic resources, into a "rentier class" (Boone 1990), which lives parasitically off the state. In a rent-seeking system, companies lobby the state for contracts, advantages, and bureaucratically created opportunities (such as access to import quotas), while would-be entrepreneurs satisfy themselves with state-derived appointments. The president is not eager to be challenged by independent economic power. Thus he adopts policies that thwart private accumulation, such as nationalizations, price controls, and burdensome regulations. Hence, African bourgeoisies have historically tended to lack the development impulse often associated with bourgeoisies elsewhere. As with poor governance, the neopatrimonial economic system is resistant to reform, as rulers want to keep their control over economic resources so as to retain the tools of controlling their fractionalized societies (van de Walle 2001:52).

Many of the pathologies of African statehood thus result from the practice of neopatrimonialism. Their revenues stolen, states endure a "systematic fiscal crisis" (van de Walle 2001:53). As governments borrow to make up their deficits, their budget woes soon turn to unsustainable debt levels and create structural dependence on foreign capital. Debt servicing steals from other forms of public spending, with health and education often the first victims. Meanwhile, people seek to escape

the burdens of regulation and corruption by resorting to informal transactions, further depriving the state of resources. African regimes
become ensconced in "permanent crises" (van de Walle 2001). These
features are explored in much greater detail in Chapter 6.

From a political point of view, there is a sheer lack of direction.
Comparing politics to a ship, Jackson and Rosberg (1984:430) note
that African rulers do not steer purposefully. They are not commanders,
but seamen, "rulers who are not nearly as preoccupied with the problem of going somewhere as with the task of keeping themselves and
their regimes afloat." Goran Hyden (2006) uses the same metaphor,
suggesting that African states "float" but do not "navigate." State institutions are hollowed out by neopatrimonialism. Mark Beissinger and
Crawford Young (2002:22) speak of a "vacuum of purpose and agenda"
and of the "evasion of authority within society." Little by little, neopatrimonialism may lead to state failure and, in some cases, to collapse and
conflict (see Chapter 7).

Critiques of Neopatrimonialism

"Neopatrimonialism" is but a word. It is not in and of itself a theory. As
a word, it does not have any particular analytical merits. Most often, it
is merely a shortcut to describe the features of the modal African
regime. However, these features can be explained, as we have seen, in
terms of culture, history, or rational decisionmaking by elites. Similarly,
an understanding of the neopatrimonial nature of the African state can
help us make sense of some of its most salient deviances. As such, the
concept contributes significantly to an analytical and theoretical understanding of African politics.

Yet as popular as the concept of neopatrimonialism has become
among scholars of African politics, it is far from unanimously endorsed.
Its critiques fall into several categories. Authors in the Marxist or "radical" tradition tend to dismiss the concept as justification for a neoliberal assault on the state (Olukoshi 1999). A more recent strand of critiques has argued that neopatrimonialism might not be as inimical to
development as we suggested earlier, and that, in other regions and time
periods, it has been associated with better economic performances. For
David Booth and Tim Kelsall (2010), for example, some Southeast
Asian countries also display features of neopatrimonialism, yet have
managed much more significant economic transformations than have
the majority of their African counterparts. Thus neopatrimonialism does
not necessarily lead to underdevelopment. The difference, Booth and

Kelsall suggest, lies in its degree of centralization and in the time horizon of elites. The more centralized the practice of neopatrimonialism (the more its networks of extraction and redistribution are controlled by the president and his inner circle), and the longer their time horizon (their expectation to remain in office), the more developmental neopatrimonialism can be.[3] In much of Africa, neopatrimonialism suffers from its polycentric nature: there are too many patrons, too many factions, too many endlessly reproduced and renegotiated reciprocal exchanges, with the result that economic operators cannot factor in the costs of the system and remain vulnerable to its unpredictability. Moreover, because expectations of power are relatively short in time (on account of the historical prevalence of coups and other turnovers), those in positions of authority tend to practice a more intense form of neopatrimonial rule than elsewhere. Booth (2012) later noted, however, the presence of developmental neopatrimonialism in Ethiopia and Rwanda after the mid-1990s, and linked it in part to the insecurity of these regimes, which they seek to alleviate by creating legitimacy out of development (see also Kelsall 2013), which favors the centralization of rents. Daniel Bach (2011, 2012) has developed a similar argument, comparing "regulated" and "predatory" forms of neopatrimonialism, and suggesting that the former is not necessarily inimical to development.

Anne Pitcher, Mary Moran, and Michael Johnston (2009:132) are also concerned about the indiscriminate use of the term "neopatrimonialism," lamenting that "at one time or another, scholars have labeled nearly every African government as patrimonial or neopatrimonial." They too show that there are variations in regime type and development among African nations that seem uncorrelated with patrimonialism. In particular, Botswana, one of Africa's few developmental success stories, managed to democratize and grow despite patrimonial politics. Its leaders, "deeply rooted in the traditional life of village and countryside," used "personal power and a range of reciprocities to solidify their legitimacy as a ruling class," while also solidifying their own financial well-being (145). Pitcher and colleagues use this example to show that neopatrimonialism need not be overly deterministic of regime type or development performance. They also stress that Weber did not mean the term to describe dysfunctional or deviant types of government, which "neopatrimonialism" has often come to include. For Weber, they stress, patrimonialism was a means of broadcasting authority rooted in personalistic and familial ties, and was perceived as legitimate by those on the receiving end of it.

Kelsall, Pitcher, and others call our attention to the existing variation in democratic and economic performance among African regimes, despite the near-universality of neopatrimonialism. Although this diversity should not be exaggerated (as a group, African states remain different from many states in other regions), it does suggest either that neopatrimonialism is not the only factor affecting performance in Africa or that there are several forms of it, varying in their intensity and effects. This latter perspective is the one adopted by Daniel Bach (2011), for whom African neopatrimonialism ranges from "integral," where state institutionalization is exceedingly weak (e.g., Mobutu's Zaire), to "regulated," where some administrative capacity remains and public policies are produced (e.g., Côte d'Ivoire under Houphouët-Boigny, Kenya under Jomo Kenyatta). Bach does not explain, however, what might account for these variations.

Gero Erdmann and Ulf Engel (2007) offer a different critique. They argue that scholarly usage of neopatrimonialism puts too much emphasis on the "patrimonial" dimension of African politics and not enough on the "neo" part—that is, the formal bureaucratic element in African politics. As a result, the concept of neopatrimonialism gives us a biased and worsened view of Africa. Failing to incorporate rational dimensions of rule limits neopatrimonialism's operational utility. As a result, Erdmann and Engel call for more scholarly emphasis on the study of the functioning of formal African bureaucracies in relation to the informal behavior of their agents.

It is also fair to ask to what extent neopatrimonialism remains as important to understanding African politics in the twenty-first century as it was in the late twentieth. After all, an increasing number of African countries have moved toward greater constitutionalism and democracy, a topic to which we return at length in Chapter 5. Such a process would seem to involve a relative increase in formal rules. There has so far been little systematic research on whether the rise of democratic forms of government has reduced the neopatrimonial nature of rule in Africa. This might be the case. For sure, several personal rulers have had to factor in the new rules of succession in office, and many seem to have incorporated them. Daniel Posner and Daniel Young (2007) show, for example, that an increasing number of rulers either respect formal rules of succession or try to bypass them by using, in turn, formal procedure.

Yet while a trend toward institutionalization has been undeniable, there are numerous forces that maintain patrimonial rule at the core of African regimes, even democratic ones. To return to the words of Emmanuel Terray (1986), the introduction of "air conditioners" (formal spaces of rational politics) into African systems has not necessarily reduced the continued importance of the "verandas" (the parallel informal structures of power) in politics. Even in South Africa, with its diversified capitalist economy and robust bureaucracy (especially relative to other African states), there has been a marked escalation of corruption and the personalization of power, particularly after Jacob Zuma assumed the presidency in 2009 (Lodge 2014). By the time he was forced to resign in 2017, Zuma was the personification of the neopatrimonial practices that had come to characterize modern South African life, including the use of public powers for private use, heightened factionalism, rampant corruption, and private gain through public resources. As Staffan Lindberg (2003) carefully illustrated in the case of Ghana, neopatrimonialism might be just as prevalent with democracy as it was before, if not more potent. Using a survey and personal interviews of members of parliament (MPs), Lindberg finds that they "wake up almost every morning to face a queue of constituents (often 10–20 persons) that expect them to take time to address their concerns and provide various sums of money" (129). Lindberg shows how Ghanaian MPs act as patrons, whose clients (the voters) use elections as their "harvesting season," expecting their patrons to give them "rewards" and grant them personal favors even before the actual election of these MPs takes place. Since more candidates are in the running and the game is zero-sum, Lindberg shows that clients can take advantage of the situation with "electoral blackmail." When the MPs do not have the resources to fulfill the demands of their constituents, corruption can increase. Conversely, the MPs can do what they want in terms of policy, because their accountability is determined only by their patronage handouts. Yet they apparently have little time for policy or for keeping the government accountable, as they have to spend the majority of their days finding ways to meet the demands of their constituents.

Lindberg shows that democracy does not necessarily deflate neopatrimonialism, and that it might in fact exacerbate it. His survey findings show that Ghanaian MPs' patronage spending increased dramatically under democracy: the proportion who spent at least 25 percent of their budget on patronage rose from one-third in 1992, to half in 1996, to more than half in 2000 (2003:131). We will explore the relationship between neopatrimonialism and democracy further in Chapter 5.

Political Parties

How relevant are political parties to the functioning of African political life? Chronologically, there are distinct phases to the evolution of political parties in Africa. In the late colonial period and early years of independence, parties often played an important role in political mobilization and in the rise of African elites. Soon after independence, however, the generalization of personal rule led to a widespread shift either toward single parties structured around the person of the president and some loose nationalistic and sometimes socialist ideology, or toward military regimes, which often banned political parties altogether. The spread of competitive elections in the late 1980s and early 1990s marked a return to political pluralism and a concomitant resurgence of political parties. In the ensuing couple of decades, however, a number of countries witnessed an evolution toward dominant parties anchoring loose alliances around presidents, reminiscent in some ways of the trend in the 1960s toward single parties. At the same time, other countries witnessed a shift to multiparty competition with a range of political parties. As we note later, recent scholarship indicates that contemporary African political party systems are far more diverse than previously assumed.

The Early Stages of Party Politics

Parties have existed in Africa since the early twentieth century, though the majority of them sprang up after 1945, when the decolonization sequence began to unfold with the first elections and the expansion of voting rights. Some parties were established early on with the aim of unifying entire nations to represent Africans toward the colonizers (although, in practice, some of these parties represented certain social groups more than others). In anglophone Africa, Ghana's Convention People's Party (CPP, established by Kwame Nkrumah in 1949), the Kenya African Union (KAU, created by Jomo Kenyatta in 1947), and the Tanganyika African National Union (TANU, formed by Julius Nyerere in 1954) are examples of such mass movements that would soon embody the decolonization struggle. In francophone Africa, the Rassemblement Démocratique Africain (RDA) was founded in 1946. Although a somewhat more elitist organization than its anglophone counterparts, it covered most of France's West and Central African possessions and affiliated with France's communist party (and later with its socialist party). All of these parties still exist in one form or another today.

Following independence, many of the nationwide political parties turned into single parties and provided the foundation for the one-party states that characterized most neopatrimonial states. This was true of the CPP in Ghana, Kenya's KAU, Tanzania's Chama Cha Mapinduzi (CCM), and the national parties that had split out from the RDA, such as the Parti Démocratique de Côte d'Ivoire (PDCI) under Félix Houphouët-Boigny and the Parti Démocratique de Guinée (PDG) of Ahmed Sékou Touré. What characterized many of these party-states was the belief that they had "a right of representation [of the nation] that had been permanently conferred" to them (Suttner 2004:6). They were "all-encompassing" (Mozaffar and Scarritt 2005:409). Yet as Mathias Basedau, Gero Erdmann, and Andreas Mehler (2007) argue, these were not truly "mass parties," but rather institutional appendages to personal rulers (see also Zolberg 1966). The role of the party organization was, in fact, negligible (Wallerstein 1966; Bienen 1967, 1971), apart from mobilization in favor of the leader. They had "loose membership systems and organizational structures" and were more "coalition[s] of disparate groups . . . united behind a president they [hoped would be] in a position to dispense various rewards" (Suttner 2004:8). The mass involvement, courted by the leaders in the decolonization phase, was progressively toned down thereafter. Not only did personal rule turn these parties into appendages of the leader, but it also emptied them of policy substance as the decisionmaking process was shifted to the presidency.

In most countries, as the party-states consolidated around the person of the president, other parties were either banned outright (as in the military regimes of Burkina Faso, Ghana, and Uganda) or assigned a very limited role, with opponents most often co-opted and opposition parties merged into the dominant one (Mozaffar and Scarritt 2005:400). The typical party-state became a "plebiscitary" regime where elections continued to be held, but with little more intent than to legitimize the authoritarian ruler (as was the case, for example, in Benin, Gabon, and Kenya). The exceptions were very few: Botswana, Gambia, and Mauritius were the only countries to consistently tolerate multiple parties over the 1960–1990 period (Upper Volta had a brief democratic episode with multiparty elections from 1978 to 1980 under Sangoulé Lamizana, sandwiched between two military regimes). Gambia saw a dramatic authoritarian reversal in 1994, however, with the consequence that only Botswana and Mauritius (with a combined population of about 3 million) have been consistently democratic since independence; but even so, Botswana has never witnessed a change of party in power.

In contrast to these national unity parties, some countries initially experienced regional parties, which heralded future problems of national integration. In Nigeria, Igbo nationalist Nnamdi Azikiwe created the National Council of Nigeria and Cameroon (NCNC) as early as 1944, an initiative followed by the establishment of the Northern People's Congress in 1949 by the sardauna (sultan) of Sokoto, Ahmadu

Bello, to unite the Hausa-Fulani, and of the Action Party in 1951 by Chief Obafemi Awolowo to represent the Yoruba. In Belgian Congo, parties were created much later, because the colonizers long refused to allow political activities. Yet when parties were authorized, they also took on ethnoregional qualities. The Alliance des Bakongo (ABAKO), created as a cultural association in 1950, became a political party in the late 1950s under the leadership of Joseph Kasavubu and represented the interests of the Bakongo. Similarly, the Confédération des Associations Tribales du Katanga (CONAKAT), a largely Lunda-based Katanga party, was established in 1958 by Moïse Tshombé. In contrast, however, the Mouvement National Congolais (MNC) of Patrice Lumumba, also created in 1958, had national ambitions. It might have helped that Lumumba himself came from a rather small ethnic group, the Tetela, and did not live in his region of origin.

In countries with pre-independence factionalism, as in Nigeria and Congo, there were military takeovers (on which more later), which usually banned parties. In Nigeria, the political system was subsequently characterized by military overthrows, volatility, and bouts of democratic rule. In Congo, military dictator Mobutu Sese Seko, who took over in 1965, civilianized his regime and established his own single party, the Mouvement Populaire de la Révolution (MPR), in 1967, which incarnated the nation and to which every Congolese belonged from birth. Soon the Congolese system also became plebiscitary, with the MPR controlling almost everything, including the state, provinces, unions, youth movements, and student organizations (Young and Turner 1985).

The Spread of Multiparty Politics

The end of the Cold War brought about sweeping changes to African politics. Single-party systems suffered from the collapse of their role models from the Soviet Union and Eastern Europe, while Western donors, long highly tolerant of friendly authoritarian regimes, began demanding democratic reforms (Monga 1997:156). These changes brought about the "resurgence" of political parties throughout Africa (Mozaffar and Scarritt 2005:401).

The fates of the ruling single parties or incumbent regimes varied. Some were ousted in pro-democracy military coups (as in Mali and Nigeria), others were voted out (as in Benin, Congo-Brazzaville, and Malawi), while still others completely transformed while in power and managed to manipulate the new electoral environment (as did Côte d'Ivoire's PDCI or Cameroon's Rassemblement Démocratique du Peuple

Camerounais [RDPC]). Coalitions that united in opposition to the ruling parties, however, also tended to absorb members from the old government who had defected. In Kenya, for example, the National Rainbow Coalition (NARC) included many former associates of the Daniel arap Moi regime (Suttner 2004:8). Matthew Shugart (1998) maintains that the character of the transition to democracy explains the character of the resulting parties. If the transition was gradual and constitution-drafting was put off by the ruling regime until after semicompetitive elections were held (what Shugart calls the "decompressive" model), countries were subjugated by insiders and their parties are now weak. If the transition was followed by a newly created provisional government that first held elections and then drafted the constitution (the "provisionary" model), strong parties resulted.

Whatever the form of transition, the number of political parties exploded almost everywhere on the continent. In the Democratic Republic of Congo, for example, more than 200 parties registered within months after Mobutu introduced multiparty politics in April 1990. In most countries, many one-man parties soon disappeared, but in some the number of parties has remained extremely high. As of 2007, there were 130 recognized political parties in Côte d'Ivoire, 103 in Burkina Faso, 94 in Mali, and 41 in Nigeria, to name a few (IDEA 2007). And in the DRC, as of August 2017, there were still over 50 registered parties.

Features of Post-1990 Political Parties

While there had been a degree of consensus among scholars of African political parties, this has changed in recent years. Today there are disagreements about the degree in which African political party systems are exceptional when contrasted with the usual characteristics of parties in Europe or North America. In reviewing the scholarship on African party systems, Anja Osei (2016:38) notes the parties "were commonly described in terms of their deficits: weak links to civil society groups, no convincing programmatic appeals, and weak or non-existent formal party structures." Recent empirical work on African political parties has greatly nuanced and broadened the understanding of African politics. In this section, we will survey the common elements identified in the literature examining African political parties since the democratic resurgence of the 1990s, paying particular attention to the major points of debate within the scholarship.

First of all, as just mentioned, there tend to be a large number of political parties in many countries, often several hundred registered ones. Most tend to be very small and revolve around one person and his or her close entourage. A large number of them "do not possess even the minimum amount of electoral support required to win one seat" (Mozaffar and Scarritt 2005:413). Far from favoring the democratic game, this multiplicity "contributes to fragmentation rather than the possibility of meaningful competition with or in opposition to the ruling party" (Randall and Svåsand 2001:11). In Mali, for example, the large number of small parties became conducive to a politics of consensus building and co-optation under Amadou Toumani Touré, which eventually led to sterilization of the opposition and low levels of electoral participation, which contributed to the political crisis that resulted in Touré's overthrow in 2012 (Bleck and Michelitch 2015).

Second, and importantly, it has typically been assumed that many African parties are based on ethnic or regional loyalties (Decalo 1998; Erdmann and Engel 2007; Widner 1997), or that ethnicity is the general organizing principle and that ethnic politics is inimical to the development of democracy. In some cases, the ethnic affiliation of parties might be explicit, if allowed by law. In Nigeria, for example, the Odoua People's Congress is a purely Yoruba affair. Similarly, the Oromo People's Congress, the All-Amhara People's Organization, and the Afar Revolutionary Democratic Unity Front of Ethiopia are, as their names respectively indicate, Oromo, Amhara, and Afar political parties. More often, ethnicity is implicit. One "knows" in Côte d'Ivoire, for example, that the RDR is a "Dioula" party, while the FPI is controlled by Bété interests and the PDCI is mainly Baoulé. Similarly, in the 2010 presidential elections in Guinea, the Union des Forces Démocratiques de Guinée (UFDG) was perceived as representing the interests of the Peul, whereas the Rassemblement du Peuple de Guinée (RPG) was perceived as representing those of the Malinké. Ethnic parties tend to enter politics to defend the interests of their ethnic group in the national system. They mobilize their electorates with appeals to these interests or by invoking some threats to the group (e.g., the capture of the state by some other ethnicity), and with the promise of clientelism. Yet not all parties are narrowly ethnic. As Erdmann (2007:56–57) argues, Africa also counts "ethnic congress" parties, which are based on ethnic coalitions or alliance. The Malawi Congress Party (MCP) is an example of such a coalition party, bringing together Chewas and Nyanjas.

Recently, Sebastian Elischer (2013) questioned the belief that ethnicity is the primary force behind African politics and party formation. Elischer's study indicates that African political party systems are far more diverse than normally assumed and he offers a useful typology, noting five ideal types: mono-ethnic parties, which promote the interest of an ethnic group; ethnic-alliance (or "congress") parties, which create alliances of convenience to promote diverse group interests; ethnic catch-all parties attempting to transcend ethnic politics; programmatic parties promoting particular ideas or ideologies; and personalistic parties built around the promotion of a particular leader or elite group. His work indicates that ethnic parties (mono-ethnic and alliance) have been more prevalent in Africa—roughly 25 percent more than nonethnic parties— and that personalistic and programmatic parties "are not sustainable over time" (2013:183). Importantly, Elischer observes not only that ethnic parties are not necessarily inimical to the development of democracy (as evidence by Benin's democratic development), but also that ethnic parties and party systems tend to become less ethnic over the course of successive multiparty elections. His comparative study leads him to conclude that, with the notable exception of Kenya, "nothing suggests that multiparty competition fosters ethnic division over time" (2013:221).

What explains the salience of ethnic parties in some countries but not in others? Elischer's study refutes the standard variables found in the literature: economic growth, economic inequality, electoral systems, party-system characteristics, and the quality of democratic elections. Rather, Elischer argues that the main causal factor is ethnic structure. Specifically, he finds that countries lacking a core ethnic group foster nonethnic parties when ethnic factionalization is low, but ethnic parties when that factionalization is high. Countries with a core ethnic group and low ethnic fragmentation tend to foster nonethnic parties and low political saliency for ethnicity. Elischer finds this is caused by a "bandwagon effect" in which the core group is divided across several parties and smaller ethnic groups are incentivized to join them rather than trying to beat them. Thus, over the course of multiparty elections, dominant ethnic groups tend to become co-opted and dispersed into competing political parties.

A third characteristic of African parties that has been noted in the literature is their relative lack of political programs. This could partly reflect the fact that, as Thandika Mkandawire (1999) argues, African democracies are essentially "choiceless"—that is, there is a very limited range of policy choice available to their governments given the constraints of debt servicing, donor conditionality, and primary-commodity reliance. Nevertheless, the policy vacuum of many African parties can be stunning and is usually reflected in their names, which invoke "national unity," "popular rally," and "patriotic movement" for development and democracy. Political platforms are thus of little assistance when one is prompted to choose between, say, the hypothetical Rally for National Unity and Party for Patriotic Development. As E. Gyimah-Boadi (2007) suggests, it might not be in the parties' interests to offer anything new in terms of policy. If their goal is to unite ethnic groups or ethnic coalitions, any reference to specific policies could be more divisive than useful. Hence, being "issueless" is an optimal strategy. The lack of programmatic dimension also reflects the aspirations of politicians within a neopatrimonial system. Not all party leaders want to govern. Some only want to take advantage of the perks of office (Monga 1997).

Fourth, most African political parties suffer from very limited institutionalization. Their bureaucratic organization is feeble and often temporary. They are often unable to provide accurate membership information, either because of a lack of any formal membership or because their members also belong to other parties (Erdmann 2007). Their funding base tends to be narrow, and most often comes from the private wealth of their founder, or from limited funds from democracy-promotion donor programs. As a result, their formal ties to society are also poorly developed (Erdmann 2007). They do not typically fulfill the representation and participation roles that parties often play elsewhere. In fact, citizen involvement in them is very limited between elections. This is even true of the large pro-democracy movements that arose in the early 1990s and became ruling parties, such as the Movement for Multiparty Democracy (MMD) in Zambia and the Alliance pour la Démocratie au Mali (ADEMA). These parties do not have membership rosters, procedures for gathering members' monetary support, activities between elections, or militant volunteers. Instead, most of their activists and supporters "expect upfront monetary payment, payment in kind, or future material reward in return for services rendered to the party" (Gyimah-Boadi 2007:25).

One needs, however, to distinguish from the mass of parties the remnants of the old single parties, some of which have managed to maintain strong and organized bureaucracies, such as Tanzania's CCM, the Zimbabwe African National Union–Popular Front (ZANU-PF), and the Frente de Libertação de Moçambique (FRELIMO). For these parties that stayed in power, it is common to have far greater organizational and bureaucratic features than do the parties of their opponents. Moreover, their access to the state also tends to guarantee significant funding.

Fifth, it has generally been assumed that the lack of organizational structure of African parties correlates with their patronage features. Many of them are based on informal relations between their members and their leaders that revolve around personal rule and clientelism. Leader loyalty is paramount. Its absence will often lead to expulsion and the likely creation of a new party by the expelled individual. This loyalty to the leader translates into a deficit of democracy: internal debate is lacking or repressed (Gyimah-Boadi 2007:25; Erdmann 2007). In the case of Tanzania, Tim Kelsall (2003:60) found that party membership is "disproportionately composed of young men looking for patronage, rather than dues-paying members," a view shared by M. Anne Pitcher (2012) in her examination of parties in Zambia. At the same time, many parties have limited life expectancy, as they depend upon the fate of their leaders (Monga 1997).

The final characteristic is the severe imbalance between the party or parties in power and those in opposition. The ruling party tends to dominate. It also usually resorts to state funds and makes the most of government structures to carry out its goals. Bratton (1998) speaks of near-total supremacy of the ruling party, citing the examples of Zimbabwe, Botswana, Kenya, and Tanzania. The domination of a single party harkens back to the era of the one-party systems of the 1960s. Then, as now, proponents assert that such systems can provide effective governance, facilitate representation through broad-based inclusivity, and actually foster the development of democracy, because, in the words of Renske Doorenspleet and Lia Nijzink (2014:14), "they seem to be better in preserving stability and promoting much needed socio-economic development." Critics note that one-party dominance constrains democracy by closing off alternative policy options, silencing of majority voices, increasing factionalism, limiting dissent, increasing authoritarian practices, and diminishing accountability. As Doorenspleet and Nijzink (2014:173) observe in their comparative study, the lack of prospects for party change in the executive office and legislature limits the strategic incentives for the ruling party to represent the varied interests of the electorate; thus, "the lack of party system competitiveness is diminishing government accountability and responsiveness."

This is not to imply that opposition parties are always powerless. Looking at Kenya, Zambia, and Zimbabwe, Adrienne LeBas (2012) suggests that the presence of pro-democracy "mobilizing structures," such as trade unions, strengthens opposition parties in hybrid regimes. For Leonardo Arriola (2013), opposition parties are able to reach across ethnic constituencies and form broad coalitions if they can raise funds from an autonomous private financial sector (ethnic group leaders must be bought up front), a strategy he illustrates with the case of Kenya (in contrast to Cameroon's fragmented opposition).

In the end, it has been argued that most of these features of African parties relate to neopatrimonialism. While lacking formal strength,

African parties are nevertheless anchored in society through informal patron-client relations and adopt their characteristics. Erdmann (2007:51) says clientelism and patronage "provide legitimacy for a party leadership and . . . can even contribute to the stabilization of a democratic regime" and "may provide a functional equivalent to some of the formal institutions or politics." Many have argued that the neopatrimonial nature of politics is inimical to the consolidation of party pluralism. As Shaheen Mozaffar and James Scarritt (2005:403) note, democratic consolidation in Africa "tends to produce dominant parties that are able to win elections with overwhelming majorities." Nicolas van de Walle (2003) has also pointed out the increased trend among African political parties toward renewed presidentialism and the rise of quasi-single parties. The neopatrimonial logic of politics encourages parties in power to grow larger and drag in co-opted competing elites, while the personal clientelistic nature of politics promotes the existence of numerous tiny parties with no long-term hope aside from rallying to those in power.

As should be clear from this brief discussion, most scholars of African political parties have tended to view them through the prism of neopatrimonialism, assuming them to be secondary to the politics of personal rule. But recent scholarship and events in a handful of African countries have provided interesting developments. Rather than assuming the dominance of informal personalized networks, for example, Osei's (2016) work on Ghana illustrates the importance of formal structures, and the complex ways in which the formal and informal coexist and interact at the national and constituency level. Osei finds that ethnic and regional factionalism plays only a minor role, while informal relations vary greatly between different Ghanaian parties.

It is important to note that several months after the publication of Osei's work, Ghana experienced a peaceful transfer of power when the presidential incumbent, John Mahama of the National Democratic Congress, was defeated by Nana Akufo-Addo of the New Patriotic Party, the first time a sitting president had failed to win a second term in Ghana. The preceding year, in Nigeria, presidential incumbent Goodluck Jonathan was defeated by Muhammadu Buhari, marking the first time a president had lost reelection in that country as well. Perhaps even more remarkable, in Gambia, opposition candidate Adama Barrow defeated long-serving incumbent Yahya Jammeh in presidential elections in 2016, marking the first electoral transfer of power in that country's history. These events challenge a number of the dominant assumptions about African political parties and electoral competition, furthering the need for a nuanced understanding of the complicated and diverse ways in which party politics are practiced across the continent. At the very least, they raise questions about the consolidation of stable, balanced, and competitive democratic systems within a neopatrimonial context. We return at length to this issue in our discussion of regime hybridity in Chapter 5.

Militaries

Although African states wage war against each other relatively rarely, militaries have been ubiquitous actors in African societies since independence. One may travel extensively through England, France, or the United States and never see a soldier. But it takes only a few minutes spent on the streets of Conakry, Kinshasa, or Nairobi to spot soldiers. And traveling between cities will often reveal many more, manning the multiple roadblocks along the way.

Just as they populate Africa's physical space, military personnel of different grades also populate its political space. Ever since the 1960s, Africa has had a history of military intervention in politics, with a greater propensity for coups d'état and military regimes than any other continent (Collier and Hoeffler 2007). By 2019, Africa had seen at least 200 coup attempts. Some countries have been afflicted by systematic instability and have experienced up to half a dozen coups. Guinea-Bissau, for example, had five coups (more coups than it had elections) from 2002 to 2012, with no president having ever completed a full term since the country became independent in 1974. Others have experienced only one or two coups and have endured the long rule of a military dictator, sometimes later metamorphosed into a civilian leader. Nigeria, the continent's largest economy and most populous country, has spent more of its post-independence history under military rule than under a civilian president. Very few have experienced no coup or coup attempt at all. For sure, as the following pages make clear, the propensity for coups that characterized the first three decades of independence was somewhat subdued by the democratic transitions of the 1990s. Yet the African coup is far from dead, and remains a common mode of political transition, including, paradoxically, the transition to democracy.

Patterns of Military Intervention

Pat McGowan and Thomas Johnson (1984:634), who have studied the question of African military coups at great length, regard a coup as an event in which the existing regime is illegally removed from power by groups "in which members of the military, police, or security forces of the state play a key role, either on their own or in conjunction with a number of civil servants or politicians." For the first three decades of African independence, they note, the military coup was the principal form of regime change on the continent. As of the end of 1985, Africa had experienced 61 successful coups and 73 failed attempts (compiled from McGowan and Johnson 1984:634 and 1986:541). By December 2001, when McGowan updated their study, the numbers of successful and failed coups had risen respectively to 80 and 108, with an additional 139 reported coup plots (McGowan 2003). Thirty states had experienced at least one successful coup, and eighteen states had experienced multiple coups. At the time of writing, Burkina Faso ranks as the most coup-prone country with ten (of which six have been successful), followed by Nigeria with eight. Despite the addition of three new countries to the continent since the 1985 count (Eritrea, Namibia, and South Africa), the total number of countries that had not experienced either a successful or a failed coup fell to six: the three newly independent states just mentioned, as well as Botswana, Cape Verde, and Mauritius (McGowan 2003:345–346). Of the previously immune states, Lesotho saw its government overthrown in a coup in January 1986, as did Côte d'Ivoire in 1999 (which eventually led to a major civil war), while Djibouti experienced a civil war from 1991 to 1994 and Malawi suffered from apparent coup attempts in 2001 and 2008.

As of early 2019, the same six countries remained free of military intervention. Yet, continent-wide, the practice of coups has not relented since McGowan's latest study. Counting only successful coups, nine countries experienced a total of fifteen coups from 2002 to December 2018: Burkina Faso (2014 and 2015), the Central African Republic (2003 and 2013), Guinea (2008 and 2009), Guinea-Bissau (2003, 2009, and 2012), Mali (2012), Mauritania (2005 and 2008), Niger (2010), Togo (2005), and Zimbabwe (2017).[4]

Interestingly, this trend seems to vindicate McGowan and Johnson's earlier assessment of West Africa as "the region par excellence of the military coup d'état" (1984:649). In contrast, before the 2017 coup in Zimbabwe, Lesotho was the only country in Southern Africa to experience a successful coup. More important, these figures also suggest that military intervention has remained widespread on the continent despite post-1990s democratization. For McGowan, "coup behavior in [sub-Saharan Africa] exhibits no clear increasing or decreasing trend" (2003:352). Indeed, as of the end of 2018, there had been thirty-one successful coups in twenty countries and more than seventy attempts since the return of multiparty politics to Africa in 1990.[5] Yet, what may have changed is a normative shift rejecting the acceptability of military coups, as evidenced by the pressure brought by the African Union, including suspension and sanctions, which forced the collapse and reversal of the 2015 coup attempt in Burkina Faso.

The continued use of military coups suggests that democratization might not have altogether de-legitimized the practice (Clark 2007). Positive popular reactions to coups in places such as Mauritania in 2005, Guinea in 2008, Niger in 2010, and Zimbabwe in 2017 indicate that Africans sometimes see military intervention as a solution to political deadlocks (whether they still see it that way a few months or years after the coup is another question). For what outside observers see as a breakdown of the political system comes sometimes in the wake of a deeper paralysis. When Colonel Ely Ould Mohamed Vall seized power in Mauritania in August 2005, it was to put an end to the regime of Maaouya Ould Sid'Ahmed Taya, which had endured since 1984 and made a mockery of democratization. Captain Dadis Camara in Guinea similarly seized power after twenty-four years under the oppressive regime of Lansana Conté. In Niger, Salou Djibo and the army stepped in, on 18 February 2010, after incumbent Mamadou Tandja, in power for ten years, had embarked upon a forceful attempt to manipulate the constitution and state institutions in order to maintain himself in power indefinitely. And in Zimbabwe, the military placed Robert Mugabe under house arrest, ending his almost four decades in power, and definitively resolving a power struggle between his wife, Grace, and the recently deposed vice president, Emmerson Mnangagwa. In their analysis of military coups in Africa, Paul Collier and Anke Hoeffler (2007:15) found that, if the president's term has a time limit, the risk of a coup is about 1.4 percent, whereas it rises to 3.2 percent in the absence of a finite term. As they put it, and as the likes of Tandja found out, those who try to change the law to extend their stay "are inviting trouble."

Some of these coups were examples of a new breed of military intervention, post-1990, that we might well label the "democratic coup." The first instance of the military taking power from a dictator in order to set up a transition to electoral democracy probably took place with the overthrow of Moussa Traoré in Mali in 1991 and the establishment of the Comité Transitoire pour le Salut du Peuple (CTSP) by General Amadou Toumani Touré, which returned power to elected politicians by 1992. This coup took place after days of pro-democracy street protests had been violently repressed by the Traoré regime. A similar instance happened in Nigeria in 1998. After dictator Sani Abacha's sudden death, Abdulsalami Abubakar, another general, took over and restored the last civilian constitution of 1979 before supervising the first democratic election in two decades the following year, which was won by Olusegun Obasanjo (a former general himself). More recently, the coup in Mauritania in 2005 and the one in Niger in 2010 fit the same bill, with the same holding true in Zimbabwe, with elections held a few months after the military deposed Mugabe.

It is hard to make sense of coups without taking into account the dynamics of the regime that is being overthrown. By the time the army intervenes, it is not unusual that a given regime has experienced significant instability for some time or has moved considerably away from its original democratic commitments. Yet whether a military coup can usher in a genuine democratization (instead of hanging, like the sword of Damocles, over the new regime's head) remains to be answered. In Mauritania, after Colonel Vall engineered the transition to democracy, the new elected ruler, Sidi Mohamed Ould Cheikh Abdallahi, installed in 2007, was promptly ejected by the army after he tried to dismiss some of the top brass in 2008. Once the military intervenes to put an end to a regime, however unjust, it sets a precedent that undermines control of the armed forces by civilian authorities, a principle of democratic governance, and thus keeps hostage subsequent elected governments. It is noteworthy that in Zimbabwe's newly installed regime, Mnangagwa filled much of his cabinet with top military leaders involved in the coup against Mugabe.

Why Do African Militaries Intervene?

What explains the relatively high propensity for military intervention in African politics? Most scholars seem to agree that, at the very least, continued poverty and the frequent dismal economic performance of most regimes provide fertile ground for army takeovers. One hypothesis is that low or negative growth undermines the legitimacy of incumbents. As McGowan and Johnson (1984:658) put it, "failure has been a setting conducive to coups and political conspiracies." Correlating some measure of military intervention with per capita gross national product (GNP), they found that the countries that managed to grow quickly had a much lower incidence of military intervention than did their poorer counterparts. Collier and Hoeffler (2007) also found, in a multivariate quantitative analysis of coups in Africa, that they tend to occur more often after prolonged periods of low income and slow growth. Botswana, Mauritius, and South Africa, three of the remaining consistently civilian regimes, are indeed also the three wealthiest countries on the continent. Similarly, the twenty countries that have experienced a successful coup since 1990 grew at a cumulative rate of 20 percent from 1995 to 2017, while the rest of the continent grew at 80 percent (though the order of causation might work both ways).[6] Zimbabwe's 2017 coup came at the end of a sustained economic crisis, fueled in part by foreign sanctions against Mugabe's regime as well as years of corruption and economic mismanagement.

Beyond poor economic performance, however, there is also a more fundamental propensity for military coups inscribed in the very functioning of neopatrimonialism. As discussed earlier, neopatrimonialism produces factionalism and regime instability (Jackson and Rosberg 1984:430). Conspiracies are often engineered by those who are kept outside the prevailing networks of neopatrimonial redistribution. Dadis Camara's coup in Guinea in 2008, for example, represented in part an attempt by junior officers at the bottom of patron-client networks to displace existing patrons from the Conté regime. The immediate justification for the Zimbabwe coup was to resolve the factionalism within the ruling ZANU-PF party between two clientelistic networks vying for ascendancy.

Philip Roessler (2011, 2016) offers an additional perspective on such conspiratorial politics and their effects on coups. He suggests that multiethnic coalitions, which he shows are the modal regime in Africa, rapidly run into problems of credible commitment in government among representatives of different ethnic groups. The incumbent might then circulate potential contenders in and out of office, but as mutual suspicions rise, power concentration within one faction becomes more likely. Roessler shows that such concentration, when successful, is likely to displace political violence from coups to civil war as the excluded group falls back on its natural constituency to regain access to the state. Until then, however, the process is intrinsically unstable, with coups and countercoups likely outcomes.

What motivates military conspiracies are the opportunities for access to resources brought about by political office. In the end, coup-staging is a form of rent-seeking behavior, as the revenues from foreign aid and natural resources are "rents to sovereignty" that coup plotters might seek to appropriate. Collier and Hoeffler (2007:16) find that the level of development aid from the top five bilateral donors is a statistically significant positive predictor of coups. "Hence," they conclude, "part of the explanation for the higher incidence of coups in Africa is that it receives more aid." Of course, there are some rather important implications of this finding—if confirmed—in terms of aid. Although many donors wish to promote democracy in Africa, their aid might in fact be counterproductive by increasing the material returns to military takeover. This would be mitigated, however, by policies of conditional aid that cut off support in cases of authoritarian reversal. For example, donors suspended all but humanitarian assistance to Guinea-Bissau and Mali after their regimes were overthrown in 2012. Yet even in such circumstances, coup leaders can often negotiate some sort of privileged status for themselves, even if they must relinquish power to civilians, and they generally manage to appropriate some portion of the rent from the aid, which tends promptly to resume. The Zimbabwe case offers an interesting contrast, as the country's foreign aid had been severely limited before the coup, but increased after the removal of Mugabe.

Profiles of Militaries and Military Regimes

Not all military interventions result in military regimes. Some coups actually usher in transitions toward electoral democracy. Others bring in a military ruler who later runs for office himself, in sham or honest elections, or merely civilianizes his regime over time. In other countries, praetorianism (excessive or abusive military rule) prevails, and soldiers run the country, occasionally replaced by other factions from within the ranks. This kind of military rule is often characterized by high degrees of authoritarianism, arbitrariness, and corruption (McGowan 2003:340). The regimes of Major-General Ibrahim Babangida in Nigeria from 1985 to 1993 and of his ruthless successor, Sani Abacha, from 1993 to 1997 provide salient illustrations.

Apart from bullying people and stealing from them, African military regimes are rarely good at anything. They do not in general have a better governance record than their civilian counterparts, nor are they able to create order, despite their theoretical comparative advantage in this domain. The words of Samuel Decalo (1976:14–15) seem to hold largely true to this day: "many African armies bear little resemblance to a modern complex organisational model and are instead a coterie of armed camps owing primary clientelist allegiance to a handful of mutually competitive officers of different ranks seething with a variety of corporate, ethnic, and personal grievances. One direct corollary is that when the military assumes power it is frequently not able to provide an efficient, nationally oriented and stable administration."

The weakness of military regimes is largely due to the character of the militaries themselves. In the words of Herbert Howe (2001), African militaries are typified by "unprofessionalism." Because rulers are more worried about their political loyalty than about their capacity, African militaries tend to lack skills, technical expertise, and combat-readiness, and often put their interests and those of their patrons ahead of those of the state. As Howe suggests, however, such weakness rarely turns into significant liability, for "an African military only needs to be mediocre by first world standards when facing manifestly incompetent opponents" (3). Since 2001, however, the rise of competent opponents, such as al-Qaeda in the Maghreb, al-Shabaab in Somalia, and powerful militias in places such as eastern Congo, has significantly increased the cost of incompetence for African militaries. While foreign actors, such as the United States, have spent considerably on attempts to professionalize numerous African militaries, there has been little to show for their efforts. Undoubtedly, the pervasiveness of personal rule has largely contributed to weakening military professionalism and has eroded the division between the civilian and military spheres, just as it has eroded other dimensions of governance. "Military mercantilism," or the use of the military for financial gains, has become common (5). Decalo (1990:24) goes so far as to suggest that the "prime characteristic" of African armies is their pursuit of their own corporate interests. This point is illustrated by the extraction of considerable resources in the Democratic Republic of Congo by occupying African militaries—from Uganda and Rwanda to Angola and Zimbabwe—during that country's civil war.

Examples of failed African military regimes abound. In Nigeria, military regimes from 1983 to 1998 brought about unprecedented mismanagement, theft, and squandering of oil resources. Peter Lewis (1996) argues that, under Babangida and Abacha, the regime went from prebendalism to sheer predation. In Mali in the 1970s, the military regime stole drought relief aid. In 2012, the Malian military seized power again under the pretext that the civilian regime was mismanaging the conflict with the Tuareg insurgency in the north. Yet in a manner of weeks the new rulers had lost half the country's territory to the rebels. In Guinea, under Dadis Camara, troops killed more than a hundred pro-democracy demonstrators, while raping numerous women. In Sudan, the military set up its own "trading, transport and industrial ventures" (McGowan 2003:341). In Gambia, the military undid two decades of democratic rule in 1994 to produce the arbitrary and erratic regime of Yahya Jammeh. And in Guinea-Bissau, the regime ushered in by a coup in 2003 turned the country into a drug-trafficking platform, bringing about gang wars that resulted in both the president and the military chief of staff being assassinated in 2009. Over and over again, African militaries have demonstrated their lack of capacity to govern. Over and over again, they have undermined, while in office, their claim to rule.

Even when not directly in power, African militaries often contribute to the low quality of African governance. Rulers tend to keep them at a safe distance and prefer to protect themselves with presidential guards that are directly accountable to them. As a result, militaries are deployed all over the country and often left to their own devices. With salaries paid irregularly and partly hijacked by the hierarchy, soldiers can become a burden to local populations. Zaire's President Mobutu explicitly instructed his soldiers to live off the land. African militaries also suffer from ethnically biased recruitment, a feature that dates back to colonialism (Howe 2001). Rulers privilege recruitment from their regions and ethnic groups. When they depart from power, their successors follow the same logic, with the consequence that militaries become plagued with ethnic factionalism. In Zimbabwe, Robert Mugabe unleashed the mostly Shona Fifth Brigade against the Ndebele civilian populations in the early 1980s in an attempt to terrorize the opposition into compliance with his regime (Mnangagwa was minister of state security at the time). In the process, an estimated 20,000 Ndebele were killed at the hands of their own national army (see Compagnon 2010).

The problematic nature of African militaries compounds the new security threats faced by African states, including the spread of Islamist insurgencies in the Horn of Africa and the Sahel (see Chapter 7). It also calls into question the strategy of some donors, including the United States, to train some of them, as such programs are almost certain to be hijacked by special interests within the ranks or the regime (Peltier 2010).

The Branches and Practice of Government

Executives and Administrations

African executives are characterized by a high degree of centralization and presidentialism. Authority and resources tend to be concentrated within the central government, with relatively little autonomy for local branches (Wunsch and Olowu 1990). In addition, within the central government, most of the authority is concentrated in the person of the president. Even in regimes that have democratized and in which decentralization reforms have taken place, the relative powers of the president and of the central government continue to dwarf those of other institutions. Table 4.1 shows the remarkable bias of African constitutions toward presidentialism, meaning systems where a directly elected president appoints and controls the government (as opposed to parliamentary systems, where the

Table 4.1 Features of Government in Africa

	Executive Type	Legislative Elections	Judicial Independence Index (Mo Ibrahim)	Corruption (%)[a]
Angola	Presidential	PR	23.4	48.9
Benin	Presidential	PR	56.4	33.4
Botswana	Parliamentary	Plurality SMD	74.0	7.3
Burkina Faso	Presidential	PR	40.2	8.5
Burundi	Presidential	PR	11.9	31.2
Cameroon	Presidential	Mixed[b]	24.8	45.6
Cape Verde	Presidential	PR	87.5	6.0
Central African Republic	Presidential	Majority SMD	38.4	41.8
Chad	Presidential	Mixed[b]	12.5	38.0
Comoros	Presidential (rotating)	Mixed[c]	35.4	n/a
Congo, Democratic Republic of	Presidential	Mixed[d]	20.0	50.4
Congo, Republic of	Presidential	Majority SMD	16.4	81.8
Côte d'Ivoire	Presidential	Plurality SMD & MMD	33.5	29.2
Djibouti	Presidential	Plurality MMD	25.1	n/a
Equatorial Guinea	Presidential	PR	0.8	n/a
Eritrea	Parliamentary	Plurality SMD	4.3	0
Eswatini	Monarchy	Mixed[e]	21.3	17.0
Ethiopia	Parliamentary	Plurality SMD	36.6	8.3
Gabon	Presidential	Majority SMD	31.2	41.8
Gambia	Presidential	Mixed[e]	25.3	52.4
Ghana	Presidential	Plurality SMD	83.3	24.3
Guinea	Presidential	Mixed[d]	30.1	48.7
Guinea-Bissau	Presidential	PR	43.2	63.1
Kenya	Presidential	Plurality SMD	71.8	28.2
Lesotho	Parliamentary (nonpolitical monarchy)	Mixed-member PR	64.6	13.8
Liberia	Presidential	Majority SMD	52.1	52.8
Madagascar	Presidential	Mixed[d]	30.6	43.1

continues

Table 4.1 continued

	Executive Type	Legislative Elections	Judicial Independence Index (Mo Ibrahim)	Corruption (%)[a]
Malawi	Presidential	Plurality SMD	60.8	16.6
Mali	Presidential	Majority SMD & MMD	49.5	43.9
Mauritania	Presidential	Mixed[f]	25.5	27.8
Mauritius	Parliamentary	Plurality MMD, minority quotas	88.4	5.9
Mozambique	Presidential	PR	38.1	14.8
Namibia	Presidential	PR	94.0	4.6
Niger	Presidential	Mixed[d]	45.9	29.4
Nigeria	Presidential	Plurality SMD	71.9	55.3
Rwanda	Presidential	PR	54.5	6.2
São Tomé	Presidential	PR	51.5	n/a
Senegal	Presidential	Mixed[d]	63.5	6.3
Seychelles	Presidential	Mixed[d]	67.2	n/a
Sierra Leone	Presidential	Plurality SMD	43.6	46.0
Somalia	Parliamentary	Appointment quotas	6.2	n/a
South Africa	Parliamentary	PR	96.5	15.1
South Sudan	Presidential	n/a	22.1	36.1
Sudan	Presidential	Mixed[d]	7.3	5.8
Tanzania	Presidential	Mixed[g]	62.6	20.0
Togo	Presidential	PR	37.0	6.2
Uganda	Presidential	Plurality SMD	63.1	27.8
Zambia	Presidential	Plurality SMD	63.1	9.5
Zimbabwe	Presidential	Plurality SMD	45.6	14.4

Sources: Classification of executive type and legislative elections adapted from Poupko 2011. Judicial Independence scores adapted from http://www.moibrahimfoundation.org/en/section/the-ibrahim-index. Corruption scores from http://www.enterprisesurveys.org.

Notes: a. Percentage of firms that expected needing to give gifts to public officials "to get things done." b. Majority SMD and modified bock voting/PR. c. Majority SMD and indirect election. d. Plurality SMD and PR. e. Plurality SMD and executive appointment. f. Majority SMD/MMD and PR. g. Plurality SMD with minority quotas. PR = proportional representation; SMD = single-member district; MMD = multiple-member district; n/a = data not available.

government is responsible to parliament). No fewer than forty out of sub-Saharan Africa's forty-nine states have presidential executives. This centralization bias originates in part in colonial administration, which was not inclined to delegate, and in part from the prevalence of personal rule and the forceful integration of African societies into the postcolonial mold.

In addition to being centralized, African governments are rather large. The average cabinet in 2018 numbered around thirty members (for contrast, France's has twenty-two).[7] With a cabinet of seventy-eight members, Uganda topped the list, as each of its ministries had both a minister and a secretary of state. Its government included ministers for microfinance and "national guidance," and some without portfolio. Other countries had ministers for disaster management, leisure, religious affairs, small and medium enterprises, sports, state reform, and African integration. Comoros had the fewest ministers, twelve. The average number for the continent seems to mark a significant increase over earlier periods. Nicolas van de Walle (2001:104) recorded average cabinet sizes of 19.1 for 1979, 20.9 for 1986, and 22.6 for 1996. He also observed a correlation between cabinet size and a country's degree of ethnic heterogeneity. The use of coalition cabinets in postconflict situations (e.g., Côte d'Ivoire, the DRC) or post-electoral deadlocks (e.g., Kenya, Zimbabwe) might account in part for the rising continental average.

Despite their large governments, African executives do not have excessively large bureaucracies, at least if one considers formally employed civil servants (other forms of public administration are considered later). Although many countries lack data, government spending (the bulk of which is accounted for by the civil service) hovers around 20 percent of gross domestic product (GDP), which is comparable to government spending in other regions. Looking at data from the early 1990s, van de Walle (2001:92) estimated that general government public employment amounted to 2 percent of total population (in twenty African countries), compared to 4.7 percent worldwide and as much as 7.7 percent in Organisation for Economic Co-operation and Development (OECD) countries.

More interesting than what African governments and administrations look like is the question of what they actually do. Of course, as in every other region of the world, they govern and administer, which includes public policy design and implementation, problem solving, service provision, and the like. Yet in comparative terms and on average, African governments suffer from rather weak capacity to do these things. Recall from Chapter 2 that the average score for Africa on the Fragile States Index is 88 (in a range of 0 to 120, with higher scores being worse), while the rest of the world averages 61. While African governments have registered remarkable successes in terms of national integration and preservation of their territorial integrity, they have not developed particularly efficient bureaucracies or social services, and have a mixed record in promoting the welfare of their citizens.[8]

This relatively weak capacity derives to some extent from their high degree of centralization: local state agents are often loath to take initiatives without the explicit orders or approval of central agents; the latter might hesitate to take action without the endorsement of their hierarchy, which in turn prefers to wait for instructions from ministers, who await orders from the president. Ministers themselves might learn of their appointments and dismissals on the radio (see Nyamnjoh 1991). Altogether, dependent as it is on the person of the president, the executive machinery is often slow and hesitant, with little propensity for quick policy response.

Although this is certainly not true of all governments at all times, weak administrative capacity might also derive from a degree of institutional mimicry of the practices of former colonial powers, which exists in several African countries. Similar ministries, agencies, and codes are created, and the trappings, ranks, statuses, and privileges of official functions are reproduced, without necessarily responding to specific policy needs. In these instances, matters of ministerial perks and privileges, of rank and status, can trump actual policy responsibilities. Thus Francis Nyamnjoh (1999:106) stresses that, in Cameroon, "every presidential decree of appointment concludes with an emphasis on the benefits of the position to the individual concerned, but hardly ever with the responsibilities that go with the office." Moreover, the desire to occupy the political domain and control the everyday lives of citizens is at times more determinant than the will to implement policy and provide services. Therefore, African governments might have overdeveloped security services while seriously lacking other dimensions of governance.

Weak capacity also results from grassroots administrative practices. Compared to the large number of more or less abstract studies of the state in Africa, there is actually relatively little scholarship on the day-to-day functioning of African administrations.[9] Dominique Darbon and Yvan Crouzel (2009:73) note the irony that African administration is an understudied topic while "every reform . . . since the 1970s put administration at the heart of development." To some extent, this shortage results from the fact that scholars of organizations and public administrations have not focused much on Africa, while political anthropologists have until recently been more interested in rural and customary settings than in the workings of public administration. This situation has undergone progressive change since around 2000, in part because of local empirical analyses carried out in West Africa by researchers associated with Niamey's Laboratoire d'Études et de Recherches sur les Dynamiques Sociales et le Développement Local (LASDEL), and because of the work of anthropologists such as Theodore Trefon (Trefon with Ngoy 2007), Brenda Chalfin (2010), and Charles Piot (2010).

The picture of African administrative services that emerges from the few available studies is not flattering. Summarizing ethnographic research from Benin, Niger, and Senegal, Jean-Pierre Olivier de Sardan (2009b:43) describes a "pervasiveness of clientelism at all levels, enormous discrepancy between the formal organisational charts and actual division of tasks, 'privilegism,' [a] 'culture of impunity,' 'areas of suspicion,' 'every man for himself–ism,' the widespread exchange of favours, systemic corruption, habitual contempt for anonymous service users, the lack of motivation among the civil servants, low productivity and command of 'double-speak.'" He finds that appointments in public administration are based more often on party militancy than on competence or experience; meetings are rare; there is "no real control of the quality (and sometimes the reality) of the services provided" (46); a significant degree of distrust prevails, particularly toward those making financial disbursement decisions (almost always suspected of embezzlement); and the public service user is seen as "an intruder, a troublemaker or a prey" and treated with contempt, unless he or she benefits from connections (43–48).

Corruption is a dominant theme in studies of African administration. Some of it is high-profile and plagues the highest reaches of executive authority. In the Democratic Republic of Congo, for example, President Joseph Kabila and his entourage set up largely fictitious companies in the British Virgin Islands, to which the state then sold mining rights at a deep discount, which the companies then resold to genuine mining companies. A British All-Parliamentary Group on the Great Lakes Region of Africa estimated the loss to the Congolese people at more than $5 billion in 2011 (http://appggreatlakes.org; see also Africa Progress Panel 2013:55–58, 100–106). In Nigeria, an audit of the oil sector revealed that $9.8 billion in revenue went missing from 1999 to 2008, including an estimated $4.7 billion owed by the state-owned Nigerian National Petroleum Corporation (NNPC). Similar unpunished corruption scandals have taken place in many other African countries over the years, such as the ClearStream affair in Kenya (Wrong 2010), the $900 million the IMF found missing from the Angolan budget in 2002 (Pearce 2002), the $1 billion the late Nigerian dictator Sani Abacha left behind in Swiss banks (Pallister 2000), the millions siphoned from the coffers of Zaire by Mobutu and his associates, and the millions reportedly taken out of Angola illegally by members of President José Eduardo dos Santos's family before his departure in 2017. When Cameroon finally moved up from last on Transparency International's worldwide corruption rankings, Cameroonians joked that the government must have bribed Transparency International.

Corruption scandals are, of course, universal. Looking at local administrative practices, however, there is also a more common form of "quiet corruption" (World Bank 2010) with possibly more negative consequences on the quality of public administration and the daily lives of Africans. This everyday corruption relates to the failure by public servants to perform their duties according to professional standards, as when "police exert their influence to extract benefits from the disorganized mass of road users; doctors do not show up in public facilities and instead provide services privately; teachers do not show up in classes since they have a second job and their impunity is guaranteed by their superiors in exchange for other favors, and so forth" (World Bank 2010:3). Olivier de Sardan (2009b:49–50) similarly notes the widespread practice of "commissions for illicit services, gratifications, string-pulling, undue remuneration of public services, tributes, sidelines, embezzlement, etc.," and calls our attention to the frequent necessity of providing "motivation" to civil servants in order for them to perform their functions. As the World Bank study makes clear, absenteeism is a common feature of African administrations. Studies of the education sector in Kenya, Uganda, Tanzania, and Zambia found rates of absenteeism among teachers ranging from 20 to 30 percent. In public health services, absenteeism reached up to 37 percent in Uganda (World Bank 2010:7, 10). Embezzlement is also widespread, with dramatic consequences for the quality of public services. A study found that only 13 percent of supplies intended for Ugandan schools actually reached them because of diversion by education authorities (World Bank 2010:8–9).

Although it is certainly not unique to the continent, corruption is a hallmark of African civil service and of its relations with citizens and firms. An average of 27.8 percent of African firms, as opposed to 22.5 percent of firms worldwide (including Africa), expect needing to give gifts to public officials to "get things done" (see Table 4.1 for specific country numbers). This number exceeds 50 percent in six out of forty-three reporting countries and reaches extreme proportions in some (82 percent in the Republic of Congo). Despite this overall picture, however, there are several examples of greater public probity on the continent, including Burkina Faso, Botswana, Cape Verde, Eritrea (whose number seems implausibly good), Ethiopia, Mauritius, Namibia, Rwanda, and Senegal. And it is worth noting that these figures are generally an improvement since the publication of the first edition of this volume.

In a recent work, Kristof Titeca and Albert Malukisa Nkuku (2018) examine the ways that civil servants in Kinshasa, the capital of the Democratic Republic of Congo, "fend for themselves" in the absence of a state salary. In a rich, empirical study they focus on a range of spaces across the city, such as public transportation, traffic police stops, markets, soccer clubs, and bars. They find that corruption and predation are not only individual phenomena, but also vertically organized practices that extend the power of elites across social spaces. Connections are extremely important, in terms of both protection and increasing extraction. Ultimately, they find that even though conflict and instability are features of the system, the system itself is quite stable and accepted. Similarly, Theodore Trefon and Balthazar Ngoy's (2007) work on local administrative practices in the Katanga province of the DRC asks how the administration endures in times of state failure and conflict, with the resulting answer: "exploitation of the people is the dominant explanation" (14). Services that generate revenues are the ones that receive priority in staffing and become de facto "privatized" by those who occupy them (15). Moreover, it is not uncommon for civil servants to have to pay their superiors a regular commission in exchange for revenue-generating administrative positions. Achille Mbembe (2000:80, 84) refers to such practices as "private indirect government," a system where "functions supposed to be public, and obligations that flow from sovereignty, are increasingly performed . . . for private ends. Soldiers and policemen live off the inhabitants; officials supposed to perform administrative tasks sell the public service required and pocket what they get. . . . Traffic in public authority . . . is such that everyone collects a tax from his or her subordinates and from the customers of the public service."

What are the causes of the relative inefficiency and weakness of Africa's public administrations? There are some straightforward but very partial explanations, such as the material precariousness of often unpaid or irregularly paid civil servants, or the general lack of sufficient human capital in countries with limited educational opportunities and few schools of public administration. But there are also more structural factors, with external and domestic origins, that impede the progress of African administrations. Among the former, it is necessary to single out the colonial roots of African administrations and their original design as instruments of command and control more than of public service (Young 1994a; Mbembe 2000). It is no doubt difficult to overcome the traditions of domination and the absence of accountability that existed between the administrators and the administered in colonial times. Olivier de Sardan (2009b:61) sums up the problem eloquently: "whereas in Europe modern bureaucracy developed more or less in parallel to the emergence of citizenship and democracy throughout the 19th and 20th centuries, in contrast, in Africa it has gone hand in hand with inequality, violence and contempt, in the absence of any real civic or egalitarian tradition, even since independence." To some extent, in some parts of Africa, to become an administrator is still to become something of a colonizer. One of the authors of this book once heard community leaders in a Congolese provincial city address newly appointed local administrators with, "Now that you are the whites . . ."

Setting aside their colonial roots, one can also focus on the imported nature of African administrations. Mamadou Dia (1996:vii), for example, argues that "the institutional crisis affecting economic management in Africa is a crisis of structural disconnect between formal institutions transplanted from outside and indigenous institutions born of traditional African culture." Disconnected institutions are inefficient, he contends, because they fail to generate loyalty and ownership and are therefore presumably conducive to opportunism. Darbon and Crouzel (2009:88), while significantly broader in their approach, also recognize the "superimposed" nature of African administrations, which hampers their capacity to regulate social relations and promotes administrative "superficiality."

The problematic nature of Africa's administrative institutions has led to successive waves of reforms that, paradoxically, might have also contributed to their enduring weaknesses. After promoting a retrenchment of the state with structural adjustment programs in the 1980s (see Chapter 6), donors presided over multiple waves of civil sector and governance reforms, the most recent being a push for decentralization, while also increasingly working with nonstate service providers. These different and sometimes contradictory emphases have not facilitated public administration. They have led to a sedimentation of institutions and policies that undermines consistency (Darbon and Crouzel 2009:87). Beyond the reforms themselves, foreign assistance to improve Africa's institutional capacity might have had unintended negative consequences. Todd Moss, Gunilla Pettersson, and Nicolas van de Walle (2006) articulate several of these. For example, reliance on aid reduces the necessity for tax revenue, which in turn reduces accountability of public institutions; hiring locals in development projects cannibalizes African civil services (because of the significantly higher wages paid by donors); and building "cells" of expertise within ministries or agencies weakens nonassociated services (see also van de Walle 2005).

Authors focusing on domestic variables have also pointed to Africa's propensity for "normative pluralism" as an explanatory factor (Darbon and Crouzel 2009). To an extent, the behavior of civil servants falls under norms of rational-legal administration, of efficiency, accountability, and process. Yet African civil servants also face other normative expectations. Reciprocity, for example, and solidarity with their community might be powerful norms dictating behaviors that are antithetical to bureaucratic expectations (Hyden 1995). Expectations of clientelistic redistribution also plague African bureaucrats and reinforce the neopatrimonial understanding of positions of authority as opportunities for access to resources. Everyone in civil service is to some extent a patron, with relatives and others who are lower on the social ladder forming expectations about the extent to which they will be taken care of. In times of necessity, particularly, generosity will be expected. Olivier de Sardan (2008) makes a similar claim with the notion of "practical norms," which coexist with formal behavioral expectations but make their transgressions acceptable. These can derive from existing societal norms (e.g., gift giving) or from practical arrangements developed within bureaucracies to facilitate work (e.g., contempt for anonymous users).

The tendency for absenteeism in African administrations, described earlier, offers an illustration of the normative pluralism argument. In many parts of Africa, funerals constitute an occasion of significant social pressure for absenteeism. The death of a family member, even a loosely related family member, often requires traveling back to the deceased's village of origin for burial ceremonies, which can last several days. Because such occasions also require the family of the deceased to look after multiple guests, they can be very costly, with the consequence that people with limited income might look for alternative ways to help pay for burial expenses, including calling upon relations of patronage in public service and requesting the requisitioning of public assets (see Anders 2009 for an example from Malawi). A survey of Zambian civil service in the 1990s made very clear the power of these societal norms. Slightly under 30 percent of surveyed civil servants in half a dozen ministries expected a three-week leave (outside regular leave time, and thus effectively constituting absenteeism) for funerals of family members. Another 30 percent expected a leave of two weeks, and yet another 30 percent one week. The author notes that "social obligations . . . are widely viewed as an acceptable excuse for absenteeism in Zambia" (Dia 1996:70). The survey also showed strong resentment of those interested in rapidly ascending the career ladder "at the expense of the group," and a near-unanimous opinion that bureaucratic decisions should "stress group harmony." Moreover, no less than 65 percent of civil servants were engaged in additional employment outside the civil service (71–74).

Whatever its causes, weak administration has spun a series of adaptations among both bureaucrats and service users. Specifically, a class of intermediaries has developed in many African countries who either substitute for absentee workers or facilitate the interaction between the public and largely unresponsive and arbitrary services.[10] These intermediaries often allow services to go on and adapt them to local norms. The use of substitutes is particularly prevalent in education sectors with "volunteer teachers" (see Tama 2009 for examples from Benin, and Poncelet, André, and de Herdt 2010 for some from the DRC). Substitutes have also been identified in public health, wildlife management, justice, and even the police. These "volunteers" allow the official office holders to engage in other occupations. In exchange, while lacking status, the substitutes tend to receive direct payments from service users or to help themselves to opportunities that may occur. Moreover, many substitutes hope that their work situation might one day be officialized and thus consider their "volunteer" activities at least partly an investment in the future.

Facilitators constitute a different category. This type of intermediation is a common entrepreneurial activity in countries characterized by arbitrariness and predation. The goal of the intermediary is to offer their customers an escape from bureaucratic unresponsiveness and a reduction in the transaction costs of dealing with state authority in exchange for payment. Facilitators may arise through personal connections or because of the comparative advantage of their social or geographical position. In the DRC, where facilitators are ubiquitous, such services are usually referred to as "protocol" (Englebert 2009:89–91). In Cameroon, as Dickson Eyoh (1998:272) describes, a private administration made up of "hordes of document merchants and providers of clerical services [is] found in front of ministerial and other government buildings." Daniel Smith (2007:60) notes that because many Nigerians "find navigating government bureaucracies frustrating," people "frequently rely on the aid of intermediaries. Indeed, at almost every major bureaucracy that provides essential services, one finds a small army of intermediaries to expedite one's business." Similarly, Giorgio Blundo (2001:82) imputes the "omnipresence of administrative brokers" in Senegal to the "opaque" nature and "exceedingly large discretionary powers" of public administration. "Armed with a briefcase and rubber stamps of occasionally dubious origins, the broker . . . stakes out the entrance of the justice palace or of the administrative building to intercept the user upon his arrival. He offers him either to facilitate acquisition of an act delivered by public authority, or to speed up some procedure" (see also Tidjani Alou 2006). Most of these brokers play a facilitating role between the administration and the citizen. Intermediation extends the benefits of public employment to nonstate actors, acting as a multiplier of the rents derived from positions of sovereignty (Englebert 2009). Intermediation also makes the state and its administration more bearable, manageable, and negotiable to the majority of users.

Although corruption is a widespread feature of African administrations, and a correlate of neopatrimonialism, it is not a uniformly shared one (see Table 4.1). Why do some countries display significantly less corruption than others? What can we learn from them that might be of use to others? While Africanist scholarship has not historically focused on these questions, one can find elements of answers here and there, as well as in the broader political economy literature that deals with variations in institutional quality among countries.

In an article comparing Brazil, Congo (Zaire), and Japan, Peter Evans (1989) suggested that efficient administrations display a high degree of "embedded autonomy" from society. Autonomy is required for them to act without being captured by nonstate interests. Embeddedness, or the identification of elite interests with those of capitalist development at large, prevents such autonomy from turning predatory. This theory might help us make sense of the low level of corruption in Botswana, where the political leadership has historically been associated with the dominant economic class of cattle herders (see Samatar and Oldfield 1995).

A related possibility, touched upon earlier in this chapter, is that corruption varies as a function of the political necessity of neopatrimonial strategies for elites and administrators. When "transplanted" states and institutions (Dia 1996) display a certain degree of congruence with precolonial practices, they might be more efficient and rulers might feel less pressure to use the state apparatus as a tool of clientelistic redistribution (Englebert 2000b). In this respect, Botswana, Cape Verde, Ethiopia, Mauritius, and Rwanda, all of which have relatively low corruption, display limited pre- and postcolonial institutional conflict. Similarly, the more ethnically heterogeneous a country, the greater the pressure to use administration for patronage in order to buy the compliance of certain groups (Easterly and Levine 1997).

There might also be situations in which it is in the interest of rulers to promote and enforce rules of administrative probity. We mentioned earlier the suggestion of David Booth (2012) and Tim Kelsall (2013) that the physically vulnerable governments of Ethiopia and Rwanda can derive political benefits from adopting the features of "developmental states," where corruption is at least centralized and constrained. Conversely, governments that have relatively few resources and are highly dependent on foreign aid, such as Burkina Faso, Cape Verde, Ethiopia, and Malawi, might find the exchange of corruption control for aid advantageous.

Governance by nonstate actors. With African administrations generally weak and not always inclined to provide public services, it comes as no surprise that an increasing number of nonstate actors have become involved in the provision of these services on the continent, sometimes on their own, sometimes in partnership with the state. Thus, a research agenda focused on "effective governance" has developed that studies how public services and collective action are organized "for real" at the local level. This literature stresses the hybridity of governance and its negotiated nature among different state and nonstate actors. A consequence of shared governance has been the blurring of the public-private divide among African institutions and the rise of more ambiguous "twilight" institutions (Lund 2007).

Aid donors, particularly donor-sponsored development projects, often provide their own measure of local governance and public service delivery. Although their time horizons are finite, they typically have some staff and equipment, and deliver specific services. These can vary from small-scale (e.g., drilling boreholes or building schools in villages) to much larger interventions, such as national immunization campaigns sponsored by the World Health Organization (WHO) or by United Nations security provision in postconflict environments. As a result, many African citizens actually receive a significant share of their public services not from their government but from donors. To some extent, this delegation exonerates African governments from their failure to provide some public goods. Many of them seem glad to delegate such policy responsibilities to donors, while at the local level a cottage industry of project "brokers," entrepreneurs trying to attract development projects to their region or village, has grown (Olivier de Sardan, Bierschenk, and Chauveau 2000).

The most common institutional form that local actors pursuing donor interventions or seeking to organize public services adopt is the nongovernmental organization, discussed in Chapter 3. African countries count thousands of NGOs and it is not rare for villages to have dozens. In 2006 it was reported that Togo alone had 5,000 registered NGOs (Piot 2010:133). While NGOs (which usually require government registration) dominate, there are also other, more or less formal, types of associations. Church groups are among the former and have long been associated with provision of healthcare and education all around the world. In Africa's weak states, these functions have been particularly salient. Parents' associations, age-group associations, and the like, make up the latter. Either as donor intermediaries or as their own local structures, these associations have become one of the main alternative providers of public service and often complement and collaborate with local state agencies. For example, associations of parents of schoolchildren might pool their resources to build a school, with the government providing the teacher. Or they may pay the public teacher, whose salary may be in arrears. In Chad, education is largely based on indigenous local associations, which have been responsible for the addition of 835,000 school seats to the national education system since 1980, in contrast to 45,000 seats from the government (Fass and Desloovere 2004:156). In the DRC, the Catholic Church has been the main provider of education for many decades (Poncelet, André, and de Herdt 2010).

In his survey of the modes of governance in Africa, Olivier de Sardan (2009a:16–17) notes that local associations are characterized by "abundance and ephemerality" and are constrained by their frequent aim to attract finance from development outfits. To be sure, some of these associations, particularly of the NGO type, are "ventriloquist" (van de Walle 2005), in the sense that they tend to reproduce the language and expectations of donors and appropriate the rents from aid that come from programs of development of civil society and the like. Yet there is also a relatively dense network of genuine grassroots organizations that structure local social life in Africa. Whatever structural weakness they suffer from, they have come to constitute the bulk of the institutional landscape on much of the continent, and have become particularly salient in countries and regions where the state is weakest. Contrary to the state, however, their governance focuses on specific groups rather than on all citizens (Joireman 2011).

As in many more-developed countries, the for-profit private sector also increasingly provides public services in Africa. Under the impetus of donors and as part of programs of economic or public sector reform (partly to combat corruption and raise revenues), some countries have seen the functions of specific state agencies contracted out to private providers. Thus, as noted by Darbon and Crouzel (2009:83), customs, finance, utilities, road tolls, and more might be managed autonomously from the main public administration by private companies. This can also be true of security services.

Aside from associations and private contractors, customary chiefs constitute the category of quasi-public actors that might have the strongest historical claim for participating in governance and service delivery. Yet although many chiefs derive legitimacy from the connection they can claim to precolonial times, they are often the product of colonialism and the postcolonial era, being for the most part appointed by governments, and are often considered part and parcel of its administration in rural areas. Chiefs typically retain considerable powers in the domains of land allocation and management, arbitration of local disputes, matrimonial relations, and the adjudication of cases involving witchcraft. While chiefs were often marginalized in the earlier years of the post-independence period as part of policies to deny ethnicity, they have made a comeback as tools of governance since the early 1990s, in parallel with efforts at democratization and decentralization (Baldwin 2016; Vaughan 2005). There are, however, variations in the degree of formal integration of chiefs into administration. In some countries, they are an official level of state administration (e.g., Niger or some rural areas of Congo). In others, their status is more informal. At times, they manage to straddle the worlds of the customary and of the postcolonial by getting themselves elected or appointed to local positions of state authority.

Kate Baldwin (2016) has argued that the inclusion in Zambia of traditional chiefs has strengthened democracy in that country by improving politicians' responsiveness to the needs of local communities. Likewise Richard Sklar (1999) finds that the integration of chiefs into effective governance, in what he calls "mixed polities" or "mixed government," provides increased legitimacy and stability to African states. In contrast, Olivier de Sardan (2009a:10–15) notes that chiefly power tends to be characterized by patrimonialism, confusion of powers, predation and corruption, clientelism, lack of accountability (chiefs, being generally appointed for life, are not accountable to their subjects), aristocratic and ostentatious behavior, and rivalry. Mahmood Mamdani (1996) also singles out the "despotic" tendencies of chiefs, and Sandra Joireman (2011) notes that customary authority and law can be detrimental to women and migrants in matters of land rights. These studies call for caution in perceiving chiefs as the necessary legitimate agents of local communities and grassroots interests, and question their potential role in democratic and decentralization reforms.

Finally, a word about rebel governance, which can be relevant in failed and collapsed states. While rebel organizations are usually effective at controlling territory and raising revenue from the populations they control, their record of administration is more mixed. Most of the time, rebels do not provide any significant governance and tend to maintain in place the local agencies of the state they combat (Tull 2004). Zachariah Mampilly (2010) suggests that the degree to which rebels provide governance is a function of previous state penetration in the area (which conditions the public demand for state services), the nature of the rebel-population rapport (mediated by ethnic homogeneity), and the degree of penetration by international NGOs, which may relieve insurgents of some duties and affect their institutional dynamism. Yet there are examples of limited rebel governance. In Liberia in the early 1990s, Charles Taylor's insurgency developed a currency and banking system, managed an international airport, and ran a radio and television network. In Angola, the União Nacional para a Independência Total de Angola (UNITA) ran schools and farms, while Eritrean rebels in the 1980s and early 1990s were engaged in light manufacturing (Spears 2004:26–27). In Uganda, Yoweri Museveni's National Resistance Army organized "resistance councils" in liberated villages in the 1980s, which took over local administration with some degree of direct democracy. Yet these tend to be the exceptions, with rebels typically more intent on controlling civilians than on providing them with governance. In South Sudan, for example, the Sudan People's Liberation Movement (SPLM) did little beyond initiating what would remain a largely embryonic justice system. Its administrative structures "existed largely in name only" (Crossley 2004:143; see also Rolandsen 2005). Adam Branch and Zachariah Mampilly (2005) concur and argue that building a government was not a goal of the SPLM, a rather paradoxical situation for a movement intent on gaining its own sovereignty.

This survey of nonstate governance actors illustrates the actual hybridity of African governance and administration. While the formal state might be all-powerful in law, its real nature is much more "negotiated" than imposed, with multiple other institutional partners (Lund 2007). While studies of formal African bureaucracies might lament their ineffectiveness, real governance is probably better understood in this shared, hybrid sense. In this respect, not only does it represent a testimony to the adaptive power of Africans and their institutions, but it also contributes to the evolution of the postcolonial state and to the creation of a new, syncretistic institutional landscape. This is therefore a very fruitful area of research for the study of the African state as it exists.

Decentralization. Although personal rule and neopatrimonialism are conducive to centralized political systems, there have been widespread decentralization reforms across Africa since the early 1990s. These reforms have come largely as a result of donor pressure, either to accompany democratization, with the expectation that more proximate administration would be more accountable to citizens, or to promote better governance and greater ownership of public institutions by Africans. The intended benefits of decentralization include improved service delivery, improved responsiveness and accountability, and increased economic stability and development at the local level (Dickovick and Wunsch 2014). Although a few countries were already decentralized (e.g., Botswana and Senegal) or federal (Nigeria) before the 1990s, most others only began to decentralize in that decade or later. As of 2019, there were four federal states in Africa (Comoros, Ethiopia, Nigeria, and Sudan), and there was hardly a state without either a decentralization law or a "local government act," although there was variety in constitutional approaches (Kuperman 2015). Although South Africa is constitutionally a unitary state, its governance comes close to the federal model in practice. Some constitutions still claim the unitary nature of the state, while making some general decentralization statement, the details of which are left to subsequent laws (e.g., Burkina Faso, Burundi, the Central African Republic, Congo, Gabon, Rwanda, Senegal, and Mozambique). Some assert the "unitary decentralized" character of the state (e.g., Cameroon, the DRC). Others provide more detailed decentralization blueprints (e.g., Madagascar, Ghana, Chad, Cape Verde, Uganda), while a few articulate explicit distributions of power between the central and local states (e.g., the DRC and federal countries). Similarly, there are variations in the degree to which customary chiefs are formally integrated into decentralization reforms, with a degree of participation or at least recognition in Chad, Ghana, Lesotho, Malawi, Nigeria, South Africa, and Togo (Fau-Nougaret 2009:15).

There is also variation in degree of implementation of existing constitutional provisions and laws. In the furthest-reaching cases, decentralization reforms have led to the establishment of elected local councils and administrations at municipal, district, provincial, or other levels. Uganda's local councils, for example, particularly at the subcounty and district levels, have significant budgetary, programmatic, and personnel authority, and retain 50 percent of the taxes they raise (Wunsch and Ottemoeller 2004:182; see also Lambright 2010). In other cases, however, and sometimes simultaneously with successful reform, the effective scope of decentralization has been more limited and initial progress has been reversed by central governments intent on keeping their control (see Ribot, Agrawal, and Larson 2006 for the cases of Senegal and Uganda).

Variations in decentralization performance seem to be due to several factors. Typically, reforms have made the least progress in francophone countries, partly as a result of the strong centralized tradition of French administration. Countries with a dominant political party at the center also typically fall short of significant reforms, as local institutions are captured by party clients (which is also the case with federalism in Ethiopia). Decentralization also often moves ahead in the immediate wake of conflicts, sometimes as part of peace agreements, and might stall thereafter.

Despite these variations, the overall trend tends toward very lukewarm reform and limited effective decentralization. In a survey of decentralization on the continent, Stephen Ndegwa (2002) gave countries a score for their extent of political, administrative, and fiscal decentralization. Of the thirty countries for which he was able to compile data, only two (South Africa and Uganda) scored above 3 on a scale from 0 to 4, with a larger score indicating greater decentralization. Of those scoring 2 to 3, the majority were former British colonies or mandates (Kenya, Ghana, Nigeria, Namibia, Tanzania, Zimbabwe, and Zambia). Ethiopia, despite being formally federal, scored only 2.4, an illustration of the frequent gap between constitutions and the practice of politics in Africa.

More recently, a study of ten African countries (Botswana, Burkina Faso, Ethiopia, Ghana, Mali, Mozambique, Nigeria, South Africa, Tanzania, and Uganda) with some of the most decentralized institutions also found evidence of mixed progress (Dickovick and Wunsch 2014). Some of the greatest progress has taken place in the formal devolution of legal authority to subnational governments and in the organization of local elections. Significant fiscal responsibilities, on both the expenditure and revenue sides, have also been transferred to these subnational units. Ultimately, however, this study finds that decentralization in these countries represents a "paradox"; effecting little change in governance at the local level but strengthening or entrenching national-level actors. The study indicates that decentralization appears to have helped stabilize and maintain several African regimes that would have been precarious otherwise. In other cases, it seems to help entrench certain ruling parties, particularly those in dominant party systems. The study concludes that "decentralization has strengthened central authority as much as it has weakened it" (2). In general, decentralized institutions remain more accountable to central governments than to local communities, showing the remarkable resilience of centralized patterns of authority in Africa. The relatively weak capacity of local institutions, where the level of human capital is often below that of central government and where infrastructure is often lacking, further hampers decentralization.

In addition, whatever the actual advances of decentralization in Africa, it is empirically unclear whether local government agents are any more responsive to citizen demands than their central counterparts (Bratton 2010:6–7). The lack of local accountability and responsiveness probably derives in large part from the weak effective implementation of decentralization reforms and the capacity of many African states, however weak, to retain their control of local politics despite donor pressure. In a comparative study of Senegal, Côte d'Ivoire, and Ghana, Catherine Boone (2003a:356) shows that decentralization is as likely to "strengthen local power brokers and state agents" as to empower local citizens. Local patterns of institutional development, she argues, remain very similar to patterns of the pre-decentralization period, as power configurations in rural societies and the manner in which central governments engage with local elites have changed less than the formal reforms might suggest, in part as a result of capture of reforms by local notables (370) (see also Wunsch 2001).

The recent case of decentralization in Kenya has offered rich insights. In 2010, two-thirds of the voters approved a referendum for a new Supreme Court, Bill of Rights, and decentralization measures that provided for forty-seven elected county governors and assemblies. The 2013 elections ushered in this new system, transforming the country's political landscape. While the existing literature on decentralization noted earlier would lead one to assume that "recentralization" by the national government or capture of the new subnational levels by local elites would occur, Cheeseman, Lynch, and Willis (2016) find that neither has occurred. Rather, the newly elected governors appear capable and willing to resist co-optation from the national government and defend county interests. As these authors note, "decentralization in Kenya has generated a political system with a more robust set of checks and balances, but at the expense of fostering a new set of local controversies that have the potential to exacerbate corruption and fuel local ethnic tensions in some parts of the country" (2). To this last point, d'Arcy and Cornell (2016) have found that Kenyan decentralization has exacerbated rent seeking and patronage practices at the local level through the expectation that it is now "everyone's turn to eat," while simultaneously increasing the political marginalization of some ethnic minorities.

Despite some three decades of donor pressure, the general timidity of the decentralization reforms in Africa speaks loudly of the resilience of centralized state power on the continent. Most African states either pay lip service to decentralization or adopt partial elements of it. The resulting hybridization of the African state, rather than transformation, is one of the hallmarks of decentralization. We saw this hybridity earlier in discussing the negotiated nature of effective governance. We will see it again when discussing democratization (Chapter 5) and economic reforms (Chapter 6).

Legislatures

While most African legislatures were for a long time little more than the rubber stamps of personal rulers, many of them have taken on a new life and more significant roles in the wake of the democratization trend of the early 1990s (see Chapter 5). In some instances they have overseen significant legislative reforms, such as the introduction of a new family code in Mali (subsequently suspended by the president) and the introduction of mining codes and land reforms in numerous other countries. In several more cases, legislatures have also stood up to incumbent regimes and acted as custodians of the constitution, as in Nigeria when parliament defeated the attempts of President Olusegun Obasanjo to allow himself a third term in office. Generally, they have provided some opponents with the protection of their status as legislators and allowed them to exercise checks and balances on incumbents if only through the use of committee oversight.

A research project on African legislatures in "emerging African democracies" has explored their features in Benin, Ghana, Kenya, Nigeria, South Africa, and Uganda and found that, within this sample, legislative power is not correlated to a country's overall degree of democracy (Barkan 2009a). In addition, former English colonies tend to have stronger legislatures, possibly because the British established legislative councils in colonial times, which created a popular expectation of legislative power (10). In the former French and Portuguese colonies, the legislatures created at independence were more easily dismantled and face greater challenges today in establishing independence and credibility. Nevertheless, in several African legislatures, "coalitions for change" have arisen since 1990, wresting significant control away from the government, including budget control, and building legislative capacity independently of the executive.

Research on African legislatures generally indicates that both citizens and MPs tend to place a higher emphasis on representation and constituency service than on legislating and government oversight, reflecting the clientelistic nature of African politics. Furthermore, the form of electoral system via which a country selects its MPs affects the relationships between MPs and the public, and between MPs and their parties, as well as the structure of political parties themselves. By and large, proportional representation strengthens political parties and allows MPs to spend more time in the capital (potentially legislating), while single-member districts allow MPs the chance to build a geographically determined political base, weakening the role of political parties and requiring more visits to one's base (potentially reducing the time available for legislating). As Table 4.1 shows, thirteen of Africa's countries have pure proportional representation systems, while another eight have mixed systems with proportional elements. Most others have majority or plurality single-member districts.

Finally, the amount of resources available for MPs plays a large role in determining the quality of the legislature. In countries where MP salaries are substantial, and where parliament has the funding to be in session more days of the year with permanent support staff (e.g., Kenya or South Africa), the frequency and quality of both committee and constituency service are higher, while in countries where the central government controls MP salaries (e.g., Ghana), parliamentary effectiveness can be crippled by low wages. Such findings might be slightly biased by the sample of countries in consideration, however. In the Democratic Republic of Congo, not included in the study of African legislatures, MPs have repeatedly raised their official salaries (from about $2,000 a month in 2006 to $13,000 by 2018) and other material perks while producing minute legislative achievements. The work of Staffan Lindberg and Yongmei Zhou (2009) on Ghana's parliament also suggests that other factors besides control of salaries by the executive might cripple the effectiveness of the legislature. They argue that Ghana's parliament has developed a comparative advantage in the provision of private goods through clientelistic networks rather than as a legislating body, because personal assistance and community development are what citizens hold their MPs most accountable for.

Several African countries also use parliamentary structures, including second chambers, to facilitate the inclusion or co-optation of customary powers into the political system, providing thereby some degree of formalization to the "mixed" nature of African government (Sklar 1999). These are, however, almost always purely advisory. Examples include Botswana's House of Chiefs, South Africa's National House of Traditional Leaders, Ghana's National House of Chiefs and its several Regional Houses of Chiefs, Nigeria's regional chiefly assemblies (such as the House of Traditional Rulers in Edo state), Zambia's House of Chiefs, Uganda's Buganda Parliament, and Namibia's Council of Traditional

Leaders. Somaliland's House of Elders is the only one to function as a genuine legislative upper house. In some countries, however, seats are also reserved for chiefs in regular assemblies. In Lesotho, for example, twenty-two members of the thirty-three-seat senate are "principal chiefs" (Salih 2005:18). In Ghana, authorities reserve 30 percent of the seats of district assemblies for chiefs (Ray 1998). Finally, KwaZulu-Natal chiefs in South Africa occupy 20 percent of the seats on KwaZulu regional councils, a number adopted so that each of the estimated 260 traditional leaders in the province would have a position (M. Williams 2000). This incorporation has allowed traditional leaders to expand their roles to new domains such as development projects and fundraising.

Although they invoke tradition, these assemblies are mostly new and the visible outcome of a process of resurgence of customary authorities that has come in the wake of the democratization wave of the 1990s. Ghana's house was established in 1992, Zambia's in 1993, South Africa's in 1996, Namibia's in 1998, and Zambia's in 2003. In addition, one can hardly avoid noticing that all of these countries are anglophone. While many former French colonies resorted to national conferences akin to France's "estates general" in their democratization process, kingship has played a greater role in the democratization of former British colonies. It could be that British indirect administration contributed to preserving the existence and integrity of some groups, whereas French direct rule was more emasculating. But there may well also be a Buckingham effect at play. Borrowing the political toolbox of the former colonial overlord, anglophone Africans might find monarchical and chiefly traditions to be useful means of political resistance or advancement.

Finally, as noted in Chapter 3, legislatures are one place where African women have increased their presence in the public sphere. Women's legislative representation almost tripled in Africa between 1990 (7.8 percent) and 2015 (22.2 percent). By 2016, twelve African state legislatures had women speakers of the house. These trends have been accompanied by the increased presence of women in local governments, as well as in the executive, judiciary, and bureaucracy. These changes have been accomplished by the introduction of electoral quotas in over 65 percent of African countries, as well as collective women's mobilization across the continent (Tripp 2016).

Judiciaries

While it would be hard to imagine a textbook on US politics that would not include at least a significant chapter on the role of courts, and particularly of the Supreme Court, the judiciary branch of government tends to be much less significant in African politics. This is partly because of the more informal nature of power in Africa, the degree of presidential centralization, and the prevalence of personal rule, all of which reduce the influence and autonomy of judicial institutions. Neopatrimonialism is largely inimical to the rule of law. As a result, African courts have not typically evolved as checks and balances on executive power. Even when constitutions give them powers such as judicial review, as in most anglophone countries, they have typically refrained from using them (Mingst 1988:141). It comes as no surprise, therefore, that there has been relatively little scholarship on African judiciaries, particularly before 1990. As Karen Mingst (1988:136) put it, "Neglect of judicial research stems not only from the parochialism of the research community, but also reflects the relative insignificance of the topic in modern African societies."

Post-1990 democratization increased to some extent the salience of the rule of law and brought judicial systems more to the forefront. By and large, however, African judiciaries still often lack power and autonomy, and rarely challenge governments. Although constitutional and other high courts might have heard more frequent cases as they occasionally became involved in challenges to electoral results, more often than not they have sided with the incumbents who appointed their judges in the first place. For example, the Constitutional Court of Zimbabwe upheld the controversial 2013 election, offering further evidence of the ruling party's manipulation of the judiciary (Southall 2013). In a surprise move, however, Kenya's Supreme Court flexed its autonomy by annulling the results of the 2017 presidential election (which was won by incumbent Uhuru Kenyatta), requiring a reelection (also won by Kenyatta).

Nevertheless, there is more variation in judicial autonomy among African regimes today than there was before 1990. Peter VonDoepp (2009) found, for example, less judicial autonomy in Malawi and Zambia than in Namibia. He suggests that the legacy of the pre-democratic period matters. In Namibia, under the South African–controlled apartheid regime, the judiciary was somewhat independent from the regime; in Zambia, under Kenneth Kaunda, it occasionally checked the excesses of the regime; in Malawi, however, under Hastings Banda, the courts were "removed from any meaningful role in the political system" (7). The degree of party dominance also matters. The de facto single-party system in Namibia gives few opportunities for challenges, unlike the more fractured party systems of Malawi and Zambia. Finally, the extent of neopatrimonialism also has an impact. Neopatrimonial regimes are

willing to weaken state institutions, including the judiciary, to maximize power. Yet their own weak capacity prevents them from doing so
directly. As a result, they tend to use bribery and informal pressure,
which allows judicial institutions to retain some potential influence to
eventually challenge rulers.

The continued prevalence of neopatrimonialism across most
African states, despite democratic reforms, hints at the extent to which
African judiciaries might suffer from corruption. The Mo Ibrahim
index of judicial independence, which assesses the extent to which
courts function free from the influence of rulers or powerful groups
and individuals, averages 44.3 for sub-Saharan Africa as a whole, on a
scale of 0 to 100, with a larger score indicating greater independence
(see Table 4.1 for country-specific scores). There are interesting
regional variations. Despite Zimbabwe's poor performance, southern
Africa places well ahead of other regions, with a score of 58.4 (down
almost 8 points from the first edition of this book). West Africa benefits from Ghana's outstanding performance, as well as Senegal and
Nigeria's decent record, scoring 50.9. Central Africa is at the bottom,
with a score of 24.5, with East Africa scoring 36.

Anecdotal evidence abounds. Citing a government report, Kenya's
Daily Nation revealed in 2003 the existence of a rising scale of payments
that affected about half of Kenya's judges, with the cost of a favorable
judgment rising with the seniority of the judge and the severity of the
case. While a magistrate's decision could be bought for as little as $50 or
as much as $1,900, it cost from $636 to $20,356 for favorable sentencing
at the high-court level, and $19,800 at the appellate-court level (*BBC
News* 2003). In Niger, where bribing judges is also common practice,
Mahaman Tidjani Alou (2006:147) recalls the words of a user of the
court of Kandi according to whom "the person who has spent the most
money is right; there is no justice, it's like a public auction." In Zimbabwe, both the chief justice and the minister of justice acknowledged
in 2012 that corruption in the judiciary was a problem. The minister
mentioned constituents' complaints about "rampant corruption in the
courts involving all key players in the justice delivery system, [includ-
ing] judicial officers and support staff, clerks, interpreters and . . .
police investigating officers, prosecutors, lawyers in the private sector,
not to mention touts who impersonate lawyers, prison officers, [and the
like]" (Madava 2012).

Partly as a result of their weak capacity and lack of autonomy, and
because of an absence of commitment from their rulers, African courts
have not generally become important actors in the worldwide struggle to

promote and defend human rights, even though many victims of human rights abuses are Africans. It is certainly a positive development that, as of 2018, thirty-three African countries—more countries than in any other region—were parties to the Rome Statute, which established the International Criminal Court (ICC) and permits African domestic courts to hear of ICC indictments for war crimes and other crimes against humanity. But in 2016, three countries (Burundi, Gambia, and South Africa) announced their intent to withdraw, though the latter two later rescinded. By 2018, Kenya, Namibia, and Uganda were also debating withdrawal from the ICC, criticizing the fact that the overwhelming majority of its investigations and indictments have been in African countries.

In domestic cases, African courts are more likely to side with the regime than with opponents or human rights activists. Many governments still see such activism as opposition. When it comes to the prosecution of international crimes, diplomatic considerations and lack of financial means often represent considerable obstacles to the administration of justice. The case of Hissène Habré, former president of Chad, provides a fitting illustration. Habré, who ruled Chad from 1982 to 1990, was indicted by a Belgian court, endowed with universal jurisdiction (the capacity to judge people anywhere in cases of war crimes or crimes against humanity), in 2005 for the killing of some 40,000 individuals by his regime and multiple cases of torture. He was then put under house arrest by the authorities of Senegal, where he had lived in exile since 1990. Despite repeated demands from Belgium and the European Parliament, Senegal refused to extradite Habré to Belgium. Instead, it set up an ad hoc war crimes tribunal under Senegalese law in 2008, which required amending the constitution. The Senegalese government then demanded 27 million euros from donors in order to proceed with the trial. In 2012, the Senegalese parliament finally passed a law for the creation of an international tribunal to try Habré, with judges to be appointed by the African Union. In July 2013, twenty-three years after being kicked out of office, Habré was finally arrested in Dakar ahead of his trial. In May 2016, he was found guilty and sentenced to life imprisonment, making him the first former head of state to be convicted for human rights abuses in the court of another nation.

Habré's trial and conviction challenges the established precedent in which African rulers enjoyed impunity for actions performed while in office. Ethiopian dictator Mengistu Haile Mariam, for example, has been living in exile in Zimbabwe since his overthrow in 1991. In 1997, Congo's Mobutu Sese Seko fled to Togo and then on to Morocco, where he died a few months later. And several high-ranking officials of the criminal Ivorian regime of Laurent Gbagbo (himself detained at the ICC) live across the border in Ghana. Yet there have been a few exceptions, such as the arrest of former Liberian president Charles Taylor in 2006 in Nigeria, where he had originally been granted exile, followed by his subsequent extradition to Liberia. Although it is less dramatic than the indictment of former heads of state, one must also single out the South African judicial system for its autonomy toward political authorities and its consistent defense of human rights. In 2012, for example, a South African court held Zimbabwean politicians liable for arrest in South Africa for crimes against humanity (including torture) perpetrated against opponents in Zimbabwe. On March 2018, South Africa's director of public prosecutions announced that former president Jacob Zuma would face eighteen charges of corruption, including more than 700 counts of fraud and money laundering.

Notes

1. In two contributions on the origins and analytical usefulness of neopatrimonialism, Daniel Bach (2011, 2012) evokes these authors and others in the genealogy of the concept.

2. The concept itself was actually coined by Samuel Eisenstadt (1973), whose work was not specifically limited to Africa, but it eventually resonated with Africanist scholars. Among the latter, it was Jean-François Médard (1982), a French scholar, who most formally and usefully articulated the concept (distinguishing it from germane notions such as clientelism, which neopatrimonialism includes) and its relevance to the region.

3. One can also find a more general discussion of the benefits of the centralization of corruption in Bardhan 1997, and of those on governance of longer time horizons in Olson 1993.

4. São Tomé and Príncipe experienced a successful military coup in July 2003, but after a week the coup plotters restored the president in exchange for a general amnesty.

5. See http://www.systemicpeace.org/africa/ACPPAnnex2b.pdf, updated past 2004 by the authors.

6. Authors' dataset, based on World Bank, *World Development Indicators,* http://data.worldbank.org/indicator.

7. See https://www.cia.gov/library/publications/world-leaders-1/index.html. We removed ambassadors to the United Nations and the United States from the Central Intelligence Agency listings.

8. The reader will find ample and detailed quantitative information on the quality of African governance and state capacity through the World Bank's Worldwide Governance Indicators project (http://info.worldbank.org/governance/wgi), Fund for Peace's Fragile States Index (http://fundforpeace.org/fsi), and the Mo Ibrahim Foundation's index of African governance (http://iiag.online).

9. Nigeria is an exception. See Adamolekum 1986, 1999; and Adebayo 2000.

10. This phenomenon is present in other less developed countries too, as illustrated in Banerjee and Duflo 2011.

5

Regime Types
Across the Spectrum

What explains why some states are more democratic than others? Why
have some African states managed to transition to multiparty democracies, while others have slipped back into authoritarianism? Are there
variations in the types of authoritarian regimes across Africa? What
accounts for changes in the nature of regimes over time? What role have
elections played in the transition to democracy and its consolidation?
What motivates African voters? Do they make calculations different
than voters in other parts of the world?

This chapter begins with a continent-wide democracy report of sorts,
providing a largely descriptive overview of the main trends and distribution in African democracy over time and in the most recent period. By
and large, the main pattern is one of stable authoritarian regimes for the
first three decades of independence, followed by rapid, widespread, but
uneven improvements in democracy in the first half of the 1990s, leading
to a new apparent equilibrium with a handful of democratic regimes and
a vast majority of hybrid, semidemocratic, or semiauthoritarian ones
since about 1995 (Tripp 2010). In recent years, there has been a slight
deterioration of political freedoms across Africa, reflecting the broader
trend in their erosion globally (Freedom House 2018). The chapter then
takes a more analytical approach and asks what accounted for regime
change over time in the aggregate and what explains current variations in
democratic performance. Studying democracy in Africa is useful not just
for making sense of African regimes, but also because African experience is rich in general theoretical insights and challenges much of the
received wisdom about democracy, democratization, and democracy
consolidation. For example, how can countries as poor as Benin or Cape
Verde, without genuine middle classes and with relatively low levels of

literacy and urbanization, not only have democratized but also have sustained their democratic performance over time? After this more theoretical section, the chapter concludes with an analysis of the most common African regime, the semiauthoritarian one, in which certain liberties and frequent elections coexist with authoritarian control by the government and a lack of effective alternation in leadership. In this analysis, we bring back neopatrimonialism as an essential factor in understanding the nature and limitations of African democratic transitions.

The Evolution of African Regimes

Most African countries inherited democratic constitutions during the decolonization process, introduced by the departing colonial powers that had paid little attention to developing democratic practices beforehand. Perhaps unsurprisingly, given the shallowness of these democratic roots, few independent African states managed to maintain their democratic institutions. Botswana and Mauritius are the only two countries that were born democratic and have remained so through the years, although it bears saying that the same political party has been in power in Botswana since independence in 1966.[1] The vast majority of other countries followed a path that consisted of a few years of democratic multiparty systems, frequently characterized by political deadlocks and constitutional crises, followed by the progressive establishment of single-party regimes or military takeover. For example, institutional paralysis led to military intervention in Congo in 1961; infighting among contenders for the presidency brought the military to power in Togo in 1963; regional tensions provoked a series of coups and countercoups in Nigeria beginning in 1965; and labor unrest brought the army into politics in Upper Volta (now Burkina Faso) in 1966, where it remained for almost five decades. Meanwhile, incumbent presidents ushered in single-party systems in Côte d'Ivoire as soon as 1960, Zambia in 1962, Tanzania in 1963 (when it was still Tanganyika), and Senegal in 1966, to name but a few. This rapid failure of democracy on the continent bears pondering, especially in light of the post-1990 efforts by donor countries to promote democracy in Africa. It is, indeed, too often ignored that most African countries already had some experience with democracy earlier in their history, and some lessons might be gleaned from understanding why that original episode was usually so short.

By and large, formal democratic institutions proved incompatible at the time with the rise of personal rule and neopatrimonialism, which formed the common African ruler's response to the weakness of the postcolonial state and the heterogeneous and mixed allegiances of their societies. As the state became a resource for allies and an element in strategies of co-optation of potential opponents, redistribution progressively trumped representation as the essential function of politics. Formal institutions lost their importance and power concentrated in a close circle around the personal ruler (Jackson and Rosberg 1984). Many of these rulers then organized single parties, mass mobilization movements that were then seen as plausible instruments of nation building, and umbrella organizations in which to dissolve potential societal polarization (Morgenthau 1964; Zolberg 1966; Glickman 1965). Tanzania's Julius Nyerere famously asserted that multiparty competition was "un-African." Thus, to some extent, formal liberal democracy was generally sacrificed for political stability, although at the time it was not infrequently argued that democracy could flourish in single-party systems.

Whatever the merits of these claims for national unity, the practical result for the majority of Africans was the rise of authoritarianism and the erosion of their newly gained rights as citizens. Many rulers argued that allegedly traditional African values such as consensus-seeking and loyalty to a single chief justified the adoption of regimes otherwise seen as dictatorial across the continent. The African modal regime became the plebiscitary dictatorship, where elections usually with a single candidate, the president, were held regularly as rituals of renewal and proclamation of loyalty (Bratton and van de Walle 1997). Of course, as discussed in Chapter 4, neopatrimonial regimes also display significant elements of instability, particularly in their tendency to foster factionalism among networks of clients. Thus, coups were common, as were military regimes, some of which civilianized over time while others did not seek to build any institutions.

Despite undermining formal institutions of accountability, neopatrimonialism involves some degree of representation. It does contribute to national unity by identifying the elites of specific communal and interest groups and using them as intermediaries in the co-optation of these groups' loyalty. For example, Nic Cheeseman (2015:63) has argued that, under Jomo Kenyatta, Kenya's patron-client systems generally enabled local communities to "hold their leaders accountable on the issues they cared most about." Thus, to some extent, these groups are "represented" in the regime, in a manner that somewhat echoes the "consociational" model derived by Arendt Lijphart (1977) for some multicultural societies of Western Europe. Yet this is not a representation based on citizenship, political preferences, ideologies, or policy issues, but more typically on identity or other characteristics. Moreover, the communal elites at the top of the patron-client pyramid are not necessarily linked to their communities or the groups they lead by relations of accountability and responsiveness. As Nicolas van de Walle (2001) has suggested, neopatrimonial redistribution is not very profound, making the democratic scope of neopatrimonial representation rather limited.

Within a few years of independence, most continental democratic aspirations had thus been stifled. When Freedom House began measuring political rights and civil liberties in countries around the world in 1972, African countries averaged around 6 on a scale from 1 (perfectly democratic) to 7 (completely authoritarian), well above the average of about 4 for the rest of the world and of nearly 5 for other developing countries (see Figures 5.1 and 5.2). This authoritarian performance continued largely unabated throughout the 1970s and 1980s. There were a few exceptions, of course. Senegal, for example, returned to a limited multiparty system in 1974. In 1978, General Sangoulé Lamizana of Upper Volta (now Burkina Faso), who had seized power in a military coup in 1966, put his regime to the electoral test and squeezed by in the second round of a surprisingly competitive election (he was overthrown two years later). In Gambia, a somewhat free electoral democracy survived from 1965 to 1994 under President Dawda Jawara (elected or reelected five times) despite several coup attempts. But apart from those, authoritarian regimes of one stripe or another dominated the continent. In fact, the apparent equilibrium qualities of authoritarianism in Africa are worth noticing. Whatever the merits of the cultural arguments of some African elites to justify their domination, the relative ease with which African dictatorships persisted for two decades or more suggests that many countries shared conditions favoring this type of regime. One was probably the dependence of their economies on primary commodities, which often prevented the rise of an independent bourgeoisie and civil society and favored government control over the economy (Ross 2012), whose rents fed the neopatrimonial redistributive machinery. Foreign aid probably had a similar effect. Finally, international patrons of African regimes during the Cold War were often willing to sacrifice democracy in the pursuit of their own security and economic interests. They would even intervene on behalf of authoritarian regimes (as did France in Zaire in 1977) in order to ensure they remained loyal geopolitical clients.

The dramatic change brought about by the end of the Cold War and collapse of the Soviet Union was a crucial determinant of the shift away from the authoritarian equilibrium in African politics. There were other, more domestic reasons for this transition, as discussed in the next section, but the correlation with the end of the Cold War is undeniable. As Figure 5.1 illustrates, the average African regime went from a score of

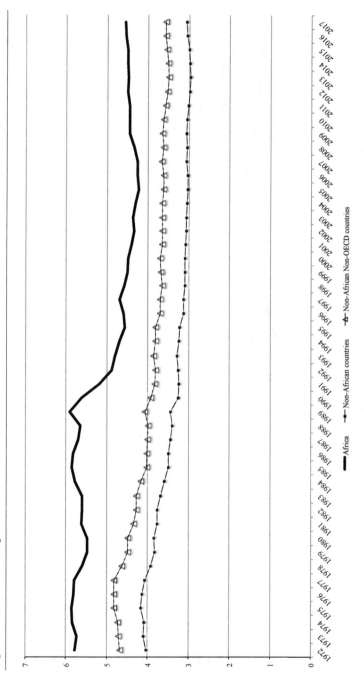

Figure 5.1 Political Rights in Africa, 1972–2017

Source: Freedom House 2018.
Note: 1=free; 7=not free.

Figure 5.2 Civil Liberties in Africa, 1972–2017

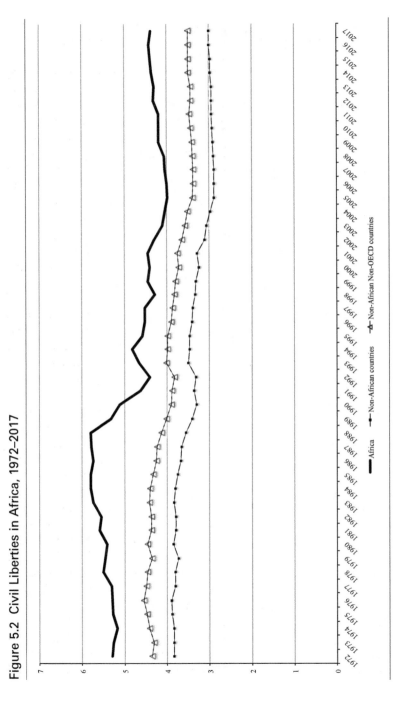

Source: Freedom House, 2018.
Note: 1=free; 7=not free.

6 to below 5 on the Freedom House scale within five years of the end of the Cold War. These changes were not uniformly distributed, however, nor have they endured everywhere.

Focusing first on the immediate post–Cold War period (1989–1995) and relying on Freedom House's indicators of political rights, we can identify a small group of countries, namely Benin, Cape Verde, Malawi, Mali, Mozambique, São Tomé and Príncipe, and the Seychelles, that showed dramatic improvements in democracy. To these we can add Namibia, which became independent as a democracy in 1991, and South Africa, which transitioned from apartheid to democracy from 1991 to 1994. A second, much larger group of countries displayed more moderate but still positive changes. None of them qualified as democratic in that period, but all adopted dimensions of multiparty politics and increased civil liberties. Some of them, such as Angola, Burkina Faso, Cameroon, Chad, Ethiopia, and Togo, at best qualified as "semiauthoritarian." Others, such as Congo-Brazzaville, Gabon, Ghana, Tanzania, and Zambia, leaned more toward "semidemocratic" (Tripp 2010). A third group achieved very limited progress and quickly regressed (the Democratic Republic of Congo, Côte d'Ivoire, Equatorial Guinea, Guinea, Mauritania, Rwanda, Somalia, Uganda, and Zimbabwe), and a fourth group actually underwent greater authoritarianism, often linked to some form of conflict (Burundi, Djibouti, Gambia, Kenya, Liberia, Nigeria, Sierra Leone, and Sudan). Of countries in these last two groups, some, such as Kenya and Nigeria, embarked on their democratic transition a few years later.

Some of these regimes engineered their own transitions, with incumbents ushering in democratic reforms, as in Ghana, Mozambique, and Zambia. In other countries, groups outside the regime forced the change. In Mali, for example, the army staged a coup against the regime of Moussa Traoré, who had used violence against demonstrators. In several francophone countries, beginning with Benin, and then Chad, Congo-Brazzaville, Niger, and Gabon, opposition groups managed to pressure the government into accepting "national conferences," sorts of general estates, which had more or less radical effects on subsequent democratization (Eboussi-Boulaga 1993; Robinson 1994; Heilbrunn 1993; Clark and Gardinier 1996). In Benin, the government of Mathieu Kérékou completely lost control of politics at this occasion and he was sidelined in favor of a transition prime minister, Nicéphore Soglo, who won the subsequent elections (Magnusson 2001). In Congo-Brazzaville, dictator Denis Sassou-Nguesso was also sidelined into the minority and had to publicly apologize to the nation for his years of misrule (Clark 2008). In places such as Chad and Gabon, however, incumbents shrewdly maneuvered and avoided losing control of the proceedings and of their power, essentially engineering harmless transitions (Buijtenhuis 1993). In several other countries, genuine democratic reforms followed earlier phases of cosmetic changes. In Kenya, for example, it was only after Daniel arap Moi retired from politics that real competition took place among parties, with the opposition winning its first victory in 2002. In Nigeria, an initial transition controlled by the military regime was canceled in 1993 after it yielded the "wrong" outcome (Suberu 1997). It was not until 1997 and the death of military dictator Sani Abacha that bona fide multiparty politics took over (Lewis 1999).

In general, democratic progress stalled considerably across the continent after 1995. By then, politics had stabilized again in most countries. Starting in 2005, the world witnessed a slow deterioration of democracy and political freedoms, what Larry Diamond (2015) has dubbed a "democratic recession." As Figures 5.1 and 5.2 indicate, the gains in civil liberties and political rights in Africa peaked in 2006. While the wave of democratization of the 1990s occurred alongside the backdrop of the end of the Cold War, the stagnation and reversals of the twenty-first century corresponded to the global ascendancy of China, which became an option for economic assistance to many repressive regimes, and the increased security concerns of the United States linked to its global counterterrorism strategies, which decreased its attention on democratic reform in Africa and elsewhere. While the Obama administration gave lip service to the virtues of democracy, that rhetoric largely disappeared under Trump, contributing to a global environment less supportive of, if not downright hostile to, the advancement of democracy and political freedoms.

The 2018 regime distribution across the continent identified nine "free," twenty-two "partly free," and nineteen "not free" countries, a slight decrease from the first edition of this book, which listed eleven "free" countries. But two of those "free" countries—Lesotho and Sierra Leone—had only recently joined that category and have subsequently regressed back to "partly free." Thus, while the world has seen a general erosion of democracy, the broader image in Africa is that democratic distribution has been more or less steady for almost two decades. On the one hand, this stabilization illustrates the remarkable consolidation of most democratic regimes. About 90 percent of the countries that were or had become democratic by 1995 were still democratic in 2018 (Benin, Botswana, Cape Verde, Ghana, Mauritius, Namibia, São Tomé and Príncipe, Senegal, and South Africa). Only Malawi slipped back, and Mali suffered a brief coup, amid a civil war, in 2012. Though, in keeping with global trends, there were notable decreases in political freedoms between 2008 and 2018 in the Central African Republic, Mali, Burundi,

Ethiopia, Mauritania, Gabon, Congo-Brazzaville, Niger, Rwanda, Eritrea, Guinea-Bissau, and Kenya (Freedom House 2018:10).

On the other hand, the overall stability of the rankings suggests that few other countries have made sustained democratic progress over the past two decades. With the notable exception of Ghana, the majority of the initially timid reformers have remained at best partial democracies, better qualified as "semidemocratic," "semiauthoritarian," or "hybrid" (Joseph 1998; Diamond 2002; van de Walle 2003; Tripp 2010). They hold regular multiparty elections and grant their citizens some political and civil rights, yet they often keep effective control, make sure they win elections, and do not shy away from repression. Similarly, none of the countries that failed to transition in the first period subsequently democratized (with the precarious exception of Sierra Leone). Some, such as Liberia and Uganda, made some limited subsequent progress. Most, however, including the DRC, Equatorial Guinea, Gambia, Mauritania, Rwanda, and Sudan, have remained largely authoritarian. Côte d'Ivoire became increasingly repressive until its government was overthrown with French support in 2011, ushering in a partly democratic regime that has still to demonstrate its sustainability. Burundi's tentative drive toward democracy was undercut by President Pierre Nkurunziza's unconstitutional decision to run for a third term in 2015, further entrenching his increasingly repressive rule (van Acker 2018). In contrast, recent developments in Gambia, where the 2016 presidential vote resulted in a surprise victory for opposition candidate Adama Barrow (and an equally surprising, though short-lived, acknowledgment of this victory by the incumbent), are grounds for some small degree of optimism. Altogether, if we rely on Freedom House data, some two-thirds of total democratic change across the continent from 1989 to 2018 actually took place in the 1989–1995 period.

The Freedom House data for 2005–2018 also indicates a striking divergence among regions, with western and southern Africa improving their democratic governance, but central and eastern Africa facing substantial declines. Since 2000, every country in East Africa has experienced a stagnation or decline in democratic governance, while much of western Africa (save those countries of the Sahel) has improved (Temin and Summers 2018). Moreover, recent moves by heads of state to hold on to power by changing or ignoring term and age limits have eroded democratic norms in numerous countries. Just between 2015 and 2018, leaders of four African countries—Burundi, Congo-Brazzaville, Rwanda, and Uganda—changed constitutional limits in order to perpetuate their rule, corresponding with a decline in each country's political freedoms. The regime of Joseph Kabila in the Democratic Republic of Congo also attempted to change the constitutional term limits, but ultimately failed.

It is also noticeable that a significant number of African elections, particularly in the latest and least of the democratizers, have been accompanied by serious violence. In Zimbabwe, the 2008 elections and post-election period also saw massive violence, mostly perpetrated by agents of the Robert Mugabe regime against opposition supporters, with nearly a hundred dead. In the Democratic Republic of Congo, both the 2006 and 2011 elections were marred by violence, including heavy artillery and machine-gun fire in 2006 and the killing of demonstrating opponents in 2011. Burundi's controversial 2015 presidential election was accompanied by intense political violence, particularly in the capital, Bujumbura (van Acker 2018). And in the 2007 Kenyan elections, after incumbent Mwai Kibaki manipulated the vote count from the Kikuyu region to give himself a narrow majority, some supporters of his regime and of opponent Raila Ondinga went on reciprocal rampages that left more than a thousand dead and half a million displaced. But nothing so far has matched the destruction brought about in the wake of the November 2010 presidential election in Côte d'Ivoire, where the refusal of incumbent Laurent Gbagbo to concede defeat, despite losing 46 percent to 54 percent to his rival, Allassane Ouattara, led to a renewal of general warfare between the two clans and some 3,000 casualties. We return to these questions of electoral violence in Chapter 7.

Upon reflection, the democratic wave of the early 1990s is not so dissimilar from the first few years of independence when democracy also briefly prevailed. The most notable difference is that more countries have stayed democratic after 1990 than after 1960. As Mattes and Bratton (2016) note, "more than half of all Africans today live in functioning multi-party electoral democracies that are demonstrably freer than the military or one-party regimes that previously dominated the continent." Of course, the difficulty for democracy to take root in Africa invites further scrutiny.

Explaining Authoritarianism and Democracy in Africa

In this section we seek some explanations for the variation in regimes across Africa and for the wave of democratization in the early 1990s and the subsequent weakening of these transitions (Carothers 2002). We begin with the variables usually connected with democracy and democratization around the world and investigate how useful they are for Africa. We then turn to some Africa-specific theories. We end with a more focused examination of the characteristics of the modal African "hybrid" regime.

The Limits of Democratization Theory

There is no shortage of theories of democratization and democratic consolidation around the world (Ingelhart 1997; Przeworski et al. 2000; Ingelhart and Welzel 2005; Acemoglu and Robinson 2005, to name but a few). Yet few of them have shown great robustness when applied to regime variations within Africa. The handful of quantitative studies that have focused specifically on African democratization have found few significant variables (Bratton and van de Walle 1997; Dunning 2004; Lindberg 2006). To some extent, the puzzle with democratic theory for Africa is to explain variation in democracy when there is little variation in its usual correlates.

Income, usually one of the most reliable predictors of democracy, seems to have no effect in Africa, where the correlation between per capita income levels and political rights scores is statistically insignificant (–0.237 between 2011 and 2017). To our knowledge, only one study (Jensen and Wantchekon 2004) finds a positive relationship between income and growth and democracy in Africa. Although some of Africa's richest countries, such as Botswana, Mauritius, and South Africa, are democracies, the former two were already democratic before becoming rich, and the latter had one of the continent's most repressive regimes while being possibly its richest country until 1994. Some of Africa's most democratic countries, such as Benin and Cape Verde, are also among the poorest in the world. Although Adam Przeworski and colleagues (2000) have shown that democratic transitions can happen at any level of income, they also suggest that consolidation usually does not take place in countries with incomes below $6,000 per capita, which is well above the average for African democracies.

To some extent, the lack of correlation between income and democracy in Africa derives from the nature of the continent's economies. While the effects of income on democracy are supposed to be mediated by the development of industrialization and the rise of a middle or entrepreneurial class, African national incomes and episodes of growth are more often the result of extractive economic activities and variations in commodity prices (see Chapter 6). Unlike manufacturing, extractive industries are often capital-intensive expatriate-dominated enclaves, more likely to promote authoritarian regimes than democracies (Ross 2001). As a result, variations in income in Africa are as likely to move with as against variations in democracy.

Focusing only on dimensions of economic performance that are more likely to correlate with democracy, such as the share of manufacturing in gross domestic product, yields little additional insights, however. Daron Acemoglu and James Robinson (2005) have suggested that elites who have invested in manufacturing capital are loath to see it destroyed and thus more likely to compromise about democracy. Yet in Africa, the correlation between the share of GDP accounted for by manufacturing and the Freedom House political rights score is statistically insignificant (0.12 between 2011 and 2017). To a large extent, this lack of relation is due to the very limited range of manufacturing (and of other economic indicators) in Africa. This problem also applies to education, which is expected to lead to the acquisition of tolerant and democratic values. The correlation between adult literacy and political rights is not significant either (−0.25 between 2011 and 2017).[2]

Among economic variables, only the availability of mineral resources seems to hold some predicting power on the nature of regimes in Africa. Resources are thought to limit the likelihood of democratization because governments can use their rents to finance extensive networks of patronage or fund internal security efforts used for repression, or both (Ross 2001). Success stories of democratic consolidation on the continent seem indeed to be more likely among resource-poor countries. Benin, Cape Verde, Mauritius, São Tomé and Príncipe, Senegal, and Seychelles are relatively resource-poor (or have been until recently). Conversely, resource-rich countries such as Angola, the Republic of Congo, Gabon, and Sudan have remained steadfastly authoritarian over the years. Several studies seem to confirm the presence of a "resource curse" in Africa, with countries that are more mineral-rich being less likely to democratize (Jensen and Wantchekon 2004; Omgba 2009; Ross 2012), with Ghana a significant exception (Phillips, Hailwood, and Brooks 2016; see also Heilbrunn 2014).[3]

Resource wealth still falls short, however, of explaining the continent's paradoxical regime distribution. For one, Botswana—one of Africa's democratic stalwarts—is a mineral economy. So are Sierra Leone and South Africa. In addition, a lack of mineral resources is in no way systematically associated with democracy, as witnessed by countries such as Côte d'Ivoire, Kenya, and Zimbabwe. More important, however, resource-curse types of explanations do not account for hybrid consolidation, which occurs as much among resource-rich as among resource-poor countries. Thus, resource exports make a more ambivalent contribution to regime distribution in Africa than suggested by the simplest form of the resource-curse argument. Nevertheless, they are part of the story.

Moving away from economic variables, it is not possible to discuss democracy in Africa without questioning the impact of ethnic configuration on regime type. As discussed earlier, the rise of personal rule is often imputed to the necessity for rulers to cope with the heterogeneity of their societies. As a result, more culturally homogeneous countries are expected to have an easier time democratizing and staying democratic than are their more heterogeneous counterparts, as they face less acute demands for patronage and redistribution. In addition, the more homogeneous a population, the more similar its policy preferences, which lowers the stakes of the democratic game (Bates 1983; Easterly and Levine 1997). Yet the data on ethnic diversity by country introduced in Table 3.1 show no significant correlation with measures of either democratic change or consolidation in Africa (Bratton and van de Walle 1997; Lindberg 2003).

There may be good reasons for this lack of relationship. Although discussions of African politics almost always refer to ethnicity, this issue is, as we saw in Chapter 3, a lot more complex than appears at first, and ethnic theories of African politics are fraught with problems. The first problem, in relating ethnicity to democracy, is that despite the equilibrium properties of semiauthoritarianism, African countries have tended to display different regimes at different times, especially taking the early 1990s into account, whereas their ethnic configuration has remained much more stable over time. In other words, we cannot explain, say, Mali's long authoritarian period (1960–1992), its dramatic democratization (1992–1995), its subsequent slow descent toward hybridity (1995–2012), its return to praetorian politics with a coup (2012), and its subsequent fledgling re-democratization (2013–2018) by referring to its ethnic configuration, which hardly changed over that period. Second, as scholars such as Daniel Posner (2005) have shown, the salience of ethnicity in Africa is more likely to be a function of the rules of the political system than the other way around. In Zambia, the switch from single- to multiparty politics reduced the effective degree of ethnic heterogeneity in the country. In Burundi, the postconflict political system seemingly reduced the saliency of ethnic identity, making most political conflict inter-Hutu affairs (Vandeginste 2014). Moreover, the work of James Habyarimana and colleagues (2009) suggests that ethnicity is more likely to function as a facilitator of collective action within groups rather than as a factor of polarization across them. Thus, whether one chooses a more primordial or a more instrumental perspective, the key to democratic performance in Africa seems unlikely to be found in ethnicity.

For similar reasons, linking democratic performance with "civic culture" (Almond and Verba 1963) is also problematic. The civic culture argument, an old staple of comparative politics, suggests that some societies have a greater disposition toward democracy than others because they share values that are propitious to compromise, communication, consensus, and diversity. Robert Putnam (1992) offered a more recent incarnation of this theory in which levels of social capital—social trust, horizontal social relations, associate life—correlate with democracy. Some of this argument echoes the notion of civil society, and we return to the latter's connections with democracy in the next section. With respect to its cultural dimensions, however, civic culture suffers from the same problem as ethnicity to the extent that there is little cultural variation over time. It is also hard to measure and, therefore, to verify. Moreover, the little work that has been done on social capital in Africa has actually found that there was less of it in democratic Botswana than in more authoritarian Uganda (Widner and Mundt 1998). And arguments that have equated trust with ethnic homogeneity have not fared better for Africa (Keefer and Knack 1997).

Despite the difficulty in deploying a rigorous cultural theory of democracy and democratization, culture remains a recurrent theme in explanations of Africa's problems with democracy. A frequent argument, in this respect, is that African societies' predilection for 'Big Man' politics is inimical to rule of law and democracy (Diamond 2008; see also Moss 2011). Michael Schatzberg (2001), for example, argued that political legitimacy in Africa was tied to widespread cultural understandings rooted in paternalism and personal rule, rather than democratic elections. Whether it is a cultural feature or not may be hard to establish, but there might indeed be a pattern of personal rule, even among democratically elected politicians and longtime democracy activists, that suggests a relative lack of constraints on the behavior of rulers and of restraint in their exercise of the office. The prevalence of Big Man politics might partly explain why some democratic transitions revert to authoritarianism. Laurent Gbagbo of Côte d'Ivoire is a case in point. As a longtime exile in France, he actively militated for democracy in his country. After returning home he was jailed by President Felix Houphouët-Boigny. Yet after winning a controversial election in 2000, he maintained himself in power for another ten years without elections, undermined the country's institutions, unleashed political assassinations against his opponents, and adopted an extravagant lifestyle. Less dramatically, Abdoulaye Wade of Senegal, after running three times unsuccessfully for the presidency, finally won in 2000 and then developed several of the trappings of Big Man politics, including grooming his son to succeed him (at which he failed) and promoting a personality cult. In Zambia, former union activist Frederick Chiluba was swept to power on a wave of social unrest in 1991, but then developed authoritarian and corrupt ways.

On the one hand, we should be wary of the potential tautological nature of arguments correlating Big Man politics with authoritarianism. Indeed, rulers might develop the Big Man syndrome for the same reasons that democracy fails to take root rather than as a cause of its failure, and it is risky to explain democratic performance by the alleged democratic qualities of leaders assessed afterward. On the other hand, while cultural features per se are unlikely to cause democracy or authoritarianism, it is nevertheless likely that they contribute to providing the context, and the constraints, that promote or undermine the unfolding of democratic institutions. In this respect, a different type of factor might be associated with a broad interpretation of civic culture. Although political cultures have significant indigenous elements, it is also true that African countries tend to maintain certain characteristics of the countries that colonized them. For example, former French colonies tend to have more centralized authority than do their former British counterparts. This could partly be a function of whether or not colonial powers resorted to indirect rule. Sandra Joireman (2001) found that common-law countries fared somewhat better than civil-law countries in a study of the effects of different colonial legacies on the rule of law in Africa. Yet the same effect is not visible with civil liberties or political rights as dependent variables: British colonies do slightly better but not significantly so. Magnusson and Clark (2005) also suggest that an original institutional design helped Benin's transition, while a system copied on France's Fifth Republic proved inadequate for Congo.

Another explanation for democratic variations in Africa has focused on the holding of elections. Staffan Lindberg has proposed that the very practice of holding elections (even if sponsored and organized by foreign donors) helps spread democratic values in society and contributes to improvements in civil liberties (Lindberg 2006; Lindberg and Zhou 2009; Lindberg and van Ham 2018; Edgell et al. 2018). This argument finds antecedents among theories that democratic change is more likely to occur in nations where past regimes held regular elections, even more so if they allowed some degree of competition among parties, however superficial such allowances were (yet such theories do not explain why some countries held past elections and others not). Michael Bratton and Nicolas van de Walle (1997:141) argue that regimes that held regular elections, even if it was a single-party state, institutionalized a tradition of mass participation, wherein elites and the masses became socialized to accept participatory political roles. Related, Robert Bates (2008:163) finds that "the longer a country has been subject to a no- or single-party system, the less likely it is to change to a multiparty system," a trend he terms "historisis."

Lindberg's work has extended this logic to inform our expectations about democratic consolidation and current variations in democratic levels across the continent. According to him, variations in democracy in Africa can be traced to a self-reinforcing democratic power of holding consecutive multiparty elections, however flawed and unfair they might be. The practice of elections, he argues, promotes the creation of a virtuous lock-in mechanism through the spread of democratic values. From this perspective, some countries might have democratized more than others because of the path-dependence that came from organizing elections earlier (which can be partly accidental and partly a function of still-unexplained domestic features). African democratic countries might remain so because they reached a level of civil liberties through their elections at which this lock-in mechanism took hold. Interestingly, while Lindberg and others have found evidence that successive multiparty elections are associated with incremental democratization in Africa, the data from other regions are much less encouraging, suggesting that this might be a case of African exceptionalism (Edgell et al. 2018).

Lindberg's argument contrasts with the finding of Philip Roessler and Marc Howard (2009) that authoritarian regimes that hold consecutive elections do not become more democratic but instead less liberal and more stable. As for hybrid regimes (which Roessler and Howard refer to as "electoral democracies"), they rarely become full-fledged democracies, despite holding regular elections. Likewise, research by Bogaards (2014:37) questions the prospects of democratization through elections and suggests the durability of authoritarian practices, concluding that "most electoral autocracies do not only remain autocratic, but also become more autocratic over repeated elections. Most liberal democracies do not only stay free, but become freer over time. Electoral democracies, in contrast, appear vulnerable to regression and breakdown."

Finally, some scholars of statebuilding have observed an interesting historical connection between war, statemaking, and democratization (Tilly 1992; Bermeo 2003; Huang 2016; Wantchekon and Neeman 2002). The general argument assumes that conflict produces more effective states and a concurrent demand for greater accountability among the populace. Much of this scholarship is based on European experiences of statebuilding, but when applied to Africa, the evidence suggests otherwise. For example, Nic Cheeseman, Machaela Collord, and Filip Reyntjens (2018) contrast three "high-conflict" cases (Burundi, Rwanda, and Uganda) with two "low-conflict" cases (Kenya and Tanzania) in East Africa. Rather than finding a positive relationship between war and democracy, they note the ways in which domestic conflict undermines three key elements of the democratization process: the quality of political institutions, degree of elite cohesion, and civil-military relations. Their findings suggest that "the combined effect of these three mechanisms helps to explain why Kenya and Tanzania have made significantly greater progress towards democratic consolidation than their counterparts" (2018:31). All of this suggests that the dominant theories of democratization and democratic consolidation fall short in explaining African experiences; or, to reframe that statement, comparative political science still has much to gain from studying Africa.

Democratic Transitions in Neopatrimonial States

As mentioned in the previous chapter, while neopatrimonialism is a common feature of African politics, it varies both quantitatively and qualitatively between regimes and within regimes over time. Thus, the relationships between neopatrimonialism and democratization are difficult to discern, if a relationship exists at all. While contemporary wisdom might suggest that neopatrimonialism would be inimical to democratization, Rachel Sigman and Staffan Lindberg (2017) find no clear evidence that neopatrimonialism impedes the advancement or survival of democracy. Indeed, recent work indicates that democratization in the neopatrimonial context can advance civil rights and greater political freedom (Lindberg 2006; Edgell et al. 2018), the institutionalization of constitutional rule (Posner and Young 2007), and wider distribution of public goods (Burgess et al. 2015). Moreover, some have argued that neopatrimonialism may actually promote democracy and development (Pitcher, Moran, and Johnston 2009; Booth and Golooba-Mutebi 2012; Kelsall 2013).

These works tend to take as their starting points the influential contributions of Bratton and van de Walle (1994, 1997), who proposed that neopatrimonialism and its dynamics of inclusion and exclusion might best explain the specificities of African democratic transitions. Writing relatively early in the post–Cold War period, their work on Africa contrasts with much of the democratic transition literature of that time, which tended to focus on Latin America, where corporatist regimes prevailed. African neopatrimonial regimes, Bratton and van de Walle note, produce different types of transition. Hence, the authors start from the premise that the nature of the preexisting regime affects the nature (or the existence) of the transition to democracy. One of the first empirical patterns they identify is that African transitions tend to originate in protest over fiscal crises rather than from reformist elements within the regime. Neopatrimonialism, they suggest, drains the state coffers and provokes fiscal crises while impeding economic growth. People who are kept outside the circle of regime insiders suffer declining living standards and resort to protesting because they lack internal mechanisms of accountability. With the ruler unable to dole out patronage to such large numbers, a crisis of legitimacy develops. Two elements intrinsic to neopatrimonialism therefore contribute to the rise of protest. First, it is a system based on faction and thus on exclusion; at any given time, some factions are excluded from the inner sanctum of power and await their turn in the wings of the political system. At the time of the crisis, the outsiders are likely to ally with the protesters in order to secure their reinsertion in the system. Second, it is a system that produces its own chronic fiscal crisis, as it relies on the redistribution of state resources to purchase allegiance. Compounded by the austerity policies of the stabilization and structural adjustment programs of the 1980s, this propensity for fiscal crisis thoroughly deprived rulers of their favored instrument of compliance by the end of the decade. Without resources to hand out, neopatrimonial regimes are dramatically short on policy instruments to deal with rising discontent at the economic crises and swiftly fall back on the tools of coercion. However, having ruled on the basis of personal loyalty rather than broad accountability, leaders fail to recognize the need to maintain popular legitimacy and are soon overwhelmed as the magnitude of popular protest expands and repression fails. To some extent, the lack of civil society comes back to haunt them, as there are few formal channels to harness protest.

While protests rage in the streets, the regime also fractures from within as the spoils of power become increasingly limited for insiders due to the state's bankruptcy. As the crisis unfolds, insiders who challenge the ruler are excluded from the regime and cross over to the opposition. Bratton and van de Walle make the interesting point here that the distinctly neopatrimonial way of punishing insider dissidents by making them outsiders is a reason that so many African opposition movements are led by former regime insiders and so many post-transition rulers were once pre-transition regime insiders.

With so much power concentrated in the hands of the personal ruler, the fate of the transition soon "hinges on the fate of the dictator" (Bratton and van de Walle 1997:84). Protests radicalize as opponents seek the overthrow of the incumbent, fearful that any other arrangement would be manipulated by a ruler who puts himself above the laws. Little room is left for the regime to absorb the protests, assimilate its leaders, and engage in its own reforms. Thus, neopatrimonial transitions are unlikely to be negotiated affairs based on compromise. The winner-take-all nature of the system promotes resistance until either final defeat or successful survival of the regime.

Where does democracy fit into these transitions? As protest is primarily about the economy and is led by former and even recent regime insiders, it does not seem at first that demands for democracy should figure prominently in such movements. Yet opponents seek democratic rules as a way to wrest power from the president, who relies on the lack of institutions and personal networks to stay in charge. Opponents may also employ the rhetoric of democratic reform in order to gain external support from the international community, or at least undermine the incumbent's patronage from external states and donors. Thus, the successful establishment of democratic rule and institutions is sure to considerably weaken the political advantage of the incumbent. It is no surprise then that many African opposition movements and parties of the late 1980s and early 1990s seemed to have the promotion of democracy as their sole objective, rather than specific policies or ideological orientations (e.g., the Alliance for Democracy in Mali and the Movement for Multiparty Democracy in Zambia). They sought a change in the rules of the game so as to secure their access to it.

Particularly enlightening in Bratton and van de Walle's argument is that pro-democracy elites are no different from incumbents in their characteristics and goals. They want power and they want resources, and most likely they once had both. They demand elections as a path to power. In addition, the authors help explain why democracy might not flourish after transitions, especially if foreign aid resumes or continues. To the extent that pro-democracy protests are economic protests at their core, the subsequent failure of democracy to provide sufficient material rewards reduces its appeal, especially after new elites have incorporated the circle of regime insiders. Thus, transitions are rapid and sudden, but replacement elites have few incentives to maintain the democratic reforms that they demanded as outsiders. Hence it is likely that the new regimes will progressively hybridize into semiauthoritarian regimes, reincorporating elements of personal and neopatrimonial rule. Moreover, as Patrick Chabal and Jean-Pascal Daloz (1999:37) later made clear, neopatrimonialism itself is not usually challenged by the protesters: "It is the decline in the resources available for patronage rather than dissatisfaction with the patrimonial order *per se* which has undermined the legitimacy of political elites on the continent." It is no surprise then that neopatrimonialism finds ways to endure despite transitions.

Once the transitions get going, they vary as a function of the degree of electoral competition and political participation of the pre-transition regimes. For as Bratton and van de Walle note, there are variations among neopatrimonial regimes, with some allowing varying degrees of electoral competition and participation in regime-friendly organizations. When both competition and participation are low, as in military oligarchies, there is no prearranged institutional path for change and the dictator tends to hang on to power for fear of reprisal. Such regimes are thus affected by protracted struggles that can turn violent and are unlikely to lead to subsequent democratic consolidation.

In regimes that tolerate participation but stifle competition, which Bratton and van de Walle label "plebiscitary one-party" systems, transition actors might capitalize upon the participatory traditions to organize some large forum capable of inheriting legitimacy from the regime, such as the sovereign national conferences that took place in many francophone regimes. The outcome of such transitions depends upon the residual strength of the leader and his capacity to manipulate the proceedings (Mathieu Kérékou and Denis Sassou-Nguesso of Benin and Congo, respectively, were unable to control their conferences, whereas Idriss Déby and Omar Bongo of Chad and Gabon managed to empty theirs of any significant threat to their power). It is in more competitive one-party systems, Bratton and van de Walle argue, that prospects are best for democracy to emerge, because of their traditions of participation and competition. Yet the examples of Côte d'Ivoire, whose transition collapsed into civil war, and Zambia, where democratic change soon stifled into semiauthoritarianism, challenge this contention.

At any rate, the essential contribution of Bratton and van de Walle is the recognition not only that democratic transitions are possible in neopatrimonial regimes, but also that they tend to follow specific trajectories that contrast with transitions in other regions. While these authors acknowledge the precipitating effects of factors such as donor-induced economic reforms and the end of Cold War patronage, they focus mainly on domestic dimensions and single out the weakness of neopatrimonial regimes in the management of protest as a key element. To some extent, their argument suggests that, for all its equilibrium qualities, neopatrimonialism contains the fiscal seeds of its own predicament and is poorly equipped to control the crises that it itself engenders. As we examine later in this chapter, their analysis also suggests that neopatrimonial transitions to democracy might face serious contradictions in the consolidation phase.

Extraversion and Instrumentalization

It is possible to add another layer to our understanding of democratic variations in Africa by considering the extent to which democracy might also be an element of some countries' foreign policy.[4] This approach need not contradict the more domestic focus of theories structured around neopatrimonialism, but can complement them as well as offer a rationale for the apparent willingness of once-dictatorial regimes to democratize and for the subsequent limits of democratization.

As will be made clearer in Chapter 8, most African countries engage in foreign relations, at least in part, based on seeking the patronage of rich countries, offering diplomatic allegiance and strategic benefits in exchange for resources, political support, and noninterference in domestic affairs (Jackson 1990; Clapham 1996). Jean-François Bayart (1993, 2000) has shown that such instrumentalization of their international dependence by African regimes (which he labels "extraversion") has been a recurrent theme in African history (see also Frederick Cooper's notion of "gatekeeper" state [2002:157]).

During the Cold War, it was not uncommon for African countries to exchange their allegiance to one of the superpowers, or to France, which maintained a close neocolonial relation with many of its former colonies, for material and strategic resources (Clapham 1996). At the end of the Cold War, the countries that were dependent on the Soviet Union lost their foreign patron, while those that relied on the United States or France faced unprecedented demands for democratization (Cheeseman 2015; Carothers 2006). Depending on their other sources of revenue or strategic advantages, regimes became more or less vulnerable to these new conditions and experienced the shock differently. Those with little to exchange became increasingly vulnerable to donor demands. They tended to be the countries closest to fiscal bankruptcy and debt default, most associated with the Soviet Union, and least endowed with natural resources. For the thirteen African clients of the Soviet Union identified by Thad Dunning (2004), the average time from the fall of the Berlin Wall in November 1989 to the adoption of multiparty politics was fourteen months.[5] For other African countries, it was thirty-three months (some, such as Eritrea, still have not adopted multiparty politics), a statistically significant difference.

It comes as no surprise, therefore, that the number of former Soviet clients is particularly high among the strongest democratizers. The Beninese regime had adopted Marxism-Leninism in the 1970s. It abandoned it in December 1989. Cape Verde and São Tomé too had been Soviet clients, while Mali and Seychelles had historical ties to the communist bloc. The Mozambican government was dependent on the Soviet Union for military equipment and oil. It too abandoned Marxism-Leninism in 1989.

French patronage did not require adjustments as costly as those of its Soviet counterpart. After 1990, the French government did demand some political changes of its African clients, but France did not disappear and its Africa policy retained other considerations besides democracy promotion. Benin and Mali democratized, but other French clients, particularly those well endowed in natural resources such as Cameroon and Gabon, or those with a more strategic location such as Chad and Djibouti, faced significantly less pressure or were better able to resist it. Vulnerability to the democratic demands of Western donors was thus not uniformly distributed across African countries, with the consequence that the regime trajectories they experienced immediately after the Cold War differed substantially (Cheeseman 2015; Dunning 2004; Bratton and van de Walle 1997).

Regime vulnerability to the demands of patrons continued to vary after the initial transitions. The regimes that have remained most vulnerable include some of the continent's consolidated democracies (e.g., Benin or São Tomé). These regimes, however, have managed to instrumentalize democracy to their own benefit. Ruling elites in most of the strongest democratizers were able to either stay in or rapidly return to power under the new democratic dispensations. Van de Walle (2003:300) found that "at the end of 2002, the single party in power before 1989 remained there in 15 of the region's multiparty political systems." In other words, being able to navigate the formal trappings of democracy afforded them international support, as they were playing by the new rules the donors had laid out, as well as the personal political and economic rewards that come with holding significant positions of domestic power. Often, elections were not particularly competitive or incumbents held a clear advantage (sometimes funded by foreign aid). Finally, it is important to note the decreasing importance that donors have placed on democracy promotion in recent years. This is partly due to the increasing influence of China and its economic support for African regimes regardless of their domestic practices. While the West tried to establish democratizing conditions to their aid after the Cold War, China tends to function without such pretenses. Moreover, the West's emphasis on democracy has also faded in recent years, as Europe and particularly the United States focus more on their own security issues.

Ultimately, the idea that democratization is part of an extraversion strategy for some African ruling elites is but one hypothesis. It provides insights into the nature of some transitions and consolidations, but it would be a step too far to see such instrumentalization in all regimes at all times. In the end, the study of democratization in Africa has as much to offer comparative politics as it has to gain from it. Conventional variables, particularly of the modernization type, have limited currency. The internal dynamics of neopatrimonialism and the propensity for regime extraversion, however, provide significant analytical mileage.

African Democracy in Practice

Beyond the dynamics of transition, what do African regimes look like? How do African democracies actually function? What differences exist between African regimes? What are the range of their characteristics? What are Africans' preferences in, and perceptions of, their political systems? Finally, what is the weight of ethnicity in the voting choices of Africans?

Hybrid Regimes

As mentioned earlier, the modal African regime can be characterized as hybrid, or comprising some democratic and some authoritarian dimensions. Partly, such hybridity is the result of either incomplete initial democratic reforms or the progressive erosion of initially successful transitions. One of the most remarkable characteristics of contemporary African politics is indeed the degree to which authoritarian neopatrimonial regimes have been able to adapt to the formal trappings of electoral democracy. Thus, to a large extent, neopatrimonialism has proved compatible with democracy rather than having dissolved in it. It has endured and reproduced despite a generalized change in the formal rules of politics.

What does hybridity look like? In general, sitting halfway between the ideal-types of democracy and authoritarianism, hybrid regimes tend to display the following characteristics: they hold regular elections, but these are often manipulated to the benefit of the incumbents; they provide some civil and political liberties, yet more or less frequently repress their exercise; they are not hegemonic, as they contain spheres of public life where opposition can organize and express itself, including the media, civil society, and legislatures, yet these groups lack autonomy and face considerable difficulties in asserting themselves; although not as easily repressed as in pure authoritarian regimes, their members remain more vulnerable than in democracies; the ruling party tends to dominate all other parties and to dwarf them in size; the security apparatus operates with few institutional and legal constraints and is often focused on domestic opponents; and formally democratic institutions are partly decoys and patronage is rampant (see Tripp 2010:12 for an excellent table summarizing and comparing the main features of democratic, hybrid, and authoritarian regimes).

Aili Tripp (2010:11–15) suggests that the category of hybrid regimes is too loose and should be broken down into two subtypes—semidemocratic and semiauthoritarian regimes—so as to better capture regime variations.[6] Semidemocracies "allow for changes in party dominance and the alternation of the presidency." In semiauthoritarian regimes, in contrast, leaders "do the absolute minimum to democratize" and "do not allow for genuinely competitive elections" (13). In the former category, she includes such states as Liberia, Malawi, Senegal, Tanzania, and Zambia; in the latter, Angola, Burkina Faso, the Central African Republic, Congo-Brazzaville, Guinea-Bissau, Kenya, Rwanda, and Uganda (20). One of the main arguments

222 *Inside African Politics*

she makes is that, while there are few democracies on the continent, the shift from previously pure authoritarian regimes to hybrid regimes represents significant progress and appears to be stable.

What is particularly noticeable about hybrid regimes is their seeming stability, their apparent equilibrium qualities. Although some might revert to full-fledged authoritarianism (e.g., Mali in 2012) and an occasional one might yet democratize (e.g., Ghana in the mid-1990s and possibly Gambia post-2016), they generally do not appear engaged in any transition but may have reached a point of stasis. Bogaards (2014:36) notes that if they do change, it tends to be semidemocracies (what he calls "competitive authoritarianism") becoming more authoritarian. Though their domination is more nuanced than that of their pure authoritarian counterparts, hybrid regimes are able to neutralize most agents of change, either through co-optation of the opposition, the manipulation of social and student movements, the intimidation of media, or even the wielding of spiritual powers when necessary. This stability is particularly noteworthy given Marina Ottaway's (2003:16) observations that these regimes are institutionally weak: "The semi-authoritarian regimes cannot develop the institutions they would need to perpetuate the allocation of power without causing the democratic façade to crumble. Nor can they allow the democratic institutions to function without hindrance, without putting the continuation of their control in jeopardy. Semi-authoritarian regimes, thus, constantly undermine their own institutions, usually by generating and exercising much power outside their realm, or more rarely by manipulating them endlessly. . . . Semi-authoritarian regimes have institutions, but the semi-authoritarian regime itself is not institutionalized."

In general, these regimes produce within the populace a disenchantment with politics and a lack of hope, which occasionally translates into a propensity for outbursts of grassroots protest and social violence without long-term mobilization or agenda. So, what is the meaning of being an opponent in such regimes? Clearly, in the vast majority of cases, the political opposition has little hope of replacing the party in power. So what do they fight for? For one, political opposition in semiauthoritarian regimes can actually provide some degree of constraint on the behavior of rulers and particularly limit their abuses and arbitrariness. In the DRC, for example, under the Joseph Kabila regime after 2006, human rights activists, media, and several NGOs, while generally very weak, nevertheless managed to limit the number of disappearances, arbitrary arrests, and political assassinations. Although responsibility eluded the top brass, several state agents were brought to court for human rights violations. Thus, to a degree, opposition and civil society contribute to maintaining what little accountability hybrid regimes have and prevent them from reverting to authoritarianism. This is no small achievement. In a book on the opposition in Burkina Faso, Mathieu Hilgers and Jacinthe Mazzocchetti (2010) provide evidence not only of the alienation of opponents and citizens in a semiauthoritarian state, but also of the different types of utility people can derive from standing up to such a regime. There are no doubt opportunities to be found in opposition (an attitude not dissimilar to the defection of regime stalwarts during transitions identified by Bratton and van de Walle). One can find a job or become co-opted if one can be a sufficient nuisance. This might also sometimes work as a strategy of individual extraversion: in some countries, people who take to the streets when demonstrations are banned, with the near-guarantee of being physically beaten, are said uncharitably by some to be seeking a visa to a Western country. But for others, however, there is a question of personal integrity and dignity. People demonstrate, vote, and voice their opposition at times more out of principle than for change. In this perspective, as Hilgers (2010) makes clear, there is an attempt to fight alienation, to be recognized and, simply, to be.

If democratic mechanisms are more apparent than real in hybrid regimes, how do they reproduce and maintain power? By and large, like their predecessors, they resort to a heavy dose of neopatrimonialism. According to van de Walle (2003), even African democracies remain pervaded by presidentialism and clientelism. There is limited effective political competition, as the politician who won the first democratic election is most often still in office. The dominant party in parliament tends to co-opt and absorb the smaller parties along some loose "presidential majority" coalition, usually built around the distribution of public resources. Personal politics remains salient (most small parties are really the weak organizational appendage of those who have or aspire to Big Man status). Thus hybridity, particularly in regimes that began with significant reformist impulse, such as Museveni's Uganda, suggests that there is something nearly unavoidable about neopatrimonialism as a mode of political regulation in Africa, and that its progressive encroachment cannot easily be resisted.

The case of Mali, a full-fledged democracy by most accounts until the 2012 coup, illustrates the limitations of African democracy and the resilience and adaptation of Big Man rule, while also suggesting different ways to think about accountability and representation in hybrid systems. Most observers agree that Mali's democratic transition, which endured for twenty years after 1992, was one of the most successful in Africa. Susanna Wing (2008), for example, shows that Malian democracy thrived on a tradition of open political dialogue embedded in an original and inclusive constitution. She argues that its success derived in part from the extent to which constitutional provisions echoed local Malian traditions of community organizations and rule by discussion. Nevertheless, Wing, like others, acknowledges that Malian democracy had many of the pitfalls of hybrid systems: it remained weak, it coexisted with personal rule and corruption, and its institutions functioned haphazardly, all of which contributed to the feelings of frustration that facilitated the army takeover in 2012. For example, by the time of the coup, people's satisfaction with Malian democracy had reached a low point (only 31 percent of the populace expressed satisfaction contrasted with 63 percent a decade before), with the majority of citizens expressing little to no faith in the electoral commission (Haïdara and Isbell 2018). Moreover, Mali had largely slipped back over time into a quasi-single-party system, with the president relying on clientelistic networks to collect some 70 percent of the votes while popular participation in elections was limited (voter turnout in 2007 was only 36 percent). Yet Céline Thiriot (2002) shows that Mali contained multiple parallel participatory innovations that allowed for other forms of association and control of authority. Albeit sometimes symbolic, these initiatives helped engender citizen participation in politics, and reflected a particularly strong civil society by African standards. In fact, fostered by conservative religious organizations, Malian civil society mobilized in 2010 against a recently adopted family code that gave women equality of rights, and against the abrogation of the death penalty, which led the president to refuse to sign these laws. Whatever one might think of the substance of these issues, few African societies are strong enough to make their governments backtrack on already passed legislation.

The 2012 Malian coup occurred weeks before scheduled elections, in the context of low public confidence in democracy and an ongoing insurgency in the north. But the army was forced to relinquish control after losing much of the country to the insurgents and under strong pressure from the regional Economic Community of West African States (ECOWAS) organization, which imposed sanctions and a blockade in order to restore the democratic constitutional order. Presidential elections were held in 2013 and again in 2018, reflecting a tentative return to a hybrid democracy.

Of course, democracies everywhere function below optimal expectations, and Mali reminds us that African democracy is a fragile proposition. But the lesson from Mali may also be a story about a normative shift among African organizations to defend the institutions of democracy across the continent. Since its founding in 2002, the African Union has proclaimed a position of zero tolerance for unconstitutional changes of government by force. Just as the Malian coup failed under pressure from the African Union and neighboring ECOWAS states, ECOWAS sent troops to force Gambia's long-term ruler, Yahya Jammeh, to accept electoral defeat in 2016. During that time, Nigeria, the strongest state in ECOWAS, witnessed its first defeat of a sitting incumbent in the 2015 election. That same year, ECOWAS and the AU were instrumental in forcing coup makers in Burkina Faso to return to the barracks and restore the constitutional order, the country being on the verge of a shaky transition to democracy after almost three decades of Blaise Compaoré's repressive rule. This normative shift privileging democratic institutions in the face of military coups was tested in November 2017 when the Zimbabwean army ousted Robert Mugabe. The African Union and the regional Southern African Development Community (SADC) condemned the coup, but accepted the appointment of Emmerson Mnangagwa as president, effectively supporting the pretense that a military coup did not really happen. Ultimately, African democratic experiments, like democracy and political freedoms across the globe, remain precarious works in process.

African Perceptions of Politics and Democracy

What do Africans think of democracy and other political issues? For a long time, in contrast to most other regions, the study of African politics lacked input of the opinions of Africans themselves, as few large–sample size comparative surveys existed. This situation dramatically improved with the creation of the Afrobarometer (www.afrobarometer.org) and such online platforms as YouGov.org. Created in 1999 and housed at Michigan State University, Afrobarometer is a joint venture of that university, the Center for Democratic Development in Ghana, and the Institute for Democracy in South Africa. As of 2018 it had conducted numerous rounds of careful quantitative surveys in thirty-six countries across the continent, which has provided scholars with a much better knowledge of African public opinion on a range of political, economic, and social issues.[7] Equally important, numerous researchers (including students) have been able to access Afrobarometer's rich data at multiple levels of disaggregation in order to test a wide range of hypotheses on African politics, many of which are referred to in these pages.

So, what is Africans' assessment of democracy? According to Afrobarometer surveys, Africans have exhibited a growing commitment to democratic ideals. In 2014, and utilizing Afrobarometer survey data from thirty-four countries, Bratton and Housessou (2014) noted that seven out of ten Africans prefer democracy to other political regimes. The proportion of those who also reject authoritarian alternatives (e.g., presidential dictatorship, military rule, and one-party regimes), and were thus considered "deeply committed democrats," has risen steadily over the preceding decade. Thus, while there has been a global "democratic recession" since 2005, evidence from the Afrobarometer surveys indicates a strong demand for democracy in Africa, particularly for high-quality elections and leadership accountability. This has led to a general democracy deficit within hybrid regimes. That is, the demand for democracy is exceeding the supply.

These findings were consistent with more recent findings by Mattes and Bratton (2016). While their findings, based on more recent Afrobarometer surveys, confirmed a steady demand for democracy, they noted that large proportions of respondents were skeptical that their demands were being met by current political leaders. Yet they also found that large differences existed between African countries. For example, three-quarters of respondents in Mauritius, a fairly stable and free democracy, were committed to democratic forms of government, while the same could be said of only less than one in ten Mozambicans. Interestingly, of the thirty-four countries included in Afrobarometer's two most recent surveys to date, popular demand for democracy decreased in fourteen countries. The surveys also found that, comparatively, demand for democracy was highest among males, urban dwellers, university graduates, and those with middle-class employment. Finally, Mattes and Bratton (2016:4) found that the quality of past elections was significant: "African countries with high-quality elections are more likely to register increases in popular demand for democracy than countries with low-quality elections."

Do Africans Vote Ethnically?

It is often assumed that ethnic considerations are as dominant in voting choices as they tend to be in other dimensions of African political life. At the dawn of the wave of democratization in the 1990s, for example, Donald Horowitz (1993) warned that elections in ethnically divided societies would be tantamount to "ethnic censuses," mere headcounts of individuals along ethnic lines. It has indeed been the fact that, in several African countries, ethnicity has been salient in electoral contests. In Nigeria, the main political parties have long identified with regions and ethnic groups. In South Africa, blacks prefer the African National Congress while whites tend to vote for the Democratic Alliance (Ferree 2006), though recent leadership turnovers may be changing that slightly. In Guinea, the two leading candidates in the 2010 elections, Alpha Condé and Célou Diallo, explicitly associated with Malinké and Peul ethnicities respectively. In the 2010 elections in Côte d'Ivoire, Dioulas from the north overwhelmingly voted for their coethnic Allassane Ouat-tara, while the Bété stuck with their man, Laurent Gbagbo. And in Kenya, the perceived manipulation of the 2007 presidential results by incumbent Mwai Kibaki, a Kikuyu, at the expense of opponent Raila Odinga, a Luo with Kalenjin support, led to massive ethnic-based vio-lence that left more than a thousand dead.

In addition, the ethnic narrative of African elections seems backed by a large body of empirical studies that find a significant effect of ethnic affiliation on voting behavior (e.g., Ferree 2006; Young 2009; Gibson and Long 2008; Norris and Mattes 2013). In general, this effect is stronger for the ruling candidates (Bratton, Bhavnani, and Chen 2013). Thus, people are more likely to vote for a coethnic when the latter is already in power than if that person is an opposition candidate. This finding suggests that ethnic voting should not be understood as a mere expression of the strength of identity in African politics. It might also reflect more practical considerations: because of the limited range of ideological competition among African parties and the generally uncontroversial desires of voters for greater welfare, Africans might vote for the politicians most likely to look after them, and shared ethnicity might provide a clue for such behavior. Since incumbents are more likely to have access to the goods of patronage, voting for a coethnic in the opposition is a less efficient strategy to improve one's lot. Finally, people who share ethnicity also likely share policy preferences, as they may experience similar material conditions. Thus, ethnic voting might become a proxy for policy voting, with policy preferences defined along ethnic lines. There might be some plausibility to this, especially since policy in Africa is often reduced to the provision of public goods, which might be regional in distribution (roads, wells, schools, and the like).

Yet one needs to add many nuances to the ethnic theory of voting. As discussed in Chapter 3, it is not necessarily useful to point to ethnic-ity as a voting foundation, since ethnic identity can aggregate at different levels. In the Democratic Republic of Congo, for example, which counts more than 200 ethnic groups, the 2006 elections saw the country split along largely regional rather than ethnic lines, with the east voting for incumbent Joseph Kabila, most of the west for challenger Jean-Pierre Bemba, and the Bandundu province for veteran politician Antoine Gizenga. Of course, in such a country as in most, no single candidate could have been elected by relying only on the votes of his own ethnic group. A recent study by Englebert, Calderon, and Jené (2018) notes that decentralization in the DRC seems to have had the unintended conse-quence of heightening ethnic allegiances within the provinces, which have shrunken in size but increased in number (from eleven to twenty-six).

Thus, at the regional level, the saliency of ethnic affiliation may have increased, but at the national level, the necessity of electoral coalitions dilutes the importance of ethnicity and makes it more difficult to predict voting behavior. In the 2010 elections in Côte d'Ivoire, for example, a significant number of Akan voters, from the center of the country, rallied to northerner Ouattara in the second round. Remember, in this respect, Daniel Posner's (2004b) insight that Chewa and Tumbuka identities were sharply demarcated in Malawi, where each group had a sufficient relative size to send representatives of its own to parliament, but were blended in Zambia, where they needed to pool their forces to compete with other large groups. Of course, such argument does not deny that people were voting to be represented by people from their ethnic group; it merely shows that such groups are somewhat fluid and people may identify at different levels of ethnicity.

Moreover, if ethnicity is the main driver of voting in Africa, how does one explain the absence of ethnic considerations in some countries' elections, even in the presence of significant ethnic heterogeneity? In a recent work, Dominika Koter (2016) seeks to explain the varying degrees of ethnic appeal between and within African countries. She suggests that one factor is the effectiveness of local leaders to act as intermediaries for electoral mobilization. Where the ties are strong, such as in Senegal, Koter finds very little evidence of politicians utilizing ethnic appeal. Where the ties are weak, as in Benin, politicians appeal to ethnic background, and electoral campaigns become framed as competition between ethnic groups over control of national resources. Koter thus explains the high degree of ethnic appeal in countries such as Kenya and Guinea, because traditional institutions that serve as intermediaries elsewhere have been undercut and destroyed by the colonial powers, as well as early independence leaders. For example, Guinean political parties and candidates in the 2010 presidential elections identified clearly as either Peul or Malinké and appealed to their relative interests.

Yet in neighboring Mali, Malian parties have not historically formed along ethnic lines, and ethnicity appears largely irrelevant to voting in Mali even though it is an important part of social life. While Koter would suggest the significance and effectiveness of Malian traditional leaders, Thad Dunning and Lauren Harrison (2010) argue that "cross-cutting ties" among people of different ethnic groups, derived from the common practice of "joking kinship," help account for the relative unimportance of ethnicity in voting. In Mali as in several other African countries, some people enjoy relations of "cousin" (*cousinage*) with people from other groups, characterized by the practice of friendly teasing, whose origins go back to historical family alliances, which prevent differences from turning into conflict. Last names can indicate to an individual whether another person stands in such "cousin" relationship to them. Using experiments, Dunning and Harrison (2010:2) found that although Malians favor coethnic politicians, "cousinage alliances counteract the negative impact of ethnic differences on candidate evaluations. . . . [S]ubjects' evaluations of candidates who are cousins from a different ethnic group are statistically indistinguishable from their evaluations of candidates who are noncousins from their own ethnic group."

Examining the ethnic voting patterns in Kenya's presidential elections illustrates both the extent and the limitations of the ethnic theory of voting in Africa. In the 2007 contest, Raila Odinga was a Luo, Mwai Kibaki a Kikuyu, and Musyoka Kalonzo a Kamba. Very clearly, each of the candidates received the vast majority of the votes among his coethnics, close to 100 percent actually for Odinga. Yet each one also appealed to other ethnic groups, some of which are culturally "close" to their own group or particularly polarized with that of another candidate. Almost 90 percent of the Kalenjin, for example, favored Odinga, while the Meru, closely related to the Kikuyu, voted for Kibaki (Gibson and Long 2008). In 2013 and again in 2017, however, Kalenjin politicians allied with Kikuyu candidate Uhuru Kenyatta, strongly suggesting that such alliances are sometimes more instrumental than culturally determined. Hence, while voting has pronounced ethnic dimensions, it goes beyond simply voting for someone of one's own ethnic group. In addition, the data for Kenya seem to support an understanding of voting along shared preferences, as there is a significant degree of intraethnic homogeneity in voting. Only in a couple of instances, among the Kisii and the Maasai, is there much candidate pluralism within a group.

Moreover, there is ample evidence on other dimensions of African voting that mitigates the pure ethnic approach. Daniel Young (2009) has found that party affiliation, change in personal circumstances, and "job approval" (retrospective evaluation of government performance) are stronger predictors of voting than ethnicity (which remains nevertheless significant). Using Afrobarometer data from sixteen countries, Michael Bratton, Ravi Bhavnani, and Tse-Hsin Chen (2013) have shown that both ethnic and economic considerations motivate African voters. Ethnic support is robust for the group in power, but evaluation of government performance with respect to unemployment, inflation, and income distribution appears a more important consideration. Staffan Lindberg and Minion Morrison (2008) have also found that evaluation of past performance and campaign promises are more robust predictors of voting than ethnicity. These findings make Africans very "normal" voters and de-exoticize the continent's politics.

Asking how people vote implies also questioning what they vote for. We know that in Africa, ideological differences carry relatively little weight in voting decisions (van de Walle 2003). But do African voters care about national issues, or do they seek to elect politicians who will bring "development" or resource transfers to their region? If the latter, then ethnicity is more likely to matter, as a politician from their region makes for a more credible patron. Leonard Wantchekon (2003) went a long way toward answering this question with an experiment he carried out in Benin in which he exposed voters in selected electoral districts—with the complicity of the real candidates—to clientelistic and broad public policy platforms. In the former case, the voters were told that the candidate, whose coethnicity was made explicit, would bring development to their region and jobs for them in the administration; in the latter, voters were told that he would reform education and healthcare nationally, fight corruption, and promote social peace across the country (410–411). Wantchekon found that the clientelistic treatment had a significant and positive effect for all candidates, while the public policy treatment more often had a negative effect. Thus it is partly the predilection for clientelism that determines the importance of ethnicity in African electoral politics. In Wantchekon's experiment, when a candidate switched from clientelistic to public policy platforms, support from his coethnics dropped (419).

All of this may lead one to conclude that ethnic affiliation, in and of itself, is not a strong predictor of voting behavior. But when it does factor in, it does so along the lines suggested by the instrumentalist approaches to ethnicity discussed in Chapter 3.

Notes

1. For more details on Botswana's democracy, see Holm 1987; Molutsi and Holm 1990; and Good 2008.

2. All data in this paragraph are based on World Bank, *World Development Indicators,* http://data.worldbank.org/indicator.

3. While not looking at the impact of natural resources on regime type, Luc Désiré Omgba (2009) finds that the presence of oil reserves has positive effects on the tenure in power of African authoritarian leaders.

4. This section is adapted from Peiffer and Englebert 2012.

5. The thirteen countries are Angola, Benin, Cape Verde, Congo-Brazzaville, Ethiopia, Guinea, Guinea-Bissau, Madagascar, Mali, Mozambique, Seychelles, Tanzania, and Zambia.

6. There are many terms in the literature used to name hybrid regimes, including "competitive authoritarianism," "electoral autocracies," "virtual democracies," and "pseudo-democracies" (for a sample, see Diamond 2002).

7. The thirty-six African countries are Algeria, Benin, Botswana, Burkina Faso, Burundi, Cameroon, Cape Verde, Côte d'Ivoire, Egypt, Gabon, Ghana, Guinea, Kenya, Lesotho, Liberia, Madagascar, Malawi, Mauritius, Morocco, Mozambique, Namibia, Niger, Nigeria, São Tomé, Senegal, Sierra Leone, South Africa, Sudan, Swaziland (as of 2018, Eswatini), Tanzania, Togo, Tunisia, Uganda, Zambia, and Zimbabwe.

6

The Economic Dimensions of African Politics

IT IS FREQUENTLY ASSUMED THAT THE PURPOSE OF GOV-ernment is to organize society and the economy, to provide public goods and services, to allow for the flourishing of individual activity and exchange. These are no simple tasks for any government in any part of the world. But nowhere might governing be more of a challenge than in Africa, where many weak states, with limited capacity, often face overwhelming material constraints and stark human needs. Put simply, there are few options, few choices, and none of them easy, in trying to overcome, or simply cope with, the obstacles brought upon Africans by history and the material world. It is thus cruelly ironic that, at least until recently, African governments have proved to be among the most dysfunctional and probably the least able to face the challenges they have inherited. It is even crueler that their policies, over the years, have often exacerbated the predicament of their populations. African governments' weaknesses and policy failures led to a frequent delegation of economic policy to outside actors, first among them the World Bank and the International Monetary Fund. Yet for all their technical competence, these external actors have also largely failed to bring about greater welfare for Africans. Moreover, African economies have often suffered from the cruelties of a global economic system that, at times, seems to actively thwart African development. Recent scandals and revelations have drawn attention to the ways that African economies have suffered from massive tax evasion by multinational firms and wealthy individuals. In 2018, for example, the United Nations Economic Commission for Africa (UNECA) reported that the continent loses at least $50 billion a year from illicit financial flows.

In this chapter we first review the historical and material constraints facing Africans. In most cases, it would be hard to think of more inauspicious circumstances to run an economy. We then turn to the actual policies of government and their international partners. Testifying probably to the cluelessness of both African governments and their international patrons, development policy in Africa has been characterized by a succession of shifts, from an early promotion of markets, through an emphasis on governance, to (for now) a near–fully fledged subsidization of the African state by donors. Throughout, conditionality, or the exchange of aid for policy, has been a structuring force, and aid has taken on a greater and greater role in African economies, with possibly more consequences for the continent's level of indebtedness than for its prospects for economic development. Still, there have been notable improvements—and stumbles—since the turn of the century, and we end the chapter by investigating recent claims of "Africa rising."

The Weight of History and Nature

In terms of their development prospects, it is undeniable that African states embarked upon independent rule under the harshest of circumstances. Very little predisposed them to efficient agriculture or industrialization, and they lacked the other foundations of rapid growth such as human capital and stable property rights. From precolonial times, they inherited the consequences of the slave trade, including low population densities and distorted social fabrics; from colonialism, outward-oriented economies and commodity dependence; and from nature, a harsh climate and debilitating diseases.

Economic Consequences of the Slave Trade and Colonization

Events that took place long ago can still matter today. The African slave trade, which terrorized Africans from about 1400 to 1900, stands as a telling example of the weight of history, as it continues to exact a crushing toll on their welfare. There were several slave trades. The trans-Atlantic one was the largest and took slaves from western, central, and eastern Africa to be shipped to the Americas. There were also smaller and more regional slave trades across the Sahara, the Red Sea, and the Indian Ocean. In pathbreaking research, Nathan Nunn (2008) carefully computes the number of slaves who were traded from each contemporary African country, using port shipment data and other documents reporting their ethnicities, and observes that the countries from which the most slaves were taken are the poorest today, a relationship that is particularly strong and robust to alternative hypotheses. Importantly, he finds that the regions that are poorest today and where the most slaves came from were actually among the most developed initially. He can rule out, therefore, the idea that the weakest societies invited the most slave raids and continued to be weak to this day.

What are the possible mechanisms through which the slave trades might affect contemporary societies? Nunn suggests two hypotheses. First, the raids and continuous warfare as well as the associated demographic depletion resulted in weakened and underdeveloped existing political structures. By the end of the nineteenth century, the countries from which most of the slaves were taken had the most underdeveloped political structures. Second, by pitting communities against each other, the trades prevented the formation of large ethnic groups and increased fractionalization. The most ethnically fragmented regions of Africa today are indeed those from which most slaves originated. In other words, the communal divisions brought about by slave trading continue to affect intercommunal relationships today. In another paper, Nunn and Leonard Wantchekon (2009) add recent household survey data to show that individuals whose ancestors suffered from the heaviest raids during the slave trades are less trusting nowadays of their neighbors, relatives, and local governments. In other words, the authors suggest a link between the intensity of slave trading and contemporary cultural individual features that are believed to correlate with economic welfare.

The overall economic effects of the slave trades, as estimated by Nunn (2008), are nothing short of astounding. According to his calculations, had the trades not occurred, 72 percent of the income gap between Africa and the rest of the world (and 99 percent of the gap with the rest of the developing world) would have been wiped out. Of course, there are methodological and other caveats to his findings, but their sheer scope suggests that the consequences of slave trading several hundred years ago continue to devastate Africa today.

Things hardly improved for Africans after the slave trade ended, for colonization followed in short order. We can simplify the impact of colonization on African development by broadly distinguishing two categories of effects: direct economic ones and those mediated through political and institutional processes. We have already touched upon the former in Chapter 2. Some of the worst effects, particularly in the first phase of colonialism, were a degree of human exploitation that led to a vastly increased mortality and the vast plundering of local natural resources. In general, the colonial economic transformation of Africa involved a high degree of outward orientation as colonial economies were geared toward the satisfaction of the needs of the colonizers. Thus, African economies became extractive, with very limited processes of transformation, and most infrastructure development served the needs of the export market. Massive amounts of labor coercion turned economies into monocultures at the cost of decreasing their capacity to produce foodstuffs. Networks of trade that had promoted some degree of economic integration on the continent were reorganized to link each colony monopolistically to its colonizer. Under colonialism, the economic structures of African societies were fundamentally altered, ceasing to be self-sufficient as they imported manufactured goods and basic foodstuffs while exporting raw materials. To this day, the perceived comparative advantages of many African economies are little more than their colonially derived specializations, even though export agriculture had begun to develop in late precolonial times (Austin 2010).

There were some variations in the economic regime as a function of whether the colony encouraged agricultural production by Africans, served the settlement of Europeans, or relied on mineral extraction. In places such as Senegal or Ghana, the colonizers made arrangements to promote the production of, respectively, peanuts and cocoa by local farmers, leading to the creation of a relatively powerful class of agricultural producers. Although they became dependent on these commodities, these economies also witnessed significant growth in trade. Ghana and Nigeria, for example, saw twentyfold increases in trade volumes between 1897 and 1960 (Austin 2008). In settler economies, as in Kenya or Zimbabwe, in contrast, Europeans stole large amounts of land from Africans and became themselves the dominant agricultural class, at the cost of much greater and lasting inequality. In countries that had mineral resources, such as gold and diamonds in South Africa, or natural endowments in other coveted commodities, such as rubber and ivory in Congo, profitable exploitation required significant labor coercion and repression. In Congo this was taken to such an extreme as to provoke a substantial and long-lasting population reduction (Hochschild 1999). Some colonies, which initially had very little in terms of either agricultural or mineral endowments, such as Upper Volta or Chad, became reservoirs of migrant labor for other colonies. This too had lasting consequences. To this day, for example, some 2 million Burkinabé migrants (over 12 percent of the population) are estimated to live in Côte d'Ivoire.

By and large, although colonial transformation ushered African economies into the modern world system, it did so at considerable cost and by putting them into a long-lasting inferior and dependent position.

African economies were forcefully integrated into a European-dominated capitalist trading system in a subservient position, structured to benefit the economic development of their colonial rulers at their own detriment. For authors such as Walter Rodney (1981) and Samir Amin (1972, 1976), these transformations amounted to a capitalist penetration that, while fueling the economic development of Europe, permanently "underdeveloped" Africa. Rodney is particularly eloquent about these effects. The economic exploitation of the colonial period, he writes, underwrote an expatriation of African economic surplus through forced labor and repressed wages in the plantation and cash-crop regimes. The supposed benefits—infrastructure or hospitals—did not amount to much, and were biased toward the whites. Roads and railways, for example, existed to enhance extraction, connecting mines and plantations to the ports. The negative consequences were many, including loss of power, increased destitution of women, tribalism, trade diversion, enclave formation, commodity dependence, monoculture development, "chronic undernourishment," and other forms of "alienation." The general point of these authors is that Africa is not so much undeveloped as *under*developed, the result of colonial policies and practices that are directly related to the wealth of the first world. The latter engenders the former. African poverty is not accidental, nor is it the consequence of African conditions; it is the product of the continent's dependent insertion into the world capitalist system courtesy of the colonial episode.

There is little for us to add to the well-trodden literature on the direct economic transformations brought about by colonialism. Since the 1990s, more authors have turned their attention to explaining the institutional outcomes of colonization and their effects on contemporary economic well-being (Hopkins 2009). Daron Acemoglu, Simon Johnson, and James Robinson (2001), although their work is not directly focused on Africa, argue that the current institutional performance of former colonial economies, measured by the stability of property rights (which correlates with economic performance), can be traced back to health conditions at the time of colonization around the end of the nineteenth century. Specifically, they suggest that different rates of settler mortality across colonies provoked different degrees of settlement. In countries such as Sierra Leone, known as the "white man's grave," few colonizers settled, whereas the pleasant and healthy conditions of, say, the Kikuyu plateau of Kenya were much more inviting. In a rather dramatic historical shortcut (see Hopkins's 2009 critique), the authors suggest that the degree of settlement is related to the type of colonial institutions that developed. Where whites settled, property rights developed, as the settlers sought to create, or reproduce from home, the conditions for their economic success. Note that these property rights did not apply to Africans, who were typically expropriated as a prerequisite for colonial settlement. In countries with less salubrious conditions, a weak skeleton of colonial administrators managed economies of extraction based on the exploitation of Africans and little attention was provided to the development of property rights or other institutions of accountable rule. Institutions endure, and the strength of property rights at the dawn of the twentieth century correlates with their strength today, the authors argue, affecting contemporary economic performance.

This argument rests on the assumption that no economic salvation occurs without European-inspired institutions. White settlement alone seems conducive to growth in the postcolonial world. Yet Botswana, the greatest African economic success and the fastest-growing country in the world from 1966 to 1985, is also possibly the African country that was least transformed by colonialism, keeping many of its precolonial institutions.[1] The argument also suggests that African countries bequeathed with extractive institutions face overwhelming odds. The key, according to this argument, lies in the degree to which the colonizers re-created the legal conditions that prevailed at home. In this respect, Acemoglu and colleagues pay empirical attention to the "neo-Britains" (Australia, Canada, New Zealand, and the United States), none of which developed in Africa.

In contrast, Ola Olsson (2007) argues that it is the length of colonial rule that mostly allows for the development of good institutions (see also Grier 1999 on the impact of duration and Mahoney 2010 for a similar argument with illustrations from Latin America). From this point of view, colonialism in Africa was too short and insufficiently transformative to rid the continent of existing inefficient institutions and evolve development-oriented ones. Here, too, there seem to be few options for building on indigenous institutions, and economic development is regarded as an exclusively European product.

Environmental Challenges: Climate and Geography

The burden of history on African economic development is compounded by particularly unpropitious natural conditions. As early as 1848, classical economist John Stuart Mill (1987 [1848]:102) wrote that "the most evident cause of superior productiveness is what are called natural advantages," among which he listed "fertility of soils" and "a favourable climate." Tropical climate, which prevails over the vast majority of sub-Saharan African countries, is a powerful obstacle to productivity in and of itself, all the more so since farming is such an essential activity. Africa's propensity for alternate dry and rainy seasons provokes an unstable water supply, which makes farmers and cattle herders vulnerable to wide variations in output, compounded by the scarcity of irrigated agriculture (only 4 percent of all African agricultural land is irrigated). Even in normal times, many regions of Africa experience relative food shortages as the reserves accumulated during the rainy season dwindle by the end of the dry season. Should rains be late or insufficient, such shortages can easily turn critical, occasionally to the point of famine. Food supply can drop dramatically and rapidly, leaving rural residents with shortages and urban residents with rising food prices, sometimes prohibitively so. In regions of livestock herding, the shrinkage of pastures induced by drought can lead to the death of many animals, conflict over remaining forage, and even destitution as herders become refugees. Africa has a higher mortality rate from droughts than any other region. In the mid-1970s and again in the mid-1980s, several countries of western Africa (particularly Mali, Mauritania, and Niger) as well as Ethiopia suffered severe drought-induced famines (Derrick 1977, 1984; de Waal 1991).[2] Famine hit Niger again in 2005 and 2010. Several southern African countries, particularly Mozambique, have also suffered from cycles of droughts and floods since 2000. Between July 2011 and August 2012, a severe drought ravaged eastern Africa. Since 2016, eastern and southern Africa have faced three consecutive years of drought, affecting seventeen countries and putting over 38 million people at risk, with Cape Town in South Africa facing the prospect of completely running out of water in early 2018. Even when it does not trigger floods, the frequently forceful nature of rain in Africa erodes topsoil and reduces its fertility.[3] This problem is compounded by desertification caused by drought and by the collection of firewood for domestic use (see Oba 2016).

Tropical climate also favors the spread of infectious diseases (to which we return later), as well as pests and parasites, all of which have negative effects on productivity. Moreover, put simply, the tropical climate is too hot. Anyone who has worked in the middle of summer with no air conditioning can empathize with the fate of tropical African farmers and the conditions they endure, day in and day out. It is easier to be productive in the temperate climates of Europe and North America than in the tropical zones of Africa, where heat inhibits work (Landes 1999).

In addition to climate, several African countries face other geographical obstacles. No less than fourteen African countries are landlocked (Botswana, Burkina Faso, Burundi, Chad, the Central African Republic, Ethiopia, Malawi, Mali, Niger, Rwanda, Uganda, South Sudan, Zambia, and Zimbabwe). Given that African economies greatly rely on commodity exports to distant countries (rather than on regional trade), being landlocked is a significant liability (more so than for, say, Switzerland), which considerably adds to transaction costs and puts these countries at a competitive disadvantage. Although Africa counts many large rivers, hardly any of them are suitable for navigation over long distances. Thus, in most cases, transport to the oceans relies on trucks or freight trains, many of which, running on colonial-era tracks, are in need of repair. For some light-bulk commodities, air transport is an option. The passage of borders alone, with the attendant bureaucratic nuisance, represents an economic burden and wastes time.

Looking at eighty-three countries worldwide from 1965 to 1990, Jeffrey Sachs and Andrew Warner (1997:187) found that a country entirely under a tropical climate grows on average 0.8 percent more slowly annually than an entirely nontropical country, whereas landlocked countries lose a mean 0.6 percent each year in growth compared to their counterparts with access to the sea. In a subsequent piece, Sachs (2000) highlighted a couple of additional factors linking tropical climate to lesser productivity. First, many new technological developments in agriculture are geared toward temperate zones and are hard to transfer to tropical production. And second, the combination of health problems associated with tropical climate that increase morbidity, and the labor-intensive nature of much tropical agriculture, slow the demographic transition to lower fertility rates.

Countries with a temperate climate not only have better economic performance than tropical countries, but also have better institutions. Kenneth Sokoloff and Stanley Engerman (2000) addressed this variation by looking at North versus South American economies. Their findings are relevant to Africa. They suggest that land endowments in Latin America are good for commodities that need economies of scale or that can benefit from the use of slavery in production. Such circumstances lend themselves to the adoption of plantation agriculture, which favors land concentration in a few hands. The landowners then promote institutions that accept and reproduce inequality but hamper long-run growth by depriving many people of economic opportunities. In the United States, in contrast, temperate climate favored commodities grown on family farms, fostering the rise of a middle class that demanded inclusive institutions, which in turn favored the subsequent industrial revolution. Other authors (Diamond 1997; Acemoglu, Johnson, and Robinson 2001; Olsson 2003) have offered variations on the theme of geography's effect on institutions and development. William Easterly and Ross Levine (2003) found that an index measure of settler mortality, latitude, crops, and landlocked status had a significant effect on another index that measured dimensions of governance such as bureaucratic quality, contract enforcements, and property rights.

Although African economies are put at a disadvantage by much of the continent's current climate, climate change is widely expected to make things worse. Of particular concern is the increased risk of drought in regions that are already at the edge of sustainability. The Sahel, which stretches east to west across the continent south of the Sahara and north of the more forested areas of the Gulf of Guinea and central Africa, is one such region. Researchers at Princeton University have predicted that average Sahelian temperatures could rise by 6.3 degrees Fahrenheit (Miguel 2008:12) and that rainfall could drop by as much as 25 percent in the second half of the twenty-first century (Held et al. 2005). Their colleagues at Stanford University have generated climate change models indicating that crop production in the Sahel could fall by up to 10 percent for sorghum, wheat, and rice by 2030 (with millet output likely rising, however), while in southern Africa corn output might fall by nearly 30 percent and wheat by 15 percent. In addition to a direct drop in the local availability of food and the significant danger of famine, reduced rainfall can also bring about resettlement and conflicts over land (Toulmin 2009). A 2007 report by the United Nations Environment Programme suggested, for example, that the conflict that raged in Darfur, Sudan, after 2003 was driven by climate change and environmental degradation, which increased competition over land for local communities, and predicted more such conflicts to come (UNEP 2007).[4] We discuss further the connections between the environment and human insecurity in Chapter 7.

After over two decades of negotiations, in December 2015 the global community reached an agreement to combat climate change. Given that Africa is extremely vulnerable to the impact of climate change (seven of the ten most vulnerable states are African), the Paris Agreement was important to Africa, helping provide the continent with funding and technology to mitigate climate change. Climate change has already led to a decrease in rainfall over large parts of the Sahel, and eastern and southern Africa, with an increase in parts of central Africa. Over the past several decades, the number of climate-related disasters, such as floods and droughts, has doubled. By 2080, it is estimated that 5 to 8 percent of land in Africa will become arid and semiarid land and 75 percent of the African population will be at risk of hunger. It is often noted that Africa is the region most vulnerable to, but least responsible for, human-made climate change, and we are only now beginning to grasp the challenges that lie ahead (Burke et al. 2016; Dinar et al. 2014).

A Particular Case of Commodity Dependence:
The Resource Curse

It is a particularly frustrating paradox that many African economies are remarkably well-endowed with natural resources, yet have been unable to use them in breaking free of poverty. The relationship between dependence on commodity exports and poor economic (and political) performance is known as the "resource curse." Ever since their colonial restructuring, most African economies have been characterized by the production of a handful of mineral commodities (e.g., cassiterite, cobalt, coltan, copper, diamonds, gold, petroleum, uranium, zinc) or agricultural commodities (e.g., cocoa, coffee, cotton, tea, nuts, rubber, sugar, spices, tobacco) for export. In quite a few cases the existence of these commodities actually contributed to the region's appeal for the colonizers.

Often, there has been limited transformation of the nature of economic output since colonial times. For sure, all around Africa, the service sector has grown, in large part reflecting growth of government employment. But the dominance of the primary (extractive and agricultural) sector over manufacturing has endured almost everywhere. Table 6.1 lists each sub-Saharan African country's primary export, and as it illustrates, most African countries remain largely natural resource–exporting economies, and their fortunes have varied with the fate of these commodities. Table 6.1 also lists each country's GDP per capita as of 2017. And while such measurements are notoriously suspect, these figures reflect a wide range of the levels of wealth generation across the continent. When commodity prices have risen, African economies have been able to accumulate significant revenue. But when these prices have fallen, so has their income. Until recently, the overall economic outcome has been paltry. What has generally not taken place is the utilization of the income from natural resources (usually referred to as "rents") to fuel the transformation, and particularly the industrialization, of Africa. Take the example of cotton, which was introduced by colonialism in several African countries, from Mali to Mozambique, where the locals dubbed it "the mother of poverty" (Isaacman 1995). There are complex linkages between cotton production and poverty, but several African countries continue to supply it to textile and garment mills in Europe and beyond, yet have failed to develop an indigenous manufacturing sector (Sneyd 2015). Why haven't Africa's natural resources made a greater contribution to African development?

The resource-curse literature is dominated by the work of Michael Ross. In his first contribution to the topic, Ross (1999) identified several potential liabilities of commodity-exporting economies, including

Table 6.1 Primary Exports and GDP per Capita in Africa

	Primary Exports, 2016 (percentage share)	GDP per Capita, 2017
Angola	petroleum (89); diamonds (8)	$4,170
Benin	gold (34); cotton (18)	$830
Botswana	diamonds (73)	$7,596
Burkina Faso	gold (70); cotton (12)	$671
Burundi	gold (60); coffee (23)	$320
Cameroon	petroleum (30); cocoa (15)	$1,447
Cape Verde	fish (67)	$3,210
Central African Republic	wood (37)	$418
Chad	petroleum (82); gold (11)	$670
Comoros	cloves (55); vanilla (12)	$797
Congo, Democratic Republic of	copper (52); cobalt (17)	$458
Congo-Brazzaville	petroleum (54); copper (31)	$1,658
Côte d'Ivoire	cocoa (46)	$1,662
Djibouti	charcoal (28); coffee (20)	$1,928
Equatorial Guinea	petroleum (69); natural gas (19)	$9,850
Eritrea	copper (42); gold (26)	$583[a]
Eswatini	drink concentrates (25); sugar (15)	$3,224
Ethiopia	coffee (24); gold (13)	$768
Gabon	petroleum (70); manganese (12)	$7,221
Gambia	wood (33); nuts (17)	$483
Ghana	gold (57); cocoa (13)	$1,642
Guinea	gold (50); aluminum (32)	$825
Guinea-Bissau	nuts (77)	$724
Kenya	tea (23); flowers (14)	$1,508
Lesotho	clothes (40); diamonds (22)	$1,182
Liberia	rubber (65); gold (17)	$456
Madagascar	vanilla (19); nickel (14)	$450
Malawi	tobacco (59); sugar (8); tea (8)	$339
Mali	gold (77); cotton (9)	$825
Mauritania	iron (36); gold (17)	$1,137
Mauritius	fish (12); sugar (10)	$10,547
Mozambique	aluminum (22); coal briquettes (13)	$416
Namibia	diamonds (20); copper (17)	$5,227
Niger	uranium (30); petroleum (20)	$378
Nigeria	petroleum (73); natural gas (15)	$1,969
Rwanda	gold (21); tea (13)	$748
São Tomé	cocoa (71); iron (7)	$1,913
Senegal	gold (14); petroleum (12)	$1,033
Seychelles	fish (65)	$15,505
Sierra Leone	diamonds (63); cocoa (22)	$499
Somalia	goats (32)	$500

continues

Table 6.1 continued

	Primary Exports, 2016 (percentage share)	GDP per Capita, 2017
South Africa	gold (20); diamonds (10)	$6,161
South Sudan	petroleum (99)	$237
Sudan	gold (57); petroleum (13)	$2,899
Tanzania	gold (35); tobacco (7)	$936
Togo	gold (31); cement (6)	$617
Uganda	gold (25); coffee (14)	$604
Zambia	copper (80)	$1,510
Zimbabwe	gold (32); tobacco (14)	$1,080

Notes: Data for primary exports from UN Comtrade, https://comtrade.un.org and https://atlas.media.mit.edu. Data for GDP per capita from World Bank, *World Development Indicators*, https://data.worldbank.org/indicator.
   a. Last available figures from 2011.

price and revenue volatility (which makes budgeting difficult), a lack of easy linkages to other sectors of the economy, and the danger of "Dutch disease," which refers to an overvaluation of the currency and the rise in costs of production across an economy as a result of a booming commodity sector. In addition, he noted that the windfall profits from commodity exports (which are usually nationalized) remove all budget constraints to governments in the short run and might lead to "policy myopia." Examining the case of oil, John Heilbrunn (2014:26) notes the ways in which the extractive colonial legacy impacts the resource curse, arguing that states with histories of routine violence will continue to experience high levels of unrest afterward. As these emerging petrostates capture and nationalize mineral rights, corruption increases both within and outside the state, undermining effective state institutions as the state is incorporated into the global regime dominated by oil companies (see also Yates 2012). In Nigeria, for example, the oil boom of the late 1970s and early 1980s led to a flurry of ill-advised and cost-inflated projects that ended up making a minimal contribution to growth but a massive one to national debt (Lewis 2007).

   The resource-curse literature observes that there might also be significant indirect effects. The income from the resource exports might underwrite subsidies for infant industries that progressively become ensconced and oppose subsequent trade liberalization (more open trade is associated with greater growth). It is also possible that the export sector becomes so powerful that it "captures" the state, dictating policy and hampering the development of broadly accountable institutions. Finally, governments that benefit from commodity rents are under less pressure than others to raise funds through the taxation of their citizens and are thus less likely to develop accountability toward the latter (Ross 2012).

The question of institutions is thus relevant once more. Clearly, countries with strong and legitimate political and economic institutions have little to fear from resource endowment. Norway has not suffered from having oil. But for countries with weak property rights, inefficient and corrupt bureaucracies, and unaccountable governments, natural resources can rapidly become a curse. This was the apprehension when significant reserves of oil were discovered in Chad in the early 1990s. Since Chad is landlocked, its government had to build a pipeline through Cameroon to the sea. Not having the necessary resources to embark on such a project, nor the creditworthiness to find private financing, it had to turn to the World Bank, which seized this opportunity to demand a set of institutional constraints on the exploitation and management of the oil with the intention of shielding Chad from the resource curse. The agreement between the World Bank and the government stipulated that the majority of the revenues from oil, which had to be deposited in offshore escrow accounts, were to go to poverty reduction projects overseen by a committee composed of religious, community, and political leaders. The government also set up a "future generations fund" in which it was to save 10 percent of its oil revenues for poverty reduction programs (see Soares de Oliveira 2007:278–286; Pegg 2006; and Massey and May 2005 for more details). In effect, the Bank was using its financial leverage to create institutional constraints on government behavior and limit its predation.

The Bank's efforts did not prove successful, however. Oil production began in 2003, but just three years later Scott Pegg (2006:12–13) was already pointing to serious shortcomings, including the omission of indirect revenues (such as taxes) among the escrowed funds, the loose definition of poverty reduction projects, and the lack of capacity building of government accounting institutions. Yet these turned out to be rather mild problems in contrast to what happened in late 2005, when the Chadian government, eager to buy weapons to combat a rebellion, unilaterally passed a law in violation of its loan agreement with the Bank that abolished the "future generations fund" and relaxed the government's spending restrictions (to include the security sector among its priorities and increase the share of nonpriority spending from 13.5 percent to 30 percent). The Bank briefly froze Chad's assets in the escrow account but, under pressure from France, the United States, and the oil companies operating there, soon caved in and allowed Chad to redefine the terms of the agreement.

By 2008, Chad was entirely in control of the use of its oil resources (Pegg 2009). Chad has since remained mired in conflict and, while its budget has greatly benefited from the boom in oil prices, there is as yet limited evidence that it has brought about any sustainable development.

Chad illustrates the complexities of reining in African governments that exercise sovereign authority over their resources with little accountability to their citizens or donors. It conforms to the available evidence, which suggests that oil-producing countries are less likely to be democratic because the rents from oil do not incentivize their governments to seek popular legitimacy by developing accountability (Ross 2012). Yet the recent case of Ghana, a country with much stronger democratic practices and institutions than Chad, has provided an interesting counterpoint. Examining Ghana, Phillips, Hailwood, and Brooks (2016:28) reject the resource-curse conclusions, arguing that "oil discoveries do not trigger the rupture in economic and social affairs that is commonly attributed to the resource." Likewise Heilbrunn (2014:228), while conceding some aspects of the resource-curse argument, concludes that oil production in Africa "leads to an expansion of a country's economy, and resource revenues increase societal wealth."

Beyond oil, additional scholarship has suggested a causal linkage between the availability of diamonds (and other similar minerals that require little infrastructural development) and the presence of conflict in low-income and weakly institutionalized countries, triggering books, movies, and much public advocacy on "blood diamonds." Paul Collier and Anke Hoeffler (2001) estimated that once the ratio of "lootable" primary commodity exports to GDP reaches 30 percent, it shows a statistically significant association with conflict. Protracted civil wars fought over, and financed by, diamonds in Sierra Leone and the Democratic Republic of Congo in the 1990s and into the 2000s provide illustrations of this plight. Yet it is not always clear whether the rebels seek access to the resources to begin with or find the use of these resources convenient for waging insurgencies motivated by other considerations, a topic we discuss in Chapter 7.

In Africa, the purported resource curse is yet another obstacle on the path of policymakers. If true, the very comparative advantage of many African nations, largely derived from the initial economic decisions of colonizers, might well be inimical to sustainable and balanced development. In Asian countries such as South Korea or Taiwan, the relative lack of natural resources contributed to strategies of development based on labor-intensive manufacturing, which progressively empowered labor and eventually led to both democracy and development. In Africa, government reliance on commodity rents, with encouragement from donors such as the World Bank, has contributed to an ambiguous development and political record and to the relative exclusion and alienation of citizens from the development process. Even if the "curse" is an illusion, it has impacted governance in Africa. As Phillips, Hailwood, and Brooks (2016:27) have observed: "Oil is so closely associated with corruption in countries such as Nigeria, Angola and Equatorial Guinea, that the *idea* of the resource curse has become a powerful narrative in a number of new oil-producing states in Africa, including Ghana. . . . Oil discoveries bring an influx of not only major oil companies, but also innumerable advisory bodies, donors, consultants and NGOs versed in the international best practice of oil sector management."

Health

Africa's tropical climate is conducive to infectious diseases. Particularly widespread is malaria, a parasitic disease that is transmitted through the bite of the Anopheles mosquito. Currently, malaria affects around 190 million Africans each year and kills nearly half a million of them, mostly children, as adults develop some immunity over their lifetime. According to the World Health Organization (WHO 2017), forty-four African countries account for about 90 percent of the world's malaria cases and deaths, with the burden largely on fourteen countries.[5] Reported cases of malaria had been falling since 2010, but that decline stalled and has even reversed in some places since 2014. By some estimates, malaria can shave up to 1.3 percent off a country's annual rate of growth. It also represents a formidable burden on health expenditures and infrastructure, accounting for 30 to 50 percent of hospital admissions in some countries. Other prevalent African infectious diseases include schistosomiasis (a serious disease of the liver contracted from parasitic worms found in fresh water), amoebiasis (a gastrointestinal infection), and hookworm disease (caused by a soil-transmitted parasite that colonizes the intestines and triggers anemia and malnutrition). There have been some public health successes on the continent. Of note is a significant decline in the number of deaths from measles thanks to vaccination campaigns. Similarly, a thirty-year campaign has all but eradicated onchocerciasis, or river blindness, from western Africa, allowing people to resettle previously abandoned fertile land near rivers.

Africa has also experienced some devastating epidemics, including recent outbreaks of the deadly Ebola virus. The first recorded outbreak was in 1976 in a Congolese village near the Ebola River (hence the name). The disease is transmitted between humans through direct contact with blood, bodily fluids, and broken skin of those infected, as well as through surfaces and objects contaminated by the fluids. The most widespread outbreak of Ebola took place in western Africa between 2013 and 2016. By the time it was contained in 2016, conservative estimates indicate that there were over 28,000 confirmed and suspected cases in Guinea, Liberia, and Sierra Leone, resulting in over 11,000 deaths (WHO 2016). In addition to the loss of life, the economic costs to the region were severe. The World Bank estimated a loss of $1.6 billion in productivity for the three countries, roughly 12 percent of their combined GDP. Observers noted that what began as a health crisis quickly escalated into a humanitarian, social, economic, and security crisis with long-term implications (McInnes 2016). In 2018, there was another outbreak of Ebola in the Democratic Republic of Congo, its tenth since the first outbreak of the virus, and the most deadly to date.

As significant as Ebola, malaria, and other health challenges have been, they are dwarfed by the devastation wrought by the human immunodeficiency virus (HIV), responsible for the epidemics of acquired immunodeficiency syndrome (AIDS). Since the mid-1980s, many African countries have been hit by HIV, making the continent the most affected region in the world. HIV most likely originated in western equatorial Africa (Cameroon, Congo, Gabon) and probably finds its origins in a similar virus found among chimpanzees (Iliffe 2006:5). The earliest, retrospectively documented, positive case of HIV was for a male Kinshasa resident in 1959, but it is not known with certainty when the disease began. The spread of HIV/AIDS was slow, as its transmission is relatively difficult (requiring the exchange of blood, genital fluids, or human milk) and its incubation long, but it started displaying exponential growth in the 1980s. By 1981, HIV prevalence among patients in antenatal clinics in Kinshasa was 3 percent; by 1984, it was closer to 7 percent (Iliffe 2006:12–13). Across central Africa, the prevalence of the disease among those aged fifteen to forty-five rose to the high single digits by the late 1980s. Rapid partner change and careless use of needles and injections seem to have been contributing factors. From its central African origins, the disease spread to other regions and struck eastern and southern Africa most virulently.

Since its epidemic onset in the early 1980s, AIDS has taken a terrifying toll on African lives. Altogether, more than 20 million Africans have died of it since the beginning of the epidemics, and about 15 million children are AIDS orphans across the continent (UNAIDS 2018). In 2017, an estimated 25.7 million adults and children were living with HIV in Africa (out of 36.9 million globally). Southern and eastern

Africa are the areas most affected by the HIV epidemic, accounting for roughly 53 percent of the people living with HIV globally, and 45 percent of the world's HIV infections. In 2017, 1.2 million Africans became newly infected and 660,000 died of it (representing about 66 percent of the global rate). More women than men live with the disease; of Africans with HIV, roughly 56 percent are female. Yet the mortality rate for men with HIV is higher. In 2017, an estimated 300,000 men in Africa died of AIDS-related illness compared to 270,000 women.[6]

There are variations by subregion, with the worst rates of infection by far occurring in southern Africa, followed by eastern Africa. In 2017, 800,000 people acquired HIV, with 380,000 dying from AIDS-related illnesses. South Africa represented 33 percent of those new infections and 29 percent of the deaths, followed by Mozambique with 16 percent of the new infections and 18 percent of the deaths. Including Tanzania, those countries accounted for more than half of new HIV infections and deaths from AIDS-related illness in the region in 2017. For a long time, western Africa seemed somewhat spared the worst of the infection, but rates increased in that region at the beginning of the century. By 2017, western and central Africa accounted for 21 percent of the world's new HIV infections and 30 percent of global deaths from AIDS-related illness, with Cameroon, Côte d'Ivoire, and Nigeria together accounting for over 70 percent of new infections in the region. Nigeria alone accounted for more than half of those deaths and new infections.

The toll of AIDS in Africa has been catastrophic. After decades of progress, life expectancy (the median age to which one can expect to live) became stuck at fifty years on average for the continent from 1987 to 2002 (it had risen to sixty in 2016), whereas it is over eighty years in the developed world. In Botswana, one of Africa's economic success stories, life expectancy collapsed from sixty-three in 1987 to forty-nine in 2001, before slowly rising to sixty-seven in 2017.[7] In the rest of southern Africa, life expectancy still hovers well-below sixty years. In addition, the epidemic has further weakened already fragile public health infrastructures and crowded out human and material resources for other patients and diseases.

Despite such statistics, AIDS trends in Africa have actually shown dramatic improvement in recent years, as the upturns in life expectancy suggest. Rates of new infections (incidence) seem to have peaked in the late 1990s, and rates of prevalence (total numbers infected) have declined. As bad as the statistics remain for southern African countries, they were worse in 2004, when prevalence was an astounding 37 percent in Botswana and Swaziland (as of 2018, Eswatini), 27 percent in Zimbabwe, and 21 percent in South Africa. Unfortunately, some of these improvements are due to the deaths of infected individuals. Yet it is taken as a measure of some success that the newly infected no longer outpace the dying. According to the Joint United Nations Programme on HIV/AIDS (UNAIDS 2018:5), HIV incidence fell by more than 25 percent from 2001 to 2009 in twenty-two sub-Saharan African countries (and in another eleven countries in other regions), including those with the biggest epidemics in absolute numbers (Ethiopia, Nigeria, South Africa, Zambia, and Zimbabwe). In recent years, the improvements have been even more notable, with the AIDS-related mortality declining by 42 percent from 2010 to 2017 in eastern and southern Africa and 24 percent in western and central Africa. The prevalence ratio of eastern and southern Africa was 0.04 in 2017, reflecting a steep decline since 2010 and moving toward the epidemic transition (UNAIDS 2018:23). These achievements are largely due to successful coordination between African governments, civil society, international donors, and the research community. Despite these significant improvements, the scale of the HIV epidemic in Africa remains massive.

It is worth pondering what effects the AIDS epidemic has had on African economies and politics. What changes in perceptions of life and behavior might be brought about by such curtailment in one's hope to remain alive, and how do these changes aggregate? Since many AIDS victims are adults who would otherwise be at the peak of their productivity, who has replaced them and their income? Who works in their fields? Who takes care of their children? To some extent, beyond its immediate consequences for the victims and their families, it is puzzling that AIDS has not so far exerted a greater toll on African economies. In Botswana, for example, GDP per capita has continued to grow at an average of about 4 percent per year since the early 1990s, and Africa in general has seen some of its best economic performance since around the turn of the century. Maybe the relative lack of drop in output can be explained by the existence of surplus labor and low productivity in agriculture, and the mineral- and capital-intensive nature of many African economies. In other words, and this can be construed as an indictment on the extent to which economic statistics truly measure the welfare of Africans, a population reduction due to deaths from the AIDS epidemics could result in greater GDP per capita for an economy whose output largely derives from a few extractive activities rather than from the productive work of many. Of course, longer-term consequences might still be felt in years to come.

Politically too, AIDS has not brought about the convulsions that a crisis of this magnitude could be expected to wreak on a country. In an article written at the peak of the crisis, Alex de Waal (2003) wondered how reduced life expectancy might affect governance in the form of the behavior and experience of bureaucrats. He suspected that absenteeism "due to illness, attending funerals and caring for the sick" would sap morale and hurt institutional effectiveness, thus undermining the developmental goal of promoting greater state capacity (12). And might corruption not increase as "people have greater needs for resources, less time to accumulate them, and feel less pressure from sanctions" (12)? One could imagine an impact on all important sectors of society: civil society could be weakened by the death or incapacitation of its leaders; military forces could see more casualties from reduced life expectancy than from combat; the education sector could dwindle as teachers fall sick. Meanwhile, governments would be unable to afford the necessary tenfold increases in their health budgets (13–17). The lack of commitment and dedication to the crisis by African rulers, as gerontocrats ruling young societies, would not help (20–22).

Yet in a rich and insightful subsequent volume, de Waal (2006) noted that few of the dire political AIDS predictions had come to pass and made two particularly striking arguments. First, while acknowledging the pessimism of such a perspective, he wondered whether one reason African polities can absorb the negative impact of AIDS might be that "they are already so dysfunctional at providing the basic functions of governance" that "the losses and stresses of HIV/AIDS are no worse than the misgovernment and war that have disfigured the continent for so long" (79). Second, he suggested that there can be political mileage in the struggle against AIDS for many African leaders, particularly as it facilitates relations with donor countries and aid flows, with the result that routine international procedures of collaboration have been put in place, with much actual treatment and intervention delegated to outside actors, and AIDS largely becoming "politically domesticated" (119).

It is worth stressing that the policies of some African governments have done little to mitigate the AIDS crisis and have probably at times worsened it. For several years in the 1980s in Congo, Mobutu Sese Seko banned all public discussion of the disease (Iliffe 2006), hardly a responsible approach to a public health threat. In South Africa, President Thabo Mbeki for many years denied a link between HIV infection and the onset of AIDS, depriving many of his citizens of health policies that could have made antiretroviral drugs available earlier. Mbeki's promiscuous successor, Jacob Zuma, while on trial for alleged rape (of which he was acquitted), acknowledged that showering after intercourse was his preferred prophylactic method. What accounts for the few country-specific successes and overall retreat of the disease? No doubt donor policies subsidizing antiretroviral drugs—including the President's Emergency Plan for AIDS Relief (PEPFAR) of the United States—have had an impact. Leadership matters too. As Amy Patterson (2006) notes, the openness and willingness of presidents to lead by example can make a big difference in changing public attitudes about AIDS, especially in countries where the weight of patriarchy favors the spread of the disease (Siplon 2005). Uganda's early successes in fighting AIDS have often been credited to President Yoweri Museveni's head-on public confrontation of the disease from the 1980s onward, a commitment that has since eroded. Evan Lieberman (2009), for his part, observes that AIDS-related public policies are more effective in countries where institutions do not reinforce ethnic divisions. And others have found that responses from civil society groups, particularly churches, have at times had a significant impact (Patterson 2011; Trinitapoli and Weinreb 2012).

The Management of African Economies and the Development Agenda

Africa's Economic Profile

Africa's economic performance since 1960 can be summarized in three phases: expansion until the mid-1970s, decline from the mid-1970s to the mid-1990s, and expansion again since the mid-1990s (see Figure 6.1). As of 1994, the average GDP per capita among African countries stood at the same level as in 1965 (when fewer countries were independent and thus included in the average), essentially suggesting that no economic progress had been made in thirty years. Yet as of 2017, it stood around 33 percent higher than in 1994 and invited assessments of a continent-wide turnaround. Over the entire almost sixty-year period, 1960 to 2017, per capita GDP grew by 54 percent, or a little over 1 percent per year, which remains the slowest growth rate of any region in the world (despite Africa starting as the poorest region). Altogether, the average African still earned only $639 in 2011, or less than two dollars a day (in 2000 dollars).[8] And even such paltry figures are misleading, for a large part of Africa's output is from mineral commodities, the income from which might not directly accrue to citizens. It should be noted, however, that African output figures are notoriously unreliable and tend to underestimate new sectors (for a provocative critique of the study of African economies, see Jerven 2015). When Ghana revised its national accounts methodology in 2010, its GDP increased by 70 percent (Jerven 2013:26).

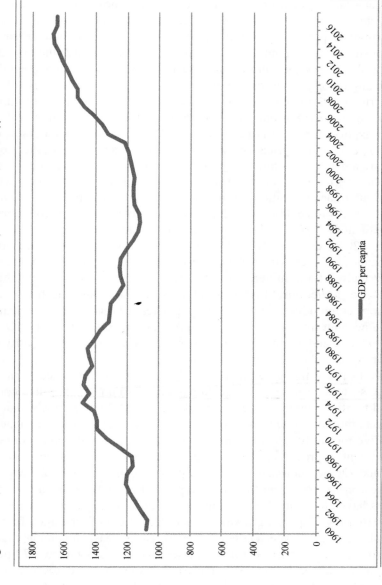

Figure 6.1 Africa's Economic Performance, 1960–2017 (constant 2010 US$)

Source: World Bank, *World Development Indicators*, http://data.worldbank.org/indicator (accessed August 2018).

Failure to industrialize has been an essential characteristic of almost all African economies. For sure, there were many attempts in many countries, especially in the 1960s and 1970s, to develop a manufacturing sector. Yet aside maybe from breweries, few manufacturing projects returned consistent output. Value added in African manufacturing hovered around a mean of 17 percent of GDP from the 1960s to the 1990s, and has since fallen steadily to around 10 percent as of 2017. In contrast, the primary sector, defined as agriculture and extractive industries, has remained the basic engine of growth (or lack thereof). The contribution of agriculture to Africa's GDP has slowly decreased from the low 20 percent range throughout the 1980s and 1990s to 16 percent in 2017, but this decline (like manufacturing's) is partly due to the rise of GDP as a result of surging commodity prices (on which more later), and does not therefore capture a genuine decline of agriculture's relative output. Nevertheless, Africa's agriculture, largely based on small household producers who use limited mechanization and irrigation, remains less productive than it could be. As for extractive industries, they have increased from about 13 percent of Africa's GDP (without South Africa) in the early 1980s to around 20 percent in 2017.[9] It is in the foreign sector, however, in the exchanges between Africa and the rest of the world, that the domination of agricultural and mineral commodities is most obvious. Altogether, exports of agricultural raw material, ores and minerals, and fuels—all primary commodities involving no significant process of transformation—account for about two-thirds of Africa's exports. The rest of GDP (between 30 and 40 percent) derives from services, the vast majority of which reflects the government sector.[10]

Not surprisingly given weak overall economic performance, Africa's social sectors—health and education—have also underperformed compared to other regions since independence. As of 2016, Africa's under-age one mortality rate was 53 per thousand live births, while its under-age five mortality rate stood at 78 per thousand. These numbers mark significant improvement over 1970, when they stood, respectively, at 133 and 226 per thousand. Nevertheless, they remain high. Public expenditures on health amount to about 2 percent of GDP. African governments have also struggled to promote the education of their citizens. As of 2016, only 57 percent of women and 72 percent of men aged fifteen and above were literate. These numbers might increase in coming years, as gross primary school enrollment rates have progressed from 70 percent as recently as 1990 to 98 percent in 2016. Yet these enrollment figures are inflated, as they include children of all ages who attend primary schools; do not necessarily indicate completion; and provide no information as to how much actual learning takes place in the classroom. While there has been a slow increase over the past few decades, gross second-ary school enrollment rates remain dire, with only 42 percent of the relevant age group attending.[11]

The development effects of the large donor contributions in support of African economies might be debatable (and are much debated, as shown later), but there is no doubt that they have created a situation of aid dependency. Foreign aid plays a pivotal role in defining the relationship between African countries and donors, and it also largely structures domestic policy and development agendas. The extent to which aid is an intrinsic part of life in Africa cannot be overstated. From ministries down to village associations, would-be entrepreneurs seek funding for projects. Bringing "development" (i.e., funded projects) to one's village or region is what politicians are elected for, and a class of "development brokers"—intermediaries between recipients and donors—has emerged (Olivier de Sardan, Bierschenk, and Chauveau 2000; Swidler and Watkins 2018). Todd Moss (2011:138) makes a telling comparison between aid to Africa and the Marshall Plan, which underwrote US assistance to European reconstruction after World War II. While funds from the Marshall Plan never exceeded 3 percent of the GDP of a single recipient country, for-eign aid to Africa (excluding South Africa) averaged 5.8 percent of the region's GDP from 1960 to 2010, with a peak of 12.5 percent in 1994 and a trough of 2.5 percent in 1970.[12] Moreover, in the early years of the twenty-first century, twenty African countries had levels of foreign aid in excess of 10 percent of their GDP (148.4 percent for Liberia), and thirty-one in excess of 5 percent (Moss 2011:139). And while the level of aid relative to the region's GDP has been declining for much of the past decade, there was an uptick in 2015 and 2016. The intensity of aid to Africa and its permanent character are essential in making sense of the continent's economies, economic policies, and external relations.

A final notable characteristic of African economies is their largely uncaptured dimension. Away from official data and financial flows, in avoidance or defiance of burdensome regulations, ineffective policies, and exploitative officials, many Africans toil in subsistence or in the "infor-mal" sector. The informal economy refers to productive and exchange activities that are undocumented and untaxed. They are illegal in the sense that informal economic operators do not have the required permits to exercise their activities, nor do they pay taxes on them (Moore, Prichard, and Fjeldstad 2018). But they are not criminal, in the sense that informal activities are similar in their economic nature to formal ones. For exam-ple, street vending is a common informal activity in Africa. There is also a criminal economic sector in Africa, which often revolves around state agents, and which is briefly discussed in our analysis of state failure in Chapter 7. But it is distinct from the informal sector and of much less significance to understanding African economies than the latter.

By virtue of its very informality, the importance of the informal sector is difficult to estimate. Most actors are self-employed or small-scale household enterprises with low levels of organization and little capital. Moreover, many Africans may be active in both the formal and informal sectors of the economy, reminding us that these are not discrete and different domains (see Raeymaekers 2014). Nevertheless, using surveys and inference from national accounts, researchers have estimated the size of informal economic activities in several African countries to be as high as 41 percent of nonagricultural GDP (Becker 2004:20). According to Nigeria's National Bureau of Statistics, the informal sector in Lagos was valued at around $7 billion in 2016, employing an estimated 5.5 million people (Rotinwa 2018). In some cases, the informal sector provides an important "safety net" for the many Africans who use it to supplement their formal economic activity. The informal sector is also particularly successful at absorbing "surplus" labor, people who cannot find formal employment. Up to 80 percent of nonagricultural employment (92 percent for women) might take place in the informal sector (ILO 2002). While the informal sector provides employment and survival opportunities for the economically most vulnerable individuals, it also deprives governments of revenues, prevents the rise of a relationship of accountability between government and economic actors, and shields a large part of output and exchange from policymaking, rendering the latter more complicated and adding to its own self-inflicted woes, to which we now turn.

The Weight of Bad Policies

Africa suffers from structural disadvantages within the global economy and other constraints on development, but the economic policies of its governments since independence have often compounded rather than solved these problems. One occasionally gets the impression that the welfare of citizens, growth, and the delivery of public services have been among the least-important concerns of some African governments. In fact, African governments have increasingly delegated a great part of policy and service delivery to other actors, mainly donors, international organizations, and nongovernmental organizations. And when policy is made, whether by local elites, donors, or both together, it has a long record of ineffectiveness.

The economic policies of the 1960s and 1970s can be best character-ized as involving a fair amount of economic engineering, increasing the size and scope of government involvement in the economy, promoting industrialization, and introducing numerous distortions with the aim of harnessing the behavior of individual producers and consumers into state-designed plans. Nationalization of foreign companies, most of which were involved in mineral extraction, became near-universal (Quinn 2002). Botswana's diamond industry might have been the only case where majority foreign ownership (of South Africa's De Beers) was maintained. Agricultural production was redesigned from its traditional structure of small household producers. Everywhere, monopolistic pub-lic marketing boards, often inherited from colonial days, purchased the entire production of cash crops at state-established fixed prices, system-atically appropriating the agricultural surplus, initially with the declared intent to reinvest it in industry. State farms were also established and, in some cases, as in Tanzania, entire villages were forced to relocate into larger units in the name of economic efficiency (Hyden 1980). In addi-tion to their interventions in production, governments recruited heavily to bolster their administrative ranks, and the public sector rapidly became dominant. In many African countries, until the 1980s, university graduates were guaranteed public employment upon graduation.

To be fair, there was a relatively broad consensus among donors and African governments on the need for these policies. Keynesianism, with its call for active management of the economy by the public sector, was in vogue. Although there were early dissenting voices criticizing the excesses of government intervention and the penalization of agriculture (Dumont 1966), many believed that shortcuts to industrialization and development could be engineered with forceful public intervention in markets. That African governments were particularly weak and still ill-equipped in terms of human capital to carry these reforms through, and that such policies harmed the most productive sector of their economies—agriculture—were not seen as impediments by most. Moreover, socialism was a popular ideology in many African countries at the time, from the Afro-Marxism of the likes of Angola, Congo-Brazzaville, Guinea, and Mozambique (Ottaway and Ottaway 1986) to the milder "African social-ism" of rulers such as Julius Nyerere in Tanzania and Léopold Senghor in Senegal, and it was encouraged through the patronage that the Soviet Union then provided to several African regimes. In this ideological context, grand schemes of state control were a common blueprint, for the state was believed to be more capable of producing desirable social outcomes than were markets (see Scott 1999). Even those who were committed to a more capitalist path favored "state capitalism," a hybrid system of private property with a large or dominant state sector.

Interventionist policies and state control of the economy were also logical economic manifestations of neopatrimonialism. Neopatrimonial regimes are endlessly hungry for cash that can accrue to those in positions of political or administrative authority and their clients, and willing to tax their productive sectors in order to appropriate it. Given the paucity of income taxes per se in Africa's low-income environments (Moore, Prichard, and Fjeldstad 2018), the most common mechanism for the transfer of revenues to the government is the creation of rents (artificially generated profits, which accrue to their beneficiaries without any compensating productive activity). In Africa, governments produce rents by taking over sectors of the economy, introducing regulatory distortions in production and exchange, manipulating prices and exchange rates, and the like.[13] There was thus, from the beginning, a remarkable coincidence between the financial needs of neopatrimonialism and the economic and ideological commitments of many African countries. No doubt many governments were genuinely interested, at least at first, in engineering the transformation of their economies toward development. But the necessities of buying allegiance and staying in power hijacked these policies and soon led to another type of development: that of vested interests among politicians, bureaucrats, and state-dependent economic actors, who demanded the continuation of these policies, irrespective of their negative economic impact.

Robert Bates (1981) addresses the uses of economic policies for political objectives in Africa. He asks what explains the choice of ineffective agricultural policies (in the sense that they reduce output) by African governments. Bates begins his inquiry by noticing that African governments have inherited public marketing boards from the colonial era, the purpose of which, besides price stabilization, is to pay farmers below-world-market prices for their commodities and appropriate the difference to finance the state, industrialization, and bureaucracies. As the revenue imperative of the independent governments increased under pressure from redistribution from multiple constituencies, governments soon instructed these boards to make concessionary loans to them, few of which were repaid, and bureaucracies began appropriating a larger and larger share of these funds for their staff and their perks and to feed corruption (Bates 1981:20–26).

While governments were able to relatively easily extract the agricultural surplus of a disorganized, heterogeneous, and largely uneducated rural class, they had to be more careful about pleasing their urban constituencies, who were more likely to unionize, demonstrate, or even launch coups.[14] Thus African governments typically subsidized food, either by operating their marketing boards at a loss or by manipulating exchange rates to undervalue the price of food imports, with the consequence that the relative price of food exports rose, further penalizing farmers because this reduced the competitiveness of their products. Farmers responded to these policies by "using the market against the state" (Bates 1981:87). Farmers decreased quantities produced, altered their production mix, and used the labor market and migrated. While the actions of the farmers failed to challenge the system, those who benefited from these policies organized to keep them in place, with the result that they were soon rather unshakable: "the mix of policies chosen to secure economic development has permitted the entrenchment of enormously powerful private interests, and . . . this fact has become an important source of the durability of policy commitments" (97). The rents, appropriated by bureaucrats for themselves or distributed for political support, feed the creation and reproduction of clientelistic networks.

While Bates focuses on agriculture, the mechanisms, distortions, and rents he identifies also took place in other sectors of African economies. Neopatrimonialism relies indeed on the creation and maintenance of rents, such as those derived from trade restrictions, and a preference for distribution over long-term investments. More generally, neopatrimonial policies led to widespread distortions in market mechanisms in order to allocate resources along political rather than economic criteria. As Richard Sandbrook (1986:321) put it, "the political requirements of regime and personal survival take precedence over and contradict the economic policies and practices needed to promote sustained economic expansion." Trade, foreign exchange, and price distortions were typical areas of predation. Neopatrimonial policies also favor current government consumption at the expense of investments in physical and human capital, which have few, if any, short-term returns to the ruling elite in terms of power.

As a result, the policy performance of neopatrimonial African states tends to be systematically worse than that of other developing countries, in the sense that African states are more likely to choose policies that retard growth (World Bank 1981:4; Ndulu and van de Walle 1996:6; Englebert 2000a; Moss 2011:98–100). In the first three decades of independence, African governments spent more on items such as wages and their own consumption as a proportion of their economies than did governments of other developing countries. They invested less in infrastructure and education (they kept children in school only about half as long as did other developing countries), the benefits of which accrue over the long run and are thus less useful for patrimonial redistribution. They also introduced so many financial distortions (and promoted reckless lending by state-controlled banks) that their banking systems ended up with serious liquidity shortages.

Neopatrimonialism not only biases economic policies away from development but also weakens a country's institutional architecture and undermines the quality of governance. When the political elite purposely keeps institutions weak, when personal rule thwarts checks and balances, when public and private monies are interchangeable, one cannot expect predictable bureaucracies, stable rule of law, or corruption-free governance. It is not surprising therefore that by the 1980s, African countries scored significantly worse than other developing countries on measures of corruption, institutional quality, and overall governance.

For sure, these aggregate measures fail to reveal the variations that existed in policy and institutional performance among African countries. While Ghana, Tanzania, and Uganda were early policy catastrophes, Botswana, Mauritius, and a few others did considerably better. There is an interesting literature on explaining the relative exceptionalism of Botswana (Samatar 1999) and Mauritius (Bräutigam 1999). Nevertheless, their policy performance was still unexceptional by world standards (although Botswana's growth was the fastest in the world from 1966 to 1985) and, as a group, African countries performed significantly worse on average than other regions.

Common across Africa was neopatrimonialism, which "saps the capacity of the state and fosters a climate in which public officials make decisions on short-term political or self aggrandizing grounds and with scant regard to their long-term economic consequences" (Sandbrook 1986:325). Bureaucratic norms are not internalized, and administrative capacity deteriorates. Corruption becomes the accepted norm. Marketing boards exploit farmers to create the necessary resources for the patronage games. Inefficient state-owned enterprises flourish (Herbst 1990a:950–951). As Sandbrook (1986:326) notes, the corrosion of bureaucratic and legal rationality, the misallocation of resources, and the discouragement of investments brought about by political decay fundamentally undermine African economies.

Although it took a while for the consequences of these economic policies to be felt, African governments backed themselves into a corner as the structures of their economies became cumbersome, inefficient, distorted, and eventually largely unresponsive to policymaking (as private economic agents sought to disengage from state predation through informal or subsistence activity). By stifling growth and encouraging profligate spending, neopatrimonialism eventually led to economic decay and crisis. As an economic system, neopatrimonialism contains the seeds of its own demise, and it can only be reproduced over the long run through life support in the form of aid flows or export revenues. Fed in part by demand for Africa's primary commodities, growth remained respectable across the continent until the mid-1970s. But when the oil crises of 1974 and 1979 hit, African economies were unable to adapt and went into freefall. For the 1980s alone, Africa's real per capita GDP contracted by about 0.7 percent per year. Altogether, despite growth earlier in the period, per capita GDP in Africa rose at an annual rate of less than 1 percent for the first three decades of independence, as against 2.3 percent for other developing countries (a result partly due to Africa's faster rate of population growth). Comparative studies of economic growth around the developing world have since amply demonstrated the critical negative role of policies and governance in Africa's slow growth. Jeffrey Sachs and Andrew Warner (1997) have shown the effects on African growth of lack of openness to trade, excess government spending, and poor institutional quality, while Robert Barro (1997) has singled out the importance of the ratio of government consumption to GDP in explaining African economic performance. Neopatrimonial policies embodied the characteristics identified by these economists as distinguishing African economic performance from that of other regions.

The Fiscal Pressures of Neopatrimonialism, Structural Adjustment, and External Debt

Compounded with the external shocks of the 1970s, neopatrimonialism brought many African economies to near-bankruptcy by the early 1980s. Interestingly, this unprecedented economic crisis provoked two types of responses. Among Africans, some were unwilling to challenge the centrality of the state in their economies and saw greater state intervention as part of the solution. Particularly, the Organization of African Unity proposed the Lagos Plan of Action in 1980, which called for an expansion and strengthening of state institutions to drive development. External donors, riding the surging wave of neoliberalism in the early 1980s in the Western world, called for a radical curtailing of state intervention in the economy. Particularly influential in this respect was the so-called Berg Report, a World Bank publication authored by Eliot Berg titled *Accelerated Development in Sub-Saharan Africa: An Agenda for Action* (World Bank 1981). It called for freer trade, privatization of state enterprises, liberalization of agricultural producer prices, and the jettisoning of agricultural subsidies, among other policy reforms. As C. S. Whitaker

(1991:341) noted, "from a historical African perspective, the Berg Report represented a radical reformulation of the role of the state, while the Lagos Plan was a call to perpetuate the status quo." Yet the Berg Report ignored the question of political incentives, assuming the benevolence of rulers and their desire to maximize public welfare (342). It did not question the root of the existing economic distortions. This lack of political economy was common in most of the World Bank's documents until the 1990s and would plague its policies in Africa over the decade.

As the OAU had no money to lend, it was the World Bank's agenda that set the tone for policy reform in Africa. The Lagos Plan was relegated to a historical footnote, while the Berg Report became the template for the African development agenda for years to come. Desperate for loans to maintain their systems afloat, African governments were indeed largely squeezed out of commercial lending and had to rely on the World Bank, and to a lesser degree on its sibling institution, the International Monetary Fund, for financing.[15] In order to cope with what it saw as the multiple structural impediments to growth of African economies (and of other economies around the world in similar situations), the World Bank designed packages of reforms that became known as structural adjustment programs (SAPs). In exchange for committing to adopt these reforms, African governments became eligible for structural adjustment loans (SALs). The loans, in baskets of foreign currencies, could be used by recipient countries any way they wished, although the policy parameters of the SAPs theoretically limited the uses to which these funds could be put. In general, they went to pay for imports and for the servicing of debt payments. The underlying idea was to facilitate the adoption of reforms by African governments through the availability of cash, to rescue them from their immediate bankruptcy in exchange for their adoption of the neoliberal policy steps seen as necessary for preventing a return to the same situation again.

Typical SAP policies or conditions of the loans (hence the expression "conditional lending") almost systematically included a currency devaluation to make imports more expensive and exports more competitive, with the aim of undermining implicit subsidies to urban consumers and encouraging agricultural production for export; privatization or liquidation of state companies to reduce opportunities for rents and public employment, which were large drains on state budgets; trade liberalization in the form of reduction of tariffs and quotas, also as a means to derive growth benefits from trade, to reduce the rents from trade controls, and to increase the efficiency of whatever little domestic industry existed by exposing it to international competition; reduction of budget deficits (typically by cutting social spending and laying off civil servants) to decrease the relative size of governments in the economy and their indebtedness; and finally, reduction of the growth in money supply (a result of the propensity to use domestic credit to fund government), with the goal of taming inflation.

From a political point of view, all these policies shared the property of undermining the foundation of neopatrimonialism (Herbst 1990a). This was not the explicit goal of the World Bank, for little if any political analysis had gone into the elaboration of these programs. The World Bank saw "too much state" and too many distortions, and sought to reduce both. It did not intentionally seek then to fundamentally restructure the African state, only to shrink it. But in fact, SAPs did represent a major challenge to the way African politics functioned. As a result, African governments found themselves in a peculiar situation, willing to agree to stringent and sometimes politically suicidal conditions for the associated cash, but much less willing to actually implement the required policies. What resulted from this contradiction became known as the "partial reform syndrome" (van de Walle 2001:60–63). African governments committed to adjustment; signed the necessary documents and received the first installments of their loans; adopted some of the easier conditions, such as privatizing state enterprises (often purchased at steep discounts by regime insiders) and implementing some mild devaluation; and then stalled (Hutchful 2002). Other conditions were either adopted in much reduced form after considerable foot-dragging or bypassed altogether. In Christopher Clapham's (1996:177) words, African governments were trying to get "as much aid as possible . . . while delivering as little policy reform as possible in exchange." And when people took to the streets to complain about reduced subsidies or rising import prices, governments said their hands were tied and that the World Bank and the IMF had forced them to adopt these policies.

Driven by their own internal logic and agendas, the World Bank and other foreign donors would often continue allocating funds to programs that were clear failures and to African governments that proved unable or unwilling to implement serious reforms. Sometimes, at least for bilateral donors, their motivation was political (such as providing assistance to valued but corrupt Cold War allies). At other times, it was ideological (such as steadfastly maintaining an adherence to economic policies despite their obvious failures). But a blinding bureaucratic mentality also prevailed among policymakers (Easterly 2002; Calderisi 2006). Moreover, even the weakest of African governments had some leverage toward the World Bank and other donors (Mosley, Harrigan, and Toye 1995; Clapham

1996:173–176). Bank representatives, under significant internal pressure to lend, visited recipient countries at regular intervals to monitor their progress. When confronted with implementation shortcomings, they were often unwilling to contemplate program failure. Instead, they tended to negotiate reduced conditions and extended the time frame of the loans, releasing additional funds to ease the burden of adjustment. In many cases, even in the rare instances when noncompliance led to program suspension, new loans were extended (the typical duration of a structural adjustment loan was eighteen months). Some countries ended up with a dozen or more successive SALs. Senegal had fifteen (van de Walle 2001:2). On average, probably fewer than 50 percent of the loan conditions were implemented (Killick 1998; van de Walle 2001:67). Loan after loan, program after program, contained similar if not identical conditions. Todd Moss (2011:115) recalls how the Kenyan government committed to privatizing the management of Kenya Railways on twenty different occasions, without ever actually doing so. Similarly, despite repeated commitments, it took the Zambian government twenty years to privatize Zambia Copper and Cobalt Mining. Adjustment programs became the default policy condition of African governments. Their economies were perpetually adjusting, but never quite adjusted.

With African per capita growth negative throughout the 1980s, the worst since independence, it became progressively clear to everyone that SAPs were not delivering on their promise of accelerated African development. As Nicolas van de Walle (2001:3), probably the most careful observer and analyst of this period in Africa's political economy, argues at the beginning of his seminal book *African Economies and the Politics of Permanent Crisis:* "At the dawn of the twenty-first century, most of sub-Saharan Africa remain[ed] mired in economic crisis despite two decades of donor-sponsored reform efforts." Critics of the World Bank and IMF questioned the underlying ideological assumptions underpinning the SAP policies, often challenging the liberal economic premises behind those policies and, in some cases, suggesting that SAP policies were economic "poison" for African societies, increasing the continent's dependence and leaving the poor even more vulnerable (see Danaher 1999; Easterly 2007; Woods 2007). Adjustment supporters blamed African governments for the failure of the programs, calling attention to the poor degree of implementation of most (e.g., World Bank 1994). But the World Bank was an accomplice in this implementation failure, as conditionality did not function properly and enabled African governments to get away with insincere reform. In retrospect, one of the most startling features of the adjustment decade is that it allowed African neopatrimonialism to survive by keeping it on life support while failing to engineer its reform (van de Walle 2001).

If one compares the policy performance of African countries at the onset of the 1980s with that of a decade later, there is indeed only limited evidence of a changed policy environment. There was progress on inflation and on exchange rates, devalued everywhere except in the former French colonies of the franc zone, which had to wait until 1994 to see their fixed peg to the French franc reduced by 50 percent. There was also significant price liberalization, deregulation, and reduction of the power of agricultural marketing boards. But there was much less progress on trade liberalization, privatization of significant state enterprises, and civil sector reform, with the number of civil servants actually increasing in many countries. Moreover, government consumption also increased, from 15 percent to 17.5 percent of GDP (excluding South Africa), by 1990.[16] So did spending on wages and salaries (compounded by the frequent accumulation of salary arrears for civil servants), interest payments, and overall subsidies and transfers. The size of militaries and of government cabinets, both a function of patronage, also increased in the 1980s, as did the size of legislatures, the number of presidential commissions, and the size of presidential slush funds. On the other hand, government capital expenditures decreased. As van de Walle (2001:96) put it, "most African states . . . responded to the crisis by looking out for themselves. . . . [A] common state response to economic collapse [was] to protect its own position and to lessen instead its developmental ambitions."

During the 1980s, the African state largely withdrew from the business of development, as a result of both the economic crisis of neopatrimonialism and the donor-mandated adjustments. Unwilling to adopt policies that would bring about their own downfall, African rulers selectively implemented adjustment programs in a manner that preserved essential features of the neopatrimonial system, while largely sacrificing the interests of their population. When stalling was no longer possible, they "instrumentalized the reform process" (van de Walle 2001:159). They recentralized their personal authority by taking direct control of some of the reforms and bypassing their own administrations, and they largely withdrew from development and social services, delegating these sectors to donors and NGOs (159–166). A considerable body of literature blames the World Bank for decreases in health and education services in Africa (e.g., Cornia, Jolly, and Stewart 1989; Mkandawire and Olukoshi 1995; Mohan et al. 2000; Riddell 1992). Yet it is worth noting that African governments were complicit in these decreases, as they often willingly sacrificed these sectors at the expense of others.

In retrospect, the greatest change to African economies brought about by the adjustment period was a formidable increase in levels of foreign indebtedness (ironically the exact opposite of adjustment's intended results). As the Bank and the IMF made large loan packages available without succeeding in jump-starting growth, African economies were left with the burden of unprecedented debt and few means to service their obligations. Moreover, every time the Bank and the IMF approved a new adjustment program, other donors plunged in too with policy support of their own, with a resulting multiplier effect on the flow of funds to African countries. Some bilateral donors extended grants, but funds from the Bank and the IMF were not gifts. They had to be paid back, with interest. And their servicing could not be rescheduled. As Figure 6.2 illustrates, the total stock of external debt for sub-Saharan Africa (excluding South Africa) rose from some 20 percent of gross national income (GNI) in the 1970s to above 100 percent in the 1990s (read on for the story of the subsequent decline).[17] According to Oxfam (1995), sub-Saharan African countries transferred $13.4 billion annually to external creditors from 1990 to 1993, or four times as much as they spent on health services and education combined.

Throughout the 1980s and 1990s, many African countries became progressively unable to service their debt. By 2001, the total debt of sub-Saharan African countries reached a staggering $209 billion. In that year, those countries borrowed $11.4 billion, but paid $14.5 billion in debt service—$9.8 billion as principal repayment and $4.7 billion as interest—resulting in a negative "net transfer" of $3.1 billion. The African debt crisis occurred later than the Latin American one (which had unfolded in the early 1980s) because most African economies were significantly less exposed to commercial loans and therefore remained more shielded from the rise in interest rates of the early 1980s (although several of them did start getting into trouble around that time). World Bank loans to low-income African countries were highly concessional. They had low, fixed interest rates (often negative in real terms) and maturities of forty years with ten-year grace periods. Middle-income African countries faced higher interest rates but these too were fixed with long maturities. Nevertheless, despite these concessions, the volume of loans accumulated to such a degree that by the late 1980s it suffocated African economies. What little increased export revenues accrued from reform seemed to go to debt payments, and more and more of the new loans were spent on paying the old ones.

The initial donor reaction was timid, at best. Some bilateral donors forgave African countries chunks of debt, but the bulk of multilateral

Figure 6.2 Africa's External Debt, 1970–2017 (constant 2010 US$)

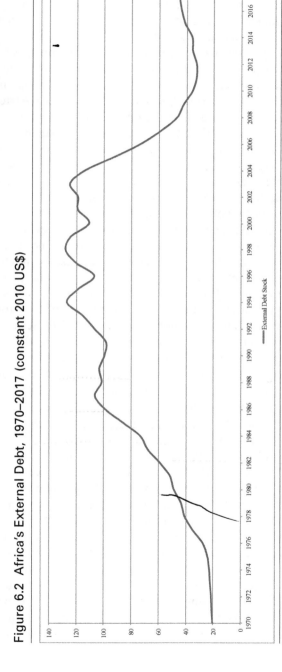

Source: World Bank, *World Development Indicators*, http://data.worldbank.org/indicator (accessed December 2018).
Note: Unweighted average.

obligations were not negotiable. Until recently, a condition for borrowing from the World Bank and the IMF was the agreement to treat obligations to these organizations as priority debt that could be neither forgiven nor rescheduled. Instead, the Bank tried to ease the burden of debt on African countries by organizing roundtables for governments that were making progress on the reform front, at which other donors were encouraged to forgive or reschedule their loans. These "Paris Group" meetings of sovereign creditors occurred frequently and tweaked African debt obligations in such a manner that default was often (but not always) avoided and the system could go on, with the full payment of African debt pushed forward into a distant and largely hypothetical future.

The reality of Bank-sponsored rescheduling agreements is that they managed the African debt crisis without resolving it at all. Just as it had become common practice for African governments to borrow one loan after another, it became common practice to engage in one rescheduling after another. Most African countries went through several of them, sometimes year after year, while their debt service did not appreciably shrink. This meant that African regimes were able to meet their obligations to their creditors, but often at the expense of domestic spending and investment. According to Thomas Callaghy (1987a:158), debt service in Congo (then Zaire) in 1985 amounted to 56 percent of its budget. Not surprisingly, governments so indebted often failed to actually reimburse all of their loans, even after rescheduling. Instead, they accumulated arrears (in other words, they were late with their payments or partially defaulted on them). Arrears represented implicit additional debt rescheduling for many African governments, but they came at a high cost, because arrears were typically capitalized (added to the principal of debt, and thus liable to interest) and often reduced the eligibility of the government to borrow more from the same creditor.

It took until the mid-1990s for Africa's debt crisis to reach its peak and become the object of some concerted solution, a topic we return to later in this chapter. Until then, the increased significance of foreign aid in African economies and their related increased dependence on debt and donor financing transformed both the relations of African countries with the rest of the world and their own domestic functioning. The politics of aid and debt created a regime of relations between African and donor countries characterized by the incessant pursuit of foreign exchange by African governments. While relatively little policymaking and effective administration took place in African governments, a lot of fundraising did. Presidents and ministers traveled the world begging for money, debt rescheduling, and debt relief. Callaghy

(1987a:148) stresses how foreign relations of African states during the 1980s were consumed with "wrestling with the burdens of debt service and the rigors of rescheduling" and with endless negotiations. Few projects took place without foreign financing, and budgets were largely conditioned by expected aid flows. Rich countries, in turn, acted almost only as "donors," which, incidentally, largely reproduced the African domestic relation of patronage in international relations (see Clapham 1996, as well as our discussion in Chapter 8).

While securing and managing the flow of aid and repayments absorbed the energies of African governments, little was left for internal purposes, and the domestic management and ownership of the process were at best haphazard. Even with willing governments, which was rarely the case, conditionality was difficult to implement and heavily taxed the thin layer of human capital of African administrations. As Callaghy (1987a:152) wrote, "African debt use and management capabilities [were] on average the worst in the world." One of the authors of this book, who worked as a junior consultant at the World Bank in the early 1990s, remembers being tasked with helping the government of Guinea-Bissau identify its stock of debt and servicing obligations in view of facilitating negotiations for a rescheduling. At the far end of the finance ministry, in a decrepit colonial building, after a maze of hallways, this consultant found a windowless out-of-the-way office where two well-intentioned civil servants sat somewhat idly facing tall stacks of loan documents (some from countries no longer in existence, such as East Germany), unable to process them for lack of computers, lack of knowledge of actual payments by each ministry, and sheer insufficiency of human resources. The truth was, Guinea-Bissau did not know the total amount of its debt and was unable to budget future payments appropriately. Debt was central to relations between African states and donors, but weak African states had little internal control or even grasp of the extent of their obligations or how to manage them.

The Governance Agenda and the Rise of Political Conditionalities

It took a while but the World Bank and other donors eventually came to realize the magnitude of the obstacles in their path and the complexity of Africa's political economy (Husain and Faruqee 1993; World Bank 1994, 2001). Without fanfare, the Bank began in the early 1990s a process of progressive transformation of the adjustment framework, which put greater emphasis on the institutional context of policies. Coincidentally, the Cold War ended at around the same time and led Western donors to reconsider their relation with African countries and the type of regimes they were supporting. The Bank's new focus produced an emphasis on the role of governance in Africa's economic development, one that paralleled the new interest of donors in promoting democracy and imposing political conditionality for their aid to African countries.

The Bank's disengagement from SAPs in Africa was progressive and partial. At first, it maintained these programs while also developing sectoral adjustment programs, which sought to be less ambitious by tackling distortions and inefficiencies in specific sectors of the economy, like agriculture, education, and energy. Simultaneously, however, an increasing number of Bank staff began to recognize the necessity of considering the broader social and political environment of African economic policies. It was no longer just a matter of less state, but of better state. To some extent, the previous failures of SAPs were an important impetus in generating new thinking on these issues at the Bank. But this evolution also followed new developments in scholarship and, particularly, the rising influence of "new institutional economics," which, while it does not challenge the neoclassical and market foundations of mainstream economics, stresses the importance of institutional factors, such as property rights, norms, and bureaucratic quality, in overall economic development. Simultaneously, Africanist scholars, inspired by the social mobilizations that led to the downfall of authoritarian regimes in Eastern Europe, began placing increasing emphasis on the role of civil society in African politics (see Chapter 3). This development too affected the Bank, where some began thinking that greater accountability of African governments might lead to a better institutional environment for economic policy.

This is how the notion of governance—the "manner in which power is exercised in the management of a country's economic and social resources for development" (World Bank 1992:1)—became a central component of development policy for the World Bank and most other donors. In some ways, the Bank had realized that the success of SAPs had been hindered by the nature of African politics, but its own statutes prevented it from meddling with the politics of member states. Article IV of the Bank's Articles of Agreement, its founding treaty, states that "the Bank and its officers shall not interfere in the political affairs of any member; nor shall they be influenced in their decisions by the political character of the member or members concerned. Only economic considerations shall be relevant to their decisions." Yet the governance discourse allowed the Bank to push its conditionality beyond economic policy and into the realms of institutions without explicitly engaging in politics. Some observed that the World Bank agenda became more encompassing, politicized, and intrusive, reconstructing a wide-range of economic, political, and social practices according to the logic of neoliberalism (Pereira 2016).

The Bank's first explicit foray into governance came in one of its regular reports on African economic performance, this one titled *Sub-Saharan Africa: From Crisis to Sustainable Growth—A Long-Term Perspective Study* (1989). Many observers rapidly remarked on its change of tone from previous publications, including sentences such as "history suggests that political legitimacy and consensus are a precondition for sustainable development" and "underlying the litany of Africa's development problems is a crisis of governance" (60). A subsequent report (World Bank 1992) focused explicitly on issues of accountability and the rule of law.

The emphasis on governance did not immediately lead to new policy instruments, but it did promote a switch beyond market mechanisms and merely "getting prices right." Reforms of the civil service sector took center stage, and the fight against corruption gained importance. The Bank thus started financing projects to streamline public service, increase its accountability, and improve the training and recruitment of civil servants. Some loans went to specific branches of administration. For example, the Bank financed projects to improve the professionalism of tax and customs agencies and shield them from the social pressures it identified as being at the root of inefficiencies, through training, better salaries, and other incentives.

The governance agenda would eventually lead to more significant transformations in the relationship between the Bank and African aid recipients. First, the Bank began measuring and tracking the governance performance of member states (this was not a uniquely African focus). Starting in 1996, it released semiannual (and later annual) indicators of accountability, government effectiveness, regulatory quality, rule of law, and control of corruption, among other factors (Kaufman, Kraai, and Mastruzzi 2010). Second, these indicators became central in new mechanisms of conditionality, as access to Bank resources was increasingly predicated upon improvements in governance performance. For example, approval of poverty reduction strategy papers (PRSPs), by and large the successor of structural adjustment programs after 1999, required the adoption of explicit mechanisms of accountability and "ownership" of reforms, including popular consultations. Similarly, since the mid-1990s, eligibility for debt forgiveness has been based on governance conditionality, particularly on country performance on a set of variables, aggregated in a Country Policy and Institutional Assessment (CPIA), including measures of regulatory environment, property rights, rule of law, transparency, accountability, and corruption.

This new conditionality coincided with the rise of bilateral political conditionality after 1990. Whereas the nature of an African political regime had little bearing on levels of aid before 1990, bilateral aid became increasingly tied to democratization afterward. Democratic conditionality is different from governance conditionality, as the latter can accommodate multiple regime types. Their joint development, however, led to a radical transformation of the aid environment for African countries, and to significantly more difficult access to aid resources than before. As a result, there was a dramatic decrease in aid to Africa, in terms of percentage of GNI, in the 1990s (it is also true, however, that the rise of conflict on the continent in that period reduced effective opportunities for aid-giving).

It is difficult to assess the success of donor efforts to reform African governance. As with the policy conditionality of SAPs, however, the capacity of weak African states to resist attempts by outsiders to change them is debatable. Although there has been a significant, albeit limited, average shift of the continent toward more democratic regimes, there is no evidence of similar general improvements in governance. For sure, some countries, such as Ghana and Rwanda, have made much progress in the transparency, predictability, and rule-based nature of their economic governance, but each such success seems to be matched by at least one opposite case of significant worsening, such as Gambia or Zimbabwe. For the continent as a whole, the governance picture remains one of stagnant underperformance. As Figure 6.3 illustrates, there has been no visible average improvement in African governance since the mid-1980s.

To some extent, although scholarship is not as developed in this respect as it is in the fate of adjustment programs, governance conditionality is probably as hard to implement as policy conditionality. Here too, the conditions go to the core of regime survival and are likely to be opposed, shirked, and manipulated by incumbent regimes. Although the World Bank and other donors realized that "bad" policies were rooted in a specific institutional and political logic, they did not necessarily have the tools to affect or undermine this logic despite confronting it more explicitly than before. As with policies, "bad governance" is partly the outcome of the neopatrimonial equilibrium of African politics. It is not so much an affliction of African systems or rule as an intrinsic part of these systems. As with economic policies, therefore, attempts at improving African governance undermined the political foundations of African regimes and met with resistance (Whitaker 1991:345). Governments set up anticorruption commissions and the like to please donors, but these typically accomplished little (see Wrong 2010 for the vividly illustrated case of Kenya). Similarly, rule of law was superficially improved with the passing of investment codes, land titling, and other self-restraining legal devices, but in practice this new legal environment could still easily be bypassed when necessary by actors connected to the state. Moreover, the willingness of donors to see African governance become more accountable to social forces suffered from the intrinsic contradiction that social relations based on patronage might not always actually be propitious to good governance (Williams and Young 1994).

On the donors' side, many of the earlier contradictions also endured. The World Bank remained under considerable pressure to lend funds irrespective of the actual performance of recipients, largely devaluing in practice the effectiveness of conditionality. Often it endorsed what was little more than lip service by African governments. Reviewing the PRSP for Ghana, Lindsay Whitfield (2005:651) makes clear that government ministries cared little about the intended participatory process, and that civil society participation amounted to little more than a one-day "public hearing with a cross section of society present, plus donors." She concludes that "the methods adopted to operationalise participation are better

Figure 6.3 African Governance Indicators, 1985–2017

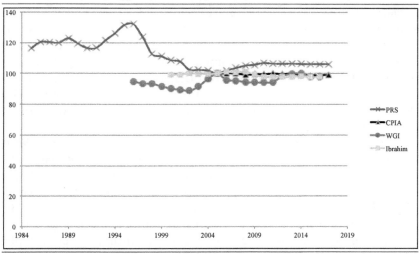

Sources: CPIA data from World Bank, World Development Indicators, http://data .worldbank.org/indicator (accessed July 2018); WGI data from www.govindicators.org (accessed July 2018); Ibrahim data from http://www.mo.ibrahim.foundation/iiag, (accessed August 2018); PRS data purchased from Political Risk Service by the authors.

Notes: All indicators have been rescaled to equal 100 in 2005. PRS = Political Risk Service, CPIA = Country Policy and Institutional Assessment, WGI = World Governance Indicators, Ibrahim = Mo Ibrahim Index.

understood within the larger context of existing practices that masquerade under the labels of participation and consultation, policy forums and dialogues" (653). For their part, bilateral donors are often willing to look the other way when their strategic interests compete with their official stance on governance, further reducing the effectiveness of reform attempts.

Altogether it comes as little surprise that the governance agenda did not yield greater aggregate improvements in the way African economies are managed. Being vaguer than the earlier policy reform agenda, its implementation was also looser. Donor commitment to good governance in Africa wavers as other priorities compete. African governments, for their part, largely pay little more than lip service to reforms that would threaten their political survival.

The Great Aid Debate

Although African policy and governance reform remained lukewarm, the continent's continued economic crisis, compounded by the spread of conflict and an increasing number of "failed states" (see Chapter 7), led donors to renew and enhance their commitment to African development from the late 1990s onward and to commit increasingly large amount of aid to it, reversing the trend that had unfolded earlier in the decade. The lobbying efforts of Western-based NGOs, particularly on matters of debt forgiveness, were influential in this respect, as was the favorable economic climate in the wake of sustained expansion among donor economies. During this time, scholars also engaged in what some dubbed the "Great Foreign Aid Debate," focused on the efficacy of development aid, with the *New York Times* characterizing it as a "ferocious intellectual debate" (18 April 2010; for a critical appraisal of this "debate," see Engel 2014).

A concerted effort for debt reduction and forgiveness among Western civil society activists led the march toward the post-1990s "big push" in aid. While supporters of the World Bank continued to criticize African regimes for failing to adequately implement the policy reforms they considered necessary to achieve development, others pointed out that the foreign donors were often complicit in providing assistance to corrupt African regimes that absconded with the development aid. For example, at the end of Mobutu Sese Seko's thirty-two-year reign in Congo/Zaire, the country's foreign debt in 1997 was around $14 billion, while it was estimated that Mobutu and his allies had pocketed between $4 billion and $10 billion of the country's wealth, pillaging the government's operating budget, its mineral export revenues, and much of its development assistance (Ndikumana and Boyce 1998). Despite ample evidence that foreign aid was not being used for legitimate purposes, foreign creditors continued to provide Mobutu and other corrupt regimes with large loans. Thus, critics pointed out that African debt was "odious," having not been incurred for the benefit of the general people, but contracted without their consent by corrupt African regimes and complicit foreign creditors (see Danaher 1999; Woods 2007). Others also noted that Africa's debt was exacerbated by existing terms of trade, characterized by continuing Western agricultural subsidies and trade barriers that thwarted the continent's economic development (see Oxfam 2003; Ritchie et al. 2003; Watkins and von Braun 2002).

Concerned with increasing levels of foreign debt in the wake of adjustment programs, and with the unwillingness of the World Bank and the IMF to reschedule or forgive their own loans, organizations such as Jubilee 2000, religious groups, and bilateral donors increased pressure on the Bretton Woods organizations to provide more systematic relief. Attention was focused on the so-called heavily indebted poor countries (HIPCs), forty-one countries (thirty-four of which were from sub-Saharan Africa) whose median debt-to-exports ratio was estimated to be around 340 percent. HIPC governments owed private creditors 17 percent of their debt, official bilateral ones 64 percent, and multilaterals 19 percent (Claessens et al. 1997). The HIPC initiative was made possible after member states found new ways to back up the creditworthiness of the World Bank and the IMF, which allowed them to face default from their borrowers (Callaghy 2009). Originally started in 1996, the HIPC initiative became the first instance of multilateral debt forgiveness and opened the door for the most dramatic reduction in African levels of indebtedness ever (refer to Figure 6.2). To become eligible, a low-income country must first qualify for Paris Club bilateral debt relief, which requires unsustainable debt levels and an approved policy reform package. After this first step, it is allowed to apply for HIPC forgiveness. Here again, the sustainability of debt levels and policy performance are taken into account. Qualified countries first reach a "decision point" at which temporary relief is offered, then, after continued good policy behavior, a "completion point" at which permanent debt relief is offered. In 2005, the level of HIPC debt forgiveness was brought to 100 percent of debts accrued toward the IMF and the World Bank, a development known as the Multilateral Debt Relief Initiative. Eventually, the HIPC initiative wrote off billions of dollars of debt to thirty-six of the poorest countries in the world, of which thirty were African. This led some to observe that "debt is no longer a problem for most [African] countries (at least for now)" (Moss 2011:157, 163).

The shrinking of African debt was an event of historic proportion, greatly changing economic dynamics across the continent and relations between African governments and donors, and possibly having facilitated the region's spurt of growth since 2000. It has freed up large amounts of funds for African governments to allocate to other budget items. From an accounting point of view, it is equivalent to a new flow of aid and, as such, has contributed to the continent-wide increase in aid since the late 1990s that peaked in 2011 but has since been in decline (see Figure 6.4). In addition to debt relief, a broader movement unfolded after 2000, including several Western governments and numerous nonstate activists, to provide substantially higher levels of aid to Africa with the intention of putting an end, once and for all, to enduring economic crisis and poverty on the continent. This was a somewhat unusual effort to the extent that it did not follow in the wake of a catastrophic event, such as a famine, and did not correspond to parallel efforts by African governments. It seemed to derive largely from Western, rather than African, dynamics. The year 2005 was the high point of this movement, and the United Kingdom provided its hub. British prime minister Tony Blair declared 2005 the "Year of Africa" and set up the Commission for Africa in anticipation of the Group of Eight (G8) summit in Gleneagles, Scotland, and the British rotating presidency of the European Union that year. The commission assembled sixteen African and non-African "experts" (including pop singer Bob Geldof and Ethiopian president Meles Zenawi), who produced a report titled *Our Common Interest* (Commission for Africa 2005), the recommendations of which were endorsed and promoted by the Blair government. The report called for a new "compact" between Africans and donors whereby Africans would take greater responsibility for their governance failures while donors would commit to greater assistance. Specifically, the report anticipated a rise in aid to Africa of $25 billion per year as of 2010 (almost a doubling), to be further increased by another $25 billion by 2015 if necessary. Because of its connection to the G8 and Blair's high international profile, the commission's work had an impact well beyond the United Kingdom and contributed to a more favorable climate toward Africa among donors the world over.

The British efforts came in the wake of a new aid initiative in the United States in the form of the Millennium Challenge Corporation (MCC) and its Millennium Challenge Account (MCA). The MCC was set up by the George W. Bush administration as a new aid agency in 2004. Its aid was based on the principle of selectivity: recipient countries must score above the median on a range of governance and policy indicators to become eligible. In addition, they must design specific growth-enhancing or poverty-reducing projects based on national priorities and are responsible for project implementation. While the Millennium Challenge Account

Figure 6.4 Foreign Aid to Africa, 1960–2016

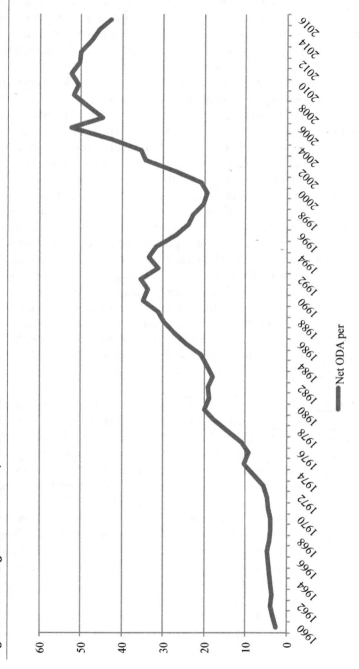

Net ODA per

Source: World Bank, *World Development Indicators*, http://data.worldbank.org/indicator (accessed December 2018).
Note: Unweighted average.

is not uniquely geared toward Africa, the plurality of countries eligible for its grants were African from the beginning. It was part of a broader effort by the United States to increase both volumes and effectiveness of foreign aid, and its funding rose from $650 million in 2004 to $2 billion in 2007.

These government initiatives coincided with a large mobilization of NGOs in the West, and particularly again in the United Kingdom, for intensifying the fight against poverty in the world. Launched in 2003, the "Make Poverty History" campaign was the work of many NGOs, including Oxfam, Action Aid, Christian Aid, and Save the Children (Harrison 2010). A few days before the Gleneagles summit, in 2005, Bob Geldof organized several simultaneous concerts in donor countries, known as Live 8 (he had been involved in concerts—Band Aid and Live Aid—in response to Ethiopian famines in the 1980s). That same year, Jeffrey Sachs released *The End of Poverty,* a book in which he argued that poverty could be eliminated worldwide by 2025 with sufficient aid. Sachs's claims were made particularly popular by the celebrity activism of Bono, another pop music celebrity. These efforts also came in the wake of the adoption of the Millennium Development Goals (MDGs) by the United Nations at its Millennium Summit in 2000. The aims of the MDGs included the eradication of extreme poverty, reductions in child mortality, universal primary education, and curbing diseases, by 2015, through the development of a global partnership between rich and poor countries. Increased aid was a large component of the MDGs, as they were designed in part as a response to declining levels of development assistance in the 1990s.

Not surprisingly, in the wake of all these initiatives, aid flows to Africa significantly increased following their drop in the early 1990s, reaching unprecedented levels ($52.48 per capita in 2011 as against $19.50 in 2000).[18] Including both new disbursements and debt relief, official development assistance (ODA) to Africa in 2011 amounted to $51 billion, out of a total of $136 billion for all developing countries, more than for any other region.[19] Asia came in second at $38 billion, but with almost four times Africa's population. In per capita terms, therefore, Africans receive far more aid than any other region.[20] These aid levels marked a strong progression from historical trends. Using constant 2015 dollars, average annual levels of ODA to sub-Saharan Africa amounted to $10.5 billion in the 1970s, $20.4 billion in the 1980s, $21.8 billion in the 1990s, $31.3 billion in the 2000s, and $43.2 billion from 2010 to 2016. These increases appear linked to public opinion mobilization and scholarly developments in donor countries more than to an improved governance or democratic record among recipient countries.

While volumes of aid increased, the nature of aid to Africa also evolved. The relative failure of adjustment conditionality and the concerns of donors over issues of governance produced a new aid regime beginning in the late 1990s in which selectivity and ownership figure prominently. Selectivity makes aid eligibility conditional upon past or current performance. Rather than giving aid in exchange for future behavior, the new aid regime means to reward those governments that already demonstrate a commitment to better policy. HIPC debt relief was based on selectivity, as it required, in principle, a track record of "good macroeconomic policy management" to reach "completion point" or full forgiveness. Similarly, only countries that score above the median on a set of governance, policy, and social indicators are eligible for Millennium Challenge Account grants. In practice, however, the enforcement of selectivity was haphazard. Countries with only minimal policy improvements received billions of dollars in debt forgiveness, while smaller Millennium Challenge Account grants were made available to countries that might not have met the selection criteria but that nevertheless displayed some improvements in the reference indicators (so-called threshold countries).

In parallel with selectivity, ownership became the dominant demand of donors in terms of substantive recipient government behavior. The idea of ownership of reforms derives from the observation that many African governments only paid lip service to donor demands, agreeing to reforms to obtain financing but subsequently neglecting their commitment. It was the donors' hope that governments that were committed to reforms would achieve a better record of implementation, though there is still concern about the Bank's willingness to look the other way as long as the established poverty reduction strategy papers conform to its views (Booth 2003; Whitfield 2005). Budget support, or the direct transfer of cash payments from donors to the treasuries of recipient countries, is related to the ownership agenda, and became an important dimension of aid to Africa after 2000. As of 2007, some 49 percent of all World Bank lending to African countries, or all of the PRSP crediting, was channeled through budget support (Barkan 2009b). Many European donors also favored this approach, while the United States largely shunned it. Once budget support is disbursed, donors do not have any direct control of where it is allocated, and it funds in part the daily functioning of governments. As an aid method, it is supposed to reduce transaction costs, facilitate coordination between donors and government and among donors, and, most important, favor ownership of reforms and accountability by African governments. By bringing aid under the centralized budget accounts of the government, it seeks to avoid the tendency for aid to develop parallel institutions and structures of governance, and to provide incentives for different ministries to "engage directly in the national budget process" (de Renzio 2009:21).

The record of budget support is still ambiguous. A European Union report found that countries with large budget support performed significantly better on several Millennium Development Goals (Beynon and Dusu 2010). In Tanzania, as reported by Andrew Lawson and colleagues (2005), budget support, which contributed 20 percent of public expenditure at the time, was associated with a large expansion of health and education services, but there were few signs of greater efficiency in public spending, service quality remained doubtful and poverty impact uncertain, and there was only limited democratic accountability in spending. In Uganda, as shown by Joel Barkan (2009b), budget support did not prevent a significant deterioration of governance. Yet although the empirical record remains hard to assess, there has been no shortage of criticism on budget support. Some of the potential flaws of this form of aid will be evident to the readers of this textbook who have familiarized themselves with the functioning of African political systems. Particularly, Tim Unwin (2004) has noted that the opacity and patronage of African politics contradict the expectations of participation and transparency of budget support. As Barkan (2009a:74, 77) argued: "Within broad limits, recipient governments can pretty much do as they choose," with the conclusion that budget support "is a significant provider of political finance."

To a large extent, directly financing the budgets of central governments reinforces the relative position of the state in society and the economy. The desire to promote ownership and capacity naturally leads to strengthening the centrality of the state in social processes. Recent developments in aid thus depart dramatically from the emphasis on "less state" of the 1980s and from the attempts to bypass the state and work with NGOs that were popular in the 1990s. This pattern is reinforced by the focus of several donors on postconflict state reconstruction and on mitigating state fragility (to which we return in Chapter 7). Donors have thus largely made their peace with the African state and have placed most of their development eggs in its basket (Swedlund 2017). As a result, the power of the state and its role as a locus of wealth and income have increased.

It is possible, however, that the developmental capacity of African states has not concurrently improved. As discussed earlier and illustrated by Figure 6.3, there has been no visible improvement on average since the mid-1990s in government effectiveness, bureaucratic red tape, rule of law, or the prevalence of corruption. In short, while they remain at times powerful vis-à-vis their societies, African states show no sign of being any more able to deliver public goods to their people. Paradoxically, there might be a causal link between aid meant to improve governance and lack of progress on the latter. Some have suggested that because African governments have been able to more or less continuously rely on aid, their incentives to develop effective and accountable institutions have been reduced (Moss, Pettersson, and van de Walle 2006; see also Moore 2004).

In addition, the powerful role of aid donors in African administrations and economies has come to represent at times a quasi-takeover of the main functions of governance by external actors, which induces further institutional weakness of the state. Budget support, particularly, has created a more intimate connection between ruling elites and donors, first as they collaborate in drawing and approving policy programs, and second as aid seamlessly transforms into domestic budgetary resources. In practice, this new partnership means that the management of African economies is largely relegated to the circles where donors have influence, if only through the process of selecting worthy recipients (see de Renzio 2009:22). In the long run, this bias might prevent both greater state capacity and greater accountability.

Africa Rising?

Given the ambiguous results of Africa's successive economic reform programs, it is particularly surprising that the continent has recorded its longest and most significant period of growth since 1995, and particularly so after 2000. Since then, Africa's GDP has more than quadrupled, rising from $367 billion in 2000 to $1.65 trillion in 2017. With a real per capita GDP increasing by an annual rate of around 4.8 percent from 2000 to 2017, this dramatic improvement led to a discourse of "Africa Rising" (OECD 2018). For the six-year period between 2002 and 2008, the average growth reached a stunning 5.6 percent, making Africa the second fastest-growing continent in the world. In 2011, *The Economist* called Africa the "hopeful continent," a decade after having dubbed it "hopeless" (2011, 2000a), while others spoke of "Africa's moment" (Severino and Ray 2010) or "Africa's turn" (Miguel 2009; see also World Bank 2010). Anecdotally, over the past two decades, we ourselves have witnessed the growth of high-rises, shopping malls, and an urban middle class from Accra to Kampala. But where did this growth come from? Is it trickling down to average Africans? Does it reflect any structural change in Africa's economies? And what are the odds that it will last?

It is generally argued that Africa's recent economic performance is related to four factors: a boom in commodity prices; increased trade with newly emerging partners, especially China; debt relief; and diversification strategies in some countries (OECD 2018:37). The boom in commodity process is probably the most decisive factor in Africa's economic growth. The price of crude oil, for example, more than tripled over the 2000–2014 period. In January 1999, the price of a barrel of crude oil was below $20, before launching on a fifteen-year run that peaked at $161 per barrel. A similar boom occurred in other commodity markets. During this same time, for example, the price of copper quadrupled. The price of iron ore rose from $12 per metric ton in 2000 to over $180 per metric ton in 2011. The prices of agricultural commodities rose, too, like coffee (tripled) and cocoa (quadrupled). Figure 6.5 provides a snapshot of this trend. Although it uses a price index that averages the value of all African exports, this index correlates largely with the value of the continent's main primary commodities, as the latter still represent 80 percent of all African exports. From a value of 100 in 2000, the index jumped to beyond 550 by 2010, only to take a substantial decline immediately afterward.

For some countries, this commodity boom has triggered unprecedented and potentially transformative rates of growth. Floating on oil, Equatorial Guinea recorded a per capita cumulative growth rate of around 1,200 percent from 1995 to 2014.[21] In other words, the average per capita income in Equatorial Guinea increased more than thirteenfold over this nineteen-year period. The other top oil producers with booming economies include Angola, Sudan, and Chad. But other, non-oil-producing economies have also witnessed highly favorable terms of trade. Mozambique, which exports aluminum, prawns, and cashews, experienced a 1,200 percent rise in export prices from 1995 to 2014; Sierra Leone, highly dependent on diamond exports, witnessed its export value index rise from 100 in 2000 to 14,708 in 2013. During this time, other non-oil-producing countries experienced smaller yet significant surges in export prices (above 300 percent), including Lesotho, Uganda, and Zambia.

The boom in commodity prices was largely driven by worldwide expansion in demand, specifically by Chinese interest in the continent's resources. As we discuss in Chapter 8, China's presence in Africa has greatly increased over the past two decades, and there is significant evidence that Chinese (and to a lesser extent Indian) economic involvement in Africa has positively impacted its overall economic performance. Chinese demand stimulated African output, as did Chinese investments in infrastructure on the continent and the increased emigration of Chinese entrepreneurs to Africa. Figure 6.6 reflects the substantial growth in

281

Figure 6.5 The Value of Africa's Exports, 1980–2016

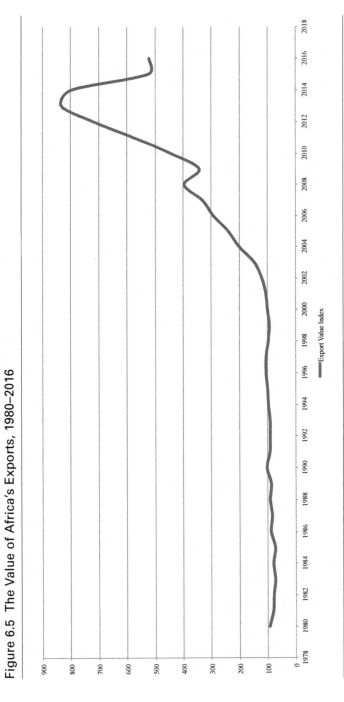

Source: World Bank, *World Development Indicators*, http://data.worldbank.org/indicator (accessed September 2018).

African trade with China—exports and imports combined—soaring from about $10 billion in 2000 to a peak of $215 billion in 2014. Collectively, the European Union has been Africa's largest trading partner, but in terms of individual countries, China surpassed the United States as Africa's largest trading partner in 2009. As of 2017, the World Bank reported that China accounted for around 16 percent of Africa's exports and was the source of over 17 percent of the continent's imports (South Africa is China's largest trading partner, importing over $20 billion in goods from China in 2017). Other leading trading partners include India, the United States, and Germany, but China's engagement with the continent has been regarded as a key driver of its recent economic growth. Africa supplies China with 22 percent of its crude oil (second after the Middle East), with Angola, Congo, and South Sudan the primary African suppliers.[22]

Chinese investment in Africa has been significant as well. From 2003 to 2010, the total amount of Chinese investment in Africa amounted to $11 billion (Weisbrod and Whalley 2011:7–8). China's direct investment in Africa just between 2009 and 2012 grew at an annual rate of over 20 percent. Since 2009, Chinese investment in the continent has consistently been between $2 and $4 billion a year, exceeding US foreign direct investment (FDI) in 2011, 2012, and 2015. Between 2000 and 2015, the Chinese government, banks, and contractors extended around $94.4 billion in loans to African governments, with Angola receiving $19.2 billion during this time. And while the United States announced in 2014 (prior to the election of President Trump) a commitment to invest $14 billion in African aid over the next decade, China committed $175 billion over that same period, underscoring China's increased importance for African economies. There is some debate about the actual impact of China's engagement, with some suggesting that it is overstated. For example, looking at a sample of thirteen African recipient countries from 2005 to 2007, Aaron Weisbrod and John Whalley (2011) found that the contribution of Chinese FDI to growth ranged from close to zero in Botswana, Ghana, and Kenya to 0.4 percent in Niger, 0.5 percent in Sudan, 0.6 percent in Nigeria, and 1.0 percent in Zambia, which does not indicate a strong continent-wide impact. Others have noted that many Chinese investments are linked to mining projects and focus largely on related material and social infrastructure, both of which favor increased productivity but with limited social impact (see Bräutigam 2015; Cheru and Obi 2010; Taylor 2009).

Chinese investments are only a fraction of total FDI to the continent, however. Probably attracted by rising commodity prices, net flows of FDI into Africa soared from $6.9 billion in 2000 to $46.3 billion in

Figure 6.6 Africa's Trade with China, 2000–2016

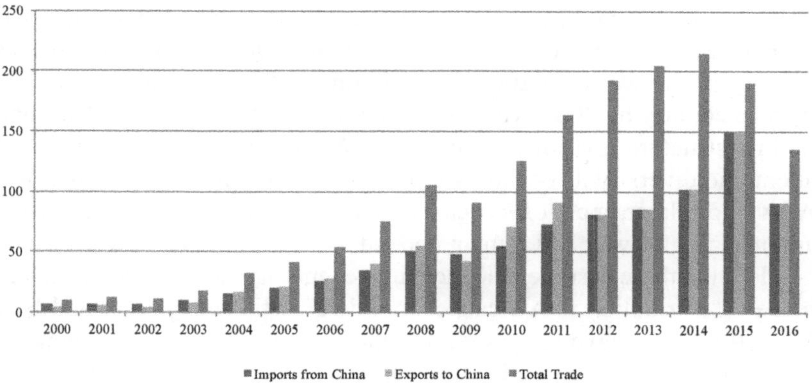

Source: China-Africa Research Initiative, http://www.sais-cari.org/data-china-africa
-trade (accessed November 2018).

2015.[23] Yet the majority of new FDI to Africa went to only a handful of countries, particularly South Africa, Nigeria, Angola, Kenya, and Ghana. Notably, there has also been a marked rise in intra-African FDI, driven largely by South Africa, Kenya, and Nigeria (Ernst and Young 2012:7).

In addition to the commodity price boom and the increased engagement of China, India, and other emerging trading partners, the dramatic reductions in debt levels since 2000 are credited with contributing to Africa's growth. The relief freed many African countries from a crushing debt burden, providing much needed revenue that had long been siphoned out of the domestic economy for debt repayment. The post-2000 big aid push might also partly account for growth, particularly for those countries with fewer expensive commodities. For some small countries, aid levels have made a visible difference in growth. GDP in Cape Verde, which averages $257 of per capita aid, grew by 62 percent between 2000 and 2017. In São Tomé and Príncipe, with $210 per capita in aid, GDP grew by 51 percent. In the Seychelles, with $2,067, GDP grew by 46 percent.

The final factor sometimes cited to explain Africa's recent economic growth are the diversification strategies and technological advances taking place in some countries. Ethiopia is frequently cited as an exemplar of these developments, as its government launched an industrial development strategy focused on promoting agriculture and industrial development, particularly exports in labor-intensive areas such as textiles, garments, leather, sugar, and cement, coupled with a strong public infrastructure drive (OECD 2018:52; Moller and Wacker 2017; Moller 2015). The country enjoyed a GDP growth averaging almost 11 percent between 2004 and 2014, moving from the second poorest country in the world in 2000 to being on track to becoming a middle-income country by 2025. Yet despite the fanfare, the actual levels of public infrastructure investment have been rather low. Moreover, Ethiopia's attempt to diversify its economy represents an exception on the continent. As we note later, most of Africa's economies have failed to diversify in any meaningful way and remain dependent on commodity markets.

Finally, there is some evidence that technological improvements have made a contribution to Africa's economic growth. Jenny Aker and Isaac Mbiti (2010:39) have suggested that the spread of cellular telephones in Africa has reduced transaction costs and facilitated local agricultural markets by efficiently spreading price information. In the first decade of the twenty-first century, the number of cell phone subscribers in Africa rose from 16 million to over 400 million, with 75 percent of Africans holding cell phone subscriptions in 2015. Moreover, the growth in mobile banking in Africa has far outpaced that of the rest of the globe over the past decade, with one in five Africans having a mobile money account in 2017, nearly twice the share in 2014 (World Bank 2018). Mobile money apps, such as M-Pesa and M-Shwari, are radically redefining the ways in which everyday Africans access and utilize money and credit.

While the past two decades have certainly witnessed remarkable levels of growth in Africa, have these developments improved life for average Africans? Here the picture is somewhat murky. On the one hand, the final report on the Millennium Development Goals released in July 2015 concluded that the project was "the most successful anti-poverty movement in history" (United Nations 2015:3). Thus, the United Nation's 2001 Millennium Development Goals evolved into the 2015 Sustainable Development Goals (SDGs) with a sense of optimism. Partly spurred by Africa's economic growth, the poverty rate in developing regions reportedly plummeted from 47 percent in 1990 to 14 percent in 2015, with global hunger reportedly cut in half during that time. Yet some observers have raised questions about the validity of these claims, regarding both the numbers and the methodologies behind them (see Hickel 2016 and 2017; Briant Carrant 2017). Moreover, while rates of extreme poverty (measured as an income of less than $1.20 per day) decreased from 45 percent in 1990 to 35 percent in 2013, more Africans are actually living in poverty (less than $1.90 per day), rising from 280 million in 1990 to 395 million in 2013 (OECD 2018:35). In 2018, Nigeria became the "poverty capital of the world," with more than 86 million citizens living in extreme poverty despite its abundant resources and $1,968 GDP per capita. A recent OECD report (2018:40) suggested that, when looking at a range of measurements, Africa's recent GDP growth has not increased well-being for most of the populations. In contrast, in his study of eighteen non-oil-producing African countries, Steven Radelet (2010) of the Center for Global Development found that growth has been accompanied by improvements in social sectors (health and education), a reduction of the poverty rate, better governance, and improved policies.

One apparent consequence of Africa's recent growth is the rise of a middle class. In 2011, the African Development Bank (2011a) estimated that the number of middle-class Africans was over 300 million (or roughly one-third of the continent's population). The following year the number was adjusted up to 500 million, with a stunning 240 percent increase over the past decade. Yet there is some controversy about these claims, given the definition of middle class as an individual with a daily income/expenditure of between $2 and $20. One can note the problematic nature behind the subjective claim that a person living on $1.90 a day is in poverty, while another earning 10 cents more is somehow middle class.

Yet the greater visibility of middle-class lifestyles over recent decades is apparent to those who travel to or reside on the continent. Most African cities have far more apartment buildings, shopping centers, private schools, car dealerships, ice cream parlors, and other trappings of middle-income lifestyles than ever before. Yet the African Development Bank's numbers should be treated with suspicion. For one thing, a large chunk of the observed African middle class live in the five countries of North Africa. If we look at sub-Saharan Africa and take into account only individuals who spend from $10 to $100 a day, the size of the African middle class shrinks to 32 million (Wonacott 2011), or less than 4 percent of the population.

Setting aside the debate over their size, one may well wonder where this new middle class comes from. Given the lack of growth in Africa's manufacturing sector, one can hypothesize that only a small proportion might come from the industrial sector. Some, however, will come from the construction sector, which tends to boom with GDP growth. Similarly, given the prevalence of poverty and subsistence activities among Africa's farmers, it is also unlikely that many members of the new middle class are in the agricultural sector. It is thus most probable that the members of Africa's new petty bourgeoisie are in the service sector. Some of them are public servants, although many of these will have been middle class before. But the majority of the growth might come from the private services sector, such as banking, transportation, retail, telecommunications, private education, and the like. The expansion of this sector might reflect an increase in domestic demand for all these services as a function of overall growth. To some extent, even if triggered by commodity exports, the additional income of countries might at least partly trickle down through the rest of the economy through induced demand for goods and services. The demand for goods might be met with increased imports, but the demand for services is more easily satisfied domestically. It is thus possible that a new class of service providers has developed and accrued additional income as a function of rising commodity prices. This class will also have benefited from the more propitious policy and legal environment in many countries, which makes private transactions considerably easier than they used to be.

If this analysis is correct, it could suggest that Africa's middle class is not yet economically transformative. Not quite parasitic, it might be less the engine of Africa's growth than its result. However, it could progressively generate its own demand and promote further growth. At any rate, however modest, the rise of a middle class in Africa will more likely than not encourage regime change. One of its consequences might be that the availability of economic opportunities outside the state will reduce the appeal of the latter in private strategies of accumulation and economic survival. As such it may decrease demand for patronage and corruption and might undermine the reproduction of neopatrimonialism. In addition, a stronger middle class is likely to demand more pro-market and pro-growth policies, and to keep governments more accountable, further reinforcing democracy and possibly dislodging regimes from their hybrid equilibriums.

One final question—and perhaps the most important question—is whether or not Africa's recent economic growth represents a major transformation for the continent. Does it represent a turnaround in Africa's fate? Sadly, we would argue that it does not. There has not been a transformation of the structure of African economies and, as we are already seeing since 2014, recent growth is clearly reversible. This is because Africa continues to be dependent on a few primary commodities and remains highly susceptible to price fluctuations. When the commodity markets tumbled in 2008 following worldwide recession, many African economies took a serious hit, underscoring their vulnerability to volatile markets (refer to Figure 6.5). Ian Taylor (2016, 2014) has noted that almost a quarter of African countries rely on a single commodity for 50 percent of their export earnings, and nearly three-quarters rely on three commodities for the majority of their export earnings. For Taylor, rather than altering the continent's subservient and precarious position within the global capitalist system, the past few decades have pushed Africa further into underdevelopment and dependency. As he notes, "the story of 'Africa Rising' is just that, a story, where growth-for-growth's sake replaces development and the agenda of industrialization and moving Africa up the global production chain has been discarded. Instead, Africa's current 'comparative advantage' as a primary commodity exporter is reinforced, even whilst such dynamics reproduce underdevelopment" (Taylor 2016:22).

At the same time, there is evidence that many African regimes have failed to learn the lessons of the past and are driving their countries toward a new debt crisis. Since 2014, numerous African countries have been forced to engage with the IMF to address debt-servicing difficulties. African governments, encouraged by global lenders and following the logic of neoliberalism, are increasing their borrowing, without strict regulatory mechanisms in place to avoid another debt crisis (Bassett 2017). In 2017, it was revealed that Mozambique had accrued around $1 billion in secret debt, bringing its total debt to over $2 billion, which it subsequently informed its creditors it was unable to service. The debt, driven by neopatrimonial practices and accumulated with international lenders and IMF complicity, wiped out the country's budget and crippled what was a growing economy. While Mozambique appears to be the worst case, other African countries have been engaging in what some regard as reckless borrowing. The debt reduction schemes of the early twenty-first century managed to drop African debts to an average of 25 percent of GDP, but that figure had grown to over 45 percent in 2017 and is rapidly moving toward 50 percent. In 2013, nine African countries' debt-to-GDP ratios were greater than 50 percent. By 2016, that number had increased to twenty. Unlike the previous debt crisis, when the debt was largely handled by the IMF and World Bank, now the creditors are mostly commercial entities or state financial organizations unlikely to be so accepting of restructuring or writing off that debt (Reid 2018). It is very likely that many African countries will soon be fully immersed in a new, and potentially more detrimental, debt crisis. Thus, while the twenty-first century has brought about significant economic growth across the continent, two key factors of its economic condition—its dependence on export commodities and the prevalence of neopatrimonialism—continue to be powerful forces.

Notes

1. In a subsequent book (Acemoglu and Robinson 2012), they acknowledge that Botswana's "inclusive institutions" contributed to its development.

2. For a broader comparative study of famines, including other causes than drought, see Sen 1982.

3. In her book *The Poisonwood Bible,* which takes place in the Democratic Republic of Congo, Barbara Kingsolver (1998) dramatically illustrates the struggle between agriculture and the elements in Africa.

4. For a different point of view, see Kevane and Gray 2008.

5. Those fourteen countries—Nigeria, the DRC, Mozambique, Ghana, Mali, Burkina Faso, Niger, Uganda, Tanzania, Cameroon, Côte d'Ivoire, Guinea, Rwanda, and Malawi, in order—account for 70 percent of the world's cases of malaria (WHO 2017:35). All data on malaria in this section are from WHO 2017.

6. All data in this and the following two paragraphs are from UNAIDS 2018.

7. World Bank, *World Development Indicators,* http://data.worldbank.org/indicator.

8. It is important to recognize that these figures, and the general discourse around development, are contested. As Jason Hickel (2016) has noted, in recent years the World Bank has redefined the poverty threshold, as well as its measurement for hunger, resulting in what some regard as an underestimation of the scale of global poverty and hunger. For critical discussions about the definitions of and methodologies around development, poverty, and hunger, see also Havnevik, Oestigaard, and Tobisson 2015; Jerven 2015; and Hickel 2017.

9. Because no such variable is contained in the World Bank's *World Development Indicators,* we infer the value of extractive industries by subtracting manufacturing output from overall industrial output.

10. All data in this paragraph are from World Bank, *World Development Indicators,* http://data.worldbank.org/indicator.

11. All figures in this paragraph are from World Bank, *World Development Indicators,* http://data.worldbank.org/indicator.

12. World Bank, *World Development Indicators,* http://data.worldbank.org/indicator.

13. Although they are avid users of rents, African governments are not alone in relying on these distortions, and the scholarship linking rents to negative welfare outcomes originally focused on India and Turkey (Krueger 1974).

14. On the "urban bias" of African policies, an antecedent theory to Bates's, see Lipton 1977.

15. Although the World Bank and the IMF are distinct institutions with separate lending programs, their policies and the conditions of their loans became largely intertwined in their dealings with Africa in the 1980s. As a result, in this book, we do not distinguish the specific agenda of the IMF, which had greater emphasis on fiscal and monetary policy, from that of the World Bank.

16. World Bank, *World Development Indicators,* http://data.worldbank.org/indicator. Apart from government consumption, all other data and trends in this paragraph are summarized from van de Walle 2001:64–112.

17. Simple average of country data. Sample size varies from year to year.

18. World Bank, *World Development Indicators,* http://data.worldbank.org/indicator.

19. All figures in this paragraph are derived from OECD 2013.

20. In absolute numbers, the top ten African recipients of foreign aid in 2011 were the DRC, Ethiopia, Kenya, Tanzania, Mozambique, Ghana, Nigeria, Uganda, Côte d'Ivoire, and Rwanda. The top five donors were the United States, the European Union, the World Bank (through its International Development Association), France, and the United Kingdom.

21. All data in this paragraph are derived from World Bank, *World Development Indicators,* http://data.worldbank.org/indicator.

22. Unless noted otherwise, the data in these paragraphs come from the China-Africa Research Initiative of the Johns Hopkins School of Advanced International Studies, available at http://www.sais-cari.org.

23. All data in this paragraph are derived from World Bank, *World Development Indicators,* http://data.worldbank.org/indicator.

7

War, Conflict,
and Security

SINCE AFRICAN STATES GAINED THEIR INDEPENDENCE,
the vast majority have endured at least one devastating war. More than
seventy wars have been fought in Africa since the early 1980s. In the
twenty-first century alone, twenty-two sub-Saharan states were affected
by armed conflict. This has led to the common perception that the continent is rife with violence and insecurity. Although Africa has not been
short on armed conflicts, it would be a mistake to overgeneralize. For
every war-torn country like the Democratic Republic of Congo, there
are stable, peaceful countries like Botswana and Ghana. Even in the
Democratic Republic of Congo, where instability remains rife in the
east and resurfaces occasionally elsewhere, the vast majority of the
country is at relative peace and was so during most of its devastating
war. Moreover, some countries that were once at war have made impressive recoveries, such as Angola and Rwanda. Nevertheless, it is true that
political violence is a problem throughout much of Africa. It is also true
that once-peaceful countries have been wrecked by political violence,
such as Côte d'Ivoire. It is thus essential to understand the nature, patterns, and causes of African conflicts, and what liabilities might expose
some countries to violent decay.

The average length of African conflicts is twenty-two years, seven
years longer than the global average (Huggins and Clover 2005:1).
Around 64 percent of African conflicts last five years or less, while
almost a quarter of them last eleven years or more (Straus 2012).[1]
Across the continent, armed conflict has heightened insecurity and promoted the militarization of the state, which has often come at great
social cost. In 2015, South Sudan spent 10.9 percent of its GDP on the
military, the highest in Africa and second in the world, while spending

only 1.8 percent on health (CIA 2018). From 2008 to 2018, several countries such as Angola and Chad spent about twice as much on defense as on health.[2] Some have argued that conflict is among the most important factors in accounting for Africa's poor economic performance during much of the twentieth century (Bloom, Sachs, and Collier 1998; Addison, le Billon, and Murshed 2001).

What explains the outbreak of conflict in contemporary Africa? How and why has the nature of armed conflict changed over the years? What are the different types of conflicts that have affected Africa? What are the main reasons Africans go to war, and what mechanisms have been developed to bring those conflicts to an end? In this chapter, we begin by examining the different types of conflict in Africa, before exploring the ways these have evolved over time. We then turn to a survey of the theories offered to explain their causes. After exploring various experiences with conflict resolution, peacekeeping, and postconflict justice, we end the chapter by conceptualizing security in Africa more broadly.

A Typology of African Conflicts

In this section, we delineate the four major forms of African conflicts—national liberation, interstate, secessionism, and domestic insurgency—while observing variations within each category. We also note that different forms of conflict can coexist to produce composite conflicts.

National Liberation Wars

Although most of the continent reached independence peacefully, a few of its colonized societies waged war against colonial and white minority rule. The most significant liberation wars were the Mau Mau uprising in Kenya in the 1950s; the wars in Angola, Mozambique, and Guinea-Bissau/Cape Verde against the Portuguese from 1960 to the mid-1970s; the Rhodesian/Zimbabwean war of 1965–1980; and the antiapartheid struggle in South Africa, whose violent phase extended from the mid-1960s to 1990.

Some scholars do not regard the Mau Mau uprising as a war of national liberation due to the internecine nature of the violence. The uprising (or "Kenya Emergency," as it was also called at the time) took place from 1952 to 1960. According to some participants, the insurgents never referred to themselves as Mau Mau, but as the Kenya Land and Freedom Army. Predominantly made up of dispossessed Kikuyu, the group operated in the forest areas of the Central Province and in the foothills around Mount Kenya, attacking police stations and government offices, as well as the occasional settler farms. The true extent of the conflict remains unclear, but the fighting resulted in over 10,000 African fatalities and the death of thirty-two white settlers. While militarily unsuccessful, the conflict set the stage for Kenya's independence in 1963 by furthering the divisions between the British Home Office and the white settlers in Kenya. London ultimately came to accept moderate African nationalists, such as Jomo Kenyatta, who became independent Kenya's first leader in 1963. There remains substantial scholarly debate about the nature and interpretation of the conflict, particularly given that the uprising was carried out almost exclusively by the Kikuyu, who lived in the agriculturally rich Central and Rift Valley provinces and were the most affected by the colonial government's expropriation of land for white settlement and cultivation (Branch 2009; Githuku 2016; Maloba 1998). The Kikuyu had resisted colonial conquest, with at least three sustained armed insurrections from 1920 to 1940. Yet Kikuyu society was deeply divided and not everyone supported the armed revolt. Indeed, the movement lacked widespread support among the wider African population in Kenya, with some regarding it as either a Kikuyu-British conflict or an intra-Kikuyu struggle (Branch 2009). Regardless, Mau Mau would go on to serve as a potent symbol of anticolonial resistance across Africa and the third world.

All three of Portugal's continental colonies experienced sustained wars of liberation, primarily because the Portuguese military government refused to join the European decolonization during the 1950s and 1960s. Instead, the Portuguese regime moved to strengthen its control and extractive economic practices, pretending its colonies were overseas provinces (Bender 1978). In response, Africans in each country launched armed struggles for independence. Unlike the Kenyan case, these liberation struggles tended to be multiethnic affairs, drawing in urban and rural participants, and producing conflicts that were more large-scale and geographically dispersed than the Mau Mau uprising. In Guinea-Bissau and Cape Verde, the struggle was led by the Partido Africano da Independência da Guiné e Cabo Verde (PAIGC), founded and led by Amílcar Cabral. In Mozambique the Frente de Libertação de Moçambique (FRELIMO) was founded in 1962 as a merger of exiled nationalist movements. FRELIMO succeeded in establishing liberated zones in northern and central Mozambique, which forced it to develop an administrative capacity alongside guerrilla actions (Bowen 2000). Things were more complex in Angola, where the anticolonial struggle was fragmented among several groups, including the Movimento Popular de Libertação de Angola

(MPLA), the Frente Nacional de Libertação de Angola (FNLA), and the União Nacional para a Independência Total de Angola (UNITA). The divisions between the groups derived partly from personal competition, ethnic cleavages (with the MPLA associated with the Mbundu, the FNLA with the Bakongo, and UNITA with the majority Ovimbundu), and interventions by foreign states. Indeed, the anticolonial wars in all three Portuguese colonies must be understood through the prism of the Cold War and the proxy wars carried out by the United States, the Soviet Union, and their allies. Angola's war was particularly susceptible to external interventions as Portugal, the United States, the Soviet Union, China, South Africa, Zaire, and others sought to enhance their positions in the country and region, while destabilizing the interests of others. It was not until the overthrow of the dictatorship in Lisbon (because of frustrations with the high cost of the colonial wars), in April 1974, that Portugal moved quickly to extract itself from its African colonies. Over a million people associated with the colonial occupation abruptly left for Portugal as the colonies were granted independence. In Angola and Mozambique, bitter civil wars quickly followed (Marcum 1978; Finnegan 1993).

The national liberation war in Zimbabwe (then Southern Rhodesia) was markedly different because it was not aimed at the colonial power, Britain, but at the white settler population, who had issued a unilateral declaration of independence in 1965. White settlers' concerns about their future had been growing even before British prime minister Harold Macmillan's speech to the South African parliament in 1960, in which he announced Britain's intention to follow the "wind of change" and grant independence to its African colonies. Led by Ian Smith, the white settler minority, composing less than 5 percent of the entire population, declared Rhodesia independent in November 1965. The black African population in the country increasingly believed that armed struggle was the only way to secure genuine independence, but the nationalist movement split into two factions: the Zimbabwe African People's Union (ZAPU), led by Joshua Nkomo and supported primarily by the Ndebele, and the Zimbabwe African National Union (ZANU), led by Robert Mugabe and largely identified with the Shona. The two groups fought separate struggles against Smith's white minority government, while also occasionally fighting each other. The war was predominantly a rural struggle, though it did become intertwined with the conflict in neighboring Mozambique and was influenced by the Cold War. By the late 1970s, the war had succeeded in severely disrupting the Rhodesian economy and breaking the morale of the white minority. In the end, the conflict resulted in over 30,000 fatalities, with acts of striking brutality committed by all sides

(Martin and Johnson 1981; Bhebe and Ranger 1995). The war ended in 1979 with the Lancaster House Accords, through which power was transferred back to Britain, which then declared the independence of majority rule Zimbabwe. Robert Mugabe became president in democratic elections the following year, a position he held for almost four decades.

The final two national liberation wars involved white-ruled South Africa. During World War I, South Africa occupied the neighboring German colony of South West Africa (Namibia). After the end of the war, South Africa administered the colony as a League of Nations mandate territory, formally on behalf of Britain. Though never officially incorporated, South West Africa was treated as a de facto province. With the creation of the United Nations, which superseded the League of Nations, international pressure was placed on South Africa to surrender the territory, which it steadfastly resisted. After the UN General Assembly formally revoked South Africa's mandate and the International Court of Justice declared South Africa's occupation of future Namibia illegal in 1966, the South West Africa People's Organization (SWAPO) launched an armed nationalist struggle. This struggle also became intertwined with the Cold War and the war in neighboring Angola, where Cuban forces had been dispatched to support the MPLA government in 1975 and again in 1988. In one of the clearest and earliest signs of the end of the Cold War, the Soviet Union and the United States successfully intervened in the late 1980s to bring about a comprehensive regional plan between South Africa, Angola, and Cuba. In return for Cuba's promise to pull its troops out of southern Angola, South Africa agreed to withdraw from Namibia, which became independent in March 1990 (Crocker 1993).

South Africa's withdrawal from Namibia occurred as the apartheid regime was slowly collapsing. South Africa had been ruled by a white minority since independence in 1910. With the election of the Nationalist Party in 1948, white rule and privilege were further entrenched within a legal system of segregation known as *apartheid* (Clark and Worger 2004), an Afrikaans word meaning "living apart." The primary force of opposition among the black majority population was the African National Congress (ANC), which formed in 1923. In 1961, as white rule became increasingly entrenched and the possibility of ending racial discrimination through legal means became hopeless, the ANC formed a military wing, the Umkhoto we Sizwe (Spear of the Nation), to engage in a war of liberation. In contrast to more formal liberation armies, the ANC's struggle was limited to sporadic guerrilla strikes (which led the United States to list the ANC as a terrorist organization until 2008), largely due to the vastly superior South African military and police forces. Yet ANC violence and international pressure ultimately led to the dismantling of the apartheid regime in 1991 and the election of ANC leader Nelson Mandela to the country's presidency in 1994.

Interstate Warfare

Interstate wars, involving at least two sovereign states in sustained combat, have been rather rare in Africa. This low incidence has struck many scholars as anomalous: Why should African states be less disposed to interstate conflicts than their European counterparts over the past several centuries? While some might celebrate the relative absence of interstate warfare in Africa, Jeffrey Herbst (1990b) has argued that this has negatively affected the continent's development. He notes that interstate warfare has not served the same developmental functions for the state in modern Africa as it did for Europe. In Europe, war helped consolidate the developing states in multiple ways: causing the states to become more efficient in their revenue collection, forcing political leaders to improve their administrative capabilities, and creating social rituals and symbols around which a disparate population could unify as a collective (Tilly 1990). In Africa, the majority of African states gained their independence without having to resort to combat and have not faced serious national security threats from neighboring states since independence. For Herbst, because interstate warfare has not been a feature in modern Africa, development has been "stunted" by the very problems that war helped European countries resolve.

Whether a blessing or a curse, the low incidence of African interstate wars can largely be credited to the general stability of the continent's political boundaries. Recall from Chapter 2 that leaders in Africa after independence agreed to maintain the boundaries they inherited from the colonial powers, a principle known as *uti possidetis*. They recognized that redrawing those boundaries would open a Pandora's box of territorial realignments that would be ultimately destructive for existing states and challenge their own hold on power. *Uti possidetis* was formalized with the establishment of the Organization of African Unity in 1963, which reaffirmed on several occasions the integrity of colonial borders and outlawed most attempts to change them.

The fear that territorial restructuring could lead to destabilization proved quite prescient, as the few attempts to substantially alter boundaries resulted in wars. The first major African border restructuring did not take place until 1993, with the carving of the independent state of Eritrea out of Ethiopia. Though the separation was peaceful at the time, the two states found themselves in the midst of a horrific war just a few short years later. The conflict that erupted in May 1998 was triggered by unresolved border issues between the two states, particularly regarding the Badme region (Iyob 2000). Attempts to demarcate the precise border relied on colonial-era treaties between Italy and Ethiopia, yet no agreement on interpretation of those treaties could be reached. Without a clear colonially created boundary, tensions increased until the outbreak of armed conflict. The resulting war, which lasted until June 2000, caused an estimated 70,000 deaths and severely crippled both countries' economies (Negash and Tronvoll 2000; Fessehatzion 2003). The conflict did not formally end until 2018, when Ethiopia's new prime minister, Abiy Ahmed, declared an end to hostilities as part of his radical reforms. The second major restructuring of Africa's international borders, the creation of South Sudan in 2011 (also born out of a successful secessionist struggle over decades), was followed by skirmishes with Sudan over disputed boundaries, leaving some observers pessimistic about a peaceful future between the two countries (Natsios 2012).

Universal adoption of the colonial map has also been credited with removing the impetus for wars of territorial conquest. The only two major wars of conquest in Africa have ended in failure: the Libyan invasions of Chad in the 1970s and 1980s, and Somalia's invasion of Ethiopia in the Ogaden War of 1977–1978. In the first case, Libya laid claim to the Aouzou Strip in northern Chad and invaded four times: 1978, 1979, 1980–1981, and 1983–1987. The Libyans were finally routed by a unified Chadian front supported by the French. In 1977, Somalia invaded neighboring Ethiopia in an attempt to secure the disputed Somali-populated Ogaden region. Somalia was initially supported by the Soviet Union, with the United States heavily committed to the Ethiopians. However, in one of the more unusual chapters of the Cold War, the Ethiopian regime was overthrown by a Marxist-Leninist military junta a few months before Somalia's scheduled invasion, and the Soviet Union found itself funding both sides of the conflict. After its failure to end the conflict, the Soviet Union shifted its support unequivocally toward Ethiopia, which, alongside Cuban troops, repelled the Somali invaders by March 1978. Tensions between the two states remain high. Ethiopia invaded Somalia in 2006 and again in 2011, not to conquer territory, but in order to back up Somalia's transitional federal government in the ongoing civil war there.

The majority of interstate wars have been primarily motivated by the desire to achieve regime change. For example, Tanzania invaded Uganda in 1979 in order to overthrow Idi Amin. The war actually began in 1978 when Ugandan troops pursued a group of mutinous soldiers to the Tanzanian border. Angry with the fact that Tanzania had been harboring anti-Amin exiles, including deposed president Milton Obote, Amin declared war on Tanzania. With his regime crumbling around him, Amin invaded and attempted to annex part of the Kagera region. Tanzania responded by repelling the invading force and then, much to the shock and public outrage of African leaders in the Organization of African Unity, proceeded to invade Uganda itself, resulting in the ousting of Amin and restoration of Obote. Yet Tanzania never expressed any interest in conquering territory, and the existence of the Ugandan state was never in question (Chatterjee 1981). Likewise, apartheid-era South Africa's undeclared war against the so-called Front-Line States (Angola, Botswana, Mozambique, Tanzania, Zambia, and Zimbabwe) from 1976 to 1987 was primarily concerned with destabilizing those neighboring states and disrupting their ability to support the ANC, as opposed to conquering and controlling them.

Secessionist Civil Wars

Secessionist civil wars are waged in order to substantially alter the territorial integrity of an existing state, usually with the goal of achieving independent sovereign status for a particular region. Although there have been a few notable cases of secessionist civil wars in Africa, their number is perhaps surprisingly low. However, the recent successful secessions of Eritrea (1993) and South Sudan (2011) could herald a change of norm, though these two cases also highlight that secessionism does not necessarily improve the well-being of the citizenry (de Vries, Englebert, and Schomerus 2019).

The first secessionist civil war in Africa occurred in Congo when the provinces of Katanga and South Kasai broke away immediately following independence. Shortly after Congo became independent on 30 June 1960, several units in the Congolese army mutinied, demanding promotions, pay raises, and the removal of white officers. Belgian troops stationed in Congo intervened and actively engaged the Congolese army and civilians. On 11 July, Moïse Tshombe, the regional leader of the southern province of Katanga, who had been denied a seat in the ruling coalition, announced his region's secession and successfully sought Belgian support. Tshombe framed the secession as a combination of ethnic nationalism and claimed that the Congolese prime minister, Patrice Lumumba, was a communist. The secession did not enjoy full support within the region and was largely driven by the desire to preserve both Belgian economic interests and Katanga's comparative wealth. Though the Congolese government enlisted UN military assistance, the multinational force that was sent to Congo did not move to dislodge Belgian troops, nor did it initially engage with secessionist Katanga. In fact, Lumumba would eventually be captured by mutinous troops and flown to Katanga, where he was handed over to the secessionist forces, beaten, tortured, and murdered. The Belgian soldiers initially provided direct support for Tshombe's breakaway government, along with French, Rhodesian, and South African mercenaries, and were able to repel UN forces until January 1963 (Gérard-Libois 1963; Gérard-Libois and Verhaegen 1961; O'Brien 1966; Kennes and Larmer 2016).

The neighboring province of South Kasai had also declared its independence shortly after Congolese independence, in part because of a deep rivalry between its leader, Albert Kalonji, and Lumumba. It renamed itself the Great Mining State of South Kasai, with Kalonji proclaiming himself "Mulopwe" (King of the Luba) (Kalonji Mulopwe 2005; Hoskyns 1965). Lacking the level of foreign support that Katanga enjoyed, Kasai fell to the Congolese military at the end of 1961 after a brutal four-month war. Despite the employment of ethnonationalist rhetoric, both secessionist provinces were driven largely by the political and economic interests of Congolese political elites and, in the case of Katanga, their foreign business associates.

While ethnic impetus for the secessionist civil wars in Congo may have been rather limited, it was far more pronounced in Nigeria's civil war, the Nigerian-Biafran War of 1967–1970. Nigeria had become independent in 1960, but regional and ethnic cleavages proved volatile as the country was divided among the more populous Hausa and Fulani in the north, the Yoruba in the southwest, and the Igbo in the southeast. Independence and democracy meant that the north enjoyed a significant advantage over the south, which had been more privileged under British colonialism. In January 1966, a primarily Igbo-led military coup took place, resulting in the deaths of many northern political leaders, including Prime Minister Abubakar Tafawa Balewa. A few months later, northern soldiers staged a countercoup, further fueling ethnic tensions and causing the deaths of tens of thousands of civilians in the following months. The eastern region voted to secede on 26 May 1967 and the regional military government declared itself the Republic of Biafra. Driven in large part by ethnic tensions, the secession was exacerbated by the presence of large amounts of oil in the region. After a brutal war in which more than a million people died in battle or from starvation and disease, Biafra was defeated in 1970 and reintegrated into Nigeria (see Achebe 2012).

In contrast to Nigeria and Congo, where post-independence secessionist struggles failed, modern South Sudan and Eritrea were both born of successful secessionist civil wars. In both cases, however, it must be borne in mind that the rump state acquiesced to the separation, which provided these secessions with validity in international law. In the case of South Sudan, independence was achieved in 2011 after a series of armed struggles in 1955–1972 and 1983–2005. As part of a comprehensive peace agreement, laboriously negotiated over several years under international patronage, a referendum on independence was held in southern Sudan in January 2011, with over 98 percent voting in favor of secession (Walker 2017). Soon after their separation, both Sudans briefly engaged in a shooting war over disputed border regions. More disastrous, however, was the eruption of an armed struggle within the ruling regime in South Sudan. In December 2013, violence broke out between supporters of President Salva Kiir Mayardit and supporters of former vice president Riek Machar Teny, plunging the newly created country into a violent civil war that by 2018 had killed tens of thousands and displaced over 4 million. A power-sharing agreement collapsed in July 2016, with another attempt signed in August 2018, which is tentatively holding at the time of this writing (Walraet 2017; Rolandsen 2011; Johnson 2003).

An Italian colony since 1890, Eritrea was administered by the British after the 1941 defeat of the Italians. Federated with Ethiopia under a UN mandate in 1951, it was progressively assimilated as a province by Addis. The Eritrean People's Liberation Front (EPLF) launched an armed struggle in 1961. It waged a thirty-year civil war, eventually joining with the Tigrayan People's Liberation Front (TPLF) to defeat the Mengistu regime in Addis in exchange for a referendum on independence, which it won handily. Eritreans gained their formal sovereignty in 1993, in what was the first successful secession in modern Africa (Iyob 1997; Pateman 1998). In 1998, as discussed in the previous section, tensions with Ethiopia over unresolved border issues erupted into a full-blown conflict, claiming tens of thousands of lives.

In addition to Eritrea and South Sudan, recent or ongoing secessionist attempts include the Casamance conflict in Senegal, the Oromo and Ogaden rebellions in Ethiopia, the Azawad movements in Niger and Mali, the struggle over Cabinda in Angola, the restless Niger Delta in Nigeria, and the unilateral withdrawal of Somaliland from the rest of Somalia since 1991 (de Vries, Englebert, and Schomerus 2019). This list, however, represents nearly all the instances of secessionist attempts in Africa since independence. As Pierre Englebert and Rebecca Hummel (2005) observe, separatist warfare is relatively rare across the continent. If one were to add all the years of conflict in every country from 1960 to 2002, 27 percent of that total in Africa would have separatist content, compared to 44 percent in the Middle East and North Africa, 47 percent in Asia, and no less than 84 percent in Europe.

There might be several reasons for this scarcity. First, the rules of territorial integrity promoted by the Organization of African Unity might inhibit separatist movements by reducing their chances of recognition (Jackson and Rosberg 1982). It is also possible that the bonds of nationalist feelings generated through shared colonization and five decades of independence have durably cemented Africa's territories to their populations (Young 2002). A third answer suggests that artificial and heterogeneous African states have been integrated and kept together thanks in large part to the distribution of state resources to group elites, which has brought about their "fusion" (Sklar 1963; Boone 2003b) or "reciprocal assimilation" (Bayart 1993). Finally, it is possible that institutions of sovereign statehood represent a political and material resource for communal elites and populations at large, the benefits of which outweigh the potential returns of separatist nonsovereign alternatives, leading to greater acquiescence with the postcolonial state than one might otherwise expect (Englebert and Hummel 2005; Englebert 2009).

Insurgency Conflicts

The most common type of conflict in Africa is the domestic insurgent war. Unlike secessions, guerrilla insurgencies are waged largely with the goal of attaining power within the existing state. Over thirty African countries have experienced one or more nonseparatist conflicts since 1960. What explains the persistent existence of these armed guerrillas in Africa? Historically, African insurgencies have recorded a rather poor success rate, at least if measured only by the degree to which they have been able to overthrow and replace existing regimes (which might not always be their goal). With the exception of the anticolonial struggles, no African insurgency was ever successful until Hissène Habré's Forces Armées du Nord (FAN) seized state power in Chad in 1979. The second successful insurgency did not occur until Yoweri Museveni's National Resistance Army (NRA) captured the Ugandan state in 1986. The rate of success improved somewhat afterward with successful insurgencies in Rwanda, Ethiopia, Congo, and Liberia. Yet only around 10 percent of African armed groups have achieved victory. Christopher Day (2019) has made an important argument that the success of African insurgencies is related to the degree in which they are embedded in the patronage networks of existing state authority structures. In short, groups led by disenfranchised elites fair far better than those comprising political outsiders.

In his seminal work *African Guerrillas,* Christopher Clapham (1998a) makes a distinction between "reform" and "warlord" insurgencies. In his typology, reform insurgencies were highly disciplined formations, with a clear ideology and structure, which had as their goal the creation of a very different kind of state within an existing national territory from that which currently governed. Recent examples include the NRA in Uganda, the RPF in Rwanda, and the TPLF in Ethiopia. In each of these three cases, the movements were successful and their leaders were hailed by some Western observers as "new Africans," who would help initiate democracy and development on the continent (Ottaway 1999). But a few years later, this "new African" ideal had collapsed and the hope that insurgent warfare might lead to a progressive "reform" of the African state was increasingly regarded as bankrupt (Clapham 2007).

In contrast, "warlord insurgencies" are neither reformist, secessionist, nor liberationist. They tend to lack an ideological structure, and are typically characterized by their highly personalized leadership. Examples include Foday Sankoh's Revolutionary United Front (RUF) in Sierra Leone, Charles Taylor's National Patriotic Front of Liberia (NPFL), and Joseph Kony's Lord's Resistance Army (LRA) in Uganda. By employing the label "warlord," Clapham sought to emphasize the leadership of movements, though the level of actual control varied a good deal from case to case. His contention was that the underlying social and economic conditions were exploited by political entrepreneurs who benefited from the conflict. As will be discussed later, these movements sometimes drew heavily on the spiritual or religious beliefs of the societies in which they operated, as did the LRA and the Holy Spirit Movement in northern Uganda and the various factions in Liberia.

William Reno (2011) offers another category of insurgent, the "parochial rebels" who fight for local, circumscribed communities. Reno notes that these vary from the warlord rebels because, for a range of reasons, they must heed the interests and values of local communities. As such, parochial rebels tend to administer areas under their control and develop political programs reflecting local grievances. Yet their aspirations are often restricted and the capture of the central state is beyond their ability or interest. Examples include western Nigeria's Oodua People's Congress (OPC) and northwestern Liberia's Lofa Defense Force (LDF), both of which emerged in the 1990s to protect local communities from predation by the state and competing rebels, respectively. The numerous self-defense militias still active in eastern DRC, commonly known as "Mayi-Mayi," are further examples. With their numerical strength ranging from a few dozen to several hundred, these Mayi-Mayi groups base their existence on protecting local, often ethnic, communities and advancing a circumscribed political agenda (Verweijen 2016; Vlassenroot and Verweijen 2017).

Borrowing from Mancur Olson, Thandika Mkandawire (2002:199–207) has made an interesting distinction between stationary and roving insurgencies. In this typology, stationary guerrillas establish physical enclaves, often building rudimentary structures of governance and control. An example of a stationary insurgency is the Forces Nouvelles, which controlled the northern section of Côte d'Ivoire during the 2001–2011 war. Roving guerrillas, conversely, are constantly on the move. Kony's LRA is an example of a roving insurgency, as it has never established any substantial "liberated" zone, but has shifted its activities from northern Uganda and southern Sudan, into the Democratic Republic of Congo and the Central African Republic (Cakaj 2016; Dunn 2017). Though no movement completely fits into either category, the distinction between stationary and roving insurgencies illuminates variations in the relationships between guerrillas and locals, as well as providing a way to understand the different methods used by movements to finance their rebellions. Stationary insurgents tend to rely heavily upon the local communities in their "liberated" zones. Parochial rebels such as the locally based Mayi-Mayi in eastern DRC are a case in point. In some instances, however, these insurgents are stationary in order to secure physical control over valuable resources. Angola's UNITA is a good example of a movement that became stationary in order to control the diamond-extraction economy. Roving bands, in contrast, tend to resort to predation and pillaging while they are on the move. Zachariah Mampilly (2010) and Jeremy Weinstein (2006) have both offered a rich investigation of the different forms of governance established by insurgents, and the challenges faced by constructing alternative forms of rule. They argue that the context of rebellion largely constrains the organization and strategies of violence employed by insurgents (see also Arjona, Kasfir, and Mampilly 2015).

Morten Bøås and Kevin Dunn (2007; 2017) suggest a further distinction in focusing on *how* African insurgents roam. Do these groups follow the main roads, as was mainly the case in Liberia? Or do they predominantly roam in the bush, like the LRA in northern Uganda or as the RUF once did (in the periods 1993–1995 and 1998–1999)? The authors suggest that this distinction can have important implications for the organization, structure, and goals of various armed groups. Road-roaming guerrilla movements tend to engage in a struggle to capture state power (either regionally or nationally), tend to fight using conventional tactics, and are hierarchically organized. Bush-path insurgents tend to be less interested in immediate capture of the central government, tend to employ nonconventional tactics (such as ambushes), and are less hierarchically organized. These are movements that often appear incomprehensible to Western observers, and their seeming lack of a recognizable strategy or political vision is sometimes taken as further proof of their primitivism. Yet Paul Richards (2005a) notes that these movements can be understood as "enclave formations," engaged in producing an alternative "world order" based on narratives of betrayal and exile, which are reinforced by their existence in such an enclave formation. As the case of the LRA and its more than three-decade-long conflict so vividly shows, these insurgencies can be very hard to defeat.

Composite Conflicts

Sometimes a conflict involves a combination of two or more motivations or strategies. For example, the linked armed conflicts of southern Africa in the 1970s and 1980s combined anticolonial nationalist struggles in Angola, Mozambique, and Namibia with indirect interstate Cold War warfare fought via proxies such as Cuba and Zaire and direct interstate warfare waged by apartheid South Africa (and to a lesser extent Rhodesia) against its neighbors.

Another and perhaps more poignant example is the so-called Africa War One or Great African War that took place in the DRC (formerly Zaire) from 1996 to 2003 (Clark 2002; Prunier 2009; Reyntjens 2009; Stearns 2011; Turner 2007). Ostensibly a struggle for control of the Congolese state, the conflict became the largest war in modern African history. Its immediate roots can be traced back to the aftermath of the 1994 Rwandan genocide, when some 2 million Rwandans—a mix of civilians, Interahamwe (the militia largely held responsible for the genocide), and members of the defeated Rwandan military (the Forces Armées Rwandaises [FAR])—sought refuge in then-Zaire, after the RPF took power in Kigali. The refugee camps became controlled by the Interahamwe and FAR, which over the next couple of years, with the blessing of Mobutu Sese Seko's central government and regional strongmen, began launching attacks into neighboring Rwanda and against the Tutsi (Banyamulenge) population in South Kivu. Frustrated by international inaction, the Rwandan government and local Banyamulenge launched a multipronged attack in 1996 against the refugee camps, Interahamwe, and Zairian army. Largely orchestrated by the Rwandan and, to a lesser extent, Ugandan governments, the rebels united as the Alliance des Forces Démocratiques pour la Libération du Congo-Zaire (AFDL), led by Laurent-Désiré Kabila, a Katangan involved in the "Simba" rebellions of the 1960s, who had since lived semiclandestinely and occasionally in exile. The rebels quickly swept westward, gaining control of the country's mineral resources. As they moved toward Kinshasa, Angolan government troops poured across the border to assist them in the overthrow of Mobutu, who fled in May 1997. By the following year, however, Kabila's relations with his Rwandan and Ugandan mentors had soured, and he demanded that they withdraw their troops immediately. More important, various local conflicts concerning land and identity in the east continued to find violent expression. Putting together another group of disenfranchised Congolese (some of whom had ties or were members of Mobutu's former regime), Rwanda and Uganda orchestrated another rebellion in eastern Congo—this time with the goal of deposing the man they had put in power a year earlier. By early August 1998, the rebels were making territorial gains through the east and, leaping across the country in a captured aircraft, deployed in Bas-Congo and threatened Kinshasa. In a desperate attempt to cling to power, Kabila convinced Zimbabwe, Namibia, and Angola to shore up his regime by sending troops (Dunn 2002). This intervention occurred under the guise of Southern African Development Community solidarity, but John Clark (2002) notes that each state was motivated by self-interest. A stalemate ensued and within a few months the rebels in the eastern part of the country had splintered, and eight neighboring countries had been brought into the fray. Although outright military victory proved impossible, Kabila repeatedly thwarted attempts to realize a negotiated settlement, until a lone bodyguard assassinated him on 16 January 2001. His son and successor, Joseph Kabila, eventually signed a series of agreements that removed foreign troops and brought a tentative peace to much of the country. Over 5 million people were killed in the conflicts between 1994 and 2003, mostly from disease, starvation, and other conflict-related causes, making it the deadliest war since World War II. Yet even after the 2003 peace agreement and another ceasefire in 2009, tensions and violence continue to plague the east of the country. In 2018 it was estimated that there were at least seventy armed groups in the east, along with 19,000 UN peacekeepers, with over 3 million refugees and internally displaced persons (IDPs). The complexity of the situation in the DRC reflects its nature as a composite conflict, and alerts us to be sensitive to *how* conflicts evolve over time, complicating static typologies.

Changing Patterns

Before we turn to an examination of the various theories seeking to explain why conflict occurs in Africa, it is useful to note the ways in which those conflicts have shifted since the end of colonization. In this section, we demarcate three eras: the Cold War, the immediate post–Cold War, and the new millennium.[3]

The Cold War in Africa

Early African armed guerrilla movements, which took place during the Cold War, were largely characterized by their anticolonial nationalism. Examples include the Mau Mau uprising in Kenya in 1952–1957, the armed rebellion of the Union des Populations du Cameroun in 1955–1960, and the Kwilu and Simba rebellions in Congo in 1963–1967. There was little outside support for any of these movements. Moreover, although they made broad nationalist claims, these rebellions depended heavily on specific ethnic groups, which limited their eventual influence.

Beyond the commitment to national self-determination, one can question whether insurgents of this early era invoked ideology as a convenient rhetorical cover. Even in the case of the Mau Mau, there is considerable debate about whether the uprising should be understood as a sustained armed revolt born out of anticolonial nationalist sentiments or as a Kikuyu revolt bent on capturing state power (Maloba 1998; Branch 2009; Githuku 2016). While Amilcar Cabral of Guinea-Bissau and Pierre Mulele, who led the Kwilu rebellions in Congo, both staked out strong ideological positions, they stand out as exceptional. Most armed movements were less ideologically coherent. In contrast to Mulele, for example, most of the leaders of the Congo's early eastern rebellions had localized agendas, born out of the immediate politics of place fueled by the alienation and anger of marginalized youths who directed their violence toward state representatives and other privileged elements of society, such as intellectuals, with deadly results (Weiss 1966; Willame 1972; Hoskyns 1965).

Secessions provided the other main type of conflict at the onset of independence. There was the Katanga and Kasai secession in Congo, followed by Nigeria's brutal Biafran civil war, during which the southeast section of the country attempted to break away. Moreover, armed groups in Western Sahara and Eritrea fought for territorial liberation (or secession, depending on one's perspective) against an annexing African state, Morocco and Ethiopia, respectively. The burst of secessionism in the 1960s might have derived from the relative lack of entrenchment at the time of the principle of postcolonial sovereignty. But the UN intervention in Congo and the lack of foreign recognition of the breakaway states affirmed the principle of territorial integrity of African states and doomed these experiments. The secessionist momentum of the early 1960s subsided. It is worth noting, however, that while the main secessionist wars started during the Cold War, the only two successful secessions took place afterward.

By the 1970s, the Cold War context began exerting a notable influence on African armed conflicts, as the participants tended to be more ideologically oriented (at least superficially) and external support became pronounced. Though most African states had gained independence by the end of the 1960s, those that had not—namely the Portuguese colonies of Angola, Mozambique, and Guinea-Bissau, and white-ruled Rhodesia and South Africa—experienced prolonged wars that were informed by Cold War geopolitical machinations. Likewise, the handful of African interstate conflicts, such as the Ogaden War, between Ethiopia and Somalia, were often played out against the backdrop of proxy conflicts between the United States and the Soviet Union, the two competing superpowers.

Given the ideologically saturated framing of the Cold War by both superpowers, it is not surprising that African armed insurgents increasingly employed revolutionary discourses usually grounded in variations of Marxism-Leninism and Maoism. Taking their cues from contemporary Asian anticolonial insurgencies, as well as Mao Zedong's successful revolution in China, these armed groups drew upon the emerging doctrine of guerrilla warfare. Of course, many armed groups espoused certain ideological commitments in part to secure financial and military aid from like-minded patrons. The rapidity with which many of these leaders dropped their ideological trappings at the end of the Cold War suggests the shallowness with which they embraced their "causes" in the first place. Regardless of their ideological orientation, these armed guerrillas were able to take advantage of external supporters, occasionally from neighboring states but more often from the Cold War superpowers and their allies, which enabled them to fight protracted guerrilla wars regardless of their popularity among the domestic population. One can think of Mozambique's Resistência Nacional Moçambicana (RENAMO) and Angola's União Nacional para a Independência Total de Angola (UNITA) as relevant examples.

The Cold War also witnessed the increased militarization of many African states. Due to the geopolitical jockeying, weak regimes enjoyed external support that effectively shored up and entrenched neopatrimonial rule across the continent. The superpowers also made it possible for African states to use scarce foreign exchange for weapon purchases (Howe 2001). In many cases, Cold War aid both empowered and circumscribed African states. On the one hand, superpower support provided African leaders with international legitimacy and access to valuable resources, which often meant that their survival was not contingent on domestic legitimacy. On the other hand, these African regimes privileged militarization over economic development to ensure their own survival. Witness the evolution of US aid during the Cold War. In 1973, 78 percent of US bilateral aid to sub-Saharan Africa was for development, and 22 percent for political and strategic purposes. But by 1985 the numbers had almost reversed, with 67 percent of aid going for political and strategic purposes and only 33 percent for development (Spero and Hart 2003:204). This situation probably primed many African societies for the violent domestic collapse that several experienced once the Cold War system ended.

Immediate Post–Cold War Era: The Emergence of "New Wars"?

The structural shift from bipolarity to multipolarity at the end of the Cold War arguably impacted the nature of conflicts around the world. While intrastate wars have always been common, in the twenty-first century they now account for 95 percent of all the world's armed conflicts. While the immediate post–Cold War era witnessed a decrease in armed conflicts in most of the developing world, Africa actually experienced a significant increase. Each year during the 1990s, the average number of armed conflicts in Africa was twice that of the previous decade. At the end of the 1990s, more Africans were dying in armed conflicts than were people in the rest of the world combined, with the continent accounting for more than half of the globe's major armed conflicts (Williams 2011:5). What explains the increase? How were these conflicts different than those of the Cold War?

The sudden end of the Cold War dramatically altered the ideologically encoded geopolitical landscape, as the existing ideological frameworks, particularly the seemingly discredited leftist ideologies, suddenly seemed irrelevant. As William Reno (2007:72) noted, armed insurgents now adopt "contemporary-sounding generic labels typical of development and human rights NGOs," such as in Liberia, home to Liberians United for Reconciliation and Democracy (LURD) and the Movement for Democracy in Liberia (MODEL). As such, formal political ideas across a left-right dimension seem to be less relevant in Africa's armed struggles than other political motivations.

The collapse of the Cold War altered the financial landscape of insurgency as well. External support virtually vanished overnight. The

United States, for example, no longer found it necessary to fund groups such as Jonas Savimbi's UNITA in Angola or RENAMO in Mozambique. These groups had to find other sources of funding or seek a negotiated accommodation with their adversaries. Soon after the collapse of the Soviet Union, several Cold War–era African conflicts either dissipated or were resolved by diplomatic initiatives. In those cases, the superpower lifelines that kept the conflict alive quickly dried up, making a continuation of the struggle problematic for the parties involved. Yet in other cases, long-running conflicts entered their second or even third decade. These tended to be struggles that were peripheral to the Cold War, such as the LRA conflict, receiving relatively little attention from either the Soviet Union or the United States.

The end of the Cold War also heralded a brief second wave of African secessionist movements. The partition of the Soviet Union and Yugoslavia altered the international norms regarding territorial integrity, leading to a resurgence of autonomy-seeking activities by regional leaders around the world, Africa included. Moreover, external pressure from Western donors advancing electoral democracy had the effect of undermining several authoritarian regimes, emboldening opposition forces pursuing self-determination. The de facto secessions of Somaliland and Puntland occurred after Somalia had all but collapsed as a functional state. Senegal's Casamance conflict, although it had begun in 1982, also took on renewed military vigor in 1990. Tuareg secessionism emerged as a violent political project in both Niger and Mali. By the middle to late 1990s, however, Western donors, faced with increased conflicts in the developing world, returned to policies supporting state integrity rather than self-determination, which contributed to largely closing this second window of separatist opportunity (Englebert and Hummel 2005).

The international small-arms market burgeoned in the wake of the Cold War's collapse, with cheap weaponry becoming readily available (Muggah 2002). There is little doubt that groups that came to control mineral-rich areas, such as the RUF in Sierra Leone, the various Liberian factions, and insurgency groups in eastern Congo, used these minerals to tap into emerging international weapon markets. Armed groups were also able to take advantage of new advances in communications technology. The ubiquity of cell and satellite phones on the African continent increased the ability of guerrillas to communicate on the battlefield and with the international community. In Congo, Laurent Kabila's men used cell phones to coordinate their assault against Mobutu's shrinking forces in 1996–1997. Satellite phones also enabled rebel leaders to communicate with the international media. Both Foday Sankoh and Sam Bockarie of the RUF, for instance, used them to connect directly to the British Broadcasting Corporation's Africa outlet. For other groups, the Internet provided another tool by which to communicate with external audiences. Websites were created, often by external supporters in Europe or the United States, in order to champion the causes of rebel groups, circulate their agendas, network with external supporters, and raise funds.

A number of scholars argued that the complexity of African conflicts significantly increased during the 1990s and, with it, the difficulties in making sense of them. Paul Richards (2005b) argued that modern African conflicts are part of broader ongoing social processes, making it difficult to distinguish between situations of war and peace, but with much of Africa existing in a liminal stage between the two. Within this increasingly ambiguous context, some authors characterized the post–Cold War conflicts as "new wars" to call attention to the changing characteristic of these conflicts as well as their connectivity to the processes of globalization. Mary Kaldor (1999) argues that "new wars" are the antithesis of the old ones, which were conducted between states with a monopoly of violence within their own territories and with professional armies behaving according to accepted rules of combat. So-called new wars take place in weakened states, with little to no monopoly of violence, unable to exert their authority across their territory. Armies are no longer professionalized, and compete with private security forces, civilian militias, and armed gangs of bandits. There appear to be no frontlines, no separation of civil from military, and no agreed-upon rules of combat.

Kaldor and others argue that these "new wars" are driven by the collapse or disintegration of states that have buckled under the pressures of globalization, fueling corruption, criminality and an increased propensity for violence. Conflict becomes increasingly privatized as paramilitary groups grow and nonstate actors undermine the legitimacy of the state. The "new wars" thesis posits that these conflicts are made possible because many governments are unable to exercise many of the functions traditionally ascribed to the Westphalian state model. In the context of contemporary globalization, these new wars are decentralized and combatants finance themselves through plundering resources and accessing informal economic networks, and thus a reliance on the local population is greatly diminished. Globalization has also meant that combatants acquire their weaponry directly or indirectly through the global arms market, making access to the tools of violence significantly easier than before.

In contrast, Ian Clark (1999) argues that globalization is not undermining the state as much as transforming it. Under the demands of globalization, the domestic bargains about what the state is able to provide and what citizens are prepared to sacrifice are being renegotiated. This is evident in the types of security arrangements that governments are willing to provide, and their ability to pursue them unilaterally. For Clark and others, globalization is leading states not to wither away but to transform themselves to deal with a wide range of challenges and opportunities.

Other observers stress the regional and transnational nature of many contemporary African conflicts. Chris Huggins and Jenny Clover (2005) note the complex interrelationship between nontraditional actors, reflected in the complicated networks of insurgents and criminal gangs in recent conflicts in the Horn, the Maghreb, and parts of West Africa. With the rise of humanitarian interventions to address these conflicts, aid organizations, UN agencies, armed forces, and private security firms are often networked as well (Autesserre 2010). These responses indicate the complex ways in which African conflicts are becoming increasingly regionalized.

Observers have also paid attention to the *character* of violence employed in modern African conflicts. Many have noted the high prevalence of child soldiers in African conflicts (Brett and Sprecht 2004; Annan and Blattman 2008). During the Sierra Leone civil war, it was estimated that nearly 70 percent of the combatants were under the age of eighteen (Brocklehurst 2007). For many, the use of child soldiers further illustrates the belief that Africa's "new wars" are characterized by decentralized violence, brutality, and horrific atrocities. Armed insurgencies in Sierra Leone, Liberia, and Uganda, for example, became infamous for their use of torture and mutilation, often against unarmed civilians. For some observers, these acts of brutality were regarded as evidence of inherent irrationality, savagery, and a "coming anarchy" (Kaplan 1994). The cases of Sierra Leone and Liberia produced multiple interpretations of the conflicts and the reasons for their marked brutality (see Richards 1996; Abdullah 1998; Bøås 2001; Richards 2005b; Fithen and Richards 2005). In his examination of Sierra Leone, Ibrahim Abdullah (1998:204, 207) argued that socially marginalized youth were "prone to criminal behaviour, petty theft, drugs, drunkenness and gross indiscipline." Lacking opportunities, they took up arms in pursuit of a "radical alternative" to the existing regime. Thandika Mkandawire (2002:181) suggests that the excessive violence in that conflict was driven by an innate hostility of urban youths against rural peasants. Other scholars sought to explain the rationality for the brutality, often suggesting that it reflected patterns of violence already embedded within society (Jabri 1996:22–23). Anthropologist Rosa Ehrenreich (1998) argued that the brutality of Uganda's LRA is grounded in established social and spiritual beliefs of the region. In fact, the LRA illustrates the spiritual dimensions of many modern African conflicts. In his work on the Liberian civil war, Stephen Ellis (1999) examined the ways in which spiritual symbols and religious beliefs were employed, specifically how secret societies influenced the ways power was understood and violence enacted.

Another notable characteristic of contemporary African conflicts is the fact that armed insurgents are overwhelmingly young men and the violence that they engage in has gender dimensions, including rape, sexual violence, and mutilation of women's bodies. Thus, an understanding of contemporary African insurgencies requires a critical examination of social factors, including the complex role of masculinity and violence upon women's bodies (Baaz and Stern 2013; Baaz 2017). Yet one should avoid assuming that only African conflicts are gendered, as well as resisting overly simplistic gendered readings of African conflicts. In Sierra Leone, for example, armed groups with more women in their ranks committed more rapes than groups with fewer women, with women participating in roughly a quarter of the rapes committed (Cohen 2013). Likewise, sensitivity to the generational dimension of African conflicts, and the role of youth, is needed (Utas and Vigh 2017).

Finally, many scholars emphasize that Africa's "new wars" fundamentally challenge state-centric assumptions about conflict and security. For example, Mark Duffield (1998) argued that the traditional statist focus on thinking about conflict obscures the fundamental nature of contemporary conflicts, where the goal is often not to impose political authority over a territorial space in the traditional sense. Duffield speaks of "postmodern conflicts" to illustrate that emerging substate conflicts blur traditional social, political, and military categories, thus making responses grounded in traditional state-to-state strategic assumptions deeply flawed. Others have employed the term "post-Westphalian wars" to characterize conflicts such as those in the DRC, Somalia, and Sudan in which the state's monopoly of violence has been significantly challenged from the outside and inside, leading to conflicts that are fought primarily between militias, paramilitaries, warlord armies, private security firms, and criminal gangs.

A New Millennium

Arguably the post–Cold War era can be demarcated further by noting significant developments since the turn of the century. In the first few years of the twenty-first century, Africa had the highest number of major armed conflicts, thirteen, of any region in the world. Yet more than half of those conflicts came to an end by 2008, and by the end of the decade, Africa was home only to one-fifth of the world's major conflicts (Williams 2011:5). Within the past few years, however, new wars have broken out in Mali, South Sudan, and the Central African Republic, with conflicts continuing in Nigeria, Somalia, and the Democratic Republic of Congo.

But while the new millennium initially witnessed a drop in the number of armed conflicts, this era was also shaped by the events of 11 September 2001, as the US-driven "war on terror" has become a new frame by which many Western policymakers and scholars engage with contemporary African guerrilla movements. Even though the label "war on terror" has dropped from fashion, the United States and the European Union continue to be highly concerned about "failed states" and "ungoverned zones" as breeding grounds for international terrorism, and with "countering violent extremism." As we discuss in Chapter 8, Western states' concerns about terrorism, failed states, and illegal immigrants have come to dominate their engagement with the continent in recent years, influencing the character of African international relations.

It should be noted that this new geopolitical framework has also provided opportunities and resources for African political elites (Dunn 2008b; Jourde 2006). America's focus on combating terrorism has led to substantial increases in military support for select African states, as well as an increased US military presence on the continent. Moreover, some African leaders have publicly linked their own struggles against domestic insurgencies to the US-led "war on terror." Ugandan president Yoweri Museveni, for example, frequently situates his government's war with the LRA in this larger context. Other states have used anti-terrorist rhetoric and practices to justify repressive measures against their domestic opposition. Leaders such as Charles Taylor and Robert Mugabe, among others, frequently labeled their opponents as "terrorists" in order to justify their detention and the stifling of dissent (Adebajo 2003:181).

Finally, while African armed groups in the immediate post–Cold War era were largely devoid of defining ideological orientations, by the beginning of the twenty-first century Islamic jihadism was becoming a significant feature of many emerging insurgencies, from al-Qaeda in the Islamic Maghreb to Nigeria's Boko Haram to al-Shabaab on the Horn of Africa. Indeed, recent years have witnessed the spread of armed Islamic jihadist groups in countries assumed to be immune to such developments, such as Kenya, Uganda, and Mozambique. While these groups are sometimes characterized—by themselves and their opponents—as part of a global jihad (with AQIM and al-Shabaab pledging allegiance to al-Qaeda, and Boko Haram proclaiming itself the Islamic State's West African Province)—the degree to which religious beliefs are a causal factor in these conflicts is debatable. In their comparative work on African insurgencies, Bøås and Dunn (2017) argue that these groups appropriate the global discourse of Islamic jihad while remaining rooted in the local cleavages that drive the conflict, reflecting a complex global-local nexus. Bøås and Dunn also draw attention to the dynamic of "brands" and "branches." Like most scholars, they reject the notion that these groups represent African branches of an organized global jihadist movement. Rather, they argue that groups such as AQIM, Boko Haram, and al-Shabaab employ a global jihadist ideology in many ways akin to a "global brand." Positioning themselves as part of a global jihadist struggle, these movements seek to connect their local and regional struggles within a recognizable "brand" that provides them with significant resources at home and from abroad. Such a framing also provides an easy and recognizable shorthand for the complicated and unique sociopolitical dynamics informing the insurgency, while also making local movements appear much more powerful and threatening. AQIM's international significance, for example, changed greatly once it attached itself to al-Qaeda, making it more feared than it had previously been. Boko Haram's choreographed courtship with the Islamic State was driven in large part by the desire to enhance its global stature and exaggerate its power, making it look more powerful than it actually was in the face of regional counter-offensives. There are risks to employing a global brand, however, from the dilution of local support to the rise of unwanted attention, such as drone attacks by the United States.

While the rise of Islamic jihadist movements reflects the growing complexities of local/global connections that characterize contemporary African insurgencies, they also represent new challenges because such movements often reject the modern state and the system of sovereign states. No matter how brutal, chaotic, and violent an insurgency such as Sierra Leone's Revolutionary United Front was, the international community could still enter into negotiations with it because the RUF recognized the legitimacy of Sierra Leone as a state, as well as that of the international state system. In contrast, groups such as AQIM and Boko Haram reject the very notion of the modern state. As such, they have little interest in being integrated into the established social and political order. Given this, and the fact that they engage in asymmetrical warfare where the goal is to outlast their opponents, they are proving to be very hard to defeat.

At the same time, from Nigeria to the DRC, Africa is witnessing an increase in parochial rebel groups. Protecting local communities from predation, particularly from the central state, some of these groups reject not just the legitimacy of the central government, but also the legitimacy of the state itself. Thus, the concomitant rise of Islamist insurgencies and parochial rebels may signal important developments in the evolution of African conflicts for the decades to come.

Theories of War in Africa

There have been numerous theories offered to explain why conflicts occur in Africa. Some approaches seek to uncover similarities across conflicts, while others emphasize the uniqueness of each conflict. Some approaches emphasize a single primary causal factor, while others attempt to consider a multiplicity of factors. In his work on African conflicts, Paul Williams (2016:9) offered a culinary metaphor, arguing that one should "think about the many different recipes for making wars and the multiple ingredients which go into them." The metaphor is useful because, as Williams notes: "First, wars are complex social systems and, like particular dishes, are comprised of multiple ingredients. Second, because the ingredients can be combined in a variety of different ways, recipes, like wars, don't always turn out as planned and, as with wars, it pays to have the correct instruments to hand at the right time or else the recipe will be ruined. Third, like wars, recipes don't make themselves—there must be cooks, and it is important to know whether one is dealing with a novice or a master chef." In this section, we identify and discuss some of the primary "ingredients" that have been identified by scholars of African conflicts.

Resource Scarcity

War-prone countries tend to be poor today. The poorest one-sixth of humanity endures about four-fifths of the world's civil wars. In seeking to explain this pattern, some scholars assume that poverty magnifies inequality, making it a powerful cause of armed violence. Some recent research, dubbed "Malthusian" or "neo-Malthusian" by proponents and critics alike, examines the relationship between conflict and scarcity. Thomas Homer-Dixon (1994) has been influential in this respect, suggesting three hypotheses. First, decreasing supplies of physically controllable resources would provoke interstate "simple-scarcity" conflicts or "resource wars." Michael Klare (2001) has asserted that competition and control over critical natural resources will be the guiding principle behind the use of military force in the twenty-first century. Second, environmental scarcity might lead groups to migrate and produce "ethnic" conflict between newcomers and established communities (this has happened in Burkina Faso, for example, where many Mossi have moved to the country's southwest region in search of land). Finally, Homer-Dixon (1999) argued that environmental scarcity would not only impoverish people but also weaken institutions such as the state and cause "deprivation conflicts." In short, increased scarcity will lead to resource capture by those with the means to do so, and marginalization of those without. African states' lack of "adaptive capacity" (Homer-Dixon and Blitt 1998:9) might make them particularly susceptible to these forces. The claim is that economically poor states, lacking both financial and human capital and being ethnically diverse, are less likely to be able to manage severe environmental challenges that lead to scarcity.

Approaches that make causal links between scarcity and violent conflict have been strongly challenged by other scholars. Paul Richards (1996), for example, has roundly rejected what he labels the "Malthus with guns" thesis by pointing out that it fails to note the possibility that resources have nonmaterial dimensions and that the causal factor might be scarcity not of resources but of justice in resource allocation. Scholars have noted that the relationship between environmental scarcity and contextual factors is highly interactive, making it impossible to determine the relative power of environmental scarcity as a cause of violence in specific cases. Moreover, there are a number of empirical studies that suggest that environmental change rarely causes conflict directly and only occasionally does so indirectly (Kahl 2006; Derman, Odgaard, and Sjaastad 2007; see also Kevane and Gray 2008). Thus, one should be cautious in inferring a simple relationship between increased environmental scarcity and warfare.

While neo-Malthusian assumptions and causal claims generate a fair amount of scholarly controversy, they do raise important considerations about the role of scarce resources, such as land, in the development of armed conflicts. On a continent that remains overwhelmingly agricultural, land continues to lie at the heart of social, economic, and political life. Moreover, there remains a lack of clarity regarding property rights in contemporary Africa, and land tenure continues to be deeply contested on much of the continent (Nustad 2015; Odgaard 2006; Peters 2004). The potential for disputes over land to contribute to the outbreak of armed conflict has been of central concern. Citing such examples as Burundi, Côte d'Ivoire, Rwanda, and Zimbabwe, the World Bank acknowledged in its 2003 report *Land Policies for Growth and*

Poverty Reduction that "deprivation of land rights as a feature of more generalized inequality in access to economic opportunities and low economic growth have caused seemingly minor social or political conflicts to escalate into large-scale conflicts" (Deininger 2003:157). The Social Conflict in Africa Database identified almost 2,000 reports of land-related conflicts between 1990 and 2016 (SCAD 2017).

The degree to which land insecurity is assumed to be a cause of conflict varies among scholars. The *Small Arms Survey* (2013:104) noted that "almost every armed conflict in Africa has had a land dimension to it, but very few are concerned solely with land issues. In almost all cases, land is one of many contributing factors—such as economic inequality, political competition, discrimination, and exclusion—that fuel violence." Much, of course, depends on the specific case under examination. Land scarcity can function as a structural or proximate cause of conflict. In the latter case, land disputes, tenure insecurity, and inequality in land access are combined with other factors that contribute to the outbreak of violence, as was arguably the case with the 1994 Rwandan genocide (André and Platteau 1998). Of course, land insecurity does not, in and of itself, necessarily lead to armed conflict. Not all countries suffering land scarcity or inequality in landownership experience conflict. Yet in Africa and elsewhere, access to land is often interwoven with ethnic dimensions. Land use patterns and customary land tenure systems have historically had an ethnic basis, something colonialism institutionalized in many parts of Africa. This has meant that important issues around citizenship and migration—specifically claims of autochthony—come into play and can gain powerful salience.

Autochthony, literally meaning "emerging from the soil," implies localist forms of belonging, and can inform debates about the electoral eligibility of candidates as well as violent struggles over landownership (Bøås and Dunn 2013; Geschiere 2004). The presence of such controversies on the African continent is not a new phenomenon. Their origins are found in both precolonial practices and ideas about the politics of place embedded in the colonial project. After independence, many African states introduced citizenship laws to determine who legitimately lived within the borders of their territories, and could therefore enjoy the privileges of belonging, and who did not. Land issues became particularly vulnerable to the politics of identity and belonging, especially where two or more groups "shared" the land. In this case, one group might claim autochthony or "son of the soil" status, presenting the others as "newcomers," "immigrants," or "strangers." Debates over "who belongs" and who has access to resources, including the ability to vote, can become politicized, particularly by aggressive political entrepreneurs. Of course, claims of autochthony need not necessarily lead to violence (Geschiere 2009; Dunn 2009; Jackson 2006; Bayart, Geschiere, and Nyamnjoh 2001).

Abundance

In contrast to the resource-scarcity hypothesis, a number of scholars have focused on how an abundance of resources contributes to conflict. Paul Collier (2000, 2007), for example, suggests that the calculations of costs and gains made by leaders of a rebellion are shaped by the revenues to be generated by control of natural resources, the availability of young men, and low levels of economic development, all of which, he argues, make conflict more likely. For Collier, economic greed (or opportunity cost) and control over resources are far stronger explanatory factors than political grievance. Collier and others often imply that African wars are fought not over political issues but in order to gain access to profits. Thus, conflict is regarded as driven by the pursuit of personal wealth instead of political power (though one may argue that these are the same things in neopatrimonial societies). Philippe le Billon (2005) has noted that, as natural resources gain in importance for combatants, the nature of the conflict itself changes, as military activities become centered on areas of economic significance. No longer is the Maoist tactic of winning over the peasantry important. Rather, insurgents often seek to establish permanent strongholds or areas of "insecurity" wherever resources are located. The state then typically deploys troops to the area, who often join in the plunder, making it hard to distinguish between rebels and soldiers (who might well collaborate) and displacing civilian populations. Cases in point include the so-called sobels of Sierra Leone and the multiple violent actors in eastern Congo after 2003.

The "greed" thesis suggests that contemporary African conflicts are explained primarily by economic considerations. Some observers have suggested that the goal of many armed conflicts in Africa is not necessarily the defeat of the enemy in battle, but the institutionalization of violence for profit (Berdal and Malone 2000). Combatants gain access to wealth not just by looting but also by maintaining resource-rich territories that are linked to international trading networks. This brings us back to the "resource curse" of Chapter 6, which associates an abundance of natural resources, particularly mineral exports, with poor economic performance and greater socioeconomic inequalities and conflict (Ross 1999 and 2004; Cilliers and Dietrich 2000). One oft-cited example of the resource curse is the presence of oil in the Niger Delta, which has caused a number of states to expand control over oil and oil revenues against a backdrop of increased demands for self-determination (and access to resource-generated profits) from minorities in the region (Soares de Oliveira 2007). In recent years, the region has seen the rise of armed groups and militant youth movements that have contributed to fueling violence (Adunbi 2015; ICG 2009; Watts 2005). An umbrella movement for several militant groups, the Movement for the Emancipation of the Niger Delta (MEND), has blown up pipelines, kidnapped foreign oil workers, and killed government troops. Its main demands are control over oil and reparations for environmental damage. The group's popularity can be partially understood given that, despite billions of dollars in revenue from decades of oil production, many of the inhabitants of the Niger Delta remain impoverished. But in keeping with the "greed not grievance" thesis, it can be suggested that the impetus for the commencement of violence has more to do with economic profitability than with political marginalization. For example, several other militant groups have joined MEND in the region, arguably taking advantage of the foreign oil companies' willingness to negotiate with kidnappers and pay large ransoms (usually around $250,000) for captured workers.

Critics such as Richards (2005b) and Bøås and Dunn (2007) have argued that the "greed not grievance" approach assumes that theft and predation are the *reasons* for the guerrilla struggle, mistaking effect for cause. While such an approach may help explain how some conflicts are sustained, they fail to explain why conflicts start in the first place. There is clearly merit in the argument that economic rivalries greatly complicate and prolong a number of wars, the case of the Angolan civil war being the clearest example. But the "greed not grievance" thesis primarily offers the observation that economic factors are necessary but not sufficient conditions for conflicts to occur. It would be a mistake, for example, to assume that the recent wars in central and western Africa started as competition over control of alluvial diamonds, coltan, or other natural resources. In fact, in both Sierra Leone and the DRC, extraction and marketing of natural resources became significant components only after the conflicts were well under way. Obviously, economic agendas are an integral part of African wars, as elsewhere. But the desire to accumulate (or, for grassroots combatants, to merely escape poverty), while an important motivation, is not the only one. Even authors closely associated with the "greed" thesis have later argued that to focus excessively on material explanations and the greed of actors may lead to one-sided explanations of conflict (Collier, Hoeffler, and Rohner 2009; Berdal 2003, 2005). Ultimately, resources—either scarce or abundant—do not cause conflicts in and of themselves, but depend on political conditions and circumstances.

Modernity

Some observers have asserted that African conflicts emerge because of a crisis of modernity. Specifically, they argue that African societies are incompatible with Western modernity and civilization (Huntington 1993; Kaplan 1994). These explanations employ evocative "Heart of Darkness"-style imagery of Africa and Africans being incapable of existing in the "modern" world, with particular attention given to "barbaric" practices of violence and the employment of witchcraft and other forms of religious spirituality. The underlying assumption is that Africa and Western modernity are somehow incompatible. Cold War competition and the balance of nuclear terror kept local conflicts in check, but now endemic hostilities have reasserted themselves. A case in point is Robert Kaplan's (1994, 1996) discussion of the RUF conflict in Sierra Leone, which he explains in terms of the dissolution of Africa's social fabric and the inherent inability of Africans to develop into a modern society. While roundly dismissed by most academics, this line of explanation continues to reassert itself in popular accounts of contemporary African conflicts.

A different angle is taken by scholars who argue that the crisis is with the project of modernity itself, and not with an incompatibility of cultures (Appadurai 1999; Dunn 2009). For some, the Westphalian state system—the representation and vehicle for Western modernity as it was exported to the rest of the world—has become increasingly challenged as a concept, an institution, and a practice. The reasons for this are varied, but the point is that these institutions and practices are failing to meet the needs within the lived experiences of most of the world's population, including Africans. Again, the concomitant increase in locally focused parochial rebels and caliphate-oriented Islamist groups may reflect a growing challenge to the legitimacy of existing states and of the state system itself. At the same time, conflicts can emerge as the institutions and practices of Western modernity are reinterpreted, reinvented, and reemployed. This point will be revisited later in our discussion of state collapse.

Elite and Factional Competition

Political competition in any country is typically driven by political elites, usually of different backgrounds and policy perspectives, jockeying for access to political power and the various institutional resources associated with the state. Given the nature of neopatrimonial rule, the stakes for the winners and losers of elite competition can be quite high in Africa. Political leaders such as Felix Houphouët-Boigny, Mobutu

Sese Seko, and Jomo Kenyatta were masterful at managing elite competition to their own advantage. Problems often emerge, however, when political elites feel that the existing system thwarts their ability for political engagement. In such cases, the employment of violence may become increasingly acceptable for frustrated elites and their supporters (Bayart 1993; Reno 1995).

In Africa, as elsewhere, many armed groups either are led by or contain large numbers of people who once enjoyed the fruits of state power and now seek to recapture those benefits through force of arms. Many former Mobutists, excluded from access to the formal and informal political system of post-Mobutu Congo, picked up arms under the banners of the Rassemblement Congolais pour la Démocratie (RCD) or the Mouvement de Libération du Congo (MLC). Likewise, some of the leaders of the Forces Nouvelles in Côte d'Ivoire were political elites excluded by the post-Houphouët state. It is worth noting that frustrated political elites who pick up arms are often interested in capturing the state and the spoils that come with it, while guerrilla leaders who are external to the established political elite (such as the LRA's Joseph Kony) are usually less interested in capturing the central government. In this line of analysis, many African conflicts can be understood as physical manifestations of the breakdown of the existing political system and its ability to successfully manage elite competition nonviolently (Bayart 1993; Day 2019; Mkandawire 2002).

Factional conflicts tend to emerge when competing elites mobilize their constituents in a struggle with other groups for scarce state-controlled resources (Chazan et al. 1999:201; Roessler 2016). This occasionally happens when an electoral faction decides that success is more likely through armed struggle than through the established legal system. Such was the case when Jonas Savimbi's UNITA restarted its armed struggle in 1992 after failing to win an outright majority in elections. Likewise, elements of Mozambique's RENAMO renewed their armed struggle in 2013, twenty years after the end of the civil war, in response to their diminishing electoral success. Armed conflict is more likely to emerge from factional competition when the basis of mobilization is driven by feelings of social marginalization or regional disenfranchisement (Kuperman 2015). Around the world, regions or social groups that feel they are being marginalized by the central state have contributed to fostering the emergence of armed insurgencies. Africa is no different, as is evidenced by current armed conflicts in such places as the anglophone region of Cameroon and the northern and Delta regions of Nigeria.

Identity Conflicts

As noted in Chapter 3, Africa's ethnic and religious diversity is sometimes treated as a causal factor in explaining African conflicts. But it is fairly easy to dismiss the idea that differences in identity alone cause conflicts. As Paul Williams (2016:141) observed: "ethnicity does not cause armed conflict; rather so-called ethnic wars are usually the result of political power struggles between elites whose actions do not simply reflect static ethnic identities but instead shape identities and the political consequences that flow from them." The same can be said for religious and other forms of communal conflicts. Ultimately, identity differences do not cause conflicts, but they can be politicized to justify all sorts of actions, including political exclusion and violence.

So-called identity conflicts in Africa have typically been driven by subnational groups raising fundamental questions about, and challenges to, existing power relations within a state. In many cases, the nature and territorial existence of the state may be challenged. All postcolonial African states, with the exceptions of Swaziland (as of 2018, Eswatini) and Lesotho, have internal communal subdivisions, which provide fertile soil for the expression of political aspirations tied to subnational identities (Posner 2005). Donald Horowitz (1985) has argued that ethnic conflict is at the center of politics in divided societies, straining the bonds that sustain civility and often igniting violence. Philip Roessler (2016) has argued that, given the ethnic diversity in most African states, those in power must constantly balance the challenge of sharing power with ethnic rivals, who may seize power through a coup, versus excluding those groups and risking civil war. Yet it should be stressed that the expression of communal identities, whether they be ethnically, racially, or religiously defined, does not necessarily lead to armed conflict. In fact, many African states with diverse populations, such as Tanzania, have not experienced significant ethnic or subethnic conflicts. Communal struggles tend to emerge in states that have several large geographically distinct ethnoregional groups, such as Nigeria, Sudan, Angola, and Congo, or a dominant group and an extremely cohesive, culturally distinct, and usually economically more advantaged minority, such as in Ethiopia.

As discussed in Chapter 3, the European colonial project relied on the institutionalization, reification, and in some cases invention of ethnic identities (Nasong'o 2015). Under colonialism, perceived cultural identities often became the foundation for political identities, which were enforced within the territorial state and reproduced through the mechanism of the law as singular and unidimensional entities. For example, colonial rule in Rwanda turned the historically porous categories of Tutsi and Hutu into discrete and rigid political categories (Mamdani 2001). Across postcolonial Africa, electoral competition has sometimes contributed to politicizing ethnic and other subnational identities (Ottaway 1999). As Peter Geschiere and Francis Nyamnjoh (2000) have noted, political liberalization can lead to fierce debates on who belongs where, violent exclusion of "strangers," and a general affirmation of roots and origins as the basic criteria of citizenship and belonging. In many cases, political liberalization has contributed to fostering a markedly illiberal move toward closure and exclusion. For example, the 1991 national conference in Zaire not only introduced highly stringent citizenship laws but also denied the Banyarwanda delegation access to the conference.

Crawford Young (1976) observed that democratic competition rewards the numerically superior ethnoregional groupings, leaving the minorities—who, due to colonial practices, were often more educated and economically advanced—feeling underrepresented, marginalized, and disempowered. In some postcolonial African states, feelings of inequality and discrimination were exacerbated by elites constructing systems of patronage and political rewards based on shared ethnic identities. For example, Igbo fears of disempowerment and discrimination at the hands of the larger Hausa-Fulani led to Biafran secession and war. As discussed in Chapter 3, almost all postcolonial African states have had to contend with the possibility of subnational communal conflict, be they ethnically or religiously defined. Given the continent's subnational diversity, most modern African states have actually been quite successful in managing possible identity conflicts.

Yet some scholars, such as Edmond Keller (2014 and 1996), have asserted that one of the defining features of the post–Cold War era is the emergence or resurgence of subnationalism, particularly ethnicity, in multiethnic states. While this does not necessarily lead to armed conflict, many modern African conflicts are framed as identity conflicts. Chapter 3 explores the issues of ethnicity in African politics and notes the difference between the theoretical approaches of primordialism, constructivism, and instrumentalism. We will not replay those differences here, but we note that, regardless of your theoretical approach, communal identity is a quite real phenomenon, given that it can serve as symbolic justification for very concrete political and economic interests. Yet the degree to which ethnicity and identity are "ingredients" in African conflicts remains highly debated among scholars.

Crises of the African State

If one assumes that most armed conflicts involve struggles over power and access to state resources (from sovereignty to state coffers), it is worth noting the ways in which some African states have entered an era of crisis and how that relates to the emergence of armed conflicts. After 1990, some African states faced multiple challenges, from increased geopolitical marginalization in the wake of the Cold War to the eroding of established neopatrimonial systems, leading to the outright collapse of Somalia, Sierra Leone, Liberia, and the DRC. Recent scholarship has focused on three related aspects of state crisis that are relevant here: the bankruptcy of neopatrimonial systems, the emergence of fragile states, and the existence of collapsed states.

As discussed in Chapter 4, neopatrimonialism is a common characteristic of African politics, producing seemingly stable and long-lasting regimes in states that appear simultaneously both "strong" and "weak." Historically, neopatrimonialism has produced weak states with remarkably stable regimes, such as the Mobutist regime in Zaire. Yet the 1990s and early 2000s witnessed crises emerging in many of the existing neopatrimonial systems. In some cases, the patrimonial logic became so dominant that it lost its integrating and legitimating aspects, making it difficult, if not impossible, for the reciprocal assimilation of elites. Neopatrimonial systems rely on the ability of political elites to fulfill the expected vertical redistribution of resources through the patron-client relationship, and when they fail to do so, the legitimacy of existing leaders is undermined and their position of power becomes increasingly challenged. While this is often the traditional trajectory in the emergence of armed insurgencies against the ruling elite, what became significant in recent years is the perceived bankruptcy of the neopatrimonial state model itself in some contexts. This is evident in the rise of Islamic jihadist groups such as AQIM and al-Shabaab, but also true for secular groups such as the numerous militias in eastern DRC that carve out and maintain structures of governance as alternatives to the existing neopatrimonial state (Raeymaekers 2014). During the Liberian war, the Lofa Defense Force (LDF) and the United Liberian Movement for Democracy in Liberia–Kromah faction (ULIMO-K) were seen as movements attempting to protect their people against the backdrop of the collapsed neopatrimonial order (Ellis 1998; Reno 1998; Bøås 2005).

For some observers, the collapse of existing neopatrimonial systems can be regarded as either a cause or an effect of the rise in "weak" or "fragile" states across the continent. While scholars may employ different terms, such as "weak," "fictive," "fragile," and "shadow," the shared assumption is that state institutions continue to exist but are unable to function effectively for various reasons (Sandbrook 1985; Cruise O'Brien 1991). There are multiple dimensions and degrees of state fragility, suggesting a complex concept. As discussed in Chapter 2, some authors argue that the postcolonial African state was created structurally weak (Jackson and Rosberg 1982). For them, African political leaders and their external supporters have no interest in altering the status quo, and thus African weak states persist. For others, the African state has been made "weak" by the practices of African political elites. In many states, political leaders have used extrastate instruments to maintain their power, such as the employment of private military contractors (O'Brien 2000). Many political leaders have also protected their privileged positions through the creation of private armed militias. In some cases, militias are directly loyal to the regime in power, as in Côte d'Ivoire, where the Jeunes Patriotes and other militias in the southern part of the country were closely connected to the presidency of Laurent Gbagbo through an informal shadow-state structure. Similarly, in the Republic of Congo, former president Denis Sassou-Nguesso used his private militia, the Cobras, to return to power in 1997 (Clark 2008). In other situations, "freelance" militias are employed by the state to do their dirty work. This is one way to interpret the Sudanese government's handling of the crisis in Darfur, and the same analysis can also be applied to the employment of so-called former freedom fighters by the Zimbabwean regime in its land-grabbing schemes.

Whether inherent or created, the weakness and fragility of the African state might contribute to the rise of armed conflicts. As state institutions no longer prove effective instruments of power, new opportunities become available both to individual officials and to other "strongmen" whose interests often run counter to those of the ruler (Bøas and Dunn 2017; Utas 2012; Reno 1998). As the state shrinks and political competition can no longer be managed through legitimate channels, armed conflict emerges and the possibility of outright state collapse increases.

State collapse refers to situations in which the state's structure and authority cease to function in a recognizable way, with the result being that established law and political order fall apart and require reconstitution. While fragile states are able to perform the expected functions of states on some level, a collapsed state fails to practice its sovereign authority, perform its institutional role as a tangible organization of decisionmaking or its intangible role as a symbol of national identity, or operate as the guarantor of security for the population within its territory. William Zartman (1995:2–3) has argued that state collapse in

Africa has occurred in two waves. The first took place during the second decade of independence, "when regimes that replaced the original nationalist generation were overthrown, carrying the whole state structure with them into a vacuum." He points to the examples of Chad in 1980–1982, Uganda in 1979–1981, and Ghana in 1979–1981. The second wave occurred in the immediate post–Cold War era and continues to the present, exemplified by Liberia in the 1990s and Somalia today.

Collapsed states reflect those situations when the state experiences complete loss of control over political and economic space. Perhaps the most widely cited author in the literature on this topic, Zartman (1995:8) argues that state collapse is a "long-term degenerative disease," with the emergence of armed insurgents regarded as a symptom, not a cause, of the collapse. Armed insurgents and internal conflict, however, can accelerate the process of state collapse. As the state loses control over its political space, neighboring states and dissident groups involve themselves directly in the vacuum left by the collapsed political order. But what causes a state to collapse? Zartman conceives of the process as a long-term slippery slope in which the established political and social orders are slowly worn away, often by societal pressures. René Lemarchand (1997) argues that states experience turning or breaking points, such as a major influx of refugees into their territory, highly disputed transition elections, or the intervention of the military into state affairs. These triggering events often sharpen the edge of a conflict and can accelerate the process of internal decomposition, as happened in Zaire and Rwanda in the 1990s.

Implicit, and sometimes even explicit, in the state-collapse literature is a state-centrism that privileges strong institutional structures. Yet many have noted that state collapse has not been brought about by the anarchic tendencies of populations, but often by political elites trying to protect their privileges within the status quo. In Sierra Leone, for example, President Valentine Strasser reconfigured the bases of political authority and reshaped political networks in his favor, pursuing a strategy that intentionally destroyed state agencies and hastened state collapse (Reno 1995). The destruction of state institutions may not reflect so much the deterioration of political authority as dramatic shifts in the bases of political structure. Moreover, while many proponents of the collapsed-state approach advocate the strengthening of state structures (Chesterman, Ignatieff, and Thakur 2005; Zartman 2005), others question whether large centralized states can be reformed to serve the interests of the masses or are even the best instruments for economic and social development in Africa (Autesserre 2009; Longman 1998). Underpinning the state-collapse literature is an assumption that all states are constituted and function in a similar way: on a spectrum from good to bad. This begs the question: For whom is the state failing and how? Rather than trying to determine whether or not an African state is "failing" or "collapsing," one could investigate how political order is constituted and reconfigured, as Theodore Trefon (2004) did in Kinshasa and Timothy Raeymaekers (2014) did in eastern DRC. Ultimately, such studies illustrate that different actors within the state have different interests, and that what is good for some, such as informalized power structures that enable elite consolidation of power and profit, may not be good for ordinary citizens. In fact, the goal of the regime may be to create and sustain structures and power relations that are generally considered the consequences of state failure. Gérard Prunier and Rachel Gisselquist (2003), for example, portray Sudan as a "successfully failed" state, an intentionally hollowed-out entity sustained almost entirely by oil revenue.

From the perspective of conflict and security, collapsed states can exacerbate regional insecurity, as neighboring states worry that domestic dissidents will seek refuge in the vacuum of the collapsed state. This can be seen in the contemporary case of Somalia. Widely regarded as a collapsed state, the country has effectively been without a functioning central government since 1991. In 2018, the government remained ineffective and was only able to tentatively control what little territory it could through the military assistance of its neighbors. Much of the country is under the control of armed militias, including al-Shabaab. Practices of maritime piracy continue off the coast of Somalia, leading the North Atlantic Treaty Organization (NATO) to actively patrol the coastline. The United States has focused considerable attention on Somalia, as it fears that al-Shabaab is receiving support from al-Qaeda and training potential terrorists (Lindley 2009). In October 2011, neighboring Kenya sent hundreds of military personnel into Somalia, to secure the border region and thwart kidnappers who were launching incursions from Somalia. In response, al-Shabaab expanded its activities into Kenya, launching over a hundred acts of violence, including the 2013 Westgate Mall terrorist attack and the 2015 Garissa University College massacre, representing a significant regionalization of al-Shabaab's campaign (Menkhaus and Gore 2017).

Peacekeeping and Conflict Resolution

Postconflict African societies often illustrate the truism that peace is fragile. In many cases, a precarious balance exists between renewed conflict and sustained peace, which makes the term "postconflict" more than a little misleading. Some scholars have coined the term "conflict trap" to illustrate that many societies emerge from conflicts with only a fragile "negative" peace in which the structural causes of the conflict, such as underdevelopment and social inequality, go unaddressed (Collier and Sambanis 2002; Collier et al. 2003). It is estimated that half of the countries that are in their first decade of postconflict peace will fall back into conflict within that decade (Walter 2004). How do African conflicts end? What can be done to facilitate the cessation of hostilities? How can a lasting peace be established?

During the Cold War era, conflicts tended to end through the outright victory of one side over the other. Geopolitical competition between the superpowers exacerbated this situation, given that their approach to resolving conflicts was often to increase support for their beneficiaries. In the post–Cold War era, however, emphasis tends to focus on negotiations, consensus, and compromise. As such, increased attention is given to concepts such as peacekeeping and conflict resolution.

Johan Galtung (1975) distinguishes between peacekeeping, understood as halting violence of a conflict through military intervention; peacemaking, understood as reconciliation through mediation, negotiation, arbitration, and conciliation; and peacebuilding, which achieves social change through socioeconomic reconstruction and development. While the former two can address direct violence, peacebuilding is necessary, Galtung argues, to confront "structural violence" ingrained in such issues as long-term insecurity, economic injustice, and the culture of violence. Galtung's work has had a profound impact on the field of conflict resolution. A more recent theorist, John Paul Lederach (1997), built upon it to argue for the need to move away from a concern with resolving specific issues and toward a focus on restoring and rebuilding relationships. Not confusing effects for cause, the goal for Lederach is the sustainable transformation of societies.

But how does one balance the practical demands of ending an immediate conflict with the long-term aspirations of remaking a society? What mechanisms are available to Africans for these tasks? To what degree have theories of African conflicts informed conflict resolution and peacebuilding? In recent years, there have been a variety of strategies employed for conflict resolution across the continent: diplomatic mediation and negotiations, armed intervention by international organizations such as the United Nations, armed intervention by regional organizations such as the Economic Community of West African States, armed intervention by multinational forces, arms-control verification, humanitarian assistance, election supervision, and post-conflict reconstruction.

International Interventions

The era of African independence coincided with an increasingly interventionist United Nations. One of the UN's first experiments in peacekeeping occurred within the context of the 1960 Congo crisis. In the wake of Katanga's secession and the unauthorized deployment of Belgian troops across the country, the Congolese government requested UN intervention and assistance. The subsequent United Nations Operation in the Congo (ONUC) was initially authorized by the Security Council to use force only in self-defense, not to become a party to the internal conflict. It was only after increased violence and the murder of Prime Minister Patrice Lumumba that the Security Council chose to become further engaged, transforming ONUC from a noninterventionist peacekeeping force into an active participant in the conflict. While some consider ONUC a success, the situation in Congo grew considerably worse after ONUC arrived, and its mandate had to be altered before the conflict ended. ONUC helped keep Congo together but its intervention did not resolve any underlying cause of state failure or conflict in the country, as subsequent years would show.

After its intervention in Congo, there was considerable suspicion of the UN across Africa, and the Security Council became less willing to involve its members in African conflicts. During the Cold War, neither superpower was particularly interested in promoting the involvement of multinational peacekeeping forces in what were often regarded as Cold War proxy wars. Thus the 1970s and 1980s witnessed a relative absence of UN-led interventions in Africa, despite numerous armed conflicts. A substantial shift occurred toward the end of the Cold War, when the two superpowers worked together and through the UN to bring about resolution of the seemingly intractable conflict involving Angola, Namibia, and South Africa.

The end of the Cold War reinvigorated humanitarian interventions and UN peacekeeping operations around the globe. From 1987 to 1994, the UN Security Council quadrupled the number of resolutions it issued and tripled the number of peacekeeping operations it authorized. Significantly, it positioned itself as the global guardian of peace and security by expanding the legitimate reasons for intervention to include protracted civil wars and humanitarian crises (Otunnu and Doyle 1998). A significant expansion of the UN's role was in the peace enforcement mission, regarded by some as "third-generation" peacekeeping. First-generation is usually understood as traditional peacekeeping, in which lightly armed UN forces are stationed between warring factions to monitor a truce or troop withdrawal. Second-generation peacekeeping operations are multidimensional, with the UN becoming more involved in implementing peace agreements, from disarming former combatants and training new security forces to repatriating refugees and monitoring elections. Peace enforcement operations, in contrast, are effectively war-making missions, including enforcement of ceasefires but also military operations to protect the delivery of humanitarian assistance or repel aggression (Doyle and Sambanis 2006; Karlsrud 2015).

The humanitarian crisis that gripped the collapsed state of Somalia provided the UN Security Council with its first large-scale third-generation peacekeeping intervention in Africa since ONUC in the 1960s. After President Siad Barre fled Somalia in January 1991, a power vacuum existed in the country that none of the warring factions could completely fill. With the collapse of the state, a civil war raged and widespread famine engulfed the country. In response to the growing humanitarian crisis, the Security Council authorized military intervention through its United Nations Operation in Somalia (UNOSOM I). Warring factions agreed to a ceasefire within the capital, Mogadishu, for the delivery of humanitarian assistance, but when the operation was expanded into rural areas, the small contingent of UNOSOM forces came under fire and the situation worsened. The operation was then taken over by the Unified Task Force (UNITAF), a United States–led, UN-sanctioned multinational force tasked with providing a peaceful environment for the distribution of humanitarian assistance. While initially driven by humanitarian motives, there was substantial confusion about the scope of the mission. Initially, the United States sought to limit its involvement to just securing the delivery of food, while the UN Secretary-General argued for a broader role that would include disarming the warring militias. After UNITAF was dissolved, UNOSOM II was established, also with US leadership but with an expanded mandate from the Security Council. UNOSOM II took on a more aggressive role, including engaging in a full-scale war with one local warlord, General Farah Aidid. The operation faced considerable opposition, including several battlefield victories for Aidid's forces, which led the United States to withdraw in March 1994 and UNOSOM II to abandon the country the following year. The failure of the UNOSOM missions raised substantial questions about the efficacy of peacekeeping operations in general, and the conflation between peacekeeping and peace enforcement operations. Moreover, it raised concerns that military interventions in the context of collapsed states offer few solutions unless tied to long-term programs of "nation building."

When the Rwandan genocide unfolded in 1994, the UN Security Council was paralyzed, in part because the United States refused to become involved in another African conflict that it claimed not to comprehend (Powers 2003). Within the UN itself, nonintervention was frequently touted as the only ethical response, even though there was already a small UN contingent on the ground as part of the Arusha peace process (Barnett 2003). Eventually, the UN was severely criticized from some corners for its inability or unwillingness to intervene in the Rwandan genocide, which contributed, in turn, to a more proactive engagement in subsequent conflicts. At the UN World Summit of 2005, all member states endorsed the doctrine of Responsibility to Protect (known as R2P), which now obligates individual states and the larger international community to protect populations from mass atrocities and human rights violations, such as genocide, war crimes, ethnic cleansing, and crimes against humanity. The doctrine provides a framework for global response strategies, including authorizing the use of force via the UN Security Council as a measure of last resort.

On the one hand, R2P has provided the framework for the UN's involvement in several major peacekeeping operations in Africa. By the beginning of 2019, those included operations in the Central African Republic, the DRC, Mali, South Sudan, Sudan-Darfur, Sudan-Abyei, and Western Sahara. Today, roughly 80 percent of all UN uniformed peacekeepers are in Africa, twice as many as were deployed a decade earlier. Since the publication of this book's first edition, the UN closed peacekeeping operations in Burundi, Côte d'Ivoire, and Liberia. It is worth noting that the operations in the Central African Republic, the DRC, and Mali represent a significant evolution in the UN's peace enforcement mandates, as these are the first cases in which UN missions were authorized to use force targeting specific groups, which may have long-term implications for the UN and its role as impartial arbitrator (Karlsrud 2015; Rhoads 2016; Tull 2017).

On the other hand, R2P has generated a fair degree of criticism for its perceived failures and shortcomings. In his comparative study, Kurt Mills (2015) notes that international interventions failed to adapt to the complexities in the DRC, complicated an ongoing conflict in Uganda by the intervention of the International Criminal Court, and have been unwilling to confront Sudanese state authorities regarding atrocities in the Darfur region. The ICC has been a major feature of the R2P doctrine, but it too has come under considerable criticism, which we will discuss later.

In addition to the more formal roles played by international organizations, civil society groups such as international nongovernmental organizations (INGOs) are often significant actors in both preventive diplomacy and conflict resolution. They frequently serve the vital role of providing early warnings of the outbreak of hostilities, refugee flows, and human rights abuses. They can also be instrumental in facilitating dialogue between parties to ensure that disputes do not become full-fledged conflicts. Likewise, they frequently serve as vital actors in conflict resolution, largely because they are perceived to be neutral by the warring parties. The US-based Carter Center, for example, was instrumental in facilitating the negotiated settlement of the Ethiopia-Eritrea war. INGOs have also been fruitful in "second track" diplomacy efforts at resolving African conflicts, as was the Catholic Church in the Mozambican civil war. At the same time, some observers have noted that the different roles that INGOs and militaries play in peace operations can lead to organizational breakdown and potentially harmful outcomes. For example, Severine Autesserre (2010) and Theodore Trefon (2011a) have both illustrated how peacekeeping operations in the DRC have been debilitated by the cacophony of interests, with NGOs, international peacekeepers, and domestic interests often undermining each other and occasionally working at cross-purposes.

Regional Organizations and Solutions

Shaped in part by the relatively poor record of UN intervention in African conflicts, a shift in peacekeeping occurred in the 1990s toward regional intervention and finding "African solutions to African problems" (Mac Ginty and Richmond 2013). As we elaborate in Chapter 8, it is often assumed that regional organizations are quicker to respond (given their smaller size) and more in tune with the conflict at hand (given proximity and shared cultural background). Neighboring states are likely to suffer the impacts of armed conflict, so they may have a personal interest in maintaining security and stability within their region.

The African Union's Peace and Security Architecture. The Organization of African Unity resisted taking on peacekeeping operations largely due to its founding precept of noninterference in the domestic affairs of member states, though budget constraints were also a consideration. The OAU's only substantial peacekeeping operation was a failed 1981 intervention in Chad. The transformation of the OAU into the African Union—discussed in Chapter 8—reflected a "fundamental change in the vision, objectives, and responsibilities entrusted in the organization" (Engel and Porto 2009:82). While the AU was to be guided by the same core principles as the OAU—noninterference and peaceful resolution of disputes—other principles were enshrined in the AU's constitution, such as respect for democratic practices and promotion of human rights. Noting the potential conflict between these principles, the Assembly of Heads of State and Government gave the AU authority to intervene in the affairs of member states in "grave circumstances," namely war crimes, genocide, and crimes against humanity, with a later amendment adding "serious threats to legitimate order" (Baimu and Sturman 2003). Since its creation, the AU has been involved in armed peacekeeping operations in six member states: Burundi (2003–2004 and 2007–present), the Central African Republic (2013–2014), Comoros (2006 and 2008), Mali (2013–present), Somalia (2007–present), and Sudan (2004–2007 and jointly with the UN 2007–present).

Central to the transformation of the AU was the creation of the African Peace and Security Architecture (APSA). Established in 2002, the APSA includes the Peace and Security Council (PSC), the Military Staff Committee, the Continental Early Warning System (CEWS), and the Panel of the Wise. It also relies on its African Standby Force (ASF), composed of approximately 20,000 soldiers drawn from five regional brigades.[4] The APSA has faced some practical challenges in fulfilling its broad mandate, which includes peace promotion, conflict prevention, postconflict reconstruction, fighting international terrorism, and developing a common AU defense policy (Engel and Porto 2009). Like all AU organs, it lacks resources. Isiaka Badmus (2015:11) observes that "while the AU has demonstrated strong commitment towards implementing the APSA, it is overshadowed by its capacity limitations and the lack of political will among AU member states." Moreover, differences among the constitutive regional organizations regarding expectations, perceptions, and operating cultures have led to different strategic approaches (Söderbaum and Tavares 2009:71–72).

Even before the official launch of the PSC, the African Union engaged in its first peace operation in Burundi (AMIB), with some 3,500 troops from Ethiopia, Mozambique, and South Africa, in 2003. AMIB faced uncertainty regarding its mandate, financial constraints, and political difficulties due to neighboring states supporting different factions. Yet within a year it had helped stabilize the majority of the country and was generally regarded as a success. The following year, the AU embarked on its mission in Sudan (AMIS), a far larger operation that deployed in Darfur after Sudan rejected a UN intervention. Despite some limited successes, AMIS was ultimately unable to bring stability to the region due to the familiar problems regarding contested mandates, coordination issues, challenges of operating within an ongoing conflict, and lack of resources. The AU also authorized a peacekeeping operation to Comoros (AMISEC) in 2006, composed of 400 troops, mainly to create a stable environment and monitor elections. Despite the relatively smooth results, the democratic process broke down shortly thereafter. South Africa tried to resolve the situation through diplomatic negotiations, but in March 2008 the AU authorized a 1,350-strong force to remove the regime of Mohammed Bacar. While the operation was a success, the government of South Africa criticized it for undermining diplomatic negotiations, while others noted that the AU did not engage in similar actions against coups in other states. In 2013 the AU sent troops to Mali following France's military campaign against Islamist insurgents in the north. Later that year it sent troops to the Central African Republic in response to the civil war. That mission was folded into a larger UN operation the following year.

Perhaps the most significant AU peace operation has been the mission in Somalia (AMISOM), which was launched in 2007 with a six-month mandate. It was still continuing in 2019. Perhaps the biggest challenge was securing troops for the mission. Until Burundian troops arrived in December 2007, Uganda was the only country to deploy soldiers to AMISOM. Despite scolding from AU commissioner Alpha Konare, member states were extremely reluctant to fulfill their promise of dispatching troops into the Somali conflict zone. The operation has also been undermined by Ethiopia and Kenya, both of which have sent troops into Somalia to pursue their own agendas. Though there were plans to create a UN-supported Internationalization Force in 2008, it never materialized. In 2010, the African Union expanded AMISOM's mission beyond peacekeeping to peace enforcement, with the mandate of directly engaging al-Shabaab. After an increase in forces, in 2011 Kenya agreed to rehat its troops as AMISOM forces and increase its troop commitment. In 2013, following the Westgate Mall terrorist attack, Kenya integrated its forces into AMISOM. These developments led to modest improvements against al-Shabaab, though the Somali government remains weak and victory elusive. In 2019, AMISOM is constituted by troops from Burundi, Djibouti, Ethiopia, Kenya, and Uganda, and police forces from Ghana,

Kenya, Nigeria, Sierra Leone, Uganda, and Zambia. For some observers, the AU's decade-long engagement in Somalia stands as an unnecessary strategic blunder (Williams 2009).

Regional interventions. The post–Cold War era has also witnessed a greater emphasis on peacekeeping and security by African regional organizations, with interventions by the Economic Community of West African States (ECOWAS), in Liberia (1990–1998 and 2003), Sierra Leone (1997–2000), Guinea-Bissau (1998–1999 and 2012), Côte d'Ivoire (2003–2004), Mali (2013), and Gambia (2017–present); the Southern African Development Community (SADC), in Lesotho (1998) and the DRC (1998); the Economic and Monetary Community of Central Africa (CEMAC), in the Central African Republic (2002–2008); and the Economic Community of Central African States (ECCAS), also in the Central African Republic (since 2008).

Peacekeeping operations by regional organizations have faced challenges related to command-and-control, poor coordination between participating states, weak political will, debates around mandates, and limited resources (Hentz, Söderbaum, and Tavares 2009). There have also been significant allegations of corruption and abuse of civilians by ECOWAS Ceasefire Monitoring Group (ECOMOG) peacekeepers (Obi 2009). Some Liberians relabeled the mission "Every Car or Moving Object Gone." Of course, allegations of abuse and corruption are not limited to regional missions and have also characterized international operations, as evidenced by charges of rape and abuse by UN troops in the DRC and elsewhere. Finally, it should be noted that regional peacekeeping operations are often seen as vehicles through which regional states strengthen their hegemony and pursue their own foreign policy agendas behind the facade of multilateralism. In the case of ECOMOG, Nigeria clearly played the leading role, while also providing an estimated 80 percent of the troops and 90 percent of the funding, and sustaining the bulk of the casualties (Adebajo and Mustapa 2008). Regardless, regional organizations have become a major mechanism for peacekeeping operations across the continent, a point we return to in Chapter 8.

Postconflict Justice

Postconflict societies tend to experience periods of intense political upheaval. The vast majority of conflicts in the world today occur in countries that experienced civil conflict within the past three decades.

One of the challenges for postconflict societies is the disarmament, demobilization, and reintegration (DDR) of combatants. Since the end of the Cold War, DDR programs have evolved into large-scale endeavors that are often internationally funded, but with mixed results (Muggah 2009; Söderström 2015). Another quandary is whether the crimes and atrocities that were committed during the conflict should be prosecuted or forgotten. Will recalling and prosecuting those crimes contribute to or undermine reconciliation? What mechanisms should be used in the attempt to balance the competing demands for accountability and reconciliation?

In many contemporary postconflict societies, a focus is placed on achieving transitional justice, which comes in different models (Bassiouni 2002). The International Criminal Tribunal for Rwanda (ICTR), created by the UN to prosecute crimes committed during the 1994 genocide, provides an example of the international judicial model. The government of Rwanda initially supported its creation, but became the only country to vote against approving the ICTR's mandate. During its existence, the ICTR was criticized for its high cost, extremely slow pace, and limited prosecutions. Officially closed in 2015, the ICTR operated over the objections of the government of Rwanda, which chose to focus on its *gacaca* justice institutions (Gahima 2012; Ingelaere 2018; Jones 2010).

Partly in response to the Rwandan genocide, the international community established the permanent International Criminal Court in 1998. The ICC can investigate and prosecute international crimes only, namely genocide, crimes against humanity, war crimes, and the crime of aggression, and only in cases where a state's domestic judicial system is unable or unwilling to do so. Since its creation, the ICC has received complaints concerning crimes in well over a hundred countries, but before 2016 had only investigated African cases, specifically in the Central African Republic, Côte d'Ivoire, the DRC, Kenya, Libya, Sudan, and Uganda. There have been thirty-two arrest warrants to date, the first of which was for Joseph Kony, the leader of Uganda's Lord's Resistance Army, and four of his lieutenants. There have been verdicts reached in six cases, with convictions in cases concerning Mali and the DRC. Notable cases include charges against Sudan's President Omar al-Bashir (accused of crimes in Darfur) and Kenya's President Uhuru Kenyatta and his vice president, William Ruto (concerning election-related violence in 2007–2008). The case against Kenyatta and Ruto collapsed spectacularly in 2016, little attempt has been made to arrest al-Bashir, and the arrest warrant against Kony effectively scuttled the peace negotiations occurring at the time (Sharma 2015; Nouwen 2013). In 2011, Côte d'Ivoire's ousted Laurent Gbagbo became the first former head of state to appear at the ICC, charged with four counts of crimes against humanity. While many welcomed the prosecution of Gbagbo, it underscored to some that the ICC was predominantly, if not exclusively, prosecuting Africans, leading several African leaders to threaten withdrawal from the ICC.

The Special Court for Sierra Leone (SCSL) follows the mixed judicial model. The pursuit of postconflict justice in Sierra Leone has employed two concurrent transitional justice mechanisms. On the one hand is the domestic, quasi-juridical Truth and Reconciliation Commission, based upon the South African model. On the other hand is the UN-approved SCSL. This was the first hybrid international court, jointly administered by the United Nations and the government of Sierra Leone. Though the international community largely considered the dual mechanisms in Sierra Leone a success, especially given the conviction of Charles Taylor in 2012, some have been critical of the ways in which the victim-perpetrator dichotomy has been employed. This dichotomy resulted in the further alienation of young, lower-ranking ex-combatants, whose social marginalization contributed to the conflict in the first place, and served as an obstacle for their reintegration into postconflict Sierra Leonean society (Shaw 2010; see also Kelsall 2009).

Unlike the international juridical model, the national juridical model pursues transitional justice through a state's domestic legal system (Perry and Sayndee 2015). For example, Ethiopia's transitional government established a special office to prosecute the crimes committed by the military council that had ruled from 1974 to 1991. These were known as the "Red Terror" trials, and were aimed primarily at establishing accountability and exacting revenge for those crimes (Tiba 2011). The best-known example of quasi-judicial transitional justice is South Africa's Truth and Reconciliation Commission (TRC), an innovative and ambitious courtlike institution established in 1995 to investigate human rights offenses that took place within the country during the apartheid era, specifically from 1960 to 1994. Victims were invited to testify about their experiences, with a focus on restoring their dignity and assisting their rehabilitation. The perpetrators of violence were also invited to give testimony and could request amnesty from prosecution. Thus, the goal of the TRC was to promote restorative justice, with the focus on uncovering the truth about past abuses, using amnesty as a mechanism rather than punishing the perpetrators.

Former president F. W. de Klerk appeared before the commission and offered his apologies for the suffering caused by apartheid, but his predecessor, P. W. Botha, refused, dismissing the reconciliation process as a "circus." Generally regarded as a pivotal mechanism in the nonviolent transition to a post-apartheid South Africa, the TRC has also been criticized for offering only the illusion of reconciliation and for failing to hold the most serious perpetrators of violence accountable (du Bois and du Bois-Pedian 2008).

Partly due to frustrations with the traditional models of transitional justice, there has been a recent shift toward customary law and other forms of local justice to complement tribunals and truth commissions (Shaw and Waldorf with Hazan 2010). For example, in northern Uganda, local elites have employed (and reinvented) Acholi rituals to cleanse, integrate, and reconcile former LRA combatants (Allen 2006; Baines 2007). One of the most notable, and controversial, local customary justice mechanisms has been the aforementioned *gacaca* system in Rwanda. Based on reinterpretation of a traditional structure employing community participation, *gacaca* was aimed both at prosecuting genocide suspects, of whom approximately 20,000 were already detained in jails across the country, and at helping to reconstruct Rwanda's damaged social fabric (Clark 2010; Gahima 2012; Ingelaere 2018). *Gacaca* faced a number of obstacles, not the least of which was dealing with a confused, fearful, and deeply traumatized population. The Rwandan state was accused of coercing participation in the trials and interfering with the hearings in order to collectivize the guilt of all Hutus (Ingelaere 2008). Moreover, *gacaca* has been regarded as extremely one-sided given the complete absence of prosecution of crimes committed by the Rwandan Patriotic Front (Straus 2008).

Critiques of Conflict Resolution

Peacekeeping attempts in Africa have been criticized in part because of their failure to consider insights provided by the theories of African conflict. Some authors, such as David Shearer (1997), wonder whether international mediations and negotiations may prolong conflicts in warlord insurgencies such as in Sierra Leone. Likewise, Christopher Clapham (1998b) has expressed concern that the accepted standardized mechanism for conflict resolution has been defined by, and in the interests of, neoliberal democratic states. Clapham argues that in the post–Cold War era, sovereign states and their territorial integrity have lost their privileged status, democratic values and neoliberal under-standings of human rights have been accepted as universal values, and all parties in a conflict have been granted a standing in peacemaking processes. As such, two models of conflict resolution have become dominant: the installation of a constitution based on multiparty democracy (e.g., Angola and Mozambique) and the creation of a coalition government (attempted in Liberia and Somalia). By looking at the Rwandan case in the early 1990s, in which variants of both approaches were applied with disastrous consequences, Clapham suggests that the assumptions in the dominant conflict resolution model are inherently flawed, particularly the notion that combatants might share common values and that mediators are neutral. For Clapham, these assumptions contributed to fostering the conditions from which the 1994 Rwandan genocide emerged.

Mark Duffield (2007) has suggested that contemporary conflict resolution enables Western regulation of the developing world, by stressing that conflicts stem from localized misunderstandings or dis-agreements, and ignoring issues of inequality, economic growth, and resource distribution. For Duffield, international conflict resolution projects are actually Western interventions that function as new forms of imperialism in which the structural divisions between global devel-opment and underdevelopment are maintained and policed. Moreover, Pierre Englebert and Denis Tull (2008) have shown that international interventions tend to underappreciate the domestic political logic of African conflicts and might be overly optimistic about their chances of effectively shaping local outcomes.

Inherent in practices of contemporary conflict resolution is the assumption that government institutions need reforming and strength-ening. Indeed, there is an uncritical assumption of the need for a strong state. Even when there is general agreement that the central state is one of the main sources of insecurity among the population, externally imposed projects of postconflict restructuring privilege the strengthen-ing of the state. In her work in postconflict DRC, for example, Sever-ine Autesserre (2010) notes that most NGOs and international actors recognize that the Congolese state is a negative force in most people's lives, yet they continue to support state-centric notions of reconstruc-tion that work to strengthen the central state and increase human inse-curity on the ground. Indeed, the conflict in the DRC highlights the variances in defining "security" and arguably illustrates the need to shift focus more toward "human" security.

Human Security and Insecurity

Traditionally, national security has been about protection from external military threats or from internal subversion of the established political order. In Africa as elsewhere, national security is often more narrowly equated with regime security. In recent decades there has been a shift in how security is conceived to include a range of other considerations. Barry Buzan, in *People, States, and Fear* (1983), claimed that security should be defined to include political, economic, societal, and environmental aspects. Others have argued that we need to move beyond regarding the state as the primary, if not exclusive, referent for discussions about security. The state, after all, is but one form of social organization that changes over time and place (as the African cases so aptly illustrate). Many scholars and activists have argued that more appropriate referents of security are the biosphere and the individual, together linked by the concept of "human security." This position was embraced by the OAU, which released the Kampala Document in 1991 on security, stating: "The concept of security . . . embraces all aspects of the society including economic, political and social dimensions of individual, family, and community, local and national life. The security of a nation must be construed in terms of the security of the individual citizen to live in peace with access to basic necessities of life while fully participating in the affairs of his/her society in freedom and enjoying all fundamental human rights" (OAU 1991). Of course, this is a far cry from what most African states have achieved in practice.[5]

Human Security, Gender, and Development

Feminist security analysis has tended to focus on patriarchal structures of privilege and control that effectively legitimize various forms of violence (Parpart and Thompson 2012; Turshen 2016). From this perspective, the concept of "national security" has been used to preserve the male-dominated order, rather than protecting the state from external attack (Enloe 1989; Hooper 2001). To what extent is the security discourse gendered? Do women experience security/insecurity differently than men? How does taking a gender analysis of the concept of human security illuminate the different ways women might conceive of and experience insecurity in Africa?

Young men continue to make up the majority of armed combatants in conflicts in general, yet women often bear the brunt of these armed conflicts, and sometimes in ways that are different from men's experience. It has often been noted that women frequently experience armed conflict as victims of rape, torture, and sexual slavery. Up to half a million women were raped during the 1994 Rwandan genocide, and the high levels of sexual violence during the conflicts in the DRC led a UN official to dub the country the "rape capital of the world" (Baaz and Stern 2013). Because women, and women's bodies, become sites upon which violence is inflicted by men during armed conflict, warfare is gendered at the most basic level (Baaz 2013; Baines 2007). Yet African women regularly experience violence, rape, and sexual assault in their daily lives, regardless of whether or not they find themselves in a war zone. In 2009, South Africa's Medical Research Council reported that more than a quarter of men in that country admitted to having committed rape, with almost half of those reporting multiple assaults. Reportedly, 60 percent of boys over age eleven believe that forcing someone to have sex is not an act of violence. The study concludes with the observation that "rape is far too common, and its origins too deeply embedded in ideas about South African manhood, for the problem to be predominantly addressed through strategies of apprehension and prosecution of perpetrators" (Jewkes et al. 2009:2). When Jacob Zuma stood trial in 2006 for raping a family friend, he defended himself in court by arguing that the woman "was dressed provocatively and that it was against Zulu culture for a man to leave a sexually aroused woman unsatisfied" (Lindow 2009). For many feminist activists, his acquittal highlighted both the often violent patriarchal structures of African society and the difficulty in finding legal protection, the combination of which increases women's daily insecurity.

Sources of insecurity for African women are also generated by the gender inequalities in control over resources. Women's access to land and other types of property is legally limited in many parts of Africa, and a significant proportion of married African women do not enjoy control over their own earnings. With regard to basic human needs, the UN notes that "more than half of rural households and about a quarter of urban households in sub-Saharan Africa lack easy access to drinking water, and most of the burden of water collection falls on women" (United Nations 2010:xi). The burden of meeting basic needs, such as food, clothing, and shelter for themselves and their families, often falls on the female and thus becomes a major source of insecurity. This is often exacerbated by the gender inequalities in power and decisionmaking.

More generally, a number of scholars working from a human security approach have noted the link between development and insecurity.

Indeed, it has become commonplace to assert that one cannot have development without security, or security without development. The argument is often made that conflicts are frequently driven by poverty and underdevelopment, with a corollary assumption being the developed world must assist in reducing poverty and developing unstable regions of the world. Human security has thus been increasingly framed in terms of protecting and improving the livelihood of the world's poor and marginalized (UNDP 1994; King and Murray 2001). Yet scholars such as Mark Duffield (2001, 2007) have challenged this assumed connection, suggesting that traditional approaches to development, along with humanitarian intervention, function less as a vehicle of change and more as tools for maintaining global inequality.

Human Security and the Environment

Setting aside the contested "neo-Malthusian" assertion that environmental degradation leads to a rise in violent conflict, scholars have explored the ways in which environmental change may be impacting human insecurity, examining the sources of and possible responses to environmental insecurity (Deudney and Matthews 1999; Myers 1989, 1993; Ohlsson 1999; Dalby 2002, 2009; Barnett 2001). With respect to climate, Africa has the smallest carbon footprint of all continents. In 2016, for example, emissions of carbon dioxide (CO_2) for all of Africa stood at 1 ton per capita, in comparison with a world average of 4.8 tons per capita, Chinese emissions of 7.5 tons per capita, and US emissions of 15.5 tons per capita.[6] Yet Africans are among the most vulnerable to climate change, and among the most ill-equipped to respond to it. Many scientists predict that Africa will face increased environmental insecurity as crop production is affected by increased temperatures, changes in rainfall, rising sea levels, and extreme events such as floods and landslides. Temperatures are expected to rise across Africa, which will increase the risk of drought and further stress agricultural production. Given that a high proportion of Africans rely on crops and livestock for their livelihoods, human security on the continent is highly vulnerable to environmental changes. For example, Uganda's Department of Meteorology warned in 2007 that even a slight temperature increase could wipe out most of the country's coffee crop, which is essential to the country for generating export revenues (Republic of Uganda 2007:12–13).

Water remains an extremely important resource in Africa, for people, crops, livestock, and energy generation. Changes in the availability of water would have substantial impacts on many aspects of life for both rural and urban dwellers. Rainfall is expected to decline significantly across most of Africa, including in the Sahara desert. For a stunning example, one can look at Lake Chad, which was once the continent's fourth largest lake with an area of about 26,000 square kilometers. By 2017, it had shrunk to less than 1,000 square kilometers due to climate change. Even where rainfall is predicted to increase, as in eastern Africa, much of this will come in the form of heavier and more torrential conditions, leading to destructive runoff and erosion. During 2007, Africa experienced its worst flooding in three decades, with more than a million people affected in twenty countries. Heavy rains and flooding destroyed homes and crops, leaving many communities extremely short of food and vulnerable to substantial health risks. But such floods have become the new norm, with eastern Africa experiencing its worst flooding in early 2018, resulting in hundreds of deaths and displacing thousands.

There is also concern that deforestation, due to both climate change and overclearing driven by economic pressures, will increase desertification and soil erosion. In many parts of Africa, forests are vital for local livelihoods, yet people's ability to manage, control, and even access these resources is often legally constrained. African forests are also becoming a global commodity, whether as a resource for carbon emission reduction in the attempts to address climate change or as a source of raw materials such as timber, fuel, and pulp (Toulmin 2009:85). Global climate changes will affect the human security of not just rural Africans but also urban dwellers, given the expected increases in heat waves, flooding, and pollution, and the expected rise in sea levels. Those most at risk are the poor majority, who already live in a precarious situation with extremely limited access to water, sanitation, and government services. To be clear, the effects of climate change are already being felt across Africa. Despite the fact that Africa will likely suffer the brunt of problems associated with global climate change, it has been powerless to address these security issues in the global arena. This is partly due to the divergent agendas and opinions among African states, but also due to their position within world affairs. It is to these concerns—particularly African agency in world affairs—that we turn next.

Notes

1. Africa's higher average may be partly explained by such lengthy outliers as the conflicts in Sudan and Ethiopia.

342   *Inside African Politics*

2. World Bank, *World Development Indicators,* http://data.worldbank.org/indicator.

3. For excellent general overviews of the development of African warfare, see Reno 2011 and Williams 2011.

4. The five brigades are to be established, one each, by the Economic Community of West African States (ECOWAS), the Southern African Development Community (SADC), the Economic Community of Central African States (ECCAS), the Eastern Africa Standby Force (EASFCOM), and the North African Regional Capacity.

5. It is worth noting that some scholars find the "human security" concept problematic due to its potentially expansive nature (Paris 2001:88). Other criticisms include the concern that the concept might cause more harm than good, in the sense that a "human security" approach may raise expectations and be too moralistic to be attainable. Finally, the Copenhagen school of international relations theory has raised considerable concern about the process of "securitization," in which politicians and policymakers increasingly frame a wide range of social issues and practices through the lens of security (Waever et al. 1993; Huysmans 2000).

6. Data from the European Commission's Emissions Database for Global Atmospheric Research available at http://edgar.jrc.ec.europa.eu.

8

The International Relations of African States

IN WRITINGS ABOUT AFRICAN INTERNATIONAL RELATIONS, it is not uncommon to find the claim that Africa exists at the margins of world affairs. But to what extent is this an accurate claim? How has Africa functioned historically in the development of the international system? What agency do its states have in the international era today? To what extent do African states work together? What have been the main challenges for achieving cooperation among them? What issues and themes have characterized African states' relations with their former colonial powers? How did African states navigate the Cold War competition between the United States and Soviet Union? How have relations with the United States, Russia, and China evolved in recent years? In this chapter we examine the development of intra-African relations from independence, to the creation of the Organization of African Unity, to the OAU's reinvention as the African Union. We then turn to an exploration of external bilateral relations, tracing the evolution of relations between African states and European powers, global superpowers, and emerging middle powers. We then look at African states' agency within a range of international organizations, from the UN to the World Trade Organization (WTO), before concluding with a discussion of the privatization of African international relations. But first we begin with a discussion of this idea that Africa exists at the global margins.

This representation of marginalization is often articulated in one of two ways: Africa is politically and economically marginalized within the practice of world politics, and Africa is ignored or marginalized by theorists of world politics. The first suggests that Africa and Africans exist on the margins of the world stage, seemingly besieged by a plethora of unanswered and underreported "crises," ranging from war, poverty, famine,

343

corruption, and disease to environmental degradation. For some, the "external world" largely ignores these tragedies, denying Africans the adequate media coverage and policy attention they might need to find solutions to their predicaments. In some corners of the Western popular press, Africa is repeatedly portrayed as a helpless, collapsing continent in need of saving but, at the same time, as seemingly beyond comprehension and salvation (Kaplan 1994; *The Economist* 2000a). This portrayal is often underpinned by an assumption that Africans and African states have very little political or economic weight in world affairs. From this position, an image emerges of Africa at the margins of world affairs, with external forces (be they foreign states, markets, or institutions) acting upon the continent unimpeded because of Africa's negligible agency.

That Africa suffers rather severe problems associated with poverty and underdevelopment cannot be dismissed. Yet it would be a mistake to conclude that Africans or African states lack agency in their own affairs or on the world stage. As noted throughout this book, ordinary Africans are neither passive nor powerless actors. Likewise, while it may be easy to note the many ways in which external political and economic actors exert influence on the continent, it would be a mistake to assume that Africans are somehow marginal to, or even outside of, world affairs.[1] As Tukufu Zuberi (2015:1) quipped, "any conceptualization of world history is incomplete without a consideration of Africa's role." Much of this chapter will illustrate that, as Jean-François Bayart (2000:267) put it, "the discourse on Africa's marginality is a nonsense."

The second claim about marginality concerns the ways in which theorists of world politics think about Africa and its place in international relations. The argument is that the academic field of international relations (IR) has largely ignored Africa and has little to say about African experiences (see Cornelissen, Cheru, and Shaw 2012; Vale, Swatuk, and Oden 2001). A few scholars claim that the inability of IR theory to accurately address African experiences is due to African exceptionalism (Neuman 1998). Others argue not so much that Africa is unique, but that the concepts and assumptions that traditional IR theory makes are flawed, and that these failures are thrown into stark relief when placing African experiences at the forefront of one's analysis, something most IR theorists fail to do (Abrahamsen 2016; Dunn 2013; Dunn and Shaw 2001; Odoom and Andrews 2017). While there is considerable variation among these Africanist critics, a common argument is that the accepted tools of Western social scientific analysis fail to capture the political processes at work on the continent. As Bayart (2000:229) bemoans, "much of what happens in Africa [is made] invisible to outsiders." This may be due to failures in the approaches, assumptions, and conceptualizations that are dominant in Western IR theory.

William Brown (2006) contends that the claims of Africanist critics do not apply to the field of IR in general, but primarily to the dominant North American paradigm of realism (though one might also include liberalism and the matching "neorevisionist" approaches of both).[2] Yet a number of Africanists have continued to champion the insights generated by realism and other traditional IR approaches (Clark 2001; Solomon 2001; Schraeder 1994, 2004; Ayoob 1998). Douglas Lemke (2011) argues that IR theories such as realism and neorealism appear inconsistent with African political reality not because of flaws in the theory, but because IR scholars fall into a state-centric trap that ignores African experiences with nonstate actors. According to Christopher Clapham (1996:246), the greatest source of scholarly "distortion" of African international relations concerns the privileging of the state and faulty assumptions about the state, which has obscured more than illuminated the relationship between the political elites in control of state institutions and those they seek to govern. As Engel and Olsen (2015:54) assert, "what clearly has failed is the postcolonial social construction and related academic imagery of the state in Africa." As a corrective to the reputed deficiencies within the IR discipline, scholars working in the field of African politics have long provided a more nuanced and sophisticated way of thinking about the sovereign state. Many have critically examined the ways in which international sovereignty became the pretext for ensuring external support for the maintenance of a growing cadre of corrupt and repressive regimes across the continent (Englebert 2009; Reno 1998). Others have explored the numerous ways in which Africans resisted or avoided the state and its attempts to exert control over the populace, creating alternative forms of governance (Raeymaekers 2014; Trefon 2004).

As earlier chapters noted, many African states are detached to varying degrees from their domestic societies while, at the same time, being dependent upon external sources of support and legitimacy for their survival. Frederick Cooper (2002:141) has argued that this is not a recent development, but was a characteristic of colonialism, as European states were unable to completely extend their rule over the African population but used the colonial state to control "the interface of national and world economies." After independence, African leaders inherited and perpetuated these "gatekeeper states." This has produced what Clapham (1996:256) calls the "privatization" of Africa's relations with the rest of the world "not only through their subversion by private interests of politicians both inside and outside the continent, but through the displacement of traditional state-to-state relations as a result of the processes of globalization." We explore this development at the end of the chapter.

Finally, it should be noted that there is considerable divergence of opinion about the nature of the international system and Africa's place within it. For instance, different IR approaches place differing levels of emphasis on structural forces, be they the anarchical nature of the international system or the hierarchical relations between states. Different assumptions are also made about the possibility of conflict and cooperation between states, and debates exist about the malleability of state behavior and the historically constructed nature of world politics in general. Because we do not want to foreclose fruitful paths of interrogation and analysis, we attempt to maintain a position of theoretical pluralism in this chapter. We reject, however, the notion that the international system represents a timeless structure largely untouched by human agency (Waltz 1977). Rather, we recognize that the international system is both a historical artifact and an ongoing project. As such, it is important to acknowledge the varied ways in which African political elites, as well as ordinary Africans, exert agency in world affairs, engaging Western conceptions, theories, and practices of IR on their own terms and within their own agendas (Abrahamsen 2016; Brown 2012; Brown and Harman 2013). Such insights highlight once again the fallacy of Africa's marginalization and assumptions about any lack of agency among Africans. As a next step, it is useful to briefly investigate the history of Africa within the contemporary international state system.

Africa in the World

Jean-François Bayart (2000:234) observed that "Africa is in no sense extraneous to the world." To speak of Africa's relationship "with" the world is to ignore that Africa is "of" the world, and of the myriad ways in which the continent has been actively engaged in the events, processes, and shifting configurations of power that have historically evolved across the globe (Taylor and Williams 2004b; Brown and Harman 2013). African societies were active participants within the various world systems and economies long before the development of today's international state system. For example, the communities along the Swahili coast were integrated into political, social, and economic systems to the east as early as the second century. Likewise, northern and western Africa have been connected to European societies for millennia. There has been lengthy interaction between European and African societies, continuing even after the trans-Saharan trade routes became controlled by Islamic communities moving westward and into Europe beginning in the seventh century (Abun-Nasr 1987). The colonial portrayal of a European "discovery" of Africa is a massive myth reliant on a case of active historical amnesia.

What this myth suggests is that European-African relations were largely driven by changes within Europe itself. For instance, the Enlightenment significantly altered how Europeans saw themselves and their relationship with non-Europeans, while also changing economic patterns in Europe, not the least of which was the rise of industrial capitalism. While it is true that internal European dynamics helped drive the trans-Atlantic slave trade and the rise of the European colonial project overseas, there is substantial scholarly evidence that highlights the role of African agency in shaping relations between Africa and Europe (Bayart 2000; Cooper 2014; Marks 2006; Northrup 2008; Thornton 1998). Simply put, assuming Europeans determined the interactions between themselves and Africans during colonialism denies African agency, ignores historical evidence, and obscures the multiple ways in which Africa and Europe have historically been connected by a constant ebb and flow of ideas and goods.

Yet by the eighteenth century, Europeans, given their technological advantage, frequently enjoyed positions of asymmetric power compared to non-Europeans. With the ascendancy of the capitalist economic system and territorial state system in Europe, European powers established informal empires in parts of the African continent. With the opening of the Suez Canal in 1869 and the perceived threat of the rise of Egyptian nationalism, Britain contributed to initiating the transformation to more formal empires and the scramble for Africa among European powers (Robinson and Gallagher 1961).

The Berlin Conference of 1884–1885 was held largely to mitigate the detrimental effects that the scramble for Africa had unleashed. Recognizing that competing European interests in Africa could lead to violent confrontations between the colonizing parties, Germany's Otto von Bismarck heeded Portugal's call for a meeting to formalize the process of territorial conquest. With all major European powers in attendance, the Berlin Conference established the principle of effective occupation, which required the imperial powers to prove possession of their colonies, either through treaties with local leaders or through direct physical administration of the territory, as well as economic use of their possessions. As noted in Chapter 2, in the aftermath of the Berlin Conference, European imperial powers quickly established a direct, but largely superficial, physical presence to support their territorial claims across the continent, with the only substantial subsequent alteration being Germany's loss of its colonies at the end of World War I. Following World War II, the United States and the Soviet Union slowly began to exert their influence in Africa as the continent became part of the emerging geopolitical landscape upon which Cold War competition was projected. As the European imperial powers engaged in the process of decolonization throughout the 1960s, both superpowers—either proactively or reactively—increased their interests in Africa. In general, the Soviet Union was driven by the desire to establish friendly relations with the newly emerging states, especially those with strongly anti-imperialist regimes, while the United States was primarily interested in thwarting perceived Soviet expansion on the continent and maintaining the systemic status quo in the context of decolonization.

The Cold War loomed large over the African continent, as nationalist struggles and internal insurgencies were often caught up in the geopolitical machinations between the two superpowers and their allies. The Cold War competition also provided African political leaders with new opportunities for leverage within world affairs. Throughout, both superpowers actively supported regimes that they regarded as friendly, while occasionally seeking to destabilize those they considered threats. Significantly, the economic networks established during colonialism persisted and new commercial ventures further intertwined Africa and Europe. At the same time, the economic crises of the 1970s severely impacted the African continent, and contributed to reshaping its relationships with Western powers and, in particular, international financial institutions such as the International Monetary Fund and the World Bank.

As evidenced in several earlier chapters, the sudden collapse of the Cold War altered the geopolitical landscape for African states. Deprived of considerable military and financial support, to say nothing of the bargaining power they enjoyed by playing off the desires and fears of the superpowers, many African leaders found themselves adrift. Some regimes quickly collapsed, such as that of Siad Barre in Somalia, while others managed to radically transform themselves, such as that of Jerry Rawlings in Ghana, and still others engaged in survival strategies that further eroded already fragile states, such as that of Mobutu Sese Seko in Zaire. In recent decades, Africa has been affected by the ongoing processes of global economic restructuring, including the adoption of neoliberal restructuring policies required for access to funding from the international financial institutions, but has also benefited from the rise of global commodity prices. While some African leaders have complained about the continent's perceived marginalization in the post–Cold War era, the presence of oil and other valued resources has ensured continued commercial interest by external forces. The end of the Cold War bipolarity has also increased opportunities for emerging powers such as China and India to engage with Africa. Moreover, the growing importance of international organizations in the post–Cold War era has provided platforms for African interaction with external actors, further belying the myth of marginality.

Intra-African Relations

What have been the primary divisions between African states? To what extent have they been able to cooperate and achieve coordinated foreign policies? In this section, we examine the principle on Pan-Africanism and how it shaped attempts at coordination between newly independent African states. After discussing the creation of the continental Organization of African Unity, we examine its reinvention as the African Union in 2000. We then explore African experiences with regional organizations, from regional economic communities to regional collective security organizations.

Pan-Africanism and the Organization of African Unity

As African states moved toward independence, there was a fair amount of rhetoric around Pan-Africanism. As Crawford Young (1986:425–426) noted, "The doctrine of Pan-Africanism was at once a global creed of racial solidarity, a doctrine of shared solidarity in the task of freeing all of Africa from alien rule, and—for a visionary though initially influential minority—an imperative of continental unification." The concept was rather vague, implying a level of continental unity, if not integration, in the postcolonial era. There was general agreement that all African societies across the continent should be free of European colonial control and enjoy national self-determination, but there was tremendous disagreement about the level to which postcolonial African states should be integrated with each other or the degree to which policies should be coordinated. Within a few years, the term "Pan-Africanism" was broadly employed to convey a vague continental consensus of mutual support, often without any specific policy prescriptions.

    In many respects, the political rhetoric of Pan-Africanism was shaped by a desire for continental coordination in the face of shared dependence within the global economic system. Given the Cold War context, African states also found strength in numbers as they navigated the bipolar terrain that was dominated by the two competing superpowers. Claims for Pan-Africanism helped shore up domestic political support for new African leaders, while covering over the often quite close relationships they maintained with the former colonial powers. Pan-African solidarity also ensured respect for the "rules of the game" in the newly emerging African state system, and thus minimized possible sources of conflict. Given the artificiality of the state borders and the potential chaos that could emerge by beginning a process of redrawing international boundaries, African leaders were quick to endorse the sanctity of those boundaries. Indeed, it was the drive to protect the sovereignty of the new African states that led African leaders to both reject proposals for continental integration on the one hand, and champion a limited degree of coordination among their fellow African states on the other.

The drive for African continental coordination and integration was largely championed by President Kwame Nkrumah of Ghana. In 1958, one year after Ghana gained its independence, Nkrumah hosted the first Conference of Independent African States, in Accra. Bringing together Egypt, Ethiopia, Ghana, Liberia, Libya, Morocco, Sudan, and Tunisia, as well as nationalist activists from several colonies, the conference was in many ways the foundation of formal postcolonial inter-African relations. That same year, Nkrumah helped establish the Ghana-Guinea Union, renamed the Union of African States, with the intention of putting Pan-Africanism into practice. In 1961, Mali joined the union, but the integration experiment started showing fissures over the states' different ideological orientations and independent foreign policy agendas. By the next year, after Ghana moved closer to the United States against the wishes of its Marxist-leaning partners, the union had collapsed (Davidson 2007).

In December 1960, a conference of most of the francophone African states was held in Brazzaville. The following year, the so-called Brazzaville Group formed the African and Malagasy Union, with the goals of developing closer economic and political cooperation and common foreign policies and defense coordination, while simultaneously strengthening its members' relationship with France. The union was crippled, however, by the inherent tension between establishing greater self-reliance among the group and continuing dependence upon France (Endeley 2009:3–10). At the 1960 conference, the Brazzaville Group, led by Côte d'Ivoire's president, Félix Houphouët-Boigny, signaled a markedly conservative orientation in its foreign policy agenda, siding with France in the Algerian war of independence. It also stated its opposition to the spread of communism in Africa and supported the Congolese factions that had overthrown Patrice Lumumba.

Largely in response to the Brazzaville Group and its policies, seven other states—Algeria, Egypt, Ghana, Guinea, Libya, Mali, and Morocco—met in Casablanca in January 1961. This "Casablanca bloc" voiced support for the Front de Libération Nationale (FLN) in Algeria and pledged its support for Lumumba in the ongoing Congo crisis. While both the Brazzaville Group and the Casablanca bloc employed the rhetoric of Pan-Africanism, their divergent views on the Algerian and Congo conflicts illustrated the range of African agendas in world affairs, particularly between radical and conservative political leaders. At the same time, the limited success in speaking with a collective voice to advance foreign policy positions, especially at the UN's General Assembly, underscored the attractiveness of continental coordination. The question remained, however, about how much coordination was desirable or even possible. The Casablanca bloc generally supported formal continental integration through a federation of all independent African states (see Nyerere 1963). In contrast, the new Monrovia Group, led by Léopold Senghor of Senegal and made up of Ethiopia, Liberia, Nigeria, Senegal, and most of the francophone African states of the Brazzaville Group, rejected political federation in favor of economic cooperation and gradual integration. These divergent views were also driven by a rivalry between Ghana and Nigeria for regional, if not continental, leadership (see Endeley 2009; Harris 1994; Sesay, Ojo, and Fasenhun 1984).

To resolve these differences, Emperor Haile Selassie of Ethiopia hosted a conference in May 1963 in Addis Ababa, which resulted in the founding of the Organization of African Unity. The twenty countries that made up the Monrovia Group had met earlier to articulate five core principles: absolute equality and sovereignty of all African states, the right of each member state to exist and not to be annexed by another, the right of states to enter into voluntary unions with each other, noninterference in the domestic affairs of fellow member states, and the pledge not to harbor dissidents from other member states. Despite other differences between the subregional groups, these principles were widely accepted by all independent African states,[3] and became the foundation of the OAU Charter. The charter reflected a largely defensive statist agenda, as it was concerned first and foremost with preservation of the established, territorially defined sovereign African states and of their leaders. Issues of good governance and democracy were steadfastly avoided, while the security of the state and its leadership was privileged. As a result, the principles of the OAU worked as an insurance policy to create a mutual-preservation society (Makinda and Okumu 2008:11–27; Amate 1986).

But how to realize these principles given the diversity of opinions among the leadership of the newly independent African states? The Monrovia Group was strongly opposed to the federalist structure advanced by Nkrumah and the Casablanca bloc. Through some significant diplomacy, the resulting structure was a compromise of the two visions. The principal institutions of the OAU would be the Assembly of Heads of State and Government, the Council of Ministers, the General Secretariat, and the Commission of Mediation, Conciliation, and Arbitration.[4] The Assembly, which was to meet every year, was the ultimate mechanism for taking action, with each member state given a single vote and with resolutions passed by a two-thirds majority. Significantly, the resolutions passed by the OAU's Assembly had no binding force whatsoever, as the charter lacked any provision for establishing an enforcement mechanism. Thus the OAU was routinely criticized as being little more than a toothless "talking club" for African heads of state (Naldi 1989), as it repeatedly failed to stop destructive civil wars or serious human rights abuses. Yet the OAU was purposely created to be incapable of intervening in the internal affairs of member states. Indeed, its history of protecting African leaders while ignoring the rights and liberties of citizens led the organization to be dubbed a "dictators' club" (Adejo 2001; Amate 1986).

The OAU's privileging of juridical statehood ensured that most African states enjoyed a supportive international environment, both inside and outside the continent. Embodying the principles of nonintervention and respect for territorial integrity, the OAU helped provide stability and security for most of the states on the continent. Wars of aggression during the first few decades of the OAU were rare, and the handful of potential African conflicts, such as between Algeria and Morocco over Western Sahara, were usually defused by a small group of senior African heads of state.[5] Importantly, the OAU established the principle that whoever controlled a state's capital was effectively the government of that state and thus enjoyed the privileges accorded to member states. Though this was tested in 1966 when the OAU's founding father, Kwame Nkrumah, was overthrown in a military coup, the adoption of this norm helped remove a number of potential conflicts.

Yet the OAU fell short of a number of its goals. It was powerless to liberate southern Africa from colonial and settler rule, and was almost completely absent in the processes that eventually led to the independence of Angola, Mozambique, Namibia, and Zimbabwe. When it was capable of speaking with one voice on foreign affairs, it was rarely able to ensure policy compliance, such as the attempt to collectively sever diplomatic relations with the United Kingdom in response to Rhodesia's 1965 unilateral declaration of independence. The only time that the OAU was successful in convincing its member states to adopt a common foreign policy was the breaking of diplomatic relations with Israel in 1973. Even though a number of states were reluctant to do so (and would reestablish relations afterward), African states fell in line largely because Israel had violated the territorial integrity of Egypt, an OAU member state, thus transgressing one of the core principles of the organization.

By the 1990s, the failure of the OAU to live up to its promises and aspirations was evident. The organization continued to be incapable of responding to a new generation of wars erupting across the continent. Despite its attempts at creating the African (Banjul) Charter on Human and Peoples' Rights in 1981, it sat passively by while human rights abuses remained rampant and Africa became synonymous with bad governance. Indeed, with its ineffectual wording and lack of implementation, this charter was seen as symptomatic of the structural ineffectiveness of the OAU (Evans and Murray 2008). Likewise, the OAU's attempts to enhance economic union and development across the continent, perhaps best encapsulated by its 1980 Lagos Plan of Action (see Chapter 6), proved to be nothing more than empty rhetoric.

Part of the OAU's failure to live up to expectations was due to the divergent foreign policy interests of member states. Representing over fifty countries, it was clear that Africa rarely spoke with one voice. Likewise, African leaders' fixation with their own survival further undermined the OAU's ability to serve as anything more than an advocate for juridical statehood, privileging the principles of territorial integrity and nonintervention above all else. The OAU also faced a massive cash crisis due to the nonpayment of membership dues. Finally, it was unrealistic to expect much from an organization that was intentionally created to be structurally ineffective, with no mechanism for enforcing its resolutions. By the end of the Cold War, with increased globalization, the crisis of neopatrimonialism, and the spread of fragile states, there emerged a consensus that the OAU needed to be reformed to meet the needs of Africans in the twenty-first century. It was against this background that it held an extraordinary summit in Libya in September 1999 and agreed to metamorphose into the African Union the following year. But before we address the creation of the AU, let us examine a related but preceding development, the establishment of the New Partnership for Africa's Development (NEPAD).

The New Partnership for Africa's Development

At the turn of the twenty-first century, the OAU sought to create a development program to jump-start Africa's economic renewal, and tasked the leaders of Algeria, Egypt, Nigeria, Senegal, and South Africa to produce a framework. The result was the New Partnership for Africa's Development, launched in October 2001. NEPAD's four primary objectives are to eradicate poverty, promote growth and sustainable development, integrate Africa into the world economy, and accelerate the empowerment of women. The final version of NEPAD was largely a merger between two competing visions: the development-focused Omega Plan, put forth by Senegal, and the Millennium Africa Recovery Plan (MAP), put forth by South Africa, Algeria, and Nigeria, with its explicit engagement with good governance and African "ownership and responsibility."

NEPAD was promoted as a major initiative of African leaders, and, as a blueprint, struck a much different tone than the 1980 Lagos Plan of Action, which had not offered any criticism of African leaders or suggested that they might share responsibility for the continent's poor economic situation. NEPAD was devoid of any direct criticism of the developed world or reference to Africa's colonial legacy. In return for promises of increased neoliberal reforms and good governance, African leaders requested more equitable terms of trade within the World Trade Organization, as well as a slight increase in development aid (NEPAD Secretariat 2001; Chabal 2002; Adésína, Graham, and Olukoshi 2005; Taylor 2005a). Some observers noted that these positions were far weaker than those advocated by UN agencies, such as the United Nations Conference on Trade and Development (UNCTAD). Some also noted that NEPAD was yet another in a long line of plans, frameworks, agendas, and declarations produced by African leaders aimed at promoting development without any substantial policy prescriptions (Taylor 2005a). Yet NEPAD was praised by world leaders for offering a frank self-examination of the continent's problems and Africans' role in creating them.

In order to provide specific mechanisms for the realization of "good governance," the AU's July 2002 summit established the Declaration on Democracy, Political, Economic, and Corporate Governance, known as the Durban Declaration (African Union 2002). The following year, the African Peer Review Mechanism (APRM) was established. The APRM was designed to improve African governance systems through a combination of public consultation, expert review, and diplomatic peer pressure. This was celebrated as an important step in establishing a much-needed enforcement mechanism for compliance of NEPAD principles (Maloka

2005). The APRM's process was based on a "self-assessment" question-naire and four types of reviews: a base review, conducted within eighteen months after a country joins the APRM; a periodic review, conducted every two to four years; a requested review, conducted at the request of a member country for whatever reason; and a crisis review, conducted at the early signs of an emerging crisis (APRM 2003). The reviews are con-ducted by individual review teams, who are appointed by a panel of seven "eminent" persons, who are themselves appointed by the APRM's Com-mittee of Heads of States. By 2017, thirty-five countries had acceded to the APRM, with seventeen peer reviews completed or in process. Com-mon conclusions reflected concerns around corruption, poor infrastruc-ture, unemployment, and gender discrimination. There is little evidence that they have had much impact to date.

As with most international institutions, NEPAD has been criticized for its slow decisionmaking process and byzantine bureaucracy. One of its founders, Senegalese president Abdoulaye Wade, publicly criticized it in 2007 for wasting hundreds of millions of dollars and accomplishing noth-ing. Some outside observers have argued that, because it fails to reflect the neopatrimonial character of African political reality, NEPAD will inevitably fail to live up to its expectations (Chabal 2002). Many Africans criticized the top-down approach of NEPAD's creation, arguing that there was a fundamental lack of consultation with African citizens, especially regarding elements of civil society (African Scholars Forum 2002).

Proponents of NEPAD praised it for focusing global attention on poverty and its societal impacts. Yet while NEPAD has been promoted largely as a "poverty reducing" development framework, it actually offers no discernible antipoverty strategy (Adésína 2006). Moreover, some critics argue that NEPAD represents an abdication toward interna-tional donor organizations such as the World Bank and the IMF, while ignoring Africa's experience with almost three decades of their man-dated structural adjustment programs and associated policies (Taylor 2005a). As these critics point out, poverty across the continent escalated during the period when African economies were under detailed manage-ment by the Bretton Woods system. Yet NEPAD and the various related reports largely ignore and absolve these external agents of any respon-sibility, prescribing more of the same while appointing collective blame to African policymakers alone. As Ian Taylor (2005b) notes, rather than offering an alternative, or even a challenge, to existing global power relations, NEPAD actually works to strengthen and legitimize them. While NEPAD's record remains mixed, its creation reflected a larger ideological shift that was further exemplified by the replacement of the

OAU with the AU. Indeed, NEPAD (and the APRM) has now fully been integrated into the African Union, with a coordinating agency based within the AU bureaucracy.

The Rise of the African Union

Just as the debates that shaped the founding of the OAU were characterized by the power struggles between Nigeria and Ghana, rivalries among Africa's regional hegemons, namely Nigeria, Libya, and South Africa, influenced the development of the AU. Libya's Muammar Qaddafi laid claim to the legacy of Nkrumah's Pan-Africanism with his advocacy of a "United States of Africa," but ultimately Qaddafi proved to be a divisive figure, anathema to the neoliberal and democratic ideals that the new AU purportedly advances (Mathews 2008). Nigeria's Olusegun Obasanjo carried significant weight in the proceedings, in part because of his perceived status as a senior African statesman, but primarily because of Nigeria's considerable economic, political, and military weight. South Africa's Thabo Mbeki was one of the primary architects of the AU, not just because of South Africa's clout on the continent, but also given Mbeki's association with the much touted "African renaissance"—the concept that contemporary African problems can be overcome through self-empowerment and self-discipline (Mbeki 1996; Touray 2016; Vale and Maseko 1998)—and his earlier success in bringing about NEPAD.

In many ways, the AU represented a continuation of the OAU's objectives and principles. It maintained the OAU's dedication to securing "sovereign equality and interdependence among member states" and pledging "respect of borders existing on achievement of independence." Yet the creation of the AU was also the product of the post–Cold War democratization wave and of changed donor expectations, which privileged an increased role for civil society as well as political and economic liberalization (Adejo 2001). While the OAU was characterized by its statism, for example, the AU sought to achieve "greater unity and solidarity" among states and African peoples, primarily by incorporating elements of African civil society through such organs as the Economic, Social, and Cultural Council (ECOSOCC), the African Peer Review Mechanism, and the Pan-African Parliament (PAP).

As noted, the OAU was characterized by its ineffectiveness, hampering its ability to intervene in the face of the numerous armed conflicts across the continent. Its irrelevance in such matters had been highly visible during such humanitarian disasters as the Rwandan genocide and the devastating collapse of Somalia. In response, the AU established the African Peace and Security Architecture, discussed in Chapter 7. Central to the APSA was the proposed 20,000-strong African Standby Force. As mentioned, the Assembly of Heads of State and Government gave the AU the authority to intervene in the affairs of member states in cases of "grave circumstances," namely war crimes, genocide, and crimes against humanity, with a later amendment adding "serious threats to legitimate order" (Baimu and Sturman 2003). In contrast to the OAU's record of inaction, the AU, in the first few years of its existence, found itself involved in several armed peacekeeping operations across the continent, though its failure to construct a coherent response to the collapse of Libya and the post-election violence in Côte d'Ivoire sparked significant internal criticism (Badmus 2015).

Arguably what set the AU most apart from the OAU was its role as a norm entrepreneur, understood as a leader who encourages others to uphold a range of norms (Murithi 2012). While issues of good governance, political liberalism, and democratization were notably absent in the founding of the OAU, such concepts were explicitly incorporated into the AU's Constitutive Act, reflecting a shift away from the established principle of noninterference. The act declared the AU's commitment to "promote and protect human and peoples' rights" largely through the African Commission and the African Court on Human and Peoples' Rights, based in Arusha, Tanzania. Pledging to "promote democratic principles and institutions, popular participation and good governance," the AU also actively assumed a role in observing and monitoring elections across the continent.[6]

Currently, the AU counts eighteen organs. Primary among them is the AU Assembly, which comprises heads of state and government or their representatives and is similar to the OAU's Assembly of Heads of State and Government. The AU Assembly meets twice a year (January and June, as well as in extraordinary sessions), with each state having one vote and resolutions requiring a two-thirds majority, while procedural issues pass by simple majority. Below the AU Assembly is the Executive Council, which is functionally similar to the OAU's Council of Ministers. One innovation of the AU was the creation of the aforementioned Pan-African Parliament, which was officially established in 2004 but remains largely ineffective. The PAP consists of five legislators nominated from each member state, and is slated to evolve into an organ with full legislative powers, but it has been the target of serious challenges and criticism, not least of which is Nigeria's complaint of inequality given that it has a population of almost 200 million yet has the same number of legislators as São Tomé and Príncipe, which has a population of around 200,000. Finally, it is somewhat dubious whether AU member states will one day harness the political will to actually live up to their commitment to build the PAP's legislative powers. The extent to which many of them curtail parliamentary roles at home augurs ill for the chances for a stronger African parliament.

The creation of the AU was also meant to establish three financial institutions—the African Central Bank, the African Investment Bank, and the African Monetary Fund—though these still remain to be realized. Nor has the AU's stated goal of establishing a single currency come to fruition. Financial considerations are one of the most significant issues facing the AU, just in terms of its own institutional survival. The OAU was beleaguered by membership payment defaults, corruption, and mismanagement, and similar challenges face the AU, whose annual budget is more than fifteen times larger. The proposed budget for 2019 was $682 million, which actually represents a 12 percent decrease from the previous year. This reduction reflects the stated goal of reducing partner funding and having 100 percent of the AU's operational budget and 25 percent of the peace operations generated from member states by 2020 (with a commitment from the UN to pay the remaining 75 percent). In 2012, member states contributed to only 3 percent of the AU's budget, though that figure had risen to 14 percent by 2017. Given its large bureaucracy and multiple activities, it remains unclear how the institution will financially sustain itself, though there is currently a proposal for all member states to impose a 0.2 percent levy on imports with the proceeds going to fund the AU.

Finally, a major characteristic of the AU is its relations with Africa's numerous regional organizations. In the decades since independence, the continent has seen enormous growth in the number of regional organizations and initiatives, especially regional economic communities. While the OAU sought to create a continent-wide community, the ensuing reality has tilted more toward fragmentation and regional integration schemes. The AU has sought to strengthen its working relationship with the numerous regional organizations for the promotion of security, stability, and economic development. While some coordination exists, there also remains a degree of incoherence and tension between the AU and regional organizations.

Regional Organizations

The Constitutive Act of the African Union called for the union to "coordinate and harmonize policies between existing and future" regional groupings. Despite the popular rhetoric of continental unity, the reality for many states was that the OAU, with more than fifty members, was too large and cumbersome to be effective. In response, a variety of regional and subregional organizations emerged in the decades following independence. Some were based on geography, others on shared official language, while still others were dedicated to specific issues. As a result, significant overlap developed, triggering duplication, inefficiency, and struggles over limited resources.

The move to establish formal regional institutions was driven largely by two related goals. One, African leaders hoped that economic development could best be achieved at the regional level, reflecting a realization that a state's success in the context of globalization was best achieved through cooperation and integration, largely mimicking the EU model (Bach 2015). And two, toward the end of the Cold War, as conflicts spread across state borders, security concerns became framed in regional terms. Often, the framing of both security and development discourses happened simultaneously, strengthening the move toward regionalization.

Regional economic communities. Developmental regionalism reflects efforts by a group of states within a geographic region to improve the efficiency of the regional economy and its collective position in the global economy (Hettne 2001). Since African independence, a number of regional development schemes have emerged, most notably the Economic Community of West African States (ECOWAS), the Southern African Development Community (SADC), the Intergovernmental Authority on Development (IGAD), and the East African Community (EAC). ECOWAS, formed in 1975, seeks to promote cooperation and integration among its fifteen member states through the elimination of customs duties; abolition of quantitative and administrative restrictions on trade among member states; establishment of common customs tariffs and commercial policies toward other developing states; abolition of obstacles to free movement of persons, services, and capital among member states; harmonization of agricultural policies; and implementation of collective schemes for development of transport, communication, energy, and other infrastructures. The fifteen-member SADC was formed in 1980 (originally as the Southern African Development Coordination Conference [SADCC]), while IGAD was originally created in 1986 as the Intergovernmental Authority on Drought and Development (IGADD) before reforming itself into a nine-member development organization for the Horn of Africa. The EAC was originally created in 1967 among Uganda, Kenya, and Tanzania, but collapsed a decade later. The regional organization was revised in 2000 and now includes the original three states, as well as Rwanda and Burundi. In 2008 the EAC and SADC joined the preexisting Common Market for Eastern and Southern Africa (COMESA) to form a twenty-one-member free trade zone. In 2018, forty-four countries agreed to a Continental Free Trade Area (CFTA), though it is largely aspirational at this point.

In examining the growth of African regional economic communities, one may wonder what relatively weak African states could effectively offer each other. A cynical but not altogether incorrect answer is "not much." Due to the effects of European colonialism, independent African economies remain overwhelmingly geared toward Western markets, rather than each other. Today, formal trade remains largely structured toward the former ruling colonial powers. The challenges to inter-African trade can be seen in the continent's physical infrastructure, which reflects the colonial priorities of resource extraction and only minimally links neighboring African countries. Under colonialism, there was little to no commercial interest in promoting intraregional trade. Moreover, telecommunications and air transport were developed to service intercontinental rather than intraregional trade. Until recently, for example, it was almost always faster for a courier letter from Nigeria to Senegal to go through Europe than to travel directly (Uche 2001). After independence, many African states advanced transport infrastructure development schemes, one of the most ambitious being the Trans-African Highways network. Yet, three decades after its creation, an examination of the cross-border links in this network found that 33 percent were unpaved roads in various states of serviceability, and only 38 percent were paved roads in good or fair condition (UNECA 2005).

In reality, little formal trade takes place between African states, though it has been increasing slightly in recent years. For most African states, the former colonial power and other foreign markets continue to represent their primary trading partners. As of 2018, only 10–12 percent of African trade was within Africa, compared to 40 percent within the region in North America, 60 percent in Western Europe, and roughly 59 percent in Asia (Ngepah and Udeagha 2018:1192). Intra-African trade in manufacturing decreased from 18 percent in 2005 to 15 percent in 2015 (African Development Bank 2017). Even within this small amount, there are substantial disparities. For some relatively weak countries, such as Djibouti, limited agricultural exports to the African region represent a significant proportion of GDP. For large inter-African traders, such as South Africa (with an estimated $70 billion in exports in 2016) and Nigeria ($40 billion in 2017), exports within the region still represent less than 4 percent of their GDP.

Despite talk of strengthening intra-African trade through increased integration, in most cases there has been little to actually integrate and little effective desire to do so. Some observers have argued that the emphasis should not be put on trade but on integrated regional economic development. The belief is that future-oriented development schemes, enacted at the regional level, have a greater chance of success for larger numbers of Africans than trying to restructure the limited existing patterns of intra-African trade (Thisen 1989). Yet there have been severe challenges to this goal. Historically, African leaders have been reluctant to lessen the sovereignty of their states by abdicating control to any supranational body. Also, about 30 percent of the revenues for African states come from taxes on trade. While structural adjustment programs broke this statist disposition, they also resulted in the further integration of African national economies into the global economic system at the expense of strengthening intra-African trade and development (see Chapter 6).

Regional economic organizations have also been debilitated by intraregional competition. At times, this competition occurs on the personal level as African leaders compete for greater regional and international prominence. At other times, this competition can take an ideological angle. The first attempt to construct the East African Community collapsed, largely because of divergent views between capitalist-leaning Kenya and socialist-leaning Tanzania, though personal conflict between Tanzania's Julius Nyerere, Kenya's Jomo Kenyatta, and Uganda's Idi Amin also played a role. Concerns about hegemonic ascendancy can affect Africa's regional economic organizations. The creation of ECOWAS was largely driven by Nigeria, reflecting its aspirations to dominate West Africa's economy. South Africa was originally excluded from SADC, but has since come to dwarf other members of the organization. It can be argued that in both ECOWAS and SADC, the larger, more developed countries benefit disproportionately (Alden and le Pere 2006; Clapham 1996:119). Resentment by the smaller states over the privileged position of regional hegemons has certainly been a concern within those organizations.

Perhaps the biggest challenge to regional economic development is the tension between regional aspirations and domestic political interests. The reality is that a government's commitment to a regional organization is overshadowed by its obligations to domestic stakeholders and the need to address internal economic and political crises. In almost every case, domestic considerations trump regional ambitions, no matter how noble. Take, for example, the political expediency of xenophobia in the form of anti-immigration legislation to shore up domestic political support. Despite the commitment of ECOWAS to the free movement of persons and labor in West Africa, Nigeria expelled West African workers in 1983 and Côte d'Ivoire disenfranchised "foreigners" at the turn of the twenty-first century, which contributed to the country's plunge into civil war.

One reason member states often lack the political will for meeting their responsibilities to regional organizations is that, unlike the case for membership in the European Union, states often are not required to meet any admission criteria. In the case of ECOWAS, membership is automatically guaranteed because of geography. As a result, member states do not contribute significantly to the funding of ECOWAS, and generally lack the political will to adhere to the rules and regulations of the organization (Uche 2005). Yet despite these failures, some proponents counter that regional economic organizations represent nascent sites of transregional governance. These institutions impact state behavior, reconstitute the nature of interest definition and bargaining, and contribute to the construction of behavioral and jurisdictional norms and regimes (Keohane 2002; Krasner 1983). Given the pressures of contemporary globalization, Africans have little choice but to increase regional economic integration (Bach 2015).

While state leaders talk about formal integration, economic regionalization is already being driven by the active informal sector. Scholarship associated with the "new regionalisms" approach has sought to capture the multitude of interrelated and complex structural transformations of the contemporary global political economy, leading some to conceive of regions beyond territorial spaces bounded by states and markets (Engel and Zinecker 2016; Hanson 2016; Hettne 1999; Mittelman 1999). This approach has also illustrated the interconnectedness of (human) security, power, and region, offering a reconceptualization of the processes of regionalization and the notion of region itself. The new regionalisms literature reminds us that, in addition to formal institutions and regulatory landscape, informal patterns of regionalization emerge via the daily practices of ordinary Africans, especially through the evolving contours of informal economic activities within the global economy.

The fact that the informal economic sector is so highly regionalized across the continent points to perhaps the clearest explanation of why Africa's regional economic groupings have failed to yield any meaningful successes, and are likely to continue their poor record. The problems that have contributed to the entrenching of underdevelopment, namely weak state institutions, poor management, and nonexistent infrastructures, also contributed to preventing such institutions from achieving their objectives. Despite considerable rhetoric about the need for infrastructural development by African states and the international financial institutions, very little has actually been achieved to make the continent a desirable destination for foreign investment, aside from the presence of primary commodities. For example, in Nigeria it is jokingly accepted that foreign firms need to "BYOI": Bring Your Own Infrastructure. Thus, Cadbury's food-processing plant in Lagos, Nigeria, generates its own electricity and drills for its own water, adding an estimated 25 percent to its operating costs (*The Economist* 2000b). Perhaps it is overly optimistic to expect weak state institutions to successfully integrate divergent and poorly managed economies into something greater than their sum.

Regional collective security organizations. The proliferation of regional organizations across the continent has also resulted from a growing recognition that conflicts can spread easily across national borders, creating regional zones of insecurity. In the terminology of Barry Buzan (1991:190), the post–Cold War era has witnessed the emergence of "regional security complexes" in which the "primary security concerns [of a group of states] link together sufficiently closely that their national security cannot realistically be considered apart from one another." The increased role of regional organizations in African security matters has been a response to the rise of these regional security complexes. Moreover, given the relatively poor record of UN intervention in African conflicts, some hoped that regional organizations would be best able to manage potential conflicts and find "African solutions to African problems."

In recent years, African leaders have turned to several regional economic communities to address security issues. Instead of inventing new organizations, the mandates of these organizations were expanded and some regional economic communities developed their own mechanisms for conflict prevention and peacekeeping intervention. For example, ECOWAS established several institutional mechanisms, namely the Defense and Security Commission, the Security and Mediation Council, the Council of Elders, the Peace and Security Observation Early Warning System, and its Ceasefire Monitoring Group (ECOMOG), which transformed the community from an organization based on self-reliance and economic development into a collective regional security regime. The creation of ECOMOG in 1990, to reestablish peace and stability in West Africa, was central to this transformation. Since then, ECOWAS has been the most active regional organization on the continent, with interventions in Liberia (1990–1998 and 2003), Sierra Leone (1997–2000), Guinea-Bissau (1998–1999), and Côte d'Ivoire (2003–2004). While SADC played important roles in conflicts in Angola and Congo, it has been besieged with problems related to a lack of common values, vague structural arrangements, and weak state institutions (Nathan 2016; Schoeman and Muller 2009).

Regional groupings are considered to have some comparative advantages over the AU in undertaking certain peace initiatives (Söderbaum and Tavares 2009). Not least, they may be quicker to respond given their smaller size. They are also assumed to be more in tune with the conflict at hand, given proximity and shared cultural background, and their heads of state might be able to draw upon their personal relationships to foster dialogue and diplomacy. Finally, since neighboring states are likely to suffer the impacts of armed conflict, there is a personal investment in maintaining security and stability within the region.

Yet regional security organizations have often been met with suspicion and criticized for being vehicles through which regional states strengthen their hegemony by pursuing their own foreign policy agendas behind the facade of multilateralism. SADC's Lesotho intervention, for example, in which 700 South African troops invaded to quell a suspected coup d'état, was regarded by many as an example of South Africa's hegemonic pursuits (the expected Botswana troops reportedly got lost on their way to the small mountainous country) (Likoti 2007). Arguably, this was also partly the case with Senegal's intervention on behalf of ECOWAS in Gambia in 2017. As mentioned in Chapter 7, Nigeria has clearly played the leading role in ECOMOG interventions, yet some have noted that the structure and culture of African regional organizations have actually made it difficult for regional powers to establish their hegemony (Clapham 1996:121). On one level, the very idea of regional hegemony contravenes the commitment to equality of African states, which has been strongly entrenched within the culture of African international relations. But perhaps more important, small African states have been able to counter the influence of would-be regional powers by engaging foreign patrons. For example, a number of small francophone states in West Africa have maintained close relations with France in part to keep Nigeria in check.

In some respects, African regional organizations have been more successful with security than with economic matters. While they have largely failed to foster increased intra-African trade, integrate regional economies, or improve their collective position in the world's economy, they have had slightly better results in monitoring elections, facilitating conflict resolution, and mounting peacekeeping operations. Yet while African regional security organizations can point to some limited successes, such as in Sudan (Williams 2009), Lesotho (van Nieuwkerk 2012), and Burundi (Boshoff 2004), the track record so far has definitely been less than stellar. Part of the reason is structural, given the regional organizations' own institutional limitations. For example, ECOMOG's activities in West Africa have been plagued by substantial command-and-control problems, logistic shortcomings, and poor coordination between member states, field commanders, and ECOWAS (Obi 2009). Similar criticisms have been made of IGAD's interventions in Sudan and Somalia (Murithi 2009) and SADC's intervention in the Democratic Republic of Congo, which was characterized by some as a "logistical nightmare" (Schoeman and Muller 2009). These limitations have been exacerbated by the lack of human, material, and financial resources (Hentz, Söderbaum, and Tavares 2009). Regional organizations often have strained relations with the African Union and United Nations, which tend to regard these organizations as a second-best option, turning to them only when the situation is either too complex or too risky to be dealt with by the larger institutions. As João Gomes Cravinho (2009:200) observes, this practice "actively contributes to weakening regional organizations by involving them only when the chances of success are poor." Thus, Africa's regional security organizations have often found the purposes and goals of specific operations to be unrealistic and beyond their limited capabilities.

External Bilateral Relations

In this section, we examine the evolution of African states' relations with their former colonial powers, as well as major global powers such as the United States, the Soviet Union/Russia, and China, in addition to other significant external actors. Just as these foreign powers each pursue their own individual interests—interests that have varied over time and circumstances—African states are each driven by their own unique agendas and capabilities, resulting in a complicated and constantly shifting terrain of African international relations.

Former Colonial Rulers and the European Union

Given that modern African states are products of European colonialism, it is unsurprising that relations with their former colonial powers tend to be the most significant feature of African foreign policies (Wright 1999). The structure and ideology of the dominant nationalist movement was a determining factor in the initial relationship between newly emerging African states and the former colonial powers. In some cases, such as in Guinea-Conakry, strident anticolonialism ensured a hostile relationship between the two. But for most independent African countries, rapport with the former metropole has been characterized by a mix of conflict, cooperation, and bargaining. Given the myriad ways in which African societies remained bound to the former European powers, some have characterized the post-independence relationship as a form of neocolonialism in which Europeans continued to exert influence over the affairs of Africans (Amin and McDonagh 1975; Leys 1975; Yates 1996). This seems particularly true for former French colonies. But while substantial economic and cultural connections continue to exist beyond their reach, African leaders have also found opportunities to exert agency in relations with their former colonial power.

Unsurprisingly, the ex-colonizers continued to have considerable political, economic, and cultural interests within Africa. More often than not, African leaders benefited from maintaining close economic ties, as they and their associates were brought into partnerships that gave them access to a share of profits and privilege. European leaders have often tended to view their former colonies as part of "their" Africa, which meant giving former colonies preferential treatment. This could include military support to ensure territorial integrity and regime security, but also preferential trade practices and developmental aid. The bulk of African aid assistance from former European powers, for example, continues to go to those countries they once controlled or had a historical interest in. Of course, some European states, such as France and Britain, have enjoyed greater capacity for maintaining an effective post-colonial relationship with their former African colonies. Belgium, Portugal, Italy, and Spain have found themselves largely marginalized on the continent by other powers, though this has changed somewhat for Portugal in recent years, as its economic relationship with Angola has increased in importance for both states.

France's sense of self has long been tied to its presence in Africa. More than any other European power, France pursued a colonial policy of assimilation and integration, tightly binding its holdings culturally, economically, and politically to the metropole. During World War II, this proved invaluable for the survival of General Charles de Gaulle and the Free French (Grovogui 2004). Afterward, de Gaulle took great pains to preserve the close relationship with *l'Afrique française*. After the devastating anticolonial war in Algeria (and Indochina), however, France's desire to hold on to its African empire began to dissipate. In 1958, de Gaulle, then president, offered a choice to the African colonies: join the "French Community" as autonomous and largely self-ruled junior partners, or receive total independence from France by immediately severing all links and access to support (see Chapter 2). Only Guinea broke with France. It was made to pay a high price, as the French left en masse, taking with them not only their technical expertise, but also government files and equipment, including telephones and lightbulbs from government offices (Singer and Langdon 1998). The rest of francophone Africa opted to maintain close relations with France, and most colonies enjoyed peaceful transfers to independence two years later.

The first generation of postcolonial African leaders, such as Léopold Senghor and Félix Houphouët-Boigny, had previously represented their territories in the French national assembly and enjoyed close personal relationships with France's political and economic classes. De Gaulle and his successors nurtured an atmosphere of "family" among these francophone African leaders, which helped bind them closely to France and French elites, providing them with important resources for their own political survival (Le Vine 2004; Golan 1981). In return, France enjoyed a level of access and influence on the continent unmatched by other former colonial powers or the Cold War superpowers. Moreover, by constructing a common currency in francophone Africa, the CFA franc,[7] France ensured both a degree of influence and monetary stability in its former colonies (Stasavage 1997). When France converted to the euro in 1992, the CFA franc was in turn pegged to the new European currency with French treasury support.

France has also continued close military relations with its former colonies. It maintains military bases across the continent and has directly intervened on multiple occasions, beginning with its 1964 incursion in Gabon to restore the pro-French dictator Léon M'ba. Since then, France has directly intervened militarily (sometimes on multiple occasions) in the affairs of Chad, the Republic of Congo, the Democratic Republic of Congo, the Central African Republic, Togo, Comoros, Rwanda, Somalia, Libya, Côte d'Ivoire, and most recently Mali. In many cases, France has sought to shore up a besieged client regime, but it has also removed African leaders it was unhappy with. This has occurred either passively, such as in the April 1974 coup in Niger, which took place when all French security personnel were curiously off-duty (Charlick 1991), or actively, as when French troops invaded the Central African Empire (as the Central African Republic was then briefly named) in 1979 to remove the international pariah Emperor Jean-Bédel Bokassa (Bigo 1988). In December 2012, France declined requests by the government of the Central African Republic to help it battle insurgents (who overthrew the regime in March 2013), but weeks later sent military forces to Mali to battle advancing Islamist forces. French policy in Africa has also been informed by Paris's desire to strengthen its position against what it regards as Anglo-Saxon dominance on the continent. For example, France secretly funneled weapons to the Biafran secessionist regime during the 1967–1970 Nigerian civil war, possibly prolonging the devastating conflict by at least eighteen months, in an attempt to dismantle the largest anglophone state in West Africa (de St. Jorre 1972). It also supported the *génocidaire* regime of Juvenal Habyarimana in Rwanda in 1994, in part for fear of the Rwandan Patriotic Front's anglophone connections. Over the past several decades, France has continued to supply large quantities of weapons to Africa, both to its own client states and to Libya, Nigeria, Kenya, Somalia, and South Africa, making it the foremost Western arms merchant on the continent.

Though the relationship can easily be regarded as one of paternalistic dependency, a number of African states (francophone and nonfrancophone alike) have actively courted close relations with France. For their part, African leaders gain development assistance, technical expertise, and in some cases invaluable military assistance and protection. While the United States has attached numerous and unpopular conditionalities to its limited assistance, France has proven to be the most accessible and willing Western supporter of African political leaders, with less concern for ideological orientation or regime type. Despite electoral turnovers, Paris's policies toward Africa have been quite consistent. This is particularly remarkable given that these policies have been under the control of the French presidency and the Cellule Africaine (African Unit), located in the Elysée palace, and not the Ministry of Foreign Affairs. Whether Gaullist, liberal, or socialist, and despite each promising to behave differently, French governments have largely adhered to similar policies toward Africa, while seeking to extend France's sphere of influence. This has been accomplished partly by the close personal relationships that exist between French and African elites. These connections (often referred to as *la Françafrique*) and French policy in general have even weathered a number of corruption scandals that have shed light on the shadowy aspects of Franco-African relations (Heilbrunn 2005; Verschave 1999). For example, in 2011 it was uncovered that several African leaders, including Omar Bongo, Téodoro Obiang Mbasogo, and Denis Sassou-Nguesso, regularly contributed millions to French politicians in an established system of kickbacks that existed under former presidents Georges Pompidou, Valéry Giscard d'Estaing, François Mitterrand, and Jacques Chirac (*Le Monde* 2011; Vampouille 2010). Historically, France's policies toward Africa have been managed by a small, tightly knit community of politicians, diplomats, and businessmen surrounding the president, who have also enjoyed close personal and financial interests in various African states (Taylor 2012; Smith and Glaser 1992). Guy Martin (1993:3) has noted that, given these connections, France's policy stance toward Africa has been "primarily motivated by a narrow conception of its national interests, and blatantly disregards African concerns and interests." Of particular note has been the role of French interest in African oil, driven by French companies Elf and TOTAL, which has influenced both France's policies toward Africa and the domestic politics of African rentier states (Yates 1996, 2009).

To strengthen its interactions with *l'Afrique française,* in 1973 France initiated an annual Franco-African summit, which has grown to include nonfrancophone states as well. In fact, starting in 1985, France decided to devote the first day of the summit exclusively to francophone states to ensure the "family" feeling of the privileged elite. As the expansion of the Franco-African summit illustrates, France's engagement with Africa is not limited to its former colonies. Paris has actively sought to incorporate the former Belgian colonies of Central Africa, particularly the DRC (formerly Zaire), into its sphere of influence (Trefon 1989; Bach 1986; Smith and Glaser 1992). Even after the end of the Cold War, as the United States and Belgium distanced themselves from the Mobutu regime in Zaire, France remained on friendly terms and was its most important international supporter—despite the assassination of French ambassador Philippe Bernard in January 1993 by Mobutu soldiers. Yet France had few investments in Zaire and its trade was far behind that of Belgium and the United States (Huliaras 1998). Support for Mobutu, as well as for the Habyarimana regime in neighboring Rwanda, was driven by a desire to maintain its so-called *chasse gardée* (private estate) in Central Africa. In this case, France sought to counter what it regarded as US ambitions to supplant French influence (Willame 1998). This fear was frequently exploited to great effect by African leaders, most notably Mobutu in Zaire and Hissène Habré in Chad. In response to fears of growing anglophone influence in the region, and in the face of the international community's belated recognition of the scope of the genocide in Rwanda, the French government took the lead in proposing an interventionist force, eventually acting unilaterally to send troops under Operation Turquoise in June 1994 (Massey 1998). Rather than being praised for its decisive humanitarianism, France was seen as complicit in the genocide and Operation Turquoise was regarded as an attempt to stall a victory by the Rwandan Patriotic Front and protect the retreat of the former Rwandan government, its army, and the Interahamwe, which France had trained and supported (Evans 1997; Gourevitch 1998; McNulty 1997).

In the wake of the collapse of the Mobutist state and the Rwandan genocide, there were signals that French policy toward Africa was beginning to change. This recalibration was also engendered by the impact of a number of political scandals and the emergence of a new generation of French leaders who proclaimed that an overhaul of Franco-African policies was needed (Kroslak 2004). In 1997, for example, Prime Minister Lionel Jospin announced that France would begin to remove its troops from Africa and close many of its military bases on the continent, signifying a substantial change in the country's Africa policy. The following year, he announced the dismantling of the Ministry of Cooperation and its incorporation into the Ministry of Foreign Affairs. France also launched a capacity-building program, Renforcement des Capacités Africaines au Maintien de la Paix (RECAMP), to shift the military burden of peacekeeping operations onto African states in an attempt to reduce French involvement and make African militaries more self-sufficient (Berman and Sams 2000). The Jospin government also announced its intention to integrate French policy toward Africa within a multilateral European framework, which represented a radical shift in practice.

Yet pronouncements advocating increased multilateralism have been belied by Paris's continued bilateral dealings with African states. Jospin's good intentions notwithstanding, the Cellule Africaine reasserted its authority. With the notable exceptions of the multilateral intervention in the Ituri region of the DRC and the 2011 bombing campaign in Libya, the governments of Presidents Jacques Chirac, Nicolas Sarkozy, François Hollande, and Emmanuel Macron have all sought a middle ground between the reforms introduced in the immediately preceding administrations and the more established policies regarding France's *chasse gardée,* tilting toward the latter more often than not. Despite institutional reforms, the established mechanisms remain and continue to exert significant influence on French policy toward Africa. In recent years, a string of political scandals (such as "Angolagate" and the established practice of kickbacks mentioned earlier) illustrated how oftensecret relations continue to characterize much of Franco-African affairs. The deployment of French troops in the DRC, Côte d'Ivoire, and Mali seems to represent a return to form for France's engagement with Africa. Indeed, though he campaigned as a reformer, Macron has exerted France's soft and hard power in Africa as part of his explicit campaign to boost France's global influence.

In sharp contrast to the Franco-African postcolonial relationship, the anglophone relationship has been notable for its looseness. Britain has provided neither the level of protection for its former African colonies and their leaders nor the degree of dependence experienced by francophone states. This was largely due to the different colonial relationships and postcolonial priorities pursued by France and Britain. Whereas France had engaged in a colonial policy of assimilation and incorporation, Britain's colonial project was predicated on the assumption that its African colonies would eventually become distinct and independent entities. While both European states developed close political, economic, and cultural linkages with their African colonies, France's sense of global self-identity was more tied up in its African empire than was Britain's, which had selectively privileged India and the white settler colonies of Kenya and Rhodesia. Britain created a vast economic empire based on extracting raw materials from its colonies, yet the direct economic ties between Great Britain and its African colonies were weaker than those in the Franco-African relationship. There are fewer major British corporate interests in sub-Saharan Africa, and those that exist lack the close relationship to political power found in France. Likewise, anglophone African leaders are not as personally connected to the ruling classes of London, as British colonial policy was largely driven by technocrats. The limited degree of personal connection and investment in Africa has shaped London's quasi-detached attitude toward Africa.

In the postcolonial era, Britain sought to enhance its global status by attaching itself to the United States. After the debacle of French and British engagement against Egypt in 1956, when the two European powers clumsily intervened on the side of Israel to seize the Suez Canal from Gamal Abdul Nasser's forces, the United States expressed its anger that its European allies had acted on their own and behind Washington's back. France was largely undeterred in pursuing its interests unilaterally in Africa, but Britain more or less fell in line with its US benefactor (Verbeek 2003; Gorst and Johnman 1997). As such, London has subsequently tended to prioritize its "special relationship" with Washington over its historical connection with Britain's African colonies.

This is not to imply that Britain has not been engaged in Africa, but the degree and characteristics of that engagement are in marked contrast to French engagement with the continent. For example, Britain has not maintained large numbers of troops on the continent. Nor has it displayed a willingness to intervene on behalf of besieged African clients or to remove embarrassing thorns in their sides. Where France moved to oust Emperor Bokassa (admittedly only after he ceased to be a useful ally), Britain did little regarding Idi Amin, dictator of Uganda and self-proclaimed "Last King of Scotland." At times when it was overtly drawn into African domestic politics, as with Rhodesia's unilateral declaration of independence and the eventual transformation of that country into majority-ruled Zimbabwe, it did so begrudgingly. As Christopher Clapham (1996:88) notes, British policymakers tended to regard Africa as "a source of trouble rather than of opportunity."

The United Kingdom's limited engagement with Africa during the Cold War is evidenced by its economic interaction with the continent. By the late 1980s, British economic interests in Africa were minimal. Only slightly more than 3 percent of British exports went to the continent, and only 1.9 percent of the UK's imports came from Africa (Ravenhill 1991). Moreover, British development aid to Africa was relatively negligible, having shrunk over the previous decades. Relative to gross national product, the total British development aid to Africa started at the relatively high figure of about 0.5 percent in the mid-1960s, then went into fairly steep decline through the mid-1970s. Though there was a slight rise in the second half of the 1970s, it continued to decline gradually but significantly during the 1980s and into the 1990s to around 0.3 percent. This decline in the 1980s and 1990s was related to ideological shifts within the British government following the victory of Conservative prime minister Margaret Thatcher, who viewed development assistance as "handouts" (Lumsdaine 1993:162). It is worth noting that while Britain increasingly disengaged from Africa during the Conservative years, it remained an important supplier of weapons to a number of African states, including regimes noted for their human rights abuses and undemocratic practices, such as Sierra Leone (Williams 2004).

The Commonwealth of Nations (formerly the British Commonwealth), an intergovernmental organization of former British colonies that holds biennial meetings of heads of government, has constituted one of the main mechanisms of postcolonial Anglo-African relations. Even here, however, the contrast with France is revealing. Whereas France frequently uses its annual Franco-African summits to push certain policies and maintain its paternalist relationship with Africa, the Commonwealth's summits are more likely to be used by former British colonies as forums to air their grievances and attempt to exert some influence over their former colonizer. For example, independent African states used the 1961 Commonwealth meeting to force out South Africa and pressure Britain to impose sanctions on the apartheid regime. Likewise, after Rhodesia's 1965 unilateral declaration of independence, the Commonwealth became a forum for African leaders to cajole Britain regarding its policies toward Africa.

While it is true that Britain expanded the Commonwealth to include a few non-anglophone African states, such as Rwanda and Mozambique, it has not reaped substantial benefits from it. Again, this was largely because Britain did not enjoy (or pursue) the strong economic, political, and personal connections that characterized France's relationship with its former colonies. While French corporate interests such as Elf and TOTAL were closely connected to Paris's policies toward Africa, British corporations with interest in Africa, such as Lon-Rho, were kept at a distance and viewed with suspicion by policymakers in London (Cronje, Ling, and Cronje 1976). More often than not, London appeared to its former African colonies as a reluctant patron with limited, but valued, resources.

Anglo-African relations experienced a significant change in the twenty-first century, due almost entirely to the rise of New Labour with the election of Tony Blair in 1997 (Taylor 2010). Signaling an ideological shift away from the Thatcher years, the new prime minister described Africa in 2001 as a "scar on the conscience of the world" and proclaimed "a sustained effort on the part of the British government to work harder, and to spend more on reducing poverty in Africa" (Blair 2001). Under the Tony Blair and Gordon Brown governments, aid to Africa increased significantly (though was still far below the UN's recommended target of 0.7 percent of a country's gross national income). The UK's overall aid to Africa primarily focused on poverty reduction, and reflected both the neoliberal economic orthodoxy and New Labour's dedication to helping African countries meet the UN's much-touted Millennium Development Goals. For example, overall aid to Nigeria in 2010 was £140 million, an increase of £40 million from 2008. The growth in development assistance and the rhetorical attention to African issues such as poverty relief were undoubtedly driven by Clare Short, British secretary of state from 1997 to 2003, who accorded significant priority to development policy (Gallagher 2009; Vereker 2002). While British exports to sub-Saharan Africa during the first four years of New Labour decreased slightly (from £3.5 million in 1997 to £3.4 million in 2001), imports from the continent doubled (from £2.8 million in 1997 to £5.6 million in 2001). Yet British commercial links to Africa remained dominated by South Africa, which represented over 40 percent of British exports and imports to the African continent (Williams 2004:52–53).

One major development was the decision by the Blair government in May 2000 to send a thousand British troops to Sierra Leone. A few months before, the UN had deployed its mission to Sierra Leone (UNAMSIL) in order to enforce the terms of the Lomé peace accord, but it proved ineffective. After the RUF rebels captured 500 UN troops and their equipment in an advance on the capital, Blair sent British troops to help evacuate foreign nationals. Yet the troops stayed on after the evacuation, helping to turn the tide against the RUF by providing support for UNAMSIL, training government troops, and even helping capture RUF leader Foday Sankoh. Under Blair, Sierra Leone became the UK's most important commitment in Africa, with more aid going there than to any other African country (Jackson and Albrecht 2011).

One should not overplay the changes in Anglo-African relations brought about by New Labour, however. Africa was still not a top priority to British policymakers, who were more focused on Europe, the former Soviet Union, and East Asia. Even within its marginal engagement with Africa, British policy continued to concentrate upon a few key states, namely Sierra Leone, Nigeria, South Africa, Kenya, Zimbabwe, and Uganda. Importantly, New Labour's policies toward Africa largely relied on development NGOs, such as Oxfam and Save the Children, and multilateral institutions, such as the United Nations, the IMF and World Bank, the European Union, and the Group of Seven (G7) and Group of Twenty (G20). Thus, even though Africa enjoyed a slightly elevated status in the rhetoric of British foreign policy under Prime Ministers Blair and Brown, the continent's place in British policies overall was still marginal. As Paul Williams (2004:58) observed, the core characteristics of British policies remained unchanged, namely "extracting profits and preventing 'their' problems ending up 'over here.' In this sense, Britain has still not moved beyond a damage limitation approach." In the wake of Britain's 2016 decision to leave the EU (so-called Brexit), however, Africa has risen slightly on London's radar as Conservative prime minister Theresa May works to establish new trade arrangements for the post-Brexit era. In 2018, she visited South Africa, Kenya, and Nigeria (UK's biggest trading partners in Africa) to proclaim a new "partnership," reflecting the increased leverage that at least those three countries have in the evolving Anglo-African relationship, with Britain losing economic opportunities in Europe and being overshadowed by China and the United States on the global scale.

Other former colonial powers largely lacked the capacity or political will to maintain an effective postcolonial relationship with their former African colonies, and thus were eclipsed on the continent by other powers. Belgium was traumatized by both the sudden collapse of Congo-Kinshasa, the colony in which Belgians had invested a vast amount of effort, and its inability to control events in the ensuing chaos. Though they were instrumental in the removal of Congolese prime minister Patrice Lumumba, Belgian leaders were unable to realize the goal of Katangese secession, as they were pushed aside by the United States and the United Nations (Dunn 2003). After Brussels failed in its attempt to exert influence over an independent Congo, it largely detached itself from its former colonial holdings, though a number of substantial links remain, especially in the formal and informal economic sectors. It did intervene militarily during the 1977 and 1978 Shaba invasions in order to shore up the Mobutu regime, but by then it was largely playing a supporting role to France. This reflected the fact that after independence, Belgium's former colonies of Congo, Rwanda, and Burundi chose to develop closer links to France. Perhaps symbolic of Belgium's reduced role on the continent, its contingent of UN-mandated troops proved extremely ineffectual in either stopping the outbreak of the 1994 Rwandan genocide or convincing the international community to intervene. Nevertheless, Belgium played a small part in Congo's multiple transitions. In the early 1990s, it was a member, with France and the United States, of the "troika" that unsuccessfully tried to steer the country toward democracy. Belgian academics also helped draft Congo's 2006 constitution, and the king of Belgium attended the ceremonies for the fiftieth anniversary of Congo's independence in 2010. Although Belgium carries limited effective influence in Congo nowadays, there remains a significant, at times familial, relationship between Belgian and Congolese elites. Belgian public actors in Congo continue at times to behave as if at home, and the Congolese government gets easily frazzled when it perceives snubbing or rejection from its former colonial overlord.

As for Portugal, its African colonies, particularly Mozambique and Angola, gained their independence after long and brutal wars that set the tone of their initial postcolonial relationship. After its 1974 coup, Lisbon focused on developing its Euro-Atlantic relations, though substantial economic ties persisted between it and its former colonies (Teixeira 2003). Since Portugal joined the OECD's Development Assistance Committee in 1991, it channeled most of its official development assistance toward its former African colonies via the OECD and the European Union. But by 2015, in the wake of its own economic crisis, its aid had dropped to less than 0.2 percent of its gross national income, far below the EU donor's target of 0.7 percent. While trade between Portugal and the lusophone countries has increased in recent years, it has largely been led by investments by the former colonies into Portugal. By 2012, Angolan investment in Portugal outpaced Portuguese investment in Angola, as capital investment in Portugal by the Angolan ruling elite (enriched from oil revenue and several decades of neopatrimonial rule) rose thirty-five-fold over the preceding decade.

Relations between the European Union and Africa have been dominated by issues of trade, aid, and, increasingly, security. The incorporation of all of Africa's former colonizers into the European Community (EC) and European Union (EU) broadened the linkages between the two continents and provided African elites with some leverage in world affairs. This and some residual sense of responsibility and entitlement that the former European colonial powers felt toward Africa were reflected in the 1957 Treaty of Rome, which, in establishing the European Community, preserved the special trading privileges between the former colonizers and the colonized. The desire to create a postcolonial framework of cooperation, especially in the fields of trade and aid, resulted in the first of the Lomé Conventions (Lomé I), in 1976, between the European Community and the African, Caribbean, and Pacific (ACP) countries. The convention was aimed at providing preferential access to European markets for specific exports, as well as guaranteeing increased levels of assistance and investment from the European Community. The convention was renegotiated and renewed three times. Lomé II (1981–1985) sought to almost double the amount of aid and investment from the EC. Lomé III (1985–1990) altered the provisions around trade and further increased EC aid. Lomé IV was signed in 1989 and was supposed to cover the next ten years (Crawford 1996; Cosgrove 1994). However, in 1995 the United States successfully charged that the preferential trade agreements institutionalized by the Lomé Conventions violated the World Trade Organization's rules, and effectively brought the string of renegotiation and renewal to an end.

The impact of the Lomé Conventions on African development was largely negligible, but the assistance did provide African states with a significant source of income. The Lomé Conventions also gave African states alternative points of access to Western European markets, while giving the EC/EU an institutionalized mechanism through which to pursue individual and collective interests in Africa. Interestingly, the Lomé I negotiations provided one of the few opportunities in which African states were able to engage collectively with external powers on relatively equal footing (Ravenhill 1985). Yet this position of strength was short-lived in a geopolitical and economic landscape that altered significantly, leaving the ACP states with restricted influence in the subsequent negotiations of the Lomé Conventions. As Clapham (1996:101) notes, "the renegotiations of the Convention from Lomé II onward essentially consisted in the EC telling the ACP states how much aid they were going to get, and the ACP complaining that it wasn't enough."

The end of the Cold War provided the EC/EU with increased opportunities to play a more pronounced global role. Such global aspirations were captured in the 1992 Maastricht Treaty, which formally created the EU and stated that one of the Union's objectives was "to assert its identity on the international scene." Yet the end of the Cold War meant that the EU's global priorities shifted away from the South to the "Near Abroad," in particular Central and Eastern Europe, and the Mediterranean. At the same time, the weakened geopolitical position of Africa led to the further politicization of EU development policy as aid became increasingly tied to good governance, human rights, and democratization (Mayall 2005). Moreover, EU development cooperation shifted from aid to trade policies. Thirty-three African countries are considered least-developed countries (LDCs) and thus most of their goods are granted duty-free access to the EU under the "Everything but Arms" initiative. And while there was a renewed commitment to poverty eradication in the context of the UN's Millennium Development Goals, it was largely assumed that these goals would be realized through private sector–led growth and the liberalization of African states and markets (Bretherton and Vogler 2006). Such assumptions were entrenched in the Cotonou Agreement of 2000, which aimed to set out EU-ACP relations for the next two decades in the post-Lomé era.

In most respects, African elites have found the terms of trade between the EU and Africa steadily worsening over the past several decades, while at the same time intrusive conditions have been attached to shrinking levels of development assistance (Lister 1997). With the EU focused on Eastern Europe and other global interests, aid to ACP countries dropped from 63.5 percent of the entire EU aid budget in 1989 to 29 percent by 1998 (Hurt 2004). Many observers noted that this resulted in the increasingly supplicant position of African states in relation to the EU (Hurt 2003; Brown 2002; Raffer 2001; van de Walle 1999). While this dynamic altered in the twenty-first century with the surge in African commodity prices, EU-Africa relations have continued to be characterized by a confused and contradictory rhetoric of "partnership" and "cooperation" that seems unconnected to reality (Carbone 2011).

While recent improvements in Africa's economic performance and the demand for its natural resources have provided African states with greater leverage, EU-African relations have recently shifted due to

European concerns about security in Africa and with stifling the flow of immigrants (Haastrup 2013). While the EU has been instrumental in helping the AU develop autonomous capabilities for addressing security concerns and lessening refugee flows, these attempts have been hampered by the competing interests of individual EU member states.

The United States

The vast majority of African states became independent during the Cold War's superpower competition. As such, the United States viewed Africa mainly as a geopolitical battleground. In many ways, the United States was constrained by its superpower role. On the one hand, it celebrated national self-determination and the end of colonialism. On the other, it held a deep distrust of revolutions and political unrest, preferring to champion the maintenance of the status quo (Hunt 2009). It thus treated Africa's anticolonial movements with a degree of apprehension, especially as African nationalism challenged the hegemony of its Western allies and raised the specter of communism on the continent. This apprehension seemed to be confirmed when the newly independent Congo collapsed into violence and civil war in 1960. Fearing that Prime Minister Lumumba was moving Congo toward the Soviet Union, the US Central Intelligence Agency (CIA), at the direction of President Dwight Eisenhower, hatched a plot to assassinate him. Lumumba was eventually cut off from his power base, arrested by US-backed Congolese dissident troops, taken to the secessionist province of Katanga, and murdered. The extent to which the CIA was involved in the murder of Lumumba remains a topic of debate, but the event marks the direct entrance of the United States into African affairs in order to counter the rise of radical nationalism (Dunn 2003; de Witte 2001). Soon after, US-backed Colonel Joseph Mobutu seized power in the Congo, beginning a three-decade reign characterized by his close relationship with the United States. Over the next several decades, the United States would ensure Mobutu's political survival, illustrating that Washington was willing to support corrupt and oppressive authoritarian regimes as long as they proved to be anticommunist allies in the geopolitical Cold War competition (Schatzberg 1991; Kelly 1993).

Despite its involvement in the Congo, the United States initially played a role on the continent secondary to that of the Europeans. By the 1970s, however, US interests in Africa increased as the Soviet Union and its allies were regarded as challenging Western power throughout the developing world. But even then, African issues rarely reached the level of senior policymakers in the United States. In his discussion of the country's Cold War foreign policy toward Africa, Peter Schraeder (1994:2) claims that US policymakers "tended to ignore the African continent until some sort of politico-military crisis grab[bed] their attention." While this is largely true, one should be careful not to overstate the case. US actions had tremendous implications on the ground, from the maintenance of African Cold War allies such as Mobutu in Zaire to the attempted undermining of Marxist-Leninist regimes in places such as Angola and Mozambique, from the impact of structural adjustment programs implemented by the US-influenced World Bank to the more complicated effects of US private economic actors, particularly regarding commodities such as oil, gold, diamonds, coffee, and tea (Dunn 2008b; Hentz 2004; Clough 1992).

US support for the status quo meant some African states were able to access material support by proving to be loyal or of geostrategic importance. In other cases, however, African insurgencies fighting pro-Soviet regimes benefited from US funding and support. This was the case in Angola, where the United States provided substantial assistance to UNITA. Ironically, the MPLA regime was supported by Cuban troops, who were directly involved in protecting oil facilities run by the US company Gulf Oil against attacks by the US-backed UNITA rebels (George 2005; Frynas and Wood 2001). Similarly, after US-backed Haile Selassie was overthrown by Marxist-Leninists in Ethiopia, neighboring Somalia was able to extract US support even though it had been a Soviet client state until the Soviet Union shifted its allegiance to the new regime in Ethiopia. In general, however, the United States did not have a deep engagement with the continent, preferring to follow the lead of its European allies and using international financial institutions to promote its economic agenda on the continent.

James Hentz (2004) has argued that US engagement with Africa has always been framed by the three competing master narratives that have shaped American foreign policy in general: realpolitik (which focuses on balance-of-power strategies within a zero-sum power struggle), "Hamiltonianism" (which privileges global order through the creation of international legal and financial structures that promote US interests), and "Meliorism" (or "Wilsonianism," reflecting a humanitarian impulse to make the world a better place economically, culturally, and politically). For Hentz, the history of US engagement with Africa has been shaped by these competing currents, with the Hamiltonian tradition being the longest, strongest, and default option. Moreover, the policies of the United States, unlike its European allies, which tend to coordinate their policies toward Africa through a specific agency, are often the product of a cacophony of voices. Primary among those voices are the White House, the State Department, the Pentagon, the US Agency for International Development (USAID), the Commerce Department (working particularly through the World Bank and the IMF), and private economic and humanitarian aid actors. The multiplicity of actors often means that the United States engages with the African continent in varied and at times conflictual ways.

Hentz also notes that there have not been strong domestic constituents influencing US policies toward Africa, as have shaped US relations toward other states and regions. As Peter Schraeder (1994) stresses, US policy toward Africa has traditionally been driven by bureaucrats. This has resulted in Africa being largely relegated to the margins of US strategic interests since the Cold War. Yet Piers Robinson (2002) has observed that focused media coverage plays a role in persuading US politicians to pursue particular policies at times when those politicians lack certainty or direction. This "CNN effect" has arguably impacted US policies toward Africa, most notably in the case of President George H. W. Bush's decision to send troops to Somalia in 1992 (Cohen 2000). Likewise, US foreign policy toward Sudan was partly influenced by domestic evangelical Christian constituencies, who often regarded the Muslim regime in Khartoum as victimizing southern Christians (de Waal 1998; Gulford 2011; Love 2006).

With the end of the Cold War it seemed as if the African continent would slip further off the US foreign policy agenda. While private economic actors remained engaged, with emerging markets in minerals such as coltan joining long-standing interests in oil and diamonds, the formal apparatus of US power seemed less interested in Africa. As a result of the ideological shift caused by the Republican congressional electoral success in 1994, USAID and the State Department became less engaged. Established allies, such as Mobutu Sese Seko in Zaire and Jonas Savimbi in Angola, lost favor with Washington and were left to suffer the consequences of their actions alone. After a perceived disastrous defeat in Somalia, the United States swore off direct military engagement in Africa, often playing a more subdued role in African affairs, particularly during the 1994 Rwandan genocide and the slow implosion of Zaire. The post–Cold War era seemed to be characterized by what one observer referred to as America's "benign neglect" of the continent (Booker 2001).

But the events of 11 September 2001 marked the beginning of a shift in relations between the United States and Africa, with the administration of George W. Bush and subsequently that of Barack Obama focused on two goals in sub-Saharan Africa: accessing African oil and other material resources and combating terrorism. In 2002 the *Washington Post* observed: "Africa, the neglected stepchild of American diplomacy, is rising in strategic importance to Washington policy makers, and one word sums up the reason—oil" (quoted in Hentz 2004:23). In 2011, over 16 percent of US oil imports came from sub-Saharan Africa (largely from Angola and Nigeria), contrasted to the 18 percent coming from the Persian Gulf. Since 2011, Nigeria and Angola have been among the top ten exporters of crude oil to the United States, offering the United States an attractive alternative to oil from the Middle East. By 2016, however, the amount of imported African oil had dropped significantly, reflecting the Obama administrations' attempts to lessen US dependence on foreign oil.[8]

In addition to its interest in accessing African oil, the United States established numerous programs, such as the African Growth and Opportunity Act (AGOA), to provide incentives for African countries to open their economies and build free markets. In exchange for adopting neoliberal economic policies, African countries were promised preferential access to US markets. Non-oil exports from sub-Saharan Africa to the United States grew from $1.4 billion in 2011 to $4.1 billion in 2015. A number of critics, however, argued that AGOA merely reproduced the conditionalities of adjustment programs and privileged regional integration schemes (Adebajo 2003; Hentz 2001). While the United States was Africa's major trading partner for many years, it was displaced by China in 2009. Indeed, exports from sub-Saharan Africa to the United States fell by 66 percent between 2006 and 2016, with exports growing by only 7 percent. In 2015, it was estimated that US-African trade flows accounted for $53 billion, which was dwarfed by the $188 billion in Sino-African trade. Exacerbating the waning trade interests of the United States with Africa, the future of AGOA is very much in question given the Trump administration's hostility to existing trade deals.

Even before the election of Donald Trump, the United States was decreasing its development assistance to the continent and demanding greater African self-responsibility. In 1985, for example, state-to-state aid was $2.4 billion, but by 1990 that figure was cut in half, to $1.2 billion, and remained at this level throughout the decade, with a slight increase to about $1.4 billion by 2001. While the figure increased over the following decade, to $7 billion in 2011 (OECD 2011a), it has been dropping significantly under the Trump administration. A major vehicle for aid has been the Millennium Challenge Corporation, created in 2004 as an independent agency, separate from the State Department and USAID. To be eligible for MCC aid (known as a Millennium Challenge

Account), a country is evaluated along third-party indicators (such as those established by the United Nations Educational, Scientific, and Cultural Organization [UNESCO], Freedom House, and the Heritage Foundation) covering seventeen governance and economic conditions. In its first year of implementation, seventeen countries were deemed eligible for an MCA, the majority being in Africa.

While President George W. Bush's 2003 promise of $10 billion to combat AIDS in Africa and the Caribbean became a significant component of his administration's engagement with the continent (Radelet 2003; Dunn 2008b), and the Obama administration created the Young African Leaders Initiative (YALI) for educating and networking young African leaders, Africa and the issue of development largely suffered from neglect under Obama, and active disdain under Trump. Trump has disparaged African states as "shit-holes." His administration has slashed budgets for African-related agencies. The initial target budget for the Millennium Challenge Corporation, for example, had been $3 billion, but that was reduced to $800 million in Trump's proposed 2019 budget. Moreover, he has refused to fill over half of the vacancies in the State Department, negatively impacting US diplomacy and crippling numerous initiatives across the continent (Stremlau 2017). In addition to significantly decreasing overseas development aid and attempting to gut the State Department's US Agency for International Development, the Trump administration also supplanted the Overseas Private Investment Corporation with the newly created US International Development Finance Corporation to provide loans to US companies willing to do business in African and other developing nations. And while the United States had pledged $14 billion in aid to Africa over the next decade, that figure is dwarfed by China's pledge of $175 billion over the same period.

US foreign policy interest in Africa has long focused on issues of security and geopolitics, but since 9/11 counterterrorism and security concerns have come to dominate its agenda on the continent. Three years before the events of 11 September 2001, terrorists bombed the US embassies in Dar es Salaam and Nairobi, killing 224 people (including 12 Americans) and injuring over 4,500. Since then, many US policymakers have been concerned that Africa was becoming, in the words of one top US diplomat, "the world's soft underbelly for global terrorism" (House Committee on International Relations 2001). For Washington, sub-Saharan Africa contains a potentially dangerous mixture of forces—weak and failing states, poverty, political repression and alienation, and social disintegration—that lends itself to radicalism and the emergence of terrorism. The emergence of violent Islamist groups in the Horn and in West Africa has caused concern in Washington.

In 2002 the United States established the Pan-Sahel Initiative, which increased training, equipment supplies, and cooperation with the militaries of Mali, Niger, Chad, and Mauritania as part of the US global "war on terror" (Ellis 2004). Much of US counterterrorism strategy has focused on the Horn, given its proximity to the Middle East, its predominant Muslim population, and Somalia's position as the world's preeminent failed state, but there is also significant US military activity in Sahelian West Africa, particularly in Niger. Since 2007, the United States has directed its support in the region to the African Union peacekeepers (AMISOM), but also the Ethiopian military, which along with the Kenyan military currently operates within Somalia against Islamist militias. Both the Bush and Obama administrations increased levels of US military engagement in Africa, especially through the Combined Joint Task Force–Horn of Africa (CJTF-HOA) program. At the center of this presence is Camp Lemonier in Djibouti, home to over 1,800 US personnel. Camp Lemonier is the only true military base that the United States maintains on the African continent, but as of 2017 there were roughly 6,000 active US military personnel spread across the continent. While most of those are concentrated in just a handful of countries, with the majority in Djibouti, almost every African country has a US military presence of some size on its soil (Watson 2017). Additionally, the US military maintains at least a dozen drone bases across Africa.

Through programs such as the Africa Crisis Response Initiative (ACRI), the African Contingency Operations Training and Assistance (ACOTA), and the Trans-Saharan Counterterrorism Partnership (TSCTP), the United States has sought to strengthen Africa's military capability by training special units from several African states, as well as providing arms and equipment to these forces. While these programs are limited and relatively minimal, they have impacted the military landscape given the access of African militaries to US training and equipment. US engagement on military matters has also resulted in the increased privatization of security in Africa, as the United States has promoted the use of private militaries and US-based security firms (Reno 2011, 2001; Hentz 2004).

In what was heralded as a major development in US-Africa relations, the Pentagon created the US Africa Command (AFRICOM) in 2007 to oversee US military activities on the continent. Previously, the continent was divided among three other regional commands: European, Central, and Pacific (Egypt remains part of the US Central Command, known as CENTCOM, which covers the Middle East region). The goal was to improve the coordination of US military operations and relations on the continent, though critics feared an increase in both the militarization of African politics and US interference in domestic affairs (Bah and Aning 2008; Moeller 2010). AFRICOM has over 1,500 military and civilian personnel based in Stuttgart, Germany. Despite the original intention of basing AFRICOM in Africa, there was little interest among African states to host it. Initially AFRICOM sought to integrate personnel from other government agencies, such as USAID and the State Department, to create a more holistic approach to policy and planning. But in recent years it has reverted into a more traditional combatant command center, reflecting the increased militarization of US policies toward Africa (Piombo 2015). Yet, even America's military engagement with Africa has decreased in recent years, as the Trump administration has moved to reduce its commitments to African allies. By early 2019, it had cut the number of its commandos in Africa by a quarter and closed seven of eight elite counterterrorism units operating on the continent.

Despite Washington's long-standing rhetorical commitment to democratization, US foreign policy toward Africa has never delivered substantially on that promise. During the Cold War, the United States was content to support authoritarian regimes that it regarded as important geostrategic allies. Likewise, in the post–Cold War era the United States has been reluctant to criticize undemocratic allies, such as Uganda's Yoweri Museveni, focusing instead on pursuing its strategic concerns, namely combating terrorism and accessing African oil (Grey 2006). This has become even more pronounced under President Trump.

It is worth noting that African governments have negotiated US power in a variety of ways. After the events of 11 September 2001, several states capitalized on leveraging their support for the US-led invasion of Iraq. One of the biggest beneficiaries was strategically located Djibouti, which currently hosts the only true US base on the continent. Other states, such as Nigeria, have been able to increase the amount of military aid and assistance by cooperating with the United States and its various anti-terrorism initiatives. ACOTA, which provides military training and standardized attack equipment (such as assault rifles, machine guns, and mortars), is linked to the training centers of the Joint Combined Arms Training System (JCATS). In many ways these programs represent a return to Cold War–era practices, according to which African political elites pledge support to the superpower in return for military assistance, training, and technology.

While the global strategic needs of the United States have certainly provided some African elites with opportunities, many leaders are slightly wary of engaging with the superpower. Across the continent one encounters at times a latent hostility to the United States. While there was optimism over the presidential election of Obama in 2008, many were disappointed by what could be considered his administration's benign neglect of the continent. Trump's active disdain and hostility has soured US-African relations, leading many African leaders to embrace China as an alternative to US and Western influence. Yet, presidential blustering aside, the reality is that US engagement with Africa is increasingly militarized and, as such, conducted by the Pentagon.

Russia

While Russia had established diplomatic relations with Ethiopia and South Africa prior to its communist revolution, it was not until the Cold War competition escalated in the 1950s that Russia figured prominently on the continent. As the superpowers turned Africa into a geopolitical chessboard, the Soviet Union enjoyed a certain advantage. While both superpowers advocated anticolonialism, the credibility of the United States was somewhat compromised by its close alliance with the former European colonizers. The Soviet Union was not burdened by such attachments. Of course, this also meant that the Soviet Union did not enjoy any of the inherent advantages the United States gained via its friendly relations with the former metropoles. For the most part, the Soviet Union was outside the continent, waiting for invitations and opportunities for engagement. This provided African leaders with a certain degree of agency.

For Africans, the Soviet Union was a potential counterweight to Western powers. Even the establishment of a Soviet embassy could be used as leverage against the West (Clapham 1996). The Soviet Union also offered valuable resources for anticolonial movements and newly independent states. In addition to financial and military assistance, it provided industrial tools and technical expertise. During the Cold War, the Soviets trained at least 200,000 Africans on the continent, while about 53,000 Africans were trained in Soviet universities, with thousands more attending military and political schools. Alumni include past presidents of Angola, Cape Verde, Mali, Mozambique, and South Africa (Shubin 2004). The Soviet Union also offered an alternative model of development, particularly given its own success with rapid industrialization. Soviet experience with state control of the economy, and the utilization of a one-party state, appealed to many African leaders, not least because it provided the means through which those leaders could increase access to the resources needed to maintain and strengthen their own neopatrimonial systems of rule.

For the Soviet Union, Africa offered opportunities to advance its global struggle against imperialism and to improve its geostrategic position vis-à-vis the United States. Early Soviet engagement with the continent was initiated by African leaders who had run afoul of their European colonial powers, namely Guinea's Ahmed Sékou Touré. After Guinea's dramatic break with France in 1958, the Soviets were happy to provide substantial amounts of aid and assistance, such as road-building equipment (which might have inexplicably included snow-plows),[9] in exchange for a foothold on the continent and access to the young generation of African radicals active in anticolonial movements. However, as the incident with the snowplows illustrated, Soviet engagement was often characterized by incompetence, ignorance, and heavy-handedness. Sékou Touré grew increasingly frustrated and distrustful of the Soviet Union, eventually expelling the Soviet ambassador. But for a time, Sékou Touré found engagement with the Soviets to be a useful bargaining chip as he played the two superpowers off each other to maximize aid. This pattern would be used by a number of independent African leaders throughout the Cold War era. For the Soviets, their initial foray into African affairs left them temporarily wary of what was regarded as the "unpredictability of African personalities and events" (Legvold 1970:129).

As more African states became independent in the 1960s, many African elites used the Soviet Union to access valuable resources and distance themselves from their former European metropoles. For their part, the Soviets scaled down their ambitions on the continent and seemed content to merely establish diplomatic relationships with as many African states as possible. This was driven by their desire to be recognized as a global superpower, exerting influence diplomatically as opposed to sponsoring revolutionary movements across the continent. Indeed, during the 1960s, it was China that provided material support for Africa's more radical states and nationalist movements, charging the Soviet Union with betraying the revolutionary cause for more conservative pursuits. This charge was predominantly true, as the Soviets competed with the United States and China for influence in Africa by establishing something of a middle ground between the two. This relatively restrained approach meant that they were often unwilling to directly intervene to protect ideologically compatible client regimes, such as Algeria's Ahmed Ben Bella, Ghana's Kwame Nkrumah, and Mali's Modibo Keita (all of whom were overthrown from 1965 to 1968), but were also happy to extend assistance to nonsocialist African states, such as Nigeria (which the Soviets supported with large amounts of military assistance during the Biafran War). Arms deliveries emerged as the Soviets' principal instrument of influence, with Russia becoming the largest supplier of arms to Africa by the 1970s.

Perhaps the greatest opportunity for Soviet engagement with Africa came with Portugal's stubborn struggle to maintain its African colonies. Because Portugal was considered a valued NATO ally, the United States was unwilling to provide support to the nationalist movements in Guinea-Bissau, Angola, and Mozambique. This had the effect of further radicalizing the anticolonial struggles in those countries, as they had no other option but to turn to the Soviet bloc (and China) for weapons, advice, and assistance. These revolutionary movements provided the Soviet Union with unprecedented opportunities for influence on the continent. Thus, by the time the Portuguese colonial empire collapsed in 1975, three new African states professing Marxism and enjoying close relations with Moscow emerged on the continent. While this afforded the Soviets an improved position in their geostrategic competition with the United States, it also came with significant obligations, especially in Angola. Initially showing restraint in the Angolan civil war, the Soviet Union eventually threw its massive military support behind the MPLA after interventions by the United States, South Africa (both supporting UNITA), and China (supporting both UNITA and the FNLA), and only then because Soviet premier Leonid Brezhnev faced political pressure domestically (Albright 1980). In 1975, US-backed Zaire sent combat troops into Angola to support the FNLA while apartheid South Africa invaded from the south in a coordinated effort with Jonas Savimbi's UNITA. The MPLA would certainly have been crushed without the intervention of its Soviet-bloc allies. But even then, the driving force behind the Soviet bloc's support for the MPLA was not the Kremlin, but Cuba and Fidel Castro. More than 35,000 Cuban troops were dispatched to Angola from November 1975 to January 1976 at Cuba's own expense and without the Soviet Union's prior knowledge or approval. The Soviets begrudgingly accepted the massive Cuban operation, yet they did not play an active role in the operation for several months (George 2005). The Cuban troops proved vital to the survival of the MPLA regime several times, remaining in the country until their negotiated withdrawal in 1991.

The Soviet Union's engagement in the Horn was similarly driven by opportunism and African initiatives. The Soviet Union had sought an active diplomatic presence in the region for geostrategic reasons, given its proximity to the Red Sea and the Middle East. Its most promising client state was Somalia, to which the Soviets began shipping weapons after Siad Barre's "scientific socialist" regime seized power in 1969. In return, Barre allowed the Soviets to use naval installations in Berbera. The military aid was vital to the Somalis as they prepared for a confrontation against US-backed Ethiopia over the disputed Ogaden region. When Ethiopian emperor Haile Selassie was overthrown by a Marxist-Leninist military regime in 1975, however, the situation became increasingly complicated for the Soviets, especially after the new Ethiopian regime turned to the Soviets for support. When the Somalis invaded Ethiopia in 1977, the Soviet Union cautiously tried to balance its support between its two allies, a position that angered Barre, who tore up the Soviet-Somali friendship and cooperation treaty. After this rebuff, the Soviets reluctantly threw their weight behind Ethiopia. Over the next two years, they dispatched nearly $2 billion in arms and between 10,000 and 15,000 Cuban troops and Soviet military advisers to Ethiopia, repelling the Somalis from the Ogaden region and representing the largest Soviet commitment in Africa. Though they were able to use the naval facilities in the Dahlak Islands (replacing their loss of the Berbera base, now occupied by Barre's new US benefactor), they derived little benefit from their relationship with Mengistu Haile Mariam's Ethiopia. Rather, their patronage proved to be a costly endeavor as they poured military weaponry into the country to shore up Mengistu's increasingly shaky and besieged regime. By the time Mikhail Gorbachev assumed power, the Soviets had effectively "retired" their support for Mengistu (Grachev 2008).

As the cases of Angola and Ethiopia illustrate, the Soviets began to extract themselves from burdensome obligations on the continent during the waning days of the Cold War. In general, their failure to forge more substantial Afro-Soviet relationships highlighted both the extent to which African economies were integrated into the Western capitalist economic system and the continuing pattern of external dependence established by colonialism. The Soviet Union was incapable of replacing the economic linkages between Africa and Western markets. Perhaps the most lasting contribution the Soviet Union made to Africa was the enormous flow of armaments into the continent. Indeed, the militarization of Africa and over-abundance of weaponry are arguably the most significant legacies of the superpowers' Cold War engagement with the continent.

With the collapse of the Soviet Union, Russia further detached itself from Africa. The Afro-Soviet trade volume decreased from $1.3 billion in 1988 to $740 million by 1994, and cultural and scientific relations were also cut back (Fidan and Aras 2010). In 1991, Russian president Boris Yeltsin suspended aid and demanded that African countries repay their debts. In response, the latter demanded that Russia either erase or reduce the debts they owed to the now-defunct Soviet Union. With Russia-Africa relations greatly damaged and reduced, Africans increasingly referred to Russia as "the land that turned its back on the continent" (Solodovnikov 2000:6).

Immediately after the Cold War, Russia pursued a close working relationship with the West, but it did not last (Shubin 2004). In recent years, an emboldened Russia has resuscitated its diplomatic contacts with former allies and reached out to other potential partners. In 2006, Vladimir Putin paid a high-profile visit to the continent, proclaiming that Russia was "returning" to Africa. This corresponded with Russia's inclusion in the so-called BRICS—Brazil, Russia, India, China, and South Africa—five emerging economies that are playing a more activist role in world affairs (Taylor 2014). Driving Russia's reengagement was not just a desire to increase its geopolitical position, but also an interest in African natural resources. Russian trade with Africa has steadily increased in recent years, accounting for $3.6 billion in 2017, up from $2.2 billion in 2015. Most of this activity has been in the gas, aluminum, manganese, and diamond industries, though Africa is also an important supplier of rubber, fish, cocoa, coffee, and tea. Moreover, Russian companies, such as Lukoil and diamond-mining Alrosa, are increasing their presence in Africa.

Further signaling its "return," according to OECD figures, Russia's annual average development assistance to Africa from 2011 to 2015 was roughly $30 million. But while Cold War–era assistance flowed only to Soviet clients, current Russian aid goes to nearly every African country. And in a symbolic return to Cold War–era exchanges, African students are being educated in Russia, many at the expense of the Russian government. In 2007, there were 4,500 African students in Russia, but by 2017 the number had risen to 15,000. Significantly, Russia has returned to its previous role as a major supplier of weapons to Africa. It is currently the leading arms exporter to the region, accounting for 30 percent of all arms trade (Lavrov 2018). Moreover, in 2017, it signed $1 billion worth of defense cooperation agreements with Angola and Nigeria, further reflecting its increasing engagement with the continent at a time when interest from its former Cold War competitor is waning.

China

China's initial engagement with Africa was largely the result of its Cold War competition with the Soviet Union. When the Sino-Soviet dispute escalated in the late 1960s and 1970s, China sought to leverage its image as an alternative to the Soviet Union in order to increase its own geopolitical position. In some cases, China and the Soviet Union created rival client networks in Africa and funded competing liberation movements in southern Africa, such as in Angola and Zimbabwe. This provided several newly independent African states with a useful source of aid, especially for large infrastructural projects such as road and railway systems. For example, China was instrumental in building the Tan-Zam railway between Dar es Salaam and Zambia, which freed landlocked Zambia from its dependence on white-ruled Rhodesia and South Africa. Despite such highly valued projects, China was often regarded as an option of last resort. In any case, Chinese interest in Africa dissipated after Mao Zedong's death in 1976 (Taylor 2009).

Beijing's engagement increased significantly after the 1989 Tiananmen Square crisis. While the United States and other Western powers heavily criticized China over the incident, a number of African states publicly defended China and the repressive military tactics employed. This led Beijing to rethink its global engagement, concluding that Africa and other parts of the developing world were more reliable and less critical partners of China than was the West. As Ian Taylor (1998, 2009) has argued, China's increased engagement was driven by Africa's considerable numerical standing in the United Nations, which served to quell any criticism of Beijing's human rights record and ensured that Taiwan remains unrecognized. These political considerations were augmented by China's increasing interest in African oil and other mineral resources (Yates 2012; Corkin 2011; Shinn and Eisenman 2005).

Reflective of the increased engagement has been the Forum on China-Africa Cooperation (FOCAC), a ministerial summit held first in 2000 and every three years since. For African leaders, China represents an attractive model for development, having transformed itself into a global economic powerhouse and, perhaps most important, having done so without following the prescriptions of the West. As such, China provides African leaders with development assistance, particularly for infrastructure projects, unencumbered by the neoliberal conditionalities imposed by the West. The leaders of Africa and China find themselves sharing mutually beneficial positions regarding state sovereignty, as neither makes demands on the other over democratic reform, good governance, or human rights. African states have also benefited economically from their engagement with China. In the eight years after the 1989 reengagement, Sino-African trade increased by 431 percent. In the following decade it increased another sixfold, from around $20 billion in 2000 to $120 billion by 2011 (Cheru and Obi 2010). Since 2009, China has been Africa's largest single trading partner. Even after the recent slowdown in the Chinese economy, Sino-African trade amounted to roughly $188 billion in 2017, a slight decrease since its 2014 peak. While the trade has largely been one-sided in China's favor, African exports to China have steadily increased. China, now the world's second largest oil consumer after the United States, is looking toward Africa for oil given its lack of domestic reserves. By the beginning of the twenty-first century, Chinese energy companies had established a significant presence across the continent in a range of activities, from building pipelines to oil and gas exploration (Lai 2007; Wysoczanska 2004).

Recent economic growth in Africa has been partly credited to its engagement with China (see Chapter 6). Of particular importance has been much-needed investment in Africa's aging infrastructure, executed as part of China's global One Belt, One Road construction initiative. Examples include Kenya's Standard Gauge Railway line, an electric railway line linking Addis Ababa in landlocked Ethiopia to the port of Djibouti, and international airports in Zambia and Djibouti. Some have argued that China's investments stand to benefit Africa, bringing about new services and products (Najam and Thrasher 2012; Tull 2006). Others have noted that China's trade and investments are valuable to the continent primarily because there is so little investment forthcoming from other sources (Taylor 2005b). Much of China's economic engagement with Africa has been largely self-serving, as evidenced by Beijing's claim that China should be given privileged access to African markets on the basis of South-South "solidarity." Symbolizing China's growing importance in Africa (and Africa's continued reliance on foreign powers), Beijing covered the entire $200 million cost of building the new African Union headquarters in Addis Ababa, which was inaugurated in 2012 (Bräutigam 2015).

Arguably, China's reengagement with Africa represents the most important change in Africa's external relations since the end of the Cold War. In addition to becoming Africa's primary trading partner, China has also become its largest single provider of loans, providing Africa with around $94 billion between 2000 and 2015, with Angola receiving the highest amount with $19.2 billion in loans. Moreover,

China's naval base in Djibouti (joining bases there by France, Germany, Italy, Russia, and the United States) is the country's only overseas military base in the world. These developments certainly contradict the idea that Africa is somehow marginal to global affairs (Harman and Brown 2013; Tull 2006). Because China's engagement to date is predicated on noninterference in domestic affairs, perhaps the most significant results of contemporary Sino-African relations are the consolidation of power by African leaders and the further legitimizing of the African juridical state at a time when both are being weakened by other forces (Muekalia 2004). Given increased competition for African oil and other natural resources, some African leaders have been able to leverage their strategic importance to their own benefit, such as Angola's attempt to balance with China against the West (Mason 2017; Besada and O'Bright 2017). Yet while this possible return to a Cold War–style scenario may benefit African elites, it is unlikely that economic benefits will trickle down to ordinary Africans. The flood of cheap Chinese goods, especially textiles, has had a detrimental effect on African producers, who struggle both at home and abroad. Moreover, as Ian Taylor (2009) has argued, because of the absence of civil society elements that might moderate China's activities on the continent, there is a danger that the more negative aspects of Chinese policy might hamper democracy and development on the continent. Some have raised concern that a new relationship of dependency is developing between Africa and China (Geda, Mosisa, and Assefa 2013; Mason 2017; Taylor 2014). In the DRC, the Kabila regime signed a $6 billion resources-for-infrastructure deal via the Chinese-Congolese Sicomines mining venture that proved to be highly inequitable and exploitative (Kabemba 2016). The track record is quite mixed, as many note that Chinese investments do not provide much employment for Africans, and when they do, it tends to be accompanied by low wages, poor working conditions, environmental degradation, and a lack of technological transfers (Leslie 2016:4). There are cases where African states, such as Uganda, Botswana, Malawi, and Kenya, have introduced restrictions to ensure more advantageous trade and investment agreements (Warmerdam and van Dijk 2016). Finally, given China's growing arms sales to several key oil-producing states, such as Sudan and Equatorial Guinea, and conflict-ridden states, such as Sierra Leone, South Sudan, Burundi, and the DRC, one may well be concerned that China is continuing the self-serving tradition of militarizing the continent pursued by other external powers (Benabdallah 2016).

Africa and Other External Actors

Despite the rhetoric of third world solidarity during the first decades of independence, African bilateral relations with other states in the developing world were relatively minimal, with the exception of the Middle East. This was partly due to North African states functioning as a bridge for both regions. Ten African states are members of the Arab League, and many other African states have sizable Muslim populations. Indeed, the linkages between Africa and the Middle East were deep and varied long before the intrusion of European colonialism on the continent. After independence, the common heritage of colonialism and dependency was emphasized to provide a sense of shared subjection, despite significant differences in colonial experiences. Both regions also experienced a pariah state in their midst: Israel in the Middle East and apartheid South Africa on the continent. While those two outcasts established a close and mutually beneficial relationship themselves, Afro-Arab solidarity was promoted within the campaign against both states. Though each region provided little more than symbolic support for the other's cause, it is worth noting that the only time that the Organization of African Unity was successful in convincing its member states to adopt a common foreign policy was over the breaking of diplomatic relations with Israel in 1973.

Yet the Afro-Arab relationship was fundamentally asymmetric. Middle Eastern states were clearly in a stronger position than their African counterparts in almost every respect. The oil wealth of most Middle Eastern states enabled the region to enjoy economic, political, and military power on the world stage that was far beyond the means of Africans. This wealth has occasionally meant that the Middle East functions as a potential source of economic assistance, military protection, and diplomatic support for a number of African states. At the same time, Africa provides a venue for Middle Eastern states to project their influence. The Afro-Arab relationship was put to the test after the 1973 Arab-Israeli War, when the rise in oil prices greatly enriched oil-producing states in the Middle East but crippled the oil-dependent states of Africa. The Arab world attempted to respond by creating the Arab Bank for Economic Development in Africa to distribute aid to the continent. Yet the total amount distributed was far lower than the sum lost by African states due to the increased oil prices, and many Africans remained deeply resentful of what they perceived was Arab wealth generated at their expense (Wai 1983).

Moreover, many non-Muslim African states have been suspicious about the spread of Islam across the continent, especially the rise of

Islamic fundamentalism (see Chapter 3). This suspicion has often been exacerbated by Arab states' engagement in conflicts in the Horn, most notably by Saudi Arabia and Yemen in Somalia and Eritrea, as well as the actions of Libya's Muammar Qaddafi, who directly and indirectly undermined neighboring African states throughout his decades in power. While championing both Arab nationalism and African integration, Qaddafi was both celebrated and distrusted across the continent, reflecting the contradictory impulses within the Afro-Arab relationship. Qaddafi's relations with Uganda are perhaps illustrative. Qaddafi championed Idi Amin's 1971 rise to power in hopes of creating a fellow Islamic and anti-Israeli African state, sending several hundred troops to support Amin. When Tanzania invaded Uganda in January 1979, Qaddafi airlifted 2,500 troops, as well as tanks, armored personnel carriers, and artillery, to thwart the invasion. While Qaddafi's assistance to Amin did little to endear him to most Ugandans, he later provided Museveni's insurgent army with much-needed funds, arms, and training. After Museveni's victory, Libyan companies invested heavily in Uganda and Qaddafi erected his towering namesake national mosque in Kampala. Yet Museveni always remained deeply suspicious of Qaddafi, even to the point of fearing that the Libyan leader might try to assassinate him. In the end, Qaddafi's 2011 overthrow and murder were met with a mix of contradictory and confused responses from across Uganda and Africa in general (Vokes 2011). In many ways, this reflected the complex nature of contemporary Afro-Arab relations, made even more complicated given the desirability of developing African oil reserves as a counterbalance to dependence on Middle Eastern oil.

There have also been a handful of other significant countries in Africa's external bilateral relations. Arguably, these middle powers have become more important to African leaders after the Cold War, as the end of the stultifying bifurcated worldview provided Africans with increased maneuverability in their foreign policies. Yet in some cases, the end of the Cold War led some external actors to disengage from the continent. For example, while Cuba provided invaluable assistance to Angola and Eritrea during the Cold War, it no longer enjoys the privileged position it once had in those countries. Though Cuba still engages in technical cooperation with Angola and Namibia, it has largely been eclipsed by post-apartheid South Africa (Gleijeses 2006). Similarly, during the 1970s and 1980s, and often acting independently of its Soviet and Chinese patrons, North Korea ran several military assistance programs in radical African states such as Guinea, Ethiopia, Mali, Tanzania, and Zimbabwe. It trained Zimbabwe's infamous Fifth Brigade, which was used by the Robert Mugabe regime in the mid-1980s to brutally suppress dissent in Matabeleland. North Korea's engagement with Africa was largely driven by its competition with South Korea and desire to gain diplomatic recognition. It succeeded in leveraging its influence to keep South Korea from joining the Non-Aligned Movement. But after the end of the Cold War, African leaders realized that South Korea had far more economic opportunities to offer than the North, and Pyongyang's limited influence diminished.

Returning to the so-called BRICS, it is worth examining the growing engagement with both Brazil and India. Trade between Brazil and Africa increased sixfold between 2000 and 2011, from $4.2 billion to a $27.6 billion. But that pales in comparison to the growth in bilateral trade with India, which was only $914 million in 1991 before skyrocketing from $5.3 billion in 2001 to $90 billion in 2015, with African exports to India more than double Indian exports to Africa. While Chinese involvement has largely been state-backed, India's engagement has focused on encouraging entrepreneurialism and private enterprise (Taylor 2014). Like China, India offers the possibility for new forms of development cooperation and aid that are largely free of the conditionalities imposed by Western powers. In recent years, India has doubled its lines of credit and increased its assistance in human resource development, technical training and capacity building, and transfer of low-cost technology (Carmody 2013; Scott 2008; Taylor 2012). While some have suggested that India's growth will bring it into increased competition with China in a new "scramble" for African resources (Mawdsley and McCann 2010; Cheru and Obi 2010; Naidu 2010), Karolina Wysoczanska (2004) notes that India has been working with China to establish joint ventures in their search for overseas energy supplies, including in Africa, with mixed success.[10]

In recent years, Iran has also become more engaged in trade and investment in Africa, probably in response to its relative diplomatic isolation. In 2007 it opened an assembly line for a car factory in Senegal, and its trade and cooperation with Nigeria and South Africa have provided important diplomatic allies. But most significant have been Iran's close connections to Sudan, with which it shares an anti-Western ideological link. Sudan turned to Iran for military cooperation in an effort at emancipating itself from relations with China and Russia (Chimbelu 2010). Under Hugo Chávez, Venezuela sought to forge closer diplomatic ties with Africa in order to counterbalance US hegemony (Márquez 2005). These connections typically focused on political and cultural issues, but were undermined after the spectacular collapse of

Venezuela's economy began in 2014. The economic ties that connect Venezuela and other neighboring Latin American countries with the African continent largely revolve around the illicit trade of drugs. West African countries increasingly function as major hubs for drug networks moving cocaine from Latin America into Europe (Carrier and Klantschnig 2012; Ellis 2009; Scheele 2015).

Canada, despite its rather negligible economic trade with and investments in Africa, has often been at the forefront of the international community's engagement on such issues as development assistance, corporate responsibility, and the promotion of human security. David Black (2004) has argued that Canada has been driven primarily by its own self-image as a peacebroker, concerned global citizen, and champion of liberal values. Canada was a major actor in the Convention Banning Anti-Personnel Landmines; the Rome Statute, which established the International Criminal Court; and the Kimberley Process, to stem the flow of conflict diamonds. The Canadian International Development Agency (CIDA) has played a pronounced role across the continent, though substantial budget cuts have curbed its relevance in recent years (Brown and Jackson 2009; Black and Tiessen 2007). While Chris Brown (2001) has pointed out that Canada's ties are comparatively minor, Africa occupies a key place in Canada's foreign policy, particularly as Ottawa tries to present itself as an ethical player on the world stage. Its lack of a colonial legacy and threatening interests enhances its ability to play the role of a milder and more benevolent Western ally, with which a number of African states have sought to engage.

Finally, Japan has increased its engagement with Africa since the end of the Cold War. Commerce and aid have formed the key components of Japan's Africa policy. Japan's aid to Africa increased after the oil shocks of 1973, as it sought new sources of energy. In the immediate years following the Cold War, it was the world's biggest aid donor overall, and the top donor for Kenya, Ghana, Gambia, Malawi, Sierra Leone, Tanzania, and Zambia (Stein 1998). Since 1993, Japan has channeled its involvement through the Tokyo International Conference on African Development (TICAD), a multilateral fundraising initiative that has prioritized principles of African "ownership" and "self-help." Yet Japan's ability to provide aid floundered in the wake of its own sustained economic downturn since the late 1990s. By 2001, its total worldwide aid had dropped to $9.8 billion from $14.7 billion six years earlier, approximately 10 percent of Japan's total aid. At the 2013 TICAD, Japan committed itself to providing roughly $1.4 billion in direct assistance to Africa (Cornelissen 2016). South Africa remains

Japan's privileged partner. As Scarlett Cornelissen (2004:129–130) notes, the two countries "have found a synergy in their foreign policy ambitions: South Africa in its attempts to establish itself as a world paragon, and Japan in trying to attain international political prowess."

International Organizations

The United Nations is the principal outlet for most foreign policy initiatives by African states, largely because it provides a ready platform for them to exercise their diplomatic influence. African states enjoy a numerical advantage in the UN General Assembly, which as of 2019 is composed of 193 seats, of which 49 are sub-Saharan African. Because of their numbers, African states and others in the developing world are often able to set the agenda of the General Assembly and greatly influence decisions. As such, the UN has been an important venue through which African states champion various causes, most notably during the era of decolonization and the struggle against white-ruled regimes in southern Africa. The high number of African states has occasionally been used to influence the makeup of powerful UN committees. In 2001, for example, African states joined with European and Asian states to deny the United States a seat on the UN's Commission on Human Rights. This move, generated by a frustration with the George W. Bush administration's global policies and unilateralism, was a symbolic victory for the developing world and an embarrassment for the United States.

While the General Assembly offers African states a useful venue for diplomatic interaction and coordination, real power resides in the Security Council, where the five permanent members wield veto power. Of the fifteen member states in the Security Council, the ten nonpermanent members are elected to two-year terms by regional blocs within the General Assembly. The African bloc elects three members to represent the continent. This representation has afforded the continent considerable influence on Security Council deliberations, yet it has been a common criticism that the five permanent members (China, France, Russia, the United Kingdom, and the United States) enjoy asymmetric power given their exclusive use of the veto. As a result, there have been repeated attempts to reform the Security Council, including a 2004 proposal by then-Secretary-General Kofi Annan, originally from Ghana, to include Brazil, Germany, India, and Japan (referred to as the Group of Four [G4]), as well as one seat for Africa and one seat for the Arab

League. The most likely contenders for the proposed African permanent seat (Egypt, Nigeria, and South Africa) each launched diplomatic initiatives to support the reform and secure a permanent seat, though African states could not unite on this issue.

It should be noted that the United Nations also provides a valuable service for African leaders by being the source of the juridical state's legitimacy. The UN effectively grants legitimacy through recognition, providing leaders with international sovereignty and the privileges that come with it, including access to financial resources. As noted, international sovereignty is often used by African leaders as a shield behind which power is generated, practiced, and legitimized. It can also provide rulers with a legal facade to engage in partnerships with miscellaneous foreign actors. For the international community at large, the production of African sovereignty is essential because, as William Reno (1997b:56) notes, it "leaves in place an interlocutor who acknowledges debts and provides a point of contact between foreign state officials and strongmen without raising politically disturbing questions of recognition."

One notable aspect of the UN-African relationship concerns the role of peacekeeping. As discussed in Chapter 7, the UN has a mixed record, with its history of both peacekeeping interventions and post-conflict justice efforts, on the continent. Some authors, such as Stephen Ellis (2005) and Stephen Krasner (2001), argue that these interventions not only reconfigure accepted norms of sovereignty, but also represent cases of supposed "benevolent" recolonization in a modern trusteeship argument (see also Fearon and Laitin 2004). Moreover, many other observers have noted how little such interventions actually accomplish (Autesserre 2010; Englebert and Tull 2008; Diehl, Reifschneider, and Hensel 1996). At the beginning of 2019, the UN, often working with the African Union, had peacekeeping operations in the Central African Republic, the DRC, Mali, South Sudan, Sudan-Abyei, Sudan-Darfur, and Western Sahara.

African relations with the international financial institutions have also been complex and controversial. The history of Africa's interactions with the World Bank and the IMF has been discussed in detail in Chapter 6. The success and value of the structural adjustment programs and their replacement, the poverty reduction strategy papers, remain a source of considerable debate. What is clear is that after the Cold War, the IMF and the World Bank increased both the scope and the intensity of their engagement with their clients' internal affairs, resulting in a broader and more intrusive agenda (D. Williams 2000; Booth and

Lucas 2002). Caroline Thomas (2004) argued that Africa's relationship with the international financial institutions was characterized by increased subservience. At the institutional level, African member states of the Bretton Woods organizations have virtually no voice within the decisionmaking processes of these institutions, which take place through their executive boards, each composed of twenty-four executive directors. All of the sub-Saharan African member states are currently represented by only two (heavily overworked) executive directors. Moreover, given that voting within the IMF and the World Bank is based on how much a country contributes to their capital, African influence is negligible at best. At the client level, despite official attempts to increase African ownership, African states continue to have very little say in the design and application of World Bank and IMF programs. Some critics, such as Taylor and Williams (2004b:17), argue that the international financial institutions "continue to promote neo-liberal economic principles in the face of overwhelming evidence of their negative social, political and even economic consequences." Yet as Nicolas van de Walle (2001) has shown, African states are not always helpless in the face of World Bank and IMF conditionality and have been able to circumscribe or instrumentalize a good portion of it. Perhaps more significant, recent years have witnessed the rise of alternative lenders, including the China Development Bank, the Export-Import Bank of China, the African Development Bank, as well as numerous commercial lenders—all of which provide African states greater options for borrowing and, as noted in Chapter 6, have raised the looming specter of a new debt crisis.

Concerns of disempowered engagement can also be found regarding Africa's relationship with the World Trade Organization. After the 1994 adoption of the Uruguay Round agreements, the General Agreement on Tariffs and Trade (GATT) system was replaced by the WTO. Under the WTO system, international trade relations have become much more legalized, especially with the adoption of the "dispute settlement understanding" mechanism and the creation of the standing Appellate Body. The creation of the WTO also increased the number of participating states, and notably gave the participating African states, known as the African Group, a healthy bloc as they made up a quarter of the WTO membership. Yet the African Group's numerical presence has not resulted in any significant influence or benefits for African states within the WTO (Mangeni 2002). Beginning in 2001 there were several rounds of WTO negotiations aimed at lowering trade barriers. The so-called Doha Round (or Doha Development

Agenda) has reflected the significant differences between the developing and developed world around agriculture and agricultural subsidies, as well as industrial tariff and nontariff barriers. Yet the Doha Round has also thrown into stark relief the limited agency that African states, with the notable exception of South Africa, have within these WTO discussions (Anderson and Martin 2005; Chadha 2011). After more than a decade of intense negotiations on lowering trade barriers—especially involving an attempt to convince the European Union and United States to dismantle their agricultural subsidies, which effectively function as trade barriers—African participation remained negligible and negotiations ultimately unproductive. After the election of Donald Trump, the Doha Round approach, if not the viability of the WTO itself, has been thrown into question. The 2018 WTO Ministerial Conference in Buenos Aires was fraught, but also notable to the extent that African states were sidelined and their interests marginalized (Bellmann 2018).

The Privatization of Africa's International Relations

As noted throughout this book, many African states have become increasingly detached, to varying degrees, from their domestic societies, while at the same time relying more upon external sources of support and legitimacy for their survival. In the closing years of Mobutu Sese Seko's Zaire, for instance, the political authority of the central government barely extended beyond the capital, Kinshasa, while Mobutu and his cadre maintained their claim to rule through the international norm of juridical sovereignty, foreign assistance, and lucrative contracts with global economic actors. While one might regard such conditions under Zaire's slow-motion collapse as exceptional, relatively little has changed in the country two decades later (Trefon 2011a, 2011b). The case of Zaire/DRC signals a number of key points about contemporary African international relations: the importance of informal markets for both the public at large and the political elites; the complicated role of formal global economic actors in African politics, from multinational corporations to independent traders; and the increasing role of nongovernmental organizations and other global civil society actors. Taken together, these factors suggest a considerable degree of privatization of African international relations (Clapham 1996).

One component in this development has been the emergence of what William Reno (1995) labeled the African "shadow state." A product of personal rule, the shadow state exists behind the facade of formal statehood. Though it exploits accepted concepts of legitimacy and institutional manifestations of state power, it relies on the control of markets and on the ability of political elites to manipulate access to market resources for political survival. Over the past several decades, as state assets became increasingly personalized and donor conditionalities further reduced both the size and the capacity of African states, the personal networks of rule became an even more pronounced feature of African shadow states. Central to the survival of the shadow state has been the incorporation of external elements, particularly formal and informal markets. One can see numerous examples of political elites using state power to create entrepreneurial opportunities within the informal sector (Bayart 1993; Bayart, Ellis, and Hibou 1999; Reno 1997a; Trefon 2011a). In Sierra Leone, Angola, and the DRC, for example, African leaders and members of their inner circles enjoyed considerable wealth via their connections in the mining sectors (Blundo and Olivier de Sardan 2006; Reno 1995). In Liberia, President Charles Taylor created enormous wealth through the development of informal regional economic networks (Reno 2007). In most cases, these economic ties were instrumental for the vertical redistribution practices used to maintain neopatrimonial networks.

The managing of formal state power as a private business has helped maintain countless African regimes, but has also brought a wide variety of private global actors into the realm of African politics and international relations. African leaders have engaged with international companies to secure direct and indirect cash payments in exchange for preferential contracts and access to resources. For example, US and South African mining companies were intimately connected to Mobutu's regime, providing the shadow state with much-needed access to foreign exchange and other resources (Bustin 1999). In fact, the death knell for Mobutu's regime sounded when these external mining groups cut profitable deals with Laurent Kabila's rebels as they advanced across the country. By 2019, the Congolese government relied on a similar role being provided by Chinese corporations and investors. International criminal networks are also involved in the international relations of African shadow states, particularly in West Africa and the Sahel (Carrier and Klantschnig 2012; Scheele 2015). During the 1990s, Nigeria was a transit point for Asian heroin into Europe. By the beginning of the twenty-first century, drug traffickers were using Guinea-Bissau, Senegal, and Mali as hubs for bringing drugs into Europe from Latin America. In 2009, rivalries over the control of drug smuggling resulted in the murders, a day apart, of Guinea-Bissau's president and army chief of staff.

The process of privatization has also impacted the security realm, as private military contractors play a growing role in Africa (Gumedze 2008; Chesterman and Lehnardt 2007; Muthien and Taylor 2002; Musah and Feyemi 2000). Of course, mercenaries have been active in Africa since independence. For instance, a substantial number of Belgian and French mercenaries were involved in the Congolese civil war, particularly on the side of the breakaway province of Katanga. Since then, the presence of mercenaries has been a regular feature of many African conflicts. French mercenary Bob Denard became one of the world's most infamous soldiers of fortune, not just for his four attempts to overthrow the governments of the Comoros from 1975 to 1995, but also because his various exploits seemed to have the implicit approval of the French government. The use of "dogs of war" has recently become a more acceptable feature of African politics, with a growing number of African heads of state using private security firms (Gumedze 2008). As Taylor and Williams (2004b:5) note, "The period since 1989 has witnessed the increasing privatization of the instruments of military power and violence and the concomitant erosion of the state's monopoly to wield such power legitimately." Private security firms not only have been used to combat insurgents, but also have become ubiquitous in much of Africa for the daily protection of premises, often replacing the police as primary providers of security (Fourchard 2011; Baker 2010). The privatization of security has been driven both by forces of globalization and by the rise of the shadow states, but has also been the result of policies advanced by Western powers, especially the United States, which have championed the use of private security firms.

The United States and other Western states have privileged nonstate actors, such as private companies and civic associations, for ideological reasons, but also to bypass regimes they find difficult to work with. They have used the IMF, World Bank, and WTO to regulate much of their economic engagements with Africa. The United Nations and its specialized agencies, such as the United Nations Development Programme (UNDP), the United Nations High Commissioner for Refugees (UNHCR), the United Nations Children's Fund (UNICEF), the World Health Organization (WHO), and the World Food Programme (WFP), have filled in the gaps of African international relations left by the reduction in the role of external states. Part of this can be explained by the numerical power of African states within the UN, as well as the pressing needs faced across the continent. But external and African states alike have often been more than willing to relegate these activities to the multinational level, further making African international relations less state-centric.

The privatization of African international relations is also visible in the growing roles of international nongovernmental organizations. INGOs have provided important resources for both the economic survival of ordinary Africans and the fueling of the neopatrimonial networks of elites. As such, they have become the lynchpin of the so-called development machine, a network of individuals, state and international agencies, consultants, and experts engaged in development work and analysis (Crush 1995). Soon after the end of the Cold War, there were as many as 3,000 development INGOs in OECD countries, distributing from 10 to 15 percent of all aid transfers to developing countries (Mavrotas and McGillivray 2009; Smillie 1997). These associations not only represented the result of private charity, but also increasingly came to channel official development flows. By the 1990s, the US government, for example, was transferring nearly 40 percent of its aid through them (Manji and O'Coill 2002), and in 2006 the OECD estimated transfers of official developed-country aid to INGOs at more than $2 billion, more than double the 2002 amount (Allard and Martinez 2008:4; Epstein and Gang 2006). By 2008, many of the largest development INGOs controlled budgets that surpassed those of official donors (Koch 2008:1).

Thus INGOs, such as Oxfam, Save the Children, and Christian Aid, have become some of the primary participants in the conduct of Western development policies toward Africa. Official aid agencies (in both Africa and the West) have increasingly come to expect INGOs to meet the welfare needs of ordinary Africans by filling in for the state (Bebbington, Hickey, and Mitlin 2008; Ndegwa 1996; Dicklitch 1998). The Bill and Melinda Gates Foundation, for example, dedicates half of its resources to health-related programs across forty-five African states, including a pledge to spend $300 million between 2018 and 2020 to support agricultural development in conjunction with the EU. Some critics have argued that these development INGOs represent a continuation of the work by missionaries and other voluntary organizations that were instrumental in Europe's colonization of Africa. Today's INGOs, the argument goes, have taken the "missionary position" of delivering services and running projects "that are motivated by charity, pity and doing things for people (implicitly who can't do it for themselves), albeit with the verbiage of participatory approaches" (Manji and O'Coill 2002:569). Regardless of how one characterizes the role of INGOs in Africa, one cannot help but be struck by the dramatic ways in which their increasing presence reflects the privatization of both North-South relations and African politics in general.

INGOs have not merely been passive conduits for Western aid to Africa; they have also become important drivers of foreign policies, particularly around such issues as AIDS, debt, and human rights. The media-oriented advocacy group Invisible Children, for example, campaigned on college campuses in an attempt to lobby US administrations over the military defeat of Joseph Kony and the LRA, most notably through their problematic "Kony 2012" campaign (Schomerus, Allen, and Vlassenroot 2011). As discussed in Chapter 6, Jubilee 2000 campaigned for the cancellation of third world debt with considerable success (Busby 2007). Likewise, the Millennium Promise Alliance, which is cofounded by economist Jeffrey Sachs, and the Global Poverty Project have actively lobbied Western governments and international institutions to ensure the realization of the UN's Millennium Development Goals. Largely through the diplomatic pressure garnered by such INGOs as Global Witness, the international scheme known as the Kimberley Process was established in 2003 to regulate the global trade in diamonds in order to stop the sale of "blood diamonds" used to fund conflicts in countries such as Angola and Sierra Leone (Grant 2004). In 2011, Global Witness announced it was leaving the Kimberley Process to highlight what it regarded as a failure to break the link between diamond sales and violence in Africa. Nevertheless, groups such as Enough have successfully lobbied US policymakers and contributed to the adoption of the Dodd-Frank Act, which forces purchasers of some minerals to document the origins of their imports in order to avoid sponsoring the exploitation of miners in conflict zones.

Issues around environmental conservation also illuminate the ways in which African international relations have become privatized. Foreign income from tourism, particularly ecotourism, grew to over 7 percent of sub-Saharan Africa's GDP by 2017 (World Travel and Tourism Council 2017). This significantly impacts how African lands and resources are being used, with the needs and desires of foreign tourists sometimes prioritized over those of local Africans (West, Igoe, and Brockington 2006). In addition to the influence of these market forces, wildlife conservation and management policies in Africa have been shaped by external nonstate actors, such as international environmental lobbying groups such as the International Union for the Conservation of Nature and Natural Resources (IUCN) and the World Wildlife Fund (WWF). These lobbying groups, development and environmental INGOs, and international organizations such as the IMF and World Bank often end up competing with African states for the control and use of their territories. Michael Hardt and Antonio Negri (2000) suggest in this respect that the "moral force" of some INGOs substantially alters the notion of modern sovereignty, particularly in the developing world. Claiming to represent those who cannot represent themselves (in this case, the flora and fauna), these NGOs assert a universal moral call that trumps state power (Dunn 2008a; Litfin 1993).

The privatization of African international relations and the personalization of political power have raised challenges to observers of African politics. As noted at the outset of this chapter, African international relations do not often seem to fit scholarly preconceptions of world politics. Whether this is because of African exceptionalism or intellectual failures on the part of academia remains a healthy topic for debate. Regardless, this chapter illustrates the diverse challenges that African states have faced, and continue to face, in the regional, continental, and global arenas. What should be clear, we hope, is that Africans are neither marginal nor powerless in these fields or in others examined throughout this book. While they certainly do not speak with a unified voice, they remain active participants in the world around them, exercising agency in a variety of ways.

Notes

1. Some scholars have offered valuable correctives to such assumptions, including Christopher Clapham in *Africa and the International System* (1996), Frederick Cooper in *Africa in the World* (2014), and Ian Taylor in *The International Relations of Sub-Saharan Africa* (2010).

2. Political realism generally regards the world in state-centric terms, assuming that states are self-interested actors, pursuing relative gains in a context of global competition and conflict. Classical realists tend to postulate that state behavior is driven by the inherent greed of humans, while neorealists assume that state egoism is a product of the anarchical state system, in which there is no central authority to guarantee security or stability (Morgenthau 2005 [1948]; Mearsheimer 2003; Waltz 1977). Liberals and neoliberals, conversely, tend to take a less pessimistic view of world politics, arguing that international affairs are characterized more by cooperation and trade than by conflict and war, pointing to a number of elements, such as international laws and organizations, that help facilitate cooperation (Kant 1983 [1795]; Keohane and Nye 1977). Liberals and neoliberals tend also not to be as state-centric or security-focused in their approach (Baldwin 1993).

3. South Africa, officially independent since 1910, was not included due to its apartheid system.

4. The task of the Commission of Mediation, Conciliation, and Arbitration was to hear and settle disputes between member states, though it lacked compulsory jurisdiction. Significantly, it never became operational because no member state ever invoked its provisions, though its functions were performed by a number of ad hoc bodies. The General Secretariat was created solely to perform an entirely administrative role, with very

limited power beyond the procedural work of the organization. Likewise, the Council of Ministers was created largely to prepare the annual conference for the Assembly and implement its decisions.

5. Morocco left the OAU in 1984 after the majority of its members recognized Western Sahara as the independent Saharawi Arab Democratic Republic. Morocco rejoined the African Union in 2017, though the status of Western Sahara remains in dispute.

6. The AU took a serious misstep in 2005 when it refused to observe the Ethiopian elections but then endorsed the results as "free and fair," which led to days of rioting in Addis Ababa and numerous deaths. For more on the relationship between the AU and its member states, including Ethiopia, see Welz 2013.

7. The acronym initially stood for "Communauté Française d'Afrique" and later for "Communauté Financière Africaine." The West African CFA franc and the Central African CFA franc—technically two distinct currencies—share the same exchange rate, are freely convertible, and are both guaranteed by the French treasury.

8. These figures were generated from the US Energy Information Administration's interactive website "US Imports by Country of Origin," available at https://www.eia.gov.

9. The case of the snowplows is infamous, but may also be apocryphal. The Soviets later claimed they sent bulldozers equipped with plows for exhibition, while countless others (including one of our professors during our undergraduate years) claim to have personally seen the snowplows in Guinea. Regardless, it is often cited as an example of misguided development aid (see Grill 2008; Goldman 1965).

10. In 2003, the two countries agreed to work together in Sudan, where India's Oil and Natural Gas Corporation bought a 25 percent stake in Sudan's Greater Nile oil field, operated with the China National Petroleum Corporation and Malaysia's Petronas. This venture was short-lived. After South Sudan became independent in 2011, it took control of several of the oil fields located in its territory. The remaining fields in the Sudan were taken over by state oil companies after the contract expired in 2016.

Acronyms

ABAKO	Alliance des Bakongo (Bakongo Alliance)
ACOTA	African Contingency Operations Training and Assistance
ACP	African, Caribbean, and Pacific
ACRI	African Crisis Response Initiative
ADEMA	Alliance pour la Démocratie au Mali (Alliance for Democracy in Mali)
AEF	Afrique Equatoriale Française (French Equatorial Africa)
AFDL	Alliance des Forces Démocratiques pour la Libération du Congo-Zaire (Alliance of Democratic Forces for the Liberation of Congo-Zaire)
AFRICOM	US Africa Command
AGOA	African Growth and Opportunity Act
AIDS	acquired immunodeficiency syndrome
AMIB	African Union Mission in Burundi
AMIS	African Union Mission in Sudan
AMISEC	African Union Mission in Support of Elections in Comoros
AMISOM	African Union Mission in Somalia
ANC	African National Congress
AOF	Afrique Occidentale Française (French Occidental Africa)
APRM	African Peer Review Mechanism (African Union)
APSA	African Peace and Security Architecture (African Union)
AQIM	al-Qaeda in the Islamic Maghreb
ASF	African Standby Force (African Union)
AU	African Union

BRICS	Brazil, Russia, India, China, South Africa
CCM	Chama Cha Mapinduzi (Revolutionary Party) (Tanzania)
CEMAC	Economic and Monetary Community of Central Africa
CENTCOM	US Central Command
CEWS	Continental Early Warning System (African Union)
CFA	Communauté Financière Africaine (French Community of Africa)
CFTA	Continental Free Trade Area (African Union)
CIA	Central Intelligence Agency
CIC	Council of Islamic Courts (Somalia)
CIDA	Canadian International Development Agency
CJTF-HOA	Combined Joint Task Force–Horn of Africa
CNDD-FDD	National Council for the Defense of Democracy–Forces for the Defense of Democracy (Burundi)
COMESA	Common Market for Eastern and Southern Africa
CONAKAT	Confédération des Associations Tribales du Katanga (Katanga Confederation of Tribal Associations)
CONTRALESA	Congress of Traditional Leaders of South Africa
CPIA	Country Policy and Institutional Assessment
CPK	Church of the Province of Kenya
CPP	Convention People's Party (Ghana)
CTSP	Comité Transitoire pour le Salut du Peuple (Transitional Committee for the Salvation of the People) (Mali)
DDR	disarmament, demobilization, and reintegration
DRC	Democratic Republic of Congo
EAC	East African Community
EASFCOM	Eastern Africa Standby Force
EC	European Community
ECCAS	Economic Community of Central African States
ECOMOG	ECOWAS Ceasefire Monitoring Group
ECOSOCC	Economic, Social, and Cultural Council (African Union)
ECOWAS	Economic Community of West African States
EPLF	Eritrean People's Liberation Front
EU	European Union
FAN	Forces Armées du Nord (Armed Forces of the North) (Chad)
FAR	Forces Armées Rwandaises (Rwandan Armed Forces)
FDI	foreign direct investment
FLN	Front de Libération Nationale (National Liberation Front) (Algeria)

FNLA	Frente Nacional de Libertação de Angola (National Front for the Liberation of Angola)
FOCAC	Forum on China-Africa Cooperation
FPI	Front Populaire Ivoirien (Ivorian Popular Front)
FRELIMO	Frente de Libertação de Moçambique (Mozambique Liberation Front)
FRODEBU	Front pour la Démocratie au Burundi (Front for Democracy in Burundi)
G4	Group of Four (Brazil, Germany, India, Japan)
G7	Group of Seven (United States, United Kingdom, France, Germany, Italy, Canada, Japan)
G8	Group of Eight (G7 + Russia)
G20	Group of Twenty (Argentina, Australia, Brazil, Canada, China, European Union, France, Germany, India, Indonesia, Italy, Japan, Mexico, Russia, Saudi Arabia, South Africa, South Korea, Turkey, United Kingdom, United States)
GATT	General Agreement on Tariffs and Trade
GDP	gross domestic product
GNI	gross national income
GNP	gross national product
HIPC	heavily indebted poor country
HIV	human immunodeficiency virus
ICC	International Criminal Court
ICTR	International Criminal Tribunal for Rwanda
IDP	internally displaced person
IGAD	Intergovernmental Authority on Development
IGADD	Intergovernmental Authority on Drought and Development (now IGAD)
IMF	International Monetary Fund
INGO	international nongovernmental organization
IR	international relations
IUCN	International Union for the Conservation of Nature and Natural Resources
JCATS	Joint Combined Arms Training System
KAU	Kenya African Union
LASDEL	Laboratoire d'Études et de Recherches sur les Dynamiques Sociales et le Développement Local (Laboratory for the Study and Research on Social Dynamics and Local Development) (Niamey, Niger)
LDC	least-developed country
LDF	Lofa Defense Force (Liberia)

LRA	Lord's Resistance Army (Uganda)
LURD	Liberians United for Reconciliation and Democracy
MAP	Millennium Africa Recovery Plan
MCA	Millennium Challenge Account
MCC	Millennium Challenge Corporation
MCP	Malawi Congress Party
MDGs	Millennium Development Goals
MEND	Movement for the Emancipation of the Niger Delta
MLC	Mouvement de Libération du Congo (Movement for the Liberation of the Congo)
MMD	Movement for Multiparty Democracy (Zambia)
MNC	Mouvement National Congolais (National Congolese Movement)
MODEL	Movement for Democracy in Liberia
MP	member of parliament
MPLA	Movimento Popular de Libertação de Angola (People's Movement for the Liberation of Angola)
MPR	Mouvement Populaire de la Révolution (Popular Movement of the Revolution) (DRC)
NARC	National Rainbow Coalition (Kenya)
NATO	North Atlantic Treaty Organization
NCNC	National Council of Nigeria and Cameroon
NEPAD	New Partnership for Africa's Development
NGO	nongovernmental organization
NNPC	Nigerian National Petroleum Corporation
NPFL	National Patriotic Front of Liberia
NRA	National Resistance Army (Uganda)
NRM	National Resistance Movement (Uganda)
OAU	Organization of African Unity
ODA	official development assistance
OECD	Organisation for Economic Co-operation and Development
ONUC	United Nations Operation in the Congo
OPC	Oodua People's Congress (Nigeria)
PAIGC	Partido Africano da Independência da Guiné e Cabo Verde (African Party for the Independence of Guinea and Cape Verde)
PALIPEHUTU	Parti pour la Libération du Peuple Hutu (Party for the Liberation of the Hutu People)
PAP	Pan-African Parliament
PDCI	Parti Démocratique de Côte d'Ivoire (Democratic Party of Côte d'Ivoire)

PDG	Parti Démocratique de Guinée (Democratic Party of Guinea)
PEPFAR	President's Emergency Plan for AIDS Relief (United States)
POLISARIO	Frente Popular de Liberación de Saguía el Hamra y Río de Oro (Popular Front for the Liberation of Saguia el-Hamra and Río de Oro) (Western Sahara)
PREG	politically relevant ethnic groups (index)
PRSP	poverty reduction strategy paper
PSC	Peace and Security Council (African Union)
R2P	responsibility to protect
RCD	Rassemblement Congolais pour la Démocratie (Rally for Congolese Democracy)
RDA	Rassemblement Démocratique Africain (African Democratic Rally)
RDPC	Rassemblement Démocratique du Peuple Camerounais (Democratic Rally of the Cameroon People)
RDR	Rassemblement des Républicains (Rally of the Republicans) (Côte d'Ivoire)
RECAMP	Renforcement des Capacités Africaines au Maintien de la Paix (Reinforcement of African Peacekeeping Capacities)
RENAMO	Resistência Nacional Moçambicana (Mozambican National Resistance)
RPF	Rwandan Patriotic Front
RPG	Rassemblement du Peuple de Guinée (Guinean People's Assembly)
RUF	Revolutionary United Front (Sierra Leone)
SADC	Southern African Development Community
SADCC	Southern African Development Coordination Conference (now SADC)
SAL	structural adjustment loan
SAP	structural adjustment program
SCSL	Special Court for Sierra Leone
SDGs	sustainable development goals
SPLM	Sudan People's Liberation Movement
SWAPO	South West Africa People's Organization
TANU	Tanganyika African National Union
TICAD	Tokyo International Conference on African Development
TPLF	Tigrayan People's Liberation Front (Ethiopia)

TRC	Truth and Reconciliation Commission (South Africa)
TSCTP	Trans-Saharan Counterterrorism Partnership
UFDG	Union des Forces Démocratiques de Guinée (Union of Democratic Forces of Guinea)
ULIMO-K	United Liberian Movement for Democracy in Liberia–Kromah faction
UN	United Nations
UNAIDS	Joint United Nations Programme on HIV/AIDS
UNAMSIL	United Nations Mission in Sierra Leone
UNCTAD	United Nations Conference on Trade and Development
UNDP	United Nations Development Programme
UNECA	United Nations Economic Commission for Africa
UNEP	United Nations Environment Programme
UNESCO	United Nations Educational, Scientific, and Cultural Organization
UNHCR	United Nations High Commissioner for Refugees
UNICEF	United Nations Children's Fund
UNITA	União Nacional para a Independência Total de Angola (National Union for the Total Independence of Angola)
UNITAF	Unified Task Force (Somalia)
UNOSOM	United Nations Operation in Somalia
UPC	Union des Populations du Cameroun (Cameroon Populations Union)
UPRONA	Union pour le Progrès National (Union for National Progress) (Burundi)
USAID	US Agency for International Development
WFP	World Food Programme
WHO	World Health Organization
WTO	World Trade Organization
WWF	World Wildlife Fund
YALI	Young African Leaders Initiative
ZANU	Zimbabwe African National Union
ZANU-PF	Zimbabwe African National Union–Popular Front
ZAPU	Zimbabwe African People's Union

Basic Information
on African States

Country Name	Colonial/Previous Names	Colonizing Country
Angola, Republic of	Angola	Portugal
Benin, Republic of	French Dahomey/Dahomey (1960–1975)	France
Botswana, Republic of	Bechuanaland Protectorate	United Kingdom
Burkina Faso	Upper Volta had been partitioned among Côte d'Ivoire, French Sudan, and Niger, 1932–1947	France
Burundi, Republic of	part of Ruanda-Urundi	Germany, Belgium
Cameroon, Republic of	Kamerun, Cameroun, Southern Cameroons/ Federal Republic of (1961–1972), United Republic of (1972–1984)	Germany, France, United Kingdom
Cape Verde, Republic of	Cape Verde	Portugal
Central African Republic	Ubangui-Shari/Central African Empire (1976–1979)	France
Chad, Republic of	Chad	France
Comoros, Union of the	Comoros	France
Congo, Democratic Republic of	Congo Free State (1885–1908), Belgian Congo (1908–1960)/Republic of Congo (1960–1965), Zaire (1971–1997), Congo-Kinshasa	Belgium
Congo, Republic of	Congo/People's Republic of (1970–1991), Congo-Brazzaville	France
Côte d'Ivoire	Côte d'Ivoire/Ivory Coast	France
Djibouti, Republic of	French Somali Coast (until 1967), Territory of the Afars and the Issas (1967–1977)	France
Equatorial Guinea, Republic of	Spanish Guinea	Spain
Eritrea, State of	Eritrea	Italy, United Kingdom, Ethiopia
Eswatini	Kingdom of Swaziland, Swaziland Protectorate	Boer Republic, United Kingdom
Ethiopia, Federal Democratic Republic of	Abyssinia (until 1974), People's Republic of (1974–1991)	—
Gabon (Gabonese Republic)	Gabon	France
Gambia, Republic of the	Gambia	United Kingdom
Ghana, Republic of	Gold Coast	United Kingdom, Germany for Togoland part
Guinea, Republic of	French Guinea	France
Guinea-Bissau, Republic of	Portuguese Guinea	Portugal
Kenya, Republic of	Kenya	United Kingdom
Lesotho, Kingdom of	Basutoland Protectorate	United Kingdom
Liberia, Republic of	—	—
Madagascar, Democratic Republic of	Madagascar/Malagasy Republic (1965–1990)	France
Malawi, Republic of	Nyasaland	United Kingdom

Date of Independence	Official Language	Capital	Area (square miles	Population
11 Nov. 1975	Portuguese	Luanda	481,354	30,355,880
1 Aug. 1960[a]	French	Porto-Novo	43,484	11,340,504
30 Sept. 1966	English	Gaborone	224,607	2,249,104
5 Aug. 1960	French	Ouagadougou	105,870	19,742,715
1 July 1962	French	Bujumbura	10,747	11,844,520
1 Jan. 1960	English, French	Yaoundé	183,569	25,640,965
5 July 1975	Portuguese	Praia	1,557	568,373
13 Aug. 1960	French	Bangui	240,535	5,745,062
11 Aug. 1960	French	N'Djamena	495,800	15,833,116
6 July 1975	Arabic, Comorian, French	Moroni	863	821,164
30 June 1960	French	Kinshasa	905,365	85,281,024
15 Aug. 1960	French	Brazzaville	132,047	5,970,646
7 Aug. 1960	French	Yamoussoukro	124,503	26,260,582
27 June 1977	Arabic, French	Djibouti	8,958	884,017
12 Oct. 1968	Spanish	Malabo	10,831	797,457
24 May 1993	Tigrinya, Arabic, English	Asmara	46,774	5,970,646
6 Sept. 1968	English, SiSwati	Mbabane	6,704	1,343,098
never colonized	Amharic	Addis-Ababa	437,600	108,386,391
17 Aug. 1960	French	Libreville	103,347	2,119,036
18 Feb. 1965	English	Banjul	4,361	2,092,731
6 Mar. 1957	English	Accra	92,100	28,102,471
2 Oct. 1958	French	Conakry	94,926	11,855,411
10 Sept. 1974	Portuguese	Bissau	13,948	1,833,247
12 Dec. 1963	English	Nairobi	224,081	48,397,527
4 Oct. 1966	English, Sesoto	Maseru	11,720	1,962,461
26 July 1847[a]	English	Monrovia	37,743	4,809,768
26 June 1960	French, Malagasy	Antananarivo	226,658	25,683,610
6 July 1964	Chichewa, English	Lilongwe	9,367	19,842,560

continues

Country Name	Colonial/Previous Names	Colonizing Country
Mali, Republic of	French Sudan/Mali Federation (1959–1960)	France
Mauritania, Islamic Republic of	Mauritania	France
Mauritius, Republic of	Ile de-France, Mauritius/Ile Maurice	France, United Kingdom
Mozambique, Republic of	Mozambique/People's Republic of (1975–1990)	Portugal
Namibia, Republic of	South West Africa (1915–1990)	Germany, South Africa
Niger, Republic of	Niger	France
Nigeria, Federal Republic of	Nigeria	United Kingdom
Rwanda, Republic of	part of Ruanda-Urundi	Germany, Belgium
Sahrawi Arab Democratic Republic	Spanish Sahara/Western Sahara	Spain
São Tomé and Príncipe, Democratic Republic of	São Tomé and Príncipe	Portugal
Senegal, Republic of	Senegal/Mali Federation (1959–1960)	France
Seychelles, Republic of	Seychelles	United Kingdom
Sierra Leone, Republic of	Sierra Leone	United Kingdom
Somalia, Federal Republic of	British Somaliland, Italian Somalia/ Somali Republic (1960–1969), Somali Democratic Republic (1969–1980), Somaliland (north, since 1991), Puntland (northeast, since 1991)	Italy, United Kingdom
South Africa, Republic of	Cape, Natal, Transvaal, and Orange colonies/Union of South Africa (1910–1961)	Netherlands, United Kingdom
South Sudan, Republic of	Sudan[c]	Sudan, United Kingdom
Sudan, Republic of	Sudan[c]	Egypt, United Kingdom
Swaziland, Kingdom of (see Eswatini)	Swaziland Protectorate	
Tanzania, United Republic of	Tanganyika, Zanzibar/United Republic of Tanganyika and Zanzibar	Germany, United Kingdom
Togo (Togolese Republic)	German Togoland, Togo/Togolese Republic	Germany, France
Uganda, Republic of	Uganda	United Kingdom
Zambia, Republic of	Northern Rhodesia, Barotseland Protectorate (Western Province)	United Kingdom
Zimbabwe, Republic of	Southern Rhodesia, Rhodesia	United Kingdom

Date of Independence	Official Language	Capital	Area (square mil	Population
20 June 1960	French	Bamako	478,841	18,429,893
28 Nov. 1960	Arabic, French	Nouakchott	397,950	3,840,429
12 Mar. 1968	English	Port Louis	720	1,364,283
25 June 1975	Portuguese	Maputo	308,641	27,233,789
21 Mar. 1990	English	Windhoek	318,261	2,533,224
3 Aug. 1960	French	Niamey	489,191	19,866,231
1 Oct. 1960	English	Abuja	356,669	203,452,505
1 July 1962	English, French, Kinyarwanda	Kigali	10,169	12,817,400
27 Feb. 1976[b]	Arabic	—	102,703	619,551
12 July 1975	Portuguese	São Tomé	386.5	204,454
20 June 1960	French	Dakar	75,955	15,020,945
29 June 1976	Creole, English	Victoria	176	94,633
27 Apr. 1961	English	Freetown	27,699	6,312,212
1 July 1960	Arabic, Somali	Mogadishu Hargeysa (Somaliland)	246,201	11,259,029
31 May 1910	Afrikaans, English, IsiNdebele, IsiSwati, IsiXhosa, IsiZulu, Sepedi, Sesotho, Setswana, Tshivenda, Xitsonga	Pretoria, Cape Town, Bloemfontein	470,689	55,380,210
9 July 2011	English	Juba	248,777	10,204,581
1 Jan. 1956	Arabic, English	Khartoum	718,723	43,120,843
9 Dec. 1961– 10 Dec. 1963 (Zanzibar)	English, Swahili	Dodoma	364,900	55,451,343
27 Apr. 1960	French	Lomé	21,925	8,176,449
9 Oct. 1962	English	Kampala	93,104	40,853,749
24 Oct. 1964	Bemba, Nyanja, Tonga, Lozi, Lunda, Kaonde, Luvale, English	Lusaka	290,586	16,445,079
18 Apr. 1980	English	Harare	150,872	14,030,368

Sources: Africa South of the Sahara 2018; World Bank, *World Development Indicators*, http://data .worldbank.org/indicator (accessed December 2018); CIA 2018.

Notes: a. Liberia was founded by freed slaves from the United States.

b. Unilateral declaration of independence. The sovereignty of the Sahrawi Arab Democratic Republic, a member of the African Union, is recognized by about 50 countries.

c. The Republic of Sudan and the Republic of South Sudan were part of Sudan until 2011, when South Sudan won independence from Sudan.

Bibliography

Aall, Pamela. 2000. "NGOs, Conflict Management, and Peacekeeping." In Tom Woodhouse and Oliver Ramsbotham (eds.), *Peacekeeping and Conflict Resolution.* London: Cass, 121–141.

Abbay, Alemseged. 2004. "Diversity and State-Building in Ethiopia." *African Affairs* 103(413): 593–614.

Abbink, Jon. 2014. "Religion and Politics in Africa: The Future of 'The Secular.'" *Africa Spectrum* 3: 83–106.

Abdul-Raheem, Tajudeen (ed.). 1996. *Pan-Africanism: Politics, Economy, and Social Change in the Twenty-First Century.* New York: New York University Press.

Abdullah, Ibrahim. 1998. "Bush Path to Destruction: The Origin and Character of the Revolutionary United Front/Sierra Leone." *Journal of Modern African Studies* 36(2): 203–235.

Abrahamsen, Rita. 2016. "Africa and International Relations: Assembling Africa, Studying the World." *African Affairs* 116(462): 125–139.

Abramovici, Pierre. 2004. "United States: The New Scramble for Africa." *Le Monde Diplomatique,* 7 July.

Abun-Nasr, Jamil. 1987. *A History of the Maghrib in the Islamic Period.* Cambridge: Cambridge University Press.

Acemoglu, Daron, Simon Johnson, and James A. Robinson. 2001. "The Colonial Origins of Comparative Development: An Empirical Investigation." *American Economic Review* 91(5): 1369–1401.

———. 2002. "Reversal of Fortune: Geography and Institutions in the Making of the Modern World Income Distribution." *Quarterly Journal of Economics* 17: 1231–1294.

Acemoglu, Daron, and James Robinson. 2005. *The Economic Origins of Dictatorship and Democracy.* New York: Cambridge University Press.

———. 2012. *Why Nations Fail.* New York: Crown Business.

Achebe, Chinua. 1960. *No Longer at Ease.* New York: Anchor-Doubleday.

———. 1966. *A Man of the People.* London: Heinemann.

———. 2012. *There Was a Country: A Personal History of Biafra.* New York: Penguin.

Adamolekum, Lapido. 1986. *Politics and Administration in Nigeria.* London: Macmillan.

———, ed. 1999. *Public Administration in Africa: Main Issues and Selected Country Studies.* Boulder: Westview.

Addison, Tony, Philippe le Billon, and S. Mansoob Murshed. 2001. "Conflict in Africa: The Cost of Peaceful Behaviour." Discussion paper. New York: United Nations University, World Institute for Development Economics Research.

Adebajo, Adekeye. 2003. "Africa and America in the Age of Terror." *Journal of Asian and African Studies* 38(2–3): 175–191.

Adebajo, Adekeye, and Abdul Raufu Mustapa (eds.). 2008. *Gulliver's Troubles: Nigeria's Foreign Policy After the Cold War.* Durban: University of KwaZulu-Natal Press.

Adebayo, Augustus. 2000. *Principles and Practice of Public Administration in Nigeria.* Abuja: Spectrum.

Adejo, Armstrong. 2001. "From OAU to AU: New Wine in Old Bottles?" *African Journal of International Affairs* 4(1–2): 119–141.

Adésína, Jimi O. 2005. "Development and the Challenge of Poverty: NEPAD, Post-Washington Consensus, and Beyond." In Jimi Adésína, Yao Graham, and Adebayo Olukoshi (eds.), *Africa and Development Challenges in the New Millennium: The NEPAD Debate*. London: Zed, 33–62.

Adésína, Jimi, Yao Graham, and Adebayo Olukoshi (eds.). 2005. *Africa and Development Challenges in the New Millennium: The NEPAD Debate*. London: Zed.

Adichie, Chimamanda Ngozi. 2006. *Half of a Yellow Sun*. New York: Knopf.

Adinkrah, Mensah. 2015. *Witchcraft, Witches, and Violence in Ghana*. New York: Berghahn.

Adunbi, Omolade. 2015. *Oil Wealth and Insurgency in Nigeria*. Bloomington: Indiana University Press.

Africa Progress Panel. 2011. *The Transformative Power of Partnerships: Africa Progress Report 2011*. Geneva.

———. 2013. *Africa Progress Report: Equity in Extractives*. Geneva.

Africa South of the Sahara 2019. 2018. London: Routledge.

African Action. 2002. "Critique of HIPC Initiative." http://www.africaaction.org/action/hipc0206.htm.

African Development Bank. 2011a. "The Middle of the Pyramid: Dynamics of the Middle Class in Africa." Market brief, 20 April. http://www.afdb.org/fileadmin/uploads/afdb/Documents/Publications/The%20Middle%20of%20the%20Pyramid_The%20Middle%20of%20the%20Pyramid.pdf.

———. 2011b. "Russia's Economic Engagement with Africa." *Africa Economic Brief* 2(7). http://www.afdb.org/fileadmin/uploads/afdb/Documents/Publications/Russia's_Economic_Engagement_with_Africa.pdf.

———. 2012. *Annual Development Effectiveness Review 2012: Growing African Economies Inclusively*. Tunis: African Development Bank.

———. 2017. *African Economic Outlook 2017*. Paris: OECD.

African Legislatures Project. 2009. "African Legislatures Project." Cape Town: Centre for Social Science Research and University of Cape Town. http://www.africanlegislaturesproject.org.

African Scholars Forum for Envisioning Africa. 2002. "Executive Summary of the Proceedings." Nairobi: Heinrich Boell Foundation.

African Union. 2002. "Durban Declaration." Durban. http://www.africa-union.org/Official_documents/Decisions_Declarations/Decisions_&_Declarations%20Durban%202002.htm.

Afrobarometer. 2009a. "Are Democratic Citizens Emerging in Africa? Evidence from the Afrobarometer." Briefing Paper no. 70. http://www.afrobarometer.org/files/documents/briefing_papers/AfrobriefNo70.pdf.

———. 2009b. "National Versus Ethnic Identity in Africa: State, Group, and Individual Level Correlates of National Identification." Working Paper no. 112. http://afrobarometer.org/publications/wp112-national-versus-ethnic-identity-africa-state-group-and-individual-level.

———. 2009c. "Neither Consolidating nor Fully Democratic: The Evolution of African Political Regimes, 1999–2008." Briefing Paper no. 67. http://www.afrobarometer.org/files/documents/briefing_papers/AfrobriefNo67.pdf.

———. 2009d. "The Quality of Democracy and Governance in Africa: New Results from Afrobarometer Round 4." Working Paper no. 108. http://www.afrobarometer.org/files/documents/working_papers/AfropaperNo108.pdf.

———. 2012. "Trends in Popular Attitudes to Multiparty Democracy in Africa, 2000–2012." Briefing Paper no. 105. http://www.afrobarometer.org/files/documents/briefing_papers/afrobriefno105a.pdf.

Aggad, Faten. 2008. "Addressing the African Peer Review Mechanism's Programmes of Action." Occasional Paper no. 5. Cape Town: South African Institute of International Affairs.

Ahiakpor, James C. W. 1985. "The Success and Failure of Dependency Theory: The Experience of Ghana." *International Organization* 39(3): 535–552.

Ahmed, Einas. 2007. "Political Islam in Sudan: Islamists and the Challenge of State Power (1989–2004)." In Benjamin Soares and René Otayek (eds.), *Islam and Muslim Politics in Africa*. New York: Palgrave Macmillan, 189–210.

Aker, Jenny C., and Isaac M. Mbiti. 2010. "Mobile Phones and Economic Development in Africa." Working Paper no. 211. Washington, D.C.: Center for Global Development.

Akpan, Uwem. 2008. "Luxurious Hearses." In Uwen Akpan, *Say You're One of Them*. New York: Little, Brown, 87–322.

Alapiki, Henry E. 2005. "State Creation in Nigeria: Failed Approaches to National Integration and Local Autonomy." *African Studies Review* 48(3): 49–65.

Albright, David E. (ed.). 1980. *Communism in Africa*. Bloomington: Indiana University Press.

Alden, Christopher. 2005. "China in Africa." *Survival* 47(3): 147–164.

Alden, Chris, and Garth le Pere. 2006. *South Africa's Post-Apartheid Foreign Policy: From Reconciliation to Revival*. London: Routledge.

Alesina, Alberto, Arnaud Devleeschauwer, William Easterly, Sergio Kurlat, and Romain Wacziarg. 2002. "Fractionalization." *Journal of Economic Growth* 8(2): 155–194.

Alesina, Alberto, William Easterly, and Janina Matuszeski. 2011. "Artificial States." *Journal of the European Economic Association* 9(2) (April): 246–277.

Allard, Gayle, and Candace Agrella Martinez. 2008. "The Influence of Government Policy and NGOs on Capturing Private Investment." Paris: Organisation for Economic Co-operation and Development. http://www.oecd.org/dataoecd/24/33/40400836.pdf.

Allen, Timothy. 2006. *Trial Justice: The International Criminal Court and the Lord's Resistance Army of Uganda*. London: Zed.

Allott, Antony. 1974. "The Changing Legal Status of Boundaries in Africa: A Diachronic View." In K. Bingham (ed.), *Foreign Relations of African States*. London: Butterworth, 111–126.

Almond, Gabriel, and Sidney Verba. 1963. *The Civic Culture: Political Attitudes and Democracy in Five Nations*. Princeton: Princeton University Press.

Amate, C. O. C. 1986. *Inside the OAU: Pan-Africanism in Practice*. New York: St. Martin's.

Amin, Samir. 1972. "Underdevelopment and Dependence in Black Africa: Origins and Contemporary Forms." *Journal of Modern African Studies* 10(4): 503–524.

———. 1976. *Unequal Development: An Essay on the Social Formations of Peripheral Capitalism*. New York: Monthly Review.

Amin, Samir, and Francis McDonagh. 1975. *Neo-Colonialism in West Africa*. New York: Monthly Review.

Amnesty International. 2008. "2008 Annual Report for Nigeria." http://www.amnestyusa.org/annualreport.php?id=ar&yr=2008&c=NGA.

Anders, Gerhard. 2009. "Like Chameleons: Civil Servants and Corruption in Malawi." In Giorgio Blundo and Pierre-Yves le Meur (eds.), *The Governance of Daily Life in Africa*. Leiden: Koninklijke Brill NV, 119–141.

Anderson, Benedict. 1983. *Imagined Communities: Reflections on the Origin and Spread of Nationalism*. New York: Verso.

Anderson, David. 2005. *Histories of the Hanged: The Dirty War in Kenya and the End of Empire*. New York: Norton.

Anderson, Kym, and Will Martin. 2005. "Agricultural Trade Reform and the Doha Development Agenda." *World Economy* 28(9): 1301–1327.

André, Catherine, and Jean-Philippe Platteau. 1998. "Land Relations Under Unbearable Stress: Rwanda Caught in the Malthusian Trap." *Journal of Economic Behavior and Organization* 34(1): 1–47.

Annan, Jeannie, and Christopher Blattman. 2008. "Child Combatants in Northern Uganda: Reintegration Myths and Realities." In R. Muggah (ed.), *Security and Post-Conflict Reconstruction: Dealing with Fighters in the Aftermath of War*. New York: Routledge, 103–125.

Appadurai, Arjun. 1999. "Dead Certainty: Ethnic Violence in the Era of Globalization." In Birgit Meyer and Peter Geschiere (eds.), *Globalization and Identity: Dialectics of Flow and Closure*. Oxford: Blackwell, 305–324.

APRM (African Peer Review Mechanism). 2003. "Base Document." Addis Ababa: African Union.

Apter, David E. 1967. *The Political Kingdom in Uganda: A Study in Bureaucratic Nationalism*. Princeton: Princeton University Press.

Arjona, Ana, Nelson Kasfir, and Zachariah Mampilly (eds.). 2015. *Rebel Governance in Civil War*. New York: Cambridge University Press.

Arriola, Leonardo R. 2013. *Multiethnic Coalitions in Africa: Business Financing of Opposition Election Campaigns*. New York: Cambridge University Press.

Ashforth, Adam. 1998. "Reflections on Spiritual Insecurity in a Modern African City (Soweto)." *African Studies Review* 41(3): 39–67.

Asiwaju, A. I. 1984. "Artificial Boundaries." Inaugural address, University of Lagos, 12 December.

———, ed. 1985. *Partitioned Africans*. New York: St. Martin's.

AU-UN Panel. 2008. "Report on Modalities for Support to African Union Peacekeeping Operations." New York: United Nations General Assembly and Security Council. A/63/666, S/2008/813.

Austin, Gareth. 2008. "The 'Reversal of Fortune' Thesis and the Compression of History: Perspectives from African and Comparative Economic History." *Journal of International Development* 20(8): 996–1027.

———. 2010. "African Economic Development and Colonial Legacies." International Development Policy Series. Geneva: Graduate Institute.

Autesserre, Severine. 2009. "Hobbes and the Congo: Frames, Local Violence, and International Intervention." *International Organizations* 63(2): 249–280.

———. 2010. *The Trouble with the Congo: Local Violence and the Failure of International Peacebuilding.* Cambridge: Cambridge University Press.

Ayittey, George. 1998. *Africa in Chaos.* New York: St. Martin's.

Ayoob, Mohammed. 1998. "Subaltern Realism: International Relations Theory Meets the Third World." In Stephanie G. Neuman (ed.), *International Relations Theory and the Third World.* London: Macmillan, 31–54.

Azarya, Victor. 1994. "Civil Society and Disengagement in Africa." In John Harbeson, Donald Rothchild, and Naomi Chazan (eds.), *Civil Society and the State in Africa.* Boulder: Lynne Rienner, 83–101.

Azarya, Victor, and Naomi Chazan. 1987. "Disengagement from the State in Africa: Reflections on the Experience of Ghana and Guinea." *Comparative Studies in Society and History* 29(1): 106–131.

Azevedo, Mario. 1991. *Historical Dictionary of Mozambique.* African Historical Dictionary no. 47. Metuchen, N.J.: Scarecrow.

Baaz, Maria Eriksson, and Maria Stern. 2013. *Sexual Violence as a Weapon of War? Perceptions, Prescriptions, Problems in the Congo, and Beyond.* London: Zed.

Bach, Daniel. 1986. "France's Involvement in Sub-Saharan Africa: A Necessary Condition to Middle Power Status in the International System." In Amadu Sesay (ed.), *Africa and Europe: From Partition to Interdependence or Dependence?* London: Croom Helm, 75–85.

———. 2011. "Patrimonialism and Neopatrimonialism: Comparative Trajectories and Readings." *Commonwealth and Comparative Politics* 49(3) (July): 275–294.

———. 2012. "Patrimonialism and Neopatrimonialism: Comparative Receptions and Transcriptions." In Daniel Bach and Mamoudou Gazibo (eds.), *Neopatrimonialism in Africa and Beyond.* London: Routledge, 25–45.

———. 2015. *Regionalism in Africa: Genealogies, Institutions, and Trans-State Networks.* London: Routledge.

Badie, Bertrand. 1992. *L'état importé: L'occidentalisation de l'ordre politique.* Paris: Fayard.

Badmus, Isiaka. 2015. *The African Union's Role in Peacekeeping: Building on Lessons Learned from Security Operations.* New York: Palgrave Macmillan.

Badri, Balghis, and Aili Mari Tripp (eds.). 2017. *Women's Activism in Africa.* London: Zed.

Bah, A. Sarjoh, and Kwesi Aning. 2008. "US Peace Operations Policy in Africa: From ACRI to AFRICOM." *International Peacekeeping* 15(1): 118–132.

Baimu, Evarist, and Kathryn Sturman. 2003. "Amendment to the African Union's Right to Intervene: A Shift from Human to Regime Security?" *African Security Review* 12(2): 37–45.

Baines, Erin K. 2007. "The Haunting of Alice: Local Approaches to Justice and Reconciliation in Northern Uganda." *International Journal of Transitional Justice* 1: 91–114.

Baker, Bruce. 2010. *Security in Post-Conflict Africa: The Role of Non-State Policing.* London: CRC.

Bakucharsky, E. M. 2007. *Russia-Africa Relations and Russia's Image in Africa.* Moscow: RAN African Institute.

Baldwin, David A. 1993. *Neorealism and Neoliberalism.* New York: Columbia University Press.

Banerjee, Abhijit, and Esther Duflo. 2011. *Poor Economics: A Radical Rethinking of the Way We Fight Global Poverty.* New York: PublicAffairs.

Bangura, Yusuf. 1999. "New Directions in State Reform: Implications for Civil Society in Africa." Discussion Paper no. 113. New York: United Nations Research Institute for Social Development.

Barbour, K. M. 1961. "A Geographical Analysis of Boundaries in Inter-Tropical Africa." In K. M. Barbour and R. M. Prothero (eds.), *Essays on African Population.* London: Routledge, 303–323.

Bardhan, Pranab. 1997. "Corruption and Development: A Review of Issues." *Journal of Economic Literature* 35 (September): 1320–1346.

Barkan, Joel. 1979. *Politics and Public Policy in Kenya and Tanzania.* New York: Praeger.

———, ed. 2009a. *Legislative Power in Emerging African Democracies.* Boulder: Lynne Rienner.

————. 2009b. "Rethinking Budget Support for Africa: A Political Economy Perspective." In Richard Joseph and Alexandra Gillies, *Smart Aid for African Development.* Boulder: Lynne Rienner, 67–85.

Barnett, Jon. 2001. *The Meaning of Environmental Security.* London: Zed.

Barnett, Michael. 2003. *Eyewitness to Genocide: The United Nations and Rwanda.* Ithaca: Cornell University Press.

Barro, Robert. 1997. *Determinants of Economic Growth: A Cross-Country Empirical Study.* Cambridge: Massachusetts Institute of Technology Press.

Basedau, M., G. Erdmann, and A. Mehler. 2007. *Votes, Money, and Violence: Political Parties and Elections in Sub-Saharan Africa.* Uppsala: Nordic Africa Institute.

Bassett, Carolyn. 2017. "Africa's Next Debt Crisis: Regulatory Dilemmas and Radical Insights." *Review of African Political Economy* 44(154): 523–540.

Bassiouni, M. Cherif (ed.). 2002. *Post-Conflict Justice.* Ardsley, NY: Transnational.

Bates, Robert. 1981. *Markets and States in Tropical Africa: The Political Basis of Agricultural Policies.* Berkeley: University of California Press.

————. 1983. "Modernization, Ethnic Competition, and the Rationality of Politics in Contemporary Africa." In Donald Rothchild and Victor Olorunsola (eds.), *State Versus Ethnic Claims: African Policy Dilemmas.* Boulder: Westview, 152–171.

————. 1997. "Area Studies and the Discipline: A Useful Controversy?" *PS: Political Science and Politics* 30(2) (June): 166–169.

————. 2008. *When Things Fell Apart: State Failure in Late-Century Africa.* New York: Cambridge University Press.

Bates, Robert, and Steven Block. 2011. "Revisiting African Agriculture: Institutional Change and Productivity Growth." Unpublished paper, August.

Bates, Robert, V. Mudimbe, and Jean O'Barr (eds.). 1993. *Africa and the Disciplines: The Contributions of Research in Africa to the Social Sciences and Humanities.* Chicago: University of Chicago Press.

Bayart, Jean-François. 1985. *L'état au Cameroun.* Paris: Presses de la Fondation Nationale de Sciences Politiques.

————. 1993. *The State in Africa: The Politics of the Belly.* New York: Longman.

————, ed. 1996. *La greffe de l'état.* Paris: Karthala.

————. 2000. "Africa in the World: A History of Extraversion." *African Affairs* 99: 217–267.

Bayart, Jean-François, Stephen Ellis, and Béatrice Hibou. 1999. *The Criminalization of the State in Africa.* Bloomington: Indiana University Press.

Bayart, Jean-François, Peter Geschiere, and Francis B. Nyamnjoh. 2001. "Autochtonie, démocratie et citoyenneté en Afrique." *Critique Internationale* 10: 177–194.

BBC News. 2003. "'Price List' for Kenya's Judges." 3 October. http://news.bbc.co.uk/go/pr/fr /-/1/hi/world/Africa/3161034.stmftidjani.

————. 2011. "Malawi President Says UK's Expelled Envoy Insulted Him." 8 May. http:// www.bbc.co.uk/news/world-africa-13327013.

————. 2012. "South Africa Fails Pupils on Textbooks—Court." 16 May. http://www.bbc .co.uk/news/world-africa-18109452.

Bebbington, Anthony, Samuel Hickey, and Diana Mitlin (eds.). 2008. *Can NGOs Make a Difference? The Challenge of Development Alternatives.* London: Zed.

Beck, Linda. 2001. "Reining in the Marabouts? Democratization and Local Governance in Senegal." *African Affairs* 100: 601–621.

Becker, Felicitas. 2006. "Rural Islamism During the 'War on Terror': A Tanzanian Case Study." *African Affairs* 105(421): 583–604.

Becker, Kristina Flodman. 2004. *The Informal Economy.* Stockholm: Swedish International Development Cooperation Agency.

Bedasso, Biniam E. 2017. "For Richer, for Poorer: Why Ethnicity Often Trumps Economic Cleavages in Kenya." *Review of African Political Economy* 44(151): 10–29.

Bediako, Kwame. 2000. "Africa and Christianity on the Threshold of the Third Millennium: The Religious Dimension." *African Affairs* 99: 303–323.

Behrman, Lucy. 1970. *Muslim Brotherhoods and Politics in Senegal.* Cambridge: Harvard University Press.

Beissinger, Mark R., and Crawford Young (eds.). 2002. *Beyond State Crisis? Postcolonial Africa and Post-Soviet Eurasia in Comparative Perspective.* Washington, D.C.: Woodrow Wilson Center.

Bellmann, Christophe. 2018. "After the WTO Ministerial Conference, Where Next for Africa?" *Bridges Africa* 7(1): 4–6.

Benabdallah, Lina. 2016. "China's Peace and Security Strategies in Africa: Building Capacity Is Building Peace?" *African Studies Quarterly* 16(3–4): 17–34.

Bender, Gerald J. 1978. *Angola Under the Portuguese: The Myth and the Reality.* Berkeley: University of California Press.

Bénot, Yves. 1969. *Idéologies des indépendances africaines.* Paris: Maspéro.

Berdal, Mats. 2003. "How 'New' Are 'New Wars'? Global Economic Change and the Study of Civil War." *Global Governance* 9(4): 477–502.

———. 2005. "Beyond Greed and Grievance—and Not Too Soon." *Review of International Studies* 31(4): 687–698.

Berdal, Mats, and David M. Malone (eds.). 2000. *Greed and Grievance: Economic Agendas in Civil Wars.* Boulder: Lynne Rienner.

Berger, Iris. 2016. *Women in Twentieth-Century Africa: New Approaches to African History.* Cambridge: Cambridge University Press.

Berman, E. G., and K. Sams. 2000. *Peacekeeping in Africa: Capabilities and Culpabilities.* Geneva: United Nations Institute for Disarmament Research and Institute for Security Studies.

Bermeo, Nancy. 2003. "What the Democratization Literature Says—Or Doesn't Say—About Postwar Democratization." *Global Governance* 9(2): 159–77.

Bernault, Florence. 2010. "Colonial Bones: The 2006 Burial of Savorgnan de Brazza in the Congo." *African Affairs* 109(436): 367–390.

Besada, Hany, and Ben O'Bright. 2017. "Maturing Sino-Africa relations." *Third World Quarterly* 38(3): 655–677.

Beynon, Jonathan, and Andra Dusu. 2010. "Budget Support and MDG Performance." Development Paper no. 2010/01. Brussels: European Commission, Directorate General for Development and Relations with ACP States.

Bhebe, Ngwabi, and Terence Ranger. 1995. *Soldiers in Zimbabwe's Liberation War.* London: Currey.

Bienen, Henry. 1967. "What Does Political Development Mean in Africa?" *World Politics* 20(1): 128–141.

———. 1971. "Political Parties and Political Machines in Africa." In Michael F. Lofchie (ed.), *The State of the Nations: Constraints on Development in Independent Africa.* Berkeley: University of California Press, 195–214.

———. 1989. *Armed Forces, Conflict, and Change in Africa.* Boulder: Westview.

Bigo, Didier. 1988. *Pouvoir et obéissance en Centrafrique.* Paris: Karthala.

Black, David. 2004. "Canada and Africa: Activist Aspirations in Straitened Circumstances." In Ian Taylor and Paul Williams (eds.), *Africa in International Politics: External Involvement on the Continent.* New York: Routledge, 136–154.

Black, David R., and Rebecca Tiessen. 2007. "The Canadian International Development Agency: New Policies, Old Problems." *Canadian Journal of Development Studies* 28(2): 191–212.

Blair, Tony. 2001. "Speech to Labour Party Annual Conference." Brighton, 2 October.

Bleck, Jaimie, and Kristen Michelitch. 2015. "The 2012 Crisis in Mali: Ongoing Empirical State Failure." *African Affairs* 114(457): 598–623.

Bloom, D. E., Jeffrey Sachs, and Paul Collier. 1998. "Geography, Demography, and Economic Growth in Africa." *Brookings Papers in Economic Activity* 2: 207–295.

Blundo, Giorgio. 2001. "Négocier l'état au quotidien: agents d'affaire, courtiers et rabbateurs dans les interstices de l'administration sénégalaise." *Autrepart* 20: 75–90.

Blundo, Giorgio, and Pierre-Yves le Meur (eds.). 2009. *The Governance of Daily Life in Africa: Ethnographic Explorations of Public and Collective Services.* Leiden: Brill.

Blundo, Giorgio, and Jean-Pierre Olivier de Sardan (eds.). 2006. *Everyday Corruption and the State: Citizens and Public Officials in Africa.* London: Zed.

Bøås, Morten. 2001. "Liberia and Sierra Leone—Dead Ringers? The Logic of Neopatrimonial Rule." *Third World Quarterly* 22(5): 697–723.

———. 2005. "The Liberian Civil War: New War/Old War?" *Global Society* 19(1): 73–88.

Bøås, Morten, and Kevin Dunn (eds.). 2007. *African Guerrillas: Raging Against the Machine.* Boulder: Lynne Rienner.

———. 2013. *Politics of Origin in Africa: Autochthony, Citizenship, and Conflict.* London: Zed.

——— (eds.). 2017. *Africa's Insurgents: Navigating an Evolving Landscape.* Boulder: Lynne Rienner.

Bogaards, Matthijs. 2010. "Ethnic Party Bans and Institutional Engineering in Nigeria." *Democratization* 17(4): 730–749.

———. 2014. "Multiparty Elections in Africa: For Better or Worse." In Renske Doorsnspleet and Lia Nijzink (eds.), *Party Systems and Democracy in Africa*. New York: Palgrave, 22–44.

Booker, Salih. 2001. "Bush's Global Agenda: Bad News for Africa." *Current History: A Journal of Contemporary World Affairs* 100(646): 195–200.

Boone, Catherine. 1990. "The Making of a Rentier Class: Wealth Accumulation and Political Control in Senegal." *Journal of Development Studies* 26(3): 425–449.

———. 1992. *Merchant Capital and the Roots of State Power in Senegal, 1930–1985*. New York: Cambridge University Press.

———. 2003a. "Decentralization as Political Strategy in West Africa." *Comparative Political Studies* 36(4): 355–380.

———. 2003b. *Political Topographies of the African State: Territorial Authority and Institutional Choice*. Cambridge: Cambridge University Press.

Booth, David. 2003. "Introduction and Overview." *Development Policy Review* 21(2): 131–159.

———. 2012. "Development as a Collective Action Problem: Addressing the Real Challenges of African Governance." Synthesis report. London: Africa Power and Politics Programme.

Booth, David, and F. Golooba-Mutebi. 2012. "Developmental Patrimonialism? The Case of Rwanda." *African Affairs* 111(444): 379–403.

Booth, David, and Tim Kelsall. 2010. "Developmental Patrimonialism? Questioning the Orthodoxy on Political Governance and Economic Progress in Africa." Working Paper no. 9. London: Africa Power and Politics Programme.

Booth, David, and H. Lucas. 2002. "Good Practice in the Development of PRSP Indicators and Monitoring Systems." Working Paper no. 172. London: Overseas Development Institute.

Boshoff, Henri. 2004. "The United Nations Mission in Burundi (ONUB)." *African Security Review* 13(3): 57–59.

Bourges, Hervé, and Claude Wauthier. 1979. *Les 50 Afriques*. Vol. 1. Paris: Seuil.

Bowen, Merle. 2000. *The State Against the Peasantry: Rural Struggles in Colonial and Postcolonial Mozambique*. Charlottesville: University of Virginia Press.

Boyd, J. Barron, Jr. 1979. "African Boundary Conflict: An Empirical Study." *African Studies Review* 22: 1–14.

Branch, Adam, and Zachariah Mampilly. 2005. "Winning the War but Losing the Peace? The Dilemma of SPLM/A Civil Administration and the Tasks Ahead." *Journal of Modern African Studies* 43: 1–20.

———. 2015. *Africa Uprising: Popular Protest and Political Change*. London: Zed.

Branch, Daniel. 2009. *Defeating Mau Mau, Creating Kenya: Counterinsurgency, Civil War, and Decolonization*. New York: Cambridge University Press.

Bratton, Michael. 1989a. "Beyond the State: Civil Society and Associational Life in Africa." *World Politics* 41(3): 407–430.

———. 1989b. "The Politics of Government: NGO Relations in Africa." *World Development* 17(4): 569–587.

———. 1998. "Second Elections in Africa." *Journal of Democracy* 9(3): 51–66.

———. 2010. "Citizen Perceptions of Local Government Responsiveness in Sub-Saharan Africa." Afrobarometer Working Paper no. 119. http://www.afrobarometer.org/files/documents/working_papers/AfropaperNo119.pdf.

———. 2013. "Where Do Elections Lead in Africa?" In Michael Bratton (ed.), *Voting and Democratic Citizenship in Africa*. Boulder: Lynne Rienner, 17–38.

Bratton, Michael, Ravi Bhavnani, and Tse-Hsin Chen. 2013. "Voting Intentions in Africa: Ethnic, Economic, or Partisan?" In Michael Bratton (ed.), *Voting and Democratic Citizenship in Africa*. Boulder: Lynne Rienner, 79–98.

Bratton, Michael, and Richard Housessou. 2014. "Demand for Democracy Is Rising in Africa, but Most Political Leaders Fail to Deliver." Afrobarometer Policy Paper no. 11. http://afrobarometer.org/sites/default/files/publications/Policy%20paper/ab_r5_policypaperno11.pdf.

Bratton, Michael, and Nicolas van de Walle. 1994. "Neopatrimonial Regimes and Political Transitions in Africa." *World Politics* 46: 453–489.

———. 1997. *Democratic Experiments in Africa*. Cambridge: Cambridge University Press.

Bräutigam, Deborah. 1999. "Mauritius: Rethinking the Miracle." *Current History: A Journal of Contemporary World Affairs* 98(628): 228–231.

————. 2015. *The Dragon's Gift: The Real Story of China in Africa.* 2nd ed. Oxford: Oxford University Press.

Bretherton, C., and J. Vogler. 2006. *The European Union as a Global Actor.* London: Routledge.

Brett, Rachel, and Irma Sprecht. 2004. *Young Soldiers: Why They Choose to Fight.* Boulder: Lynne Rienner.

Briant Carrant, Jane. 2017. "Unheard Voices: A Critical Discourse Analysis of the Millennium Development Goals' Evolution into the Sustainable Development Goals." *Third World Quarterly* 38(1): 16–41.

Brocklehurst, Helen. 2007. *Who's Afraid of Children? Children, Conflict, and International Relations.* London: Ashgate.

Brown, Chris. 2001. "Africa in Canadian Foreign Policy 2000: The Human Security Agenda." In F. Hampson, N. Hillmer, and M. A. Molot (eds.), *Canada Among Nations 2001.* Ontario: Oxford University Press, 192–212.

Brown, Chris, and Edward T. Jackson. 2009. "Could the Senate Be Right? Should CIDA Be Abolished?" In Allan M. Maslove (ed.), *How Ottawa Spends, 2009–10.* Montreal: McGill-Queen's University Press, 151–174.

Brown, William. 2002. *The European Union and Africa: The Restructuring of North-South Relations.* London: Tauris.

————. 2006. "Africa and International Relations: A Comment on IR Theory, Anarchy, and Statehood." *Review of International Studies* 32(1): 119–143.

————. 2012. "A Question of Agency: Africa in International Politics." *Third World Quarterly* 33(10): 1889–1908.

Brown, William, and Sophie Harman (eds.). 2013. *African Agency in International Politics.* London: Routledge.

Brownlie, Ian. 1979. *African Boundaries: A Legal and Diplomatic Encyclopedia.* London: Hurst.

Bryceson, Deborah F., Jesper B. Jonsson, and Richard Sherrington. 2010. "Miners' Magic: Artisanal Mining, the Albino Fetish, and Murder in Tanzania." *Journal of Modern African Studies* 48(3): 353–382.

Buchanan, James. 1975. *The Limits of Liberty: Between Anarchy and Leviathan.* Indianapolis: Liberty Fund.

Buijtenhuis, Robert. 1991. "Des résistances aux indépendances." In Christian Coulon and Denis-Constant Martin (eds.), *Les Afriques politiques.* Paris: Editions la Découverte, 44–56.

————. 1993. *La conférence nationale souveraine du Tchad: Un essai d'histoire immédiate.* Paris: Karthala.

Burbidge, Dominic. 2014. "'Can Someone Get Me Outta This Middle Class Zone?!' Pressures on Middle Class Kikuyu in Kenya's 2013 Election." *Journal of Modern African Studies* 52(2): 205–225.

Burgess, Robin, Remi Jedwab, Edward Miguel, Ameet Morjaria, and Gerard Padró i Miguel. 2015. "The Value of Democracy: Evidence from Road Building in Kenya." *American Economic Review* 105(6): 1817–1851.

Burke, Anthony, Stefanie Fishel, Audra Mitchell, Simon Dalby, and Daniel J. Levine. 2016. "Planet Politics: A Manifesto from the End of IR." *Millennium* 44(3): 499–523.

Busby, Joshua William. 2007. "Bono Made Jesse Helms Cry: Jubilee 2000, Debt Relief, and Moral Action in International Politics." *International Studies Quarterly* 51(2): 247–275.

Bustin, Edouard. 1999. "The Collapse of Congo/Zaïre and Its Regional Impact." In Daniel Bach (ed.), *Regionalization in Africa: Integration and Disintegration.* Oxford: Currey, 81–90.

Buzan, Barry. 1983. *People, States, and Fear: The National Security Problem in International Relations.* Rev. ed. Chapel Hill: University of North Carolina Press.

Cahen, Michel. 2005. "Success in Mozambique?" In Simon Chesterman, Michael Ignatieff, and Ramesh Thakur (eds.), *Making States Work: State Failure and the Crisis of Governance.* New York: United Nations University Press, 213–233.

Cakaj, Ledio. 2016. *When the Walking Defeats You: One Man's Journey As Joseph Kony's Bodyguard.* London: Zed.

Calderisi, Robert. 2006. *The Trouble with Africa: Why Foreign Aid Isn't Working.* New York: Palgrave Macmillan.

Callaghy, Thomas. 1984. *The State-Society Struggle: Zaire in Comparative Perspective.* New York: Columbia University Press.

————. 1987a. "Between Scylla and Charybdis: The Foreign Economic Relations of Sub-Saharan African States." *Annals of the American Academy of Political and Social Science* 489: 148–163.

————. 1987b. "The State as Lame Leviathan: The Patrimonial Administrative State in Africa." In Zaki Ergas (ed.), *The African State in Transition*. Basingstoke: Macmillan, 87–116.

————. 2009. "The Search for Smart Debt Relief: Questions of When and How Much." In Richard Joseph and Alexandra Gillies (eds.), *Smart Aid for African Development*. Boulder: Lynne Rienner, 87–101.

Carbone, Maurizio. 2011. "The European Union and China's Rise in Africa: Competing Visions, External Coherence, and Trilateral Cooperation." *Journal of Contemporary African Studies* 29(2): 203–221.

Cardozo, Fernando Henrique, and Enzo Faletto. 1979. *Dependency and Development in Latin America*. Berkeley: University of California Press.

Carmody, Pádraig. 2013. *The Rise of the BRICS in Africa*. London: Zed.

Carothers, Thomas. 2002. "The End of the Transition Paradigm." *Journal of Democracy* 13(1): 5–21.

————. 2006. "The Backlash Against Democracy Promotion." *Foreign Affairs* 85(2): 55–68.

Carrier, Neil, and Gernot Klantschnig. 2012. *Africa and the War on Drugs*. London: Zed.

Chabal, Patrick. 2002. "The Quest for Good Government and Development in Africa: Is NEPAD the Answer?" *International Affairs* 78(3): 447–462.

Chabal, Patrick, and Jean-Pascal Daloz. 1999. *Africa Works: Disorder as Political Instrument*. Bloomington: Indiana University Press.

Chadha, Rajesh. 2011. "International Trade Policy and Developing Countries." *Margin: The Journal of Applied Economic Research* 5(1): 1–16.

Chalfin, Brenda. 2010. *Neoliberal Frontiers: An Ethnography of Sovereignty in West Africa*. Chicago: University of Chicago Press.

Chaliand, Gérard. 1969. *Armed Struggle in Africa: With the Guerrillas in "Portuguese" Guinea*. New York: Monthly Review.

Chandra, Kanchan. 2001. "Cumulative Findings in the Study of Ethnic Politics." *American Political Science Association—Comparative Politics* 12(1): 7–11.

Charlick, Robert B. 1991. *Niger: Personal Rule and Survival in the Sahel*. Boulder: Westview.

Chatterjee, S. K. 1981. "Some Legal Problems of Support Role in International Law: Tanzania and Uganda." *International and Comparative Law Quarterly* 30(4): 755–768.

Chazan, Naomi, Robert Mortimer, John Ravenhill, and Donald Rothchild. 1999. *Politics and Society in Contemporary Africa*. Boulder: Lynne Rienner.

Cheeseman, Nic. 2008. "The Kenyan Elections of 2007: An Introduction." *Journal of Eastern African Studies* 2(2): 166–184.

Cheeseman, Nic, Michaela Collord, and Filip Reyntjens. 2018. "War and Democracy: The Legacy of Conflict in East Africa." *Journal of Modern African Studies* 56(1): 31–61.

Cheeseman, Nic, Gabrielle Lynch, and Justin Willis. 2016. "Decentralisation in Kenya: The Governance of Governors." *Journal of Modern African Studies* 54(1): 1–35.

Cheru, Fantu, and Cyril Obi (eds.). 2010. *The Rise of China and India in Africa*. London: Zed.

Chesterman, Simon, Michael Ignatieff, and Ramesh Thakur (eds.). 2005. *Making States Work: State Failure and the Crisis of Governance*. New York: United Nations University Press.

Chesterman, Simon, and Chia Lehnardt (eds.). 2007. *From Mercenaries to Market: The Rise and Regulation of Private Military Companies*. New York: Oxford University Press.

Chimbelu, Chiponda. 2010. "Iran Makes Inroads in Parts of Africa." *Deutsche Welle*, 28 February. http://www.dw-world.de/dw/article/0,,5257032,00.html.

Chuku, Gloria. 2005. *Igbo Women and Economic Transformation in Southeastern Nigeria, 1900–1960*. New York: Routledge.

CIA (Central Intelligence Agency). 2018. *The World Factbook*. https://www.cia.gov library/publications/the-world-factbook/index.html.

Cilliers, Jakkie, and Christian Dietrich. 2000. *Angola's War Economy: The Role of Oil and Diamonds*. Pretoria: Institute for Security Studies.

Claessens, Stijn, Enrica Detragiache, Ravi Kanbur, and Peter Wickham. 1997. "HIPC's Debt: Review of the Issues." *Journal of African Economies* 6(2): 231–254.

Clapham, Christopher. 1982. "Clientelism and the State." In Christopher Clapham (ed.), *Private Patronage and Public Power: Political Clientelism in the Modern State*. London: Pinter, 1–35.

———. 1985. *Politics and the Third World*. Madison: University of Wisconsin Press.

———. 1996. *Africa and the International System: The Politics of State Survival*. Cambridge: Cambridge University Press.

———, ed. 1998a. *African Guerrillas*. Oxford: Currey.

———. 1998b. "Rwanda: The Perils of Peacemaking." *Journal of Peace Research* 35(2): 193–210.

———. 2006. "Ethiopia." In Christopher Clapham, Jeffrey Herbst, and Greg Mills (eds.), *Big African States*. Johannesburg: Wits University Press, 17–38.

———. 2007. "*African Guerrillas* Revisited." In Morten Bøås and Kevin Dunn, *African Guerrillas: Raging Against the Machine*. Boulder: Lynne Rienner, 221–233.

Clapham, Christopher, Jeffrey Herbst, and Greg Mills (eds.). 2006. *Big African States*. Johannesburg: Wits University Press.

Clark, Ian. 1999. *Globalization and International Relations Theory*. Oxford: Oxford University Press.

Clark, John. 2001. "Realism, Neo-Realism, and Africa's International Relations in the Post–Cold War Era." In Kevin Dunn and Timothy M. Shaw (eds.), *Africa's Challenge to International Relations Theory*. Basingstoke: Palgrave Macmillan, 85–102.

———, ed. 2002. *The African Stakes of the Congo War*. New York: Palgrave Macmillan.

———. 2007. "The Decline of the African Military Coup." *Journal of Democracy* 18(3): 141–155.

———. 2008. *The Failure of Democracy in the Republic of Congo*. Boulder: Lynne Rienner.

Clark, John, and David Gardinier (eds.). 1996. *Political Reform in Francophone Africa*. Boulder: Westview.

Clark, Nancy, and William Worger. 2004. *South Africa: The Rise and Fall of Apartheid*. New York: Longman.

Clark, Phil. 2010. *The Gacaca Courts, Post-Genocide Justice, and Reconciliation in Rwanda: Justice Without Lawyers*. New York: Cambridge University Press.

Clough, Michael. 1992. *Free at Last? US Policy Toward Africa and the End of the Cold War*. New York: New York University Press.

Cohen, Herman J. 2000. *Intervening in Africa: Superpower Peacemaking in a Troubled Continent*. New York: Palgrave Macmillan.

Coleman, James S. 1954. "Nationalism in Tropical Africa." *American Political Science Review* 48(2): 404–426.

Coleman, James S., and C. R. D. Halisi. 1983. "American Political Science and Tropical Africa: Universalism vs. Relativism." *African Studies Review* 26(3–4): 25–62.

Collier, Paul. 2000. *Economic Causes of Civil Conflict and Their Implications for Policy*. Washington, D.C.: World Bank.

———. 2007. *The Bottom Billion: Why the Poorest Countries Are Failing and What Can Be Done About It*. New York: Oxford University Press.

Collier, Paul, and Anke Hoeffler. 2001. "Greed and Grievance in Civil War." Working paper. Washington, D.C.: World Bank.

———. 2002. *The Political Economy of Secession*. Washington, D.C.: World Bank Development Research Group and Center for the Study of African Economies.

———. 2007. "Military Spending and the Risks of Coups d'État." Oxford: Centre for the Study of African Economics, Oxford University.

Collier, Paul, Anke Hoeffler, and Dominic Rohner. 2009. "Beyond Greed and Grievance: Feasibility and Civil War." *Oxford Economic Papers* 61(1): 1–27.

Collier, Paul, and Nicholas Sambanis. 2002. "Understanding Civil War." *Journal of Conflict Resolution* 46(1): 2–12.

Collier, Paul, et al. 2003. *Breaking the Conflict Trap: Civil Wars and Development Policy*. New York: Oxford University Press.

Collins, G. 2007. "Incorporating African Conflicts into the War on Terror." *Peace Review* 19: 397–406.

Commission for Africa. 2005. *Our Common Interest: An Argument*. London: Penguin.

Comolli, Virginia. 2015. *Boko Haram: Nigeria's Islamist Insurgency*. London: Hurst.

Compagnon, Daniel. 2010. *A Predictable Tragedy: Robert Mugabe and the Collapse of Zimbabwe*. Philadelphia: University of Pennsylvania Press.

Conca, Ken, and Geoffrey Debelko (eds.). 2002. *Environmental Peacemaking*. Washington, D.C.: Woodrow Wilson Center.

Conrad, Joseph. 1990 [1902]. *Heart of Darkness*. New York: Dover.

Cooper, Frederick. 2002. *Africa Since 1940: The Past of the Present.* Cambridge: Cambridge University Press.

———. 2014. *Africa in the World: Capitalism, Empire, Nation-State.* Cambridge: Harvard University Press.

Copans, Jean. 1980. *Les marabouts de l'arachide: La confrérie mouride et les paysans du Sénégal.* Paris: Le Sycomore.

Coquery-Vidrovitch, Catherine. 1997. *African Women: A Modern History.* Boulder: Westview.

Corkin, Lucy. 2011. "Uneasy Allies: China's Evolving Relations with Angola." *Journal of Contemporary African Studies* 29(2): 169–180.

Cornelissen, Scarlett. 2004. "Japan-Africa Relations: Patterns and Prospects." In Ian Taylor and Paul Williams (eds.), *Africa in International Politics: External Involvement on the Continent.* New York: Routledge, 116–135.

———. 2016. "Japan's Official Development Assistance to Sub-Saharan Africa: Patterns, Dynamics, and Lessons." In Hiroshi Kato, John Page, and Yasutami Shimomura (eds.), *Japan's Development Assistance: Foreign Aid and the Post-2015 Agenda.* Basingstoke: Palgrave Macmillan, 149–165.

Cornelissen, Scarlett, Fantu Cheru, and Timothy Shaw (eds.). 2012. *Africa and International Relations in the 21st Century.* London: Palgrave Macmillan.

Cornia, Giovanni A., Richard Jolly, and Frances Stewart. 1989. *Adjustment with a Human Face: Protecting the Vulnerable and Promoting Growth.* Oxford: Clarendon.

Cosgrove, Carol. 1994. "Has the Lomé Convention Failed ACP Trade?" *Journal of International Affairs* 48(1): 223–250.

Coulon, Christian. 1981. *Le marabout et le prince: Islam et pouvoir au Sénégal.* Paris: Pedone.

———. 1997. "L'exotisme peut-il être banal? L'expérience de *Politique Africaine.*" *Politique Africaine* 65 (March): 77–95.

Coulon, Christian, and Denis-Constant Martin (eds.). 1991. *Les Afriques politiques.* Paris: Editions la Découverte.

Cravinho, João Gomes. 2009. "Regional Organizations in African Security: A Practitioner's View." *African Security* 2(2–3): 193–205.

Crawford, Gordon. 1996. "Whither Lomé?" *Journal of Modern African Studies* 34: 503–518.

Crocker, Chester. 1993. *High Noon in Southern Africa: Making Peace in a Rough Neighborhood.* New York: Norton.

Cronje, Suzanne, Margaret Ling, and Gillian Cronje. 1976. *LonRho: Portrait of a Multinational.* London: Penguin.

Crossley, Ken. 2004. "Why Not to State-Build New Sudan." In Paul Kingston and Ian Spears (eds.), *States Within States: Incipient Political Entities in the Post–Cold War Era.* New York: Palgrave Macmillan, 135–151.

Crowe, Sybil. 1942. *The Berlin West African Conference, 1884–1885.* New York: Longmans, Green.

Cruise O'Brien, Conor. 1966. "The United Nations and the Congo." *Studies on the Left* 6(3): 5–27.

Cruise O'Brien, Donal B. 1971. *The Mourides of Senegal: The Political and Economic Organization of an Islamic Brotherhood.* Oxford: Clarendon.

———. 1991. "The Show of State in a Neo-Colonial Twilight: Francophone Africa." In James Manor (ed.), *Rethinking Third World Politics.* London: Longman, 145–165.

Crush, Jonathan (ed.). 1995. *Power of Development.* London: Routledge.

CSAE (Center for the Study of African Economies). 2011. "How Fast Has Poverty Been Falling in Africa?" *CSAE Newsletter* 4 (Spring): 6–8.

Curtin, Philip D. 1966. "Nationalism in Africa, 1945–1965." *Review of Politics* 28(2): 143–153.

Dalby, Simon. 2002. *Environmental Security.* Minneapolis: University of Minnesota Press.

———. 2009. *Security and Environmental Change.* Cambridge: Polity.

Danaher, Kevin. 1999. *Fifty Years Is Enough: The Case Against the World Bank and the International Monetary Fund.* Boston: South End.

Dancer, Helen. 2015. *Women, Land, and Justice in Tanzania.* Oxford: Currey.

Darbon, Dominique, and Yvan Crouzel. 2009. "Administrations publiques et politiques publiques en Afrique." In Mamoudou Gazibo and Céline Thiriot, *Le politique en Afrique: État des débats et pistes de recherche.* Paris: Karthala, 71–102.

d'Arcy, Michelle, and Agnes Cornell. 2016. "Devolution and Corruption in Kenya: Everyone's Turn to Eat?" *African Affairs* 115(459): 246–273.

Davidson, Basil. 1992. *The Black Man's Burden: Africa and the Curse of the Nation-State.* New York: Times.
———. 2007. *Black Star: A View of the Life and Times of Kwame Nkrumah.* London: Currey.
Davidson, Ogunlade, Kirsten Halsnæs, Saleemul Huq, Marcel Kok, Bert Metz, Youba Sokona, and Jan Verhagen. 2003. "The Development and Climate Nexus: The Case of Sub-Saharan Africa." *Climate Policy* 3(1): 97–113.
Day, Christopher. 2019. *The Fates of African Rebels: Victory, Defeat, and the Politics of Civil War.* Boulder: Lynne Rienner.
de Renzio, Paolo. 2009. "More Aid or Smarter Aid? Donors, Governance, and Accountability." In Richard Joseph and Alexandra Gillies (eds.), *Smart Aid for African Development.* Boulder: Lynne Rienner, 17–29.
de St. Jorre, John. 1972. *The Nigerian Civil War.* London: Hodder and Stoughton.
de Vries, Lotje, Pierre Englebert, and Mareike Schomerus (eds.). 2019. *Secessionism in African Politics: Aspiration, Grievance, Performance, Disenchantment.* New York: Palgrave Macmillan.
de Waal, Alex. 1991. *Evil Days: Thirty Years of War and Famine in Ethiopia.* New York: Human Rights Watch.
———. 1998. "Exploiting Slavery: Human Rights and Political Agendas in Sudan." *New Left Review* 1(227): 135–146.
———. 2003. "How Will HIV/AIDS Transform African Governance?" *African Affairs* 102: 1–23.
———, ed. 2004. *Islamism and Its Enemies in the Horn of Africa.* Bloomington: Indiana University Press.
———. 2006. *AIDS and Power: Why There Is No Political Crisis—Yet.* London: Zed.
de Waal, Alex, and A. H. Abdel Salam. 2004. "Islamism, State Power, and Jihad in Sudan." In Alex de Waal (ed.), *Islamism and Its Enemies in the Horn of Africa.* Bloomington: Indiana University Press, 71–113.
de Witte, Ludo. 2001. *The Assassination of Lumumba.* London: Verso.
Decalo, Samuel. 1976. *Coups & Army Rule in Africa: Studies in Military Style.* New Haven: Yale University Press.
———. 1990. *Coups and Army Rule in Africa: Motivations and Constraints.* New Haven: Yale University Press.
———. 1998. *The Stable Minority: Civilian Rule in Africa.* Gainesville: Florida Academic Press.
Deininger, Klaus. 2003. *Land Policies for Growth and Poverty Reduction.* Washington, D.C.: World Bank and Oxford University Press.
Deltombe, Thomas, Manuel Domergue, and Jacob Tatsitsa. 2011. *Kamerun! Une guerre cachée aux origines de la Françafrique, 1948–1971.* Paris: Editions la Découverte.
Deng, Francis M. 1995. *War of Visions: Conflict of Identities in the Sudan.* Washington, D.C.: Brookings Institution.
Derman, Bill, Rie Odgaard, and Espen Sjaastad. 2007. *Conflicts over Land and Water in Africa.* West Lansing: Michigan State University Press.
Derrick, Jonathan. 1977. "The Great West African Drought, 1972–74." *African Affairs* 76(305): 537–586.
———. 1984. "West Africa's Worst Year of Famine." *African Affairs* 83(332): 281–299.
Deudney, Daniel, and Richard Matthews (eds.). 1999. *Contested Grounds: Conflict and Security in the New Environmental Politics.* New York: State University of New York Press.
Deutsch, Karl W. 1953. *Nationalism and Social Communication: An Inquiry into the Foundations of Nationality.* Cambridge: Massachusetts Institute of Technology Press.
DFID (Department for International Development). 2011. "Statistics on International Development 2011: Key Statistics." http://data.gov.uk/dataset/dfid_stats_on_international_dev_2011.
Dia, Mamadou. 1996. *Africa's Management in the 1990s and Beyond: Reconciling Indigenous and Transplanted Institutions.* Washington, D.C.: World Bank.
Diamond, Jared. 1997. *Guns, Germs, and Steel: The Fates of Human Societies.* London: Norton.
Diamond, Larry. 1987. "Class Formation in the Swollen African State." *Journal of Modern African Studies* 25(4): 567–596.
———. 1996. "Rethinking Civil Society." In Bernard Brown and Roy Macridis (eds.), *Comparative Politics: Notes and Readings.* Orlando: Harcourt Brace, 207–216.
———. 2002. "Thinking About Hybrid Regimes." *Journal of Democracy* 13(2): 21–35.
———. 2008. "The Rule of Law Versus the Big Man." *Journal of Democracy* 19(2): 138–149.

————. 2015. "Facing Up to the Democratic Recession." *Journal of Democracy* 26(1): 141–155.

Dicklitch, Susan. 1998. *The Elusive Promise of NGOs in Africa: Lessons from Uganda*. Basingstoke: Macmillan.

Dickovick, J. Tyler, and James S. Wunsch (eds.). 2014. *Decentralization in Africa: The Paradox of State Strength*. Boulder: Lynne Rienner.

Diehl, Paul F., Jennifer Reifschneider, and Paul R. Hensel. 1996. "United Nations Intervention and Recurring Conflict." *International Organization* 50: 683–700.

Dinar, Ariel, Rashid Hassan, Robert Mendelsohn, and James Benhin. 2014. *Climate Change and Agriculture in Africa: Impact Assessment and Adaption Strategies*. New York: Routledge.

Diouf, Makhtar. 1988. *Sénégal: Les ethnies et la nation*. Dakar: Les Nouvelles Editions Africaines du Sénégal.

Doorenspleet, Renske, and Lia Nijzink. 2014. *Party Systems and Democracy in Africa*. New York: Palgrave Macmillan.

Doty, Roxanne Lynn. 2003. *Anti-Immigrantism in Western Democracies: Statecraft, Desire, and the Politics of Exclusion*. London: Routledge.

Dowd, Robert A. 2015. *Christianity, Islam, and Liberal Democracy: Lessons from Sub-Saharan Africa*. New York: Oxford University Press.

Doyle, Michael W., and Nicholas Sambanis. 2006. *Making War and Building Peace: United Nations Peace Operations*. Princeton: Princeton University Press.

Dressel, Carol A. 1966. "The Development of African Studies in the United States." *African Studies Bulletin* 9(3): 66–73.

du Bois, François, and Antje du Bois-Pedian (eds.). 2008. *Justice and Reconciliation in Post-Apartheid South Africa*. New York: Cambridge University Press.

du Pisani, André. 2001. "New Sites of Governance: Regimes and the Future of Southern Africa." In Peter Vale, Larry Swatuk, and Bertil Oden (eds.), *Theory, Change, and Southern Africa's Future*. London: Palgrave Macmillan, 195–218.

Duffield, Mark. 1998. "Post-Modern Conflict." *Civil Wars* 1(1): 65–102.

————. 2001. *Global Governance and the New Wars: The Merging of Development and Security*. London: Zed.

————. 2007. *Development, Security, and Unending War: Governing the World of Peoples*. Cambridge: Polity.

Dumont, René. 1966. *False Start in Africa*. New York: Praeger.

Dunn, Kevin. 2001. "MadLib #32: The (Blank) African State: Rethinking the Sovereign State in International Relations Theory." In Kevin Dunn and Timothy M. Shaw (eds.), *Africa's Challenge to International Relations Theory*. New York: Palgrave Macmillan, 46–63.

————. 2002. "A Survival Guide to Kinshasa: Lessons of the Father, Passed Down to the Son." In John F. Clark (ed.), *The African Stakes of the Congo War*. New York: Palgrave Macmillan, 53–74.

————. 2003. *Imagining the Congo: The International Relations of Identity*. New York: Palgrave Macmillan.

————. 2008a. "Environmental Security, Spatial Preservation, and State Sovereignty in Central Africa." In Douglas Howland and Luise White (eds.), *The State of Sovereignty*. Bloomington: Indiana University Press, 222–242.

————. 2008b. "Sub-Saharan Africa." In Edward Kolodziej and Roger Kanet (eds.), *From Superpower to Besieged Global Power: Restoring World Order After the Failure of the Bush Doctrine*. Athens: University of Georgia Press, 238–258.

————. 2009. "'Sons of the Soil' and Contemporary State Making: Autochthony, Uncertainty, and Political Violence in Africa." *Third World Quarterly* 30(1): 113–127.

————. 2013. "Preface: Africa's Continuing Challenge to IR Theory." In Kevin Dunn and Timothy M. Shaw (eds.), *Africa's Challenge to International Relations: Classic Edition*. London: Palgrave Macmillan.

Dunn, Kevin, and Timothy M. Shaw (eds.). 2001. *Africa's Challenge to International Relations Theory*. Basingstoke: Palgrave Macmillan.

Dunning, Thad. 2004. "Conditioning the Effects of Aid: Cold War Politics, Donor Credibility, and Democracy in Africa." *International Organization* 58: 409–423.

Dunning, Thad, and Lauren Harrison. 2010. "Cross-Cutting Cleavages and Ethnic Voting: An Experimental Study of Cousinage in Mali." *American Political Science Review* 104(1): 1–19.

Duverger, Maurice. 1959 [1954]. *Political Parties: Their Organization and Activity in the Modern State.* London: Methuen.

Easterly, William. 2002. "The Cartel of Good Intentions: The Problem of Bureaucracy in Foreign Aid." *Journal of Policy Reform* 5(4): 223–250.

———. 2007. *The White Man's Burden: Why the West's Efforts to Aid the Rest Have Done So Much Ill and So Little Good.* New York: Penguin.

Easterly, William, and Ross Levine. 1997. "Africa's Growth Tragedy: Policies and Ethnic Divisions." *Quarterly Journal of Economics* 112(4): 1203–1250.

———. 2003. "Tropics, Germs, and Crops: How Endowments Influence Economic Development." *Journal of Monetary Economics* 50: 3–39.

Eboussi-Boulaga, Fabien. 1993. *Les conférences nationales en Afrique noire: Une affaire à suivre.* Paris: Karthala.

Echenberg, Myron. 1991. *Colonial Conscripts: The Tirailleurs Sénégalais in French West Africa, 1857–1960.* London: Currey.

The Economist. 2000a. "The Hopeless Continent." 11 May.

———. 2000b. "A Survey of Nigeria: Striving amid Chaos." 15 January.

———. 2011. "Africa Rising: The Hopeful Continent." 3 December.

———. 2012. "Guinea-Bissau's Latest Coup: Sniffing a Chance." 21 April.

Edgell, Amanda, Valeriya Mechkova, David Altman, Michael Berhard, and Staffan Lindberg. 2018. "When and Where Do Elections Matter? A Global Test of the Democratization by Elections Hypothesis, 1900–2010." *Democratization* 25(3): 422–444.

Ehrenreich, Rosa. 1998. "The Stories We Must Tell: Ugandan Children and the Atrocities of the Lord's Resistance Army." *Africa Today* 45(1): 79–102.

Eifert, Benn, Edward Miguel, and Daniel Posner. 2010. "Political Competition and Ethnic Identification in Africa." *American Journal of Political Science* 54(2): 494–510.

Eisenstadt, Samuel. 1973. *Traditional Patrimonialism and Modern Neo-Patrimonialism.* Beverly Hills: Sage.

Ekeh, Peter. 1975. "Colonialism and the Two Publics in Africa: A Theoretical Statement." *Comparative Studies in Society and History* 17(1): 91–112.

Elischer, Sebastian. 2013. *Political Parties in Africa: Ethnicity and Party Formation.* New York: Cambridge University Press.

Ellis, Stephen. 1998. "Liberia's Warlord Insurgency." In Christopher Clapham (ed.), *African Guerrillas.* Oxford: Currey, 155–171.

———. 1999. *Mask of Anarchy: The Destruction of Liberia and the Religious Dimensions of an African Civil War.* London: Hurst.

———. 2004. "Briefing: The Pan-Sahel Initiative." *African Affairs* 103(412): 459–464.

———. 2005. "How to Rebuild Africa." *Foreign Affairs* 84(5): 135–148.

———. 2009. "West Africa's International Drug Trade." *African Affairs* 108(431): 171–196.

Ellis, Stephen, and Gerrie Ter Haar. 2004. *Worlds of Power: Religious Thought and Political Practice in Africa.* New York: Oxford University Press.

———. 2007. "Religion and Politics: Taking African Epistemologies Seriously." *Journal of Modern African Studies* 45(3): 385–401.

Encyclopædia Britannica. 2013. *Encyclopædia Britannica Online Academic Edition.* http://www.britannica.com.

Endeley, Isaac. 2009. *Bloc Politics at the United Nation: The African Group.* Lanham: University Press of America.

Engel, Susan. 2014. "The Not-So-Great Aid Debate." *Third World Quarterly* 35(8): 1374–1389.

Engel, Ulf, and Gorm Rye Olsen. 2015. "Authority, Sovereignty, and Africa's Changing Regimes of Territorialization." In Scarlett Cornellison, Fantu Cheru, and Timothy Shaw (eds.), *Africa and International Relations in the 21st Century.* Basingstoke: Palgrave Macmillan, 51–65.

Engel, Ulf, and João Gomes Porto. 2009. "The African Union's New Peace and Security Architecture." *African Security* 2: 82–96.

——— (eds.). 2010. *Africa's New Peace and Security Architecture.* London: Ashgate.

Engel, Ulf, and Heidrun Zinecker. 2016. *The New Politics of Regionalism: Perspectives from Africa, Latin America, and Asia-Pacific.* New York: Routledge.

Englebert, Pierre. 2000a. "Pre-Colonial Institutions, Post-Colonial States, and Economic Development in Tropical Africa." *Political Research Quarterly* 53(1): 7–36.

————. 2000b. *State Legitimacy and Development in Africa.* Boulder: Lynne Rienner.

————. 2003. "Why Congo Persists: Sovereignty, Globalization, and the Violent Reproduction of a Weak State." Working Paper no. 95. Oxford: Oxford University, Queen Elizabeth House. http://www2.qeh.ox.ac.uk/research/wpaction.html?jor_id=252.

————. 2009. *Africa: Unity, Sovereignty, and Sorrow.* Boulder: Lynne Rienner.

Englebert, Pierre, Alma Bezares Calderon, and Lisa Jené. 2018. "Provincial Tribalisation: The Transformation of Ethnic Representativeness Under Decentralisation in the DR Congo." Working Paper no. 61. London. Secure Livelihoods Research Consortium.

Englebert, Pierre, and Rebecca Hummel. 2005. "Let's Stick Together: Understanding Africa's Secessionist Deficit." *African Affairs* 104(416): 399–427.

Englebert, Pierre, Stacy Tarango, and Matthew Carter. 2002. "Suffocation and Dismemberment: Contribution to the Debate on African Boundaries." *Comparative Political Studies* 35(10) (December): 1093–1118.

Englebert, Pierre, and Denis Tull. 2008. "Postconflict Reconstruction in Africa: Flawed Ideas About Failed States." *International Security* 32(4): 106–139.

Englund, Harri. 2006. *Prisoners of Freedom: Human Rights and the African Poor.* Berkeley: University of California Press.

Enloe, Cynthia. 1989. *Bananas, Beaches, and Bases: Making Feminist Sense of International Politics.* Berkeley: University of California Press.

Epstein, Gil, and Ira N. Gang. 2006. "Contests, NGOs, and Decentralized Aid." *Review of Development Economics* 10(2): 285–296.

Erdmann, Gero. 2007. "Party Research: Western European Bias and the 'African Labyrinth.'" In M. Basedau, G. Erdmann, and A. Mehler, *Votes, Money, and Violence: Political Parties and Elections in Sub-Saharan Africa.* Uppsala: Nordic Africa Institute, 34–64.

Erdmann, Gero, and Ulf Engel. 2007. "Neopatrimonialism Reconsidered: Critical Review and Elaboration of an Elusive Concept." *Commonwealth & Comparative Politics* 45(1): 95–119.

Ernst and Young. 2011. "2011 Africa Attractiveness Survey: It's Time for Africa." Johannesburg: EYGM.

————. 2012. "2012 Africa Attractiveness Survey: Building Bridges." Johannesburg: EYGM.

Evans, Glynne. 1997. *Responding to Crises in the African Great Lakes.* New York: Oxford University Press.

Evans, Malcolm D., and Rachel Murray (eds.). 2008. *African Charter on Human and Peoples' Rights.* New York: Cambridge University Press.

Evans, Peter B. 1989. "Predatory, Developmental, and Other Apparatuses: A Comparative Political Economy Perspective on the Third World State." *Sociological Forum* 4(4): 561–587.

————. 1995. *Embedded Autonomy: States and Industrial Transformation.* Princeton: Princeton University Press.

Evans-Pritchard, Edward E. 1937. *Witchcraft, Oracles, and Magic Among the Azande.* Oxford: Clarendon.

Evans-Pritchard, Edward E., and Meyer Fortes (eds.). 1940. *African Political Systems.* London: Oxford University Press.

Eyoh, Dickson. 1998. "Conflicting Narratives of Anglophone Protest and the Politics of Identity in Cameroon." *Journal of Contemporary African Studies* 16(2): 249–276.

Ezrow, Natasha, and Erica Frantz. 2013. "Revisiting the Concept of the Failed State: Bringing the State Back In." *Third World Quarterly* 34(8): 1323–1338.

Fairhead, James, and Melissa Leach. 1996. *Misreading the African Landscape: Society and Ecology in a Forest-Savanna Mosaic.* Cambridge: Cambridge University Press.

Fanon, Frantz. 1963. *The Wretched of the Earth.* New York: Grove.

Fass, Simon M., and Gerrit M. Desloovere. 2004. "Chad: Governance by the Grassroots." In Dele Olowu and James S. Wunsch (eds.), *Local Governance in Africa: The Challenges of Democratic Decentralization.* Boulder: Lynne Rienner, 155–180.

Fau-Nougaret, Matthieu. 2009. "Originalité et convergence des phénomènes de décentralisation en Afrique Sub-Saharienne." http://afrilex.u-bordeaux4.fr/sites/afrilex/IMG/pdf/doctrine-102-58.pdf.

Fearon, James, and David Laitin. 1996. "Explaining Interethnic Cooperation." *American Political Science Review* 90(4): 715–735.

————. 2004. "Neotrusteeship and the Problem of Weak States." *International Security* 28(4): 5–43.

Ferree, Karen. 2006. "Explaining South Africa's Racial Census." *Journal of Politics* 68(4): 803–815.

———. 2012. "How Fluid Is Fluid? The Mutability of Ethnic Identities and Electoral Volatility in Africa." In Kanchan Chandra (ed.), *Constructivist Theories of Ethnic Politics.* New York: Oxford University Press, 312–340.

Fessehatzion, Tekie. 2003. *Shattered Illusion, Broken Promise: Essays on the Eritrea-Ethiopia Conflict.* Trenton: Red Sea.

Fidan, Hakan, and Bülent Aras. 2010. "The Return of Russia-Africa Relations." *Bilig* 52 (Winter): 47–68.

Filiou, Jean-Pierre. 2009. "The Local and the Global Jihad of al-Qa'ida in the Islamic Maghrib." *Middle East Journal* 63(2): 213–226.

Finnegan, William. 1993. *A Complicated War: The Harrowing of Mozambique.* Berkeley: University of California Press.

Fithen, Caspar, and Paul Richards. 2005. "Making War, Crafting Peace: Militia Solidarities & Demobilisation in Sierra Leone." In Paul Richards, *No Peace, No War: An Anthropology of Contemporary Armed Conflicts.* Oxford: Currey, 117–136.

Forrest, Joshua B. 2003. *Subnationalism in Africa: Ethnicity, Alliances, and Politics.* Boulder: Lynne Rienner.

Foucher, Vincent. 2002. "Les 'évolués,' la migration, l'école: Pour une nouvelle interprétation de la naissance du nationalisme Casamançais." In Momar Coumba Diop (ed.), *Le Sénégal contemporain.* Paris: Karthala, 375–424.

Fourchard, Laurent. 2011. "The Politics of Mobilization for Security in South African Townships." *African Affairs* 110(441): 607–627.

Frank, André Gunder. 1966. "The Development of Underdevelopment." *Monthly Review Press* 18(4): 17–31.

Freedom House. 2018. "Freedom in the World 2018." http://www.freedomhouse.org/report /freedom-world/freedom-world-2018.

French, Howard. 1996. "A Neglected Region Loosens Ties to Zaire." *New York Times,* 18 September.

Frère, Marie-Soleil. 2011. *Elections and the Media in Post-Conflict Africa: Votes and Voices for Peace?* London: Zed.

Freston, Paul. 2001. *Evangelicals and Politics in Asia, Africa, and Latin America.* Cambridge: Cambridge University Press.

Frynas, Jedrzej, and Geoffrey Wood. 2001. "Oil and War in Angola." *Review of African Political Economy* 28(90): 587–606.

Fund for Peace. 2018. *Fragile States Index.* Washington, D.C. http://fundforpeace.org/fsi/data.

Gabay, Clive. 2015. *Exploring an African Civil Society: Development and Democracy in Malawi, 1994–2014.* Lanham: Lexington Books.

Gahima, Gerald. 2012. *Transitional Justice in Rwanda: Accountability for Atrocity.* London: Routledge.

Gallagher, Julia. 2009. "Healing the Scar? Idealizing Britain in Africa, 1997–2007." *African Affairs* 108(432): 435–451.

Galtung, Johan. 1975. "Three Approaches to Peace: Peacekeeping, Peacemaking, and Peacebuilding." *Peace, War, and Defense: Essays in Peace Research* 2: 282–304.

Geda, Alemayehu, Solomon Mosisa, and Matias Assefa. 2013. "To Be or Not to Be: Dilemma of Africa's Economic Engagement with China and Other Emerging Economies." *Africa Review* 5(2): 118–38.

Geertz, Clifford. 1973. "The Integrative Revolution: Primordial Sentiments and Civil Politics in the New States." In Clifford Geertz, *The Interpretation of Cultures.* New York: Basic, 255–310.

Gellner, Ernest. 1964. *Thought and Change.* London: Weinfield and Nicolson.

———. 1983. *Nations and Nationalism.* Ithaca: Cornell University Press.

George, Edward. 2005. *The Cuban Intervention in Angola, 1965–1991.* London: Routledge.

Gérard-Libois, Jean. 1963. *La sécession Katangaise.* Brussels: CRISP.

Gérard-Libois, Jean, and Benoit Verhaegen. 1961. *Congo 1960.* Brussels: CRISP.

Geschiere, Peter. 1991. "Le poids de l'histoire." In Christian Coulon and Denis-Constant Martin (eds.), *Les Afriques politiques.* Paris: Editions la Découverte, 29–43.

———. 1997. *The Modernity of Witchcraft: Politics and the Occult in Postcolonial Africa.* Charlottesville: University of Virginia Press.

———. 2004. "Ecology, Belonging, and Xenophobia: The 1994 Forest Law in Cameroon and the Issue of Community." In Harri Englund and Francis B. Nyamnjoh (eds.), *Rights and the Politics of Recognition in Africa.* London: Zed, 237–259.

———. 2009. *Perils of Belonging: Autochthony, Citizenship, and Exclusion in Africa and Europe.* Chicago: University of Chicago Press.

———. 2015. *Witchcraft, Intimacy, and Trust: Africa in Comparison.* Chicago: University of Chicago Press.

Geschiere, Peter, and Francis Nyamnjoh. 2000. "Capitalism and Autochthony: The Seesaw of Mobility and Belonging." *Public Culture* 12(2): 423–452.

Gewald, Jan-Bart. 2001. "El Negro, El Niño, Witchcraft, and the Absence of Rain in Botswana." *African Affairs* 100(401): 555–580.

Gibson, Clark, and James Long. 2008. "What Explains the African Vote? Using Exit Poll Data from Kenya to Explore Ethnicity and Government Performance in Vote Choice." Paper presented at a meeting of the Working Group on African Political Economy, Berkeley.

Gifford, Paul. 2004. *Ghana's New Christianity: Pentecostalism in Globalizing African Economy.* Bloomington: Indiana University Press.

———. 2016. *Christianity, Development, and Modernity in Africa.* New York: Oxford University Press.

Githuku, Nicholas K. 2016. *Mau Mau Crucible of War: Statehood, National Identity, and Politics of Postcolonial Kenya.* Lanham: Lexington Books.

Gleijeses, Piero. 2006. "Moscow's Proxy? Cuba and Africa, 1975–1988." *Journal of Cold War Studies* 8(2): 3–51.

Glickman, Harvey. 1965. "One-Party System in Tanganyika." *Annals of the American Academy of Political and Social Science* 358: 136–149.

———. 1995. *Ethnic Conflict and Democratization in Africa.* Atlanta: African Studies Association.

Goetz, Anne-Marie, and Shireen Hassim. 2003. *No Shortcuts to Power: African Women in Politics and Policy Making.* London: Zed.

Golan, Tamar. 1981. "A Certain Mystery: How Can France Do Everything That It Does in Africa—and Get Away with It?" *African Affairs* 80(318): 3–11.

Goldman, Marshall I. 1965. "A Balance Sheet of Soviet Foreign Aid." *Foreign Affairs* 43(2): 349–360.

Good, Kenneth. 2008. *Diamonds, Dispossession, and Democracy in Botswana.* Oxford: Currey.

Gorst, Anthony, and Lewis Johnman. 1997. *The Suez Crisis.* London: Routledge.

Gourevitch, Philip. 1998. *We Wish to Inform You That Tomorrow We Will Be Killed with Our Families: Stories from Rwanda.* New York: Farrar, Straus, and Giroux.

Gouws, Amanda. 2016. "Women's Activism Around Gender-Based Violence in South Africa: Recognition, Redistribution, and Representation." *Review of African Political Economy* 43(149): 400–415.

Grachev, Andrei. 2008. *Gorbachev's Gamble: Soviet Foreign Policy and the End of the Cold War.* Cambridge: Polity.

Grant, J. Andrew. 2004. "Global Governance and Conflict Diamonds: The Kimberley Process and the Quest for Clean Gems." *Round Table* 93(375): 385–401.

Green, Elliott. 2010. "Patronage, District Creation, and Reform in Uganda." *Studies in Comparative International Development* 45(1): 83–103.

———. 2012. "On the Size and Shape of African States." *International Studies Quarterly* 56(2) (June): 229–244.

———. 2017. "Ethnicity, National Identity, and the State: Evidence from Sub-Saharan Africa." *British Journal of Political Science.* 1–23. https://doi:10.1017/S0007123417000783.

Grey, Robert D. 2006. "Africa." In Mary Buckley and Robert Singh (eds.), *The Bush Doctrine and the War on Terrorism.* London: Routledge, 121–132.

Grier, R. 1999. "Colonial Legacies and Economic Growth." *Public Choice* 98: 317–335.

Griffiths, Ieuan. 1986. "The Scramble for Africa: Inherited Political Boundaries." *Geographical Journal* 152: 204–216.

———. 1995. *The Atlas of African Affairs.* New York: Routledge.

Grill, Bartholomäus. 2008. "Snowplows for Guinea: Why Development Aid Has Failed and What Can Be Learned from the Mistakes." *Der Spiegel,* 6 March. http://www.spiegel

.de/international/world/snowplows-for-tropical-guinea-how-we-can-learn-from-failed-development-aid-in-africa-a-539782.html.

Grimm, Sonja, Nicolas Lemay-Hébert, and Olivier Nay. 2014. "'Fragile States': Introducing a Political Concept." *Third World Quarterly* 35(2): 197–209.

Grovogui, Siba. 2004. "The Trouble with the Evolués: French Republicanism, Colonial Subjectivity, and Identity." In Patricia M. Goff and Kevin C. Dunn (eds.), *Identity and Global Politics: Theoretical and Empirical Elaborations.* New York: Palgrave Macmillan, 103–121.

Gulford, Christopher. 2011. "Independent South Sudan Jubilant, Wobbly a Day Later." *Los Angeles Times,* 11 July.

Gumedze, Sabelo (ed.). 2008. *Elimination of Mercenarism in Africa.* Pretoria: Institute for Security Studies.

Gyimah-Boadi, E. 2007. "Political Parties, Elections, and Patronage: Random Thoughts on Neo-Patrimonialism and African Democratization." In M. Basedau, G. Erdmann, and A. Mehler, *Votes, Money, and Violence: Political Parties and Elections in Sub-Saharan Africa.* Uppsala: Nordic Africa Institute, 21–33.

Haastrup, Toni. 2013. *Charting Transformation Through Security: EU-Africa Relations.* Basingstoke: Palgrave Macmillan.

Habyarimana, James, Macartan Humphreys, Daniel Posner, and Jeremy Weinstein. 2009. *Coethnicity: Diversity and the Dilemmas of Collective Action.* New York: Russell Sage.

Hagberg, Sten. 2002. "'Enough Is Enough': An Ethnography of the Struggle Against Impunity in Burkina Faso." *Journal of Modern African Studies* 40(2): 217–246.

Hagmann, Tobias. 2005. "Beyond Clannishness and Colonialism: Understanding Political Disorder in Ethiopia's Somali Region, 1991–2004." *Journal of Modern African Studies* 43(4): 509–536.

Haïdara, Fadimata, and Thomas Isbell. 2018. "Popular Perceptions of Elections, Government Action, and Democracy in Mali." *Afrobarometer Dispatch* 219. http://afrobarometer.org/sites/default/files/publications/Dispatches/ab_r7_dispatchno219_democracy_and_elections_in_mali.pdf.

Hale, Henry. 2004. "Explaining Ethnicity." *Comparative Political Studies* 37(4): 458–485.

Hansen, Stig Jarle. 2016. *Al-Shabaab in Somalia: The History and Ideology of a Militant Islamist Group.* New York: Oxford University Press.

Hanson, Kobena T. 2016. *Contemporary Regional Development in Africa.* New York: Routledge.

Harbeson, John. 1994. "Civil Society and Political Renaissance in Africa." In John Harbeson, Donald Rothchild, and Naomi Chazan (eds.), *Civil Society and the State in Africa.* Boulder: Lynne Rienner, 1–29.

Harbeson, John, Donald Rothchild, and Naomi Chazan (eds.). 1994. *Civil Society and the State in Africa.* Boulder: Lynne Rienner.

Hardt, Michael, and Antonio Negri. 2000. *Empire.* Cambridge: Harvard University Press.

Harman, Sophie, and William Brown. 2013. "In from the Margins? The Changing Place of Africa in International Relations." *International Affairs* 89(1): 69–87.

Harnischfleger, Johannes. 2004. "Sharia and Control over Territory: Conflicts Between 'Settlers' and 'Indigenes' in Nigeria." *African Affairs* 103(412): 431–452.

Harris, Gordon. 1994. *Organization of African Unity.* Oxford: Transaction.

Harrison, Graham. 2010. "The Africanization of Poverty: A Retrospective on 'Make Poverty History.'" *African Affairs* 109(436): 391–408.

Hassan, Hussein D. 2008. "Islam in Africa." Report no. RS22873. Washington, D.C.: Congressional Research Service.

Hassan, Mai, and Ryan Sheely. 2017. "Executive-Legislative Relations, Party Defections, and Lower Level Administrative Unit Proliferation: Evidence From Kenya." *Comparative Political Studies* 50(12): 1595–1631.

Havnevik, Kjell, Terje Oestigaard, and Eva Tobisson (eds.). 2015. *Framing African Development: Challenging Concepts.* Leiden: Brill.

Haykel, Bernard. 2009. "On the Nature of Salafi Thought and Action." In Roel Meijer (ed.), *Global Salafism: Islam's New Religious Movement.* New York: Columbia University Press, 33–57.

Haynes, Jeffrey. 2005. "Islamic Militancy in East Africa." *Third World Quarterly* 26(8): 1321–1339.

Heilbrunn, John R. 1993. "Social Origins of National Conferences in Benin and Togo." *Journal of Modern African Studies* 31(2): 277–299.

———. 2005. "Oil and Water? Elite Politicians and Corruption in France." *Comparative Politics* 37(3): 277–296.

————. 2014. *Oil, Democracy, and Development in Africa*. New York: Cambridge University Press.
Held, I. M., T. L. Delworth, J. Lu, K. L. Findell, and T. R. Knutson. 2005. "Simulation of Sahel Drought in the 20th and 21st Centuries." *Proceedings of the National Academy of Sciences* 102(50): 17891–17896.
Hellsten, Sirkku. 2016. "Deconstructing the Myth of the African Middle Class." In Henning Melber (ed.), *The Rise of Africa's Middle Class: Myths, Realities, and Critical Engagements*. London: Zed, 159–169.
Hentz, James J. 2001. "Redesigning US Foreign Policy: Regionalism, Economic Development, and Instability in Southern Africa." In Kevin Dunn and Timothy M. Shaw (eds.), *Africa's Challenge to International Relations Theory*. Basingstoke: Palgrave Macmillan, 185–203.
————. 2004. "The Contending Currents in United States Involvement in Sub-Saharan Africa." In Ian Taylor and Paul Williams (eds.), *Africa in International Politics: External Involvement on the Continent*. New York: Routledge, 23–40.
Hentz, James J., Frederik Söderbaum, and Rodrigo Tavares. 2009. "Regional Organizations and African Security: Moving the Debate Forward." *African Security* 2(2–3): 206–217.
Herbst, Jeffrey. 1990a. "The Structural Adjustment of Politics in Africa." *World Development* 18: 949–958.
————. 1990b. "War and the State in Africa." *International Security* 14(4): 117–139.
————. 2000. *States and Power in Africa: Comparative Lessons in Authority and Control*. Princeton: Princeton University Press.
Hettne, Björn. 1999. "Globalization and the New Regionalism: The Second Great Transformation." In Björn Hettne, András Inotai, and Osvaldo Sunkel, *Globalism and the New Regionalism*. Basingstoke: Macmillan, 1–24.
————. 2001. "Regionalism, Security, and Development: A Comparative Perspective." In Björn Hettne, András Inotai, and Osvaldo Sunkel (eds.), *Comparing Regionalisms: Implications for Global Development*. London: Palgrave Macmillan, 1–53.
Hickel, Jason. 2016. "The True Extent of Global Poverty and Hunger: Questioning the Good News Narrative of the Millennium Development Goals." *Third World Quarterly* 37(5): 749–767.
————. 2017. "Is Global Inequality Getting Better or Worse? A Critique of the World Bank's Convergence Narrative." *Third World Quarterly* 38(10): 2208–2222.
Hilgers, Mathieu. 2010. "Identité collective et lutte pour la reconnaissance: Les révoltes à Koudougou lors de l'affaire Zongo." In Mathieu Hilgers and Jacinthe Mazzocchetti (eds.), *Révoltes et oppositions dans un régime semi-autoritaire: Le cas du Burkina Faso*. Paris: Karthala, 175–194.
Hilgers, Mathieu, and Jacinthe Mazzocchetti (eds.). 2010. *Révoltes et oppositions dans un régime semi-autoritaire: Le cas du Burkina Faso*. Paris: Karthala.
Hobbes, Thomas. 1968 [1651]. *Leviathan*. London: Penguin.
Hobson, J. A. 1902. *Imperialism: A Study*. London: Cosimo.
Hochschild, Adam. 1999. *King Leopold's Ghost: A Story of Greed, Terror, and Heroism in Colonial Africa*. Boston: Houghton Mifflin.
Hodgkin, Thomas. 1956. *Nationalism in Colonial Africa*. London: Frederick Muller.
Holm, John D. 1987. "Botswana: A Paternalistic Democracy." *World Affairs* 150(1): 21–30.
Holsti, Kalevi. 1996. *The State, War, and the State of War*. New York: Cambridge University Press.
Homer-Dixon, Thomas. 1994. "Environmental Scarcities and Violent Conflict." *International Security* 19(1): 5–40.
————. 1999. *Environment, Scarcity, and Violence*. Princeton: Princeton University Press.
Homer-Dixon, Thomas, and Jessica Blitt (eds.). 1998. *Ecoviolence: Links Among Environment, Population, and Security*. Lanham: Rowman and Littlefield.
Hooper, Charlotte. 2001. *Manly States: Masculinities, International Relations, and Gender Politics*. New York: Columbia University Press.
Hopkins, A. G. 2009. "The New Economic History of Africa." *Journal of African History* 50: 155–177.
Horowitz, Donald L. 1985. *Ethnic Groups in Conflict*. Berkeley: University of California Press.
————. 1993. "Democracy in Divided Societies." *Journal of Democracy* 4(4): 18–38.
Hoskyns, Catherine. 1965. *The Congo Since Independence*. London: Oxford University Press.
House Committee on International Relations. 2001. "Africa and the War on Global Terrorism: Hearings Before the Subcommittee on Africa of the Committee on International Relations." Washington, D.C., 107th Congress, 1st session.
Howe, Herbert. 2001. *Ambiguous Order: Military Forces in African States*. Boulder: Lynne Rienner.

Huggins, Chris, and Jenny Clover (eds.). 2005. *From the Ground Up: Land Rights, Conflict, and Peace in Sub-Saharan Africa.* Pretoria: Institute for Security Studies.

Huliaras, Asteris C. 1998. "The 'Anglosaxon Conspiracy': French Perceptions of the Great Lakes Crisis." *Journal of Modern African Studies* 36(4): 539–609.

Human Rights Watch. 2004. "Nigeria's 2003 Elections: The Unacknowledged Violence." New York.

Hunt, Michael. 2009. *Ideology and US Foreign Policy.* New Haven: Yale University Press.

Huntington, Samuel. 1993. "The Clash of Civilizations." *Foreign Affairs* 72(3): 22–49.

Hurt, Stephen R. 2003. "Cooperation and Coercion? The Cotonou Agreement Between the European Union and ACP States and the End of the Lomé Convention." *Third World Quarterly* 24: 161–176.

———. 2004. "The European Union's External Relations with Africa After the Cold War: Aspects of Continuity and Change." In Ian Taylor and Paul Williams (eds.), *Africa in International Politics: External Involvement on the Continent.* New York: Routledge, 155–173.

Husain, Ishrat, and Rashid Faruqee (eds.). 1993. *Adjustment in Africa: Lessons from Country Case Studies.* Washington, D.C.: World Bank.

Hutchful, Eboe. 2002. *Ghana's Adjustment Experience: The Paradox of Reform.* Oxford: Currey.

Huysmans, Jef. 2000. "The European Union and the Securitization of Migration." *Journal of Common Market Studies* 38: 751–777.

Hyden, Goran. 1980. *Beyond Ujamaa in Tanzania: Underdevelopment and an Uncaptured Peasantry.* Berkeley: University of California Press.

———. 1983. *No Shortcut to Progress: African Development Management in Perspective.* Berkeley: University of California Press.

———. 1984. "Administration and Public Policy." In Joel Barkan and John Okumu (eds.), *Politics and Policy Making in Kenya and Tanzania.* New York: Praeger, 93–113.

———. 1995. "Reciprocity and Governance in Africa." In James S. Wunsch and Dele Olowu (eds.), *The Failure of the Centralized State: Institutions and Self-Governance in Africa.* Boulder: Lynne Rienner, 245–269.

———. 2006. *African Politics in Comparative Perspective.* Cambridge: Cambridge University Press.

ICG (International Crisis Group). 2009. *Nigeria: Seizing the Moment in the Niger Delta.* Africa Briefing no. 74. Brussels.

Iddrisu, Abdulai. 2013. *Contesting Islam in Africa: Homegrown Wahhabism and Muslim Identity in Northern Ghana, 1920–2010.* Durham, NC: Carolina Academic.

IDEA (International Institute for Democracy and Electoral Assistance). 2007. "Political Parties in West Africa: The Challenge of Democratization in Fragile States." Stockholm.

Iliffe, John. 2006. *The African AIDS Epidemic: A History.* Athens: Ohio University Press.

ILO (International Labour Organization). 2002. *Women and Men in the Informal Economy: A Statistical Picture.* Geneva.

Ingelaere, Bert. 2008. "The Gacaca Courts in Rwanda." In L. Hoyse and M. Salter (eds.), *Traditional Justice and Reconciliation After Violent Conflict: Learning from Africa.* Stockholm: International Institute for Democracy and Electoral Assistance, 24–59.

———. 2018. *Inside Rwanda's Gacaca Courts: Seeking Justice After Genocide.* Madison: University of Wisconsin Press.

Ingelhart, Ronald. 1997. *Modernization and Postmodernization: Cultural, Economic, and Political Change in 43 Societies.* Princeton: Princeton University Press.

Ingelhart, Ronald, and Christian Welzel. 2005. *Modernization, Cultural Change, and Democracy: The Human Development Sequence.* New York: Cambridge University Press.

IRC (International Rescue Committee). 2007. *Mortality in the Democratic Republic of Congo: An Ongoing Crisis.* New York.

Isaacman, Allen. 1995. *Cotton Is the Mother of Poverty: Peasants, Work, and Rural Struggle in Colonial Mozambique, 1938–196.* London: Heinemann.

Iyob, Ruth. 1997. *The Eritrean Struggle for Independence: Domination, Resistance, Nationalism, 1941–1993.* Cambridge: Cambridge University Press.

———. 2000. "The Ethiopian-Eritrean Conflict: Diasporic vs. Hegemonic States in the Horn of Africa, 1991–2000?" *Journal of Modern African Studies* 38(4): 659–682.

Jabri, Vivienne. 1996. *Discourses on Violence: Conflict Analysis Reconsidered.* New York: University of Manchester Press.

Jackson, Paul, and Peter Albrecht. 2011. *Reconstructing Security After Conflict: Security Sector Reform in Sierra Leone.* Basingstoke: Palgrave Macmillan.

Jackson, Robert H. 1990. *Quasi-States: Sovereignty, International Relations, and the Third World*. Cambridge: Cambridge University Press.

Jackson, Robert, and Carl Rosberg. 1982. "Why Africa's Weak States Persist: The Empirical and the Juridical in Statehood." *World Politics* 35(1): 1–24.

———. 1984. "Personal Rule: Theory and Practice in Africa." *Comparative Politics* 16(4): 421–442.

———. 1985. "The Marginality of African States." In Gwendolen Carter and Patrick O'Meara (eds.), *African Independence: The First Twenty-five Years*. Bloomington: Indiana University Press, 45–70.

———. 1986. "Sovereignty and Underdevelopment: Juridical Statehood in the African Crisis." *Journal of Modern African Studies* 24(1) (March): 1–31.

Jackson, Stephen. 2006. "Sons of Which Soil? The Language and Politics of Autochthony in Eastern D.R. Congo." *African Studies Review* 49(2): 95–123.

Jega, Attahiru (ed.). 2000. *Identity Transformation and Identity Politics Under Structural Adjustment in Nigeria*. Stockholm: Nordic Africa Institute.

Jensen, Erik. 2004. *Western Sahara: Anatomy of a Stalemate*. Boulder: Lynne Rienner.

Jensen, Nathan, and Leonard Wantchekon. 2004. "Resource Wealth and Political Regimes in Africa." *Comparative Political Studies* 37(7): 816–841.

Jerven, Morten. 2013. *Poor Numbers: How We Are Misled by African Development Statistics and What to Do About It*. Ithaca: Cornell University Press.

———. 2015. *Africa: Why Economists Get It Wrong*. London: Zed.

Jewkes, Rachel, et al. 2009. "Understanding Men's Health and Use of Violence: Interface of Rape and HIV in South Africa." Policy brief. Pretoria: Medical Research Council.

Joffe, George. 1990. "Concepts of Sovereignty and Borders in North Africa." In Carl Grundy-Warr (ed.), *International Boundaries and Boundary Conflict Resolution*. Durham: Boundaries Research, 221–239.

Johnson, Douglas H. 2003. *The Root Causes of Sudan's Civil Wars*. Oxford: Currey.

Joireman, Sandra F. 2001. "Inherited Legal Systems and Effective Rule of Law: Africa and the Colonial Legacy." *Journal of Modern African Studies* 39(4): 571–596.

———. 2011. *Where There Is No Government: Enforcing Property Rights in Common Law Africa*. New York: Oxford University Press.

Jones, Nicholas A. 2010. *The Courts of Genocide: Politics and the Rule of Law in Rwanda and Arusha*. New York: Routledge.

Jordaan, Eduard. 2006. "Inadequately Self-Critical: Rwanda's Self-Assessment for the African Peer Review Mechanism." *African Affairs* 105(420): 333–351.

Joseph, Richard. 1977. *Radical Nationalism in Cameroon: Social Origins of the U.P.C. Rebellion*. Oxford: Clarendon.

———. 1987. *Democracy and Prebendal Politics in Nigeria*. Cambridge: Cambridge University Press.

———. 1997. "Democratization in Africa After 1989: Comparative and Theoretical Perspectives." *Comparative Politics* 29(3): 363–382.

———, ed. 1999. *The State, Conflict, and Democracy in Africa*. Boulder: Lynne Rienner.

Joseph, Richard, and Alexandra Gillies (eds.). 2009. *Smart Aid for African Development*. Boulder: Lynne Rienner.

Joseph, Richard, and Jeffrey Herbst. 1997. "Correspondence: Responding to State Failure in Africa." *International Security* 22: 175–184.

Jourde, Cédric. 2006. "The Role of the United States in Western Africa: Tying Terrorism to Electoral Democracy and Strategic Resources." In Charles-Philippe David and David Grondin (eds.), *Hegemony or Empire: The Redefinition of US Power Under George W. Bush*. Aldershot: Ashgate, 181–201.

Kabemba, Claude. 2016. "China-Democratic Republic of Congo Relations: From a Beneficial to a Developmental Cooperation." *African Studies Quarterly* 16(3–4): 73–88.

Kahl, Colin. 2006. *States, Scarcity, and Civil Strife in the Developing World*. Princeton: Princeton University Press.

Kaldor, Mary. 1999. *New and Old Wars: Organized Violence in a Global Era*. Oxford: Polity.

Kalonji Mulopwe, Albert. 2005. *Congo 1960: La sécession du Sud-Kasai*. Paris: L'Harmattan.

Kalu, Ogbu U. 2003. "Safiyya and Adamah: Punishing Adultery with Sharia Stones in Twenty-First Century Nigeria." *African Affairs* 102(408): 389–408.

Kandawasvika-Nhundu, Rumbidzai. 2013. *Political Parties in Africa Through a Gender Lens.* Stockholm: International Institute for Democracy and Electoral Assistance.
Kane, Ousmane. 2007. "Moderate Revivalists: Islamic Inroads in Sub-Saharan Africa." *Harvard International Review* 2: 64–68.
Kant, Immanuel. 1983 [1795]. *Perpetual Peace and Other Essays.* Indianapolis: Hackett.
Kaplan, Robert. 1994. "The Coming Anarchy." *Atlantic Monthly,* February.
———. 1996. *The Ends of the Earth: A Journey at the Dawn of the 21st Century.* New York: Random.
Kaplinsky, Rafael. 1980. "Capital Accumulation in the Periphery: The Kenyan Case Reexamined." *Review of African Political Economy* 7(17): 83–105.
Karlsrud, John. 2015. "The UN at War: Examining the Consequences of Peace-Enforcement Mandates for the UN Peacekeeping Operations in the CAR, the DRC, and Mali." *Third World Quarterly* 36(1): 40–54.
Kasfir, Nelson. 1979. "Explaining Ethnic Political Participation." *World Politics* 31(3): 365–388.
———. 1998a. "Civil Society, the State, and Democracy in Africa." In Nelson Kasfir (ed.), *Civil Society and Democracy in Africa: Critical Perspectives.* Portland: Cass, 123–149.
———. 1998b. "The Conventional Notion of Civil Society: A Critique." In Nelson Kasfir (ed.), *Civil Society and Democracy in Africa: Critical Perspectives.* Portland: Cass, 1–20.
Kassimir, Ron. 1997. "The Internationalization of African Studies: A View from the SSRC." *Africa Today* 44(2): 155–162.
Kaufman, Daniel, Aart Kraai, and Massimo Mastruzzi. 2010. "The Worldwide Governance Indicators: Methodology and Analytical Issues." Policy/Research Paper no. 5430. Washington, D.C.: World Bank.
Keefer, Philip, and Stephen Knack. 1997. "Does Social Capital Have an Economic Payoff? A Cross-Country Investigation." *Quarterly Journal of Economics* 112(4): 1251–1288.
Keller, Edmond. 1996. "Toward a New African Political Order: An Introduction." In Edmond J. Keller and Donald Rothchild (eds.), *Africa and the New International Order: New Perspectives on State Sovereignty and Regional Security.* Boulder: Lynne Rienner, 1–14.
———. 2005. "Making and Remaking State and Nation in Ethiopia." In Ricardo R. Larémont (ed.), *Borders, Nationalism, and the African State.* Boulder: Lynne Rienner, 87–134.
———. 2014. *Identity, Citizenship, and Political Conflict in Africa.* Bloomington: Indiana University Press.
Kelly, Sean. 1993. *America's Tyrant: The CIA and Mobutu of Zaïre.* Washington, D.C.: American University Press.
Kelsall, Tim. 2005. "History, Identity, and Collective Action: Difficulties of Accountability." In Ulf Engel and Gorm Rye Olsen (eds.), *The African Exception.* London: Ashgate, 53–68.
———. 2009. *Culture Under Cross-Examination: International Justice and the Special Court for Sierra Leone.* New York: Cambridge University Press.
———. 2013. *Business, Politics, and the State in Africa: Challenging the Orthodoxies on Growth and Transformation.* New York: Zed.
Kennes, Erik, and Miles Larmer. 2016. *The Katangese Gendarmes and War in Central Africa: Fighting Their Way Home.* Bloomington: Indiana University Press.
Keohane, Robert. 2002. *Power and Governance in a Partially Globalized World.* London: Routledge.
Keohane, Robert, and Joseph Nye. 1977. *Power and Interdependence.* New York: Longman.
Kevane, Michael. 2014. *Women and Development in Africa: How Gender Works.* 2nd ed. Boulder: Lynne Rienner.
Kevane, Michael, and Leslie Gray. 2008. "Darfur: Rainfall and Conflict." *Environmental Research Letters* 3(3). http://iopscience.iop.org/1748-9326/3/3/034006/pdf/1748-9326_3_3_034006.pdf.
Killick, Tony. 1998. *Aid and the Political Economy of Policy Change.* London: Routledge.
King, Gary, Robert Keohane, and Sidney Verba. 1994. *Designing Social Inquiry: Scientific Inference in Qualitative Research.* Princeton: Princeton University Press.
King, Gary, and Christopher Murray. 2001. "Rethinking Human Security." *Political Science Quarterly* 116(4): 585–610.
Kingsolver, Barbara. 1998. *The Poisonwood Bible.* New York: HarperCollins.
Kinyanjui, Mary Njeri. 2014. *Women and the Informal Economy in Urban Africa: From the Margins to the Centre.* London: Zed.

Kirk-Greene, Anthony. 1980. "The Thin White Line: The Size of the British Colonial Service in Africa." *African Affairs* 79(314): 25–44.
Klare, Michael T. 2001. *Resource Wars: The New Landscape of Global Conflict.* New York: Holt.
Koch, Dirk-Jan. 2008. "A Paris Declaration for International NGOs." *Policy Insights* 73. http://www.oecd.org/dataoecd/7/55/41159413.pdf.
Kopytoff, Igor. 1987. "The Internal African Frontier: The Making of African Political Culture." In I. Kopytoff (ed.), *The African Frontier: The Reproduction of Traditional African Societies.* Bloomington: Indiana University Press, 3–83.
Koter, Dominika. 2016. *Beyond Ethnic Politics in Africa.* Cambridge: Cambridge University Press.
Krasner, Stephen D. (ed.). 1983. *International Regimes.* Ithaca: Cornell University Press.
———, ed. 2001. *Problematic Sovereignty.* New York: Columbia University Press.
Kroslak, Daniela. 2004. "France's Policy Toward Africa: Continuity or Change?" In Ian Taylor and Paul Williams (eds.), *Africa in International Politics: External Involvement on the Continent.* New York: Routledge, 61–82.
Krueger, Ann. 1974. "The Political Economy of the Rent-Seeking Society." *American Economic Review* 64(3): 291–303.
Kuperman, Alan (ed.). 2015. *Constitution and Conflict Management in Africa: Preventing Civil War Through Institutional Design.* Philadelphia: University of Pennsylvania Press.
Lai, H. H. 2007. "China's Oil Diplomacy: Is It a Global Security Threat?" *Third World Quarterly* 28(3): 519–537.
Laitin, David. 1977. *Politics, Language, and Thought: The Somali Experience.* Chicago: University of Chicago Press.
Laitin, David, and Said Samatar. 1987. *Somalia: Nation in Search of a State.* Boulder: Westview.
Lambright, Gina M. S. 2010. *Decentralization in Uganda: Explaining Successes and Failures in Local Governance.* Boulder: Lynne Rienner.
Landes, David S. 1999. *The Wealth and Poverty of Nations: Why Some Are So Rich and Some So Poor.* New York: Norton.
Lange, Matthew. 2004. "British Colonial Legacies and Political Development." *World Development* 32(6): 905–922.
Larémont, Ricardo René. 2005. *Borders, Nationalism, and the African State.* Boulder: Lynne Rienner.
Last, Murray. 2000. "La Charia dans le Nord-Nigeria." *Politique Africaine* 79: 141–152.
Lavrov, Sergey. 2018. Interview with Foreign Minister Sergey Lavrov by *Hommes d'Afrique* magazine. Ministry of Foreign Affairs, 5 March. http://www.mid.ru/en/foreign_policy/news.
Lawson, Andrew, David Booth, Meleki Msuya, Samuel Wangwe, and Tim Williamson. 2005. "Does General Budget Support Work? Evidence from Tanzania." London: Overseas Development Institute.
le Billon, Philippe. 2005. *Geopolitics of Resource Wars: Resource Dependence, Governance, and Violence.* London: Cass.
Le Monde. 2011. "African Scandal Shakes French Republic." 13 September. http://www.presseurop.eu/en/content/news-brief-cover/943541-african-scandals-shake-french-republic.
Le Vine, Victor. 1964. *The Cameroons from Mandate to Independence.* Berkeley: University of California Press.
———. 1980. "African Patrimonial Regimes in Comparative Perspectives." *Journal of Modern African Studies* 18(4): 657–673.
———. 2004. *Politics in Francophone Africa.* Boulder: Lynne Rienner.
Leach, Melissa, and Robin Mearns. 1996. *The Lie of the Land: Challenging Received Wisdom on the African Environment.* London: Currey.
LeBas, Adrienne. 2012. *From Protest to Parties: Party-Building and Democratization in Africa.* Oxford: Oxford University Press.
Lederach, John Paul. 1997. *Building Peace: Sustainable Reconciliation in Divided Societies.* Washington, D.C.: US Institute of Peace.
Legum, Colin. 1976. *Pan-Africanism: A Short Political Guide.* Westport: Greenwood.
Legvold, Robert. 1970. *Soviet Policy in West Africa.* Cambridge: Harvard University Press.
Lemarchand, René. 1962. "The Limits of Self-Determination: The Case of the Katanga Secession." *American Political Science Review* 56(2): 404–416.
———. 1970. *Rwanda and Burundi.* New York: Praeger.
———. 1992. "Burundi: The Politics of Ethnic Amnesia." In Helen Fein (ed.), *Genocide Watch.* New Haven: Yale University Press, 70–86.

————. 1995. "Rwanda: The Rationality of Genocide." *Issue: A Journal of Opinion* 23(2): 8–11.

————. 1997. "Patterns of State Collapse and Reconstruction in Central Africa: Reflections on the Crisis in the Great Lakes." *African Studies Quarterly* 1(3): 5–22.

————. 2007. "Consociationalism and Power-Sharing in Africa: Rwanda, Burundi, and the Democratic Republic of Congo." *African Affairs* 106(422): 1–20.

Lemke, Douglas. 2002. *Regions of War and Peace.* New York: Cambridge University Press.

————. 2003. "African Lessons for International Relations Research." *World Politics* 56(1): 114–138.

————. 2011. "Intra-National IR in Africa." *Review of International Studies* 37(1): 49–70.

Lenin, V. I. 1999 [1916]. *Imperialism: The Highest Stage of Capitalism.* Chippendale: Resistance.

Leslie, Agnes Mgoma. 2016. "China-Africa Relations: Political and Economic Engagement and Media Strategies." *African Studies Quarterly* 16(3–4): 1–6.

Levitsky, Steven, and Lucan Way. 2002. "Elections Without Democracy: The Rise of Competitive Authoritarianism." *Journal of Democracy* 13(2): 51–65.

Lewis, I. M. 2003. *A Modern History of the Somali.* Athens: Ohio University Press.

Lewis, Peter. 1992. "Political Transition and the Dilemma of Civil Society in Africa." *Journal of International Affairs* 46(1): 31–54.

————. 1996. "From Prebendalism to Predation: The Political Economy of Decline in Nigeria." *Journal of Modern African Studies* 34: 79–103.

————. 1999. "Nigeria: An End to the Permanent Transition?" *Journal of Democracy* 10(1) (January): 141–156.

————. 2007. *Growing Apart: Oil, Politics, and Economic Change in Indonesia and Nigeria.* Ann Arbor: University of Michigan Press.

————. 2012. "Democracy and Economic Performance." In Ellen Lust and Stephen Ndegwa (eds.), *Governing Africa's Changing Societies: Dynamics of Reform.* Boulder: Lynne Rienner, 45–72.

Leys, Colin. 1975. *Underdevelopment in Kenya: The Political Economy of Neo-Colonialism.* Berkeley: University of California Press.

————. 1996. *The Rise and Fall of Development Theory.* Bloomington: Indiana University Press.

Lichbach, Mark, and Alan Zuckerman. 2009. *Comparative Politics: Rationality, Culture, and Structure.* Cambridge: Cambridge University Press.

Lieberman, Evan S. 2009. *Boundaries of Contagion: How Ethnic Politics Have Shaped Government Responses to AIDS.* Princeton: Princeton University Press.

Lijphart, Arendt. 1977. *Democracy in Plural Societies: A Comparative Exploration.* New Haven: Yale University Press.

Likoti, Fako Johnson. 2007. "The 1998 Military Intervention in Lesotho: SADC Peace Mission or Resource War." *International Peacekeeping* 14(2): 251–263.

Lindberg, Staffan. 2003. "It's Our Time to 'Chop': Do Elections in Africa Feed Neo-Patrimonialism Rather Than Counteract It?" *Democratization* 10(2): 121–140.

————. 2006. *Democracy and Elections in Africa.* Baltimore: Johns Hopkins University Press.

Lindberg, Staffan, and John Clark. 2008. "Does Democratization Reduce the Risk of Military Interventions in Politics in Africa?" *Democratization* 15(1): 86–105.

Lindberg, Staffan, and Minion Morrison. 2008. "Are African Voters Really Ethnic or Clientelistic? Survey Evidence from Ghana." *Political Science Quarterly* 123(1): 95–122.

Lindberg, Staffan, and Carolien van Ham. 2018. "Elections: The Power of Elections in Multiparty Africa." In Nic Cheeseman (ed.), *Institutions and Democracy in Africa.* Cambridge: Cambridge University Press, 213–237.

Lindberg, Staffan, and Yongmei Zhou. 2009. "Co-optation Despite Democratization in Ghana." In Joel Barkan (ed.), *Legislative Power in Emerging African Democracies.* Boulder: Lynne Rienner, 147–176.

Lindley, Anna. 2009. "Between 'Dirty Money' and 'Development Capital': Somali Money Transfer Infrastructure Under Global Security." *African Affairs* 108(433): 519–539.

Lindow, Megan. 2009. "South Africa's Rape Crisis: 1 in 4 Men Say They've Done It." *Time,* June. http://www.time.com/time/world/article/0,8599,1906000,00.html.

Lindqvist, Sven. 1996. *"Exterminate All the Brutes."* New York: New Press.

Linz, Juan, and Alfred Stepan. 1996. *Problems of Democratic Transition and Consolidation.* Baltimore: Johns Hopkins University Press.

Lipton, Michael. 1977. *Why Poor People Stay Poor: Urban Bias in World Development.* Cambridge: Harvard University Press.

Lister, Marjorie. 1997. *The European Union and the South: Relations with Developing Countries.* London: Routledge.

Litfin, Karen. 1993. "Ecoregimes: Playing Tug of War with the Nation-State." In Ronnie Lipschutz and Ken Conca (eds.), *The State and Social Power in Global Environmental Politics.* New York: Columbia University Press, 94–117.

Lodge, Tom. 2014. "Neo-Patrimonial Politics in the ANC." *African Affairs* 113(450): 1–23.

Loimeier, Roman. 2007. "Nigeria: The Quest for a Viable Religious Option." In William F. S. Miles (ed.), *Political Islam in West Africa: State-Society Relations Transformed.* Boulder: Lynne Rienner, 43–72.

Lombard, Louisa. 2009. "Post-Halloween Edition: Witches and Sorcerers." *Foole's No Man's Land,* 2 November. http://foolesnomansland.blogspot.com/2009/11/post-halloween-edition -witches-and.html.

Longman, Timothy. 1998. "Rwanda: Chaos from Above." In Leonardo Villalón and Philip Huxtable (eds.), *The African State at a Critical Juncture.* Boulder: Lynne Rienner, 75–91.

Love, Roy. 2006. "Religion, Ideology, and Conflict in Africa." *Review of African Political Economy* 33(109): 619–634.

Lumsdaine, David Halloran. 1993. *Moral Visions in International Politics: The Foreign Aid Regime, 1949–1989.* Princeton: Princeton University Press.

Lund, Christian (ed.). 2007. *Twilight Institutions: Public Authority and Local Politics in Africa.* London: Blackwell.

Lust, Ellen, and Stephen Ndegwa. 2012. "The Challenge of Governance in Africa's Changing Societies." In Ellen Lust and Stephen Ndegwa (eds.), *Governing Africa's Changing Societies: Dynamics of Reform.* Boulder: Lynne Rienner, 1–18.

Lyman, Princeton N., and J. Stephen Morrison. 2004. "The Terrorist Threat in Africa." *Foreign Affairs* 83(1): 75–86.

Mac Ginty, Roger, and Oliver P. Richmond. 2013. "The Local Turn in Peace Building: A Critical Agenda for Peace." *Third World Quarterly* 34(5): 763–783.

MacGaffey, Wyatt. 1986. *Religion and Society in Central Africa: The Bakongo of Lower Zaire.* Chicago: University of Chicago Press.

Madava, Tinashe. 2012. "Zimbabwe: Corruption, Partisanship Blight Judiciary." *Financial Gazette* (Harare), 12 April. http://allafrica.com/stories/201204140071.html.

Magnusson, Bruce. 2001. "Democratization and Domestic Insecurity: Navigating the Transition in Benin." *Comparative Politics* 33(2): 211–230.

Magnusson, Bruce, and John Clark. 2005. "Understanding Democratic Survival and Democratic Failure in Africa: Insights from Divergent Democratic Experiments in Benin and Congo (Brazzaville)." *Comparative Studies in History and Society* 47(3): 552–582.

Mahoney, James. 2010. *Colonialism and Postcolonial Development: Spanish America in Comparative Perspective.* New York: Cambridge University Press.

Makinda, Samuel M., and F. Wafula Okumu. 2008. *The African Union: Challenges of Globalization, Security, and Governance.* London: Routledge.

Maloba, Wunyabari. 1998. *Mau Mau and Kenya: An Analysis of a Peasant Revolt.* Bloomington: Indiana University Press.

Maloka, Eddy. 2005. "NEPAD and Its Critics." In Jimi Adésína, Yao Graham, and Adebayo Olukoshi (eds.), *Africa and Development Challenges in the New Millennium: The NEPAD Debate.* London: Zed, 86–104.

Mamdani, Mahmood. 1996. *Citizen and Subject: Contemporary Africa and the Legacy of Late Colonialism.* Princeton: Princeton University Press.

———. 2001. *When Victims Become Killers: Colonialism, Nativism, and the Genocide in Rwanda.* Princeton: Princeton University Press.

Mampilly, Zachariah. 2010. *Rebel Rulers: Insurgent Governance and Civilian Life During War.* Ithaca: Cornell University Press.

Mangeni, Francis. 2002. *African Influence at the WTO.* Lusaka: Common Market for Eastern and Southern Africa.

Manji, Firoze, and Carl O'Coill. 2002. "The Missionary Position: NGOs and Development in Africa." *International Affairs* 78(3): 567–583.

Marchal, Roland. 2004. "Islamic Political Dynamics in the Somali Civil War." In Alex de Waal (ed.), *Islamism and Its Enemies in the Horn of Africa.* Bloomington: Indiana University Press, 114–145.

Marchand, Marianne, Morten Bøås, and Timothy M. Shaw. 1999. "The Political Economy of New Regionalisms." *Third World Quarterly* 20(5): 897–910.

Marcum, John. 1978. *The Angolan Revolution.* 2 vols. Cambridge: Massachusetts Institute of Technology Press.

Marks, Robert B. 2006. *The Origins of the Modern World: Fate and Fortune in the Rise of the West.* Lanham: Rowman and Littlefield.

Márquez, Humberto. 2005. "Weaving New Alliances with Cultural Threads." *Inter Press Service,* 28 October. http://ipsnews.net/africa/nota.asp?idnews=30807.

Martin, David, and Phyllis Johnson. 1981. *The Struggle for Zimbabwe: The Chimurenga War.* New York: Faber and Faber.

Martin, Guy. 1993. "Continuity and Change in Franco-African Relations." *Journal of Modern African Studies* 33(1): 1–20.

Marut, Jean-Claude. 2002. "Le problème Casamançais est-il soluble dans l'état-nation?" In Momar Coumba Diop (ed.), *Le Sénégal contemporain.* Paris: Karthala, 425–458.

Marysse, Stefaan. 2005. "Decentralization Issues in Post-Conflict Democratic Republic of the Congo (DRC)." In F. Reyntjens and S. Marysse (eds.), *L'Afrique des Grands Lacs, annuaire 2004–2005.* Paris: L'Harmattan, 189–208.

Mason, Robert. 2017. "China's Impact on the Landscape of African International Relations: Implications for Dependency Theory." *Third World Quarterly* 38(1): 84–96.

Massey, Simon. 1998. "Operation Assurance: The Greatest Intervention That Never Happened." *Journal of Humanitarian Assistance,* 15 February. http://sites.tufts.edu/jha/archives/123.

Massey, Simon, and Roy May. 2005. "Dallas to Doba: Oil and Chad, External Controls, and Internal Politics." *Journal of Contemporary African Studies* 23(2): 253–276.

Mathews, Kay. 2008. "Renaissance of Pan-Africanism: The AU and the New Pan-Africanists." In John Akokpari, Angela Ndinga-Muvumba, and Tim Murithi (eds.), *The African Union and Its Institutions.* Auckland Park: Fanele, 25–40.

Mattes, Robert, and Michael Bratton. 2016. "Do Africans Still Want Democracy?" Afrobarometer Policy Paper no. 36. https://afrobarometer.org/sites/default/files/publications/Policy%20papers/ab_r6_policypaperno36_do_africans_want_democracy.pdf

Mavrotas, George, and Mark McGillivray (eds.). 2009. *Development Aid: A Fresh Look.* London: Palgrave Macmillan.

Mawdsley, Emma, and Gerard McCann (eds.). 2010. *India in Africa: Changing Geographies of Power.* Cape Town: Pambazuka.

Mayall, J. 2005. "The Shadow of Empire: The EU and the Former Colonial World." In C. Hill and M. Smith (eds.), *International Relations and the European Union.* New York: Oxford University Press, 292–316.

Mbeki, Thabo. 1996. "I Am an African." Address to South Africa's Constitutional Assembly, 8 May. http://www.hollerafrica.com/pdf/vol1AfricanRenSep_Oct_2004.pdf#page=9.

Mbembe, Achille. 2000. *On the Postcolony.* Berkeley: University of California Press.

McGowan, Pat, and Thomas H. Johnson. 1984. "African Military Coups d'État and Underdevelopment: A Quantitative Historical Analysis." *Journal of Modern African Studies* 22(4): 633–666.

———. 1986. "Sixty Coups in Thirty Years: Further Evidence Regarding African Military Coups d'État." *Journal of Modern African Studies* 24(3): 539–546.

McGowan, Patrick. 2003. "African Military Coups d'État, 1956–2001: Frequency, Trends, and Distribution." *Journal of Modern African Studies* 41(3): 339–370.

McInnes, Colin. 2016. "Crisis! What Crisis? Global Health and the 2014–15 West African Ebola Outbreak." *Third World Quarterly* 37(3): 380–400.

McNulty, Mel. 1997. "France's Rwanda Débâcle." *War Studies Journal* 2(2): 3–22.

Mearsheimer, John J. 2003. *The Tragedy of Great Power Politics.* New York: Norton.

Médard, Jean-François. 1982. "The Underdeveloped State in Tropical Africa: Political Clientelism or Neo-Patrimonialism." In C. Clapham (ed.), *Private Patronage and Public Power.* London: Pinter, 162–191.

———. 1991. "Étatisation et désétatisation en Afrique noire." In J.-F. Médard (ed.), *États d'Afrique noire.* Paris: Karthala, 355–365.

Melber, Henning (ed.). 2016. *The Rise of Africa's Middle Class: Myths, Realities, and Critical Engagements.* London: Zed.

———. 2017. "The African Middle Class(es)—in the Middle of What?" *Review of African Political Economy* 44(151): 142–154.

Melson, Robert, and Howard Wolpe. 1970. *Nationalism and New States in Africa.* London: Heinemann.

Menkhaus, Ken. 2007. "The Crisis in Somalia: Tragedy in Five Acts." *African Affairs* 106(204): 357–390.

Michalopoulos, Stelios, and Elias Papaioannou. 2013. "Pre-Colonial Ethnic Institutions and Contemporary African Development." *Econometrica* 81(1): 113–152.

Migdal, Joel. 1988. *Strong Societies and Weak States: State-Society Relations and State Capabilities in the Third World.* Princeton: Princeton University Press.

Miguel, Edward. 2004. "Tribe or Nation? Nation Building and Public Goods in Kenya Versus Tanzania." *World Politics* 56: 327–362.

———. 2005. "Poverty and Witch Killing." *Review of Economic Studies* 72: 1153–1172.

———. 2008. "Is It Africa's Turn? Progress in the World's Poorest Region." *Boston Review* 33(3) (May–June): 7–12.

Mikell, Gwendolyn. 1997. *African Feminism: The Politics of Survival in Sub-Saharan Africa.* Philadelphia: University of Pennsylvania Press.

Miles, William F. S. 2007. *Political Islam in West Africa: State-Society Relations Transformed.* Boulder: Lynne Rienner.

———. 2013. *Jews of Nigeria: An Afro-Judaic Odyssey.* Princeton: Markus Wiener.

Mill, John Stuart. 1987 [1848]. *Principles of Political Economy.* Fairfield, NJ: Augustus Kelley.

Mills, Kurt. 2015. *International Responses to Mass Atrocities in Africa: Responsibility to Protect, Prosecute, and Palliate.* Philadelphia: University of Pennsylvania Press.

Mingst, Karen. 1988. "Judicial System of Sub-Saharan Africa: An Analysis of Neglect." *African Studies Review* 31(1): 135–148.

Mittelman, James. 1999. "Rethinking the 'New Regionalism' in the Context of Globalization." In B. Hettne, A. Inotai, and O. Sunkel (eds.), *Globalism: The New Regionalisms and the Future of Security.* New York: St. Martin's, 25–53.

Mkandawire, Thandika. 1999. "Crisis Management and the Making of 'Choiceless Democracies' in Africa." In Richard Joseph (ed.), *The State, Conflict, and Democracy in Africa.* Boulder: Lynne Rienner, 119–136.

———. 2002. "The Terrible Toll of Post-Colonial Rebel Movements in Africa: Towards an Explanation of the Violence Against the Peasantry." *Journal of Modern African Studies* 40(2): 181–215.

Mkandawire, Thandika, and Adebayo Olukoshi. 1995. *Between Liberalisation and Oppression: The Politics of Structural Adjustment in Africa.* Dakar: Council for the Development of Social Science Research in Africa.

Moeller, Robert. 2010. "The Truth About Africom." *Foreign Policy,* 21 July.

Mohan, G., E. Brown, B. Milward, and A. B. Zack-Williams (eds.). 2000. *Structural Adjustment: Theory, Practice, and Impacts.* London: Routledge.

Mokuwa, Esther, Maarten Voors, Erwin Bulte, and Paul Richards. 2011. "Peasant Grievance and Insurgency in Sierra Leone: Judicial Serfdom as a Driver of Conflict." *African Affairs* 110(440): 339–366.

Moller, Lars Christian. 2015. *Ethiopia's Great Run: The Growth Acceleration and How to Pace It.* Washington, D.C.: World Bank Group.

Moller, Lars Christian, and K. Wacker. 2017. "Explaining Ethiopia's Growth Acceleration: The Role of Infrastructure and Macroeconomic Policy." *World Development* 96: 198–215.

Molutsi, Patrick P., and John D. Holm. 1990. "Developing Democracy When Civil Society Is Weak: The Case of Botswana." *African Affairs* 89(356): 323–340.

Monga, Célestin. 1996. *The Anthropology of Anger: Civil Society and Democracy in Africa.* Boulder: Lynne Rienner.

———. 1997. "Eight Problems with African Politics." *Journal of Democracy* 8(3): 156–170.

Moore, H., and T. Sanders. 2001. *Magical Interpretations and Material Realities: Modernity, Witchcraft, and the Occult in Postcolonial Africa.* London: Routledge.

Moore, Mick. 2004. "Revenues, State Formation, and the Quality of Governance in Developing Countries." *International Political Science Review* 25(3): 297–319.

Moore, Mick, Wilson Prichard, and Odd-Helge Fjeldstad. 2018. *Taxing Africa: Coercion, Reform, and Development.* London: Zed.

Morgenthau, Hans J. 2005 [1948]. *Politics Among Nations.* New York: McGraw-Hill.

Morgenthau, Ruth S. 1964. *Political Parties in French-Speaking West Africa.* Oxford: Clarendon.

Morrill, Constance. 2006. "Show Business and 'Lawfare' in Rwanda: Twelve Years After the Genocide." *Dissent* 53(3): 14–20.

Morrison, Donald G., Robert C. Mitchell, and John N. Paden. 1989. *Black Africa: A Comparative Handbook*. 2nd ed. New York: Paragon House and Irvington.

Mosley, Paul, Jane Harrigan, and John Toye. 1995. *Aid and Power: The World Bank and Policy-Based Lending*. 2nd ed. New York: Routledge.

Mosoti, Victor. 2006. "Africa in the First Decade of WTO Dispute Settlement." *Journal of International Economic Law* 9(2): 427–453.

Moss, Todd. 2011. *African Development: Making Sense of the Issues and Actors*. 2nd ed. Boulder: Lynne Rienner.

Moss, Todd, Gunilla Pettersson, and Nicolas van de Walle. 2006. "An Aid-Institutions Paradox? A Review Essay on Aid Dependency and State Building in Sub-Saharan Africa." Working Paper no. 74. Washington, D.C.: Center for Global Development.

Moyo, Dambisa. 2009. *Dead Aid: Why Aid Is Not Working and How There Is a Better Way for Africa*. London: Macmillan.

Mozaffar, Shaheen, and James Scarritt. 2005. "The Puzzle of African Party Systems." *Party Politics* 11(4): 399–421.

Muekalia, D. 2004. "Africa and China's Strategic Partnership." *African Security Review* 13(1): 5–11.

Muggah, Robert. 2002. *Development Held Hostage: Assessing the Effects of Small Arms on Human Development*. Geneva: United Nations Development Programme.

———, ed. 2009. *Security and Post-Conflict Reconstruction: Dealing with Fighters in the Aftermath of War*. New York: Routledge.

Murdock, George P. 1959. *Africa: Its People and Their Culture History*. New York: McGraw-Hill.

———. 1967. *Ethnographic Atlas*. Pittsburgh: University of Pittsburgh Press.

Muriaas, Ragnhild L. 2011. "Traditional Institutions and Decentralization: A Typology of Co-Existence in Sub-Saharan Africa." *Forum for Development Studies* 38(1): 87–107.

Murithi, Tim. 2009. "Inter-Governmental Authority on Development on the Ground: Comparing Interventions in Sudan and Somalia." *African Security* 2(2–3): 136–157.

———. 2012. "The African Union at Ten: An Appraisal." *African Affairs* 111(445): 662–669.

Musah, A.-F., and J. K. Feyemi (eds.). 2000. *Mercenaries: An African Security Dilemma*. London: Pluto.

Muthien, B., and Ian Taylor. 2002. "The Return of the Dogs of War? The Privatization of Security in Africa." In T. Biersteker and R. Hall (eds.), *The Emergence of Private Authority in Global Governance*. Cambridge: Cambridge University Press, 183–202.

Myers, Norman. 1989. "Environment and Security." *Foreign Policy* 47: 23–41.

———. 1993. *Ultimate Security: The Environmental Basis of Political Stability*. New York: Norton.

Naidu, Sanusha. 2010. "India's African Relations: In the Shadow of China?" In Fantu Cheru and Cyril Obi (eds.), *The Rise of China and India in Africa*. London: Zed, 34–52.

Najam, Adil, and Rachel Thrasher. 2012. Introduction to Adil Najam and Rachel Thrasher (eds.), *The Future of South-South Economic Relations*. London: Zed, 1–12.

Naldi, Gino J. 1989. *The Organization of African Unity: An Analysis of Its Role*. London: Mansell.

Nasong'o, Wanjala (ed.). 2015. *The Roots of Ethnic Conflict in Africa: From Grievance to Violence*. New York: Palgrave Macmillan.

Nathan, Laurie. 2016. *Community of Insecurity: SADC's Struggle for Peace and Security in Southern Africa*. New York: Routledge.

National Security Council. 2002. *National Security Strategy Report*. http://www.whitehouse.gov/nsc/nss.pdf.

Natsios, Andrew. 2012. *Sudan, South Sudan, and Darfur*. New York: Oxford University Press.

Ncube, Mthuli, and Charles Leyeka Lufumpa (eds.). 2015. *The Emerging Middle Class in Africa*. New York: Routledge.

Ndaywel e Nziem, Isidore. 1998. *Histoire générale du Congo: de l'héritage ancien à la république démocratique*. Brussels: De Boeck.

Ndegwa, Stephen. 1996. *The Two Faces of Civil Society: NGOs and Politics in Africa*. Bloomfield, CT: Kumarian.

———. 2002. "Decentralization in Africa: A Stocktaking Survey." Africa Region Working Paper no. 40. Washington, D.C.: World Bank.

Ndikumana, Leonce, and James K. Boyce. 1998. "Congo's Odious Debt: External Borrowing and Capital Flight in Zaire." *Development and Change* 29: 195–217.

Ndulu, Benno J., and Nicolas van de Walle. 1996. "Africa's Economic Renewal: From Consensus to Strategy." In Benno J. Ndulu and Nicolas van de Walle (eds.), *Agenda for Africa's Economic Renewal*. Washington, D.C.: Overseas Development Council, 3–31.

Negash, Tekeste, and Kjeti Tronvoll. 2000. *Brothers at War: Making Sense of the Eritrean-Ethiopian War*. London: Currey.

NEPAD Secretariat. 2001. "New Partnership for Africa's Development (NEPAD)." http://www.dfs.gov.za/events/Nepad.pdf.

Neuberger, Benyamin. 1991. "Irredentism and Politics in Africa." In Naomi Chazan (ed.), *Irredentism and International Politics*. Boulder: Lynne Rienner, 97–109.

Neubert, Dieter. 2016. "Kenya: An Unconscious Middle Class? Between Regional-Ethnic Political Mobilization and Middle Class Lifestyles." In Henning Melber (ed.), *The Rise of Africa's Middle Class: Myths, Realities, and Critical Engagements*. London: Zed, 110–128.

Neuman, Stephanie G. (ed.). 1998. *International Relations Theory and the Third World*. London: Macmillan.

New York Times. 1976. "Comoros Overkill." 15 January.

Ngepah, Nicholas, and Maxwell C. Udeagha. 2018. "African Regional Trade Agreements and Intra-African Trade." *Journal of Economic Integration* 33(1): 1176–1199.

Ngugi Wa Thiong'o. 1986. *Decolonising the Mind: The Politics of Language in African Literature*. London: Heinemann.

Niemann, Michael. 2000. *A Spatial Approach to Regionalisms in the Global Economy*. Basingstoke: Macmillan.

Nixon, Charles. 1972. "Self-Determination: The Nigeria/Biafra Case." *World Politics* 24(4): 473–497.

Nkrumah, Kwame. 1970. *Africa Must Unite*. New York: International Publishers.

Norris, Pippa, and Robert Mattes. 2013. "Does Ethnicity Determine Support for the Governing Party?" In Michael Bratton (ed.), *Voting and Democratic Citizenship in Africa*. Boulder: Lynne Rienner, 41–60.

North, Douglass. 1990. *Institutions, Institutional Change, and Economic Performance*. New York: Cambridge University Press.

Northrup, David. 2008. *Africa's Discovery of Europe, 1450–1850*. New York: Oxford University Press.

Nouwen, Sarah M. H. 2013. *Complementarity in the Line of Fire: The Catalysing Effect of the International Criminal Court in Uganda and Sudan*. Cambridge: Cambridge University Press.

Nsibambi, Apollo R. 1994. "The Restoration of Traditional Rulers." In H. B. Hansen and M. Twaddle (eds.), *From Chaos to Order: The Politics of Constitution-Making in Uganda*. London: Currey, 41–60.

Nugent, Paul. 1996. "Arbitrary Lines and the People's Minds: A Dissenting View on Colonial Boundaries in West Africa." In Paul Nugent and A. I. Asiwaju (eds.), *African Boundaries*. London: Pinter, 35–67.

———. 2002. *Smugglers, Secessionists, and Loyal Citizens on the Ghana-Togo Frontier: The Lie of the Borderlands Since 1914*. Athens: Ohio University Press.

———. 2010. "States and Social Contracts in Africa." *New Left Review* 63 (May–June): 35–66.

———. 2012. *Africa Since Independence*. 2nd ed. London: Palgrave Macmillan.

Nugent, Paul, and A. I. Asiwaju (eds.). 1996. *African Boundaries*. London: Pinter.

Nunn, Nathan. 2008. "The Long-Term Effects of Africa's Slave Trades." *Quarterly Journal of Economics* 123(1): 139–176.

Nunn, Nathan, and Leonard Wantchekon. 2009. "The Slave Trade and the Origins of Mistrust in Africa." Working Paper no. 14783. Cambridge, MA: National Bureau of Economic Research.

Nustad, Knut G. 2015. *Creating Africas: Struggles over Nature, Conservation, and Land*. London: Hurst.

Nyamnjoh, Francis B. 1991. *Mind Searching*. Lagos: Kucena Damian.

———. 1999. "Cameroon: A Country United by Ethnic Ambition and Difference." *African Affairs* 98(390): 101–118.

Nyerere, Julius. 1963. "A United States of Africa." *Journal of Modern African Studies* 1(1): 1–6.

Nzomo, Maria. 1996. "Kenya: The Women's Movement and Democratic Change." In Leonardo Villalón and Phillip Huxtable (eds.), *The African State at a Critical Juncture: Between Disintegration and Reconfiguration*. Boulder: Lynne Rienner, 167–184.

OAU (Organization of African Unity). 1964. "Border Disputes Among African States." AHG/Resolution 16(I). First Ordinary Session of the Assembly of Heads of State and

Government, Cairo, 17–21 July. http://www.africa-union.org/official_documents/Treaties
_Conventions_Protocols.

———. 1991. "Kampala Document: Towards a Conference on Security, Stability, Development, and Co-operation in Africa." http://www.africaleadership.org/rc/the%20kampala
%20document.pdf.

Oba, Gufu. 2016. *Climate Change Adaption in Africa: An Historical Ecology.* London: Routledge.

Obadare, Ebenzer. 2007. "White-Collar Fundamentalism: Interrogating Youth Religiosity on
Nigerian University Campuses." *Journal of Modern African Studies* 45: 517–537.

———, ed. 2013. *The Handbook of Civil Society in Africa.* London: Springer.

Obi, Cyril I. 2009. "Economic Community of West African States on the Ground: Comparing
Peacekeeping in Liberia, Sierra Leone, Guinea Bissau, and Côte d'Ivoire." *African Security* 2(2–3): 119–135.

O'Brien, Kevin A. 2000. "Private Military Companies and African Security 1990–98." In
Abdel-Fatau Musah and J. 'Kayode Fayemi (eds.), *Mercenaries: An African Security
Dilemma.* London: Pluto, 43–75.

Odgaard, Rie. 2006. *Land Rights and Land Conflicts in Africa: The Tanzania Case.* Copenhagen: Danish Institute for International Studies.

O'Donnell, Guillermo, Philippe C. Schmitter, and Lawrence Whitehead. 1986. *Transitions
from Authoritarian Rule.* Baltimore: Johns Hopkins University Press.

Odoom, Isaac, and Nathan Andrews. 2017. "What/Who Is Still Missing in International Relations
Scholarship? Situating Africa as an Agent in IR Theorizing." *Third World Quarterly* 38(1): 42–60.

OECD (Organisation for Economic Co-operation and Development). 2011a. "Development Aid
at a Glance—Statistics by Region: 2, Africa." http://www.oecd.org/dac/stats/regioncharts.

———. 2011b. "International Development Statistics." http://www.oecd.org/dataoecd
/50/17/5037721.htm.

———. 2013. "Development Aid at a Glance: Statistics by Regions." http://www.oecd
.org/dac/stats/World%20-%20Development%20Aid%20at%20a%20Glance%202013.pdf.

———. 2018. *Africa's Development Dynamics 2018: Growth, Jobs, and Inequalities.* Paris.

Ohlsson, Leif. 1999. *Environment, Scarcity, and Conflict: A Study of Malthusian Concerns.*
Göteborg: PADRIGU.

Olivier de Sardan, Jean-Pierre. 1999. "A Moral Economy of Corruption in Africa?" *Journal of
Modern African Studies* 37(1): 25–52.

———. 2008. "A la recherche des normes pratiques de gouvernance réelle en Afrique." APPP
Discussion Paper no. 5. London: Overseas Development Institute.

———. 2009a. "The Eight Modes of Local Governance in West Africa." Working Paper no. 4.
London: Africa Power and Politics Programme.

———. 2009b. "State Bureaucracy and Governance in Francophone West Africa: An Empirical Diagnosis and Historical Perspective." In Giorgio Blundo and Pierre-Yves le Meur
(eds.), *The Governance of Daily Life in Africa.* Leiden: Koninklijke Brill NV, 39–72.

Olivier de Sardan, Jean-Pierre, Thomas Bierschenk, and Jean-Pierre Chauveau. 2000.
Courtiers en développement: Les villages Africains en quête de projets. Paris: Karthala.

Oloka-Onyango, J. 1997. "The Question of Buganda in Contemporary Ugandan Politics."
Journal of Contemporary African Studies 15(2): 173–189.

Olowu, Dele, and James S. Wunsch. 2004. *Local Governance in Africa: The Challenges of
Democratic Decentralization.* Boulder: Lynne Rienner.

Olson, Mancur. 1971 [1965]. *The Logic of Collective Action: Public Goods and the Theory of
Groups.* Cambridge: Harvard University Press.

———. 1993. "Dictatorship, Democracy, and Development." *American Political Science
Review* 87(3): 567–576.

Olsson, Ola. 2003. "Geography and Institutions: A Review of Plausible and Implausible Linkages." Working Paper in Economics no. 106. Gothenburg: University of Gothenburg.

———. 2007. "On the Institutional Legacy of Mercantilist and Imperialist Colonialism."
Working Paper in Economics no. 247. Gothenburg: University of Gothenburg.

Olukoshi, A. 1999. "State, Conflict, and Democracy in Africa: The Complex Process of Renewal." In
Richard Joseph (ed.), *State, Conflict, and Democracy in Africa.* Boulder: Lynne Rienner, 451–465.

Omaar, Rakiya. 2004. "Peace-Building and Democracy: The Lessons of Somalia and Somaliland." In Richard Cobbold and Gregg Mills (eds.), *Global Challenges and Africa.* London: Royal United Services Institute for Defense and Security Studies, 83–92.

Omgba, Luc Désiré. 2009. "On the Duration of Political Power in Africa: The Role of Oil Rents." *Comparative Political Studies* 42(3): 416–436.

Osei, Anja. 2016. "Formal Party Organization and Informal Relations in African Parties: Evidence from Ghana." *Journal of Modern African Studies* 54(1): 37–66.

Otayek, René, and Benjamin Soares. 2007. "Introduction: Islam and Muslim Politics in Africa." In Benjamin Soares and René Otayek (eds.), *Islam and Muslim Politics in Africa.* New York: Palgrave Macmillan, 1–24.

Ottaway, Marina. 1999. *Africa's New Leaders: Democracy or State Reconstruction?* Washington, D.C.: Carnegie Endowment for International Peace.

————. 2003. *Democracy Challenged: The Rise of Semi-Authoritarianism.* Washington, D.C.: Carnegie Endowment for International Peace.

Ottaway, Marina, and David Ottaway. 1986. *Afrocommunism.* New York: Holmes and Meier.

Otunnu, Olara, and Michael Doyle (eds.). 1998. *Peacemaking and Peacekeeping for the New Century.* Boston: Rowman and Littlefield.

Owomoyela, Oyekan. 1994. "With Friends Like These . . . A Critique of Pervasive Anti-Africanisms in Current African Studies Epistemology and Methodology." *African Studies Review* 37(3): 77–101.

Oxfam. 1995. *The Oxfam Poverty Report.* Washington, D.C.

————. 2003. *Dumping Without Borders: How US Agricultural Policies Are Destroying the Livelihoods of Mexican Corn Farmers.* Washington, D.C.

Packenham, Thomas. 1992. *The Scramble for Africa: White Man's Conquest of the Dark Continent from 1876 to 1912.* New York: Avon.

Pallister, David. 2000. "Pennies from Heaven: Many of Nigeria's Missing Millions Were Laundered Through Greedy Banks in London." *The Guardian* (London), 7 September.

Paris, Roland. 2001. "Human Security: Paradigm Shift or Hot Air?" *International Security* 26(2): 87–102.

Parpart, Jane. 1989. *Women and Development in Africa.* Lanham: University Press of America.

Parpart, Jane L., and Lisa Thompson. 2012. "Engendering (In)Security and Conflict in African International Relations." In Scarlett Cornelissen, Fantu Cheru, and Timothy Shaw (eds.), *Africa and International Relations in the 21st Century.* New York: Palgrave Macmillan, 177–193.

Pateman, Roy. 1998. *Eritrea: Even the Stones Are Burning.* Lawrenceville, NJ: Red Sea.

Patman, Robert G. 1990. *The Soviet Union in the Horn of Africa: The Diplomacy of Intervention and Disengagement.* New York: Cambridge University Press.

Patterson, Amy S. 2006. *The Politics of AIDS in Africa.* Boulder: Lynne Rienner.

————. 2011. *The Church and AIDS in Africa: The Politics of Ambiguity.* Boulder: First Forum.

Pearce, Justin. 2002. "IMF: Angola's 'Missing Millions.'" *BBC News,* 18 October.

Pegg, Scott. 2006. "Can Policy Intervention Beat the Resource Curse? Evidence from the Chad-Cameroon Pipeline Project." *African Affairs* 405(418): 1–25.

————. 2009. "Briefing: Chronicle of a Death Foretold—The Collapse of the Chad-Cameroon Pipeline Project." *African Affairs* 108(431): 311–320.

Peiffer, Caryn, and Pierre Englebert. 2012. "Extraversion, Vulnerability to Donors, and Political Liberalization in Africa." *African Affairs* 111(444): 355–378.

Peltier, Jean-Philippe. 2010. "Rethinking Africa's Military." *American Foreign Policy Interests* 32: 219–228.

Pereira, Joao Márcio Mendes. 2016. "Recycling and Expansion: An Analysis of the World Bank Agenda (1989–2014)." *Third World Quarterly* 37(5): 818–839.

Perry, John, and T. Debey Sayndee. 2015. *African Truth Commissions and Transitional Justice.* Lanham: Lexington Books.

Peters, P. E. 2004. "Inequality and Social Conflict over Land in Africa." *Journal of Agrarian Change* 4(3): 269–314.

Pew Research Center. 2006a. "Pentecostalism in Africa." Pew Forum on Religion and Public Life. http://pewforum.org/Christian/Evangelical-Protestant-Churches/Overview-Pentecostalism -in-Africa.aspx.

————. 2006b. *Spirit and Power: A 10-Country Survey of Pentecostals.* Washington, D.C.: Pew Forum on Religion and Public Life.

————. 2010a. *Global Christianity.* Washington, D.C.: Pew Forum on Religion and Public Life.

————. 2010b. *Global Religious Landscape.* Washington, D.C.: Pew Forum on Religion and Public Life.

————. 2015. *The Future of World Religions: Population Growth Projections, 2010–2050.* Washington, D.C.: Pew Forum on Religion and Public Life.

————. 2017. *The Changing Global Religious Landscape.* Washington, D.C.: Pew Forum on Religion and Public Life.

Phillips, Jon, Elena Hailwood, and Andrew Brooks. 2016. "Sovereignty, the 'Resource Curse,' and the Limits of Good Governance: A Political Economy of Oil in Ghana." *Review of African Political Economy* 43(147): 26–42.

Pierce, Steven. 2016. *Moral Economies of Corruption: State Formation and Political Culture in Nigeria.* Durham, N.C.: Duke University Press.

Piombo, Jessica (ed.). 2015. *The US Military in Africa: Enhancing Security and Development?* Boulder: First Forum.

Piot, Charles. 2010. *Nostalgia for the Future: West Africa After the Cold War.* Chicago: University of Chicago Press.

Pitcher, Anne, Mary Moran, and Michael Johnston. 2009. "Rethinking Patrimonialism and Neopatrimonialism in Africa." *African Studies Review* 52(1) (April): 125–156.

Pitcher, M. Anne. 2012. *Party Politics and Economic Reform in Africa's Democracies.* New York: Cambridge University Press.

Polgreen, Lydia, and Alan Cowell. 2009. "Soldiers Kill Guinea-Bissau's President After Death of Army Chief, Diplomats Say." *New York Times,* 2 March.

Pommerolle, Marie-Emmanuelle, and Hans de Marie Heungoup. 2017. "The 'Anglophone Crisis': A Tale of the Cameroonian Postcolony." *African Affairs* 116(464): 526–538.

Poncelet, Marc, Géraldine André, and Tom de Herdt. 2010. "La survie de l'école primaire congolaise (RDC): Héritage colonial, hybridité et résilience." *AutrePart* 54: 23–42.

Posner, Daniel. 2004a. "Measuring Ethnic Fractionalization in Africa." *American Journal of Political Science* 48(4): 849–863.

————. 2004b. "The Political Salience of Cultural Difference: Why Chewas and Tumbukas Are Allies in Zambia and Adversaries in Malawi." *American Political Science Review* 98(4): 529–545.

————. 2005. *Institutions and Ethnic Politics in Africa.* New York: Cambridge University Press.

Posner, Daniel, and Daniel Young. 2007. "The Institutionalization of Political Power in Africa." *Journal of Democracy* 18(3): 126–140.

Potholm, Christian. 1979. *The Theory and Practice of African Politics.* Englewood Cliffs, NJ: Prentice Hall.

Poupko, Eliezer S. 2011. "Constitutional Design for Conflict Management in Africa: A Cross-Country Index." Paper presented at the conference "Constitutional Design and Conflict Management in Africa," Austin, October.

Powers, Samantha. 2003. *A Problem from Hell: America and the Age of Genocide.* New York: HarperPerennial.

Prescott, J. R. V. 1972. *Political Geography.* London: Methuen.

————. 1987. *Political Frontiers and Boundaries.* London: Allen and Unwin.

Press, Steven. 2015. *Rogue Empires: Contracts and Conmen in Europe's Scramble for Africa.* Cambridge: Harvard University Press.

Prozesky, Martin. 2009. "Is the Secular State the Root of Our Moral Problems in South Africa?" *Alternation* 3: 237–253.

Prunier, Gérard. 2009. *Africa's World War: Congo, the Rwandan Genocide, and the Making of a Continental Catastrophe.* New York: Oxford University Press.

Prunier, Gérard, and Rachel M. Gisselquist. 2003. "The Sudan: A Successfully Failed State." In Robert Rotberg (ed.), *State Failure and State Weakness in a Time of Terror.* Washington, D.C.: Brookings Institution, 101–128.

Przeworski, Adam, Michael Alvarez, José A. Cheibub, and Fernando Limongi. 2000. *Democracy and Development: Political Institutions and Material Well-Being in the World, 1950–1990.* Cambridge: Cambridge University Press.

Putnam, Robert. 1992. *Making Democracy Work: Civil Traditions in Modern Italy.* Princeton: Princeton University Press.

Quinn, John. 2002. *The Road Oft Traveled: Development Policies and Majority State Ownership of Industry in Africa.* New York: Praeger.

Radelet, Steven. 2003. "Bush and Foreign Aid." *Foreign Affairs* 82(5): 104–117.

————. 2010. "Emerging Africa: How 17 Countries Are Leading the Way." Washington, D.C.: Center for Global Development.

Raeymaekers, Timothy. 2014. *Violent Capitalism and Hybrid Identity in the Eastern Congo: Power to the Margins*. New York: Cambridge University Press.

Raffer, K. 2001. "Cotonou: Slowly Undoing Lomé's Concept of Partnership." Discussion Paper no. 20. Manchester: Development Studies Association.

Rakner, Lise, et al. 2004. *The Budget as Theatre: The Formal and Informal Institutional Makings of the Budget Process in Malawi*. Bergen: Christen Michelsen Institute.

Randall, Vicky, and Lars Svåsand. 2001. "Political Parties and Democratic Consolidation in Africa." Paper prepared for Joint Sessions of Workshops meeting, European Consortium for Political Research, Grenoble, 6–11 April.

Ranger, Terrence O. 1983. "The Invention of Tradition in Colonial Africa." In Eric Hobsbawm and Terrence Ranger (eds.), *The Invention of Tradition*. New York: Cambridge University Press, 211–262.

———. 1993. "The Invention of Tradition Revisited: The Case of Colonial Africa." In Terrence Ranger and Olufemi Vaughan (eds.), *Legitimacy and the State in Twentieth-Century Africa: Essays in Honour of AHM Kirk-Greene*. Oxford: Saint Anthony's College, 62–111.

Rathbone, Richard. 2000. *Nkrumah and the Chiefs: The Politics of Chieftaincy in Ghana, 1951–1960*. Athens: Ohio University Press.

Ravenhill, John. 1985. *Collective Clientelism: The Lomé Conventions and North-South Relations*. New York: Columbia University Press.

———. 1991. "Africa and Europe: The Dilution of a 'Special Relationship.'" In John Harbeson and Donald Rothchild (eds.), *Africa in World Politics*. Boulder: Westview, 179–201.

Ray, Donald. 1998. "Chief-State Relations in Ghana: Divided Sovereignty and Legitimacy." In E. Adriaan B. van Rouveroy van Nieuwaal and Werner Zips (eds.), *Sovereignty, Legitimacy, and Power in West African Societies: Perspectives from Legal Anthropology*. Hamburg: Lit Verlag, 48–69.

Reid, Cate. 2018. "Africa's New Debt Crisis." *Africa Report* 103 (September): 24–26.

Reilly, Benjamin. 2001. *Democracy in Divided Societies: Electoral Engineering for Conflict Management*. New York: Cambridge University Press.

Reno, William. 1995. *Corruption and Politics in Sierra Leone*. Cambridge: Cambridge University Press.

———. 1997a. "African Weak States and Commercial Alliances." *African Affairs* 96(383): 165–186.

———. 1997b. "Sovereignty and Personal Rule in Zaïre." *African Studies Quarterly* 1(3): 39–64.

———. 1998. *Warlord Politics and African States*. Boulder: Lynne Rienner.

———. 2001. "How Sovereignty Matters: International Markets and the Political Economy of Local Politics in Weak States." In Thomas Callaghy, R. Kassimir, and Robert Latham (eds.), *Intervention and Transnationalism in Africa*. Cambridge: Cambridge University Press, 197–215.

———. 2004. "The Roots of Sectarian Violence, and Its Cure." In Robert I. Rotberg (ed.), *Crafting the New Nigeria: Confronting the Challenges*. Boulder: Lynne Rienner, 219–238.

———. 2007. "Liberia: The LURDs of the New Church." In Morten Bøås and Kevin Dunn (eds.), *African Guerrillas: Raging Against the Machine*. Boulder: Lynne Rienner, 69–80.

———. 2011. *Warfare in Independent Africa*. New York: Cambridge University Press.

Reporters Without Borders. 2018. "World Press Freedom Index." https://rsf.org/en/ranking.

Republic of Uganda. 2007. "Climate Change: Ugandan National Adaptation Programmes of Action." http://unfccc.int/resource/docs/napa/uga01.pdf.

Reynolds, Andrew. 2002. *The Architecture of Democracy: Constitutional Design, Conflict Management, and Democracy*. New York: Oxford University Press.

Reyntjens, Filip. 2009. *The Great African War: Congo and Regional Geopolitics, 1996–2006*. New York: Cambridge University Press.

———. 2018. "Understanding Rwandan Politics Through the *Longue Durée:* From the Precolonial to the Post-Genocide Era." *Journal of Eastern African Studies* 12(3): 514–532.

Rhoads, Emily P. 2016. *Taking Sides in Peacekeeping: Impartiality and the Future of the United Nations*. Oxford: Oxford University Press.

Ribot, Jesse, Arun Agrawal, and Anne M. Larson. 2006. "Recentralizing While Decentralizing: How National Governments Reappropriate Forest Resources." *World Development* 34(11): 1864–1886.

Richards, Paul. 1996. *Fighting for the Rain Forest: War, Youth, & Resources in Sierra Leone*. Oxford: Currey.

―――. 2005a. "Green Book Millenarians? The Sierra Leone War Within the Perspective of an Anthropology of Religion." In Niels Kastfelt (ed.), *Religion and African Civil Wars*. London: Hurst, 119–146.

―――. 2005b. "New War: An Ethnographic Approach." In Paul Richards, *No Peace, No War: An Anthropology of Contemporary Armed Conflicts*. Oxford: Currey, 1–21.

―――, ed. 2005c. *No Peace, No War: An Anthropology of Contemporary Armed Conflicts*. Oxford: Currey.

Riddell, J. B. 1992. "Things Fall Apart Again: Structural Adjustment Programmes in Sub-Saharan Africa." *Journal of Modern African Studies* 30(1): 53–68.

Riker, William. 1962. *The Theory of Political Coalitions*. New Haven: Yale University Press.

Ritchie, M., et al. 2003. *United States Dumping on World Agricultural Markets*. Minneapolis: Institute for Agriculture and Trade Policy.

Robinson, Amanda Lea. 2014. "National Versus Ethnic Identification in Africa: Modernization, Colonial Legacy, and the Origins of Territorial Nationalism." *World Politics* 66(4): 709–746.

Robinson, Pearl. 1994. "The National Conference Phenomenon in Francophone Africa." *Comparative Studies in Society and History* 36(3): 575–610.

Robinson, Piers. 2002. *The CNN Effect: The Myth of News, Foreign Policy, and Intervention*. London: Routledge.

Robinson, Ronald, and John Gallagher. 1961. *Africa and the Victorians*. New York: Palgrave Macmillan.

Rodney, Walter. 1981. *How Europe Underdeveloped Africa*. London: Bogle-L'Ouverture.

Roessler, Philip. 2011. "The Enemy Within: Personal Rule, Coups, and Civil War in Africa." *World Politics* 63(2): 300–346.

―――. 2016. *Ethnic Politics and State Power in Africa: The Logic of the Coup–Civil War Trap*. Cambridge: Cambridge University Press.

Roessler, Philip, and Marc Howard. 2009. "Post–Cold War Political Regimes: When Do Elections Matter?" In Staffan Lindberg (ed.), *Democratization by Elections: A New Mode of Transition?* Baltimore: Johns Hopkins University Press, 101–127.

Rolandsen, Øystein H. 2005. *Guerrilla Government: Political Changes in the Southern Sudan in the 1990s*. Uppsala: Nordic Africa Institute.

―――. 2011. "A Quick Fix? A Retrospective Analysis of the Sudan Comprehensive Peace Agreement." *Review of African Political Economy* 38(130): 551–564.

Rolandsen, Øystein H., and Ingrid Marie Breidlid. 2012. "A Critical Analysis of Cultural Explanations for the Violence in Jonglei State, South Sudan." *Conflict Trends* 1: 49–56.

Romero, Patricia W. 2015. *African Women: A Historical Panorama*. Princeton, NJ: Markus Wiener.

Ross, Michael. 1999. "The Political Economy of the Resource Curse." *World Politics* 51(2): 297–322.

―――. 2001. "Does Oil Hinder Democracy?" *World Politics* 53(3): 325–361.

―――. 2012. *The Oil Curse: How Petroleum Wealth Shapes the Development of Nations*. Princeton: Princeton University Press.

Rotberg, Robert. 1962. "The Rise of African Nationalism: The Case of East and Central Africa." *World Politics* 15(1): 75–90.

―――. 2002. "Failed States in a World of Terror." *Foreign Affairs* 81(4): 1–13.

Rothchild, Donald. 1997. *Managing Ethnic Conflict in Africa*. Washington, D.C.: Brookings Institution.

Rothchild, Donald, and Naomi Chazan. 1988. *The Precarious Balance: State and Society in Africa*. Boulder: Westview.

Rothchild, Donald, and Letitia Lawson. 1994. "The Interactions Between State and Civil Society in Africa: From Deadlock to New Routines." In John Harbeson, Donald Rothchild, and Naomi Chazan (eds.), *Civil Society and the State in Africa*. Boulder: Lynne Rienner, 255–281.

Rothchild, Donald, and Victor Olorunsola (eds.). 1983. *States Versus Ethnic Claims: African Policy Dilemmas*. Boulder: Westview.

Rotinwa, Ayodeji. 2018. "Lagos: The Taxman Cometh." *Africa Report* 101: 28–31.

Royal African Society. 2008. "Excerpts from the Speech of Nicolas Sarkozy." African Commentaries. http://www.royalafricansociety.org/ras-publications-and-reports/416.html.

Sachs, Jeffrey D. 2000. "Tropical Underdevelopment." Working Paper no. 57. Cambridge: Harvard University, Center for International Development.

———. 2005. *The End of Poverty: Economic Possibilities for Our Time*. New York: Penguin.

Sachs, Jeffrey D., and Andrew M. Warner. 1997. "Fundamental Sources of Long-Run Growth." *American Economic Review* 87(2): 184–188.

Salih, M. A. Mohamed. 2004. "Islamic NGOs in Africa: The Promise and Peril of Islamic Voluntarism." In Alex de Waal (ed.), *Islamism and Its Enemies in the Horn of Africa*. Bloomington: Indiana University Press, 146–181.

———. 2005. *African Parliaments: Between Governance and Government*. New York: Palgrave Macmillan.

Samatar, Abdi. 1999. *An African Miracle: State and Class Leadership and Colonial Legacy in Botswana*. Portsmouth, NH: Heinemann.

Samatar, Abdi, and Sophie Oldfield. 1995. "Class and Effective State Institutions: The Botswana Meat Commission." *Journal of Modern African Studies* 33(4): 651–668.

Samatar, Said S. 1985. "The Somali Dilemma: Nation in Search of a State." In A. I. Asiwaju (ed.), *Partitioned Africans*. New York: St. Martin's, 155–193.

Sandbrook, Richard. 1972. "Patrons, Clients, and Factions: New Dimensions of Conflict Analysis in Africa." *Canadian Journal of Political Science* 5(1): 104–119.

———. 1985. *The Politics of Africa's Economic Stagnation*. New York: Cambridge University Press.

———. 1986. "The State and Economic Stagnation in Tropical Africa." *World Development* 14(3): 319–332.

Saul, John. 1979. *The State and Revolution in East Africa*. New York: Monthly Review.

SCAD (Social Conflict in Africa Database). 2017. "Social Conflict in Africa Database Version 3.3." Austin: University of Texas. http://strausscenter.org/scad.html.

Schatzberg, Michael. 1988. *The Dialectics of Oppression in Zaire*. Bloomington: Indiana University Press.

———. 1991. *Mobutu or Chaos? The United States and Zaïre, 1960–1990*. Lanham: University Press of America.

———. 2001. *Political Legitimacy in Middle Africa: Father, Family, Food*. Bloomington: Indiana University Press.

Schedler, Andres. 2006. *Electoral Authoritarianism: The Dynamics of Unfree Competition*. Boulder: Lynne Rienner.

Scheele, Judith. 2015. *Smugglers and Saints of the Sahara: Regional Connectivity in the Twentieth Century*. Cambridge: Cambridge University Press.

Schoeman, Maxi, and Marie Muller. 2009. "Southern African Development Community as Regional Peacekeeper: Myth or Reality?" *African Security* 2(2–3): 175–192.

Schomerus, Mareike, Tim Allen, and Koen Vlassenroot. 2011. "Obama Takes on the LRA." *Foreign Affairs,* November. http://www.foreignaffairs.com/articles/136673/mareike-schomerus -tim-allen-and-koen-vlassenroot/obama-takes-on-the-lra.

Schraeder, Peter. 1994. *United States Foreign Policy Toward Africa: Incrementalism, Crisis, and Change*. Cambridge: Cambridge University Press.

———. 2004. *African Politics and Society: A Mosaic in Transformation*. Belmont, CA: Wadsworth.

Scott, D. 2008. "The Great Power 'Great Game' Between India and China: The Logic of Geography." *Geopolitics* 13(1): 1–26.

Scott, James. 1999. *Seeing Like a State: How Certain Schemes to Improve the Human Condition Have Failed*. New York: Yale University Press.

———. 2009. *The Art of Not Being Governed: An Anarchist History of Upland Southeast Asia*. New Haven: Yale University Press.

Sen, Amartya. 1982. *Poverty and Famines: An Essay on Entitlements and Deprivation*. Oxford: Clarendon.

Sesay, Amadu, Olusola Ojo, and Ordobola Fasenhun. 1984. *The OAU After Twenty Years*. Boulder: Westview.

Severino, Jean-Michel, and Olivier Ray. 2010. *Africa's Moment*. Cambridge: Polity.

Sharma, Serena. 2015. *The Responsibility to Protect and the International Criminal Court: Protection and Prosecution in Kenya*. London: Routledge.

Shaw, Carolyn Martin. 2015. *Women and Power in Zimbabwe: Promises of Feminism*. Urbana: University of Illinois Press.

Shaw, Rosalind. 2010. "Linking Justice with Reintegration? Ex-Combatants and the Sierra Leone Experiment." In Rosalind Shaw and Lars Waldorf, *Localizing Transitional Justice:*

Interventions and Priorities After Mass Violence. Stanford: Stanford University Press, 111–132.

Shaw, Rosalind, and Lars Waldorf, with Pierre Hazan (eds.). 2010. *Localizing Transitional Justice: Interventions and Priorities After Mass Violence.* Stanford: Stanford University Press.

Shearer, David. 1997. "Exploring the Limits of Consent: Conflict Resolution in Sierra Leone." *Millennium* 26(3): 845–860.

Shinn, David, and J. Eisenman. 2005. "Dueling Priorities for Beijing in the Horn of Africa." *China Brief* 5(21): 1–4.

Shirbon, Estelle. 2009. "French Power Brokers Convicted over Arms to Angola." Reuters, 27 October.

Shubin, Vladimir. 2004. "Russia and Africa Moving in the Right Direction?" In Ian Taylor and Paul Williams (eds.), *Africa in International Politics: External Involvement on the Continent.* New York: Routledge, 102–115.

Shugart, Matthew. 1998. "The Inverse Relationship Between Party Strength and Executive Strength: A Theory of Politicians' Constitutional Choices." *British Journal of Political Science* 28(1): 1–29.

Sigman, Rachel, and Staffan Lindberg. 2017. "Neopatrimonialism and Democracy: An Empirical Investigation of Africa's Political Regimes." Working Paper Series 2017:56. Gothenburg: Varieties of Democracy Institute, University of Gothenburg.

Simon, David. 2003. "Regional Developmental-Environment Discourses, Policies, and Practices in Post-Apartheid South Africa." In A. Grant and F. Söderbaum (eds.), *The New Regionalisms in Africa.* Aldershot: Ashgate, 67–89.

Singer, Barnett, and John Langdon. 1998. "France's Imperial Legacy." *Contemporary Review* 27(2): 231–238.

Siplon, Patricia. 2005. "AIDS and Patriarchy: Ideological Obstacles to Effective Policy Making." In Amy S. Patterson (ed.), *The African State and the AIDS Crisis.* Burlington: Ashgate, 17–36.

Sklar, Richard L. 1963. *Nigerian Political Parties: Power in an Emerging African Nation.* Princeton: Princeton University Press.

———. 1979. "The Nature of Class Domination in Africa." *Journal of Modern African Studies* 17(4): 531–551.

———. 1993. "The African Frontier for Political Science." In Robert Bates, V. Mudimbe, and Jean O'Barr (eds.), *Africa and the Disciplines: The Contributions of Research in Africa to the Social Sciences and Humanities.* Chicago: University of Chicago Press, 83–110.

———. 1999. "African Polities: The Next Generation." In Richard Joseph (ed.), *State, Conflict, and Democracy in Africa.* Boulder: Lynne Rienner, 165–178.

Small Arms Survey. 2013. *Everyday Dangers.* Cambridge: Cambridge University Press.

Smillie, Ian. 1995. *The Alms Bazaar: Altruism Under Fire—Non-Profit Organisations and International Development.* London: IT Publications.

———. 1997. "NGOs and Development Assistance: A Change in Mind-Set?" *Third World Quarterly* 18(3): 563–577.

Smith, Adam. 1976 [1776]. *An Inquiry into the Nature and Causes of the Wealth of Nations.* Chicago: University of Chicago Press.

Smith, Anthony D. 1986. *The Ethnic Origins of Nations.* Oxford: Blackwell.

Smith, Daniel Jordan. 2007. *A Culture of Corruption: Everyday Deception and Popular Discontent in Nigeria.* Princeton: Princeton University Press.

Smith, Elie. 2016. "In Central Africa, Citizens Are Using Social Media to Build Democracy—Here's How." *Washington Post.* April 6.

Smith, Stephen, and Antoine Glaser. 1992. *Ces messieurs Afrique: Le Paris-village du continent noir.* Paris: Calmann-Levy.

Smith, Zeric Kay. 2001. "Mali's Decade of Democracy." *Journal of Democracy* 12(3): 73–79.

Sneyd, Adam. 2015. "The Poverty of 'Poverty Reduction': The Case of African Cotton." *Third World Quarterly* 36(1): 55–74.

Soares, Benjamin F. 2006. "Islam in Mali in the Neoliberal Era." *African Affairs* 105(418): 77–96.

Soares, Benjamin F., and René Otayek (eds.). 2007. *Islam and Muslim Politics in Africa.* New York: Palgrave Macmillan.

Soares de Oliveira, Ricardo. 2007. *Oil and Politics in the Gulf of Guinea.* New York: Columbia University Press.

Söderbaum, Frederik, and Rodrigo Tavares. 2009. "Problematizing Regional Organizations in African Security." *African Security* 2(2–3): 69–81.

Söderström, Johanna. 2015. *Peacebuilding and Ex-Combatants: Political Reintegration in Liberia.* New York: Routledge.

Sokoloff, Kenneth L., and Stanley L. Engerman. 2000. "Institutions, Factor Endowments, and Paths of Development in the New World." *Journal of Economic Perspectives* 14(3): 217–232.

Solodovnikov, V. G. (ed.). 2000. *Russia and Africa: A Look to the Future.* Moscow: RAN Institute for African Studies.

Solomon, Hussein. 2001. "Realism and Its Critics." In Peter Vale, Larry A. Swatuk, and Bertil Oden (eds.), *Theory, Change, and Southern Africa's Future.* New York: Palgrave Macmillan, 34–57.

Southall, Roger. 2013. *Liberation Movements in Power: Party and State in Southern Africa.* Suffolk: Currey.

Spears, Ian S. 2004. "States-Within-States: An Introduction to Their Empirical Attributes." In Paul Kingston and Ian S. Spears (eds.), *States Within States: Incipient Political Entities in the Post–Cold War Era.* New York: Palgrave Macmillan, 15–34.

Spero, Joan, and Jeffrey Hart. 2003. *The Politics of International Economic Relations.* Boston: Wadsworth.

Spruyt, Hendrik. 1994. *The Sovereign State and Its Competitors.* Princeton: Princeton University Press.

Stanley, Henry Morton. 1988 [1878]. *Through the Dark Continent.* 2 vols. New York: Dover.

Stasavage, David. 1997. "The CFA Franc Zone and Fiscal Discipline." *Journal of African Economies* 6(1): 132–167.

State Geological Committee of the USSR. 1964. *Atlas Narodov Mira.* Moscow: Department of Geodesy and Cartography.

Statistics South Africa. 2003. *Census 2001: Census in Brief.* Pretoria: Statistics South Africa.

Stearns, Jason. 2011. *Dancing in the Glory of Monsters: The Collapse of the Congo and the Great War of Africa.* New York: PublicAffairs.

Stein, Howard. 1998. "Japanese Aid to Africa: Pattern, Motivation, and the Role of Structural Adjustment." *Journal of Development Studies* 35(2): 27–53.

Strandsbjerg, Amilla. 2000. "Kérékou, God, and the Ancestors: Religion and the Conception of Political Power in Benin." *African Affairs* 99(396): 395–414.

Straus, Scott. 2008. *The Order of Genocide: Race, Power, and War in Rwanda.* Ithaca: Cornell University Press.

Strayer, Joseph. 1970. *On the Medieval Origin of the Modern State.* Princeton: Princeton University Press.

Stremlau, John J. 2017. "An Early Diagnosis of Trump's Impact on US-African Relations and on Sustainable Democracy in the US and Africa." Special report. Johannesburg: South African Institute of International Affairs.

Suberu, R. T. 1997. "Crisis and Collapse: June–November 1993." In Larry Diamond, A. Kirk-Greene, and O. Oyediran (eds.), *Transition Without End: Nigerian Politics and Civil Society Under Babangida.* Boulder: Lynne Rienner, 281–302.

Suttner, Raymond. 2004. "Transformation of Political Parties in Africa Today." *Transformations* 55: 1–27.

Swatuk, Larry. 2005. "Environmental Security." In M. Betsill, K. Hochstetler, and D. Stevis (eds.), *Palgrave Advances in International Environmental Politics.* London: Palgrave Macmillan, 203–230.

Swedlund, Haley J. 2017. *The Development Dance: How Donors and Recipients Negotiate the Delivery of Foreign Aid.* Ithaca: Cornell University Press.

Swidler, Ann, and Susan Cotts Watkins (eds.). 2018. *A Fraught Embrace: The Romance and Reality of AIDS Altruism in Africa.* Princeton: Princeton University Press.

Swift, Jeremy. 1996. "Desertification: Narratives, Winners, and Losers." In Melissa Leach and Robin Mearns (eds.), *Lie of the Land: Challenging Received Wisdom on the African Environment.* Oxford: Currey, 73–90.

Szanton, David (ed.). 2004. *The Politics of Knowledge: Area Studies and the Disciplines.* Berkeley: University of California Press.

Tama, Clarisse. 2009. "Les 'enseignants de l'ombre' ou les 'travailleurs au noir' de l'état et la co-production du service public éducatif au Bénin." Paper presented at the conference "States at Work in Sub-Saharan Africa," LASDEL, Niamey.

Tarnoff, Curt. 2011. *Millennium Challenge Corporation: Report for Congress.* Washington, D.C.: Congressional Research Service.

Taylor, Charles Lewis, Michael C. Hudson, and Bruce M. Russett. 1972. *World Handbook of Political and Social Indicators.* New Haven: Yale University Press.

Taylor, Ian. 1998. "China's Foreign Policy Towards Africa in the 1990s." *Journal of Modern African Studies* 36(3): 443–460.

———. 2005a. *NEPAD: Towards Africa's Development or Another False Start?* Boulder: Lynne Rienner.

———. 2005b. "NEPAD and the Global Political Economy: Towards the African Century or Another False Start?" In Jimi Adésína, Yao Graham, and Adebayo Olukoshi (eds.), *Africa and Development Challenges in the New Millennium: The NEPAD Debate.* London: Zed, 63–85.

———. 2009. *China's New Role in Africa.* Boulder: Lynne Rienner.

———. 2010. *The International Relations of Sub-Saharan Africa.* New York: Continuum.

———. 2012. "India's Rise in Africa." *International Affairs* 88(2): 779–798.

———. 2014. *Africa Rising: BRICS—Diversifying Dependency.* Oxford: Currey.

———. 2016. "Dependency Redux: Why Africa Is Not Rising." *Review of African Political Economy* 43(147): 8–25.

Taylor, Ian, and Paul Williams (eds.). 2004a. *Africa in International Politics: External Involvement on the Continent.* New York: Routledge.

———. 2004b. "Introduction: Understanding Africa's Place in World Politics." In Ian Taylor and Paul Williams (eds.), *Africa in International Politics: External Involvement on the Continent.* New York: Routledge, 1–22.

Teixeira, N. S. 2003. "Between Africa and Europe: Portuguese Foreign Policy, 1890–2000." In A. C. Pinto (ed.), *Contemporary Portugal: Politics, Society, and Culture.* New York: Columbia University Press, 85–118.

Ter Haar, Gerrie. 2003. "A Wondrous God: Miracles in Contemporary Africa." *African Affairs* 102(408): 409–428.

Terray, Emmanuel. 1986. "Le climatiseur et la véranda." In *Afrique plurielle: Hommage à Georges Balandier.* Paris: Karthala, 36–44.

Thiriot, Céline. 2002. "Le rôle de la société civile dans la transition et la consolidation démocratique en Afrique: Éléments de réflexion à partir du cas du Mali." *Revue Internationale de Politique Comparée* 9(2): 277–295.

Thisen, Jean K. 1989. "Alternative Approaches to Economic Integration in Africa." *Africa Development* 14(1): 19–60.

Thom, Derrick J. 1975. *The Niger-Nigeria Boundary, 1890–1906: A Study of Ethnic Frontiers and a Colonial Boundary.* Athens: Ohio University, Center for International Studies.

Thomas, Caroline. 2000. *Global Governance, Development, and Human Security.* London: Pluto.

———. 2004. "The International Financial Institutions' Relations with Africa: Insights from the Issue of Representation and Voice." In Ian Taylor and Paul Williams (eds.), *Africa in International Politics: External Involvement on the Continent.* New York: Routledge, 174–194.

Thornton, John Kelly. 1998. *Africa and Africans in the Making of the Atlantic World, 1400–1800.* New York: Cambridge University Press.

Throup, David. 1987. *Economic and Social Origins of Mau Mau, 1945–53.* Oxford: Currey.

Thurston, Alex. 2014. "Muslim Politics and Shari'a in Kano State, Northern Nigeria." *African Affairs* 114(454): 28–51.

Tiba, Firew. 2011. "The Trial of Mengistu and Other Derg Members for Genocide, Torture, and Summary Executions in Ethiopia." In Chacha Murungu and Japhet Biegon (eds.), *Prosecuting International Crimes in Africa.* Pretoria: University Law Press, 163–184.

Tidjani Alou, Mahaman. 2006. "Corruption in the Legal System." In Giorgio Blundo and Olivier de Sardan (eds.), *Everyday Corruption and the State: Citizens and Public Officials in Africa.* London: Zed, 137–177.

Tilly, Charles. 1990. *Coercion, Capital, and European States, A.D. 990–1992.* Malden, MA: Wiley-Blackwell.

Titeca, Kristof, and Tom de Herdt. 2011. "Real Governance Beyond the 'Failed State': Negotiating Education in the Democratic Republic of Congo." *African Affairs* 110(439): 213–231.

Titeca, Kristof, and Albert Malukisa Nkuku. 2018. "How Kinshasa's Markets Are Captured by Powerful Private Interests." *The Conversation,* 11 March. https://theconversation.com/how-kinshasas-markets-are-captured-by-powerful-private-interests-88602.

Toulmin, Camille. 2009. *Climate Change in Africa.* London: Zed.

Touray, Omar Alieu. 2016. *The African Union: The First Ten Years.* Lanham: Rowman and Littlefield.

Trefon, Theodore. 1989. *French Policy Toward Zaïre During the Giscard d'Estaing Presidency.* Bruxelles: Centre d'Étude et de Documentation Africaines.

———, ed. 2004. *Reinventing Order in the Congo: How People Respond to State Failure in Kinshasa.* London: Zed.

———. 2011a. *Congo Masquerade: The Political Culture of Aid Inefficiency and Reform Failure.* London: Zed.

———. 2011b. "Failed State: Can DR Congo Recover?" *BBC News,* 21 November. http://www.bbc.co.uk/news/world-africa-15775445.

Trefon, Theodore, with Balthazar Ngoy. 2007. *Parcours administratif dans un état en faillite: Récits populaires de Lubumbashi.* Paris: L'Harmattan.

Trinitapoli, Janet, and Alexander Weinreb. 2012. *Religion and AIDS in Africa.* New York: Oxford University Press.

Tripp, Aili Mary. 2000. *Women and Politics in Uganda.* Madison: University of Wisconsin Press.

———. 2001. "The Politics of Autonomy and Cooptation in Africa: The Case of the Ugandan Women's Movement." *Journal of Modern African Studies* 39(1): 101–128.

———. 2010. *Museveni's Uganda: Paradoxes of Power in a Hybrid Regime.* Boulder: Lynne Rienner.

———. 2016. "Women's Mobilization for Legislative Political Representation in Africa." *Review of African Political Economy* 43(149): 382–399.

Tronchon, Jacques. 1986. *L'insurrection Malgache de 1947.* Paris: Karthala.

Tull, Denis. 2004. *The Reconfiguration of Political Order in Postcolonial Africa: A Case Study from North Kivu (DR Congo).* Hamburg: African Studies Center.

———. 2006. "China's Engagement in Africa: Scope, Significance, and Consequences." *Journal of Modern African Studies* 44(3): 459–479.

———. 2011. "Weak States and Successful Elites: Extraversion Strategies in Africa." Research Paper no. 9. Berlin: SWP.

———. 2017. "The Limits and Unintended Consequences of UN Peace Enforcement: The Force Intervention Brigade in the DR Congo." *International Peacekeeping* 25(2): 1–24.

Turner, Thomas. 2007. *The Congo Wars: Conflict, Myth, and Reality.* London: Zed.

Turshen, Meredith. 2016. *Gender and the Political Economy of Conflict in Africa: The Persistence of Violence.* London: Routledge.

Uche, Chibuike U. 2001. *The Politics of Monetary Sector Cooperation Among the Economic Community of West African States Members.* Policy Research Working Paper no. 2647. Washington, D.C.: World Bank.

———. 2005. "Can African Institutions Finance African Development? Evidence from the ECOWAS Fund." In Jimi Adésína, Yao Graham, and Adebayo Olukoshi (eds.), *Africa and Development Challenges in the New Millennium: The NEPAD Debate.* London: Zed, 235–255.

UNAIDS (Joint United Nations Programme on HIV/AIDS). 2008. *Report on the Global AIDS Epidemic.* Geneva.

———. 2010. *Global Report: UNAIDS Report on the Global AIDS Epidemic.* Geneva.

———. 2018. *UNAIDS Data 2018.* Geneva.

UNDP (United Nations Development Programme). 1994. *Human Development Report: New Dimensions of Human Security.* New York: Oxford University Press.

———. 2007. *Human Development Report: Fighting Climate Change—Human Solidarity in a Changing World.* New York.

———. 2009. *Overview of Tourism in Africa.* New York. http://www.ticad.net/documents.

UNECA (United Nations Economic Commission for Africa). 2005. *Committee on Regional Cooperation and Integration Report: Trade Facilitation to Promote Intra-African Trade.* Addis Ababa.

———. 2010. *Assessing Regional Integration in Africa IV [ARIA IV]: Enhancing Intra-African Trade.* Addis Ababa.

UNEP (United Nations Environment Programme). 2007. *Sudan: Post-Conflict Environmental Assessment.* Nairobi.

United Nations. 2010. *The World's Women 2010: Trends and Statistics.* New York.

———. 2015. *Millennium Development Goals Report 2015.* New York.

United Nations Inter-Agency Committee on Women and Gender Equality. 1999. "Women's Empowerment in the Context of Human Security." http://www.hegoa.ehu.es/dossierra/seguridad/Womens_empowerment.pdf.

United Nations Millennium Project. 2005. *Investing in Development: A Practical Plan to Achieve the Millennium Development Goals (The Sachs Report).* London: Earthscan.

Unwin, Tim. 2004. "Beyond Budgetary Support: Pro-Poor Development Agendas for Africa." *Third World Quarterly* 25(8): 1501–1523.

US Energy Information Administration. 2011. *International Energy Outlook 2011.* Washington, D.C.

US Energy Information Agency. 2011. "How Dependent Are We on Foreign Oil?" http://www.eia.gov/energy_in_brief/foreign_oil_dependence.cfm.

Utas, Mats. 2003. *Sweet Battlefields: Youth and the Liberian Civil War.* Dissertations in Cultural Anthropology Series. Uppsala: Uppsala University.

———. 2005. "Building a Future? The Reintegration and Remarginalisation of Youth in Liberia." In Paul Richards (eds.), *No Peace, No War: An Anthropology of Contemporary Armed Conflicts.* Oxford: Currey, 137–154.

———, ed. 2012. *African Conflicts and Informal Power: Big Men and Networks.* London: Zed.

Utas, Mats, and Henrik Vigh. 2017. "Radicalized Youths: Oppositional Poses and Positions." In Morten Bøås and Kevin Dunn (eds.), *Africa's Insurgents: Navigating an Evolving Landscape.* Boulder: Lynne Rienner, 23–42.

Vale, Peter, and Sipho Maseko. 1998. "South Africa and the African Renaissance." *International Affairs* 74(2): 271–287.

Vale, Peter, Larry A. Swatuk, and Bertil Oden (eds.). 2001. *Theory, Change, and Southern Africa's Future.* New York: Palgrave Macmillan.

Vampouille, Thomas. 2010. "L'enquête sur les biens mal acquis relancée." *Le Figaro,* 9 November. http://www.lefigaro.fr/actualite-france/2010/11/09/01016-20101109ART-FIG00648-l-enquete-sur-les-biens-mal-acquis-relancee.php.

van Acker, Tomas. 2018. "From Rural Rebellion to Urban Uprising? A Socio-Spatial Perspective on Bujumbura's Conflict History." *Journal of Eastern African Studies* 12(2): 310–328.

van de Walle, Nicolas. 1999. "Aid's Crisis of Legitimacy: Current Proposals and Future Prospects." *African Affairs* 98(392): 337–352.

———. 2001. *African Economies and the Politics of Permanent Crisis, 1979–1999.* Cambridge: Cambridge University Press.

———. 2003. "Presidentialism and Clientelism in Africa's Emerging Party System." *Journal of Modern African Studies* 41(2): 297–321.

———. 2005. *Overcoming Stagnation in Aid-Dependent Countries.* Washington, D.C.: Center for Global Development.

van Evera, S. 2001. "Primordialism Lives!" *American Political Science Association—Comparative Politics* 12(1): 20–22.

van Nieuwkerk, Anthoni. 2012. "South Africa and Peacekeeping in Africa." *African Security* 5(1): 44–62.

van Rouveroy van Nieuwaal, E. Adriaan B. 1999. "Chieftaincy in Africa: Three Facets of a Hybrid Role." In E. Adriaan B. van Rouveroy van Nieuwaal and Rijk van Dijk (eds.), *African Chieftaincy in a New Socio-Political Landscape.* Hamburg: Lit Verlag, 21–47.

Vandeginste, Stef. 2009. "Power-Sharing, Conflict, and Transition in Burundi: Twenty Years of Trial and Error." *Africa Spectrum* 3: 63–86.

———. 2014. "Governing Ethnicity After Genocide: Ethnic Amnesia in Rwanda Versus Ethnic Power-Sharing in Burundi." *Journal of Eastern African Studies* 8(2): 263–277.

Vansina, Jan. 1966. *Kingdoms of the Savannah.* Madison: University of Wisconsin Press.

———. 1982. "Mwasi's Trials." *Daedalus* 111(2) (Spring): 49–70.

———. 1990. *Paths in the Rainforest: Toward a History of Political Tradition in Equatorial Africa.* Madison: University of Wisconsin Press.

Vaughan, Olufemi. 2000. *Nigerian Chiefs: Traditional Power in Modern Politics, 1980s–1990s.* Rochester: University of Rochester Press.

———, ed. 2003. *Indigenous Political Structures and Governance in Africa.* Ibadan: Sefer.

———. 2005. *Tradition and Politics: Indigenous Political Structures in Africa.* Trenton: Africa World.

Verbeek, Bertjan. 2003. *Decision-Making in Great Britain During the Suez Crisis.* London: Ashgate.

Vereker, J. 2002. "Blazing the Trail: Eight Years of Change in Handling International Development." *Development Policy Review* 20(2): 133–140.

Verhaegen, Benoît. 1966. *Rébellions au Congo.* Vol. 1. Brussels: CRISP.

———. 1969. *Rébellions au Congo.* Vol. 2. Brussels: CRISP.
Verschave, François-Xavier. 1999. *La Françafrique: Le plus long scandale de la république.* Paris: Stock.
Verweijen, Judith. 2016. *Stable Instability: Political Settlements and Armed Groups in the Congo.* London: Rift Valley Institute.
Villalón, Leonardo A. 1995. *Islamic Society and State Power in Senegal: Disciples and Citizens in Fatick.* Cambridge: Cambridge University Press.
———. 2007. "Senegal: Shades of Islamism on a Sufi Landscape." In F. S. William Miles (ed.), *Political Islam in West Africa: State-Society Relations Transformed.* Boulder: Lynne Rienner, 161–182.
Villalón, Leonardo, and Philip Huxtable (eds.). 1998. *The African State at a Critical Juncture.* Boulder: Lynne Rienner.
Vlassenroot, Koen, and Judith Verweijen. 2017. "Democratic Republic of Congo: The Democratization of Militarized Politics." In Morten Bøås and Kevin Dunn (eds.), *Africa's Insurgents.* Boulder: Lynne Rienner, 99–118.
Vokes, Richard. 2011. "Qadhafi and Uganda." *The Africanist,* 24 November. http://theafricanist.blogspot.com/2011/11/qadhafi-and-uganda.html.
Volman, Daniel. 2003. "The Bush Administration and African Oil." *Review of African Political Economy* 98: 573–584.
von Soest, Christian. 2007. "How Does Neopatrimonialism Affect the African State's Revenues? The Case of Tax Collection in Zambia." *Journal of Modern African Studies* 45(4): 621–645.
VonDoepp, Peter. 2009. *Judicial Politics in New Democracies: Cases from Southern Africa.* Boulder: Lynne Rienner.
Waever, Ole, et al. 1993. *Identity, Migration, and the New Security Agenda in Europe.* London: Pinter.
Wai, Dunstan M. 1983. "African-Arab Relations: Interdependence or Misplaced Optimism?" *Journal of Modern African Studies* 21(2): 187–213.
Walker, Rachelle. 2017. "Secessionist Conflicts and New States." In Morten Bøås and Kevin Dunn (eds.), *Africa's Insurgents: Navigating an Evolving Landscape.* Boulder: Lynne Rienner, 61–78.
Wallerstein, I. M. 1966. "The Decline of the Party in Single-Party African States." In J. La Palombara and M. Weiner (eds.), *Political Parties and Political Development.* Princeton: Princeton University Press, 201–214.
Walraet, Anne. 2017. "South Sudan: Violence as Politics." In Morten Bøås and Kevin Dunn (eds.), *Africa's Insurgents: Navigating an Evolving Landscape.* Boulder: Lynne Rienner, 197–216.
Walter, Barbara. 2004. "Does Conflict Beget Conflict?" *Journal of Peace Research* 41(3): 371–388.
Waltz, Kenneth. 1977. *Theory of International Politics.* Berkeley: University of California Press.
Wangwe, S. 2005. "Culture, Identity, and Social Integration: The Tanzania Experience in Social Integration." Paper presented at the conference "New Frontiers of Social Policy," Arusha, December.
Wantchekon, Leonard. 2003. "Clientelism and Voting Behavior: Evidence from the Field Experiment in Benin." *World Politics* 55(3): 399–422.
Wantchekon, Leonard, and Zvika Neeman. 2002. "A Theory of Post–Civil War Democratization." *Journal of Theoretical Politics* 14(4): 439–464.
Warmerdam, Ward, and Meine Pieter van Dijk. 2016. "Chinese Traders in Kampala: Status, Challenges, and Impact on Ugandan Society." *African Studies Quarterly* 16(3–4): 129–148.
Watkins, K., and J. von Braun. 2002. *Time to Stop Dumping on the World's Poor, 2002–2003. Annual Report: Trade Policies and Food Security.* Washington, D.C.: International Food Policy Research Institute.
Watson, Kathryn. 2017. "Where Does the US Have Troops in Africa, and Why?" *CBS News,* 21 October. https://www.cbsnews.com/news/where-does-the-u-s-have-troops-in-africa-and-why.
Watts, Michael. 1983. *Silent Violence: Food, Famine, and Peasantry in Northern Nigeria.* Berkeley: University of California Press.
———. 2005. "Resource Curse? Governmentality, Oil, and Power in the Niger Delta, Nigeria." In Philippe le Billon (ed.), *The Geopolitics of Resource Wars: Resource Dependence, Governance, and Violence.* New York: Cass, 50–80.
Waylen, Georgina. 1996. *Gender in Third World Politics.* Boulder: Lynne Rienner.

Weber, Max. 1978 [1922]. *Economy and Society: Outline of an Interpretive Sociology.* Berkeley: University of California Press.

Weinstein, Jeremy. 2006. *Inside Rebellion: The Politics of Insurgent Violence.* New York: Cambridge University Press.

Weisbrod, Aaron, and John Whalley. 2011. "The Contribution of Chinese FDI to Africa's Pre-Crisis Growth Surge." Working Paper no. 17544. Cambridge, MA: National Bureau of Economic Research.

Weiss, Herbert (ed.). 1966. *Congo 1964: Political Documents of a Developing Nation.* Princeton: Princeton University Press.

———. 1967. *Political Protest in the Congo.* Princeton: Princeton University Press.

Weldon, S. Laurel, and Mala Htun. 2013. "Feminist Mobilisation and Progressive Policy Change: Why Governments Take Action to Combat Violence Against Women." *Gender and Development* 21(2): 231–247.

Welz, Martin. 2013. *Integrating Africa: Decolonization's Legacies, Sovereignty, and the African Union.* London: Routledge.

West, Paige, James Igoe, and Dan Brockington. 2006. "Parks and Peoples: The Social Impact of Protected Areas." *Annual Review of Anthropology* 35: 251–277.

Whitaker, C. S. 1991. "Doctrines of Development and Precepts of the State: The World Bank and the Fifth Iteration of the African Case." In Richard L. Sklar and C. S. Whitaker (eds.), *African Politics and Problems in Development.* Boulder: Lynne Rienner, 333–353.

Whitfield, Lindsay. 2005. "Trustees of Development from Conditionality to Governance: Poverty Reduction Strategy Papers in Ghana." *Journal of Modern African Studies* 43(4): 641–664.

WHO (World Health Organization). 2016. "Ebola Virus Disease Situation Report." 10 June. Geneva.

———. 2017. *World Malaria Report 2017.* Geneva.

Widner, Jennifer. 1997. "Political Parties and Civil Societies in Sub-Saharan Africa." In I. William Zartman and Marina Ottaway (eds.), *Democratization in Africa: The Second Phase.* Boulder: Lynne Rienner, 65–81.

Widner, Jennifer, and Alexander Mundt. 1998. "Researching Social Capital in Africa." *Africa* 68(1): 1–23.

Wilks, Ivor. 1975. *Asante in the Nineteenth Century: The Structure and Evolution of Political Order.* New York: Cambridge University Press.

Willame, Jean-Claude. 1972. *Patrimonialism and Political Change in the Congo.* Stanford: Stanford University Press.

———. 1997. *Banyarwanda et Banyamulenge: Violences ethniques et gestion de l'identitaire au Kivu.* Paris: L'Harmattan.

———. 1998. "The 'Friends of the Congo' and the Kabila System." *Issue: A Journal of Opinion* 26(1): 27–30.

Williams, D. 2000. "Aid and Sovereignty: Quasi-States and the International Financial Institutions." *Review of International Studies* 26(4): 568–572.

Williams, David, and Tom Young. 1994. "Governance, the World Bank, and Liberal Theory." *Political Studies* 42(1): 84–100.

Williams, Michael. 2000. "The Struggle for Social Control in South Africa: Traditional Leaders and the Establishment of the Local State in KwaZulu-Natal." Paper presented at the annual meeting of the African Studies Association, Nashville.

Williams, Paul. 2004. "Britain and Africa After the Cold War: Beyond Damage Limitation?" In Ian Taylor and Paul Williams (eds.), *Africa in International Politics: External Involvement on the Continent.* New York: Routledge, 41–60.

———. 2009. "The African Union's Peace Operations: A Comparative Analysis." *African Security* 2(2–3): 97–118.

———. 2011. *War and Conflict in Africa.* Cambridge: Polity.

Wing, Susanna D. 2008. *Constructing Democracy in Transitioning Societies of Africa: Constitutionalism and Deliberation in Mali.* New York: Palgrave Macmillan.

———. 2012. "Women's Rights and Legal Reform in Francophone Africa." In Ellen Lust and Stephen Ndegwa (eds.), *Governing Africa's Changing Societies: Dynamics of Reform.* Boulder: Lynne Rienner, 145–176.

Wonacott, Peter. 2011. "A New Class of Consumers Grows in Africa." *Wall Street Journal,* 2 May.

Woods, Ngaire. 2007. *The Globalizers: The IMF, the World Bank, and Their Borrowers.* Ithaca: Cornell University Press.

World Bank. 1981. *Accelerated Development in Sub-Saharan Africa: An Agenda for Action.* Washington, D.C.

———. 1989. *Sub-Saharan Africa: From Crisis to Sustainable Growth—A Long-Term Perspective Study.* Washington, D.C.

———. 1992. *Governance and Development.* Washington, D.C.

———. 1994. *Adjustment in Africa: Reforms, Results, and the Road Ahead.* Washington, D.C.

———. 2001. *Aid and Reform in Africa: Lessons from Ten Case Studies.* Washington, D.C.

———. 2010. *Silent and Lethal: How Quiet Corruption Undermines Africa's Development Efforts (Africa Development Indicators 2010).* Washington, D.C.

———. 2018. *The Global Findex Database 2017: Measuring Financial Inclusion and the Fintech Revolution.* Washington, D.C.

World Travel and Tourism Council. 2017. *Travel and Tourism Economic Impact 2017: Sub-Saharan Africa.* London: World Travel and Tourism Council.

Wrong, Michela. 2010. *It's Our Turn to Eat: The Story of a Kenyan Whistle-Blower.* New York: HarperPerennial.

Wunsch, James S., and Dele Olowu. 1990. *The Failure of the Centralized State: Institutions and Self-Governance in Africa.* Boulder: Lynne Rienner.

Wunsch, James S., and Dan Ottemoeller. 2004. "Uganda: Multiple Levels of Local Governance." In Dele Olowu and James S. Wunsch, *Local Governance in Africa: The Challenges of Democratic Decentralization.* Boulder: Lynne Rienner, 101–210.

Wysoczanska, Karolina. 2004. "Sino-Indian Co-operation in Africa: Joint Efforts in the Oil Sector." *Journal of Contemporary African Studies* 29(2): 193–201.

Yacono, Xavier. 1991. *Les étapes de la décolonisation française.* Paris: Presses Universitaires de France.

Yarak, Larry W. 1990. *Asante and the Dutch, 1744–1873.* Oxford: Clarendon.

Yates, Douglas. 1996. *The Rentier State in Africa: Oil Rent Dependency and Neocolonialism in the Republic of Gabon.* Lawrenceville, NJ: Africa World.

———. 2009. *The French Oil Industry and the Corps des Mines in Africa.* Lawrenceville, NJ: Africa World.

———. 2012. *The Scramble for African Oil: Oppression, Corruption, and War for Control of Africa's Natural Resources.* London: Pluto.

Young, Crawford. 1965. *Politics in the Congo: Decolonization and Independence.* Princeton: Princeton University Press.

———. 1976. *The Politics of Cultural Pluralism.* Madison: University of Wisconsin Press.

———. 1983. "Comparative Claims to Political Sovereignty: Biafra, Katanga, Eritrea." In Donald Rothchild and Victor Olorunsola (eds.), *State Versus Ethnic Claims: African Policy Dilemmas.* Boulder: Westview, 199–232.

———. 1986. "Nationalism, Ethnicity, and Class in Africa: A Retrospective." *Cahiers d'Études Africaines* 26(103): 421–495.

———. 1994a. *The African Colonial State in Comparative Perspective.* New Haven: Yale University Press.

———. 1994b. "Evolving Modes of Consciousness and Ideology: Nationalism and Ethnicity." In David E. Apter and Carl G. Rosberg (eds.), *Political Development and the New Realism in Sub-Saharan Africa.* Charlottesville: University of Virginia Press, 61–86.

———. 1994c. "Zaire: The Shattered Illusion of the Integral State." *Journal of Modern African Studies* 32(2): 247–263.

———. 2002. "Nationalism and Ethnicity in Africa." *Review of Asian and Pacific Studies* 23: 1–19.

———. 2007. "Nation, Ethnicity, and Citizenship: Dilemmas of Democracy and Civil Order in Africa." In Sara Dorman, Daniel Hammett, and Paul Nugent (eds.), *Making Nations, Creating Strangers: States and Citizenship in Africa.* Leiden: Brill, 241–264.

———. 2012. *The Postcolonial State in Africa: Fifty Years of Independence, 1960–2010.* Madison: University of Wisconsin Press.

Young, Crawford, and Thomas Turner. 1985. *The Rise and Fall of the Zairean State.* Madison: University of Wisconsin Press.

Young, Daniel J. 2009. "Support You Can Count On? Ethnicity, Partisanship, and Retrospective Voting in Africa." Afrobarometer Working Paper no. 115. http://www.afrobarometer .org/files/documents/working_papers/AfropaperNo15.pdf.

Zartman, I. William. 1995. *Collapsed States: The Disintegration and Restoration of Legitimate Authority.* Boulder: Lynne Rienner.

————. 2005. *Cowardly Lions: Missed Opportunities to Prevent Deadly Conflict and State Collapse.* Boulder: Lynne Rienner.

Zeleza, Paul Tiyambe. 1997. "The Perpetual Solitudes and Crises of African Studies in the United States." *Africa Today* 44(2): 193–210.

Zolberg, Aristide. 1966. *Creating Political Order: The Party-States of West Africa.* Chicago: Rand McNally.

Zuberi, Tukufu. 2015. *African Independence: How Africa Shapes the World.* New York: Rowman and Littlefield.

Zunes, Stepeh, and Jacob Mundy. 2010. *Western Sahara.* Syracuse: Syracuse University Press.

Index

Abacha, Sani, 168–169, 171–172, 178–179, 206
Abbink, Jon, 105–106
Abdullah, Ibrahim, 309
Abiy Ahmed, 93, 295
Abubakar, Abdulsalami, 169
Acemoglu, Daron, 31, 209–210, 235–236, *287n*1
Acephalous societies, 18–22. *See also* Stateless societies
Achebe, Chinua, 54, 73
ACP. *See* African, Caribbean, and Pacific
Acquired immunodeficiency syndrome (AIDS), 10, 128, 246–250, 382, 404
Adinkrah, Mensah, 117, 118
Administrations: absenteeism in, 179, 182–183, 249; autonomy of efficient, 184–185; colonialism and, 26–43, 65, 94; corruption of, 178–192; decentralization, 188–192; foreign aid and, 185–192, 267–279; imported states and, 180–182; intermediaries, 183–184; nonstate actors and, 185–188, 263; normative pluralism, 182–183; reforms of, 181–192; weak, 152, 173–192; *See also* Executives
AEF. *See* Afrique Equatoriale Française
African, Caribbean, and Pacific (ACP), 376–377
African Development Bank, 124, 285–399
African Economies: agriculture in, 148, 234, 237–238, 248, 252, 255, 257, 268, 283–284, 400; aid in, 185–192, 267–279, 275*fig*; capitalism in, 46–47, 76–77, 118–120, 255–256, 347; colonialism and, 23–43, 232–236; commodity dependence, 14, 162, 209, 235–238, 240–245; commodity price boom and, 12, 240, 252, 280–283, 286–287, 348, 377; conditional lending to, 162, 232, 259–272, 277, 368, 381, 390, 395, 399, 401; debt of, 152, 162, 219, 242, 259–283, 265*fig*, 287, 389, 398, 399, 404;

disease and, 237, 245–250; economic engineering in 1960s and 1970s, 250–252, 254–259; education in, 89, 108, 249, 252, 257–258, 264, 276, 278, 285–286; environmental challenges to climate, geography, and, 236–239; forced labor in, 29–30, 36, 66*n*6, 126, 235; foreign aid in, 259–279; growth turnaround of, 4, 10, 232, 279–287; health and, 245–250; IMF and, 259–279, 287, 288*n*15, 355, 374, 398–399, 402, 404–405; informal sector of, 63–64, 127, 131, 253–254, 308, 362–363, 400–401; investment in, 4, 28, 120, 122, 257, 258, 266, 280–284, 363, 376, 391–392, 395–396; loans to, 259–279; management and development agenda, 250–287; manufacturing in,119, 188, 209–210, 240, 244, 252, 285, 360; middle-class Africans and, 12, 84, 105, 119, 124, 199, 226, 238, 279, 285–286; natural resources and, 240–245, 280–283, 286–287; neopatrimonialism and, 259–279; NGOs and, 245, 263, 272, 276, 278; overview, 250–287; performance from 1960, 250–252, 254–259; political conditionality, governance agenda and, 267–272; poverty and, 89, 104, 124, 240, 243, 269–270, 274–278, 284–285, 313, 354–355, 373, 377, 398; protest and, 215–217; regional economic communities, 359–363; rentierism in, 47, 122–123, 152, 202, 210, 240, 243–245, 256–257, 260–261, 288*n*13; resource curse, 210, 240–245, 316–317; slave trade and, 232–234; socialism of, 88, 120, 255; structural adjustment programs, 79, 128, 181, 216, 260–269, 355, 361, 379, 398 ; trade in, 4, 20, 234, 238, 242, 259–260, 273, 280–283, 281*fig*, 283*fig*, 354, 360–361, 374–377,

463